ARGUING ABOUT ART

"I welcome a book like *Arguing About Art* that presents a diversity of contemporary problems with good contemporary essays that respond to one another. I think the students like it too."

Robert J. Yanal, *Wayne State University, USA*

"Neill and Ridley have a unique approach among the aesthetics anthologies. The material included seems right for the kind of audience intended, and the use of a position and counter-position introduces the readers to the methods of philosophy as well as the issues of aesthetics . . . It fills a useful niche in the literature."

Dabney Townsend, *Armstrong Atlantic State University, USA*

"I think *Arguing About Art* nicely complements any introduction to aesthetics . . . I like all the introductions to the sections I have taught. They are brief, just setting up the issues and rehearsing the main arguments. They are also uniformly well written and engaging."

Dominic McIver Lopes, *University of British Columbia, Canada*

Arguing about Art, Second Edition is an expanded and revised new edition of this highly acclaimed anthology. This lively collection presents twenty-seven readings in a clear and accessible format, discussing major themes and arguments in aesthetics. Alex Neill and Aaron Ridley's introductions provide a balanced account of each topic and highlight the important questions that are raised in the readings. This new edition includes five new sections: *The Art of Food?*, *Rock Music and Culture*, *Enjoying Horror*, *Art and Morality*, and *Public Art*. Many of the introductions have been updated and each section includes suggestions for further reading. *Arguing About Art* is an ideal companion for any student coming to aesthetics for the first time.

The new edition:

- Provides a unique and accessible collection of readings in aesthetics. It will be a valuable companion for all students of the philosophy of art, art studies, literature, and cultural studies.
- Introduces a wide range of topics, including Sentimentality, Feminism and Aesthetics, and Appreciation, Understanding, and Nature. Three articles have been specially commissioned for the book.
- Contains concise, stimulating introductions and suggestions for further reading.
- Includes new sections on *The Art of Food?*, *Rock Music and Culture*, *Enjoying Horror*, *Art and Morality* and *Public Art*.

Alex Neill and **Aaron Ridley** are both Senior Lecturers in Philosophy at the University of Southampton.

ARGUING ABOUT ART

Contemporary Philosophical Debates

Second Edition

Edited by
Alex Neill and Aaron Ridley

London and New York

First edition published by McGraw Hill in 1995

Second edition published in 2002
by Routledge
11 New Fetter Lane, London EC4P 4EE

Simultaneously published in the USA and Canada
by Routledge
29 West 35th Street, New York, NY 10001

Routledge is an imprint of the Taylor & Francis Group

Typeset in Sabon and Frutiger by
Keystroke, Jacaranda Lodge, Wolverhampton
Printed and bound in Great Britain by
TJ International Ltd, Padstow, Cornwall

British Library Cataloguing in Publication Data
A catalogue record for this book is available from the British Library

Library of Congress Cataloging in Publication Data
Arguing about art : contemporary philosophical debates
/ edited by Alex Neill and Aaron Ridley.— 2nd ed.
p. cm.
Includes bibliographical references and index.
1. Aesthetics, Modern. I. Neill, Alex. II. Ridley, Aaron.
BH201 .A74 2001
111'.85—dc21
2001049059

ISBN
0-415-23738-6 (hbk)
0-415-23739-4 (pbk)

CONTENTS

CONTENTS

CONTENTS

CONTENTS

PREFACE

In producing a new edition of this book, our goal has been, as it was for the first edition, to provide a collection of readings that is representative of some debates in contemporary philosophical aesthetics, and one which will enable students using it to engage with and join in those debates. This new edition is in twelve parts, each presenting a topic in contemporary aesthetics. As a glance at the table of contents will show, the selection of readings and topics is very diverse, reflecting a variety of perspectives on philosophy and on art.

Three factors have influenced our selection of topics. First, we have tried to produce a collection which is representative of ongoing discussion among contemporary aestheticians. As anyone familiar with the discipline knows, contemporary aesthetics exhibits no common agenda; there is no agreed-on set of questions or concerns which defines the discipline. We have attempted to reflect the diversity of interests and concerns pursued by aestheticians today in the topics we have selected. In doing so, we have included readings which focus on a variety of art forms: painting, film, photography, music, and literature, as well as cooking and food and the natural environment. We believe that this variety will make the book usable and useful for a diverse audience, of the sort often found in courses on aesthetics: for students of literature and music, for example, as well as students of art, art history and philosophy.

Clearly, some of the topics included are more venerable than others, and we do not suggest that they are all of equal importance. However, and this is the second factor which influenced our selection, we have found that these are topics which students take up and become involved with actively and readily. All of the readings here represent good examples of serious philosophical writing about the arts, which, we have found, work well in the classroom. They generate lively discussion and a feeling of genuine engagement with and in philosophical reflection about the arts. It is of course not easy to pick readings which will be accessible to every undergraduate reader and are also of philosophical and pedagogical value. However, we believe that this collection gets the balance about right.

Third, we have tried to include topics which make concrete many of the concerns raised in more abstract form by the classic texts of aesthetics, so that this collection can serve as an effective supplement to the latter. We begin by asking whether food can be art; the essays we have included raise interesting questions about cooking and food themselves, but also provide a context for fruitful discussion of the more general question "What is art?" and associated questions such as those concerning the nature of aesthetic experience, taste, and the distinction between art and craft. The next part, on The "Authentic" Performance of Music, raises issues concerning authenticity, but also provides a context for discussion of the critical relevance of an artist's intentions. Rather different aspects of authenticity are taken up in the parts on Fakes and Forgeries, and Rock Music and Culture. Next come two topics which raise issues central in the history of aesthetics: the nature of aesthetic appreciation (here in the context of the natural environment) and representation (here in the context of photography). We then move on to two topics which focus on our emotional and intellectual engagement with art: Feelings and Fictions, and Enjoying Horror. The ethical dimension of that engagement is then picked up in parts on Sentimentality and Art and Morality. Finally, we turn to a pair of topics which bear on the institutions and the politics of aesthetics and the art world: Feminism and Aesthetics, and Public Art.

(We don't mean to suggest that the order in which the topics have been presented here is necessarily the best one. There are 479,001,599 other possible ways of ordering the twelve topics, and it is conceivable that at least some of these will make as much sense as the one which we have chosen.)

Acknowledgements

As we have thought about and worked on this anthology, we have been greatly helped in many ways by a number of people. For help with the first edition, we would particularly like to thank Jay Bachrach, Curtis Brown, Allen Carlson, Judith Cornwell, Sylvia Crisantes, David Dunham, Denis Dutton, Rick Flieger, Stan Godlovitch, Kathleen Higgins, Larry Kimmel, Flo Leibowitz, Jerrold Levinson, Doug McKenty, Marianne Neill, Ira Newman, Pat Powers, Jim Rather, Patty Rodney, Willis Salomon, Daniel Smith, Ann Spencer, Jay Thomson, Lee Thweatt, Dan Tures, Cynthia Ward, and Sue Weinberg.

For help with the second edition, we would like to thank Allen Carlson, Theresa Cook, Eva Dadlez, Stephen Davies, Denis Dutton, Ted Gracyk, Tom Kennedy, Deborah Knight, Carolyn Korsmeyer, Flo Leibowitz, Elizabeth Linehan, John MacKinnon, Ira Newman, Richard Smith, Bob Stecker, William Tolhurst, Julie Van Camp, Nigel Warburton, Sarah Worth, Robert Yanal; and at Routledge, Tony Bruce, Sarah Howlett, and Siobhan Pattinson. And, of course, we are grateful to all the writers who have allowed us to include their work here.

Alex Neill, Aaron Ridley

ACKNOWLEDGEMENTS

The editors and publisher would like to thank the following copyright holders for permission to reprint material:

Carlson, Allen, "Appreciation and the natural environment", *Journal of Aesthetics and Art Criticism* 37 (1965), 267–75. Reprinted by kind permission of Blackwell Publishers.

Carroll, Noël, "On being moved by nature", from *Landscape, Natural Beauty and the Arts*, edited by Salim Kemal and Ivan Gaskell, Cambridge: Cambridge University Press, 1993. Reprinted by kind permission of Cambridge University Press.

Carroll, Noël, *The Philosophy of Horror*, New York: Routledge, 1990. Reprinted by kind permission of Routledge, part of the Taylor & Francis Group.

Davies, Robertson, *What's Bred in the Bone*. © 1985 by Robertson Davies. Used by permission of Viking Penguin, a division of Penguin Putnam, Inc.

Davies, Stephen, "Authenticity in musical performance", *British Journal of Aesthetics* 27(1) (1987), 39–50. Reprinted by kind permission of the author and Oxford University Press.

Devereaux, Mary, "Oppressive texts, resisting readers and the gendered spectator: the *new* aesthetics", *Journal of Aesthetics and Art Criticism* 48 (1990), 337–44. Reprinted by kind permission of Blackwell Publishers.

Dutton, Denis, "Artistic crimes", *British Journal of Aesthetics* 19(4) (1965), 304–14. Reprinted by kind permission of the author and Oxford University Press.

Gaut, Berys, "The paradox of horror", *British Journal of Aesthetics* 33(4) (1965), 333–45. Reprinted by kind permission of the author and Oxford University Press.

Hein, Hilde, "What is public art? Place, time and meaning", *Journal of Aesthetics and Art Criticism* 54 (1996), 1–7. Reprinted by kind permission of Blackwell Publishers.

Horowitz, Gregg, "Public art/public space", *Journal of Aesthetics and Art Criticism* 54 (Winter 1996), 8–14. Reprinted by kind permission of the author and Blackwell Publishers.

Kelly, M., "Public art controversy", *Journal of Aesthetics and Art Criticism* 54(1) (Winter 1996), 15–22. Reprinted by kind permission of Blackwell Publishers.

King, William L., "Scruton and the reasons for looking at photographs", *British Journal of Aesthetics* 32(3) (1992), 258–68. Reprinted by kind permission of the author and Oxford University Press.

Korsmeyer, Carolyn, "The meaning of taste and the taste of meaning" from chapter 4 of *Making Sense of Taste,* in *Philosophical Topics* 25.1 (1997). Reprinted by kind permission of the author and *Philosophical Topics*.

Lessing, Alfred, "What is wrong with a forgery?", *Journal of Aesthetics and Art Criticism* 19 (1965), 461–7. Reprinted by kind permission of Blackwell Publishers.

Marquez, Gabríel Gárcia, *One Hundred Years of Solitude*. English translation © 1970 by Harper & Row Publishers, Inc.

Neill, Alex, "Fiction and the emotions", *American Philosophical Quarterly* 30(1) (1993), 1–13. Reprinted by kind permission of the American Philosophical Quarterly.

Radford, Colin, "How can we be moved by the fate of Anna Karenina?" *Proceedings of the Aristotelian Society* supplementary vol. 49 (1975), 67–80. Reprinted by courtesy of the Editor of the Aristotelian Society © 1975.

Savile, Anthony, "Sentimentality", *The Test of Time*, Oxford: Oxford University Press, 1982. Reprinted by kind permission of Oxford University Press.

Scruton, Roger, "The decline of musical culture", various extracts from *The Aesthetics of Music*, Oxford: Clarendon Press, 1997. Reprinted by kind permission of Oxford University Press.

Scruton, Roger, "Photography and representation", *The Aesthetic Understanding*, London: Routledge, 1983. Reprinted by kind permission of Taylor & Francis, plc.

Tanner, Michael, "Morals in fiction and fictional morality", *Proceedings of the Aristotelian Society* supplementary vol. 68 (1994), 51–66. Reprinted by courtesy of the Editor of the Aristotelian Society © 1994.

Telfer, Elizabeth, "Food as art", from *Food for Thought*, London: Routledge, 1996. Reprinted by kind permission of the author and Taylor & Francis, plc.

"Transcript of a hearing to decide the future of *Tilted Arc*", by various contributors, *Harper's Magazine* (July 1985).

Walton, Kendall L., "Morals in fiction and fictional morality", *Proceedings of the Aristotelian Society* supplementary vol. 68 (1994), 27–50. Reprinted by courtesy of the Editor of the Aristotelian Society © 1994.

Warburton, Nigel, "Individual style in photographic art", *British Journal of Aesthetics* 36(4) (1996), 389–97. Reprinted by kind permission of the author and Oxford University Press.

Young, James O., "The concept of authentic performance", *British Journal of Aesthetics* 28(3) (1998), 228–38. Reprinted by kind permission of Oxford University Press.

Every effort has been made to trace the copyright holders but if any have been inadvertently overlooked the publisher will be pleased to make the necessary arrangements at the first opportunity.

1

INTRODUCTION

"The discussion of art is a human activity quite as natural as the creation of art . . ."
Lionel Trilling, "Criticism and Aesthetics"

For at least two and a half thousand years, people have been arguing about art. What is the nature of art? What kind of qualities can art have, and how? What is the nature of our *experience* of art? What qualities can our experience of art have, and how? Which of those qualities are the most rewarding, and why? Disagreement about the nature and value of art, and about the nature and value of our experience of art, gives rise to philosophical debate. Someone dismisses as "sentimental slop" a novel which you love. Has one of you made a mistake? Your uncle insists on watching terrifying movies. Is he insane? The market value of a "Rembrandt" plummets when it turns out that Rembrandt didn't paint it after all. Should it? Artworks tend to portray women in certain lights. How, and why? All of these questions raise issues of the kind with which philosophical aesthetics – the subject-matter of this book – is concerned. In what follows, you will find twelve arguments which explore some of the most fundamental and enduring as well as some of the most contemporary questions in the philosophy of art.

*

But are questions like these, questions about the nature and value of art and aesthetic experience, worth arguing about? After all, aren't these things just a matter of subjective likes and dislikes, of purely personal opinion? That is itself one of the main questions in aesthetics. (It was one of the central concerns of both Hume and Kant in their writings on aesthetics, for example.) Since the very beginnings of philosophical reflection on art, people have wondered whether value judgements about works of art can be true or false, whether they are anything more than subjective statements of personal preference. We cannot hope to settle that question here. But even if it should turn out to be true that value judgements about works of art are purely subjective, that would not show that it was pointless to argue about issues in aesthetics. For one thing, not all talk about art is talk about the *value* of art.

So even if *value judgements* about art do no more than express subjective preference, that does not mean that *all* talk about art is merely subjective. For another thing, confusion and mistakes can arise when we think about subjective matters just as they can when we think about objective matters. We can be mistaken about what we like and dislike, and about why we like or dislike it. One of the most important things we try to do in aesthetics is to resolve confusions and to identify mistakes in our thinking about art and about aesthetic experience. Even if some of our talk about art does no more than express personal preference, then, arguing about art can help to clarify our understanding of important aspects of art and our experiences of it. We believe that taking up and joining in with the philosophical arguments represented in this book will bear this claim out.

*

Many of these arguments, as is often the case in philosophy, may appear rather abstract. Indeed, some of them are; they *can* be understood and taken up at a highly theoretical level. However, all of the arguments will be better understood, and more usefully taken up, if the reader resists the temptation to treat them as purely theoretical. These arguments are about aesthetic experience, and in most cases about human experience of various sorts of art. That is, they are about a kind of experience which almost everyone has had at some time. What this means is that they are arguments which will be understood best by and will be most helpful to the reader who insists on testing them against his or her own experiences of art. We hope that the arguments here will encourage the reader to develop his or her own views about some of these issues. And the reader whose thinking is informed by his or her own experiences of art will be in much the best position to make a real contribution to these debates.

Part 1

THE ART
OF FOOD?

The Fine Arts are five in number: Painting, Sculpture, Poetry, Music and Architecture – whereof the principal branch is Confectionery.

Antonin Carême, Chef, 1784–1833

[The *pièce*] stands probably four or five feet high. A froth of green foliage forms its base – leaves of mashed potato as delicate as ever grew from pastry tube. From that a Doric column, garlanded with pale full-blown flowers of lobster meat, diminishes twice.

At the top, on a pedestal edged with little shells and shrimpy rosebuds, is a pool of the clearest blue-green sugar, crystallised. And from it, with only the ankles of his tail held in the crystal, curves a fresh plump fish, every scale gleaming, his eyes popping with satiric amusement, and a beautiful umbrella of spun sugar held over his head by one sturdy fin!

M.F.K. Fisher, describing "A Culinary Fantasy:
The Cautious Carp", a confection by Antonin Carême

Cooking may be as much a means of self-expression as any of the arts.

Fanny Farmer, *The Boston Cooking School Cook Book*

We are told by Fanny Farmer that "cooking may be as much a means of self-expression as any of the arts," but that only goes to show that there is more to art than self-expression.

Monroe C. Beardsley, *Aesthetics: Problems in the Philosophy of Criticism*

IS THERE AN ART OF COOKING, of food and drink? Even a brief survey of the ways in which we often talk about food and its preparation reveals a widespread tendency to speak of great chefs, and for that matter wine-makers and distillers, as artists – thus for example according to Andre L. Simon, Antonin Carême "certainly was an artist and he also had a spark of that divine gift we call genius, the intuition and enthusiasm which alone achieve lasting results." We sometimes describe and discuss dishes and wines and whiskies in the same sort of terms that we use to describe and discuss works of art – consider for example Morton Shand on Strasbourg *pâté de foie gras*, presented "whole in rosy pink and galloantica strata framed in the alabaster filigree of a layer of goose-fat." And it is common to find the experience of good food and drink described as a variety of aesthetic experience – thus for example the food writer M.F.K. Fisher suggests that when it is combined with herb butter, "eating meat becomes not a physical function like breathing or defecating but an agreeable and almost intellectual satisfaction of the senses." In short, it is far from uncommon to find people talking about food and drink, and their preparation, in the sort of language that we typically use to discuss works of art and their production. But is this sort of talk to be taken seriously? When someone describes a particularly light and fluffy *omelette aux fine herbes* as "beautiful", or the bottle of wine that they have opened to drink with it as "a work of art", is this merely pretentious hyperbole – or could what they say be literally true?

To ask these questions is to raise the rather larger issues of what makes a practice a form of art, and a particular thing into a work of art. These issues, which have occupied philosophers at least since Plato's day, are never far below the surface in the essays in this chapter. Is our experience of food and drink ever correctly thought of as aesthetic experience? (But then what *is* aesthetic experience?) Isn't cooking better thought of as a craft than an art? (But then what does that distinction amount to?) Aren't food and drink too functional to be thought of as works of art? (But then why have people tended to think of art as somehow importantly *non*-functional?) Elizabeth Telfer raises these questions and more in the first chapter in this part, concluding that there *is* an art of food, albeit a "simple" and a "minor" one.

Telfer's reservations about the potential of food and its preparation to amount to art are explained in the final section of her chapter, where she points to what she argues are three major limitations of food in this respect: its "transience", the fact that "it cannot have meaning", and the fact that "it cannot move us". It is the second of these claims that Carolyn Korsmeyer is most concerned with, in the second chapter in this part. In sharp contrast to Telfer, Korsmeyer argues that food can indeed have meaning in at least some of the important ways in which works of art can have meaning. In doing so, she draws on a theory of art formulated by the philosopher Nelson Goodman in his book *Languages of Art*. In that work, Goodman analyses a variety of ways in which works of art may have meaning by functioning symbolically, the most significant of which are by representation, by exemplification, and by expression. (A useful introduction to Goodman's thought on these matters can be found in his essay "How buildings mean", which is listed in the Suggestions for further reading at the end of this chapter.) Korsmeyer considers each of these symbolic functions, or ways of meaning, in relation to food, arguing that all of them can be found in this context: that is, that food may be representational, may exemplify, and may be expressive. To understand what food is or can be, she argues, is thus in part to understand what it has in common with works of art.

Is there then an art of food? Both Telfer and Korsmeyer argue, though from different directions, in ways that would seem to support a positive answer to this question. Yet both hold back from answering with an unqualified "Yes!" Are they right to do so? Answering that question depends on thinking hard about the nature of art, as well as about food and drink.

2

FOOD AS ART
Elizabeth Telfer

FOOD AS ART

Might food and drink sometimes constitute an art form? Philosophers who have dealt with this topic tend to say that whereas food and drink can of course produce aesthetic reactions, it cannot be an art form or produce works of art. I shall therefore begin by examining the concept of aesthetic reactions, in general and as applied to food. I shall then consider the concepts of a work of art and an art form, and show how these concepts might be applied in the sphere of food. I shall go on to discuss the reasons which philosophers have produced for rejecting the idea of an art of food, and consider how they may be countered. Finally, I shall briefly discuss the social significance of regarding food as an art and some reasons for concluding that it is a minor rather than a major art.

AESTHETIC REACTIONS

What makes us call a reaction an aesthetic one? We naturally associate the word "aesthetic" with the arts, but we can also speak of an aesthetic reaction to natural things such as a beautiful landscape, or to man-made, non-art objects such as pieces of machinery. J.O. Urmson, in a well-known article (Urmson 1962), takes for granted that an aesthetic reaction is not a neutral reaction, but a species of pleasure. He suggests that we can best distinguish an aesthetic reaction from other kinds of reaction on the basis of the grounds for it. For example, if we react favourably to a play because it will earn a lot of money for us, because it teaches a fine moral lesson or because it is a successful venture for a playwright we know, our reaction is not aesthetic. Our reaction is aesthetic, in many simple cases, if it is based solely on how the object appears to the senses.

This appreciation of a thing for its own sake is sometimes characterised as disinterested. The use of this word is misleading: my favourable reaction to the play because

I am pleased by my friend's success might be called disinterested, but it is still not an aesthetic reaction. The point is better made by calling the reaction non-instrumental: I appreciate the thing's look or sound for its own sake, not for any benefit it brings to me or others.

Now, as Urmson himself says, it is not at all clear how this account can be made to apply to aesthetic reactions in more complex cases. For example, our appreciation of a novel does not seem to be sensual; still less our appreciation of the beauty of a logical proof (which Urmson allows as an example of an aesthetic reaction). However, his account fits those reactions which are likely to be most nearly like our reactions to food. If I admire some factory chimneys because they make a marvellous pattern, my admiration is aesthetic, whereas if I admire them because they show the factory to be powerful, it is not. Similarly, if I like the way cottage cheese contrasts in flavour and texture with rye bread, my reaction is aesthetic, whereas if I am pleased with the combination because it is low-calorie and high-fibre, it is not.

Are all cases of non-instrumental liking of a sensual phenomenon aesthetic reactions? We think of aesthetic reactions as needing also to have intensity: vaguely saying 'that's nice' without really taking something in does not seem to deserve the name. But the requirement of intensity does not imply that aesthetic reactions always involve actively paying attention to or concentrating on something. This is true of deliberate aesthetic activity, but some of the most powerful aesthetic reactions involve being impressed by some unexpected or short-lived phenomenon – perhaps something too quick to pay attention to, such as a flash of forked lightning. Nor need there be any analysis of what is seen or heard. Often analysis does take place, as when I see the fields in a landscape as forming a pattern. But suppose I lie on my back in the grass on a cloudless summer's day and gaze up into the sky, as if wallowing in the blueness. There is nothing to analyse, but surely this is an aesthetic reaction.

So far I have not challenged Urmson's assumption that an aesthetic reaction is a pleasant reaction to something. But it will not do as it stands. An aesthetic reaction need not be a favourable one, and even where it is, pleasure may not be the right charac- terisation of it. For example, we might speak of being interested or intrigued by a pattern of clouds, excited or exhilarated by lightning, moved by a panorama, awed by a natural wonder such as Niagara Falls, and so on. In none of these cases is "pleasure" the right description of our feeling, though sometimes "joy" would be appropriate.

Often we claim a kind of objectivity for our aesthetic reactions. We can say of both man-made and natural objects not only "I am excited, moved, awed by this", but also "This is sublime, beautiful, elegant, intriguing", as if attributing a quality to the object. Sometimes the second way of speaking may be only another way of expressing our own reactions, as when I say "This is nice" as I get into a hot bath. But at other times we think of the object of our aesthetic attention as in some way warranting or meriting a particular reaction, because it has qualities which other people also would appreciate or come to appreciate in it. In other words, there is often a sense of objective judgment in our reaction. This sense of objectivity need not entail a belief that some things are beautiful, graceful or awe-inspiring in themselves, regardless of how human beings see them; perhaps aesthetic qualities are capacities which some things have to arouse reactions of a certain kind in us. But it does mean that the realm of the aesthetic is not all "just a matter of what you like". We think that there can be judgments in this sphere which claim to be in some sense valid or well-founded, and that it makes sense to argue about them, even if the arguments often cannot be resolved.

It might be objected that the word "judgment" is scarcely appropriate to describe a sudden reaction to a flash of lightning. However, I did not claim that there is an element of judgment in every single aesthetic reaction. My wallowing in the blueness of the sky need not be accompanied by the thought that everyone ought to feel as I do about it, any more than my reaction to the lightning need be. But in each case judgment is possible: one might say to oneself immediately afterwards, "How beautiful!" and think of the sight as deserving one's feeling of joy.

Aesthetic judgments can sometimes be made in the absence of the non-neutral reaction which normally accompanies them. In some states of mind I can look at a landscape which would normally delight me and feel quite indifferent to it, but still see it as beautiful – meaning, perhaps, that it is the kind of thing which ought to delight people, and would normally delight me too.

The account which I have given of aesthetic reaction will not suit all cases. But I hope I have succeeded in suggesting a range of sense-experiences which fall under the description of "aesthetic reactions", and which may be characterised as non-neutral, non-instrumental, having a certain intensity and often accompanied by judgments for which the judgers claim a kind of objectivity.

How does all this apply to food and drink? Urmson is rather grudging on the matter: "It is at least reasonable to allow an aesthetic satisfaction to the connoisseur of wines and to the gourmet" (Urmson 1962: 14). There are, however, some more specific points that one would want to make.

First, it is generally agreed that there can be aesthetic reactions to tastes and smells. (There can also, of course, be visual aesthetic experiences connected with foodstuffs, as when one admires a rosy apple, but these raise no questions peculiar to food and drink.)

Second, as with the other examples of aesthetic reaction, we can distinguish liking the taste and smell of food from approving of it instrumentally on the grounds that it is nourishing, fashionable or produced by politically respectable regimes. Likewise we can distinguish the person who "enjoys his food" but does not notice what he eats, from the person whose awareness is more vivid – the latter reaction being the only one which is characteristically aesthetic.

And third, as with the other senses, the non-neutral, vivid and non-instrumental reaction to tastes and smells can be combined with a judgment for which the judger claims objectivity. I can not only like a food myself but also believe that the taste is a fine one which people ought to like, even if some of them at present do not. For example, I may not only prefer fresh grapefruit without sugar myself, but also think this preference is justified and hope to convince others of this. It is also possible for the judgment to become detached from the non-neutral reaction, as with other kinds of aesthetic reaction: I can say "These sandwiches are good" when I am aware that they deserve to be enjoyed but I am so tired that I am quite indifferent to them myself.

WORKS OF ART

As I said earlier, many philosophers argue that although food and drink can give rise to aesthetic reactions, they cannot constitute works of art. In order to examine this claim, we first need to consider what is meant by saying that something is a work of art.

Not all objects that can give rise to aesthetic reactions are works of art. A work of art is by definition a man-made thing, even if the human involvement need consist of no more than putting a natural object in a gallery and giving it a title. This much is clear, but beyond this point there are considerable complexities. One problem is that the phrase "work of art" can be used in either a classifying or an evaluative way. To use it in a classifying way is to say something about how the object is regarded, whereas to use it in an evaluative way is to say something about the extent to which it merits the label "work of art".

Urmson's definition of a work of art takes the phrase in a classifying sense: for him a work of art is "an artefact primarily intended for aesthetic consideration" (Urmson 1962: 22). Since we know from our discussion in the previous section what is meant by "aesthetic consideration", we can now expand this definition: if something is a work of art, then its maker or exhibitor intended it to be looked at or listened to with intensity, for its own sake. So if I go into a gallery of modern art, see a pile of metal pipes in a corner and wonder whether it is a work of art or some materials left behind by the central heating engineers, I am employing Urmson's sense of the phrase, wondering whether the pile is intended to be looked at with intensity. However, Urmson's use of the word "primarily" allows for the possibility that a work of art might be made for use as well as ornament. So a chair can count as a work of art if the maker intends it primarily to be looked at in the way one would look at a picture, even if he also intends it to be sat upon.

The classifying sense of the term "work of art", in the way Urmson uses it, takes the maker's or exhibitor's intentions as the criterion for deciding whether something is a work of art or not. There are, however, objects such as ethnological objects, or religious buildings, which were not intended by their makers as works of art but which are now treated as such. So we have a second classifying sense of "work of art": a thing is a work of art for a society if it is treated by that society as primarily an object of aesthetic consideration.

To grasp the evaluative use of the phrase "work of art", consider again the pile of metal pipes in the gallery. Suppose I look at it more closely, and find a notice on it saying "Modern Times" or "Metallic Three" (or even "Metal Pipes"); I may now say "That's not a work of art, that's just a pile of junk." I know perfectly well that the pile is a work of art in the first sense: that is, I know that the artist and the gallery owner intend us to gaze at it with intensity and that the public will probably oblige. But I am claiming that this object is not worth gazing at in this way, that it does not merit or repay aesthetic consideration.

People who use the phrase "work of art" in this evaluative way are from one point of view commending the things that they call works of art, but it does not follow that they consider all works of art to be good ones. Thus the person who refuses to call a collection of pipes a work of art might also say of a not very good conventional sculpture, "That is a work of art, even if it's not very good", meaning that it deserves to be appraised aesthetically, even though it may then be found wanting.

The distinction between the classifying and the evaluative senses of the phrase "work of art" is relevant to food. I shall claim that some dishes clearly constitute works of art in the classifying sense. But I shall also discuss arguments purporting to show that food does not merit aesthetic attention: in other words, that dishes cannot constitute works of art in the evaluative sense.

So far I have written as though there is no problem about what philosophers call the "ontological status" of a work of art: what kind of a thing it is, what kind of existence it has. But in fact there are many problems. Perhaps buildings, pictures and sculpture are unproblematic (though even here there are difficulties about the case of many identical etchings taken from one plate). But a piece of music is not a tangible object at all: for example, the Moonlight Sonata is not the piece of paper on which Beethoven wrote it, since there is still such a thing as the Moonlight Sonata even if that paper is destroyed. On the other hand, we do not want to identify the sonata with its performances, not only because it is one thing and they are many, but also because it would exist as a work of art even if it had never been performed. The same sort of thing can be said of plays. We therefore have to see this kind of work of art, a piece of music or a play, as an abstract thing, a kind of blueprint for performance. This point has relevance to food, as we shall see.

We can now begin to consider whether it makes sense to say that food and drink can sometimes be works of art. First I must clarify the question. It is obvious that foodstuffs can be made into visual objects which are works of art. The great pastrycook Carême – who was famous for the immensely elaborate models (known as *pièces montées*) which he made out of sugar and other foodstuffs – once said of confectionery that it was the principal branch of architecture (Quinet 1981: 164–5). It could be argued that these

13

objects are not food, since they were not intended to be eaten, but food properly so called is likewise often arranged or decorated in creative and attractive ways which constitute a visual work of art. However, the taste of food and drink as well as the look of it can give rise to aesthetic reactions, and I therefore wish to ask whether food and drink can sometimes constitute works of art of a kind peculiar to themselves, appealing mostly to the senses of taste and smell.

Our definition of a work of art, in the classifying sense, was: "a thing intended or used wholly or largely for aesthetic consideration". This is not true of run-of-the-mill food. But many meals are intended by their cooks to be considered largely in this way – to be savoured, appraised, thought about, discussed – and many eaters consider them in this way. Such meals also serve the functions of relieving hunger and providing nourishment, but they are of a kind which shows that this is not the main point of them. A meal that claims to be a work of art is too complex and long-drawn-out to be understandable in terms simply of feeding, and a cook who has cooked a work of art is not satisfied if the eaters do not notice what they eat. Such a cook aims to produce a particular kind of pleasure, one which depends upon a discerning appreciation of the flavours and how they combine and succeed one another.

To illustrate the approach of the cook who prepares a work of art, I quote from *The Good Food Guide Dinner Party Book* (Fawcett and Strang 1971). This is a book of recipes collected from some of the restaurants recommended in *The Good Food Guide* and assembled by its authors into suggested dinner-party menus.

> Guests who are particularly interested in food and cooking would enjoy this meal with a savoury beginning and fruity finale . . . The deep-fried croquettes are made of haddock and creamed potato. Serve them with sauce tartare . . . since its cold sharpness is a foil for the smoked haddock's savoury richness . . .
>
> (p. 62)

> With all this richness [roast duck with port and orange sauce or pickled pineapple or prune and Beaujolais sauce] try a green salad and the rather bland puree of potatoes and chestnuts . . .
>
> (p. 101)

> . . . the result is a homely rather than an elegant sweet, with the sharpness of the cherries contrasting with the mildness of the filling.
>
> (p. 101)

> The Jaegermeister pâté is a forceful one, with venison and liver as the basic ingredients, seasoned with mushrooms, herbs and brandy. The salad served with it is an agreeable contrast of crisp apples, celery and walnuts in mayonnaise.
>
> (p. 106)

Instead of muffling the scampi in a coating of crumbs, this recipe prescribes a delicate cream sauce, flavoured with mushrooms and brandy, which complements their flavour perfectly.

(p. 106)

These passages and many others like them illustrate the authors' desire to design dishes, courses and whole meals which present patterns of harmonious or contrasting flavours and textures. This is the approach of the cook who is designing a work of art.

ART, CRAFT, CREATION, INTERPRETATION

I have so far discussed cookery as an art, but perhaps cookery is really a craft. So we need to know what the difference is between art and craft.

Some commentators draw the distinction on the basis of the purpose to which the artefact is to be put: if it is intended for contemplation it is a work of art, if for use it is a work of craftsmanship. This distinction employs the notion of a work of art in what I called the classifying sense. But this way of drawing the distinction is not satisfactory. As we have already seen, something which is incidentally useful may be primarily intended for contemplation, and things not intended for contemplation by their makers are sometimes treated as works of art by others.

There is another possible distinction between art and craft: art is original creation, whereas craft is carrying out an instruction, following a convention or employing a technique (Whittick 1984: 47–52). This distinction is between kinds of work, rather than between the products of the work. We can apply the distinction without difficulty to some cases: for example the architect who designs the church is an artist, whereas the masons and woodcarvers who carry out his instructions are craftsmen. But other cases are less clear-cut. Painting and composing are normally thought of as original creation, but painters and composers often follow a convention: they create in accordance with a set of rules which defines a genre, such as sonata form or the conventional iconography of paintings of the Virgin Mary. If following a convention is the mark of a craftsman, then painters and composers are often craftsmen in that respect. But unlike the exact instructions of the mason, such conventions leave room for choice, so the painter's or composer's use of them is both craft and a part of the creative process. The same feature of craft in art is seen if we consider technique. Technique is a mark of craft, but the creative artist requires technique: we can distinguish creativity from skill in brushwork in painting, and creativity from mastery of orchestration in composition. Again, the painter's use of technique is both craftsmanship and part of the creative process.

The conclusion that emerges from this discussion is that the distinction between art and craft is basically not between people but between different aspects of their work, which may be blended in different proportions; if the work contains a good deal of creativity it will be thought of as art, if it contains a modest amount it will be thought of as craft, but there is no sharp distinction. The extreme case of the mason leaves no room for creativity, and so the mason is a craftsman who is not an artist at all; we might class him as a technician. But many so-called crafts, such as pottery and furniture making, leave plenty of room for creativity alongside the following of a convention and the employment of technical skill.

This blend of creation and craft applies also to interpretation. People tend to speak of composing and writing plays as creative, playing music and acting as interpretative. This way of speaking suggests that interpretation is not creative and is therefore not art. But the interpreter is in a position rather like that of a composer or writer writing in a genre with a strict convention. The music or drama that is being interpreted does not provide an exact plan of what is to be done, so interpretative artists have to make choices, have to be creative, and within an interpretative art we can distinguish between creativity and technique. In a sense, then, each performance is a work of art. If we do not use the phrase "work of art" in this context, it is perhaps because we have a sense that a work of art must be something durable – an idea to which I shall return.

So is cookery an art or a craft? It is true that it is often thought of as a craft. One reason for this is that its products are useful. But as we have seen, the usefulness of a thing does not prevent its being a work of art, so this criterion does not prevent cookery from being an art. And if the distinction between craft and art is based on the degree of creativeness, some cookery can still qualify as an art. As we saw from *The Good Food Guide Dinner Party Book*, recipes are sometimes treated as works of art, of a kind analogous to musical compositions. The cook who creates such a recipe is a creative artist. A cook can also create recipes by producing variations on someone else's recipe or on a traditional one, like a jazz composer arranging a standard tune or a classical composer arranging a folk song; cooks who do this are also creative artists.

Those who actually produce the dishes may or may not be artists. If a chef who creates such a dish gives exact orders for its preparation to his team of assistants, the assistants are technicians rather than artists, and the relationship between chef and technicians is like that between the architect and the masons. But most cooks are like neither architects nor masons. A cook following a recipe (a recipe that is a work of art, that is, like those in *The Good Food Guide Dinner Party Book*) is normally a performing artist rather than a technician, because recipes are usually vague ("season to taste", "add a pinch of ginger if desired" and so on) and need interpretation. So a particular cook's version of a recipe is an interpretative work of art, like a particular musician's performance of a piece of music. The same applies if the creator of a recipe cooks his own dish; he is an interpreter as well as a creator, like a composer playing his own compositions. (Both will of course need technique as well as interpretative artistry, such as the ability to make a white sauce without lumps, and pastry which remains in one piece.) It might seem as though the cook following recipes rather than creating them has room for artistry only when the recipes are vague. But even the cook who follows precise recipes has to make choices about the combination and sequence of dishes in a meal, and so to that degree is an artist.

DISHES AS WORKS OF ART

If cookery is an art form, what exactly is the work of art?

I said that both an original recipe and an actual dish (a particular performance of a recipe, as it were) are works of art if they are regarded aesthetically. However, sometimes there are problems about this scheme. Suppose a chef working for Marks and Spencer creates a superb pie, which is then turned out by the thousand. Are all the pies works of art, or is the abstract recipe the only work of art? The nearest analogy in the standard fine arts is probably with engraving and other forms of print-making, where the essence of the process is that it enables an artist to produce many copies of one work. Since we can call each engraving a work of art, we can call each Marks and Spencer pie a work of art, at least in the classifying sense.

There is another problem of quite a different kind about the status of dishes as works of art. Because people have to eat them to appreciate them, and because each person necessarily eats a different part of the dish, it might seem that in the sphere of food no one can appreciate a complete work of art, and no two people can appreciate the same one. I am not referring to the common thought that all viewers and listeners approach works of art from their own points of view and with their own preconceptions, and so in a sense each sees a different work of art. The present problem, if there is one, belongs particularly to food, and is more like a situation where each viewer of a picture sees only one section of it.

In fact, however, a dish of food is normally more homogeneous than this, or should be. All those who partake of it are presented with roughly the same thing. What they smell and taste is tangible stuff. But it is not a structure with parts, even if the dish is a structure with parts, like a pie, because one cannot smell or taste a structure. Admittedly there may be problems where a dish is not homogeneous enough: one diner's experience of the strength and blend of flavours may not match another's. These accidents are comparable to having a seat in a concert hall from which some of the instruments in the orchestra are inaudible: the recipe is not at fault, but the performance is.

Another apparent difficulty about treating dishes of food as works of art is this: how can there be works of art which are destroyed by the very activity, eating, which is necessary for contemplating them? This difficulty too depends on the mistaken idea that what is appreciated is a structure. As before, the answer to the difficulty is that even where a dish is a structure such as a pie, the aspect of it which is relevant to aesthetic appraisal is not the structure, which is destroyed as soon as the dish is started, but the combination of flavours, which runs right through the eating like letters through a stick of rock (Prall 1958: 185).

OUGHT FOOD TO BE AN ART FORM?

So far I have not mentioned art forms. An art form is a type of work of art, a class to which works of art in a similar medium belong. For example, sculpture is an art form, the class to which the particular works of art that are sculptures belong. So if dishes of food are works of art, then food is an art form. The term "art form" has the same two senses, classifying and evaluative, as the term "work of art".

It would be implausible to maintain that food and drink never constitute works of art in the classifying sense. People sometimes treat them as works of art, and I have argued that we can compare the creator of a recipe to a composer, and the cook who follows one to a performer. But some philosophers are willing to go further than this and claim that food deserves to be treated as art. D.W. Prall seems to be claiming this when he says:

> Like all sense presentations, smells and tastes can be pleasant to perception, can be dwelt on in contemplation, have specific and interesting character, recognizable and remembered and objective. They offer an object, that is, for sustained discriminatory attention.

> (Prall 1958: 187)

But others have claimed that there cannot be such a thing as an art of food as there is of painting or poetry. Since food is in point of fact sometimes treated as an art, these philosophers should be construed as saying that food and drink do not repay being treated as works of art: in other words, that food is not an art form in the evaluative sense. Of course, we can agree that much food is not. But I shall argue that the reasons for dismissing the whole sphere of food from being an art form in the evaluative sense are unconvincing, although I shall eventually conclude that, as an art form, food and drink are a minor one.

The first argument against food and drink as works of art in the evaluative sense concerns the usefulness of food and drink: it might be claimed that nothing useful deserves to count as a work of art, because, as Oscar Wilde said, "All art is quite useless" (Wilde 1948: 17). This argument must be fallacious: of the traditional fine arts (architecture, sculpture, painting, music, poetry) one, namely architecture, is concerned with useful objects. The proper point to make about the uselessness of art, as we saw at the beginning of the chapter, is not that works of art must be useless things, but that to appraise an object aesthetically is to consider it in abstraction from its usefulness. Whether a thing, useful or not, can be a work of art in the evaluative sense depends on whether it is worth appraising in this way.

However, perhaps those who say that food should not be treated as art because it is useful are really claiming that abstracting from usefulness is particularly difficult in the case of eating and drinking. One might reply that, on the contrary, it is all too easy to forget about usefulness (that is, nutritional value) when eating, and what is difficult to forget is the urge to simply munch away without thought. Either way, what these points would show is that it is difficult to treat food as an art form, not that it never merits being treated in that way.

Or perhaps the argument about usefulness is really that it is inappropriate to look at food aesthetically because this is treating a means as an end, and assuming food to be positively good when it is merely necessary. This argument is similar to those used to demote the physical pleasures. But it will not do. It is food as nourishment which is necessary, but the aesthetic value of food depends not on its nourishing properties but on its taste and smell. What we are valuing aesthetically is in effect a different thing from food as nourishment.

A second reason for refusing to count food as a work of art in the evaluative sense relates to the physicality of the way we appreciate food. Whereas we can see and hear at a distance, we taste something only if it actually touches the relevant parts of the body. Isn't this (it might be said) too crude to be art? We might retort that sight and hearing also require a physical link between thing perceived and the organ of perception: light waves in the one case, sound waves in the other. It remains true that the contact between the thing tasted and the taste-organ is direct in the case of food – but why should this matter? The question, surely, is not whether the way we taste things is crude but whether tastes themselves are crude. One might as well say that music played on a violin is cruder than music played on an organ because the violin is a simpler instrument.

As we shall see shortly, some philosophers do wish to argue that tastes are too crude to sustain art. But the argument from physicality, if I may so call it, might have a different origin: it might stem from a sense that the body taints what it is associated with, and that the freer we are of it the better we are. Sight and hearing, on this view are nobler senses because they are less physical, and to cultivate the more physical kinds of perception is to concentrate on unworthy objects. And of course taste is not only physical in the sense of being dependent on physical contact: normally (except at a wine-tasting or similar) we taste things in the course of making them part of our bodies. So anyone who thinks that we should as far as possible ignore the body might well feel that to dwell on any element of the processes by which it is renewed is in some way disgusting.

As was shown in Chapter 2 of my *Food for Thought* this hostility to the body is found in Plato, Aristotle in his Platonic moods and some strands of Christianity. I argued there that their arguments should be rejected. If we do this, we will reject along with them the argument that the physical nature of the sense of taste makes it unworthy.

But can combinations of flavours be sufficiently complex to constitute works of art in the evaluative sense of the phrase? Many writers think they cannot. One set of claims is that the eye and the ear are capable of finer discriminations than the senses of taste and smell; that the eye and the ear have more powers of recuperation; and that it is difficult to remember tastes (Gurney 1880: 10–11). These claims depict the limitations as being in us. Another set of claims is that tastes cannot be arranged in regular patterns, and that they do not possess form. These claims depict the limitations as being in tastes themselves.

The distinction between limitations in us and limitations in tastes is itself problematic. How can we be sure that a limitation is in the tastes and not in our perception of them? Does this distinction even make sense? But even if we accept the distinction for the sake of argument, what these considerations show is not that food cannot constitute works of art, but a much weaker thesis: that works of art based on food must be relatively simple. It is instructive that Monroe Beardsley, when discussing the possibility of works of art in food, asks why there are no "taste symphonies and smell sonatas" (Beardsley 1958, 1981: 99). Symphonies and sonatas are exceedingly complex works of art. He should have asked whether there can be taste-and-smell preludes, and the answer is by no means so obvious.

Let us start with the arguments that depict the limitations as being in us, and more particularly the claim that in taste and smell we cannot discriminate finely. It is true that our sense of smell, at any rate, is less highly developed than that of many animals. But we can still recognise a huge range of different smells and tastes. Moreover, these capacities can be developed and trained: we have only to think of the skills of the wine-taster or tea-taster. If our culture laid more stress on the importance of discrimination in food, more people would cultivate a palate, in the same way as musicians train the musical ear. The results might still be cruder than the discernments which can be made in sights and sounds, but this would not show that an art of food could not be worthy of the name. An artist can deliberately restrict his range of colours and shapes, or sounds and timbres, and still produce beautiful works.

The effect of the alleged limitations in our powers of recuperation is this: after tasting something very bitter or strongly spiced, say, we cannot for a while taste anything more subtly flavoured. But there are analogous problems in other arts. After loud ringing chords, the ear finds difficulty in focusing on small sounds; if we look too hard at a bright red shape in a picture, we find that shape, in green, floating about in front of our eyes as we look at the rest of the picture, and so on. In all these cases, artist and audience each have to make allowances. We learn not to stare at one part of a picture, and the conductor or pianist learns to leave a pause after loud chords. Similarly the chef serves a sorbet, or the diner eats a piece of bread, "to cleanse the palate" after the goulash.

There seems to be no difference in principle here, even though there may be a greater limit to the abruptness of possible contrasts in the realm of food. What these limitations suggest, if they exist, is not that there cannot be an art of food, but that such an art must be simple.

As far as our allegedly limited memory is concerned, it is not clear what the limitation is supposed to mean. If the claim is that memory is needed to enable us to appreciate the food as we eat it, we can reply that the art of food is not an art with that degree of complexity: its works of art are not as complex as a complex piece of music, such as a symphony, in which the composer may introduce into the last movement references to themes played in earlier movements. We might also make the point that, whatever may be said about food, most people's memory for music is in any case limited; the average listener – unless he has heard the work several times – cannot pick up references to the beginning of a work at the end of it. And if some feature requiring memory for its appreciation was untypically introduced into a work of art based on food, it seems likely that the expert would be as aware of it as the expert music listener would be of a reference in music – for example, the discerning diner would, like the expert listener, pick up the reference if a flavour in the savoury recalled a note, as people say, in the *hors d'œuvres*.

If, on the other hand, the claim is that memory is needed for subsequent analysis, the observation would show not that there can be no food art, but that there can be no food criticism. In fact those who write critically about food, such as food correspondents in newspapers or *Good Food Guide* inspectors, seem to be able to recall the food with as much precision as the subject-matter requires – aided no doubt by written notes, as any kind of critic might be.

I turn now to the arguments about the limitations of tastes themselves. The tenor of my reply is similar to that concerning our limitations. As before, I would say both that the claims are exaggerated and that the kinds of art which are used as the touchstone are particularly complex.

First, the regular patterns: it is said that tastes do not have an inherent sequence as colours or musical pitches do, so they cannot be arranged in "systematic, repeatable, regular combinations" (Beardsley 1958, 1981: 99). But it is not true that there are no sequences in tastes. We can arrange them in sequence from sweet to sour, for example, or from least salty to most salty. And not all art forms have "systematic, repeatable, regular combinations": this is true of music and architecture, but not of representative painting or sculpture. In any case, food does allow of systematic, repeatable, regular combinations: the cook creates the possibility for them, which the eater then realises. Suppose a diner eats in rotation mouthfuls of: duck in orange sauce; new potatoes with cream and garlic; broccoli. Is this not a systematic, repeatable, regular combination? It will be varied now and again by the introduction of mouthfuls of wine, but this does not make it indiscernible.

The second argument, the one concerning form, is that food does not allow a combination of features, as in a face or a tune; that such a combination is necessary for form (meaning something like "structure"); and that form is necessary for beauty. It is said that a chord in music, for example, is unlike a combination of flavours. A chord in music has both form (in the spacing of the pitch of the notes) and timbre (the characteristic quality of the sounds produced by the musical instrument or instruments), but flavours have only something analogous to timbre (Gurney 1880: 243–4).

This argument is puzzling. First of all, it does not seem to be true that form is required for beauty: we can say that the blue of the sky or the sound of one note on an oboe is beautiful. Perhaps the claim should be that form is required for the complexity which is involved in an art. Second, it is not clear why we may not say that some combinations of tastes have form. Take, for example, a salty biscuit, spread with unsalted butter, and topped by a very bland cheese with an anchovy or olive. Here the four elements can be arranged in order of saltiness, somewhat like a chord with notes of four different pitches. And since each of these four elements tastes of more than just salt, there is another dimension of variation, analogous to the timbre which is also present in a chord. We could also arrange the four elements according to the solidity of their texture, from the butter to the biscuit. I would not claim that form in food can be as complex as in music – for one thing the dimension of time has nothing like the impact that it has in music. But it would be a mistake to say that form is lacking altogether.

It is also claimed that tastes do not allow such things as balance and climax. I can only suppose that those who say that balance and climax are not possible in food have never planned a menu for a dinner party. Certainly a cook planning a dinner, or indeed a discerning diner choosing his meal in a restaurant, thinks partly in terms of these things. For example, he does not put the most striking dish at the beginning, leaving the rest to be an anticlimax. He will accompany elaborate dishes with simpler ones, so that attention does not get dissipated, and so on. Margaret Visser, in *Much Depends on Dinner*, conveys this point well:

> A meal is an artistic social construct, ordering the foodstuffs which comprise it into a complex dramatic whole, as a play organises actions and words into component parts such as acts, scenes, speeches, dialogues, entrances, and exits, all in the sequences designed for them. However humble it may be, a meal has a definite plot, the intention of which is to intrigue, stimulate, and satisfy.
>
> (Visser 1989: 14–15)

I conclude that there are no limitations, in us or in the nature of tastes themselves, which prevent food from giving rise to works of art in the evaluative sense of that phrase, though these will be simpler than in the arts of sight and sound.

IMPLICATIONS OF FOOD AS AN ART FORM

Why does all this matter? If food at its best deserves to be treated as a simple art form, as I have suggested, what follows?

We think of the arts as an important part of our lives. In our society, this manifests itself in at least three ways. The state spends some of its resources on support for the arts; educationalists try to inculcate some knowledge of and concern for the arts into their pupils; and individuals cultivate the arts, and regard someone with no respect for them as defective, a philistine. Should the art of food find its place in all these activities?

There are certainly people who feel that one should cultivate the art of food, eat elegantly and discerningly, "take trouble" with one's food. They regard this as part of being civilised, and hold that a person who thinks that it does not matter what one eats is at best boorish. But even if we agree that everyone should cultivate the arts, does it follow that everyone should cultivate this particular art? There are at least two reasons why we should not conclude this. First, a person cannot appreciate any art form unless it means something to him or her. It may not therefore be possible for everyone to cultivate every art, and so we cannot prescribe that everyone must cultivate one particular art form. Second, given that time and resources are limited, an individual has to choose from among the art forms that he can appreciate, and the kind of art form that food is will affect that choice. I shall argue in the next section that food represents not only a simple but also a minor art form. If this conclusion is granted for the moment, others follow. For example, it would be reasonable for a person without much time or money to decide, while fully aware of the aesthetic claims of food, that for him major arts had to come first and that food could not be an art form in his life.

Whether such a decision is reasonable partly turns on how expensive good food is; and we can now see the relevance of state subsidy. If fine restaurants were subsidised sufficiently, no one would need to reject this art form merely on grounds of cost. In fact they are not subsidised at all. Is this misguided of the state? I think we can say that it is not, for two reasons, both depending on the fact that money is limited. First, given that a choice has to be made, it is appropriate to subsidise the major arts rather than the minor ones. And second, this particular art form will survive without subsidy. With some arts, such as opera, the point of subsidy in Britain seems to be not to enable everyone to afford to share in an art form, but to prevent it from disappearing altogether. On that criterion there is no need to subsidise good restaurants.

The third way in which the importance of the arts is recognised is in the role they have in education. Teachers try to initiate their pupils into at least the rudiments of an understanding of the major arts. This would not commonly be extended to the art of food, except perhaps for those in domestic science classes. Again the problem is one of priorities: given that time and resources are limited, it seems more important to tell children about the major arts. But this decision may be short-sighted. The advantage of food from the teacher's point of view is precisely the feature which might seem to make it a disadvantage aesthetically speaking: namely, that everyone has to eat. With food, as with clothes, people have a chance to enhance an area of their everyday lives. So to that extent the aesthetic appreciation of food is not a separate, alien activity, but an aspect of what is done every day.

The universality of eating might make some argue that there cannot be an art of food: appreciation of the arts requires a cultivated understanding, but everyone eats, so there cannot be an art of food. It will by now be clear that this argument is confused. Not all eating is an aesthetic activity. Aesthetic eating, if I may call it this, is eating with attention and discernment food which repays attention and discernment. And to achieve attention and discernment may well take some practice and some instruction. On the other hand, the art of food is easier to appreciate than arts which require a lot of background information; the art of food is a possible people's art.

A MINOR ART

I must now make good my promise to show that the art of food is not only a simple art but also a minor one. At first I thought that a simple art was necessarily also minor: my argument was that something complex can support a more sustained aesthetic contemplation than something which is simple, and is therefore aesthetically more satisfying. This argument is sound if the contemplation is of an analytical kind. But there also seems to be a non-analytical kind of aesthetic contemplation, which can be sustained even when it has a simple object such as an abstract sculpture of simple shape. I therefore cannot assume that the art of food is a minor art merely on the ground that it is simple.

It might plausibly be claimed, however, that the art of food is minor because it is not only simple but also limited in three important ways: food is necessarily transient, it cannot have meaning and it cannot move us. I shall look briefly at each of these three claims.

There are two reasons why transience might make a work of art less important. One is that it limits the contemplation that is possible – a work of food art will not be around very long to be contemplated. The other reason is that transient works of art cannot acquire the stature that a long-lived work of art can have. To be a great work of art, an object must have had the chance to "speak" to different generations, as for example the Taj Mahal and the *Odyssey* have. This limitation – the inability to speak to different generations – affects food in two ways.

We have seen that in the sphere of food there are two kinds of work of art: the recipe, analogous to a musical composition, and the dish as cooked on a particular occasion, analogous to a performance. Now a recipe is not transient, because it can be written down, but despite its permanence, it may still not be able to speak to different genera-tions, not because it is impossible to note down everything with sufficient precision – the cook can interpret, as we said – but because the nature of ingredients changes: for example, farmers breed leaner animals for meat nowadays in response to modern worries about cholesterol, and varieties of fruit and vegetables are constantly changing. Performances, however, are transient. It is true that we can now record most kinds of performance, and that some performances may as a result gather the stature of permanent works of art. But a dish of food is more transient than other kinds of per-formance, because we cannot reliably record the performance of a cook. I do not only mean that we do not yet have the technology, though that is true; food loses its taste eventually, whatever means we use to preserve it. I also mean that there is a highly relevant reason why we may not be able to record a genuine cookery performance, one intended for particular eaters: if the food is any good, they will eat it all!

We must conclude that works of art in food, whether creative or interpretative, cannot gain the same stature as those of greater permanence. This is one important reason why food must remain a relatively minor art. We might say the same, for the same reason, about any art of the short-lived kind – an art of fireworks, for example, or of flower arranging. The peculiar poignancy of fireworks and flowers depends on their evanescence, and such art cannot have immortality as well.

The second claim, that food cannot have meaning, needs a word of explanation, since I mentioned in Chapter 2 of *Food for Thought* many ways in which food does have meaning: for example, it can symbolise a nation's way of life and traditions. However, what I am about to show is that it does not have the same kinds of meaning as the major art forms have.

To begin with, food does not represent anything else, as most literature and much visual art does. We can see the representational arts – painting and literature – as telling us something about the world and ourselves, and we can see the world and ourselves in the light of ways in which they have been depicted in the representational arts. But we cannot do either of these things with food. This is an important way in which some of the arts have meanings which food cannot have.

However, it might be said with justice that an art does not need to be representational in order to be a major art. Music, for example, does not represent the world so much as create another world of its own. In that respect the art of food might be said to resemble music: it creates its own world of tastes and smells. But music, although it is not in general representational, seems to be able to carry another kind of meaning, one of which food is not capable: music can express emotion. There is a philosophical problem about what it means to say that music expresses emotion, as well as a problem about how music does it, but it is at any rate clear that it does, and that food does not. And it is important to us that music expresses emotion: it is one of the things that is meant by the claim that music is a kind of communication.

The inability of food to express emotion does not mean that cooks cannot express themselves in their work. For one thing, 'expressing oneself' need not mean expressing emotion. Since cooking gives scope for taste, inventiveness and discernment, cooks can express these qualities through their cookery. For another thing, cooking can in one sense be an expression of emotion. A cook can cook as an act of love, as we have seen, or out of the joy of living. But whereas in music the emotion is somehow expressed in the product itself – the music can be sad or joyful, angry or despairing – in food the emotion is only the motive behind the product.

Lastly, food cannot move us in the way that music and the other major arts can. This claim is different from the claim that food cannot express emotion. A great building, for example, can move us without itself expressing emotion; so can some kinds of music. But is it true that food cannot move us? Speaking for myself, I should say that good food can elate us, invigorate us, startle us, excite us, cheer us with a kind of warmth and joy, but cannot shake us fundamentally in that way of which the symptoms are tears or a sensation almost of fear. We are not in awe of good food, and we hesitate to ascribe the word "beauty" to it, however fine it is. (Of course, we often say that a dish is beautiful. But that means much less. All kinds of things can be called beautiful, but very few kinds of thing can be said to have beauty, still less great beauty.) If I am right about the absence of this earth-shaking quality in the art of food, it constitutes a limit to the significance it can have for us.

If food cannot be more than a minor art form, there is a danger of being precious about it – of treating it, that is, as though it had more aesthetic importance than it does. So although food may be an art form, we should not always treat it as such. For one thing, not all food constitutes a work of art. If we carefully contemplate every meal with an eye to balance and climax, harmony and contrast and so on, not only will we often be disappointed in our aesthetic aspirations, but also we will fail to get the pleasure that we could get, both from the food and from the other aspects of the occasion. And even on an occasion where the food repays aesthetic study, we may spoil its appeal by too close a scrutiny, like someone looking for Schubertian profundity in a folk song, and also pay so much attention to it that we miss other aspects of the occasion.

This is a subtle matter. Even with Schubert, we can spoil the experience by telling ourselves, "This is art", instead of letting the song speak for itself. With the art of food, we have two problems. We need to strike a balance between the aesthetic claims of the food on a particular occasion and the social claims of that occasion. We also need to find a middle way between two unsatisfactory attitudes to the aesthetic dimension of food: we must not be so heedless as to waste a satisfying kind of aesthetic experience, but not so precious as to expect more of it than it can give.

REFERENCES

For references other than those listed here, see the "Suggestions for further reading" at the end of this part.

Fawcett, Hilary and Strang, Jeanne (1971) *The Good Food Guide Dinner Party Book*, London: Consumers' Association and Hodder and Stoughton.

Prall, D.W. (1958) "The elements of aesthetic surface in general", in Eliseo Vivas and Murray Krieger (eds) *The Problems of Aesthetics*, New York and Toronto: Rinehart & Co.

Wilde, Oscar (1948) *The Picture of Dorian Gray*, in G.F. Maine (ed.) *The Works of Oscar Wilde*, London and Glasgow: Collins.

3

THE MEANING OF TASTE AND THE TASTE OF MEANING

Carolyn Korsmeyer

Taste turns out to be a sense that is more complex, subtle, and worthy of interest than its placement in the history of philosophy would suggest. The sense of taste is an educable faculty, as the dizzying variety of eating preferences displayed across the globe testify. At the same time, as physiologists and psychologists have demonstrated, there are a number of inborn, universal preferences, such as attraction to sweet and salt and aversion to bitter. These responses not only account for common likes and dislikes but seem to be the foundation for common meanings assigned to flavors. A question that remains to be addressed is whether the educability and discrimination of taste permit a defense of its aesthetic importance. Can taste experiences be legitimately considered genuine aesthetic experiences?

This question needs to be paired with a related and equally important one concerning the status of food as art. This is not a simple question about linguistic habits, for terms such as "culinary art" are both widely used and perfectly clear. But the question persists: Is the artistic potential for food comparable in its own domain to the artistic potential for sound to be transformed into music, for pigments to become paintings, words to form poems? Opinion leans heavily to the negative. . . . Taste and food have had their advocates, however. A few brave theorists have defended the aesthetic potential for the enjoyment of taste, and yet others have gone on to argue on behalf of the artistic possibilities of food and drink. . . .

Elizabeth Telfer does make a case for food as an art form, though decidedly not a major one. The concept of art she employs considers the defining feature of an artwork to be its status as an object for aesthetic consideration. Carefully planned and presented meals organize eating sequentially, harmonizing the flavors and textures to be experienced. This kind of cooking, she believes, qualifies as the making of food as art, an art that is appreciated through aesthetic eating. The kind of art that food represents, however, is simple compared to symphonies, buildings, poems, or paintings. The medium of food has four limitations that preclude its development into a proper fine art. First of all, as Prall also notes, the formal arrangements and expressive range possible are far more restricted in food than in the fine art media.[1] Moreover, Telfer argues, food is a transient medium. While recipes may linger, actual meals are consumed and their remnants disposed of. Foods therefore cannot garner the studied appreciation over time that elevates especially fine products of more durable media such as paintings and poetry into canonicity. Third, she claims that unlike other arts, foods do not have meaning.

> To begin with, food does not represent anything else, as most literature and much visual art does. We can see the representational arts – painting and literature – as telling us something about the world and ourselves, and we can see the world and ourselves in the light of ways in which they have been depicted in the representational arts. But we cannot do either of these things with food. This is an important way in which some of the arts have meanings which food cannot have.[2]

Finally, food cannot express emotion (though a cook may "express herself" and feelings such as love for friends in the act of cooking). Nor can it move us in the way great art can. Its aesthetic and artistic limitations lead Telfer to conclude that while food affords aesthetic enjoyment and can be considered a simple art, it is also a *minor* art. This is not intended to be a criticism of food, just a recognition of its nature: "we must not be so heedless as to waste a satisfying kind of aesthetic experience, but not so precious as to expect more of it than it can give."[3] A similar sentiment is expressed by Frank Sibley: "Perfumes, and flavours, natural or artificial, are necessarily limited: unlike the major arts, they have no expressive connections with emotions, love or hate, death, grief, joy, terror, suffering, yearning, pity, or sorrow, or plot or character development. But this need not put them out of court."[4] This conclusion may be found as well in other defenses of food as an art form – but not a major art form – including that of the anthropologist Mary Douglas. Douglas believes the display function of food and its occasional dissociation from nourishment is reason to class certain types of foods with the *decorative* arts.[5] It seems that whatever pleasures food can deliver and however refined cuisine may become, it is in the end just pleasure, after all, and offers less to our minds and imaginations than do more important art forms.

Given the concept of the aesthetic Telfer employs, she has articulated a cogent and sympathetic defense of food as art. Yet it is a pallid victory if there is nothing more to be said. Gustatory delectation is a positive pleasure, and a discriminating palate is perhaps as hard to come by as a musical ear. But . . . any brief for foods that focuses on the enjoyment of the sensation of tasting alone is going to reach a limit very quickly. Without question good food is enjoyable, and a discrimination that is difficult and educable pays dividends in taste pleasures. The case that the perceptual discrimination and enjoyment of taste are at least close cousins, phenomenally speaking, to aesthetic discrimination and enjoyment is fairly easy to make. We can travel down this road to gourmet land and the haute cuisine that marks the dining possibilities of an elite, but the deeper kinds of significance granted works of art will not appear so long as refined enjoyment is the highest end of eating. Discriminating and relishing fine distinctions are only one part of aesthetic apprehension. Omitted are the insight, emotion, and deepened understanding that are expected from encounters with important aesthetic objects. Since among the latter are works of art, this merges into consideration of the status of food as art and a comparison of foods and drink with artworks. A case for comparability in this domain is harder to make, not because the grounds for comparison are absent but because of the tendency to continue attention to gourmet eating and fine dining when one seeks to understand the aesthetic qualities of food. Therefore, if we want to pursue the parallels between food and standard art forms beyond pleasant savoring and cultivated discrimination, we need to inquire about the possibilities for the cognitive dimensions of taste and food. . . .

REPRESENTATIONAL FOOD

Many philosophers, including Telfer, have concurred that food does not represent anything outside itself and thus fails in one of the standard tasks of art, to deliver understanding and insight about life and the world. The disclosure of the symbolic functions of food will dispel that misunderstanding. The most obvious example of symbolic food, what would be classified as representational food, is food that is crafted to look like something other than itself. The examples I offer may appear at first to be incidental, perhaps even frivolous, but they direct attention to the pervasiveness of meaning in foods. In fact, representational foods are quite common. Consider the following very limited list:

- Gummy bears, candy canes, sugar skulls, cinnamon hearts, candy corn, the metaphorical chocolate kiss
- Gingerbread men, hamentaschen, hot cross buns, pretzels, croissants, braided breads, chocolate Yule logs
- Radish roses, goldfish crackers, melon boats, vegetables cut and assembled into bouquets of flowers
- Easter eggs, butter lambs, molded gelatins shaped like stars, tequila sunrises, birthday cakes in the shape of basketballs, wedding cakes that look like temples, carved ice sculptures flanking a buffet table
- The bread and wine of the Christian Eucharist.

These few examples are hardly all comparable in the significance that their representations possess. Most of them appear to be more or less sui generis cases of nondenoting representations, shaped foods that are fun or witty or pleasant or decorative. (The bread and wine of the Eucharist are a striking exception and possibly appear shocking lined up with the other cases.) But they illustrate the intriguing fact that an enormous amount of what we put into our mouths represents (in some sense or other) something else. Many such instances derive from actual representations of things or events, though if their popularity persists long enough, that function may be lost to awareness and they may lose their original significance.

Consider the pretzel. In Italy, where pretzels are said to have been invented, the word denominating this food is *bracciatelli*, which translates into English as "folded arms." In the early seventeenth century, an inventive monk twisted a string of dough and baked it into the curved outline of the arms of a brother at prayer to dispense as a reward for his pupils who recited their catechism correctly.[6] In some parts of Europe pretzels are a Lenten food, and presumably there the curls of the snack are recognized to denote the folded arms of a monk. . . . When the monk representation is pointed out, the experience of eating a pretzel is transformed very slightly and perhaps achieves the aesthetic predicate "witty." The food takes on a new, expressive dimension, and the aesthetic apprehension of the pretzel expands.

Another familiar food that began its life as a symbol is the croissant. Croissants were invented in Vienna in 1683. In celebration of the successful defense of the city against the Ottoman Turks, Viennese bakers crafted little buns in the shape of the crescent moon on the flag of their enemies. In this case, not only is the crescent shape recognized as denoting the foreign enemy, but the fact that one *devours* the crescent reenacts the defeat of the invaders, and perhaps also represents Christianity conquering Islam. How long such references continue to function will vary greatly with time and place, and in this case the representational function of croissants is only a historical curiosity. But it is a curiosity with a lesson that cautions against any easy dismissal of the representational possibilities of food. The fact that crafting an item of daily bread was so readily turned to triumphant commemoration should indicate the easy commerce between food and shared social significance, a significance manifest in the symbolic use of foods.

Some of the most famous food representations have been intended to deceive, and hence qualify as a type of illusionism. Such is the case with items of the meal satirized by Petronius in his account of Trimalchio's feast in the *Satyricon*, during which apparent live boars turn out to be skins filled with birds, cooked fish seem to swim in their sauces, a hare sprouts wings, and dishes that look like piglets are really sweet cakes. But we need not rely only on such legendary excesses; a visit to a Japanese restaurant will provide plenty of examples: carrots trimmed into small turtles and fish, or radishes and onions mimicking bunches of tiny flowers. Here there are also deceptive possibilities, such as the pale-green leaf shapes that appear to the uninitiated to be bland substances such as mashed avocado but are actually puréed horseradish. Employing Goodman's idiom, we could say that these are leaf-representations that metaphorically exemplify coolness but possess furious hotness. The combination might be described as ironic. . . .

A little reflection reveals that representation in food of a similar sort, if less elaborately crafted, is fairly common, though it is most dramatic when the meal involved is part of a ceremony. (The sugar skulls in the list above are a component of the celebration of the Day of the Dead in Mexico. Their design is contiguous with the practice of serving an entire ceremonial meal to the dead.) Ceremonies provide some of the most sustained and complex instances of symbolic function ... In the European Middle Ages commemorative set pieces accompanied certain state or ecclesiastical banquets, at which the events or people being honored were represented in food sculptures displayed between courses: scenes from the Holy Land presented to knights returning from a crusade, or biblical tableaux and saints for archbishops. Often central components of such displays required that the skins of animals and birds be reassembled with their cooked contents, which presented chefs with the considerable challenge of resurrecting a peacock, deer, or swan and posing it in a convincingly lifelike posture. These creations perhaps skirt the borderland of "foods," for they were chiefly for display and parade and were not eaten, though the fact that their media were edible is part of their artistry. (Edible in theory, anyway. Revel reports that such presentations were often accompanied by an unappetizing stench from the decomposing skins into which the spiced and cooked meats were stuffed.) These creations raise the question of the boundaries of culinary art, and just where the experience of eating stops and starts. Shortly I shall address the ceremonial function of foods. At issue now, however, is the extent to which the sheer artistry of symbolic foods alone – the difficulty attendant on rendering them, the skill required, and the accomplishment of the finished product – qualifies these sorts of displays as art.

Obvious reference to objects and events make these foods representational, and to that degree the claim that foods cannot represent or refer to anything outside themselves is demonstrably false. The types of representation include denotation (reference to an existing individual or actual event) and representation-as (food that is shaped like something else but does not refer to any particular thing). The problem at this stage of analysis seems to be that such representations appear to have a frivolous, unnecessary quality that makes the food interesting and curious but not necessarily profound or important. . . . Shortly I shall supply a way to understand food that minimizes this suspicion, but even then stunt cuisine alone will not serve as a central or paradigm example of what is most important about eating. At best, it sustains the characterization of cooking as a decorative art, to use Douglas's classification. And indeed much food artistry is for decorative purposes, as traditions of techniques for carving and cutting demonstrate. For centuries before Carême noble kitchens employed carvers for the preparation of meats and fruits, and a cookbook of the twentieth century continues this tradition with an appendix devoted to garnishes that announces that "garnishes are to foods what lace collars, belt buckles, and costume jewelry are to dresses."[7] The decorative capacities of food appear to be well established. So far, however, even the extravagant displays of Carême can do little to extend the artistic value of foods beyond decoration.

Moreover, we may also note an objection to decorative food that points to an adventitious element to the representational capacities of food: the examples of symbolic function in food discussed above are largely the result of *visual* manipulation.[8]

Similarly, an Easter egg is a symbol of rebirth and renewal, partly because an egg literally houses new life but also partly because of its roundish shape – the endlessness of the edge of a sphere. The pretzel denotes a praying figure because of loops it makes that also could be made with a pencil. The churlish could complain that nothing especially "culinary" resides in these examples, and that their representational forms are simply derived from the repertoire of the objects of vision.

This objection indicates the need to extend recognition of the symbolic features of food yet further, to which task I shall turn momentarily. First, however, I acknowledge that much of the representational value of foods does indeed rely on information provided by other senses, particularly vision. To me this is not an indication of a poverty of symbolic possibility for food but an illustration of the unremarkable fact that the experience of eating involves more than one sense. We have already invited smell into the company of taste, fully considered, and texture as well, which makes use of the sense of touch. The crunch and slurp of food involves hearing (there are Japanese dishes for which audible slurping is prescribed), and the preparation of a table is carefully attuned to visual pleasure.

But more can be said by way of response, both for the fact that sometimes what is seen is also eaten and for the symbolic function of the taste sensation itself. The fact that when a croissant was eaten the defeated Ottomans were metaphorically consumed involves the medium of food intimately. The croissant is still a symbol relying on visual representation, though its edibility enters dramatically into the enactment of its meaning. Nonetheless, representation (both denotation and representation-as) is but one mode of symbol that food achieves. It is when we examine [the] concept of exemplification that the pervasiveness of the symbolic function of food is most clearly demonstrated.

EXEMPLIFICATION

Exemplification, the symbolic relation in which an object both possesses a property and refers to it, is possibly the most common symbol type that food offers, for virtually any food exemplifies. That is, it refers and calls attention to some of the properties of what is eaten, presenting them for special notice and assessment or enjoyment through direct experience. In fact, the gourmet exercising a discriminating palate is attending to the properties exemplified in food and drink. These are not simply qualities that the food happens to possess. The gourmet does not direct attention to incidental properties that do not represent the aspects of food that demand appreciation. She does not care, for example, about the weight of the sow that discovered the truffles on the plate; she cares only about the taste properties of the truffles themselves. If she cares about when they were gathered and where they were found, it is insofar as such facts account for exemplified properties of taste. Note that when the claim is put this way, it does not fall prey to the complaint that taste directs attention only to the subjective state of one's own body. Attention to exemplified properties is attention directed to the object of perception via the taste sensations that it is capable of delivering. . . . The symbolic relation of exemplification refers to qualities possessed by the object of experience. True, they are experienced in the mouth. But this is simply a signal that we are in the domain of taste.

Chicken soup, for example, possesses a variety of properties, such as flavor, saltiness, and a somewhat oily texture. The ingredients are more or less present in the final product, and the sipper of soup may attend to them appreciatively (perhaps while at the same time assuaging hunger or dosing a cold). The property of (say) a subdued hint of parsnip well cloaked by onion and dill is exemplified in the soup in much the same way that being in a minor key may be exemplified in music or being blue exemplified by certain Picasso paintings.

These aesthetic characteristics are taste's version of aesthetic savoring and are familiar under other descriptions. They are also the most frequent sorts of evaluations and encomia one encounters in food writing. Exemplification enfolds the sensuous elements of taste experience – the quality of flavor, the blends or conflicts of sensations, as well as the pleasures. Thus this particular symbolic function, inseparable from the felt qualities of sensation, recasts in other vocabulary the most common defense of the aesthetic experience of food, but makes clear that the relish and enjoyment is more than subjective delectation, though it is that as well.

Because food exemplifies a multitude of complex sensory relationships of different tastes, smells, and textures, any meal (perhaps excepting K-rations, astronaut food, and the airline snack) also possesses what Goodman terms relative repleteness – that condition in which "comparatively many aspects of a symbol are significant." "Relative repleteness" is just a way of stating that a large range of the properties available to the sense are relevant to its appreciative assessment. Interestingly, this term of the aesthetic, "repleteness," like "taste" itself, is also part of the gastronomic vocabulary.

These types of exemplified properties, all of which refer to the taste qualities to which attention is drawn, are familiar in terms of the savoring and enjoyment of eating. Exemplification extends further than taste experience per se, however, and enters into the kinds of meanings that we absorb so deeply from our cultural practice that they are often lost to conscious awareness. The sorts of foods we eat at different times of the day vary, and in fact certain kinds of foods come to "mean" the meal that they provide. Oatmeal conveys the meaning of breakfast, for example, in those cultures where cereals constitute a typical first meal of the day. Examination of this sort of meaning gives us more senses in which foods may exemplify.

Possibly the nearest relative to a cognitivist account of food has been articulated by structuralist anthropologists. They assume that human behavior falls into patterns or structures that are similar no matter what the task at hand, and that activities such as cooking and eating, and indeed choosing what is considered edible, make most sense when compared with other aspects of a society's activities and belief systems. In Claude Lévi-Strauss's famous trope, for example, "raw" and "cooked" are oppositions that are isomorphic with other binaries (such as nature–culture and male–female), which taken together illuminate the myths and social practices of vastly divergent societies.[9] Mary Douglas considers food as a "system of communication," and she speculates about how food might be understood as an art form.[10]

> If food is to be considered as an art form it would be necessary first to choose questions which could be asked equally well of other art forms, and then to identify an area of problems which are specific to the food medium. Having first distinguished what kind of art form food is amongst the others in that culture, it would then be right to ask how does the local food art compare with other food arts in other cultures.[11]

Considering eating practices in her home country, England, Douglas observes that because food has a practical function, nourishment, it is appropriately grouped with the applied arts such as clothing, architecture, and utensils, rather than with the fine arts of music, sculpture, and painting. (When food is for display, as we have already noted, Douglas classifies it more specifically as an applied decorative art.) Hence the aesthetic elements in foods are those that are distinct from nutrition and are "subject to pattern-making rules" just like the fine arts. The sensory qualities of food are a big part of its aesthetic aspect. Food can have its own distinctive patterns of acceptable textures, smells, tastes, and colors; or sometimes (as with representational foods) it borrows from the registers of other art forms. Appropriate qualities for foods may transfer from standards of social behavior: for example, smooth, refined foods for formal occasions (structurally similar to silks and satins) and rough-textured foods for informal gatherings (where denim or tweed may be worn). Eating practices are also heavily patterned by social relations and class: what people eat and when, as well as with whom, varies according to their job and economic status. Generally speaking, "if food is treated as a code, the messages it encodes will be found in the pattern of social relations being expressed. The message is about different degrees of hierarchy, inclusion and exclusion, boundaries and transactions across the boundaries."[12]

Not only can eating be analyzed according to the social patterns it manifests, single meals have their own structure as well. Which combinations of foods count as meals depend on their sequence, their mixture of liquids and solids, of meats and vegetables and starches, the utensils required for their consumption, and the time of their service. Little of these patterns is supplied by the biological need for nutrition; they are the result of accumulated traditions and practices that culminate in the recognition of certain foods as edible, as constituting meals, as tasting good. All these recognitions, exercised so routinely that they are rarely even present to awareness, demand complex "cognitive energy."[13]

Douglas's disclosure of the structures that order eating and the classification of foods is illuminating for several elements of the "meaning" of food. Particularly insightful are her discoveries about what is recognizable as edible and the isolation of "meals," as well as what we may call the social hierarchies present in eating habits: the kinds of foods eaten, who eats with whom, and so on. (One shares meals with friends and equals, for example.) The structures of eating reveal a good deal about large social patterns and are thus aptly descriptive of behavior. Often they are so inculcated in practice that they are not sufficiently obvious to consciousness to constitute an "experience" at all, but they may be brought into the focus of awareness with a little attention. Such implicit meanings may be understood as exemplified properties.

To wit: One wakes up in the morning and brews coffee. Toast, butter, and cereal complete this American-style breakfast. That the coffee is freshly ground and particularly savory, or that the toast is whole wheat rather than white this morning, may be the only exemplifications noticed by a sleepy eater. The other properties exemplified by this breakfast, however, are unnoticed only because they are habitual. Transport this person to Norway and serve him small silver fish and dark orange cheese redolent of goat, and he will surely take note of the fact that these foods do not "mean" breakfast to him. Not only are they not the types of foods he ordinarily encounters upon waking (a rather conservative time of ingestion) but they offer the kinds of tastes that seem more appropriate to lunchtime. Even more dramatic is the difference between cereal and the cooked rice dishes that he would be offered in China. Such national differences in what is eaten and when produce different exemplified properties, different "meanings" embodied in the foods. It is an obvious point, but the fact that tastes are always embedded in meanings is so often overlooked that the obvious is worth stating.

EXPRESSIVE FOODS

Exemplification has offered us two types of features of foods and their tastes: the particular properties that are savored and enjoyed in foods, which qualify conventionally as the aesthetic experience of taste according even to noncognitivist analyses; and the implicit properties that food acquires when it occupies a particular place in the rhythm of nourishment that is represented by mealtimes. We have not yet explored to any extent . . . expressive properties.

In these instances, the property possessed and referred to by the food is one that applies metaphorically. The example given earlier was the property "sinister" applied to an apple. Obviously, this is not a property that usually applies to apples, metaphorically or literally; in the context of the story of Snow White, an apple is sinister because it is poisoned and because it was malevolently prepared to bring about the death of Snow White. There are numerous cases in which expressive properties attach to foods because of the particular context of a story, but there are also more ordinary cases in which foods come to express certain properties because of the traditional or routine circumstances of their preparation.

Chicken soup, again, is a home remedy of sorts in a number of cultures. There may be some medical reason for this custom; the healthful reintroduction of salt and liquid into a body that is dehydrated from fever has been suggested. Such palliative features are not likely to be a part of the experience of the soup, however; more relevant for the expressive properties such as "soothing" and "comforting" that are exemplified by chicken soup is the very fact that it is a home remedy and *means* that one is being taken care of. The expression of care that soup exemplifies is supported by the literal properties that soup also has: a rich but not taxing flavor, ingredients that are easy to swallow, and so on. The expression of this kind of property by foods may be culturally dispersed, localized in smaller groups such as families, or even perhaps a product of the habits of individuals.

Sometimes the expressive potential of foods exploits what seem to be the natural disposition of some flavors to be liked or disliked. Sweet, as we have seen, is one of the basic flavors that all people like, whatever their differences in securing particular sweet substances. It comes as no surprise, therefore, to find that sweet foods are used in ritual ceremonies to signal prosperity or luck. At the Jewish New Year, for example, bread is dipped in honey to signal a promise of hope and prosperity for the coming year. During ritual meals Hindus offer something sweet to eat in honor of the gods. Salt is needed for survival; it is also a universally sought-after taste in moderation, as physiological studies have demonstrated. Recognition of the significance of salt is formalized in the hospitality practices of several cultures. According to traditional code, one who breaks bread and shares salt with a Bedouin thereby achieves that person's protection, a custom that has also entered into literary tradition and into the expression "to share the salt with" or to "break bread with" in English. One word for hospitality in Russian means literally "bread-salt."[14] Conversely, the Weyewa of Indonesia may quietly rebuke one who violates the social code by offering him nuts of particular bitterness.[15] Such examples confirm a certain common expressive quality recognized in the basic tastes reviewed in the last chapter, which seem to lend themselves to being considered natural symbols when deliberately employed as flavors of food and drink.

The potential for even a simple, basic flavor to convey complex propositional understanding is illustrated at some length by an old English fairy tale, which shows us something of the direct, intimate force of understanding possible by means of the sense of taste. The title of the story is the nickname of its heroine, "Caporushes." It tells of a rich man who demanded professions of love from his three daughters. "I love you as I love my life" was the satisfactory answer of the first. "Better than all the world beside," said the second, and was also approved. The youngest (and of course the prettiest) daughter avoided clichés and described her love thoughtfully with a humble kitchen comparison: "I love you as fresh meat loves salt!" she said. Believing himself slighted, the father banished her from his household. The girl wandered until she came to a fen; then, fearing robbers, she wove herself a concealing cloak and hat of rushes to cover her rich dress and jeweled hair. So disguised, she took up an anonymous life as a scullery maid in the house of a neighboring noble. Some time later the son and heir of the manor fell in love with the beautiful scullery girl, and they became betrothed. Her father, grief-stricken and now blind, was invited to the wedding feast. Knowing he would be present, the bride ordered no salt to be used in preparation of the meal. As the story is told:

> Now when the company sate down to table their faces were full of smiles and content, for all the dishes looked so nice and tasty; but no sooner had the guests begun to eat than their faces fell; for nothing can be tasty without salt.
>
> Then Caporushes' blind father, whom his daughter had seated next to her, burst out crying.
>
> "What is the matter?" she asked.
>
> Then the old man sobbed, "I had a daughter whom I loved dearly, dearly. And I asked her how much she loved me, and she replied, 'As fresh meat loves salt.' And I was angry with her and turned her out of house and home, for I thought she didn't love me at all. But now I see she loved me best of all."

And then – for it is a fairy story – "as he said the words his eyes were opened, and there beside him was his daughter lovelier than ever."[16]

This simple story illuminates several features of a discovery of a "truth" through immediate sense experience. Both literally and figuratively, the father is made to "see" his daughter's love through the taste of unseasoned meat. Moreover, what he comes to see or know through the exercise of the sense of taste is clearly an instance of propositional knowledge (that his daughter loved him and captured that love with reference to meat and salt). At the same time, what he discovers qualifies as a more or less commonplace truth, an obvious insight demanding little cogitation. The reader has had no difficulty from the start in recognizing the declaration of love in the words of the youngest daughter; the reader does not require the taste of the meat to know the meaning of her words. Everyone knows that food is more tasty with salt. What delivers the particular revelation to this sad father?

The circumstances of the wedding feast provide a context for his discovery. There is a wedding, an occasion for celebration; yet there is also grief and remorse over a lost, beloved child. We assume that the father has dwelt upon her words and his harsh response repeatedly. The sudden, unexpected, unmistakable *taste* of unseasoned meat brings home the pain of her rejected declaration of love. He *knows* viscerally, intimately, literally at a "gut level" that she loved him and that he cast her out unjustly. The sequence of events in the story and the particular position of the father focus the sense quality of saltless meat and its meaning in a discovery, an epiphany: *This* was her profession of love; *this* was my loss.

Philosophers have long struggled to reconcile two apparently opposing insights about aesthetic apprehension, especially when the object of attention is a work of art: On the one hand, art seems to afford unique, particular, and indispensable insights about life and experience. Yet on the other hand, when one is pressed to say just what a particular work of art "says," the reply is often something close to a truism. This tale helps us to see how both insights are reconcilable. It is significant that the father became blind after he banished his daughter, a signal of his stubborn refusal to recognize her love, even of his limited understanding of language, for he was expecting a more lofty statement and was not flexible enough to recognize the originality and force of her words. Through the revelation afforded him by taste, he gains wisdom, happiness, and vision both literal and figurative. He had not only to know her love "intellectually," as it were, but to *feel* the force of it. The power of the sensory experience of saltless meat can be delivered *only* through this "subjective" route: apprehending with one's whole being – mind and body – what before was recognized only intellectually. This is the force of "aesthetic" apprehension: that some truth or realization or discovery is delivered in a way that touches one intimately, that focuses and concentrates insight with the poignant immediacy of the blind father's taste of saltless meat. (So read, this little story confirms the reason taste was considered so suitable as a metaphor for aesthetic experience.) . . .

CEREMONIES AND RITUALS

The cognitive significance of food is an effect of reference, representation, expression, exemplification, and the social conditions of its preparation and serving. Not all eating has much significance, but any ceremonial meal possesses it in abundance. Virtually all cultures and religions practice ceremonial eating, and so again a few examples must suffice to demonstrate the symbolic functioning of this kind of activity.

Festival meals can be analyzed by considering their individual components, their social context, and the fact of the meal as a whole. In the United States the fall holiday of Thanksgiving supposedly reenacts and thereby refers to the survival of an early European settlement through the harsh Massachusetts winter of 1621, during which time they would have starved without the good offices of the local Indians. This allusion to a happy relationship between peoples who were often at odds is vague and romantic, and the cynical might call this a case of fictional representation rather than denotation. Nonetheless, the reference to this historical event, whatever its actual character may have been, is important and makes the entire dinner itself representational. In keeping with the idea that the meal commemorates fellowship and community, it is ideally a large dinner among family and friends. There is a limited menu that recreates what is popularly believed to be the first Thanksgiving feast, including turkey and root vegetables. The food is hot, savory, and heavy – the kind of slowly digested sustenance that ushers in cold months. Literal exemplified properties such as warmth, flavor, texture, and weight contribute to the metaphoric exemplified properties of comfort, well-being, and plenty. In commoner parlance, the meal has a languid, comforting quality that is exaggerated by the habit of putting too much on the table and inducing torpor. The menu relies very much on tradition; innovation is frowned upon. There must be a turkey with stuffing and cranberry sauce, gravy, and several pies, including pumpkin or sweet potato, harvest vegetables not ordinarily associated with dessert at other times of the year. The choice of green vegetables, breads, and additional foods is optional, but without the core turkey the meal is unrecognizable as Thanksgiving. The selection of foods is so prescribed by tradition that many are prepared only at this time.

With the Thanksgiving meal, as with many ritual occasions, the conservative combination of foods indicates the degree to which it is the entire meal itself that acts as a symbol. The various dishes contribute to the expressive quality of the whole, and some of them also refer to events of the first Thanksgiving (the turkey to a bird native to the North American woods, the squash and other root vegetables to seasonal fare and approaching winter, cranberries to a food uniquely available to the region in colonial America). Their seasonal position is experienced as part of the experience of eating, which imparts awareness of a particular time of year. The fact that seasonal festivals are repeated is a critical part of the experience of eating. One is aware of oneself participating yet again in a cyclical celebration, one that is never quite the same as festivals of time past yet retains an enduring identity over time.[17] This is an indispensable element of all rituals, that they occur over and over, that the diner takes his or her place among others participating in similar rituals of dinner; that one time is ending and another beginning. Possibly one reason why sometimes foods taste good only during their relevant festivals is that their meaning is so restricted to that time.

Another festival meal illustrates even more legislated symbolic functions for foods. The Jewish Passover seder commemorates the exodus of the Jews from captivity in Egypt, and by extension the freedom of all peoples from slavery. A religious ritual meal such as this is rich with symbolic relations manifest not only in the visual presentation of foods but also in their very tastes. In the center of the table is the seder plate, and on it are placed six foods that are part of the ceremony that opens and closes the meal: the roasted shank bone of a lamb, a roasted egg, bitter herbs, *charoses* (a mixture of ground nuts, honey, and apples), parsley or chervil, and a dish of salt water. The bitter herbs signify bondage and sorrow in Egypt. This symbolic value does not depend on visual properties; the herbs metaphorically exemplify sorrow by means of their sharp taste. The small bowl of salt water denotes (and indeed chemically replicates) the tears shed in captivity, and the parsley, indicating the renewal of spring, is dipped in the salt water and eaten. The *charoses* symbolizes with its texture the mortar the Jews used in building temples for the Egyptians, and it is eaten in combination with the bitter herbs (which may be horseradish or a sharp-tasting green herb). The egg stands for renewal of life, and the shank bone for the Paschal lamb eaten in commemoration of the passover itself, the fact that God passed over the houses of the Jews and slew the firstborn of the Egyptian captors.

No risen bread is eaten during the ten days of Passover observance, in commemoration for the flight from Egypt, which necessitated taking bread from ovens before it had time to rise. The matzoh that signifies this aspect of the exodus exemplifies the properties of unleavened bread, as opposed to merely possessing the properties, as any cracker may do. It also metaphorically exemplifies or expresses haste and urgency, and by all these means it commemorates the biblical event and its continued significance.

Some ritual foods of the seder plate are present and tasted but not actually consumed. The lamb shank bone simply sits on the plate and is raised and replaced during the ceremony. Salt water has emetic properties and cannot be more than tasted. Thus many foods with important symbolic functions are not actually to be eaten, in the sense that their role is not one of nourishment or of sensory enjoyment and delectation. Nevertheless they not only are part of the meal, they also have a significance that is manifest in the act of tasting. Passover also has standard foods that are eaten chiefly at that time, as does Thanksgiving. (Because it is a much older and more dispersed festival – many centuries old and celebrated all over the world – local customs for choice of those foods vary.) And as with many religious practices, there are also prescribed means of preparing foods, some of which alter their taste from the way they would be experienced at other seasons. (Matzoh flour, for example, must be substituted in any recipe that otherwise would call for wheat flour.) The regional differences in the enactment of the Passover seder, including the different foods considered traditional, do not disturb the identity of the ceremony.

The profound importance of foods that are not actually to be eaten as part of a meal is also illustrated by the Christian sacrament of the Eucharist.[18] This is the liturgical rendering of the Passover seder Christ held with his disciples, though the meaning of the substances and what is considered "tasting" and "eating" have altered with the change of religious belief and the circumstances in which the foods are encountered. The wafer and wine of Communion denote the body and blood of Christ. If one subscribes to the doctrine of transubstantiation, they actually become those substances, in which case the body and blood are literally re-presented: present again to the congregation. The Communion bread and wine metaphorically exemplify or express the events foreshadowed by the Last Supper – the agony in the garden of Gethsemene, the crucifixion, and the resurrection. These instances of bread and wine are both food and not food. They are tasted and swallowed, but not for nourishment. The tastes of the bread and when permitted of the wine – for not all churches allow the laity to drink of the blood of Christ – occasion reflection of the profoundest sort. The fact that the sacrament is actually taken into the body indicates the most direct participation in the mystical reenactment of God's sacrifice, one that the exercise of any sense other than taste might not render so intimate.

Not only eating but also its opposite should be considered as part of the ritual meanings of foods, for fasts as well as feasts are observances of many religions, such as Lent, Ramadan, Yom Kippur. When expedient, fasting may be incorporated into the religious practices of daily life, as with the Ethiopian church that demands one fast day a week – not only penance and self-discipline, perhaps, but prudent rationing of food resources in a country where food distribution is difficult.[19] Periods when one should neither exercise the sense of taste nor nourish the body are significant; they nourish the soul, for the assumption is that the body's comfort is a hindrance to probing reflections of the spirit. In this way the very hierarchy of the senses is incorporated into the rhythms and meanings of eating practices.

These examples indicate that the customs and beliefs of the ambient culture contribute to the meanings of foods, and reciprocally foods themselves contribute to the defining characteristics of a culture. The tea ceremony of Japan is a practice of Zen Buddhism and manifests (exemplifies) the values of that philosophy. It involves far more than just drinking tea, for the ceremony is a staged event that prescribes ideal qualities for the physical surroundings and for the utensils to be used. It invites engagement with all the senses and fosters meditation on the meaning of the experience. D.T. Suzuki describes the art of tea drinking in terms of the Zen value of simplicity. The hut for the ceremony is spare, nestled in a spot chosen for vegetation, view, water, wind. The preparation of the tea is unhurried; the tastes are delicate, indeed all the sensations surrounding the event are soft and harmonious. Here is Zen Master Takuan's description of a tea ceremony:

> Let us then construct a small room in a bamboo grove or under trees, arrange streams and rocks and plant trees and bushes, while [inside the room] let us pile up charcoal, set a kettle, arrange flowers, and arrange in order the necessary tea utensils. And let all this be carried out in accordance with the idea that in this room we can enjoy the streams and rocks as we do the rivers and mountains in Nature, and appreciate the various moods and sentiments suggested by the snow, the moon, and the trees and flowers, as they go through the transformation of seasons,

appearing and disappearing, blooming and withering. As visitors are greeted here with due reverence, we listen quietly to the boiling water in the kettle, which sounds like a breeze passing through the pine needles, and become oblivious of all worldly woes and worries.[20]

The meaning of tea in this setting – its simplicity, its harmony, its conduciveness to mental clarity and awareness of the flow of life – indicates that the taste and other experiences afforded through this ceremony should be inflected and guided by a suitable and informed philosophic attitude. Indeed, simply tasting the tea alone would be an impoverished experience. It would lack the meaning, the significance, of tea. The tea itself may be said to exemplify some of these properties, for the quality of the liquid and of its service draw attention to the delicacy and subtlety of its flavor. Like any of the single dishes served at the festival meals mentioned above, however, it is a part of a complex whole and its meaning emerges from the entire event and the philosophical tradition it embodies and perpetuates.

FOOD AND ART COMPARED

I have been presenting the case for the similarity of foods with works of art by demonstrating how . . . certain symbolic functions seem to be enacted by foods in much the same way that they are by works of art. . . . Ought we now to take the next step and conclude that foods also qualify as works of art in the full sense of the term? That they represent in their own medium the same sorts of objects as paintings, sculptures, poems, and symphonies? I do not believe we should. For one thing, the concept of art, dominated as it is today by the idea of *fine* art, is a poor category to capture the nature of foods and their consumption. While one earns a bit of stature for food by advancing it as an art form, the endeavor is apt to divert attention from the interesting ways in which the aesthetic importance of foods diverges from parallel values in art. Much of my argument has been devoted to correcting misunderstandings about the sense of taste and to defending the theoretical significance of food, but the discontinuities between meals and art should not be gainsaid. How ought we to characterize these dissimilarities without at the same time losing sight of the important similarities between foods and arts?

We may begin by considering again a possible objection to aesthetic meanings for foods that I have flagged from time to time: foods seem to be heavily dependent on either ceremonial context or personal or cultural narrative to attain their cognitive and aesthetic significance. The symbolic functions of food of the wider variety – those that involve expression and denotation in particular – seem to require a place in some cultural practice in order to come into being. Consequently, one may suspect that it is not the food itself that has meaning. Without its placement on the appropriate Thursday in

November, for instance, Thanksgiving is just another heavy meal; the food alone does not express the festival.[21] Without the surrounding story and the history of ritual, the individual items on the Passover table are just things to eat; without the tradition of Zen philosophy, displayed equally in the setting, the utensils, and the surroundings of the ceremony, the cup of tea is only a cup of tea. In short, foods and their tastes appear to depend inordinately on defining context if they are to achieve the cognitive significance that I am claiming underwrites their aesthetic standing.

Of course, one could grant this point and retreat to just one symbolic function, exemplification, as the basis for the aesthetic import of foods. Foods that are presented for the delight of the palate can be understood to exemplify their tastes. Yet it would be a sacrifice of richness and breadth for the significance of foods if this were the only grounds on which it could be aesthetically justified. It would be another way of claiming that well-prepared food tastes really good – and we knew that already. Therefore this suspicion regarding context dependence is to be taken seriously. Rather than constituting a brief against the cognitive and aesthetic dimensions of tastes and foods, however, these considerations illuminate two important discontinuities between foods and fine arts: the aesthetic functions of food exceed the qualities of the food itself, and food and art do not have parallel histories and traditions.

Consider the disparaging contrast one artist was moved to make between food and art. The composer Hector Berlioz was an acerbic critic of the music of his day, and on his travels in Italy he complained that the audiences of Milan were so boisterous and inattentive to the operas performed that one could hardly hear the music. In his *Memoirs* of 1832 he recorded this gripe: "To the Italians music is a sensual pleasure, and nothing more. For this most beautiful form of expression they have scarcely more respect than for the culinary art. They like music which they can assimilate at a first hearing, without reflection or attention, just as they would do with a plate of macaroni."[22]

One may have a higher opinion of both Italian opera and pasta and still acknowledge that Berlioz's complaint expresses an insight about the difference between eating and encountering art. It is not, however, that eating never provokes "reflection and attention," as he surmises. I hope that the examples of ritual and ceremonial eating and the complex situations in which foods and tastes exemplify metaphorical properties lay to rest the idea that tasting and eating are to be appreciated only for sensuous enjoyment. The uses of foods and drink for religious and commemorative purposes clearly foster, even force, reflection on the meaning of the event taking place, its location in culture and history, and its personal emotional import. Unlike music or other fine art, however, this sort of reflection – important as it is – is not a mark of greatness for food *as food*. Berlioz might complain about the quality of Italian comic opera, and his objection to the shallow fare served up by the composers of that genre – the fact that they appeal to the ear more than to the heart or mind – would be at the same time a complaint about the quality of the music, about whether it merits being considered "great art." By contrast, many of the symbolic features of food may be fully present in food that is not particularly tasty but still serves the significant function of being part of a ceremonial event. To be sure, this is not the case for all aspects of taste and of food. For food to be "great" *as food*, its sensuous exemplified properties – those delivered for particular attention to the thoughtful diner – need to be especially fine. But it may represent, express, and otherwise signify without being haute cuisine; without, in other words, being particularly fine insofar as the "culinary art" is considered.

This feature of food is connected to the observation that foods require extended context to achieve their denotative and expressive meanings, that the items to eat *by themselves* do not always manage to carry their ritual or traditional or cultural significance. In certain cases meaning may become so attached to particular items that they indeed do stand alone by virtue of unique association. But in most instances fuller context is required for the foods to possess their symbolic functions. The reason is both very complex and rather obvious, though it tends to be obscured by the tendency to compare works of art to items of food on a case-by-case basis: the history of art and the history of food are not parallel. Thus what art has come to be and what food has come to be in our contemporary culture are not the same. This observation could lead to some intricate historical investigation, but I shall invoke only one fairly evident distinction: In the Western tradition there has developed a concept of *fine* art that is held to contrast to craft or to applied or decorative arts. Moreover, within the tradition of fine art, we also have the recent and still powerful legacy of the idea that aesthetic value is autonomous and intrinsic, that art is valuable for its own sake alone. The influence of this historical shift on the concept of art and on aesthetics has led us to consider the various cognitive and aesthetic qualities of works of art to inhere in the works themselves, free of surrounding context. Foods have no such history. Their aesthetic qualities emerge from practice and are embedded in the festivals and ceremonies and occasions in which they take on their fullest meanings. To try to compare a single meal or individual food with any given work of art is to yank that item from its context and impoverish its aesthetic import. It directs attention only to its exemplified qualities, and not even to all of those: the ones that remain to be relished free from ceremonial practices are just those *sensuous* exemplified qualities – the savor of the tastes themselves – that for all their undeniable pleasures do not fill the terrain of deeper aesthetic significance that foods display in their practical contexts, including ritual, ceremony, and commemoration. On its own food is assessed only for a relatively narrow band of exemplified properties; art is assessed for all symbolic functions.

Thus despite the similarities between food, drink, and artworks in terms of their cognitive significance and related aesthetic dimensions, there is a lack of symmetry between the features of foods that are comparable to central aesthetic features of art and the measure of the quality of the individual objects under assessment. This is probably why those who have advanced briefs on behalf of both the aesthetic and the artistic significance of foods have fallen short of being able to assert their full status as works of art. Either food is denied the status altogether while being granted aesthetic value, as Prall argues, or foods are recognized as permitting a certain degree of artistic achievement but are relegated to a minor art form, as Telfer, Douglas, and perhaps even Revel maintain. I believe that insofar as they carry the same sort of aesthetic significance, understood as constituting a cognitive dimension in the sort of way that Goodman accommodates, food and drink merit aesthetic standing, and at the same time serve many of the same symbolic functions as do works of fine art. However, the latter role, which I believe makes foods deeply important and not just sensuously delightful, is not always paramount when the quality of cuisine is being evaluated. In this instance, the sensuous enjoyment of eating and drinking often legitimately takes the foreground, and the other symbolic functions of foods (expressive, representational, and so on) recede – unless, of course, fine cuisine is also a part of a ceremony, ritual, or commemoration. Even when the fare is scanty or poor and the sensuous enjoyment thereby lessened, however, the other symbolic functions of foods may still be of such importance that the festival, practice, or ritual of which eating is a component is in no way diminished.

So is food an art form? This does not seem to me to be the crucial question, though the commonalities between food and art are centrally significant for understanding what food is in its own right. Certainly food does not qualify as a fine art; it does not have the right history, to make a complex point in shorthand. Culinary art can still be considered a minor or a decorative art, or perhaps a functional or applied art (for we should not minimize the fact that eating is a daily aspect of living in the most literal sense of that term). The reasons advanced by Telfer, Revel, and Douglas are sufficient to support in this sense the artistic achievement of fine cooking, distilling, and winemaking. However, this warrant for the label "art" is not the most important link between food and art. It is much more significant that both form symbolic systems with similar components, though those components are not symmetrically related to the merits of the created products. The fine achievements of the cook, the winemaker, and others who prepare what we ingest are sometimes but not invariably a part of the most important aesthetic experiences of eating and drinking. These achievements need to be understood in related and overlapping ways, but ways that also acknowledge and preserve the distinctive roles that foods, tastes, and eating may assume.

Moreover, though I have disputed the dismissal of taste as a low, bodily sense from the beginning, my purpose has been not to elevate taste to the status of the distal senses but rather to point out the ways in which taste invites philosophical interest. Some portion of that interest is in the ranking of the senses itself, for the bodily element of the experience of eating has its own significance that contributes to the asymmetry between foods and fine art forms. It is not only that so many of the exemplified properties savored in food are sensuous (which is to say it tastes good). An important part of eating, drinking, and tasting is precisely that they signify the bodily, the mortal part of existence. There is only a superficial irony in this claim: part of the importance of food, eating, and awareness of tasting, swallowing, digesting is that they do direct attention to the supposedly "lower" aspect of being human – the fact that we are animal and mortal. Eating is and must be rooted in a relentless routine of hunger, swallowing, satiety, and hunger again. No wonder sometimes we do not have the time for aesthetic attention to this demand. The significance of eating is ineluctably bodily, and the constancy of the rhythms of eating remind us of the transience of the activity. (In Hegel's words, "we can smell only what is in the process of wasting away, and we can taste only by destroying.")[23] Despite the fact that tasting and eating provide fully aesthetic cognition, I do not want to try to level the senses or their objects in such a way that the traditions that rank the senses disappear altogether. It will be more illuminating to probe the meanings assigned to foods and to eating, including aspects of what may appear at first to be their negative valence. This needs to be acknowledged so that the different reflections prompted by food and by tasting and eating may be rightly understood. The inescapable cycle of hunger and eating is in a sense commemorated by the fragility of food itself, which melts, collapses, is eaten and digested, rots, molds, and decays. Because eating is a repetitive and transient experience, because food does not last but spoils, because it not only nourishes but poisons, eating is a small exercise in mortality. Rather than transcend time, as romantic ideas of art suggest is the goal of masterworks, food succumbs to time – as do we ourselves. This perhaps is the final reflection that tasting prompts: not just that it is pleasurable but that it fades so quickly.

NOTES

1 See also Carolyn Korsmeyer, "On the aesthetic senses and the origin of fine art," *Journal of Aesthetics and Art Criticism* 34(1) (Fall 1975).
2 See above, p. 25.
3 See above, p. 26.
4 Frank Sibley, "Tastes and smells and aesthetics," unpublished manuscript.
5 Mary Douglas, "Food as an art form," in *In the Active Voice* (London: Routledge & Kegan Paul, 1982), p. 107.
6 Martin Elkort, *The Secret Life of Food* (Los Angeles: Jeremy P. Tarcher, 1991), p. 100.
7 *The Village Cookbook* (Scarsdale, NY, 1948) p. 325.
8 Kevin Sweeney raised this point to me.
9 Claude Lévi-Strauss, *The Raw and the Cooked*, trans. John and Doreen Weightman (New York: Harper & Row, 1969). Lévi-Strauss is widely criticized among anthropologists – including those who share a structuralist approach, such as Mary Douglas – for imposing too rigid a structure of analysis on the phenomena under question.
10 Douglas, *In the Active Voice*, pp. 85–7. This "system" is closely connected to the social systems of rest, health and body care, clothing, and family. Ultimately, the patterns revealed in a study of such systems are heavily influenced by social power relations.
11 Ibid., p. 106.

12 Mary Douglas, "Deciphering a meal," *Daedalus* (Winter 1972): 61; reprinted in Douglas, *Implicit Meanings* (London: Routledge & Kegan Paul, 1975).

13 "Each meal carries something of the meaning of the other meals; each meal is a structured social event which structures others in its own image. The upper limit of its meaning is set by the range incorporated in the most important member of its series. The recognition which allows each member to be classed and graded with the others depends upon the structure common to them all. The cognitive energy which demands that a meal look like a meal and not like a drink is performing in the culinary medium the same exercise that it performs in language. First, it distinguishes order, bounds it, and separates it from disorder. Second, it uses economy in the means of expression by allowing only a limited number of structures. Third, it imposes a rank scale upon the repetition of structures. Fourth, the repeated formal analogies multiply the meanings that are carried down any one of them by the power of the most weighty." (Ibid., pp. 69–70.)

14 Leonard R. Kass discusses this and other aspects of hospitality in food practices in *The Hungry Soul* (New York: Free Press, 1994), pp. 111–27.

15 Joel C. Kuipers, "Matters of taste in Weyewa," in *The Varieties of Sensory Experience*, ed. David Howes (Toronto: University of Toronto Press, 1991), pp. 111–27.

16 *English Fairy Tales*, retold by Flora Annie Steel (New York: Macmillam, 1918), p. 308.

17 For observation on the nature of festivals and their continuity with art, see Hans-Georg Gadamer, *Truth and Method* (1960), trans. Joel Weinsheimer and Donald G. Marshall (New York: Continuum, 1994), pp. 122–3.

18 On the Eucharist, see Louis Marin, *Food for Thought*, trans. Mette Hjort (Baltimore: Johns Hopkins University Press, 1989), pp. 120–4.

19 This observation was suggested to me by Tereffe Asrat.

20 Takuan (1573–1645) quoted in D.T. Suzuki, *Zen and Japanese Culture* (Princeton: Princeton University Press, 1970), pp. 275–6.

21 As Barbara Salazar pointed out to me, festival timing is not open to arbitrary manipulation. During World War II President Roosevelt moved Thanksgiving up a week or two, to nationwide outrage. It was moved back as soon as the war was over.

22 Hector Berlioz, *Memoirs of Hector Berlioz from 1803 to 1865*, trans. Rachel Holmes and Eleanor Holmes, rev. Ernest Newman (New York: Tudor, 1935), p. 183.

23 G.W.F. Hegel, *Aesthetics: Lectures on Fine Art*, trans. T.M. Knox, 2 vols. (Oxford: Clarendon, 1975), 1:138.

SUGGESTIONS FOR FURTHER READING

Beardsley, M.C. (1981) *Aesthetics: Problems in the Philosophy of Criticism*, 2nd edn, Indianapolis: Hackett Publishing Company, Inc.

Brillat-Savarin, Jean-Anthelme (1970) *La Physiologie du goût*, trans. Anne Drayton as *The Philosopher in the Kitchen*, Harmondsworth: Penguin Books.

Curtin, Deane W. and Heldke, Lisa M. (eds) (1992) *Cooking, Eating, Thinking: Transformative Philosophies of Food*, Bloomington and Indianapolis: Indiana University Press.

Davies, Stephen (1991) *Definitions of Art*, Ithaca and London: Cornell University Press.

Fretter, William B. (1971) "Is wine an art object?", *Journal of Aesthetics and Art Criticism* 30: 97–100.

Goodman, Nelson (1976) *Languages of Art*, 2nd edn, Indianapolis: Hackett Publishing Company, Inc.

—— (1988) "How buildings mean", in Nelson Goodman and Catherine Z. Elgin, *Reconceptions in Philosophy and Other Arts and Sciences*, Indianapolis: Hackett Publishing Company, Inc.

Gurney, Edmund (1880) *The Power of Sound*, London: Smith, Elder and Co.

Korsmeyer, Carolyn (1999) *Making Sense of Taste: Food and Philosophy*, Ithaca and London: Cornell University Press.

Mainardi, Patricia (1973) "Quilts: the great American art", *Feminist Art Journal* 2(1): 1, 18–23. (Reprinted under the same title in an enlarged illustrated edition by Miles and Weir Ltd., San Pedro, Cal., 1978.)

Prall, D.W. (1929) *Aesthetic Judgment*, New York: Crowell. (See especially pp. 57–75, reprinted as "The elements of aesthetic surface in general", in Eliseo Vivas and Murray Krieger (eds) *The Problems of Aesthetics*, New York and Toronto: Rinehart & Co., 1958.)

Quinet, Marienne L. (1981) "Food as art: the problem of function", *British Journal of Aesthetics* 21(2): 159–71.

Telfer, Elizabeth (1996) *Food for Thought: Philosophy and Food*, London: Routledge.

Urmson, J.O. (1962) "What makes a situation aesthetic?", in Joseph Margolis (ed.) *Philosophy Looks at the Arts*, New York: Charles Scribner's Sons.

Visser, Margaret (1989) *Much Depends on Dinner*, Harmondsworth: Penguin Books.

Whittick, Arnold (1984) "Towards precise distinctions of art and craft", *British Journal of Aesthetics* 24, 1: 47–52.

Anyone interested in this topic should also read some good writing *about* food, cooking, and eating: for example, anything by M.F.K. Fisher, or Elizabeth David, or Jane Grigson, to name just three of the very best.

Part 2

THE "AUTHENTIC" PERFORMANCE OF MUSIC

Please request Herr von Seyfried to conduct my opera today; I myself want to see and hear it at a distance; by that means, at any rate, my patience will not be so severely tried, as when close by I hear my music murdered. I cannot help thinking that it is done purposely.

Ludwig van Beethoven, in a letter to Meyer

Beethoven's Violin Concerto is a lesson in the correct attitude of a composer towards a player. It was written for a virtuoso of the name of Clement, and is inscribed to him with a vile pun on his "clemency" towards the poor composer. The score assigns four staves to the violin solo, in order to leave room for alterations; and in many places all the four staves have been filled. The violinist whose criticism Beethoven took so much pains to meet produced (or, as he called it, "created") the concerto under conditions of his own making that were not considered unusual in those days. The first movement was played in the first part of the programme, the slow movement and the finale in the second part. Among the items which took place between these divisions was a sonata of Clement's own composing, to be played on one string with the violin upside down. Clement survived this performance for many years.

Donald Francis Tovey, *Concertos and Choral Works*, pp. 70–1

MUCH OF THE MUSIC THAT WE know today was composed during periods when the instruments available were very different from those we have grown used to since. The modern grand piano, for instance, with its steel strings and its sturdy iron frame, only came into existence in the last century. Mozart's and Beethoven's "piano" music was composed with the forte-piano in mind – a light-stringed, wood-framed instrument, with a distinctive light sound all its own. All of the main kinds of instrument have undergone major evolutionary changes, and these changes have brought in their train successively different approaches to the interpretation of earlier music.

What we hear when we listen to a Mozart piano concerto, then, performed on a modern piano and with modern orchestral instruments, is quite different from what we would have heard had we attended a concert given by Mozart himself, a little more than two centuries ago. The sound is different; and the style of performance is different. Recently, many musicians have attempted to give performances of old music on historically appropriate instruments, played in historically appropriate ways. These musicians – advocates of "authentic" performance practices – try to let us hear in the music of earlier ages something that more closely resembles the sounds which were originally conceived.

By themselves, of course, such efforts might represent no more than exercises in archaeological reconstruction: attempts to understand how, as a matter of fact, things were done. But combined, as they frequently are, with the evaluative claim that "authentic" performances are in some way *preferable* to "inauthentic" ones, these efforts raise a variety of important philosophical questions. For example, what precisely must a performance be like if it is to count as "authentic"? Must it be identical to some earlier performance, perhaps one approved by the composer? Must it be a performance which allows the work to be experienced in a way similar to that in which the composer's contemporaries might have experienced it? If we can answer these questions, and so decide what we *mean* by "authentic" performance, a further question arises. Do such performances have *aesthetic* advantages not possessed by "inauthentic" performances – and if so, which aesthetic advantages, and why?

Stephen Davies, in the first chapter in this part, is a determined defender of authentic performance practices. For Davies, authenticity represents an *ideal* to be aimed at, rather than an attempt to reproduce any *actual* past performance. So for instance, an authentic performance does not necessarily attempt to recreate a performance witnessed and approved by the composer or by his contemporaries. James O. Young takes a very different view, arguing that authentic performance does not even represent an ideal: if musicians wedded to the ideal of authenticity have enriched our musical experience, he says, then they have done so "not by giving authentic performances but by giving successful ones".

The controversy here is a rich one. On the face of it, the suggestion that we should perform music of the past in certain historically appropriate ways might seem unproblematic. But it turns out to be difficult to say just what is meant by "historically appropriate", and no easier to explain what the aesthetic justification for seeking such appropriateness might be. It might be suggested that aesthetic benefits arise from faithfulness to the intentions of the composer – that aesthetically successful performances are performances which do justice to what the composer *wanted*. But there are difficulties involved in this suggestion. For one thing, we often don't know what a composer did want. And for another thing, some composers may have wanted perverse or unrealizable things.

These are intriguing questions – and not only to those who are concerned with classical music. Paul Simon conceived *Bridge Over Troubled Water*, for example, with the voice of Art Garfunkel in mind. Does this mean that Simon's ballad is only "authentically" performed when Garfunkel sings it? Again, consider theatre. The kinds of performance which are given today of Shakespeare's plays are very different from those which could have been witnessed by his contemporaries, and sometimes they are performed as a kind of political or social commentary on questions important to us today, but which could not have been asked by an audience of the late sixteenth century. Questions of authenticity are as pressing here as they are with respect to the performance of classical music.

4

AUTHENTICITY IN MUSICAL PERFORMANCE

Stephen Davies

In this paper I discuss musical performances and their authenticity with respect to the independently identifiable musical pieces of which they are performances.[1] I intend my account to be descriptive rather than prescriptive (but I appreciate that, where intuitions clash, it is the location of the border between description and prescription which is at issue).

The adjective "authentic" has a number of meanings which no doubt are related. But I am not here interested in the unity of the concept, nor with the relative primacy of these different meanings. Nor shall I discuss one familiar notion of musical authenticity – that in which a performance is authentic with respect to a style or *genre*. My limited interest is in the authenticity of musical performances *as* performances of particular compositions (which are independently identified with event-specifications which, in the case of the Western cultural tradition on which I shall concentrate, take the form of musical scores). That is, if I talk of the authenticity of a performance of Beethoven's Fifth Symphony, I am interested in its authenticity as a member of the class of performances recognizable as performances of Beethoven's Fifth Symphony and not with it as a member of other classes of performances to which it may also belong, such as nineteenth-century symphony.

The view for which I argue characterizes authenticity in musical performance as follows: a performance which aims to realize the composer's score faithfully in sound may be judged for authenticity. A performance of X is more rather than less authentic the more faithful it is to the intentions publicly expressed in the score by the composer (where those intentions are determinative and not merely recommendatory of performance practice). Because the composer's score under-determines the sound of a faithful performance, the authenticity of any particular performance is judged against (the appropriate member/s of) a set of ideally faithful performances. As a commendatory term "authentic" is used to acknowledge the creative role of the performer in realizing faithfully the composer's specifications.

STEPHEN DAVIES

The paper is divided into six sections. The first four sections concentrate on the aim of faithfulness in securing authenticity; as well as an attempt to define authenticity these sections contain a characterization of what is involved in faithfully realizing a composer's intentions. In the penultimate section I discuss why authenticity in musical performance is value-conferring. In the final section I emphasize the creative nature of the performer's role.

I

In this first section I argue that the pursuit of authenticity involves the attempt to produce musical *sounds* as opposed to the social *milieu* within which those sounds originally were created.

Over the past fifty years there has been a growing interest in authenticity in musical performance. The same period also has seen a developing interest in the performance of pre-modern music. These parallel developments probably are related. Where modern music is written for modern instruments and notated in the standard fashion, a high degree of authenticity will be achieved in performance by a competent musician. But the more foreign the styles of performance and the more unfamiliar the instruments employed, the harder will it be for musicians to produce authentic performances without the benefit of scholarly advice and instruction.

A moment's reflection shows that the pursuit of authenticity in musical performance has been highly selective. The price of admission, the dress of the audience, the method by which the programme is printed – each of these and much else in the context in which music is performed is decidedly modern. The search for musical authenticity takes a very particular direction. A highly authentic performance is likely to be one in which instruments contemporary to the period of composition (or replicas of such instruments) are used in its performance, in which the score is interpreted in the light of stylistic practices and performance conventions of the time when the work was composed, in which ensembles of the same size and disposition as accord with the composer's specification are employed, and so forth.

The selectivity displayed in the search for authenticity in musical performance has been systematic in a way which suggests that the quest may be characterized as aiming at the production of a particular *sound*, rather than at the production of, for example, the social ambience within which the music would or could be presented by the composer's contemporaries. This point is effectively illustrated as follows: orchestral music composed in the latter half of the eighteenth century might standardly have been performed in wood-panelled rooms. Nowadays such works would be performed in concert halls. Modern concert halls are designed with modifiable acoustics, the adjustments being made by the use of baffles etc. In performing music of the period in

58

question, the acoustics of the concert hall would be set with a reverberation period such as one might find in a wood-panelled room containing a small audience. Although the music now is performed in a large hall in front of a large audience, the acoustic properties of the modern building are so arranged that they duplicate the acoustic properties of the sort of room in which the music would have been performed in the composer's day. Now, whilst one might prefer the intimacy of music performed in salons I take it that it will be accepted that the use of concert halls which reproduce the acoustic properties of wood-panelled rooms would be considered not *merely* as an adequate compromise between the demands of authenticity and, say, economic considerations, but, instead, would be accepted as a full-blooded attempt at authentic performance.[2] That modern acoustic technology might serve the aim of authenticity in this way suggests strongly that musical authenticity aims at the creation of a particular sound and not at the production of a particular visual, social, or other effect.

Some performances are less authentic for being given in buildings other than that for which the work was written, but this is true only of performances of works written with an ear to the unique acoustic properties of a particular building. That is, it is true of performances of Stravinsky's *Canticum Sacrum* and of many works by Andrea and Giovanni Gabrieli which were written for San Marco in Venice, and it is not true of Verdi's *Aïda* which was written for the opera house in Cairo, because, whereas the acoustics of the opera house in Cairo are not distinctively different from those of other opera houses, the acoustics of San Marco are unlike those of other buildings. These examples do not count against the point that a concern with the authenticity of a performance is a concern with its sound.

II

In this second section I suggest that one might best hope to make a performance authentic by recreating the musical sound of a performance which might have been heard by the composer's contemporaries. (Why this is a formula for success is a matter considered in the next section.) I also argue that the sound to which an authentic performance aspires is that of a possible, rather than an actual, performance; that is, authenticity in musical performance is judged against an ideal.

So far I have said that a performance is more or less authentic in a way which depends upon its sound. One might ask – the sound of what? A musical work comprises notes and relationships between them, so an authentic performance of a given work must be a performance which concerns itself with producing the notes which comprise the work. The sound of an authentic performance will be the sound of those notes.

But it is not easy to specify the set of notes which comprise a given work.[3] The notes recorded in the score often are not the notes which the performer should play; frequently there are conventions known both to composers and performers governing the ways in which the written notes are to be modified (for example by accidentals or embellishment). So an interest in discrepancies between that which is written and that which is conventionally to be played is of practical and not merely scholarly significance. Debates about the problems of *musica ficta* in music written pre-1600 reflect strongly a desire to achieve authentic performances of the music in question.

Even where the conventions by which the score is to be read are known, it is not a straightforward matter always to say which notes should be played. Consider music written at about the end of the seventeenth century when pitches were as much as a minor third lower than now. The modern performer might play the work at the modern pitch level, but vocal and wind parts will then sound strained even if sung or played brilliantly and correctly.[4] Or the performer might tune down modern instruments, as a result of which their tone will suffer, or transpose orchestral parts, in which case the sound is affected by alterations in fingerings and *embouchure*, by changes in register, by shifts to harmonics etc. In view of such difficulties it is understandable that performers have turned to the use of instruments from the period of composition, or to replicas of such instruments, so that vocal and instrumental parts "lie" comfortably to the voice and hands. The use of such instruments is justified ultimately by the resulting sound of the performance.

However, despite the use of instruments and the appeal to musical conventions from the time of composition, clearly it is inadequate to characterize authenticity in musical performance in terms of the sound heard by the composer's contemporaries. His or her contemporaries could perform the work in question in ways which were relatively inauthentic.[5] Typically this would occur where the performance contained wrong notes or where the composer's specifications were misrepresented in some other way. Probably the musicians who sight-read the overture to *Don Giovanni* from orchestral parts on which the ink was still wet gave a performance which was not as authentic as it could have been. Since the performances heard by the composer's contemporaries often were less authentic than was possible, authenticity in musical performance cannot be defined in terms of the sounds actually heard by the composer's contemporaries. This suggests that, in striving for authenticity, the performer aims at an *ideal* sound rather than at the sound of some actual, former performance.

III

In this third section I consider the relevance of the composer's intentions in an assessment of the authenticity of a performance of the composer's work. I suggest that only those intentions which conventionally are accepted as determinative are relevant to judgements of authenticity; other of the composer's intentions or wishes might be ignored in an ideally authentic performance. Because the composer's determinative intentions under-determine the sound of an ideally authentic performance of his or her work, there is a set of ideal performances (and not any single ideal performance) in terms of which the relative authenticity of actual performances is judged.

There are conventions in terms of which musical scores are to be read. The composer is able to express his or her intentions in a musical notation only because the conventions for realizing in sound that notation are known both to the composer and to the performer of the day. Those conventions provide not only a vehicle for, but also a limitation on, the intentions which may be expressed in the score. Not all of the intentions which the conventions allow to be expressed are determinative of that which can be required in the name of authenticity. Non-determinative intentions (as expressed in the score or in other ways) have the status of recommendations. I take it that exact metronome indications are non-determinative in that tempo may be varied to suit the performance conditions. Both the composer and the performing musician who is his or her contemporary are familiar with the conventions usually and know which of the expressed intentions are determinative and which are not determinative of that at which an authentic performance must aim.

The conventions by which musical scores are to be read change over time in ways which affect that which the composer may determine with respect to the performer's attempt to produce an authentic performance. Phrasing was not notationally determined in the early seventeenth century, but was notationally determined by the nineteenth century. At some time, before the convention was established, composers notated phrasings which would have been understood rightly as recommendations for, rather than as determinative of, what should be played. At that time the composer's indications of phrasing might be disregarded without any diminution in the authenticity of the performance (although the performance may have been less good as a result on other grounds). (Sometimes these changes in convention arise from composers' rebelling against the existing conventions, but such rebellions reject only a few conventions at any one time and do so against a wider background of accepted conventions.) Because conventions of determinativeness change through time, the conventions appropriate to the authentic performance of a score are those with which the composer would have taken musicians *of the day* to be familiar. It is this fact which explains that which I have emphasized in the previous section – that an attempt at an authentic performance is likely to be successful by aiming to recreate the sound of an accurate performance by the composer's contemporaries.[6]

Sometimes it is possible to infer from what is written in the score that the composer would have preferred to write something else had the instruments or the performers been capable of accommodating his or her intentions. For example, a sequential pattern might be interrupted by an octave transposition where a continuation of the pattern would have exceeded the singer's or the instrument's range. In these cases it is appropriate to talk of the composer's wishes (rather than intentions). Sometimes nowadays, with the wider range of some instruments and the greater proficiency of many musicians, these wishes could be realized and there would be a musical point to doing so. However, such wishes have no more a bearing on the authenticity of a performance than do the composer's non-determinative intentions. Both the work and the performance may be better for the modification, but not because the alteration makes the performance more authentic. If it were accepted that mere wishes could set the standards of authenticity, it would also be accepted that many works could not have been performed authentically by the composer's contemporaries and some could not be performed authentically at all.

Clearly, in taking the line that I have, I must deny that authenticity in musical performance is judged against the *sound* of some particular performance which was envisaged by the composer. I have said that not all of the composer's expressed intentions are determinative of that which must be accurately rendered in an ideally authentic performance, in which case I must also hold that the sound of an ideally authentic performance is under-determined by the intentions in terms of which its authenticity is judged. The way in which we talk of authenticity favours my view, I claim, rather than the view that authenticity is measured against the *sound* of a performance which the composer had in mind. First, in reaching judgments about the authenticity of performances we do not seem to face the epistemological difficulties which would inevitably arise if the standard for authenticity was a sound which may never have been realized. Second, rather than taking composer's performances as definitive models which performers are obliged to copy slavishly, we take them to be revealing of what we expect to be an interesting interpretation. In a performance the composer may make his or her intentions as regards the *sound* of a performance more explicit than could be done in the score, but that which is made explicit is not thereby made definitive. Other performers are left with the job of interpreting the score for themselves.[7] Third, we would not (as we do) accept that *different-sounding* performances of a single work might be equally and ideally authentic if authenticity were judged against the sound of a *particular* performance imagined by the composer. It is (a member of) a *set* of ideal performances against which the authenticity of an actual performance is judged.

This last point deserves emphasis. Because an ideally authentic performance faithfully preserves the composer's determinative intentions, and because those intentions under-determine the sound of a faithful performance, different-sounding performances may be equally and ideally authentic. For example, many combinations of vocal and instrumental resources are compatible with that which is determinative in the score of Guillaume de Machaut's *Messe de Notre-Dame*. Even if the composer wrote for a particular combination of singers and instruments (such as were to be assembled for the coronation of Charles V in 1364, perhaps) the conventions of the day allow that performances by quite different combinations would be no less authentic. As long as two performances are faithful to the score and are consistent with the performance practices in terms of which it is to be rendered, they may be equally authentic whilst sounding different. Compare, for example, performances of Beethoven's symphonies as conducted by Klemperer and Toscanini, both of whom have been praised as interpreters of the works. Klemperer tends to take the pieces at the slowest tempo consistent with Beethoven's instructions and he emphasizes the structural qualities of the music so that, for example, climaxes at relatively weak structural points receive less weight than do those in structurally important places, even where the dynamics are the same in both places. Toscanini takes the works at a brisk tempo and concentrates on the drama or beauty of each individual passage, investing every note and phrase with its full potential of power. Without Klemperer's staid approach, the grandeur and architectonic qualities of Beethoven's music could not be presented. Without Toscanini's volatile approach, the dynamism and verve of Beethoven's music could not be appreciated. So, the ideally authentic performance has no *particular* sound because it is no *particular* performance. Rather, the standard against which the authenticity of performances of a work is judged comprises a *set* of performances each of which is faithful to the composer's determinative intentions.

In view of the above I offer the following account: a performance will be more rather than less authentic if it successfully (re)creates the sound of a performance of the work in question as could be given by good musicians playing good instruments under good conditions (of rehearsal time etc.), where "good" is relativized to the best of what was known by the composer to be available at the time, whether or not those resources were available for the composer's use.

IV

In this fourth section I analyse musical performance as involving both certain intentions on the part of the performer and a relationship of invariance between the composer's sound-specification and the performer's realization of that score. Performing is contrasted briefly with improvising and fantasizing. The point of authenticity is said to be the faithful realization of the composer's score in sound.

The notion of performance must be analysed in terms of the performer's intentions. If the production of some set of sounds is to be a performance of X, then it must be the intention of the producer of the sounds to generate a sound faithful to an X-specification. However, the intention to perform X is defeasible; where the sound produced is not recognizable as a realization of the X-specification the attempt at performance has failed. The notion of authenticity operates *within* the range set on the one hand by performances which are barely recognizable as such and on the other hand by performances which are ideally accurate. The closer comes a performance recognizable as such to the sound of an ideal performance of the work in question, the more authentic is that performance.[8]

I have suggested that there must be, as well as the appropriate intentions, an invariant relationship between the composer's specification and a performance of that specification as a necessary condition of the success of the attempt at performance. There must be some common factor (or tolerance across a range of features) necessary for a performance's being a performance of X rather than of Y, and necessary for different sounding performances all to be performances of the same X. Now, clearly the standard by which an attempted performance is minimally recognizable as such falls far short of a standard which identifies the work with the totality of notes which comprise it. By this standard only a perfectly accurate performance could count as a performance of the work in question, yet we all know that the school orchestra may play wrong notes, play out of tune, and fail to play together while performing what is unmistakably Beethoven's Fifth Symphony. Clearly it is because musical works comprise large numbers of notes, not all of which contribute equally to the overall effect, that the identity of the work survives the performance of wrong notes. So what is invariant between performances of the same work is *patterns* of notes (or aspects, gestalts, emergent properties, functions of notes) plus a tolerance for deviation from these patterns. Musical works are so complex that there are patterns of notes within patterns of notes and these various patterns may remain recognizable despite changes in or omissions of individual notes. The standard of adequacy which must be met in a successful attempt to perform the composer's score need not be one that requires a high degree of accuracy.[9] It is within the gap between a set of ideally faithful interpretations of a work and of barely recognizable performances of that work that the notion of authenticity operates. A performance is the more authentic the further beyond the minimum standard of adequacy it falls. The more faithful is a musical performance to the work's specification the more authentic is that performance.

The difference between a *performance* of X, an *improvisation* on X and an X-inspired *fantasia* lies in the musician's intentions, the aim being to realize a higher level of invariance with respect to the work's specification in performance than in improvisation and in improvisation than in fantasizing. Whereas authenticity is appropriately predicated of performances of particular works, it is not appropriately predicated of improvisations or fantasias inspired by particular works; that is, authenticity applies only where there is intended to be more rather than less invariance between the specification of the work and its rendition in sound. This suggests that the notion of authenticity applies where a text (usually a written score in literate music cultures and a model rendition in oral music cultures) is interpreted by a mediator who stands between the composer and his or her audience, and where the point of the interpretation is to render faithfully to the audience that which is determined of the sound of the performance in the work's specification. Ultimately a concern with the authenticity of performances of particular works takes it interest from a more fundamental concern with the authority of authorship.

A shift of focus to music which is primarily improvisational (i.e., most jazz, a substantial amount of non-western music and some recent "classical" music) helps to bring out the point. In such music, where the composer creates a cipher which lends itself to improvisational manipulation, we are more likely to be concerned with the authenticity of the *style* of the performance of any given work than with its authenticity as a performance of that particular work. The less the sound of the performance is determined in a faithful realization of the composer's specification, the less we are concerned with the type of authenticity in performance which I have been discussing (and the more the musicians are rated above composers). The less the composer has a hand in the final outcome the less is a concern with musical authenticity a concern with the authority of authorship.

V

In this fifth section I consider the way in which authenticity in musical performance is valued. I suggest that, although such authenticity would not be valued were it not a means to an independently valued end – the end of presenting the composer's interesting musical ideas – nevertheless, authenticity in musical performance is not valued *as* a means to this end.

Beyond the level of an acceptably competent performance, authenticity is value-conferring. That is, a musical performance is better for its being more authentic (other things being equal). Because we have an aesthetic concern with the musical interest of the composer's ideas, and because those musical ideas must be mediated by performance, we value authenticity in performance for the degree of faithfulness with which the performance realizes the composer's musical conception as recorded in the score. I am not maintaining that authenticity in performance takes its value from the worth of the musical content contributed by the composer. Rather, my point is this: were it not for the fact that composers set out to write aesthetically rewarding works, and were it not for the fact that they are usually successful in this, we would not value authenticity in musical performances as we do. But, in any particular instance, authenticity in performance is valued independently and irrespective of the aesthetic value of the work itself. A performance is better for a higher degree of authenticity (other things being equal) *whatever* the merits of the composition itself. A performance praiseworthy for its authenticity may make evident that the composer wrote a work with little musical interest or merit. It is the creative skill required of the performer in faithfully interpreting the composer's score which is valued in praising the authenticity of performances of that score.[10]

65

Of course, authenticity is not the only quality for which a performance might be valued. Where a relatively inauthentic performance is highly valued, it is valued *in spite of* its inauthenticity. Thus Schnabel's recorded performances of the Beethoven sonatas are well regarded despite the wrong notes that they contain.

VI

In this final section I emphasize how creative is the role of the performer in realizing faithfully the composer's specification. In developing the point a contrast is drawn between performing and copying.

The performance transforms the notes-as-written into the notes-as-sounds. In talking casually of the notes of a piece, and so obscuring this distinction, one might easily lose sight of the creativity of the role enacted by the performer in faithfully converting the one into the other. The sounded notes created by the performer go far beyond the bare peg which the composer provides and on which the musicians hang their art. An authentic performance concerns itself with the production of the notes which comprise the piece and which the composer specified, but the notes-as-sounds produced by the performer involve subtleties of attack, decay, dynamics, tone and so on which cannot be captured in any notation that composers are likely to use. The written notes and the way in which they are played come together inseparably in the notes-as-sounds, and it is in no way to under-value the role of the composer as the specifier of the notes-as-written to acknowledge that the musician brings something original to the notes-as-written in rendering them into sound.[11] The creative role of the performer, rather than involving a departure from the concern to realize faithfully the composer's intentions, is integral to the execution of that concern.

What is more, rather than consisting of mere aggregations of notes, music comprises themes, chords, subjects, answers, sequences, recapitulations, developments, motifs, accompaniments, and so forth. These are gestalts (or aspects etc.) and not mere successions of notes. Because their articulation in sound owes as much or more to the performer as to the composer, it can be seen how extensive and important is the creative role of the performer.

One way of bringing out the creative role of the performer as a necessary intermediary between the composer and the audience is by contrasting performing and copying. Copying need not be intentional; copying may be a mechanical process performed by a machine. And where copying is intentional, the aim of faithfulness is to be contrasted with that of creativity. By contrast, performance always is intentional, because the performer must bring more than is supplied by the composer to a performance which is faithful to the composer's ideas. Performing must go beyond that which is given in order to present accurately that which is given. But nothing not present in the original needs to be brought to copying. A machine might copy a performance (for example, by recording it on tape), but performing is done only by agents.[12] And copies are authentic only in the sense contrasted with forgery or fakery, whereas performances are authentic in the sense which here has been under discussion. Authenticity is an attribute acknowledging the way in which the interpretation of a musical score is both necessary in the presentation of the music-as-sounds and is also inherently creative. Authenticity, as a praiseworthy attribute, acknowledges the ineliminability of the performer's contribution to the sound of the performance.[13]

NOTES

1 Although it might be argued, for example, that rehearsals are not performances, this is a subtlety I shall attempt to ignore.

2 As implied here, the desirability of musical authenticity may sometimes be outweighed by other factors – musical, pragmatic or even moral. (I assume that arguments against the use of trained *castrati* in *opera seria* are of the latter kind.) Of course, where the choice is between no performance at all and a less than ideally authentic performance, the latter may be preferable.

3 Some of the considerations I mention are discussed also by Paul Ziff in "The cow on the roof", *The Journal of Philosophy* 70 (1973), 713–23. Guy Sircello (in "Various variants", 723–4), and Kendall L. Walton (in "Not a leg to stand on", 725–6) reply to Ziff in the same volume.

4 Competent musicians do not usually stumble over fast passages, lose the tempo or produce gross tonal contrasts but, despite this, hard music sounds hard to play. Thomas Carson Mark makes this clear in "On works of virtuosity", *The Journal of Philosophy* 77 (1980), 28–45.

5 It might be objected to what I have said that judgements of authenticity apply only to performances which are historically removed from the period of composition or culturally removed from the place or style of composition, or in some other way distanced from the composition. On my view judgements of authenticity tend to reduce to judgements of accuracy. But this does not mean that a performance by the composer's contemporaries (for whom the score is "transparent" to the conventions by which it is to be read) are not distanced from the work in a way that leaves room for judgements of authenticity. Performance involves a creative element which is integral and not merely appended to the faithfulness of the performance. This creative element distances *any* particular performance from the work of which it is a performance.

6 The claim that the conventions of score-reading and/or performance practice establish which of the composer's publicly expressed intentions are determinative may be defeated where there are grounds for believing that the composer was not familiar with the conventions or that the composer believed that the musicians who would perform the piece were not familiar with all the relevant conventions. These double-take and triple-take situations are unusual. An example: If the composer had only ever heard violins with a thin and reedy tone and by the indication "violin" on the score meant to designate instruments of that type, then the fact that Guaneri's violins were extant at the time would not license their use in performances of the composer's works in the name of authenticity, not even if the composer had *wished* that the instruments which he or she knew as violins had a richer, fruitier

tone. (To avoid such problem cases I should relativize all claims about the role of the relevant conventions to the composer's knowledge of those conventions and beliefs about the performers' knowledge of those conventions.)

7 A pertinent discussion of musical authenticity and the relevance of composers' intentions may be found in Richard Taruskin's "On letting the music speak for itself: some reflections on musicology and performance" in *The Journal of Musicology* 1 (1982), 338–49. The status of the composer's intentions are discussed interestingly by Randall R. Dipert in "The composer's intentions: an examination of their relevance for performance", *The Music Quarterly* 66 (1980), 205–18. The philosophical literature on the subject of artist's intentions is immense. Two of my own papers bear on our topic: "The relevance of authors' and painters' intentions", *The Journal of Aesthetics and Art Criticism* 40 (1982), 65–76 and "Attributing significance to unobvious musical relationships", *The Journal of Music Theory* 27 (1983), 203–13.

8 It is controversial, I realize, to regard a barely recognizable performance as authentic. Of course, the level of authenticity expected in a *competent* performance is far higher than the minimum at which a performance is barely recognizable as such. A minimally recognizable performance is inauthentic when authenticity is relativized to a standard of acceptability at the level of a competent performance.

9 The same kind of point may be made with respect to other musical parameters. A performance on the piano of J. S. Bach's Concerto in D Minor for Harpsichord, BWV 1052, *is* a performance of it, despite the change of instrument, and not the performance of a *transcription* of Bach's work. Conventions in Bach's time allowed quite free interchange between keyboard instruments and, in view of this, merely changing the solo instrument does not transform the work enough for the performance to count as that of a transcription. (One does not transcribe a musical work merely by altering a word in its *title*, which, in effect, is what happens here.)

10 Indulging in some armchair socio-biology: it is perhaps not surprising in a social species such as ours – which is concerned with successful communication and for which there can be no guarantee that any particular attempt at communication will not fail – that that which facilitates communication becomes valued for its own sake and apart from the worth of the contents which it helps to communicate. (Not that I think that music can usefully be compared to a language with respect to its meaning – see "Is music a language of the emotions?", *The British Journal of Aesthetics* 23 (1983), 222–33.)

11 For a similar view see the end of Nigel Harrison's "Creativity in musical performance", *The British Journal of Aesthetics* 18 (1978), 300–6.

12 I do not deny that copying by hand an illuminated manuscript might require patience, skill, etc. in a way that suggests that copying is anything but mechanical in this instance. Nor do I wish to deny that there are imaginable cases in which computers are programmed to produce sounds where we would be tempted to say a machine performs. (Just as there are cases in which the musician performs *on* a violin without our saying the violin performs, so there are cases in which musicians perform *on* computers – but the example to be imagined is not of this type.) But if there were such computers, talk of them as machines would begin to look inapposite; at such a point one begins thinking in terms of intelligent or agent-like "machines".

13 A number of people have commented helpfully on versions of this paper. In particular, I owe thanks to Denis Dutton and Graham Oddie and a special debt to Denis Robinson and Jan Crosthwaite.

5

THE CONCEPT OF AUTHENTIC PERFORMANCE

James O. Young

> If you feel the seriousness of a tune, what are you perceiving? – Nothing that could be conveyed by reproducing what you heard.
>
> Wittgenstein, *Investigations*, p. 210e.

Interest in early music has increased dramatically in recent years. Anyone at all cognizant of music is aware of a constant stream of books, journals, concerts, workshops, conferences and recordings devoted to early music. The extent of interest in early music is indicated by the fact that in Britain alone there are well over one-hundred professional ensembles engaged in the performance of early music.[1] The early music movement is not so much concerned with a period of music as with an artistic ideal. Within the movement's purlieu falls the music of all periods from classical antiquity through the middle ages, the renaissance, the baroque, classical and romantic periods to the early twentieth century. "Modern" musicians, however, interpret much of this same repertoire. What distinguishes the advocates of early music is that they aim at "authentic performance".[2]

There can be no doubt that the early music movement has been of enormous value. Members of the movement have, however, been insufficiently reflective about the concept of authentic performance.[3] They believe that it is possible to give performances which are "authentic". These performances have, moreover, more than antiquarian interest. Authentic performance is supposed to represent an attractive artistic ideal. That is, an authentic performance is an artistically successful interpretation of a composition. However, had advocates of early music paused to reflect, they would have realized that authentic performance cannot be characterized in such a way that it represents an ideal which is both attainable and worth attaining. There are principled, not merely practical, reasons why authentic performance is not a realizable artistic ideal. Reflection on these reasons will provide insight into the nature of music and the experience of music.

Members of the early music movement tend to regard the quest for authentic performance as a process of solving musicological difficulties of a practical nature. They begin by compiling scores which are faithful to composers' manuscripts or to early editions. Performers of early music pay particular attention to scoring. They perform on authentic instruments and do so with an ensemble of the authentic size. Having determined a score and selected their instruments, performers of early music proceed to perform in accordance with authentic performance techniques, the techniques contemporary with a piece's composition. They also ensure that their instruments are tuned as they would have been at the time of composition. So, for example, a Beethoven piano concerto will be performed on a fortepiano (either an "original instrument" or an authentic copy) and not on a modern concert grand. The stringed instruments will be strung in gut and the wind instruments will have fewer keys and otherwise differ from modern instruments. The orchestra will be much smaller than is now common and there will be a greater balance between the strings and winds. The fast movements will be played at a tempo slower than is now common and the slow movements will be rather faster. The A above middle C will be tuned to 435 cycles per second and not to the now-standard 440. If all practical questions of score, instrumentation, tuning, and performance techniques could be resolved, performers of early music believe, authentic performance is possible.

Of course, as advocates of authentic performance recognize, some practical obstacles to authentic performance will never be overcome. We will never know precisely how bowed instruments were used to accompany mediaeval songs. No scores have survived since the accompaniment was improvised. There are insurmountable practical obstacles to giving an authentic performance of even such a familiar piece as Mozart's Clarinet Concerto. As is well known, the piece was written for Anton Stadler. What is less known is that he did not play a clarinet at all but a basset clarinet. Precisely what sort of instrument Stadler would have played is unknown and, in all probability, will remain unknown. Moreover, the manuscript of Mozart's concerto does not survive. In the first printed edition of the concerto, published ten years after Mozart's death, the basset clarinet part is rewritten so as to be playable on a clarinet. It is possible to reconstruct the original score but not with complete accuracy. But the concept of authentic performance is not problematic for practical reasons. Imagine that there is an Omniscient Musicologist, a musicologist than whom no greater can be conceived. Such a musicologist would know everything about original scores, instruments, performance techniques and tuning. But the concept of authentic performance would still be problematic.

Suppose that, with the aid of the Omniscient Musicologist, all of the practical difficulties of the early music movement are overcome. It would then be possible to give the first characterization of authentic performance:

(1) An authentic performance is a performance which reproduces music as it was heard at the time of its composition.

There are good reasons to suppose that authentic performances, so characterized, could not be given. But it should be apparent that, when conceived of in this manner, authentic performance does not even represent an artistic ideal worth attaining.[4]

The first point worth noting is that there are moral obstacles which should prevent the authentic performance of certain compositions. Consider the authentic performance of eighteenth-century opera.[5] Many of the parts were written for, and performed by, castrati. Now, the tone colour of a castrato's voice differs from that of a female alto or soprano. But not even the most committed advocate of early music will think that the ideal of authentic performance would justify the mutilation of prepubescent boys. This is, perhaps, an extreme example but it serves to demonstrate that there are moral constraints which should prohibit the realization of the ideal of the authentic performance of all music.

There are, however, no moral obstacles facing the authentic performance of many compositions. These compositions, it might be thought, could be heard as they were at the time of their composition. A problem, however, immediately presents itself. If (1) is accepted, there will be a question about how to give an authentic performance of pieces which were not performed at the time of their composition. And there certainly are pieces which were not so performed. The performance of such pieces cannot reproduce how the music sounded at the period of their composition. Or, rather, the only authentic performance is non-performance – which is scarcely an attractive artistic ideal. But most compositions were heard within a short time of their composition. It is not clear, however, why anyone would want to hear them that way again.

Music must often have sounded perfectly atrocious at the time of its composition. The instruments on which music was performed were often in very bad repair. While in the service of Esterházy, Haydn had to contend with oboes in rotten condition.[6] In 1770 Charles Burney travelled throughout France and Italy collecting material for his history of music. He wrote that "All the keyed instruments I have yet heard on the continent, except some of the organs[,] are very bad." Of the spinets he heard in Italy he wrote that "the keys are so noisy and tone so feeble one hears more wood than wire."[7] If authentic performance is to reproduce music as it was originally heard, performers of early music are committed to playing Haydn's early symphonies on rotten oboes and to performing eighteenth-century Italian domestic music on decrepit harpsichords. Surely this is enough to render unappealing authentic performance as characterized in (1).

But it gets worse. Not only were the instruments of the eighteenth century often of a poor quality, but often the musicians were as well. Many of the best-known pieces of the eighteenth century were originally performed by amateurs. Handel's Chandos Anthems were first played by the Duke of Chandos' domestic staff. One of the players was recommended because "He shaves very well & hath an excellent hand on the violin & all necessary languages."[8] However good his hand may have been on the violin, it is unlikely that he played as well as a modern professional. Even the professional musicians of the period were not up to present standards. The difficulties which Mozart had with his players were, of course, legion. Mind you, he often did not make things easy for them. He often provided them with scores only a few days or even a few hours before a performance. So, if we accept (1) as the characterization of authentic performance, it seems that performers of early music must not allow themselves to become too accomplished and must, in some cases, take care not to rehearse their parts.

Of course, not every original performance was given by poor musicians on bad instruments. But the fact that many were is enough to render (1) untenable. Authentic performance should be characterized in such a way that artistically attractive authentic performances can be given of any piece, regardless of how it may originally have sounded. Moreover, it should be clear that (1) is not in accord with the actual practices of performers of early music. In deciding how to play a composition they do not attempt to determine whether the piece was played well or poorly. Rather, they attempt to decide how the composition *should* sound. Talk about how early music should sound suggests another account of authentic performance.

Recognizing that standards of musicianship and of instrument making have not always been what they now are, one might characterize authentic performance in terms of the intentions of composers.[9] One might adopt the following account of authentic performance.

(2) An authentic performance is one in which a composition sounds the way its composer intended it to sound.

This characterization will avoid many of the objections to which (1) is subject. Unfortunately, if authentic performance is so characterized, there is no way to determine which performances are authentic. And it is not even clear that (2) represents an ideal worth attaining.

The second account of authentic performance fails because of our inability to determine all of a composer's intentions. Certainly it is possible to know with a fair degree of certainty what some of a composer's intentions were. No doubt he intended that his compositions should sound as they do when played on the instruments available at the time of composition. And, no doubt, he intended that the instruments should be tuned as was customary in the period. The Omniscient Musicologist will be able to tell us a great deal about how a composer intended his works to sound. But there is a great deal that not even an Omniscient Musicologist can know. The totality of possible musicological evidence will underdetermine the selection of one performance as more authentic than another.

There is no possible evidence which will determine precisely what a composer's intentions were with respect to all aspects of the interpretation of a piece. The possible evidence could take one of two forms. Musicologists could discover a composer's instructions about how to play a piece and reports may survive about how he actually performed one of his compositions. In practice, of course, even this evidence is often unavailable. But if it were available to an Omniscient Musicologist, it would still not determine which performances are authentic. Even complete reports of a composer's own performance of a solo piece would not be decisive evidence. There is no guarantee that even a composer's own performance realized his intentions. Not even a composer's own reports would be decisive evidence. The knowledge of how a piece is to be interpreted is, in large measure, practical knowledge, a knowledge of how something is to be done. Such knowledge, like the knowledge of how to ride a bicycle, cannot be fully captured in propositional terms. Not even the composer will be able to describe precisely what his intentions were. If we cannot know what a composer's intentions were, we cannot determine which performances are authentic and which are not and (2) is unsatisfactory.

Even if authentic performance could be characterized in terms of composers' intentions, it is not clear that, so characterized, it would be an attractive artistic ideal. Composers may not be the best interpreters of their own compositions. Once a piece has been composed, the composer's views on how it is best performed are no better than those of any qualified musician. And they may be worse. Frescobaldi left very detailed instructions on how to perform his keyboard compositions.[10] These instructions do not, of course, determine the choice of authentic performances. But even if they did, performers might be wise to disregard them. Many musicians, including those interested in authentic performance, disregard Frescobaldi's instructions simply because they believe that following them does not result in very successful interpretations.

Performers of early music might encourage another account of authentic performance by noting that they never aimed to realize the intentions of a single individual but, rather, to perform in the style of some period. The performers of some period, perhaps, never succeeded in perfectly realizing the style of their time. However, had these musicians been properly trained and had they been possessed of good instruments, the recreation of how their music sounded would be a more attractive artistic goal. These reflections give rise to the third account of authentic performance.[11]

> (3) An authentic performance makes a piece sound as it would have sounded at the period of its composition, had conditions been ideal.

This characterization of authentic performance is immune to many of the objections which cripple (1) and (2). It is, however, subject to the objection that music cannot sound to us as it would have sounded to earlier listeners, even under ideal conditions. And it is still not clear that we should want music to sound as it would have sounded under ideal conditions.

As Wittgenstein recognized, just as there is a distinction between seeing and seeing as, so there is a distinction between hearing and hearing as. All observers see the same thing when they look at a picture of a duck-rabbit.[12] And yet the picture looks one way to someone who only sees it as a rabbit and another to someone who only sees it as a duck. Moreover, the beliefs of viewers have an impact on how things look to them. Someone who has no knowledge of rabbits will not see the duck-rabbit as a rabbit. Gombrich relates a story which indicates that the same points can be made about hearing as can be made about seeing.[13] During the Second World War he was engaged in monitoring broadcasts. Many of the monitored transmissions were barely audible. Even though two listeners heard the same sounds they often heard them as different things. Any beliefs about what was being said in the broadcasts were sure to have an impact on what listeners would hear them as saying. There is no more an innocent ear than there is an innocent eye.

Suppose that listeners of some period were to hear a composition of their time performed under ideal conditions. And suppose that listeners of our time were to hear an authentic performance (as defined in (3)) of the same piece. The two groups of listeners would, on these suppositions, hear the same (or similar) sounds. But they would not hear them as the same. A few examples will make this point clear. Some intervals which are now heard as consonant were in the past heard as dissonant. In the middle ages a third was a dissonant interval. Mediaeval listeners hearing (under ideal conditions) a composition which contained a third would hear the interval as dissonant. Now, of course, thirds are no longer heard as dissonant. Modern listeners hearing the same mediaeval composition will hear the thirds as consonant. The same piece will sound quite different to modern and mediaeval ears, even under ideal conditions. Having been exposed (subjected?) to the music of the twentieth century almost nothing sounds dissonant any longer. It is even difficult for us to hear the dissonances of the eighteenth and nineteenth centuries.

The experience of music has changed in more fundamental ways as well. Eighteenth-century people had many beliefs which we do not have. These beliefs had an enormous impact on how they experienced music. Unlike those who first heard Lully's operas, we do not hear the trumpet flourishes as the trumpets of the Sun King. Lully's operas shamelessly flattered Louis XIV and we cannot but hear them as affected and sycophantic. But the courtiers at Versailles heard them quite differently. They knew the sound of ceremonial trumpets and they believed sycophancy to be normal behaviour. In the eighteenth century the rustic bagpipe and shepherd flute were still familiar. Audiences would have heard many passages for oboe or flute in Bach or Handel as recalling these instruments. Modern listeners can hear the same sounds as eighteenth-century listeners would have heard under ideal conditions. But the sounds are not heard as possessed of rustic associations.[14] Of course, we can and do learn that period listeners heard certain sounds as rustic or regal. But it is one thing to know that others heard them thus and quite another to hear them so ourselves.

Hearing, like other forms of perception, is not a passive process but an active process of interpreting vibrations of air. The music of the past could not sound to us as it did to listeners of earlier eras, we could not hear it as they heard it, unless we could interpret it as they did. We could not so interpret the music of earlier listeners unless we shared the beliefs which enabled them to hear as they did. Our experiences of music, of society and of nature are very different from the experiences of, say, listeners in the eighteenth century and so our beliefs and our interpretation of music must differ. Since our interpretation must differ so must how the music sounds to us. By listening to a great deal of their music we share some of their experiences and come to have some of their beliefs – but not all of them. Which is just as well – to do so we would have to live in an absolute monarchy – but our inability to share their beliefs makes it impossible for us to hear music of earlier periods as it was heard.

Paraphrasing Wittgenstein we might ask, if some period audience heard the regality of a tune, what were they perceiving? – nothing that could be conveyed by reproducing what they heard, or would have heard under ideal conditions. Authentic performance as characterized in (3) requires that there be authentic listeners who hear music as it was heard during an earlier period. We are not and cannot be such listeners. Since the music of earlier periods cannot sound to us as it sounded to period listeners, or would have sounded to them under ideal conditions, (3) must be rejected. Authentic performance as characterized in (3) is an unattainable goal.

There is a sense in which no listener ever hears music precisely as another does. But the experience and beliefs of two similarly educated twentieth-century listeners will be substantially the same and it is reasonable to suppose that they hear music very much as the other does. But even within the twentieth century not all listeners hear music as others do. Listening to Oriental music is, for many Westerners, like listening to a foreign language. They may, for example, fail to discern something as simple as whether a song is happy or sad. Oriental listeners, in contrast, will immediately hear a song as happy or as sad. The song sounds differently to them. The distinction between this case and that of early music is that it is possible for Westerners to acquire the experiences and beliefs which would enable them to hear as Orientals do.

It might be thought that, even if we cannot hear music as an early listener heard it, perhaps in the 'mind's ear' music could sound to us as it sounded in the mind's ear of the earlier listener. There is, however, no more an innocent mind's ear than there is an innocent ear. Indeed, the psychological evidence indicates that mental images are even more conceptualized, even more interpreted, than sensory images. The beliefs of subjects have an enormous impact on how mental images seem to them.[15]

It is not possible for musicians to give a performance which would sound to us as it would have sounded to period listeners. It is not even clear that this would be a worthwhile artistic goal if it were possible. There is much early music which we would not want to hear as it would have sounded, under ideal conditions, to period audiences.

Much great music was poorly regarded by early listeners. Burney merely reported prevailing sentiments when he found "a manifest inferiority in design, invention, grace, elegance and every captivating requisite" in Handel's late operas.[16] It is not all desirable to hear Handel's late operas as contemporaries heard them, or would have heard them under ideal conditions. We now hear Handel's late operas as full of every captivating requisite and a performance which does not let us hear them this way holds little allure.

The concept of authentic performance has one last gasp. It might be thought that the previous attempts to characterize authentic performance as an attainable and attractive goal have failed because they make reference to the subjective aspects of performing or listening: the intentions of composers or the hearing of listeners. Authentic performance can, however, be defined in purely objective terms.

> (4) An authentic performance is one which causes air to vibrate as it would have vibrated at the time of its composition, under ideal conditions.

This account of authentic performance is subject to a simple objection: a (possible) synthesizer could vibrate air in the requisite manner without providing an authentic performance. (4) can, however, be reformulated to meet this objection.

> (4′) An authentic performance is one which, by means of authentic instruments, causes air to vibrate as it would have vibrated at the time of its composition, under ideal conditions.

There may still be some doubts about whether (4′) represents an attainable goal. But even if air could be vibrated in the requisite manner, (4′) would not be an acceptable account of authentic performance.

Perhaps not even an Omniscient Musicologist could tell performers how to vibrate air as period musicians would have vibrated air under ideal conditions. Air will vibrate in the manner that air would have vibrated only if a piece is played in precisely the manner in which it would have been played. Certainly musicologists can provide a great deal of information about past performance techniques and this information will help musicians to approximate the requisite vibrations. However, any musician knows that performers' beliefs about a piece will influence their interpretation of it. To recur to an earlier example, flautists will play a passage in a certain way if they believe it to recall a shepherd's flute. And their interpretation will be influenced by whether or not they have heard shepherds piping. Just as experience and beliefs have an impact on how music is heard, so do they have an impact on how it is played and, thus, on how air vibrates. Not having the experiences and beliefs of earlier musicians, today's musicians cannot vibrate air precisely as early performers would. So it seems that (4′) is not an attainable objective.[17]

However, even if air could be vibrated in the requisite manner, (4′) fails as a characterization of authentic performance. Anyone who would characterize authentic performance as in (4′) (to the best of my knowledge no one does) has lost sight of the point of any style of performance. As a result, even if (4′) describes an attainable end, it does not represent an attractive artistic ideal. A style of performance is artistically attractive when performances in the style realize some artistic goal. There is a variety of views about what an artistic goal is. Some writers have it that the goal of art is to make certain aesthetic experiences possible. Others hold that the goal is to express emotion or to convey ideas. But, in any case, a style of performance is an attractive artistic ideal when it leads to the attainment of artistic goals, however these are conceived. A style of performance attains its goals by means of vibrating air in certain ways. But it is artistically attractive, not because air vibrates in certain ways, but because an artistic goal is attained. Because it characterizes authentic performance in terms of vibrating air, (4′) fails to characterize it as an attractive artistic ideal.

(4′) fails because it loses sight of the fact that a performance is intended to attain artistic goals, not to vibrate air. This problem is highlighted when we recall that artistic goals can be attained by means of air caused to vibrate in a variety of ways by a variety of means. Under different acoustic and atmospheric conditions it is necessary to play differently and so to vibrate air somewhat differently to attain the same musical results. This makes it clear that an artistically attractive style of performance cannot be characterized in terms of vibration in air.

It is now possible to see why the quest for an authentic performance was misguided. The problem is that the concept of authentic performance suggests that there is an ideal performance of every composition. That is, there is a suggestion that there is a single best interpretation of any piece and this is its authentic performance. It is, however, necessary for all listeners and musicians to hear and play music in their own fashion. They cannot play or hear music as people in the past may have done. Just as each generation must interpret Shakespeare in its own way, so must each age interpret Bach for itself. There is no ideal performance of a composition but, rather, many.

Authentic performance cannot be characterized in such a way that it represents an artistic ideal which is both attainable and worth attaining. The conclusion to be drawn is that the concept is not a useful one. It does not follow that the early music movement is without value. On the contrary, the movement has enormously enriched musical experience. It has done this, however, not by giving authentic performances but by giving successful ones. That is, an early music performance is valuable not because it bears some relation to past performances but because present listeners find it artistically appealing. The playing of authentic scores on authentically tuned authentic instruments in accordance with authentic performance techniques will not result in authentic performances. But performances by modern performers of early music can, and often do, attain the artistic goals of present listeners.[18]

NOTES

1 See the *Directory of British Early Music Groups* (London: Early Music Centre, 1981).

2 Robert Donington, a distinguished authority on early music, writes, for example, that "if you want the best that any music has to offer, you do well to go at it in the authentic way". "Why early music?", *Early Music* 11 (1983), 45.

3 But see three recent articles, one by a musician, one by a music critic and one by a philosopher. Ton Koopman, "Some thoughts on authenticity", *Musick*, 8(3) (1987), 2–6; Will Crutchfield, "The meanings of 'authenticity'", *Oberlin Alumni Magazine* 82(4) (1986), 4–9; and Stephen Davies, "Authenticity in musical performance", reprinted in this book.

4 Davies reaches this conclusion for reasons similar to those given here.

5 This same example is used by Davies, note 2.

6 This is reported in Christopher Hogwood, *Music at Court* (London: The Folio Society, 1977), p. 112.

7 Charles Burney, *Music, Men, and Manners in France and Italy 1770* (London: The Folio Society, 1969), p. 69.

8 Quoted in Christopher Hogwood, *Handel* (London: Thames & Hudson, 1984), p. 73.

9 The harpsichordist Ralph Kirkpatrick reports that his aim is to perform "harpsichord and clavichord music in a manner as close as possible to what could be ascertained of the intentions of the composers." "Fifty years of harpsichord playing", *Early Music* 11 (1983), 31.

10 Selections from Frescobaldi's instructions are found in *Composers on Music*, ed. Sam Morgenstern (New York: Pantheon, 1956), pp. 24–6.

11 This is essentially the account of authentic performance given by Davies. He writes that "a performance will be more rather than less authentic if it successfully (re)creates the sound of a performance of the work in question as could be given by good musicians playing good instruments under good conditions (of rehearsal time etc.), where 'good' is relativized to be the best of what was known by the composer to be available at the time, whether or not those resources were available for the composer's use." My talk of ideal conditions can be taken as shorthand for Davies's definition and the following argument will still work.

12 For a discussion and a drawing of a duck-rabbit see Ludwig Wittgenstein, *Philosophical Investigations* (Oxford: Basil Blackwell, 1963), pp. 194ff.

13 E.H. Gombrich, *Art and Illusion* (Princeton University Press, 1969), pp. 204–5.

14 These examples are taken from Hogwood. *Music at Court*, p. 59f. Hogwood would not draw the same conclusions.

15 For a discussion of the conceptualized nature of mental images see Zenon Pylyshyn, "Imagery and artificial intelligence", in *Readings in Philosophy of Psychology*, Vol. 2, ed. Ned Block (Cambridge, Massachusetts: Harvard University Press, 1981), pp. 170–94. Pylyshyn mainly discusses visual mental imagery but there is no reason to suppose that auditory imagery would be any different.

16 Quoted in Hogwood, *Handel*, p. 101.

17 In this context a remark of Julian Bream is instructive. "Looking back over many centuries of music, the problem seems to me how to remain innocent after experience. Finally, I suppose, I don't believe that to be possible." Quoted in Tony Palmer, *Julian Bream: A Life on the Road* (London: Macdonald & Co., 1982), p. 126.

18 In the course of writing this essay I profited from the comments of Bill Eastman, D.D. Todd, Sheldon Wein, and, especially, Charles Morgan. Special thanks are due to Rosemary Mountain of the School of Music, University of Victoria and an anonymous referee.

SUGGESTIONS FOR FURTHER READING

Davies, Stephen (1988) "Authenticity in performance: a reply to J.O. Young", *British Journal of Aesthetics* 28: 373–6.

—— (1988) "Transcription, authenticity and performance", *British Journal of Aesthetics* 28: 216–27.

—— (1990) "Violins or viols? – a reason to fret", *Journal of Aesthetics and Art Criticism* 48: 147–51.

Dipert, Randall (1980) "The composer's intentions: an examination of their relevance for performance", *Music Quarterly* 66: 205–18.

Donington, Robert (1989) *The Interpretation of Early Music*, New York: Norton.

Edidin, Aron (1991) "Look what they've done to my song: historical authenticity and the aesthetics of musical performance", *Midwest Studies in Philosophy* 16: 394–420.

Godlovitch, Stan (1988) "Authentic performance", *Monist* 71: 258–77.

—— (1990) "Musical performance and the tools of the trade", *Iyyun* 39: 321–38.

—— (1998) *Musical Performance*, London: Routledge.

Kenyon, Nicholas (1988) *Authenticity and Early Music*, New York: Oxford University Press.

Kerman, Joseph (1985) *Contemplating Music*, Cambridge: Harvard University Press, Chapter 6.

Kivy, Peter (1988) "On the concept of the 'historically authentic' performance", *Monist* 71: 278–90.

—— (1995) *Authenticities*, Ithaca and London: Cornell University Press.

Le Huray, Peter (1990) *Authenticity in Performance: Eighteenth-Century Case Studies*, Cambridge: Cambridge University Press.

Levinson, Jerrold (1990) "Authentic performance and performance means", in *Music, Art, and Metaphysics*, Ithaca: Cornell University Press.

—— (1990) "Evaluating musical performance", in *Music, Art, and Metaphysics*, Ithaca: Cornell University Press.

Rudinow, Joel (1994) "Race, ethnicity, expressive authenticity: can white people sing the blues?", *Journal of Aesthetics and Art Criticism* 52(1): 127–37.

Taruskin, Richard (1982) "On letting the music speak for itself: some reflections on musicology and performance", *Journal of Musicology* 1: 338–49.

Taylor, Paul Christopher (1995) "So black and blue: response to Rudinow", *Journal of Aesthetics and Art Criticism* 53(3): 313–16. (Followed by a reply from Rudinow.)

Thom, Paul (1990) "Young's critique of authenticity in musical performance", *British Journal of Aesthetics* 30: 273–6.

Part 3

FAKES AND FORGERIES

At least four of the copies of Rembrandt self-portraits are judged superior to their originals, which are nowhere to be seen. On two of these copies, the draftsmanship and brush control are finer than anything Rembrandt himself ever could accomplish. Unless, of course, the copies are by Rembrandt and all of his originals are by someone else.

This is hard to believe, as Schillig says.

Joseph Heller, *Picture This*, p. 49

"But it is superb!"

"Yes. A superb fake."

"Well – but could anybody spot it?"

"Not without a scientific examination. The panel is old and quite genuine, and it is covered in leather as old as itself. The colors are correct, made in the true manner. The technique is impeccable, except that it is rather too good for a wholly unknown painter. And this ingenious scoundrel Corniche has even seen that the *craquelure* incorporates some authentic dust. I don't suppose one observer in a thousand would have any doubt about it."

"Oh, but Meister – that observer would surely spot the old Fugger *Firmenzeichen*, the pitchfork and circle, that can just barely be perceived in the upper left-hand corner. He would pride himself on having spotted it and guessed what it is, although it is almost obscured."

"Yes. But it is a fake, my dear Max."

"Perhaps in the substance. Certainly not in the spirit. Consider, Meister: this is not imitating any known painter's work – that would be a fake, of course. No, this is simply a little picture in a sixteenth-century manner. Now what makes it different from these others?"

"Only the fact that it has been done in the past month."

"Oh, that is almost Lutheran pernickety morality! That is an unworthy servitude to chronology. Cousin, what do you say? Isn't it a little gem?"

Robertson Davies, *What's Bred in the Bone*, p. 318

SUPPOSE THAT YOU INHERIT A SMALL pencil drawing by the Swiss artist Paul Klee. Your benefactor has left the drawing to you because she knows how much you admire Klee's work, and how much you appreciate this drawing in particular. Naturally, you want to have the drawing insured, so you take it to an expert who, after examining the work, tells you that your prized Paul Klee drawing is not in fact a drawing by Paul Klee at all, but a fake! Naturally enough, you are devastated.

Of course, there are all sorts of reasons why you might be devastated by this news. For one thing, the forgery is almost certainly worth much less than a drawing by Klee, and so the fact that your drawing is a forgery might matter to you financially. For another, you had taken the drawing to be a genuine Paul Klee, so you may feel that the discovery that it is really a forgery casts doubt on your credentials as a connoisseur of modern art. These may be very important matters to you. But remember that one of the reasons that your benefactor left the drawing to you was that you had always liked it so much. And the drawing itself has not changed. So, should the fact that it has turned out to be a forgery matter to you *aesthetically*?

In the first of the chapters in this part, Alfred Lessing argues that it should not. "The plain fact", Lessing writes, "is that aesthetically it makes no difference whether a work of art is authentic or a forgery", and "The fact of forgery is important historically, biographically, perhaps legally, or . . . financially; but not, strictly speaking, aesthetically." The suggestion here is that the features of a work or object that are relevant to our aesthetic appreciation of the work are features that we can see (or hear, or feel, or even perhaps smell). The aesthetically relevant features of a work or object, that is, are *observable* features. Given that there has been no change in the observable features of your drawing, then, there should be no change in your aesthetic appreciation of it. This is not to say that there is nothing wrong with forgeries, however: as Lessing sees it, the problem with them is that they lack originality, in one important sense of that term. This lack of originality negatively affects their status as art. But since originality is not an observable feature (you cannot tell whether a work is original simply by looking at it), lack of originality cannot affect a forgery's *aesthetic* value.

But is it true that only the observable features of a work are relevant to our aesthetic appreciation of it? In the second of the chapters in this part, Denis Dutton argues against this view. Dutton suggests that all works of art can be seen as performances, and that a central part of what is involved in aesthetic appreciation is appreciation of what an artist has *achieved* in his or her performance. This achievement (or lack of it) may not be wholly observable; understanding an artist's achievement, Dutton argues, depends on knowing something about the origins of the work and about the context in which it was produced. In Dutton's view, that is, non-observable features of a work, and in particular facts about its origins, are relevant to our assessment of the achievement the work represents, and thus may well be relevant to our aesthetic appreciation of it. The problem with forgery, he suggests, is that "it misrepresents artistic achievement", by misleading us about the origins of the work in question. Although discovering that a work is a forgery may not lead us to notice any difference in its observable features, it does alter our understanding of its origins, and hence our assessment of the achievement it represents. Thus, if Dutton is right, discovering that a work is a forgery may legitimately affect our aesthetic appreciation of that work.

Clearly, discovering that your drawing is a forgery is likely to upset you. The chapters in this part suggest, however, that it is not so clear whether your reasons for being upset can include aesthetic reasons. In essence the question is this: Can the fact of forgery matter to a person whose only concern is with aesthetic value? Answering this question is an important step on the way towards getting clear about the nature of aesthetic experience.

6

WHAT IS WRONG WITH A FORGERY?

Alfred Lessing

This article attempts to answer the simple question: What is wrong with a forgery? It assumes, then, that something *is* wrong with a forgery. This is seen to be a reasonable assumption when one considers that the term *forgery* can be defined only in reference to a contrasting phenomenon which must somehow include the notion of genuineness or authenticity. When thus defined there can be little doubt that the concept of forgery is a normative one. It is clear, moreover, that it is a negative concept implying the absence or negation of value. But a problem arises when we ask what kind of value we are speaking of. It appears to be generally assumed that in the case of artistic forgeries we are dealing with the absence or negation of *aesthetic* value. If this were so, a forgery would be an aesthetically inferior work of art. But this, as I will show, is not the case. Pure aesthetics cannot explain forgery. Considering a work of art aesthetically superior because it is genuine, or inferior because it is forged, has little or nothing to do with aesthetic judgment or criticism. It is rather a piece of snobbery.[1]

It is difficult to make this position convincing to a person who is convinced that forgery *is* a matter of aesthetics. If a person insists that for him the aesthetic value (i.e., the beauty) of a work of art is affected by the knowledge that it is or is not genuine, there is little one can say to make that fact unreal for him. At most one can try to show that in the area of aesthetics and criticism we are easily confused and that his view, if carried through, leads to absurd or improbable conclusions. It is important that we do this because it is impossible to understand what is wrong with a forgery unless it be first made quite clear that the answer will not be in terms of its aesthetic worth.

Somehow critics have never understood this and have again and again allowed themselves to be forced into an embarrassing position upon the discovery of some forgery or other. Perhaps the classic, certainly the most celebrated case in point, was that of Han van Meegeren, who in 1945 disturbed the complacent tranquility of the world of art and art critics by confessing that he was the artist responsible for eight paintings, six of which had been sold as legitimate Vermeers and two as de Hooghs. It is not hard to imagine the discomfort felt by critics at that time, especially when we recall how thoroughly successful van Meegeren was in perpetrating his fraud. His *Disciples at Emmaus* was subjected to the very highest praise by the noted critic and scholar Abraham Bredius as one of Vermeer's finest achievements, and it hung in the Boymans Museum for seven years. During that time thousands upon thousands admired and praised the painting. There was no doubt in anyone's mind that this was one of the greatest of Vermeer's paintings and, indeed, one of the most beautiful works of art in the world. It was undoubtedly this universal judgment of aesthetic excellence which accounts largely for the sensational effects of van Meegeren's confession in 1945.

It is of course embarrassing and irritating for an expert to make a mistake in his field. And it *was*, as it turned out, a mistake to identify the painting as a Vermeer. But it should be obvious from the words of Bredius that there is more involved here than a mere matter of misidentification. "The colors are magnificent," he writes. "The highest art . . . this magnificent painting . . . *the* masterpiece of Vermeer": this is more than identification. This clearly is aesthetic praise. And it is just the fact that the critics heaped such lavish praise on a picture which turned out to have been painted by a second-rate contemporary artist that made the van Meegeren case such a painful affair for them. To their way of thinking, which I am trying to show was not very logical, they were now apparently faced with the dilemma of either admitting that they had praised a worthless picture or continuing to do so.

This was, of course, precisely the trap that van Meegeren had laid for the critics. It was, in fact, the whole *raison d'être* of his perpetrating the fraud. He deliberately chose this extreme, perhaps pathological, way of exposing what he considered to be false aesthetic standards of art critics. In this respect his thinking was no more logical than that of the critics. His reasoning, at least about his first forgery, *The Disciples*, was in effect as follows: "Once my painting has been accepted and admired as a genuine Vermeer, I will confess publicly to the forgery and thus force the critics either to retract their earlier judgments of praise, thereby acknowledging their fallibility, or to recognize that I am as great an artist as Vermeer." The dilemma as stated contains a difficulty to which we shall return later. What is important historically is that the critics accepted van Meegeren's dilemma as a genuine one (thereby becoming the dupes of a logical forgery as well as an artistic one), although in the public outburst of indignation, condemnation, praise, blame, analysis, investigation, and discussion which followed van Meegeren's confession, it is difficult to determine which horn of this dilemma the critics actually chose to be impaled on.

There existed, in fact, a small group of critics who never for a moment accepted van Meegeren's claim to have painted *The Disciples at Emmaus*. They argued vehemently that whereas all the other paintings in question are easily shown to be forgeries, no convincing evidence had been produced to prove that *The Disciples* (as well as one other painting entitled *The Last Supper*) was not by Vermeer and that, in fact, all evidence pointed to the conclusion that it was a genuine Vermeer. Subsequent laboratory tests using more modern techniques have finally settled the issue against these critics, but that need not concern us.

What should concern us is the fact that aesthetically it would seem to make no difference whatever whether *The Disciples* is a Vermeer or a van Meegeren. Needless to say, this is not the view of the critics. To them apparently it makes all the difference in the world. Consider, for example, the words of J. Decoen, who was one of that aforementioned group of critics that held that *The Disciples* was a genuine Vermeer:

> I must recall that the moment of greatest anguish for me was when the verdict [of van Meegeren] was being considered. The Court might, according to an ancient Dutch Law, have ordered the destruction of *all* the pictures. One shudders at the thought that one could, officially, have destroyed two of the most moving works which Vermeer has created. During the trial, at the moment of his indictment, the Public Prosecutor stated that there was in Court a man who claimed that a number of the paintings were not by van Meegeren. He made this statement because, ever since 1945, he must have realized that my perseverance had not faltered, that my conviction was deep, and that I had never changed my original statements in any respect whatsoever. These words may possibly have influenced the decision of the Court with regard to the application of the Law. If this be so, I should consider myself amply repaid for my efforts and pains, for my tenacity may possibly have ultimately rescued two capital works of the Dutch school of the seventeenth century.[2]

But what does it matter that Decoen is wrong? Could he no longer take pride in having prevented the destruction of these "capital" paintings even though they are products of the twentieth instead of the seventeenth century? The answers, it seems to me, are almost self-evident. What, after all, makes these paintings "capital works"? Surely it is their purely aesthetic qualities, such as the ones mentioned by Bredius in his description of *The Disciples*. But if this is so, then why, even if this painting is a forgery, should Decoen not be justified in his actions, since he has preserved a painting which is aesthetically important for the only reason that a painting can be aesthetically important – namely, its beauty? Are we any more justified in destroying capital paintings of the twentieth century than those of the seventeenth? To this question we are usually given the answer that the one is after all a forgery while the other is genuine. But our question is precisely: What is the difference between a genuine Vermeer and a van Meegeren forgery? It is of no use to maintain that one need but look to see the difference. The fact that *The Disciples* is a forgery (if indeed it is) cannot, so to speak, be read off from its surface, but can finally be proved or disproved only by means of extensive scientific experiments and analyses. Nor are the results of such scientific investigations of any help in answering our question, since they deal exclusively with non-aesthetic elements of the picture, such as its chemical composition, its hardness, its crackle, and so on. The truth is that the difference between a forgery and a genuine work of art is by no means as obvious as critics sometimes make out. In the case of *The Disciples*, at least, it is certainly not a matter of but needing to look in order to see. The actual history of *The Disciples* turns all such attempted *post facto* explanations into a kind of academic sour grapes.

The plain fact is that aesthetically it makes no difference whether a work of art is authentic or a forgery, and, instead of being embarrassed at having praised a forgery, critics should have the courage of their convictions and take pride in having praised a work of beauty. Perhaps if critics did respond in this way we should be less inclined to think that so often their judgments are historical, biographical, economical, or sociological instead of aesthetic. For in a sense, of course, van Meegeren proved his point. Perhaps it is a point for which such radical proof was not even necessary. We all know very well that it is just the preponderance in the art world of nonaesthetic criteria such as fame of the artist and the age or cost of the canvas which is largely responsible for the existence of artistic forgeries in the first place. We all know that a few authentic pen and ink scratches by Picasso are far more valuable than a fine landscape by an unknown artist. If we were offered a choice between an inferior (but genuine) Degas sketch and a beautiful Jones or Smith or X, how many of us would choose the latter? In a museum that did not label its paintings, how many of us would not feel uneasy lest we condemn one of the greats or praise an unknown? But, it may be argued, all this we know. It is simply a fact and, moreover, probably an unavoidable, understandable – even a necessary – fact. Is this so serious or regrettable? The answer, of course, is that it is indeed serious and regrettable that the realm of art should be so infested with nonaesthetic standards of judgment that it is often impossible to distinguish artistic from economic value, taste or fashion from true artistic excellence, and good artists from clever businessmen.

This brings us to the point of our discussion so far. The matter of genuineness versus forgery is but another nonaesthetic standard of judgment. The fact that a work of art is a forgery is an item of information about it on a level with such information as the age of the artist when he created it, the political situation in the time and place of its creation, the price it originally fetched, the kind of materials used in it, the stylistic influences discernible in it, the psychological state of the artist, his purpose in painting it, and so on. All such information belongs to areas of interest peripheral at best to the work of art as aesthetic object, areas such as biography, history of art, sociology, and psychology. I do not deny that such areas of interest may be important and that their study may even help us to become better art appreciators. But I do deny that the information which they provide is of the essence of the work of art or of the aesthetic experience which it engenders.

It would be merely foolish to assert that it is of no interest whatsoever to know that *The Disciples* is a forgery. But to the man who has never heard of either Vermeer or van Meegeren and who stands in front of *The Disciples* admiring it, it can make no difference whether he is told that it is a seventeenth-century Vermeer or a twentieth-century van Meegeren in the style of Vermeer. And when some deny this and argue vehemently that, indeed, it does make a great deal of difference, they are only admitting that *they* do know something about Vermeer and van Meegeren and the history of art and the value and reputation of certain masters. They are only admitting that *they* do not judge a work of art on purely aesthetic grounds but also take into account when it was created, by whom, and how great a reputation it or its creator has. And instead of seeking justification in the fact that in truth it is difficult to make a pure, aesthetic judgment, unbiased by all our knowledge of the history and criticism of art, they generally confuse matters of aesthetics even more by rationalizing that it is the complexity of the aesthetic experience which accounts for the difference made by the knowledge that a work of art is a forgery. That the aesthetic experience is complex I do not deny. But it is not so complex that such items of information as the place and date of creation or the name of the creator of a work of art have to be considered. The fact that *The Disciples* is a forgery is just that, a fact. It is a fact *about* the painting which stands entirely apart from it as an object for aesthetic contemplation. The knowledge of this fact can neither add anything to nor subtract anything from the aesthetic experience (as aesthetic), except insofar as preoccupation with it or disappointment on its account may in some degree prevent us from having an aesthetic experience at all. Whatever the reasons for the removal of *The Disciples* from the walls of the Boymans Museum in Rotterdam, they were assuredly not aesthetic.

And yet, we can all sympathize with, or at least understand, why *The Disciples* was removed. It was, after all, a forgery, and even if we grant that it is not a matter of aesthetics, it still seems self-evident that forgery remains a normative term implying a defect or absence in its object. In short, we still need to answer our question: What is wrong with a forgery?

The most obvious answer to this question, after the aesthetic one, is that forgery is a moral or legal normative concept, and that it thus refers to an object which, if not necessarily aesthetically inferior, is always morally offensive. Specifically, the reason forgery is a moral offense, according to this view, is of course that it involves *deception*. Reasonable as this view seems at first, it does not, as I will try to show, answer our question adequately.

Now it cannot be denied, I think, that we do in fact often intend little more than this moral connotation when we speak of forgery. Just because forgery is a normative concept we implicitly condemn any instance of it because we generally assume that it involves the breaking of a legal or moral code. But this assumption is only sometimes correct. It is important to note this because historically by far the majority of artistic fakes or forgeries have not been legal forgeries. Most often they have been the result of simple mistakes, misunderstandings, and lack of information about given works of art.

We can, as a point of terminology, exclude all such instances from the category of forgery and restrict the term to those cases involving deliberate deception. There is, after all, a whole class of forgeries, including simple copies, misattributions, composites, and works "in the manner of" some reputable artist, which represent deliberate frauds. In these cases of forgery, which are undoubtedly the most notorious and disconcerting, someone, e.g., artist or art dealer, has passed off a work of art as being something which it is not. The motive for doing so is almost always economic, but occasionally, as with van Meegeren, there is involved also a psychological motive of personal prestige or revenge. In any case, it seems clear that – if we leave out of consideration the factor of financial loss, which can of course be considerable, as again the van Meegeren case proved – such deliberate forgeries are condemned by us on moral grounds, that is, because they involve conscious deception.

Yet as a final answer to our question as to what is wrong with a forgery, this definition fails. The reason is the following: Although to some extent it is true that passing *anything* off as *anything* that it is not constitutes deception and is thus an undesirable or morally repugnant act, the case of deception we have in mind when we define forgery in terms of it is that of passing off the inferior as the superior. Although, strictly speaking, passing off a genuine de Hoogh as a Vermeer is also an immoral act of deception, it is hard to think of it as a forgery at all, let alone a forgery in the same sense as passing off a van Meegeren as a Vermeer is. The reason is obviously that in the case of the de Hoogh a superior work is being passed off as a superior work (by another artist), while in the van Meegeren case a presumably inferior work is passed off as a superior work.

What is needed, then, to make our moral definition of forgery more accurate is the specification "passing off the inferior as the superior." But it is just at this point that this common-sense definition of artistic forgery in moral terms breaks down. For we are now faced with the question of what is meant by superior and inferior in art. The moral definition of forgery says in effect that a forgery is an inferior work passed off as a superior one. But what is meant here by inferior? We have already seen that the forgery is not necessarily *aesthetically* inferior. What, then, does it mean? Once again, what is wrong with a forgery?

The attempt to define forgery in moral terms fails because it inevitably already assumes that there exists a difference between genuine works of art and forgeries which makes passing off the latter as the former an offense against a moral or legal law. For only if such a difference does in fact exist can there be any rationale for the law. It is, of course, precisely this assumed real difference which we are trying to discover in this chapter.

It seems to me that the offense felt to be involved in forgery is not so much against the spirit of beauty (aesthetics) or the spirit of the law (morality) as against the spirit of art. Somehow, a work such as *The Disciples* lacks artistic integrity. Even if it is beautiful and even if van Meegeren had not forged Vermeer's signature, there would still be something wrong with *The Disciples*. *What?* is still our question.

We may approach this problem by considering the following interesting point. The concept of forgery seems to be peculiarly inapplicable to the performing arts. It would be quite nonsensical to say, for example, that the man who played the Bach suites for unaccompanied cello and whom at the time we took to be Pablo Casals was in fact a forger. Similarly, we should want to argue that the term *forgery* was misused if we should read in the newspaper that Margot Fonteyn's performance in *Swan Lake* last night was a forgery because as a matter of fact it was not Margot Fonteyn who danced last night, but rather some unknown person whom everyone mistook for Margot Fonteyn. Again, it is difficult to see in what sense a performance of, say, *Oedipus Rex* or *Hamlet* could be termed a forgery.

Here, however, we must immediately clarify our point, for it is easily misunderstood. There is, of course, a sense in which a performance of *Hamlet* or *Swan Lake* or the Bach suites could be called a forgery. If, for example, someone gave a performance of *Hamlet* in which every gesture, every movement, every vocal interpretation had been copied or imitated from the performance of *Hamlet* by Laurence Olivier, we could, I suppose, call the former a forgery of the latter. But notice that in that case we are interpreting the art of acting not as a performing art but as a creative art. For what is meant is that Olivier's interpretation and performance of *Hamlet* is itself an original and creative work of art which can be forged. Similar comments would apply to Margot Fonteyn's *Swan Lake* and Casals's Bach suites and, in fact, to every performance.

My point, is then, that the concept of forgery applies only to the creative and not to the performing arts. It can be denied, of course, that there is any such ultimate distinction between creative and performing arts. But we shall still have to admit, I think, that the duality on which it is based – the duality of creativity or originality on the one hand and reproduction or technique on the other – is real. We shall have to admit that originality and technique are two elements of all art; for it can be argued not only that a performance requires more than technique, namely originality, but also that the creation of a work of art requires more than originality, namely technique.

The truth of the matter is probably that both performances and works of art vary greatly and significantly in the degree to which they possess these elements. In fact, their relative presence in works of art and performances makes an interesting way of categorizing the latter. But it would be wrong to assert that these two elements are inseparable. I can assure the reader that a portrait painted by me would be technically almost totally incompetent, and yet even I would not deny that it might be original. On the other hand, a really skillful copy of, for example, a Rembrandt drawing may be technically perfect and yet lack all originality. These two examples establish the two extreme cases of a kind of continuum. The copy of Rembrandt is, of course, the forgery *par excellence*. My incompetent portrait is as far removed from being a forgery as any work can be. Somewhere in between lies the whole body of legitimate performances and works of art.

The implications of this long and devious argument are as follows: Forgery is a concept that can be made meaningful only by reference to the concept of originality, and hence only to art viewed as a *creative*, not as a reproductive or technical, activity. The element of performance or technique in art cannot be an object for forgery because technique is not the kind of thing that can be forged. Technique is, as it were, public. One does or does not possess it or one acquires it or learns it. One may even pretend to have it. But one cannot forge it because in order to forge it one must already possess it, in which case there is no need to forge it. It is not Vermeer's technique in painting light which van Meegeren forged. That technique is public and may be had by anyone who is able and willing to learn it. It is rather Vermeer's discovery of this technique and his use of it, that is, Vermeer's originality, which is forged. The light, as well as the composition, the color, and many other features, of course, were original with Vermeer. They are not original with van Meegeren. They are forged.

At this point our argument could conclude were it not for the fact that the case which we have used throughout as our chief example, *Christ and the Disciples at Emmaus*, is not in fact a skillful copy of a Vermeer but a novel painting in the style of Vermeer. This threatens our definition of forgery since this particular forgery (always assuming it *is* a forgery) obviously possesses originality in some sense of the word.

The problem of forgery, in other words, is a good deal more complex than might at first be supposed, and before we can rest content with our definition of forgery as the lack of originality in works of art, we must show that the concept of originality can indeed account for the meaning of forgery as an untrue or objectionable thing in all instances, including even such a bizarre case as van Meegeren's *Disciples at Emmaus*. It thus becomes important to examine the various possible meanings that the term *originality* may have in the context of art in order to determine in what sense *The Disciples* does and does not possess it, and hence in what sense it can meaningfully and justifiably be termed a forgery.

1. A work of art may be said to be original in the sense of being a particular object not identical with any other object. But this originality is trivial since it is a quality possessed by all things. *Particularity* or *self-identity* would be better names for it.

2. By originality in a work of art we may mean that it possesses a certain superficial individuality which serves to distinguish it from other works of art. Thus, for example, a certain subject matter in a particular arrangement painted in certain colors may serve to identify a painting and mark it as an original work of art in the sense that its subject matter is unique. Probably the term *individuality* specifies this quality more adequately than *originality*.

It seems safe to assert that this quality of individuality is a necessary condition for any work of art to be called original in any significant sense. It is, however, not a necessary condition for a work to be called beautiful or to be the object of an aesthetic experience. A good reproduction or copy of a painting may be the object of aesthetic contemplation yet lack all originality in the sense which we are here considering. Historically many forgeries are of this kind, i.e., more or less skillful copies of existing works of art. They may be described as being forgeries just because they lack this kind of originality and hence any other kind of originality as well. Notice that the quality which makes such a copy a forgery, i.e., its lack of individuality, is not a quality which exists in the work of art as such. It is a fact about the work of art which can be known only by placing the latter in the context of the history of art and observing whether any identical work predates it.

As we said above, it is not this kind of originality which is lacking in *The Disciples*.[3]

3. By originality in art we may mean the kind of imaginative novelty or spontaneity which is a mark of every good work of art. It is the kind of originality which attaches to individual works of art and which can be specified in formal or technical terms such as composition, balance, color intensity, perspective, harmony, rhythm, tempo, texture, rhyme, alliteration, suspense, character, plot, structure, choice of subject matter, and so on. Here again, however, in order for this quality to be meaningfully called originality, a reference must be made to a historical context in terms of which we are considering the particular work of art in question, e.g., this work of art is original because the artist has done something with the subject and its treatment which has never been done before, or this work is not original because many others just like it predate it.

In any case, *The Disciples* does, by common consent, possess this kind of originality and is therefore, in this sense at least, not a forgery.

4. The term *originality* is sometimes used to refer to the great artistic achievement of a specific work of art. Thus we might say that whereas nearly all of Milton's works are good and original in the sense of (3) above, *Paradise Lost* has a particularly profound originality possessed only by really superlative works of art. It is hard to state precisely what is meant by this use of the term *originality*. In justifying it we should probably point to the scope, profundity, daring, and novelty of the conception of the work of art in question as well as to the excellence of its execution. No doubt this kind of originality differs from that discussed under (3) above only in degree.

It is to be noted that it cannot be the lack of this kind of originality which defines a forgery since, almost by definition, it is a quality lacking in many – maybe the majority of – legitimate works of art. Moreover, judging from the critical commentary with which *The Disciples* was received at the time of its discovery – commentary unbiased by the knowledge that it was a forgery – it seems reasonable to infer that the kind of originality meant here is in fact one which *The Disciples* very likely possesses.

5. Finally, it would seem that by originality in art we can and often do mean the artistic novelty and achievement not of one particular work of art but of the totality of artistic productions of one man or even one school. Thus we may speak of the originality of Vermeer or El Greco or Mozart or Dante or Impressionism or the Metaphysical Poets or even the Greeks or the Renaissance, always referring, I presume, to the artistic

95

accomplishments achieved and embodied in the works of art belonging to the particular man, movement, or period. In the case of Vermeer we may speak of the originality of the artist's sense of design in the genre picture, the originality of his use of bright and pure colors, and of the originality of his treatment and execution of light.

We must note first of all that this meaning of originality, too, depends entirely on a historical context in which we are placing and considering the accomplishment of one man or one period. It would be meaningless to call Impressionism original, in the sense here considered, except in reference to the history of art which preceded it. Again, it is just because Vermeer's sense of pictorial design, his use of bright colors, and his mastery of the technique of painting light are not found in the history of art before him that we call these things original in Vermeer's work. Originality, even in this more profound sense, or rather especially in this more profound sense, is a quality definable only in terms of the history of art.

A second point of importance is that while originality as here considered is a quality which attaches to a whole corpus or style of works of art, it can be considered to exist in one particular work of art in the sense that that work of art is a typical example of the style or movement to which it belongs and therefore embodies the originality of that style or movement. Thus we may say that Vermeer's *A Painter in His Studio* is original because in this painting (as well as in several others, of course) we recognize those characteristics mentioned earlier (light, design, color, etc.) which are so typical of Vermeer's work as a whole and which, when we consider the whole of Vermeer's work in the context of the history of art, allow us to ascribe originality to it.

Turning our attention once more to *The Disciples*, we are at last in a position to provide an adequate answer to our question as to the meaning of the term forgery when applied to a work of art such as *The Disciples*. We shall find, I think, that the fraudulent character of this painting is adequately defined by stating that it lacks originality in the fifth and final sense which we have here considered. Whatever kinds of originality it can claim – and we have seen that it possesses all the kinds previously discussed – it is *not* original in the sense of being the product of a style, period, or technique which, when considered in its appropriate historical context, can be said to represent a significant achievement. It is just this fact which differentiates this painting from a genuine Vermeer! The latter, when considered in its historical context, i.e., the seventeenth century, possesses the qualities of artistic or creative novelty which justify us in calling it original. *The Disciples*, on the other hand, in *its* historical context, i.e., the twentieth century, is not original, since it presents nothing new or creative to the history of art even though, as we have emphasized earlier, it may well be as beautiful as the genuine Vermeer pictures.

It is to be noted that in this definition of forgery the phrase "appropriate historical context" refers to the date of production of the particular work of art in question, not the date which in the history of art is appropriate to its style or subject matter.[4] In other words, what makes *The Disciples* a forgery is precisely the disparity or gap between its stylistically appropriate features and its actual date of production. It is simply this disparity which we have in mind when we say that forgeries such as *The Disciples* lack integrity.

It is interesting at this point to recall van Meegeren's reasoning in perpetrating the Vermeer forgeries. "Either," he reasoned, "the critics must admit their fallibility or else acknowledge that I am as great an artist as Vermeer." We can see now that this reasoning is not sound. For the notion of greatness involved in it depends on the same concept of historical originality which we have been considering. The only difference is that we are now thinking of it as an attribute of the artist rather than of the works of art. Van Meegeren's mistake was in thinking that Vermeer's reputation as a great artist depended on his ability to paint beautiful pictures. If this were so, the dilemma which van Meegeren posed to the critics would have been a real one, for his picture is undeniably beautiful. But, in fact, Vermeer is *not* a great artist only because he could paint beautiful pictures. He is great for that reason plus something else. And that something else is precisely the fact of his originality, i.e., the fact that he painted certain pictures in a certain manner *at a certain time in the history and development of art*. Vermeer's art represents a genuine creative achievement in the history of art. It is the work not merely of a master craftsman or technician but of a creative genius as well. And it is for the latter rather than for the former reason that we call Vermeer great.

Van Meegeren, on the other hand, possessed only craftsmanship or technique. His works lack the historical originality of Vermeer's and it is for this reason that we should not want to call him great as we call Vermeer great.[5] At the same time it must be recalled that van Meegeren's forgeries are not forgeries *par excellence*. *The Disciples*, though not original in the most important sense, possesses, as we have seen, degrees of originality generally lacking in forgeries.

In this connection it is interesting to speculate on the relations between originality and technique in the creative continuum which we came upon earlier. A totally original work is one which lacks all technique. A forgery *par excellence* represents the perfection of technique with the absence of all originality. True works of art are somewhere in between. Perhaps the really great works of art, such as Vermeer's, are those which embody a maximum of both originality and technique: van Meegeren's forgeries can never be in this last category, for, as we have seen, they lack the most important kind of originality.

Finally, the only question that remains is why originality is such a significant aspect of art. Now we need to note, of course, that the concern with originality is not a universal characteristic of art or artists. Yet the fact that the search for originality is perhaps typical only of modern Western art tends to strengthen the presumption of its fundamental relation to the concept of forgery. For it is also just in the modern Western tradition that the problem of forgery has taken on the kind of economic and aesthetic significance which warrants our concern with it here. But why, even in modern Western art, should the importance of originality be such that the concepts of greatness and forgery in art are ultimately definable only by reference to it? The answer is, I believe, not hard to find. It rests on the fact that art has and must have a history. If it did not, if artists were concerned only with making beautiful pictures, poems, symphonies, etc., the possibilities for the creation of aesthetically pleasing works of art would soon be exhausted. We would (perhaps) have a number of lovely paintings, but we should soon grow tired of them, for they would all be more or less alike. But artists do not seek merely to produce works of beauty. They seek to produce *original* works of beauty. And when they succeed in achieving this originality we call their works great not only because they are beautiful but because they have also unlocked, both to artists and to appreciators, unknown and unexplored realms of beauty. Men like Leonardo, Rembrandt, Haydn, Goethe, and Vermeer are great not merely because of the excellence of their works but also because of their creative originality which goes on to inspire other artists and leads through them to new and aesthetically valuable developments in the history of art. It is, in fact, this search for creative originality which insures the continuation and significance of such a history in the first place.

It is for this reason that the concept of originality has become inseparable from that of art. It is for this reason too that aesthetics has traditionally concerned itself with topics such as the inspiration of the artist, the mystery of the creative act, the intense and impassioned search of the artist, the artist as the prophet of his times, the artistic struggle after expression, art as the chronicle of the emotional life of a period in history, art as a product of its time, and so on. All such topics are relevant not to art as the production of works of beauty but to art as the production of *original* works of beauty, or, more accurately, works of original beauty. As such they are perfectly legitimate topics of discussion. But we must not forget that the search for originality is, or ought to be, but the means to an end. That end is, presumably, the production of aesthetically valuable or beautiful works of art; that is, works which are to become the object of an aesthetic experience. That experience is a wholly autonomous one. It does not and cannot take account of any entity or fact which is not aesthetically perceivable in the work of art itself. The historical context in which that work of art stands is just such a fact. It is wholly irrelevant to the pure aesthetic appreciation and judgment of the work of art. And because the fact of forgery – together with originality and greatness – can be ultimately defined only in terms of this historical context, it too is irrelevant to the aesthetic appreciation and judgment of *The Disciples at Emmaus* or any other work of art. The fact of forgery is important historically, biographically, perhaps legally, or, as the van Meegeren case proved, financially; but not, strictly speaking, aesthetically.

In conclusion, let us consider the following paradoxical result. We have seen in what sense Vermeer is considered to be a great artist. We have also seen that although *The Disciples* is indistinguishable from a genuine Vermeer, van Meegeren cannot be thus called great. And yet we would suppose that Vermeer's greatness is somehow embodied in his work, that his paintings are proof of and monuments to his artistic genius. What are we to say, then, of this van Meegeren forgery which hung in a museum for seven years as an embodiment and proof of Vermeer's genius? Are we to say that it now no longer embodies anything at all except van Meegeren's skillful forging technique? Or are we to grant after all that this painting proves van Meegeren's greatness as Vermeer's paintings do his? The answer is, I think, surprising but wholly appropriate. Paradoxically, *The Disciples at Emmaus* is as much a monument to the artistic genius of Vermeer as are Vermeer's own paintings. Even though it was painted by van Meegeren in the twentieth century, it embodies and bears witness to the greatness of the seventeenth-century art of Vermeer.

NOTES

1   Cf. Arthur Koestler, "The anatomy of snobbery," *The Anchor Review* 1 (Garden City: Doubleday Anchor Books, 1955): 1–25.
2   J. Decoen, *Vermeer-Van Meegeren, Back to the Truth*, trans. E.J. Labarre (London: Donker, 1951), p. 60.
3   A slightly more complex case is offered by forgeries (including probably some of van Meegeren's less carefully executed Vermeer forgeries) which are not simple copies of other paintings but which are composites of other paintings. While such forgeries clearly have a measure of individuality totally lacking in the simple copy, I should want to maintain that they lack only superficially the kind of originality here discussed.
4   To avoid all ambiguity in my definition of forgery, I need to specify whether "actual date of production" refers to the completion of the finished, concrete work of art or only to the productive means of such works. This question bears on the legitimacy of certain works in art forms where the means of production and the finished product are separable. Such works include lithographs, etchings, wood-cuts, cast sculptures, etc. What, for example, are we to say of a modern bronze cast made from a mold taken directly from an ancient bronze cast or a modern print made from an eighteenth-century block? Are such art objects forgeries? The answer, it seems to me, is largely a matter of convenience and terminology. Assuming that there is no moral fraud, i.e., deception, involved, whether or not to call such cases instances of forgery becomes an academic question. It depends entirely on what we take to be "the work of art." In the case of lithography or etching there may be some ambiguity about this. I myself would define "the work of art" as the finished concrete product and hence I would indeed call modern prints from old litho stones forgeries, though, assuming no deception is involved, forgeries of a peculiarly amoral, nonoffensive sort. In other arts, such as music, there is little or no ambiguity on this point. Clearly, no one would want to label the first performance of a newly discovered Beethoven symphony a forgery. In still other, e.g., the literary, arts, due to the absolute inseparability of the concrete work of art and the means of its production, this problem cannot arise at all.
5   Unless it be argued that van Meegeren derives *his* greatness from the originality of his works when considered in the context not of the history of art but of the history of forgery!

7

ARTISTIC CRIMES

Denis Dutton

The concept of forgery is a touchstone of criticism. If the existence of forgeries – and their occasional acceptance as authentic works of art – has been too often dismissed or ignored in the theory of criticism, it may be because of the forger's special power to make the critic look ridiculous. Awkward as it is, critics have heaped the most lavish praise on art objects that have turned out to be forged. The suspicion this arouses is, of course, that the critics were led to praise the forgery for the wrong reasons in the first place. Since the aesthetic object as perceived is no different after the revelation that it is forged, the implication to be drawn is that it had previously been critically valued not for its intrinsic aesthetic properties, but because it was believed to be the work of an esteemed artist.

Natural as this suspicion is, it represents a point of view I shall seek to discredit in the following discussion. Everyone recognizes that the proper identification of an art object as genuine or forged is crucial as regards monetary value, that forgery has moral implications, that there are important historical reasons for wanting to distinguish the genuine from the faked art object. But there are many who believe as well that when we come down to assessing the *aesthetic* merits of an art object, the question of authenticity is irrelevant. In this respect, the Han van Meegeren episode is an excellent test case. For van Meegeren's ambition went beyond merely monetary rewards: he wanted to wreak revenge on a critical establishment which he viewed as unjust in its assessment of his talents. And it must have been sweet, during the unveiling of the painting in 1937, to stand at the edge of a crowd in the Boymans Museum and hear one of the world's reigning experts on Dutch masters proclaim van Meegeren's own *Christ and the Disciples at Emmaus* as "perhaps *the* masterpiece of Johannes Vermeer." Not all of his subsequent forgeries received such unqualified acceptance, but it must be remembered that van Meegeren's activities did not come to light until he was arrested shortly after the war for having sold a Dutch national treasure (*The Adulteress*) to the enemy. (The buyer of that painting, Hermann Göring, was reportedly unbelieving when informed of the matter in jail, and there remained critics who continued to doubt van Meegeren's story, at least with regard to the *Emmaus*, for years.)

The van Meegeren episode is just one example of the general problem of forgery in the arts. I say "arts" in the plural because I believe that in one form or another the problem can arise in all of the arts. The problem may be stated quite simply thus: if an aesthetic object has been widely admired and it is discovered that it is a forgery, a copy, or a misattribution, why reject it? A painting has hung for years on a museum wall, giving delight to generations of art lovers. One day it is revealed to be a forgery, and is immediately removed from view. But why? The discovery that a work of art is forged, as, say, with a van Meegeren Vermeer, does not alter the perceived qualities of the work. Hence it can make no *aesthetic* difference whether a work is forged or not. At least this is how one approach to this question goes, an approach that has had such able defenders as Alfred Lessing and Arthur Koestler.[1] Koestler, for instance, insists that an object's status as original or forged is extraneous information, incidental to its intrinsic aesthetic properties. Thus the individual who pays an enormous sum for an original but who would have no interest in a reproduction which he could not tell from the original (perhaps a Picasso pen-and-ink drawing), or worse, who chooses an aesthetically inferior original over an excellent and superior forgery (or reproduction), is said to be at best confused and at worst a snob.

In a discussion largely in agreement with this, Lessing mentions that the possibility of forgery exists only in the "creative" but not the "performing" arts. While I will argue that in certain respects this distinction itself is dubious, as regards the possibility of forgery it is surely misleading. Consider for a moment Smith and Jones, who have just finished listening to a new recording of Liszt's *Transcendental Études*. Smith is transfixed. He says, "What beautiful artistry! The pianist's tone is superb, his control absolute, his speed and accuracy dazzling. Truly an electric performance!" Jones responds with a sigh. "Yeah, it was electrical all right. Or to be more precise, it was electronic. He recorded the music at practice tempo and the engineers speeded it up on a rotating head recorder." Poor Smith – his enthusiasm evaporates.

But really, ought it to? If Smith cannot with his ears discriminate the difference between the pianist's technical accomplishments and an engineer turning a knob, why *should* it make any difference to him? In fact, looking at the situation from Koestler's perspective, we will have to consider that Smith is a snob, or at least somehow confused. But surely there is something legitimate in Smith's response; surely there is more to this than can be accounted for by saying that Smith is simply letting extraaesthetic considerations influence his aesthetic response to the piano performance.

I raise this example in connection with Lessing's claim that "the concept of forgery applies only to the creative and not to the performing arts." The distinction between so-called creative and performing arts has certain obvious uses: we would not wish to confuse the actor and the playwright, the conductor and the composer, the dancer and the choreographer. And yet this distinction (often employed invidiously against the performer) can cause us to lose sight of the fact that in certain respects all arts are creative, and correlatively, all arts are performing. It is this latter fact which is of particular relevance to understanding what is wrong with forgeries. For it can be argued that every work of art – every painting, statue, novel, symphony, ballet, as well as every interpretation or rendition of a piece of music, every reading of a poem or production of a play – involves the element of performance.

When we speak of a performance we usually have in mind a human activity which stands in some sense complete in itself: we talk of the President's performance at a press conference, or a student's performance on an examination, with the intention of marking off these particular activities from the whole of a presidential administration or the quality of the student's work done throughout a course. Moreover, as these examples also indicate, performances are said to involve some sense of accomplishment, of achievement. As objects of contemplation, art works stand in differing relations to the performances of artists, depending on the art form in question. On the one hand, we have such arts as the dance, where the human activity involved in creating the object of contemplation and the object itself are one and the same thing. In such a case it would be odd to say that the object somehow represents the performance of the artist, because to perceive the object is to perceive the performance. On the other hand, we have painting, where we normally perceive the work of art without perceiving those actions which have brought it into being. Nevertheless, in cases such as the latter what we see is the end-product of human activity; the object of our perception can be understood as representative of a human performance. That arts differ with respect to how or whether we actually perceive at the moment of creation the artist's performance makes no difference to the relevance of the concept to understanding all of the arts. In fact, the concept of performance is internal to our whole notion of art.[2]

Every work of art is an artifact, the product of human skills and techniques. If we see an actor or a dancer or a violinist at work, we are constantly conscious of human agency. Less immediately apparent is the element of performance in a painting that has hung perhaps for generations in a museum, or a long-familiar musical composition. Yet we are no less in such cases confronted with the results of human agency. As performances, works of art represent the ways in which artists solve problems, overcome obstacles, make do with available materials. The ultimate product is designed for our contemplation, as an object of particular interest in its own right, perhaps in isolation from other art objects or from the activity of the artist. But this isolation which frequently characterizes our mode of attention to aesthetic objects ought not to blind us to a fact we may take for granted: that the work of art has a human origin, and must be understood as such.

We begin to see this more clearly when we consider our aesthetic response to natural beauty. In a passage in *Art as Experience*, John Dewey asks us to imagine that some object we had come to enjoy, believing it to be a primitive artifact, is revealed to us to be an "accidental natural product."[3] In Dewey's view, this revelation changes our "appreciative perception" of the object. His point is that aesthetic appreciation is "inherently connected with the experience of making." This is well taken; imagine, for instance, the sorts of things we might say of the object before and after the revelation of its natural origin. We could continue to appreciate those features from among the object's purely physical qualities which please us, such as shape and texture. But aspects of the object which we had previously assumed to be expressive will no longer be understood as such: it could still be called "angular" or "jagged" but not "energetic" or "restless"; it could still be "fragile," perhaps even "graceful," but no longer "economical" or "witty." It could in general still be described in terms of predicates indicating that it is agreeably shaped, but not in terms of predicates implying that it is well wrought. We could continue to enjoy the object, but we would no longer find ourselves admiring it in the same way: "to admire" usually means in part "to enjoy," but it also carries with it implications of *esteem* (one can even admire a work of art without particularly enjoying it).[4]

Contrast this with another object of aesthetic appreciation. Let us take as an example one which we do not usually think of in terms of performance: Schubert's setting of Goethe's "Erlkönig." Like a pleasantly shaped piece of driftwood, this song is an object of aesthetic enjoyment. But it is surely more than merely a pretty piece of music sprung from the mind of someone on an autumn afternoon in 1815. As a work of art, it is seen, for example, as a way of overcoming various problems, musical and dramatic, posed by Goethe's text. The poem presents a composer with certain possibilities and limitations; in listening to Schubert's "Erlkönig" we are listening not simply to an attractive sonic surface, but to how one man has worked within those limitations in developing those possibilities. We listen as the music modulates to extraordinarily remote keys; we note how Schubert's stresses differ from Goethe's and are yet in no way inferior to the poet's; we admire how the composer has handled the problems posed by the three voices in the poem; we consider, against the backdrop of prevailing tonal conventions in Schubert's time, the shrill minor ninths with which he has the child cry "Mein Vater"; we notice how Schubert (typically) can allow the music to modulate into major keys without destroying the dark atmosphere of the song – in fact, the song is all the more sinister with these harmonic diversions.

In all of these considerations, we treat the composition of the music itself as a performance, as an activity involving human intention. There are theorists who would of course insist on our distinguishing the song as an object of aesthetic attention from the circumstances of its origin. That such distinction is possible is self-evident. That we do not, and ought not, completely divorce these elements of appreciation is also clear. What *is* Schubert's "Erlkönig"? It is this pretty sonic experience, certain words strung together and sung in certain tones to piano accompaniment, and we can talk endlessly about the beauties of that aural surface just as we could talk of the appealing properties of the piece of driftwood. It is also a profound human achievement, something done by someone; it is precisely a *setting* of Goethe's poem, one of perhaps fifty other such settings produced in the nineteenth century. What is understood and appreciated about Schubert's "Erlkönig" is neither of these to the exclusion of the other: both are part of our understanding of this great work of art.

And so it is whenever we observe the work of an artist, be that artist a composer developing a theme, or inventing one (compare the usual performances of Beethoven with Tschaikovsky in these regards), be that artist a poet writing an elegy for his deceased parrot, be that artist a painter trying to figure out how to give some unity to the family portrait now that the duke insists on having his favorite hunting dogs included too, be that artist a playwright who must resolve a complex and tangled plot – in all of these cases, it is appropriate to speak of the performance of a task, and of the success or failure of the task at hand.

Again, in order to grasp what it is that is before us, we must have some notion of what the maker of the object in question has done, including some idea of the limitations, technical and conventional, within which he has worked. It may be perfectly true (and not necessarily obviously so) to remark that in a painting of the Madonna the pale pink of the Virgin's robe contrasts pleasantly with the light blue-gray of her cloak. But it is far from irrelevant to know that the artist may be working within a canon (as, for example, fifteenth-century Italian artists did) according to which the robe must be some shade of red, and the cloak must be blue. The demand (to juxtapose fundamentally warm and cool colors) poses difficulties for creating harmony between robe and cloak, in the face of which Ghirlandaio may reduce the size of the cloak and tone it down with gray, Perugino may depict the cloak thrown over the Virgin's knees and allow a green shawl with red and yellow stripes to dominate the composition, while Filippo Lippi may simply cover the robe completely with the cloak. To say that the resulting assemblage of colors is pleasant may, again, be true enough; a fuller appreciation and understanding, however, would involve recognizing how that pleasing harmony is a response to a problematic demand put upon the artist.

Artistic performances in general, like musical or dramatic performances in particular, are assessed according to how they succeed or fail – the notions of success or failure are as much internal to our idea of performance as the idea of performance is to our concept of art. In this respect, there is an important truth in a view such as Goethe's which insists that criticism must begin by finding out what the artist intended to do and then ask whether he succeeded in doing it. Before we can determine whether or not a particular artistic performance can be said to succeed or fail, we must have some notion of *what counts as success or failure in connection with the kind of artistic performance in question.*[5] Let us consider once again Smith's difficulties with the piano performance of the Liszt *études*. The attitude we properly take toward any artistic performance varies enormously, depending on the nature of what confronts us. There are many elements that go into a performance of a Liszt study according to which we assess it. We consider tone, phrasing, tempo, accuracy, the pianist's ability to sustain a line, to build to a climax, and so forth. Speed and brilliance may be important considerations (which is not to say that the fastest or most brilliant performance will be the best). Now part of what will count as achievement in the performance of a Liszt study is that the music be produced by the pianist's ten fingers; in piano criticism this is usually taken for granted. Given how we understand pianistry, this forms one of the expectations we take with us to our perception of the piano performance; it indicates, moreover, part of what counts as achievement in playing the piano.

Of course, I am not saying that the assessment of success or failure in piano performance need necessarily be the way I describe it. We can well imagine different manners of going about producing the aural experience to which we attend. There might come a time, for instance, when electronically produced accelerandos will become accepted procedure in piano recording. But note that this will alter our conception of what will count as achievement in a recorded piano performance. We will no longer say things like, "Didn't she play that run beautifully?" but rather, "Don't they do marvelous tempo engineering at Decca?" We may expect that engineers will be given credit on record albums, not for having (presumably) faithfully reproduced the sounds the artist has produced, but for having altered those sounds in ways previously left to the performer. I for one would not oppose this, any more than I oppose recording *Götterdämmerung* in separate sessions on various days. But just as I know, and in fact ought to know, that the resulting recording of *Götterdämmerung* will feature voices which sustain their power throughout the whole opera in a way that would be impossible in any live performance, so I ought to know that the piano recording I am listening to is a collaboration of pianist and engineer, one which, perhaps, features runs at speeds human nerve and muscle could never alone produce. Until I know this, I cannot understand the nature of the achievement before me.

Here is where the electronic accelerandos of the van Meegeren fakes have the ability to betray us, and where forgery in general misleads. In the most obvious sense, a forgery is an artifact of one person which is intentionally attributed to another, usually with the purpose of turning a profit. But what is wrong with forgeries – and forgeries of painting would stand merely as the most famous examples – is that they not only misattribute origin: because they misattribute origin, they *misrepresent achievement*. It is essential that forgeries be understood as a subset of a wider class of misrepresented artistic performances. Since all art can be seen under the aspect of performance, whether or not the art in question is conventionally called "performing," there exists always the possibility that the nature of the achievement involved in the performance may be misrepresented or misunderstood. In my example of the piano recording, Smith brings to his experience certain expectations regarding what is to count as achievement in the art in question, and these expectations are not met. The point is that Smith's experience cannot be understood as an experience of sound, such that the faster and more brilliant the sounds the better; Smith's experience of sound implies the experience of a performance, of something done in a certain way by a human being.

The fundamental question, then, is, What has the artist done, what has he achieved? The question is fundamental, moreover, not because of any contingent facts about the psychology of aesthetic perception, but because of the nature of the concept of art itself. As I have noted, Smith's initial disappointment in the piano recording may later be replaced by admiration for the skill and sensitivity with which the engineer has varied the tempi of the recording. This does not indicate that Smith's response can be understood as merely conditioned by his beliefs about what he perceives. To the contrary, Smith's beliefs are about what he takes to be a work of art, and hence are centered on what he understands to be the achievement implicit in what he perceives. Technological advances in the arts in general, the inventions of airbrushes, electric stage lighting, sound synthesizers, and so forth, have tended progressively to alter what counts as achievement in the arts; these advances have in no way altered the relevance of the concept of achievement in art or criticism and hence have not changed to that extent the concept of art *überhaupt*. Smith's mistake about the nature of the achievement before him, or the experts' mistakes about the van Meegeren Vermeers, simply requires that the question of what the achievement is be recast: indeed, the achievement of the engineer may be worthy of admiration, just as the achievement of van Meegeren was considerable. Still, the achievement of an engineer is not the achievement of a pianist, and the achievement of van Meegeren, however notable it may be, cannot be identical with that of Vermeer.

Thus I can believe that the painting before me is a Vermeer instead of a van Meegeren, and adjust my perception accordingly. But I cannot similarly believe that it makes *no difference* whether it is a Vermeer or a van Meegeren, not at any rate if I am to continue to employ the concept of art in terms of which we think about Vermeers, van Meegerens, piano virtuosi, and the rest. This is not a contingent matter of belief or taste; reference to origins is a necessary constituent of the concept of a work of art. Nor is it merely a cultural question. Cultural considerations can influence how we talk about art, can alter in various ways our attitude toward it. It is frequently pointed out, for instance, that criticism as customarily practiced in the European tradition places great emphasis on the individual artist in a way that art and criticism in the Orient traditionally do not. Modern critics in the Occident tend to care deeply, perhaps sometimes excessively, about who created a work of art. But this does not mean that, say, Chinese critics have been unconcerned with the origins of art works: it does not entail that they would be uninterested ever in distinguishing a copy from a newly invented composition, or a marvelously carved stone from one smoothed by the waters of a brook. To be sure, culture shapes and changes what various peoples believe about art and their attitudes toward it. This may be strikingly different from ours, as in the case of the elaborately carved *Malagan* of New Ireland, which is unceremoniously discarded after its one-time use. Anyone who concluded from this that the people of New Ireland had no concept of art would be open to ridicule; they may have different views about how art is to be treated – to that extent we could even say loosely that it is a "different conception of art from ours." But, limiting ourselves only to that consideration germane to the present discussion, it is a conception of art so long as according to it art is treated among other things as human performance, the work of art having implicit in it the possibility of achievement of some kind. Thus the concept of art is constituted a priori of certain essential properties. I do not propose to enumerate those features (the question of the contents of any such list lies at the heart of the philosophy of art); but I do insist that reference to origins and achievement must be included among these properties.[6] This whole issue is what gives the problem of forgery such central philosophical importance: theorists who claim that it ought to make no difference to appreciation whether a work is forged or not do not merely challenge a few dearly held cultural beliefs about what is important in art. To the contrary, they attack the very idea of art itself.

Let us take stock of what I have so far argued. I have claimed that in certain respects, differing according to the type of art in question, the concept of performance is intrinsic to our understanding of art; that works of art of whatever sort can be seen under the aspect of performance. In emphasizing the importance of the notion of performance in understanding art, I have centered attention on the extent to which works of art are the end-products of human activities, on the degree to which they represent things done by human agents. In this way, part of what constitutes our understanding of works of art involves grasping what sort of achievement the work itself represents. This takes us, then, to the question of the origins of the work: we cannot understand the work of art without some notion of its origins, who created it, the context in which the creator worked, and so forth. But now it must be stressed that our interest in origins, in the possibility or actuality of human achievement, always goes hand-in-hand with our interest in the work of art as visual, verbal, or aural surface. In its extreme forms, contextualism in critical theory has tended to emphasize the origins of the work, its status as human achievement, at the expense of attention to the purely formal properties; in its exclusive concentration on formal properties, isolationism, or formalism, has (by definition) tended to slight the importance of the human context, the human origins, of art. Both of these positions in their more extreme and dogmatic forms constitute a kind of philistinism. The more familiar sort of philistinism (the sort against which Koestler and Lessing react) has it that if a work of art is a forgery, then it must somehow be without value: once we are told that these are van Meegerens before us, and not Vermeers, we reject them, though their formal properties remain unchanged. The opposed sort of philistinism, which could well be called *aestheticist philistinism*, claims that formal properties are the only significant properties of works of art; that since questions of origins are not important, it ought to make no difference to us at all whether we are confronted with Vermeers or van Meegerens. Both positions are properly called philistine because both fail to acknowledge a fundamental element of artistic value.

In developing a view which finds the aesthetic significance of forgery in the extent to which it misrepresents artistic achievement, I have hitherto avoided discussion of a concept often contrasted with the idea of forgery: originality. It is of course easy to say that originality is a legitimate source of value in art, that forgeries lack it, and that they therefore are to be discredited on that account. This seems true enough as far as it goes, but the difficulty is that it does not go far enough. One problem centers on deciding what "original" means, or ought to mean, in contrast to "forged." Originality is often associated with novelty in art, but this sense alone will not do, since there are many fine works of art whose outstanding features have little to do with novelty. Stravinsky's musical ideas, or Wagner's, were more novel in their respective epochs than Mozart's or Bach's; yet it would be odd on that account to call the contributions of the latter composers relatively unoriginal. Furthermore, even forgeries – those putative paradigm cases of unoriginal effort – can have strikingly original aspects. Not, perhaps, with those forgeries which are mere copies; but indeed, the most interesting cases of forgery involve works which are precisely not slavish copies, but pastiches, or works in the style of another artist. Here there is room for originality. Consider the heavy-lidded, sunken eyes of van Meegeren's faces: they may be insipid, but they are certainly original, and not to be found in Vermeer. In fact, we must remind ourselves that stripped of its pretensions, each of the van Meegeren Vermeers is an original van Meegeren. For what it is worth, each of these canvases is in that sense an original work of art: my point is precisely that it may not be worth much.

A crux here is that an artistic performance can be perfectly original and yet at the same time share with forgery the essential element of being misrepresented in terms of its actual achievement. The concept of originality is important in this context because it emphasizes the importance of the origins of the work of art: part of what disturbs us about such cases as the van Meegeren episode is that aesthetically significant aspects of the paintings at issue did not have their origins with Vermeer but with an artist who lived some hundreds of years later. In that sense, we can call the van Meegeren fakes "unoriginal"; though they are original van Meegerens, elements which we especially value in them did not originate with Vermeer – and part of what would make those elements valuable is that they be the product of seventeenth-century Vermeer performances rather than twentieth-century van Meegeren performances. But even where all aspects of the performance in question did in fact originate with the single individual who is credited with it, even where the performance is in that sense pluperfectly original, it is possible for it to share with forgery the essential feature of misrepresentation of achievement. Consider an instrumental performer who announces he will play an improvisation and then proceeds to play a carefully premeditated composition of his own creation. What is performed originates entirely with the performer; it is in no sense a copy of the work of another, and one would not want to call it "unoriginal." But it is surely a performance that shares with forgery the fact that its true nature is misrepresented. (Still, even though its status as composition or improvisation is indifferent to the fact that the same person is performing, origins remain important: an improvisation is distinguished from a composition in that it is originated spontaneously, on the spur of the moment – it is heard as it is created.)

And just as there can be cases of misrepresentation of achievement which do not, strictly speaking, involve any misunderstanding of the identity of the individual with whom the art object originates, so there can be misattributions of origin which do not entail significant misrepresentation of achievement. There are stanzas counting as decent Keats which would not have to be radically reappraised in terms of the artistic achievement they represent if they were discovered to have actually been written by Shelley. The same might be said of certain canvases by Derain and Cézanne, or sonatas by Kuhlau and Telemann. (This is not to deny that there are crucial differences between these artists and many of their works: but to mistake Mozart for Haydn is not *always* a foolish or naive blunder.) In other cases, subtle and interesting shifts in our understanding of particular works might result: a piece of music perceived as run-of-the-mill Beethoven might be seen as outstanding Spohr. In such a case, however, our reassessment of the achievement involved is relative only to the career of the individual artist, and not to the historical achievement the work represents.

The significant opposition I find then is not between "forged" and "original," but between correctly represented artistic performance and misrepresented artistic performance. Originality remains a highly relevant concept here, however, insofar as it shows us that some notion of the origins of a work is always germane to appreciation. Without such concern, we cannot understand the full nature of the achievement a work represents, and such understanding is intrinsic to a proper grasp of the work of art. The predictable challenge to this involves the insistence that while I have been directing attention to human performances, what is really in question in appreciating works of art is aesthetic experience. On this account, aesthetic experience is said to refer to the visual or auditory experience of the sensuous surface of the work of art. Yet who is it who ever has these curious "aesthetic experiences"? In fact, I would suppose they are never had, except by infants perhaps – surely never by serious lovers of painting, music, or literature (the latter always a difficult case for aestheticians who like talking about "sensuous surface"). The encounter with a work of art does not consist in merely hearing a succession of pretty sounds or seeing an assemblage of pleasing shapes and colors. It is as much a matter of hearing a virtuoso perform a dazzling and original interpretation of a difficult piece of music or of experiencing a new vision of a familiar subject provided by a painter. Admittedly, there is an attraction in wanting to look past these thorny complexities to concentrate on the sensuous surface, and it is the same attraction that formalism in all its various guises has always had. It is a marvelously simple view, but (alas!) art itself is even more marvelously complex. Against those who insist that an object's status as forged is irrelevant to its artistic merit, I would hold that when we learn that the kind of achievement an art object involves has been radically misrepresented to us, it is not as though we have learned a new fact about some familiar object of aesthetic attention. To the contrary, insofar as its position as a work of art is concerned, it is no longer the same object.[7]

NOTES

1   Arthur Koestler, "The aesthetics of snobbery," *Horizon* 8 (1965): 50–53; Alfred Lessing, "What is wrong with a forgery?" reprinted in the present volume.
2   For a detailed discussion of the general relevance of the notion of performance to aesthetic criticism, see F.E. Sparshott, *The Concept of Criticism* (Oxford: Clarendon Press, 1967).
3   John Dewey, *Art as Experience* (New York: Capricorn Books, 1958), pp. 48–9.
4   In response to an early draft of this chapter presented at a meeting of the American Philosophical Association in Chicago, April 30, 1977, Kendall Walton commented on the difference between our reactions to natural and man-made beauty: "A theist may see the hand of God in a sunset or in the Grand Canyon. But if God is as powerful as he is supposed to be, his making the Grand Canyon or a sunset is hardly an achievement; in this way, one might regard the Grand Canyon as one regards Dutton's electronically accelerated performance . . . the result is too easy to be impressive." In considering the difficulties of criticizing the work of an omnipotent artist, we see the extent to which our admiration of the greatest artistic achievements of humankind involves some sense of the frailty and limitations of ordinary human intellect and imagination.
5   See also Denis Dutton, "To understand it on its own terms," *Philosophy and Phenomenological Research* 35 (1974): 246–56.
6   Cf. Leonard B. Meyer, "Forgery and the anthropology of art," in *Music, the Arts, and Ideas* (Chicago: University of Chicago Press, 1967). Meyer quotes Eliot's remark, "certain things have been done once and for all and cannot be achieved again." He then adds, "The crucial word here is 'achieved.' They can perhaps be done again, but they cannot be achieved again. Beethoven's late style is a discovery and an achievement. Someone coming later can only imitate it" (pp. 58–9).
7   Many friends and colleagues, offered interesting suggestions and comments on various early drafts of this article. In particular, I thank Palko Lukacs, Edward Sayles, Alexander Sesonske, and Kendall Walton for their valuable advice.

SUGGESTIONS FOR FURTHER READING

Bailey, George (1989) "Amateurs imitate, professionals steal", *Journal of Aesthetics and Art Criticism* 47: 221–7.

Battin, M. Pabst (1979) "Exact replication in the visual arts", *Journal of Aesthetics and Art Criticism* 37: 153–8.

Bowden, Ross (1999) "What is wrong with an art forgery?: an anthropological perspective", *Journal of Aesthetics and Art Criticism* 57: 333–44.

Cahn, Steven M. and Griffel, L. Michael (1975) "The strange case of John Shmarb: an aesthetic puzzle", *Journal of Aesthetics and Art Criticism* 34: 21–2.

Cebik, L.B. (1989) "On the suspicion of an art forgery", *Journal of Aesthetics and Art Criticism* 47: 147–56.

Clark, Roger (1984) "Historical context and the aesthetic evaluation of forgeries", *Southern Journal of Philosophy* 22: 317–22.

Courtney, Neil (1975) "The strange case of John Shmarb: an epilogue and further reflections", *Journal of Aesthetics and Art Criticism* 34: 27–8.

Currie, Gregory (1989) "Authenticity", chapter IV of his *An Ontology of Art*, New York: St Martin's Press.

Dutton, Denis (ed.) (1983) *The Forger's Art: Forgery and the Philosophy of Art*, Berkeley: University of California Press. (A very useful collection of articles on forgery. The first article, "Han van Meegeren *fecit*", by Hope B. Werness, tells the story of one of the most famous forgers in history.)

Epperson, Gordon (1975) "The strange case of John Shmarb: some further thoughts", *Journal of Aesthetics and Art Criticism* 34: 23–5.

Gardner, Howard (1982) "Illuminating comparisons: looking at fakes and forgeries", in his *Art, Mind and Brain*, New York: Basic Books.

Gerald, W.R. (ed.) (1977) *The Eye of the Beholder: Fakes, Replicas and Alterations in American Art*, New Haven: Yale University Press.

Goodman, Nelson (1976) "Art and authenticity", chapter III of his *Languages of Art*, 2nd edn, Indianapolis: Hackett.

Hoaglund, John (1976) "Originality and aesthetic value", *British Journal of Aesthetics* 16: 46–55.

Koestler, Arthur (1955) "The anatomy of snobbery", *Anchor Review* 1: 1–25.

Kulka, Thomas (1982) "The artistic and aesthetic status of forgeries", *Leonardo* 15: 115–17.

Kurz, Otto (1967) *Fakes: A Handbook for Collectors and Students*, 2nd edn, New York: Dover.

Levinson, Jerrold (1980) "Aesthetic uniqueness", *Journal of Aesthetics and Art Criticism* 38: 435–50.

—— (1980) "Allographic and autographic art revisited", *Philosophical Studies* 38: 367–83.

McFee, Graham (1980) "The fraudulent in art", *British Journal of Aesthetics* 20: 215–28.

Radford, Colin (1978) "Fakes", *Mind* 87: 66–76.

Sagoff, Mark (1976) "The aesthetic status of forgeries", *Journal of Aesthetics and Art Criticism* 35: 169–80.

—— (1978) "On restoring and reproducing art", *Journal of Philosophy* 75: 453–70.

—— (1981) "On the aesthetic and economic value of art", *British Journal of Aesthetics* 21: 318–29.

Sartwell, Crispin (1988) "Aesthetics of the spurious", *British Journal of Aesthetics* 28: 360–7.

Steele, Hunter (1977) "Fakes and forgeries", *British Journal of Aesthetics* 17: 254–8.

Part 4

ROCK MUSIC AND CULTURE

It is the banality of present-day popular music – a banality relentlessly controlled in order to make it saleable – which brands that music with its crucial trait. That trait is vulgarity. We might almost suspect that this is the most avid concern of the audience, and the maxim of their musical mentality is indeed Brecht's line: "But I don't want to be human!" Any musical reminder of themselves, of the doubtfulness and possible uplifting of their own existence, will embarrass them. That they are really cut off from their potential is the very reason why it infuriates them to be reminded by art.

Theodor W. Adorno, "Popular Music"

You know, the dangerous thing about listening [to music] is that you don't really know the effect it's going to have.

Tori Amos, rock musician

IN AN AGE OF MASS COMMUNICATION, many of us have regular opportunities to listen to almost any style of music produced anywhere in the world. One result of this is much greater disparity in musical tastes than hitherto. Another is that musical styles can spread very rapidly: for example, in 1977 hip-hop music existed only in some neighbourhoods of New York City; two years later, hip-hop recordings were available and imitated by fans in most of the world's urban centres. In short, musical culture has changed dramatically.

In the first chapter in this part, Roger Scruton argues that it has done so for the worse. Widespread indifference to "classical" music – music which demands attention for its own sake – represents nothing less than a crisis of culture. The crisis is compounded by the widespread acceptance of a different type of music as the mainstay of popular culture, music in which melody is deficient and harmonic texture is of no importance. The acceptance of this sort of music, he thinks, reflects the triumph of a culture that refuses to control the behaviour of those who cannot properly control it for themselves, and as such represents a decline in morals as well as in music.

In the second chapter, Theodore Gracyk takes issue with Scruton's arguments, maintaining that fans of rock music do practise discrimination in their aesthetic responses. While listening may be less oriented toward melody and harmonic complexity than is necessary in the "classical" tradition, a distinctively musical understanding is demanded by the music of the heavy metal band Led Zeppelin, as well as by the grunge rock of Nirvana. Agreeing with Scruton that neither blanket condemnation nor blanket acceptance is an appropriate attitude toward popular music, Gracyk offers examples that challenge Scruton's thesis of declines in listening practices and in the education of taste.

Although they disagree about a good deal, Scruton and Gracyk are united by a rejection of aesthetic relativism and aesthetic subjectivism: views which hold that there is no objective standard of taste beyond the preferences of a group or an individual, no objective basis or rule for measuring when it comes to questions of good and bad, of better and worse, that everyone is entitled to his or her own tastes, and none can be said to be any better or worse than any other. Scruton's suggestion is that it is only in a culture in which people are not invested in a properly ordered human community that relativism and subjectivism gain a hold, and it is only by accepting them – by giving up on any idea that we might be able to distinguish objectively between better and worse music – that one could embrace grunge or heavy metal music. Cultural practices that trivialize aesthetic judgement are a denial of what we are as human beings, for we are beings who structure our social lives through expressive objects that demand aesthetic discrimination. Music that does not demand aesthetic discrimination is literally "dehumanizing", and a society that allows such music to flourish is one that has ceased to be a community.

Gracyk agrees with Scruton that we should question relativism and uphold a distinction between better and worse responses to various pieces of music. However, he does not endorse the idea that some types of music are objectively superior to all others, and he attempts to show that their shared position on the culture of listening does need not to give rise to Scruton's concerns about popular music. Gracyk argues that while philosophy of music may legitimately tackle questions of how music bears meaning, Scruton is no longer engaging in philosophy when he attacks grunge and heavy metal. He accuses Scruton of relying too heavily on speculation about what the audience experiences when listening to such music. Agreeing with Scruton that the meaning of music is whatever an informed audience understands when listening to it, Gracyk challenges Scruton to investigate what popular audiences actually understand in their favourite music. He concludes with some speculations about the expression of an ideal of cultural order in some of the music that Scruton regards as clear evidence of a cultural crisis.

Does a shift in taste from Bach to Mantovani or to Nirvana represent a decline in culture, or merely a value-neutral shift in personal preferences? Is our taste in music and in art more generally a matter of purely individual interest, or might it be, as Nietzsche suggested, a measure of the *worth* of a culture? These questions are at the heart of the chapters in this part, and they represent a very deep issue in the philosophy of art.

8

THE DECLINE OF MUSICAL CULTURE

Roger Scruton

TONALITY

Perception is a natural epistemological power of the organism, which depends on no social context for its exercise. The musical experience, however, is not merely perceptual. It is founded in metaphor, arising when unreal movement is heard in imaginary space. Such an experience occurs only within a musical culture, in which traditions of performance and listening shape our expectations. And in *our* tradition – which could fairly claim to be the richest and most fertile that has yet existed – tonality has played the leading role in the building of musical space. No philosophy of music worth the name can ignore tonality, or dismiss the suggestion that it shows us part of what we hear, when we hear sounds as music. Tonality provides a paradigm of musical organization – an organization in which melody is led by harmony, and harmony in turn by melody. And attempts to depart from tonality, or to discard it entirely, seem only to confirm its authority over the musical ear.

For many musicians, however, tonality has become a "dead language", or a language that can be used only ironically – maybe even sarcastically – so as to neutralize the banality of its overexploited terms. For such musicians, the search for an alternative musical order defines the work of the composer in our time, and sets the agenda for every creative gesture.

Conceptions of tonality have ranged so widely, that it is now hard to know what is excluded from the category. George Perle, in an influential study, has described the serial music of Schoenberg and his followers as "twelve-tone tonality",[1] while Roy Travis defines as tonal any music whose "motion unfolds through time a particular tone, interval or chord"[2] – a definition that leans on metaphor, and which excludes virtually nothing.

There is a reason for these wide definitions. Seeking the essence of Western classical music, writers come up against the fact that it is always departing in some new direction. They therefore try to include within their concept of tonality not only the classical tradition, but all the harmonic experiments which it has engendered. There is a real question, indeed, whether it is possible to describe tonality in a way that allows for non-tonal music.

Putting that question aside, we can attempt to define tonality in two ways – formally, in terms of essential features, or materially, in terms of the tonal tradition. Formally speaking, tonal music is music that is organized around a tonic. Much music – perhaps all traditional music – contains privileged tones, which are emphasized by rhythm, pitch, repetition, or accent, and to which the melody returns. But not all music has a tonic. Music has a tonic only if the following conditions are met:

1   The melodic line feels fully "closed" only when it comes to rest on a certain privileged tone (the tonic).
2   The final move on to the tonic has (in standard cases) the character of a "cadence" – a loosening of tension.
3   Octaves are heard as equivalent – so that the effect of closure is duplicated at the octave.
4   Other tones are heard in relation to the tonic – as more or less distant from it, as tending towards or away from it.

Those conditions are not merely stipulative. They attempt to capture a fundamental musical experience – a feature of the intentional world of tones that has been noticed and nurtured by many musical cultures, and which led at last to the discovery of keys, modulations, and triadic harmony. As *now* understood, of course, tonality means that a piece of music is (at any given moment) in a certain *key*, or else moving between keys, a key being a self-contained melodic and harmonic system. But we should not take so parochial and time-bound an approach to the underlying phenomenon. There is much "tonicized" music which is either without harmony, or inherently resistant to it – like the folk-music of the Arabian tribes, in which voices can only double the melody at the unison or octave, leading to effects of high comedy when (as was the case in my youth) the Egyptian army would march to the sound of a military band. . . .

THE DANCE OF SYMPATHY

Sympathetic emotions are aroused as easily by imaginary as by real situations. Indeed, they are more fully released in us by fiction than by fact. In real situations our interests are at stake, and tend to eclipse our sympathies. Fictions occur at an impassable distance, in another and inaccessible world, where the pure archetypes of human feeling expand into a space of their own creation. No fiction can impede or advance my purposes: fictional characters pose no threat; nor can we change their situation. Our feelings towards them are free from the normal cost of sympathy, which is the active need to intervene. In entering a fictional world, we are *exercising* our feelings, but not *acting from* them, for the beliefs necessary for motivation have been ruled out of court. This peculiar exercise of sympathy therefore presents us with the residue of emotion, when the motive has been neutralized – the residue which distinguishes *emotion* from all the other motives in the human psyche. This residue is often referred to as "feeling"; but it is more than that. It is an active assessment of the world, as a place in which my concerns are engaged. Through the free play of sympathy in fiction our emotions can be educated, and also corrupted. And that is one reason why art matters.

Our response to music is a sympathetic response: a response to human life, imagined in the sounds we hear. However, in the absence of representation there is no precise object of sympathy – neither an imaginary human subject, nor a situation perceived through his eyes. The life in music belongs in the musical process, abstract, indeterminate, unowned except through the act whereby we listeners possess it.

Sympathy is not merely a matter of feeling things. There are sympathetic actions and sympathetic gestures. These gestures may arise in response to a real person, really feeling something – someone who needs help, encouragement, or reprimand. Or they may again arise, as in representational art, to things imagined, which are severed from the world of practical interests. Among actions of this second kind none is more remarkable than dancing. In dancing I respond to another's gestures, move with him, or in harmony with him, without seeking to change his predicament or to share his burden. Dancing is not necessarily an aesthetic response; but it has an intrinsic tendency to become aesthetic: it involves responding to movement for its own sake, dwelling on the appearance of another's gesture, finding meaning in that appearance, and matching it with a gesture of my own.

Plato and Aristotle emphasized the character-forming nature of music partly because they thought of music as something in which we *join*. When we dance to music we move with it, just as we move with other people in a dance. And although there are forms of dancing which break free from the bounds of aesthetic experience – which, by losing all restraint, spill over into erotic or violent action – there is a kind of dancing which parallels acting or singing, in being the producer and the product of an aesthetic response. This kind of dancing resembles our experience in the concert hall, which is itself a kind of truncated dance. When we listen we may tap our feet and sway subliminally; our whole being is absorbed by the movement of the music, and moves with it, compelled by incipient gestures of imitation. The object of this imitation is life – life imagined in the form of music.

When someone dances to music, he responds to the way it sounds. Someone might be "set in motion" by subdued music, or driven to a frenzy by corybantic noise. But he would be dancing *to* the music only if his movements express his attention to the music. "Dancing to", in the sense that I am considering, is the name of an aesthetic response.

The dancer who moves with the music moves also with other dancers – and this is part of what he does, even when the other dancers are imaginary. Dancing creates a "sympathetic space" whose meaning is corporate. (It is part of the pleasure of dancing that you are "joining in".)

A ballerina may say, "when I hear this music, I imagine a bird fluttering about its violated nest; that way I know how to dance to it." On the other hand, she may simply say, "This is how I dance to it", and venture no interpretation of her gestures. Similarly, a dancer may describe the music in emotional terms – as an expression of love or grief or anger – and so make sense of it, as the focus of the dance. But someone could dance the very same dance, and feel no inclination to describe the music in emotional terms. Understanding lies in the dance, not in the description.

Dance is a close relative of gesture, and in particular of the formal gestures with which we encounter one another on special occasions, such as weddings and funerals. Manners are a kind of generalized choreography. Consider the gesture of condolence: in performing this I *represent myself* to my grieving neighbour. The distinction can be made (as I shall show in more detail later) between the sincere gesture of condolence and the sentimental fake. We distinguish true compassion, which focuses on another's suffering, from the self-dramatizing pretence of it, whose aim is to display the "beautiful soul" of the performer. A sincere gesture of condolence is not an expression of grief, but an expression of sympathy for grief: its sincerity consists in its concentration on another's predicament, with a view to *relating* to the other *in* his predicament. Sincerity is therefore a matter of intention: is the gesture aimed at the other in his predicament, or is it aimed reflexively, at the person who makes it? (Contrast the person who is distressed by the victim's distress and tries to comfort him, from the person who makes magnificent display of a vicarious grief but forgets the victim entirely, and a moment later is found happily engaged in some equally dramatic emotional display towards someone else.) Conventions emerge spontaneously, as David Lewis has shown, from the complex intentions involved in communicating our states of mind.[3] The conventional gestures at a funeral make possible the sincere expressions, of regret and condolence. In learning them you enter into a common culture with your neighbours.

There is no more difficulty in describing the gestures of a dancer as sincere or sentimental than there is in so describing the gestures of condolence at a funeral. In learning the steps of the dance you are learning to represent yourself to others. And in dancing to music you respond sympathetically to an imaginary movement that is itself understood as a movement of sympathy.

Nietzsche wrote of the "birth of tragedy out of the spirit of music". More plausibly, we might refer to the birth of drama out of the spirit of dancing. Dancing is the social activity which stands nearest to the aesthetic response – a way of "being together" which achieves the absorption in the present experience and the saturation of interest, that are the familiar gifts of art. Light is cast on the expressive character of music if we see the response of the listener as a kind of latent dancing – a sublimated desire to "move with" the music, and so to focus on its moving forms.

In responding to a piece of music we are being led through a series of gestures which gain their significance from the intimation of community. As with a dance, a kind of gravitational field is created, which shapes the emotional life of the one who enters it. We move for a while along the orbit of a formalized emotion and practise its steps. Our truncated movements are also acts of attention: we do what we do in response to the sounds that we hear, when we attend to them aesthetically. If this is what it is to hear the meaning, then hearing the meaning is inseparable from the aesthetic experience. . . . The experience of musical form is an experience of movements and gestures, detached from the material world, and carried through to their musical completion. In hearing the content of a piece of music, therefore, we are also hearing the form: the life which grows and fulfils itself in tones.

But why is the "experience of meaning" (as I have described it) so important? Why is it that so many musical people deny the expressive character of music, and why is it that we find it difficult (and usually unnecessary in any case) to put the meaning of music into words – to move from an intransitive to a transitive idea of expression? . . .

The transition from the Viennese waltz, to ballroom dancing, to ragtime, to the Charleston and Tango, to swing, to rock, and on to all the successors of rock, tells us much about the moral transformation of modernity. Love, sex, and the body are perceived differently now; courtesy and courtship have disappeared from dancing just as they have disappeared from life. The Platonic campaign against the reign of Dionysus could no longer be seriously fought, since the idea of dancing as a form of *order* and self-control – the idea embodied in the Greek chorus and preserved in the formation dances of our ancestors – is dead. Dancing has become a form of social and sexual release – or else a spectator art, something that *others* do, to be contemplated in passive silence. Moreover, in a very important sense, the dances observed on the stage, as in a ballet, are not real dances, but representations of the dance. And while there are places where you can go for waltzes, polkas, or highland reels, you do not so much dance there as "dance" in inverted commas, conscious of your separation from the real life of the body in modern conditions.

There is nothing strained or unnatural in that fragment of the social history of dancing; yet it is far from being morally neutral – any more than the condemnation of modern corybantic dancing given by Ernst Bloch in *The Principle of Hope*, or by Allan Bloom in *The Closing of the American Mind*. And it shows clearly why taste in dancing is continuous with the moral life, of a piece with our taste in company and lifestyle. If therefore, our response to absolute music is a kind of latent dancing, it is surely unproblematically true that taste in music matters, and that the search for objective musical values is one part of our search for the right way to live. . . .

INSTRUMENTAL MUSIC, AND THE CULTURE OF LISTENING

. . . Music has many social uses: in worship, dancing, marching, and as an accompaniment to labour. It is plausible to suppose that dancing and singing came before silent listening in the scheme of things, and that singing for a purpose (e.g. in an act of worship, or in battle) came before the pure strophic song. Yet, by a seemingly inexorable process, instrumental music gradually took over from the voice, just as silent listening took over from song and dance. Music seemed to fulfil its destiny by freeing itself from its worldly uses, while continuing to allude to them in ever more refined and ever more suggestive gestures. After Beethoven it became impossible to think of the human voice as the source of music, or of song as the goal of melody. From Weber onwards the opera is in the process of becoming symphonic music: the voice is no longer accompanied by the orchestra, but redeemed by it, lifted free from its natural condition and remade as a member of the symphony of instruments. The voice is removed from the physical space of human action, to reappear in the acousmatic space of music.

This displacing of song and dance from the central place in music-making has a profound spiritual significance. Music is heard as though breathed into the ear of the listener from another and higher sphere: it is not the here and now, the world of mere contingency that speaks to us through music, but another world, whose order is only dimly reflected in the empirical realm. Music fulfils itself as an art by reaching into this realm of pure abstraction and reconstituting there the movements of the human soul. Only through a culture of listening can this strange transformation occur: but once it begins, it feeds on itself, each new work being conceived as a further extension of that other-worldly voice which speaks to us in tones. And the experience of this voice becomes the more important to us as the sense of a spiritual and religious community dwindles. Music is free from the obligation to represent the empirical world; hence it can gesture to the true community, precisely when that community is vanishing. The implied community which can be glimpsed in music is finer, nobler, and more generous in its feelings than anything that we could know. The encounter with it leads to the peculiar, quasi-religious reverence of the recital room and the concert hall.

It is understandable that we should be so alert to the things which pollute this higher community with the debris of our baser attitudes. The invitation to sympathy that is uttered in the voice of pure music is one that we are eager to accept; but the slightest cliché or banality, the slightest borrowing of some stock effect, makes us doubt the voice's sincerity. We encounter the temptation to pretence, and to the community established by pretence – that complicitous humbug which is the goal of sentimentality. Even if that is how our *lives* must be, we can surely be spared such an experience in art. For we enter the realm of art of our own accord and precisely so as to understand what *might* have been, had we been free from the tyranny of habit.

Instrumental music also provides us with a paradigm of order: in the great works of pure music gestures follow logically, completing one another. The musical logic shows us what it is like to live something completely and to its conclusion, without the flitting between states of mind which is the norm of sentimental compromise. It is from instrumental music that we derive our most overwhelming experience of form. And when, as in the later operas of Wagner, this experience of purely musical form gathers into itself the workings of a drama, the effect is so overwhelming that only religious language can describe it.

ABSOLUTE MUSIC

In opera and song we have representation, achieved through the words, and therefore a subject-matter *towards which* the music is inviting our response. But these cases of applied music say nothing about pure or "absolute" music, in which neither words nor drama provide an object to our emotions. We recognize that there is good and bad taste in absolute music. But does taste have the same moral resonance as it has in my examples? And if not, why should taste matter?

The theory of expression that I developed [earlier] offers an answer to that sceptical question. Music is a companion, and an object of sympathy. It *invites* us into its orbit, so as to share in its manners and outlook, and to "join in" a particular form of life. That description is of course metaphorical. But it is a natural record of something that we all know, and of which Plato had an inkling, in his impetuous desire to ban from the ideal republic all but the sober and virtuous modes of music. To understand the point it is useful to return to Plato, and also to our previous discussion of the dance.

According to Plato, music is mimetic of human character. His term *mimēsis* is crucially ambiguous between the three forms of meaning . . .: imitation, representation, and expression. Nevertheless, he believed that the presentation of character in music leads to another act of *mimēsis* in those who sing or dance to it: they "enter into" the spirit of the music, learning to imitate the character that it imitates. *Mimēsis* is the process whereby habits are acquired – both good and bad; music therefore plays a role in the education of character. People who dance or march to the Dorian mode are learning to hold themselves as honourable citizens should hold themselves; those who dance to the Phrygian mode are releasing what is lowest and wildest in their nature, and learning to imitate the intemperate soul.

Plato's theory depends upon two crucial assumptions: first that the "imitation" of character by music is the same phenomenon as the "imitation" of character by a person; secondly, that our interest in music involves the kind of engagement that is characteristic of dancing, singing along, or joining in. Although the first of those assumptions is clearly false, the second, I have argued, contains a grain of truth. And Plato is surely right to think that dancing is a reflection of social character. Listen to a gavotte from the late Renaissance, and imagine the mores of the people who danced to it. . . . Then listen to a track by Nirvana, and imagine the mores of the people who can dance to *that*. Surely, you will not be tempted to think that these two sets of people could live in the same way, with the same habits of mind and character, and the same ways of responding to each other in the circumstances of social life.

THE CONSUMER CULTURE

. . . Before concluding, it is fitting to consider popular music, and the quite peculiar condition into which music has been put, by the seeming disappearance from ordinary listening of the judgement of taste.

Plato, the reader will recall, wished to ban certain kinds of music from his Republic – particularly those associated with the wild dances of the corybants. In Plato's view, abandoned movement bespeaks an abandoned soul, and the "care of the soul" is the first task of politics. Aristotle was not so keen on banning things. Nevertheless, he too believed that music has character, and that when singing or dancing we imitate this character and make it our own. Few matters are more important to the educator than the music which his pupils sing or dance to. In this, the Greeks thought, as in every habit, we must separate virtue from vice, which means distinguishing music that fulfils our nature, from music which destroys it.

Not many people would now endorse those ancient attitudes. Perhaps only Allan Bloom, in *The Closing of the American Mind*, has been willing to stand beside Plato, in dismissing the Dionysian pop music of our times as the enemy of moral order. But Bloom's despondency about popular culture rang hollow: the music that he deplored animates the world of enterprise; it is the voice of modern America, humming in homes, offices, and factories throughout the nation, encouraging those who provide the surplus upon which Bloom and his kind depend. Only in a democratic culture can a poor child rise to the rank of tenured professor, to collect a salary consonant with his self-opinion in return for reading the Great Books, and thinking the Great Thoughts, which he would have read and thought in any case.

This democratic culture is the real meaning of the "postmodern" age. Modernism, with its priesthood of the avant-garde, was the last gasp of the aristocratic world-view. Such a view is no longer tenable, not because it is false, but because the conditions are no longer in place, which would enable us to live it. The democratic culture of America is also a geopolitical force. Turn on the radio anywhere in the world, and you will hear the sounds of rock, grunge, and Heavy Metal. American popular music flows through the ether like the voice of mankind itself; and while local attempts to block the public ear may enjoy a brief success, they depend on unsustainable efforts of coercion. If you were to ask what really brought down the Berlin Wall, the answer would surely include some reference to American popular culture, which had so captivated the hearts of the young that their impatience to join that enchanted world would brook no further delay.

Democratic culture presses us to accept every taste that does no obvious damage. A teacher who criticizes the music of his pupils, or who tries to cultivate, in the place of it, a love for the classics, will be attacked as "judgemental". In matters of aesthetic taste, no adverse judgement is permitted, save judgement of the adverse judge. This attitude has helped America to survive and flourish in a world of change. An aristocratic culture has an instinctive aversion to what is vulgar, sentimental, or commonplace; not so a democratic culture, which sacrifices good taste to popularity, and places no obstacles whatsoever before the ordinary citizen in his quest for a taste of his own. This is the culture whose "political theology" has been so carefully constructed by Rawls in his *Theory of Justice* – the culture in which "conceptions of the good" belong to the private sphere, and the public sphere has no other business than to guarantee fair treatment for everyone, without regard for private tastes.

Bloom would have agreed with Adorno in nothing besides a certain lyrical despondency. But it was Adorno who first rejected the popular scene, describing it as part of the "false consciousness" with which capitalism distracts us from the truth of our condition. He was not referring to REM, U2, or AC/DC. He was dismissing the melodious and sophisticated music of our parents and grandparents: Gershwin, Cole Porter, Rodgers and Hammerstein; Louis Armstrong, Glenn Miller, and Ella Fitzgerald. This blanket condemnation aroused no more sympathy at the time than does Bloom's today. But it also shows how important judgement is. For those things dismissed by Adorno are better in every way than the things dismissed by Bloom; and whatever argument can be levelled against grunge and Heavy Metal will surely leave the innocent melodies of our parents and grandparents quite unaffected. Castigating all popular music is not merely counter-productive; it shows the very same atrophy of judgement as the surrounding popular culture.

But how should we judge that which repudiates judgement? There *is* a literature devoted to pop music, and it frequently offers a verdict on its subject. But it is a verdict founded in acceptance, both of the music and of the lifestyle of its adherents. Writers who look for the "meaning" of Heavy Metal tend to argue in the manner of Robert Walser,[4] referring to the alienation and frustration expressed by this music – while making no real distinction between the expressive and the inexpressive instances, so removing the term "expression" from the context of aesthetic judgement. . . . Criticism gives way to the anthropology of subcultures, each of which is entitled to its "conception of the good", and none of which can be judged from a point of view outside itself.

It seems to me, however, that there is nothing very compelling in that aesthetic relativism. In a democratic culture, people believe themselves to be entitled to their tastes. But it does not follow that good and bad taste are indistinguishable, or that the education of taste ceases to be a duty. It is only the abstract nature of music that seems to rescue it from criticism: we have no difficulty in seeing why a taste for pornographic videos may be adversely judged, or why we might wish to protect our children from acquiring it. In so far as pop music is attached to words and images it may attract similar criticism – as indeed, "rap" music, with its message of sustained aggression, and the violent images of the music video have attracted criticism. But the sympathetic reader of my argument will recognize that words and images do not exhaust the meaning of music. On the contrary, they reinforce a message which is shaped and projected through tones.

We can best understand the point by once again returning music to its hypothetical origins in dance. It is obvious that dancing has social consequences – particularly on the attitudes through which men and women come together in quest of a partner. Traditional dances had to be *learned* – often by a long process which began in childhood. (Think of the gavotte, the gig, or the stately saraband.) They were not forms of abandon, but exercises in self-control. They required the dancer to understand steps, patterns, formations, and sequences; they required him to fit his gestures to the movement of his partner and to the pattern of the whole. In formation dancing, you also relinquish your partner to dance with others whom you may not know. In this way the sexual motive is moderated in its very invocation. The dancer may be prompted by desire; but he is dancing with people for whom he has no such emotion, acknowledging their existence as sexual beings with gestures of innocent courtesy. A girl might dance with her lover's friend or father, with her own brothers, uncles, and neighbours, clarifying – not in her mind only, but also in her body – her posture towards the other sex. The formation dance is dignified; but it is also lively – in the true sense of that word – far more lively than anything to be seen on MTV. (If you doubt this, then it is time to learn some Highland reels.) This liveliness is in fact the other side of dignity: it comes about when the body dances, and the soul along with it. The formation dance is also the enactment of a moral idea, a vision of peaceful community which serves to tame the sexual instinct and to overcome its impetuosity.

Formation dances gave way, in time, to the paired forms of waltz, polka, and schottische, in which only the steps need to be learned. These forms were at first regarded as immoral. Even so, they permitted the dancer to take a partner of any age or status, to dance without hint of a sexual motive, and to represent himself as an embodied person, rather than an abandoned body. The conception of the dance as a social rather than a sexual occasion lasted well into our century. It survives in the ballroom waltz, the foxtrot, and even the tango and the Charleston, which require such knowledge and control as to become a display more of skill than of sexuality – and also occasions of innocent fun. If such dances are familiar today, it is rather as flamenco is familiar. They have become forms of ballet. But ballet is not so much dancing as the *representation* of dancing. It is an activity for experts, and takes place on an elevated stage, removed from the world of the audience, who sit immobilized below.

There are now few occasions when a young man can dance with his aunt, or a young girl with her boyfriend's father. Dancing has become a sexual exhibition, since the music available for dancing has no other meaning besides release. It requires neither knowledge nor self-control, for these would impede the democratic right of everyone to enter the fray. Hence no one really dances with anyone else; instead, each dancer exudes a kind of narcissistic excitement which requires no acknowledgement from a partner besides similar gestures of display. The ethos of such a dance is well captured by the immortal words of the group Nirvana:

I lease it, lease, yeah.
Ev'ryone is how old?
Pick me, pick me, yeah.
Ev'ryone is waiting.

The dance becomes a lapse into disorder, a kind of surrender of the body which anticipates the sexual act itself. This decay of dancing is a necessary consequence of democratic culture, and an irreversible feature of the post-modern world. And it goes hand in hand with a decay in musical resources. The gestures that attend the new forms of dancing require an abdication of music to sound: to the dominating beat of the percussion, and to such antiharmonic devices as the "power chord", produced by electronic distortion. Melodies become brief exhalations, which cannot develop since they are swamped by rhythm, and have no voice-leading role. Consider the actual tune sung by the late Kurt Cobain to the words I have quoted: fragments in a kind of B minor (though harmonized for the most part with an E major chord played anyhow), with only a ghostly resemblance to melody. No movement passes between the notes, since all movement is generated elsewhere, by the rhythm guitar. And this melodic deficiency goes hand in hand with a loss of harmonic texture. In the soup of amplified overtones, inner voices are drowned out: all the guitarist can do is create an illusion of harmony by playing parallel fifths. (The number, called "Dive", the chorus of which invites the fan to "dive in me", is to be found in the album *Incesticide*.)

At the same time, this music has enormous power over its typical audience, precisely because it has brushed aside the demands of *music*, and replaced them with demands of another kind. The audience does not listen *to* the music, but *through* it, to the performers. The group members become leaders of an "imagined community" – the community of their fans. Television, which brings distant things into close-up, while holding them behind an impassable screen, emphasizes this experience, endowing the singer with the epiphanous aura of the shaman, dancing before his tribe. The relation between the musicians and their fans is tribal; and any criticism of the music is received by the fan as an assault upon himself and his identity.[5] It is not a metaphor to describe Kurt Cobain as an idol: on the contrary, he is simply one among many recent manifestations of the Golden Calf. His music exists in order to blow away the external world, to create an imaginary living-space, where the fan can move freely, endowed with miraculous powers. If the music sounds ugly, this is of no significance: it is not there to be listened to, but to take revenge on the world.

THE DECLINE OF THE MUSICAL CULTURE

Our civilization is bound up with music as no other that the world has known. In social gatherings, whether sacred or secular, formal or informal, ceremonial or friendly, music has played a dominant role. It is an invitation to join, an expression of the feelings and hopes of the participants. It lends dignity and harmony to our gestures, and raises them to a higher level, where they can be understood and emulated. Whether singing hymns in church, whistling a tune in the street, or sitting rapt in a concert hall, we are enjoying the expression of human life – but in an enhanced and perfected form, which offers a mirror to our understanding.

Of course, music is of many kinds, and not all has the expressive power or moral refinement of Bach, Mozart, and Schubert. Moreover, the gradual sundering of "high-brow" and "lowbrow", "classical" and "popular" has left a gap between the language of serious music and the ears of the young – a gap that was once filled with hymns, carols, and musicals, but which is now empty except for the works of Sir Andrew Lloyd Webber, whose popularity, however, is a vivid reminder of the continuing need for melody and harmony, in a world suborned by rhythm. This no man's land between high and popular culture was vacated only recently. Debussy bequeathed his harmonies to jazz, and jazz its rhythms to Stravinsky. Gershwin, Milhaud, Constant Lambert, and Bernstein wrote music that is neither highbrow nor lowbrow, while even the Broadway musical is grounded in harmony and counterpoint. The long tradition of musical utterance, which enabled our parents to hum with equal facility an aria by Mozart or a melody of Nat King Cole, was a precious icon of humanity. You can hear it still in the Beatles or Buddy Holly, and to sing or move to this music is to take one step across the divide between popular and classical culture. You are beginning to think and feel *musically* – with an awareness of the voice not as a sound only, but as an expression of the soul. Compare the breathless gestures of Nirvana with the melody in "She loves you", by the Beatles, in which the music moves effortlessly through the harmonic field of G major, with phrases that answer and develop their predecessors, and which open the implied harmony at every juncture on to vistas of neighbouring keys – B minor, E minor, C minor, and D.

A musical culture introduces its participants to three important experiences, and three forms of knowledge. The first is the experience of melody – of musical thinking, as it begins in tonal space and leads onwards to an apt conclusion. In singing a melody we understand the relation between phrases, the way in which tone calls to tone across the imagined space of music. Melodies have character, and in singing them we imitate the forms of human life. Musical education teaches us to be alert to this character, and to understand that the rightness or wrongness of a tone is the rightness or wrongness of a gesture. In singing we rehearse our social nature, just as we do in dancing. And it matters that we should sing in courteous and cheerful ways.

The second experience is that of harmony – of voices sounding together, moving in concord, creating tensions and resolutions, filling the tonal space with an image of community. Classical harmony provides us with an archetype of human sympathy. The ability to notice a bass-line, to feel the rightness of the notes and of the harmonies that erupt from them, is the ability to respond to a wider world, to value the other voice, and to situate both self and other in a moralized universe. There is all the difference between harmony formed through voice-leading, and harmony formed by hitting strings without regard to the relations among the inner parts – as in the characteristic figure for acoustic guitar in "Losing my religion" by REM, in which no triad is ever inverted, and nothing moves between the chords, so that all is absorbed in rhythm. . . .

The third experience is that of rhythm – by which I mean something other than the all-pervasive beat, on which the shapeless cries of the singer are hung as on wires of steel. I mean the pulse of human life, displayed in measure, syncopation, and accent. Rhythm is a play of heartbeats, which reaches to all mankind. You hear it in jazz, and in the great works of classical music – a delicate display of accents which invites us to dance. Beat is not rhythm, but the last sad skeleton of rhythm, stripped bare of human life.

Nobody who understands the experiences of melody, harmony, and rhythm will doubt their value. Not only are they the distillation of centuries of social life: they are also forms of knowledge, providing the competence to reach *out* of ourselves through music. Through melody, harmony, and rhythm, we enter a world where others exist besides the self, a world that is full of feeling but also ordered, disciplined but free. That is why music is a character-forming force, and the decline of musical taste a decline in morals. The *anomie* of Nirvana and REM is the *anomie* of its listeners. To withhold all judgement, as though a taste in music were on a par with a taste in ice-cream, is precisely not to understand the power of music.

In the first Pythian Ode Pindar evokes the lyre of Apollo, reminding us that music is god-given, and hated by the beings to whom the love of Zeus does not extend. Music soothes, cheers and pacifies; it threatens the power of the monsters, who live by violence and lawlessness. Those lonely, antinomian beings are astounded by music, which speaks of another order of being – the order which "the footstep hears, as the dance begins." It is this very order that is threatened by the monsters of popular culture. Much modern pop is cheerless, and meant to be cheerless. But much of it is also a kind of *negation* of music, a dehumanizing of the spirit of song.

Theories of cultural decline are two a penny, and it is no part of philosophy to provide them. Nevertheless, we should be doing scant justice to the subject of this chapter, if we did not, in conclusion, try to understand the process that has brought us to our present pass. Marxists typically divide culture into two components: one belonging to ideology, and serving to induce our acquiescence in existing things; one transcending ideology, to become a critical instrument, an unsettling and destabilizing force, which furthers the cause of social revolution, and prepares us for a better world. Contemporary popular culture belongs to the first of those categories: it is, in the Marxist view, the opiate of the consumer society, decadent precisely because that society is decadent. The true art of our time, according to writers like Bloch and Adorno, is the questioning, critical, forward-looking art of the avant-garde, in which the existing social realities are put in question, and the ground is prepared for something new.

Such a view is no longer believable: the consumer society is characterized by its extraordinary stability. It is able to receive the deft thrusts of history with a buoyant equilibrium, to survive all Jeremiads, to re-emerge from every downpour with the same untroubled countenance, acknowledging that the critic too deserves his place in the democratic order. Modernism did not overthrow the consumer culture: it merely inoculated it against modernism, which now floats around the system accompanied by its own friendly anti-bodies. What I have described is not the *decadence* of popular music, but its final *freedom* – its breaking-loose from the channel of taste, into the great ocean of equality, where the writ of taste no longer runs. The postmodern world denatures music only because it denatures everything, in order that each individual might have his chance to buy and sell. Popular music ceases to be music, just as sexual love ceases to be love: nothing less than this is required by the new form of life – life "in the present moment". And the alienation that comes from this life – the fear, inadequacy, and anger that attend the attempt to live without the blessing of the dead – is itself expressed by the popular culture and reabsorbed by it. The cheerlessness of so much pop music is therapeutic: an acknowledgement that we live *outside* society, that we too, in granting equality to every human type, have become monsters, and that a monster is an OK thing to be.

There is therefore more than a grain of truth in Nietzsche's view, according to which high culture belongs to the "pathos of distance" established by an aristocratic class. Culture embodies the will of that class to perpetuate its own distinction, and to glorify its power. It declines when the aristocratic class renounces the will to power, becomes rotten with guilt and self-doubt, and finally succumbs to the equalizing tendency of the herd.[6] Nietzsche implies that no *new* culture will come in place of the old, except through conquest. Democratic man is essentially "culture-less", without the aspirations that require him to exalt his image in literature and art. The postmodern world is the world that follows the death of the "last man" – the last human being who has attempted to *better* himself, and to strive towards the inequality which is the mark of the truly human.

There is an element in the picture which Nietzsche refuses to acknowledge. Like the Marxist, he attaches culture to the wrong roots – namely, to the power-relations that prevail in a society. In fact, culture is the natural elaboration of a first-person plural, which expresses itself in the first instance through religious forms and a conception of the sanctity of places and times, persons and offices, customs and rites. A culture is grounded in a religion, develops with the religion, and grows away from it only to mourn its loss. When people lose their faith, and cease to experience their social membership in sacral terms, the culture begins to wither, like the leaves on a tree that has been felled – which may, however, sprout for a year or more beyond its cutting down. Although Nietzsche is right in identifying taste with the demands of privilege, and in seeing art as perpetuating the idea of a "higher" state, he fails to see that this idea is the gift of religion, which heals the divisions of rank and class, and releases the highest aesthetic inspiration into the veins of society. The postmodern world is not merely democratic; it is essentially irreligious, since that is what "life in the present moment" requires. It has become deaf to the voice of absent generations, and lives in the thin time-slice of the now, calling over and over the same tuneless utterance – "the loud lament of the disconsolate chimera".

It is not only art and music that have undergone a fatal metamorphosis in these new conditions. The human psyche itself has been thrown out of orbit, as the world is swallowed by its own representations. The television screen has ceased to be a summary of distant episodes, and become the criterion of reality itself. Events are real to the extent that they can be captured on a videotape, and made available in playback. But when the really real is endlessly repeatable, nothing truly happens. The river of time ceases to murmur in the psychic background, and a zombie-like disengagement spreads like a fungus over the human will. Life becomes episodic, like a soap opera, and its parts can be reorganized according to a rule of substitution. Any part of life has its equivalent, which will "do just as well", and the attachment to particulars – to spouses and lovers, to projects and ambitions, to sacred places and true communities – begins to seem faintly comic, especially in playback. That is what Adorno really meant, I believe, by the "fetishization" of culture.

In such a condition it is inevitable that people should lose all sense of a sacral community, so as to become locked in the isolation of their own desires. The social world, which remains a necessary *image* – for how else can we live with our isolation? – becomes sentimentalized. It is also inevitable that the products of popular culture should be uniform and mutually substitutable – using always the same devices, the same phrases, the same references to a world that is not to be questioned, save in a sentimental and self-regarding way. It is further inevitable that the religious impulse, which finds no outlet to the transcendental, should find solace in idolatry, and that popular culture should involve the worship of idols. There, in brief is the explanation of popular music as we currently know it. In the condition in which we find ourselves, it is inevitable that popular music should be both sentimental and idolatrous.

NOTES

1 *Twelve-Tone Tonality* (Berkeley & Los Angeles, 1977).
2 "Towards a new concept of tonality", *Journal of Music Theory* 3 (1959), 26.
3 *Convention* (Cambridge 1969).
4 *Running with the Devil: Power, Gender and Madness in Heavy Metal Music* (Hanover, 1993).
5 See S. Frith, "Towards an aesthetic of popular music", in Leppert and McClary (eds), *Music and Society* (Cambridge, 1987).
6 *Beyond Good and Evil*, tr. R.J. Hollingdale (Harmondsworth, 1973), chapter 9, "What is noble?", section 257.

9

MUSIC'S WORLDLY USES, OR HOW I LEARNED TO STOP WORRYING AND TO LOVE LED ZEPPELIN

Theodore Gracyk

I

Family quarrels have a habit of dragging on without resolution. Family connections bring the combatants together on a regular basis, allowing small personal differences to build up and to solidify into impregnable opposing fortresses. So there should be no surprise in my admission that the fight I am about to pick with Roger Scruton is more likely to end in a draw than a victory, because it's really a family quarrel. Our starting-point is the same. Music does not yield its meanings to listeners outside the continuing culture that gives the music its significance. Nor will it yield its meanings to listeners positioned within its originating culture if those listeners fail to engage the music through some form of active participation. We live in a time when a great deal of the world's music is available to anyone with a computer and an Internet connection. When I sit down to write, I have the option of working to the percussive flow of a Javanese gamelan orchestra, to the bleating trumpets of a Tibetan Tantric Buddhist ritual, or to a choir trilling traditional Chinese folk songs. But that music wouldn't really yield a musical experience to me, because I don't really know how to listen to it.

I don't intend to suggest that the problem is my lack of formal training in the music of Tibet, Java, or China. Much of the time, what I actually listen to is popular music recorded between 1955 and the present. In recent months, my work has most often been accompanied by the music of Led Zeppelin (1970s rock), Yo La Tengo (1990s indie rock), Muddy Waters (1950s electric blues), Django Reinhardt (1930s jazz), and some piano music by Erik Satie (late nineteenth century). I have no formal training of any kind with any of this music, either. But as many theorists have argued, formal training and the skills of musicological analysis are neither necessary nor sufficient for understanding music.[1] What matters is whether the listener *hears* the music in the right way.

So I agree with Scruton about his central points in the philosophy of music, pulled together for the first time in his recent *The Aesthetics of Music*.[2] Yet I fear that several mysterious leaps are introduced to get him from his central position about the culture of listening to his final conclusion that recent popular music is hardly fit to be granted the status of music. The major steps of his challenge are as follows:

1   Scruton defends the intrinsic superiority of our harmonic tradition, the tradition of Western art music that reigned supreme from the Renaissance to the early twentieth century.

2   Scruton highlights the importance of the educated listener's sympathetic response to music. That response allows us to reach out of ourselves in an experience of feeling that is simultaneously free and disciplined.

3   Dancing is the paradigm sympathetic response to music, and even silent listening is "a kind of latent dancing". Because dancing is fundamentally a group or community activity, the appropriate dance response to a piece of music indicates the fundamental character of the social life of those who make and respond to that music.

4   Aesthetic response to instrumental music is the paradigm of engagement with music. Its lack of "worldly uses" (its autonomy) allows it to invite a sympathetic response with an ideal community that is finer and nobler than any that we actually encounter in this world.

5   Popular music represents a repudiation of taste, for it is deficient in the areas of melody, harmony, and rhythm. Scruton calls it "a kind of negation of music, a dehumanizing of the spirit of song". It invites a sympathetic response to a decadent, disordered community. Scruton's conclusion from this line of reasoning is that "taste in music matters, and that a search for objective musical values is one part of our search for the right way to live".

Given the many supporting arguments involved, I will not attempt here to reconstruct the entire argument and to subject it to scrutiny. Instead, I will point to several holes in the argument that allow Scruton to proceed with his uncharitable indictment of recent popular music. At the same time, I hope to show that a philosophy of music must be supplemented by honest descriptions of musical activity and listeners' comprehension before we try to establish evaluative conclusions about the state of music in contemporary culture.

II

So what do I find so right about the philosophical side of Scruton that I want to characterize our disagreements as similar to those in a family quarrel?

One important building block in the edifice of Scruton's aesthetics of music is his argument that music exists in an intentional realm. This intentional realm is quite distinct from the physical space occupied by the sound waves that reach our ears. Music arises in the listener's comprehension of those sounds. The experience of music is the experience of meaning. The basic point will be clear to anyone who's ever heard a conversation conducted in a language that he or she does not understand. One can hear the sounds made by speakers, but there is no comprehension of how one sound relates to any other. Above all, sounds that happen earlier will not be heard as establishing the rightness or wrongness of sounds that come later. And just as one can listen to a conversation without hearing it *as speech*, one can listen to music without hearing the ordered relations that must be heard to hear it *as music*. In this sense, music exists in a space or realm all its own.

It might be useful for me to say a little more about the idea that music has a basis in sound but that the music itself is, in Scruton's terminology, "constituted intentionally". Since you are reading this sentence in English, I wager that when you hear the phrase "The cat in the", your immediate expectation is that "hat" will be the fifth word in the sequence. But even if you lack background experience with the children's books of Dr Seuss, you will anticipate that either an adjective or a noun will follow "the", and that if you get an adjective as the fifth word, a noun will soon follow. The phrase "in the" demands it. None of this implies that you're consciously aware of the need for adjectives or nouns, or about the difference between direct and indirect objects. But linguistic competence implies expectations of a certain kind, allowing us to unconsciously anticipate what should and shouldn't happen next. Thanks to these expectations, we can follow the meaning of speech (and writing, where visual shapes substitute for sounds) without fussing about the rules of syntax. This is what we mean by the proposal that language is constituted intentionally by the understanding of the participants, emerging in an intentional realm that is not to be equated with the physical stuff that conveys language from one person to another.

In short, we do not hear music simply because we hear sounds which happen to be music. We hear the music when we understand the organization of the sounds and grasp what is conveyed by that organization. But what does Scruton want us to conclude from this fact? He wants us to conclude two things.

First, he wants to recognize that we grasp the intentional realm only because we are members of a community tradition. In my writing and your understanding this piece of written English, you and I participate in a community enterprise with a long history. But we do not simply participate in that community. Our participation shapes us: we think and act in certain ways because we have internalized that tradition. But if this is true of language, it is also plausible that it holds true of music. Therefore, as Plato originally recognized, our interest in music reflects engagement in a certain social life, and so it reveals something about our character.

Second, Scruton wants to conclude that when composers remind us that the sounds *are* sounds, they remind us of the physical or material conditions of music production. Such compositions redirect listeners' attention away from the tonal dimension that permits one tone to lead to another. (In much the same way, Edouard Manet's critics in nineteenth-century Paris faulted him for the unfinished quality of his paintings; artists were expected to blur and obscure the evidence of the artist's brush in finishing a painting. How can the audience look at the painting if the artist insists on calling attention to the paint?) In any case, Scruton rightly holds that there is physical gesture, and then there is gesture in the sense of something that is to be understood as conveyed through that gesture, as when one thrusts out an arm to gesture *towards* something. We should not confuse the physical movement with the intentionality of the action. But does it really follow that awareness of the material conditions of music must distract us from the intentionality of the musical experience?

In responding to these two points, I will draw on my own experiences as a fan of popular music. For many years I did not pay any attention to the music of Led Zeppelin, even though I am of just the right age to have been a fan during their creative peak in the 1970s. The fact that I heard the same five or six Led Zeppelin tracks constantly on the radio during those years might explain my lack of interest in hearing more. Like many rock fans, I assumed that popular music is best when it's located a bit further from the mainstream. As with Scruton's concerns about the band Nirvana, I had preconceptions about what it would say about me if I liked Led Zeppelin. But I had an awakening some years later, when Led Zeppelin's presence in my life had been reduced to the occasional dose of "Stairway to Heaven" or "Whole Lotta Love" on Classic Rock radio. One day I heard the song "D'Yer Mak'Er" on the radio. Hearing it with fresh ears after so many years, I realized how much humour is built into its musical arrangement.

Led Zeppelin's recording of "D'Yer Mak'Er" kicks off with a distinctively syncopated drum pattern: bam-bam-bam-BAM, pause, BAM, pause, and drum roll. The song then unfolds at a much slower tempo than the percussive introduction leads one to expect. The bass guitar provides the true tempo and the busy drums subdivide the beat. The drums lag as they emphasize the offbeat, which is complicated by frequent subdivisions of the beat that are again interrupted by brief pauses. The song's rhythmic arrangement is decidedly that of Jamaican reggae. The reggae feel is reinforced by the way that Jimmy Page's slightly distorted guitar scratches out the song's chords in the right side of the stereo mix. As with most reggae, the guitar often falls silent at moments of heightened percussive action. When it arrives, Robert Plant's vocal contribution is entirely at odds with the musical tone. The lyrics are a trite plea to a departed lover, sung with an exaggerated swoon and a frequent repetition of simple words ("oh, oh, oh") and syllables ("cry ay ay ay ay ay"). At a time when reggae was a regarded as the militant expression of Jamaican nationalism, Plant's vocal line could only come across as trite and therefore politically incorrect. In a word, it was just plain silly.

The moment that really caught my ear and made me laugh comes late in the song. The song is constructed out of two simple segments, A and B, arranged AABAABAA. After two verses and one contrasting chorus, then two more verses and the chorus, the song's logic calls for another verse. As the chord progression signals the beginning of that verse, Jimmy Page's guitar steps forward (stereo left) in place of Robert Plant's voice. But two elements of the solo are out of place. First, Page does not improvise upon the established melody or upon the chord changes, as is to be expected in such music. Instead, his lead guitar simply plays the melody that Plant has established in the verse. Second, there is the actual sound quality or tone colour of the guitar. It is not the shrieking, heroic, wailing guitar that we expect from Led Zeppelin. This guitar solo has a weak, anaemic, and distant quality, as if the guitarist were isolated in another room. One obvious response is to wonder what *this* guitar is doing in this song. The guitar solo is not merely a surprise. It is a surprising let-down. It deflates all expectations about what should appear at this point in "D'Yer Mak'Er". Here, the joke is conditional on the listener's awareness of the sound quality chosen for the arrangement. Far from turning the listener away from the experience of meaning, meaning arises from a worldly awareness of the brute fact of a guitar solo with a specific tone colour. But because the guitar solo's melody echoes Plant's vocal line, it also suggests a parody of that line, reinforcing the distance between Plant and the rest of the musical arrangement.

Humour arises in the intentional realm. (Think of how common it is for two people to hear the same joke, but for only one to see the humour in it.) Furthermore, "D'Yer Mak'Er" cannot be written off as a case where my finding it humorous is to be excused as my subjective response. In press interviews, the members of Led Zeppelin have confirmed that they intended to convey humour through the arrangement. The song's title, pronounced so that it sounds much like "Jamaica", is part of a rather silly British joke. So I seem to have independently heard in the music something that I was meant to hear in it and that is objectively there in the music.

The important point in this example is that it displays musical intelligence. However, it is not confined to the intentionality that arises from expression through expectations centred on the song's tonic. The song's arrangement is the key to its humour, rather than the movement of tones and of harmony formed through voice-leading. The song could be played and sung in a way that strips it of its humour, in which case it would emerge as the 1950s rock-and-roll ballad that is suggested by the lyric sheet's obscure mention of the "girl group" Rosie and the Originals. In fact, the guitar solo in "D'Yer Mak'Er" is very similar in sound to the electric guitar that opens "Angel Baby" by Rosie and the Originals, as if Jimmy Page is consciously reminding listeners of how electric guitars *used* to sound. This example shows that we cannot always divorce musical meaning from an awareness of the material conditions of the music. In addition to the actual sound of Page's guitar solo, part of the joke is that knowledgeable listeners do not expect Jimmy Page to play anything so obvious. Part of the joke involves recognition that Page is a guitar virtuoso. But how do we derive musical meaning from this fact if we leave music in an abstract, spiritual realm? A philosophy of music that makes no room for recognition of instrumental virtuosity is hardly a philosophy of *music*.[3]

Finally, this example confirms Scruton's belief that I participate sympathetically in a rich and fertile musical tradition. It is rich and fertile in just the way that the English language is rich and fertile. Both traditions are firmly *of this world*. Of course, I do not mean the tradition of Western art music. I mean the popular music that Scruton rejects as decadent and debased. My sympathetic response to "D'Yer Mak'Er" draws upon Caribbean rhythms that originally derive from Africa. It also draws upon the musical and lyrical conventions of popular love songs of the 1950s. (An additional dimension to the humour of "D'Yer Mak'Er" is that Led Zeppelin reminds us that reggae partially derives from Jamaican appropriations of American rock'n'roll of the 1950s.) My response also requires an ear for European harmony. But instead of aiming at the closure of the music's final tonic, this music subordinates harmony to the role of support for melody, rhythm, and language. The musical joke of the song's instrumental guitar passage assumes familiarity with multiple conventions of these traditions.[4] One cannot grasp the meanings of this music if one is deaf to the voices of the past. This music is rich in cross-reference and allusion. Its riches have nothing to do with its unworldly character or its harmonic organization and complexity.

So what does a response to this music say about those who prefer it to the European classical tradition? Or about listeners who love both? Such a response involves sympathy with the project of multiculturalism. This music is multiculturalism in action. It reveals a cosmopolitan orientation in which cultural boundaries are continually erased and then redrawn, integrating diverse traditions without erasing differences and without any expectation that one dimension of one musical culture should rule supreme. It reflects a willingness to tolerate cultural ambiguity. It betrays an orientation to finding our community here, in the empirical realm, through trial and error. It abandons the presumption that there is one musical tradition that is inherently superior to all others, and with it the view that there is only one right way to live. It deflates the utopianism of Scruton's insistence on music as a realm of pure abstraction. But the result is not that listeners are thrown back into the self-regarding narcissism of their own private desires. Music really is something into which we *join*, and all response to music is indeed a sympathetic response to a social order.

III

Two other examples interest me. Both provide a reason to wonder about the superiority of Western art music as a civilizing force. More specifically, they address the idea that dance is our best means for externalizing and demonstrating the audience's sympathetic response to music and for revealing the character of the social life of those who make and respond to that music. Let us suppose, with Scruton, that listeners simply do not understand a piece of music if they do not grasp its expressive character. Music's expressive character is the central element of anything that we might describe as music's "content". (It does not follow that listeners must be able to articulate what they thereby understand.) At the same time, understanding is not a private matter. It demands a public act that allows individuals to determine whether others have the same response. Music is objectively expressive when informed listeners are moved to respond to it in the same way. The public character of that response (laughing with "D'Yer Mak'Er" or dancing in waltz time to the verses of the Beatles' "I Me Mine" and then moving in common time to the chorus) is a defining element of our relationship to the larger community of listeners.

There is nonetheless something odd about Scruton's invitation to *imagine* what sort of dancing goes with Renaissance music and then the music of the band Nirvana, and then to extrapolate in imagination to the further social relations of people who listen to such music and dance in that (imagined) manner. Why don't we look and see? As long as we dwell on the question of how music is expressive, we are in the realm of philosophical theorizing. However, specific associations between a style of music and the gestures associated with that style are contingent facts about the world, not *a priori* truths. If we want to discuss the mores of an audience, we ought to investigate matters of fact to determine how the audience uses the music. Only then can we say what they understand when they understand it.

My first example in illustrating this point is drawn from a recent film by writer/director Cameron Crowe, best known for the 1996 movie *Jerry Maguire* (1996). While each of Crowe's film projects has employed popular music with sensitivity rivalled only by Martin Scorsese, only two have been about musicians. They are *Singles* (1992) and *Almost Famous* (2000). The scene that interests me is one of the emotional highlights of *Almost Famous*.

On one level *Almost Famous* is a simple coming-of-age story. Modelled on Crowe's own initiation into journalism at sixteen, it is Crowe's first film project to draw heavily on his own life. A bright teenager loves rock music and becomes a rock critic. Crowe calls his *alter ego* William Miller (played by Patrick Fugit). William Miller's first major assignment involves an extended road trip across the United States with a rock band that's just on the cusp of becoming major rock stars. On another level, the story of the boy's adventures is an excuse for a series of vignettes that allow Crowe to explore rock music at the point where it emerged from underground status to become the geopolitical force that so irks Scruton. Prying into different relationships among musicians, fans, music promoters, and the rock press, Crowe addresses Scruton's concern that popular music is both sentimental and idolatrous. But having observed the process first hand, Crowe sees evidence that it can be otherwise, and that it often is. Scruton sees an inevitable decline. Crowe sees both a decline and a continuing possibility for a community that finds common public expression in the popular arts.

The sequence from *Almost Famous* that interests me is one that explores Scruton's theme of musical experience as active participation in a public arena. The band's guitarist, Russell Hammond (played by Billy Crudup), has emerged as the only member of the group likely to achieve stardom, and as the tour grinds through middle America he is increasingly tempted to follow his muse and his management company and to pursue his own solo career. (Earlier rock fans will be reminded of Peter Frampton's solo career following a stint with Humble Pie or Sting's success after leaving the Police; more recent audiences might think of Jerry Cantrell's solo success after Alice in Chains.) One night Hammond flees the group, rock journalist Miller in tow, and hooks up with a group of teenagers who invite him to a party. Fuelled by alcohol and drugs, he ends up on the roof of their house, threatening to dive into the swimming pool. William gets him off the roof and into the arms of the tour manager, who hauls Hammond onto the tour bus. His band mates, the road crew, and assorted hangers-on silently observe his sullen return to their little community. No one talks. They all know that Hammond wants to leave. The radio breaks the awkward silence with a cascading piano melody, which turns out to be Elton John performing his 1971 song "Tiny Dancer". A few voices softly sing along. (It is itself a song about a girl who identifies with and sings along to a song by a pop musician.) Soon Hammond joins the singing and the tension of the group quickly dissolves. The singing grows stronger. William Miller tells the girl seated beside him that he wants to go home. "You are home", she assures him. The bus continues its journey past the farms of the American Midwest.

It is important that this is an example of a community joined in song. Scruton's emphasis on instrumental music received in rapt silence in the concert hall makes it plausible to focus on "latent dancing" as the most relevant audience response. But if we remind ourselves that most people are interested in songs, not absolute music, then it is relevant to ask how people really do respond to songs. The public activity of *joining in* is itself an expressive act, one in which we remind ourselves that we belong. In the *Almost Famous* example, the act of singing is a mending of fences, a gesture of reconciliation and mutual forgiveness. More fundamentally, raising voices in common song is a public response that creates rather than expresses community.[5] This use of song is common at sporting events and other public gatherings when the national anthem is used to unite the crowd into a common community before the other activities begin.

It is also important to consider songs because dance is primarily a response to rhythm and not a response to tonality and melodic line. Dancing to music does not reveal everything that music can express, and if it did, then tonality would play little role in the experience of musical meaning. In emphasizing dance as the paradigm of aesthetic response to music, Scruton sells short the idea that informed listeners grasp a complex intentional object that conveys a range of emotions and ideas. Consider Scruton's example of formation dancing as an enactment of social order. Suppose the audience is dancing to a song. Participants do not understand that song unless the response is to the complex whole of music and lyric. Yet there is no relationship between the ability to join in a Scottish Highland reel and the supposed superiority of European art music as a vehicle for presenting messages through tones. Nor is the formation dance really dead. The country and western line dance is immensely popular in the beer halls of America and much of the rest of the world. (By some measures, country music is more popular than rock music.) But it does not matter whether the actual song is a cheatin' song, a love song, or an assertion of working-class pride. The pattern of the dance is fitted to the tempo and the rhythm, not to the harmonies and the lyric. One does not have to understand very much about music to engage in communal dance. The audience's ability to synchronize their movements with the music's pulse and beat does not demonstrate a genuine transition from the physical to the intentional realm.

We are merely speculating about what is to be found in a certain type of music or in a specific piece of music if we do not know what knowledgeable listeners recognize in it. I once played recordings of traditional songs from Burundi for a group of American university students. According to the liner notes, a song that my students heard as salacious was really the story of a homesick man remembering his youth. Assuming that the mood of the music was appropriate to the words, then hearing a sexual dimension in it demonstrated my students' verbal *and musical* ignorance. Similarly, a listener's ability to enter into the intentional realm when presented with the music of Beethoven and the Beatles does not rule out the possibility that the same listener will misunderstand hip-hop, the music of Nirvana, and other cases of seemingly simple popular music. My next example illustrates this danger of jumping to conclusions about musical meaning when one does not know what an appreciative audience actually finds in a particular piece.

As recordable compact discs have become more common and more affordable, the Phillips electronics corporation has run a series of print advertisements and television commercials for the Phillips CD recorder. They face the challenge of making the personal CD recorder attractive without ever admitting that consumers might want to use the machines to "bootleg" music. So the Phillips advertisements emphasize the CD recorder as a way to compile music from different compact discs in one's own music collection on one disc.

One of these television commercials is particularly clever for the way that it plays with the themes of Scruton's philosophy of music. A clean-cut young man sets an elegant dining table: wine glasses, cloth napkins, candles. Large abstract paintings adorn the walls. The young man loads a recordable compact disc into his Phillips compact disc player. The doorbell sounds just as he places a single flower into an exquisite vase as the table's centrepiece. An attractive young woman is at the door. She is clearly impressed by his efforts as they sit down to dinner. He picks up a remote control unit, aims it at the CD player, and a crude, grinding, industrial noise erupts over a steady, brutal beat. A deep, growling voice joins the clanging, discordant grind of "industrial" rock. The guttural timbre of the voice is the sort that's used in horror films for characters subject to demonic possession. It rasps, "Let me call you sweetheart/I'm in love with you". Cut to a close-up of the young woman. Her eyes widen. She is confused. Then a sly smile appears on her lips. She starts moving to the rhythm of the music, and a moment later they are both swaying to the same rhythm.

The joke, of course, is the moment when her surprise gives way to delight. We are invited to think that she's horrified by his horrible lapse in taste: you can't let *this* music into *this* social exchange! But she isn't horrified. She's touched by his expression of love and by its being an expression that provides her with an opportunity for response. He has correctly provided music that gratifies her tastes and she conveys her appreciation of the musical gesture by moving joyfully with it. This style of music is just the sort that Scruton attacks as "a dehumanizing of the spirit of song". Yet the young woman is clearly responding to what the music says to her. She understands that this musical gesture is also his gesture. Had he chosen music expressing something contrary to the spirit of the evening, she would not have welcomed the music. At the same time, she might not grasp and accept the gesture if it were rendered in another musical style: a Burundi folk song or the jazz singing of Billie Holiday might convey exactly the same sentiments to a different audience, but not to her. Mere philosophizing cannot tell us whether grunge and industrial rock music are really so different from Franz Schubert and Richard Wagner when it comes to questions of musical expression.

IV

My closing argument is entirely speculative. It is the proposal that an important ideal is expressed by the abrasive eruption of beat and sounds that is characteristic of recent rock music. That ideal is the ideal of music as an expression of ordered living. But where European art music has offered that "spiritual" ideal by sublimating rhythm in favour of tonal adventure, rock music offers a more earthbound metaphor for life. Rather than "reminding" us of utopia, rock offers a continuing metaphor for the struggle to build human community.

The central insight behind this proposal is Jacques Attali's point that musical organization is a species of political organization. There are strong parallels between

Attali and Scruton, particularly in Attali's notion that "the code of music simulates the accepted rules of society," for the conditions underlying the existence of a musical culture are the condition for the creation and consolidation of every community.[6] Deviations from the communal project are literally noise. The existence of music requires the suppression of noise and a "silencing" of discordant activity. When an individual develops a taste for the musical organization typical of that individual's culture, she literally subordinates herself to the body politic.

But what of music that embraces noise, allowing it to coexist with melody and harmony and rhythm? Scruton listens to a recording by Nirvana and complains that it is deficient in melody and its "amplified overtones" drown out its inept harmonies. Scruton concludes that fans of such music cannot possibly be listening *to* the music, and so their interest must be in something else. There can be no contesting the fact that Nirvana secured a large fan base through a single song, "Smells Like Teen Spirit" (1991). The song was recently chosen as the third most significant pop song of the past forty years by *Rolling Stone* magazine and VH1 television. (Songs by the Beatles and the Rolling Stones took the number one and number two slots.)

Nirvana's recording of "Smells Like Teen Spirit" is a furious blast of rock and roll. It is also graced with an aching, sweet melody. Except for one or two songs and then the television broadcast and resulting album, *MTV Unplugged in New York* (1994), Nirvana brought together elements of heavy metal and punk rock by accompanying every song with the rapid strumming of feedback-drenched rhythm guitar. The vocals tended to be throaty, shouted rasps. The arrangements seem designed to disguise Kurt Cobain's flair for melody. But they certainly had the effect of getting audiences to listen, for it really was Cobain's way with melody that distinguished Nirvana from a thousand other punk-influenced bands and catapulted them into the ranks of major pop stars.

The melodic sense that Scruton finds so deficient in Nirvana is demonstrated by Tori Amos's version of "Smells Like Teen Spirit," recorded in 1992. Arranged only for piano and voice, it sits sandwiched on *Crucify* between similar reductions of songs by the Rolling Stones and Led Zeppelin. Presented by a classically trained pianist as if it were a piece of nineteenth-century German Romanticism, the regularity of the accompanying piano figure recalls one of Schubert's most famous lieder, "Gretchen am Spinnrade". Amos sings the same words and melody as Cobain, but without the distraction of the guitar and pounding drums we cannot help but hear the way that the pauses in the melody express hesitancy, confusion, and forbearance. Tori Amos's singing increases in projection and intensity at the end, so that the song's resolution on the anticipated tonic is a gesture of resignation.

All of these musical elements of the song are there to be heard in Nirvana's version of the song. What Nirvana's arrangement adds is, in a word, noise. Tori Amos emphasizes the song's melodic power. Nirvana makes listeners work to hear it. I suppose that non-fans will interpret this as incompetence or decadence. But if we return to our

145

earlier insight that something might be happening here that is only constituted intentionally, then we can ask what we are to understand by Nirvana's continuing decision to put melody and accompaniment into such sharp conflict. This is not speculation about Kurt Cobain's personal intentions. It is an attempt to articulate the music's aesthetic appeal as something that includes noise and not as music that is appealing despite the noise.

For listeners who hear the melody and the elements of noise as two parts of a musical complex, the refusal to let melody triumph can stand for a political refusal. As if intended as an illustration of Attali's claims about music, noise, and political organization, Nirvana refuses to "normalize" its activity in conformity to the demand that tonality must govern music.[7] There is melodic gesture. But there is not the extreme subordination of discord that has been the price of tonality in European art music. At the same time, the group displays discipline in audible acts of taming noise, of civilizing chaos, of controlling impulsive outburst of sound and energy. In live performance (documented on Nirvana's *From the Muddy Banks of the Wishkah*), virtually every Nirvana song began with a piercing wail of feedback that is suddenly interrupted by a burst of rhythmic strumming, establishing the song's pulse before the drums and bass guitar enter. Finally, we hear the voice that supplies the melody. Here, listeners are vividly reminded that music involves continuous discipline and suppression of noise. The transformation of noise into rhythm invokes Puritanism far more than decadence.

Sounding very much like Scruton, Attali believes that the "new noise" of both John Cage and the Rolling Stones represents the collapse of the old order of musical and social organization without announcing anything new.[8] I have proposed something different. John Cage may be the pinnacle of a modernist movement that rejected the logic of tonal music, but the Rolling Stones and Nirvana were never part of that legacy and so their actions are not specifically a repudiation of it. Nirvana's music may be an illustration of the tensions of bourgeois life, but their musical balancing act of noise and melody is a stand against the degree of repression that we often assume everyone must accept as the price of modern life. This public gesture is directed at society at the end of the twentieth century, not at Europe in the nineteenth. Ten years later, Nirvana's style of music is out of fashion and popular music is again awash in elaborate harmonies. We may hear the music of groups like the Backstreet Boys and 'N Sync as gestures of conformity. But let's avoid the mistake of thinking that popular music that turns its back on music dominated by the intentional world of tones (tonality as in the Western classical system) is less musical.

Nirvana's arrangement of "Smells Like Teen Spirit" employs sound to elicit an aesthetic response. It displays musical intelligence. It may be interpreted as directing us back to facts about this world and as illustrating the brutal struggle involved in the pursuit of a perfect order. However, it would be a serious mistake to suppose that philosophy reveals a correlation between immutable, objective musical values and the ideal organization of human society. Philosophy of music may well tell us that the meaning of music lies in the sympathetic response of knowledgeable listeners. But we need something more than philosophy to demonstrate that there is nothing worth understanding in "D'Yer Mak'Er" or "Smells Like Teen Spirit".

NOTES

1   See Stephen Davies, *Musical Meaning and Expression* (Cornell University Press, 1994), p. 369.
2   Roger Scruton, *The Aesthetics of Music* (Oxford University Press: 1997), portions reprinted in this book.
3   See Stan Godlovitch, *Musical Performance: A Philosophical Study* (London: Routledge, 1998), chapter 2.
4   Popular music also employs the tradition of the final move on to the tonic note. Led Zeppelin's "Stairway to Heaven" is a prime example. Musical organization in relation to the tonic is the hallmark of so-called "progressive" rock, which includes several other Led Zeppelin songs. See Edward Macan, *Rocking the Classics: English Progressive Rock and the Counterculture* (Oxford and New York: Oxford University Press, 1997).
5   Tony Kirschner, "Studying Rock: Toward a Materialist Ethnography", in Thomas Swiss, John Sloop, and Andrew Herman (eds) *Mapping the Beat: Popular Music and Contemporary Theory* (Oxford: Blackwell, 1998), pp. 247–68. See also Ellen Willis, "Crowds and Freedom", in Karen Kelly and Evelyn McDonnell (eds) *Stars Don't Stand Still in the Sky: Music and Myth* (New York University Press, 1999), pp. 153–9.
6   Jacques Attali, *Noise: The Political Economy of Music* (Minneapolis: University of Minnesota Press, 1985), p. 26. There are several essays related to this theme in Thomas Swiss, John Sloop, and Andrew Herman (eds) *Mapping the Beat: Popular Music and Contemporary Theory* (Oxford: Blackwell, 1998).
7   Attali, pp. 59–62.
8   Attali, p. 137. One of Attali's main proposals is that musical organization is prophetic in being a precursor to coming modes of political and economic organization; Cage and the Rolling Stones are merely a "liquidation of the old".

SUGGESTIONS FOR FURTHER READING

Alperson, Philip (ed.) (1998) *Musical Worlds: New Directions in the Philosophy of Music*, University Park: Pennsylvania State University Press.

Attali, Jacques (1985) *Noise: The Political Economy of Music*, trans. Brian Massumi, Minneapolis: University of Minnesota Press.

Baugh, Bruce (1993) "Prolegomena to any aesthetics of rock music", *Journal of Aesthetics and Art Criticism* 51: 23–9.

—— (1995) "Music for the young at heart", *Journal of Aesthetics and Art Criticism* 53: 81–3.

Bayles, Martha (1994) *Hole In Our Soul: The Loss of Beauty and Meaning in American Popular Music*, New York: The Free Press.

Clarke, Donald (1995) *The Rise and Fall of Popular Music*, New York: St Martin's Press.

Covach, John and Graeme M. Boone (eds) (1997) *Understanding Rock: Essays in Musical Analysis*, Oxford and New York: Oxford University Press.

Davies, Stephen (1999) "Rock versus classical music", *Journal of Aesthetics and Art Criticism* 57(2): 193–204.

Frith, Simon (1996) *Performing Rites: On the Value of Popular Music*, Cambridge, Mass.: Harvard University Press.

Gracyk, Theodore (1996) *Rhythm and Noise: An Aesthetics of Rock*, Durham and London: Duke University Press.

—— (1999) "Valuing and evaluating popular music", *Journal of Aesthetics and Art Criticism* 57(2): 205–20.

Hamm, Charles (1995) *Putting Popular Music in Its Place*, Cambridge: Cambridge University Press.

Kelly, Karen and Evelyn McDonnell (eds) (1999) *Stars Don't Stand Still in the Sky: Music and Myth*, New York: New York University Press.

Leblanc, Lauraine (1999) *Pretty In Punk: Girls' Gender Resistance in a Boys' Subculture*, New Brunswick and London: Rutgers University Press.

Lewis, Lisa (1990) *Gender Politics and MTV: Voicing the Difference*, Philadelphia: Temple University Press.

Lipsitz, George (1994) *Dangerous Crossroads: Popular Music, Postmodernism and the Poetics of Place*, New York: Verso.

Macan, Edward (1997) *Rocking the Classics: English Progressive Rock and the Counterculture*, Oxford and New York: Oxford University Press.

Nehring, Neil (1997) *Popular Music, Gender, and Postmodernism: Anger is an Energy*, Thousand Oaks: Sage Publications.

Ross, Andrew and Tricia Rose (eds) (1994) *Microphone Fiends: Youth Music & Youth Culture*, New York and London: Routledge.

Scruton, Roger (1997) *The Aesthetics of Music*, New York: Oxford University Press.

Swiss, Thomas, John Sloop, and Andrew Herman (eds) (1998) *Mapping the Beat: Popular Music and Contemporary Theory*, Malden and Oxford: Blackwell Publishers.

Van Der Merwe, Peter (1989) *Origins of the Popular Style: The Antecedents of Twentieth-Century Popular Music*, Oxford: Clarendon Press.

Whiteley, Sheila (ed.) (1997) *Sexing the Groove: Popular Music and Gender*, London and New York: Routledge.

Young, James O. (1995) "Between a rock and a harp place", *Journal of Aesthetics and Art Criticism* 53: 78–81.

Part 5

APPRECIATION, UNDERSTANDING, AND NATURE

The face of the water, in time, became a wonderful book – a book that was a dead language to the uneducated passenger, but which told its mind to me without reserve, delivering its most cherished secrets as clearly as if it uttered them with a voice. . . . In truth, the passenger who could not read this book saw nothing but all manner of pretty pictures in it, painted by the sun and shaded by the clouds, whereas to the trained eye these were not pictures at all, but the grimmest and most dead-earnest of reading matter.

Now when I had mastered the language of this water and had come to know every trifling feature that bordered the great river as familiarly as I knew the letters of the alphabet, I had made a valuable acquisition. But I had lost something, too. I had lost something which could never be restored to me while I lived. All the grace, the beauty, the poetry had gone out of the majestic river: I still keep in mind a certain wonderful sunset which I witnessed when steamboating was new to me. A broad expanse of the river was turned to blood; in the middle distance the red hue brightened into gold, through which a solitary log came floating, black and conspicuous; in one place a long, slanting mark lay sparkling upon the water; in another the surface was broken by boiling, tumbling rings, that were as many-tinted as an opal; where the ruddy flush was faintest, was a smooth spot that was covered with graceful circles and radiating lines, ever so delicately traced; the shore on our left was densely wooded, and the sombre shadow that fell from this forest was broken in one place by a long, ruffled trail that shone like silver; and high above the forest wall a clean-stemmed dead tree waved a single leafy bough that glowed like a flame in the unobstructed splendor that was flowing from the sun. There were graceful curves, reflected images, woody heights, soft distances; and over the whole scene, far and near, the dissolving lights drifted steadily, enriching it, every passing moment, with new marvels of coloring.

I stood like one bewitched. I drank it in, in a speechless rapture. . . . But as I have said, a day came when . . . if that sunset scene had been repeated, I should have looked upon it without rapture, and should have commented upon it, inwardly, after this fashion: The sun means that we are going to have wind to-morrow; that floating log means that the river is rising, small thanks to it; that slanting mark on the water refers to a bluff reef which is going to kill somebody's steamboat one of these nights, if it keeps on stretching out like that; those tumbling "boils" show a dissolving bar and a changing channel there; . . . that tall dead tree, with a single living branch, is not going to last long, and then how is a body ever going to get through this blind place at night without the friendly old landmark?

No, the romance and the beauty were all gone from the river. . . . Since those days, I have pitied doctors from my heart. What does the lovely flush in a beauty's cheek mean to a doctor but a "break" that ripples above some deadly disease? . . . Does he ever see her beauty at all, or doesn't he simply comment upon her unwholesome condition all to himself? And doesn't he sometimes wonder whether he has gained most or lost most by learning his trade?

Mark Twain, *Life on the Mississippi*

I do not think I shall ever forget the sight of Etna at sunset; the mountain almost invisible in a blur of pastel grey, glowing on the top and then repeating its shape, as though reflected, in a wisp of grey smoke, with the whole horizon behind radiant with pink light, fading gently into a grey pastel sky. Nothing I have ever seen in Art or Nature was quite so revolting.

Evelyn Waugh, *Labels* VII

A LARGE PART OF OUR AESTHETIC experience and enjoyment is experience and enjoyment of nature. Think of the ways in which we talk about and respond to things as various as pieces of driftwood and uncut quartz, patches of wildflowers growing by the highway, sunsets, rainbows, rain-forests, glacier plains, mountain ranges. It seems clear that we often regard these and other sorts of natural objects and natural environments not only as aspects of our world that give us pleasure, but as aspects of our world that are *aesthetically* important. Gazelles as well as Brancusi's sculpture *Bird in Space* are delicately graceful, bird-song as well as music can be melodious, and the Grand Tetons as well as Chartres Cathedral are majestic. Indeed, it might be said that we first learn about beauty through our engagement with the natural world. Children are likely to find rainbows beautiful long before they appreciate poetry; and the art that children learn to appreciate first is very often art which represents aspects of the natural world.

So it seems clear that natural objects and natural environments are aspects of the world which we can appreciate aesthetically. But although this may be clear, it is not so clear just what is *involved* in aesthetic appreciation of the natural world. In particular, we may wonder how similar aesthetic appreciation of the natural world is to aesthetic appreciation of works of art. Is coming to see that the Grand Tetons are majestic the same sort of process as coming to see that Chartres Cathedral is majestic? There are certain features of our experience that are clearly involved in and relevant to our appreciation of art; are the same features involved in and relevant to our appreciation of the natural world?

In the first of the chapters in this part, Allen Carlson suggests that just as our aesthetic appreciation of art is based on our knowledge of cultural history and artistic conventions, so our aesthetic appreciation of nature is based on knowledge — but in this case, knowledge of science and *natural* history rather than cultural history. For example, how we appreciate an environment comprised of a wide expanse of sand and mud will depend on whether we see it as a beach or a sea-bed or a tidal basin. If our knowledge of natural history is so poor that we think of whales as big fish rather than as mammals, then we will be unable to aesthetically appreciate whales as fully as a person who has some knowledge of the kind of creatures that they are. As Carlson says,

> to aesthetically appreciate nature we must have knowledge of the different environments of nature and of the systems and elements within those environments. In the way in which the art critic and the art historian are well equipped to aesthetically appreciate art, the naturalist and the ecologist are well equipped to aesthetically appreciate nature.

In the second chapter in this part, Noël Carroll argues that this view of appreciation is too narrow. It leaves out, Carroll suggests, "certain very common appreciative responses to nature

– responses of a less intellective, more visceral sort, which we might refer to as 'being moved by nature'." Carroll does not deny that Carlson's model captures *one* of the ways in which we may aesthetically appreciate nature, but he holds that it is not the *only* way of doing so. As Carroll says, "We may appreciate nature by opening ourselves to its stimulus, and to being put in a certain emotional state by attending to its aspects." For example, being excited by the grandeur of a waterfall may be a way of aesthetically appreciating that waterfall. On Carroll's view, that is, aesthetic appreciation of nature may be less cognitive, less dependent on knowledge of science and natural history, than Carlson suggests. Indeed, he implies, the same may be true of our aesthetic appreciation of works of art: for example, "one may find certain Surrealist paintings haunting without knowing the metaphysical, psychological and political aims of the Surrealist movement."

As these readings suggest, reflection on our aesthetic experience of and engagement with the natural world gives rise to a number of questions that are central to the philosophy of art. What exactly is it to appreciate something aesthetically? How are appreciation and understanding connected? Is aesthetic appreciation and judgement fundamentally subjective, or is it open to assessment in terms of rationality and truth? These are questions which we cannot ignore if we are to understand the importance to us of both art and nature.

10

APPRECIATION AND THE NATURAL ENVIRONMENT

Allen Carlson

I

With art objects there is a straightforward sense in which we know both what and how to aesthetically appreciate. We know *what* to appreciate in that, first, we can distinguish a work and its parts from that which is not it nor a part of it. And, second, we can distinguish its aesthetically relevant aspects from its aspects without such relevance. We know that we are to appreciate the sound of the piano in the concert hail and not the coughing which interrupts it; we know that we are to appreciate that a painting is graceful, but not that it happens to hang in the Louvre. In a similar vein, we know *how* to appreciate in that we know what "acts of aspection" to perform in regard to different works. Ziff says:

> . . . to contemplate a painting is to perform one act of aspection; to scan it is to perform another; to study, observe, survey, inspect, examine, scrutinise, etc., are still other acts of aspection.
> . . . I survey a Tintoretto, while I scan an H. Bosch. Thus I step back to look at the Tintoretto, up to look at the Bosch. Different actions are involved. Do you drink brandy in the way you drink beer?[1]

It is clear that we have such knowledge of what and how to aesthetically appreciate. It is, I believe, also clear what the grounds are for this knowledge. Works of art are our own creations; it is for this reason that we know what is and what is not a part of a work, which of its aspects are of aesthetic significance, and how to appreciate them. We have made them for the purpose of aesthetic appreciation; in order for them to fulfill this purpose this knowledge must be accessible. In making an object we know what we make and thus its parts and its purpose. Hence in knowing what we make we know what to do with that which we make. In the more general cases the point is clear enough:

155

In creating a painting, we know that what we make is a painting. In knowing this we know that it ends at its frame, that its colors are aesthetically important, but where it hangs is not, and that we are to look at it rather than, say, listen to it. All this is involved in what it is to be a painting. Moreover, this point holds for more particular cases as well. Works of different particular types have different kinds of boundaries, have different foci of aesthetic significance, and perhaps most important demand different acts of aspection. In knowing the type we know what and how to appreciate. Ziff again:

> Generally speaking, a different act of aspection is performed in connection with works belonging to different schools of art, which is why the classification of style is of the essence. Venetian paintings lend themselves to an act of aspection involving attention to balanced masses: contours are of no importance, for they are scarcely to be found. The Florentine school demands attention to contours, the linear style predominates. Look for light in a Claude, for color in a Bonnard, for contoured volume in a Signorelli.[2]

I take the above to be essentially beyond serious dispute, except as to the details of the complete account. If it were not the case, our complementary institutions of art and of the aesthetic appreciation of art would not be as they are. We would not have the artworld which we do. But the subject of this paper is not art nor the artworld. Rather: it is the aesthetic appreciation of nature. The question I wish to investigate is the question of what and how to aesthetically appreciate in respect to natural environment. It is of interest since the account which is implicit in the above remarks and which I believe to be the correct account for art cannot be applied to the natural environment without at least some modification. Thus initially the questions of what and how to appreciate in respect to nature appear to be open questions.

II

In this section I consider some paradigms of aesthetic appreciation which prima facie seem applicable as models for the appreciation of the natural environment. In this I follow tradition to some extent in that these paradigms are ones which have been offered as or assumed to be appropriate models for the appreciation of nature. However, I think we will discover that these models are not as promising as they may initially appear to be.

The first such paradigm I call the object model. In the artworld non-representational sculpture best fits this model of appreciation. When we appreciate such sculpture we appreciate it as the actual physical object which it is. The qualities to be aesthetically appreciated are the sensuous and design qualities of the actual object and perhaps certain abstract expressive qualities. The sculpture need not represent anything external to itself;

it need not lead the appreciator beyond itself: it may be a self-contained aesthetic unit. Consider a Brancusi sculpture, for example, the famous *Bird In Space* (1919). It has no representational connections with the rest of reality and no relational connections with its immediate surroundings and yet it has significant aesthetic qualities. It glistens, has balance and grace, and expresses flight itself.

Clearly it is possible to aesthetically appreciate an object of nature in the way indicated by this model. For example, we may appreciate a rock or a piece of driftwood in the same way as we appreciate a Brancusi sculpture: we actually or contemplatively remove the object from its surroundings and dwell on its sensuous and design qualities and its possible expressive qualities. Moreover, there are considerations which support the plausibility of this model for appreciation of the natural environment. First, natural objects are in fact often appreciated in precisely this way: mantel pieces are littered with pieces of rock and driftwood. Second, the model fits well with one feature of natural objects: such objects, like the Brancusi sculpture, do not have representational ties to the rest of reality. Third and most important, the model involves an accepted, traditional aesthetic approach. As Sparshott notes, "When one talks of the aesthetic this or that, one is usually thinking of it as entering into a subject/object relation."[3]

In spite of these considerations, however, I think there are aspects of the object model which make it inappropriate for nature. Santayana, in discussing the aesthetic appreciation of nature (which he calls the love of nature) notes that certain problems arise because the natural landscape has "indeterminate form." He then observes that although the landscape contains many objects which have determinate forms, "if the attention is directed specifically to them, we have no longer what, by a curious limitation of the world, is called the love of nature."[4] I think this limitation is not as curious as Santayana seems to think it is. The limitation marks the distinction between appreciating nature and appreciating the objects of nature. The importance of this distinction is seen by realizing the difficulty of appreciating nature by means of the object model. For example, on one understanding of the object model, the objects of nature when so appreciated become "ready-mades" or "found art." The artworld grants "artistic enfranchisement" to a piece of driftwood just as it has to Duchamp's urinal or to the real Brillo cartons discussed by Danto.[5] If this magic is successful the result is art. Questions of what and how to aesthetically appreciate are answered, of course, but in respect to art rather than nature; the appreciation of nature is lost in the shuffle. Appreciating sculpture which was once driftwood is no closer to appreciating nature than is appreciating a totem pole which was once a tree or a purse which was once a sow's ear. In all such cases the conversion from nature to art (or artifact) is complete; only the means of conversion are different.

There is, however, another understanding of how the object model applies to the objects of nature. On this understanding natural objects are simply (actually or contemplatively) removed from their surroundings, but they do not become art, they remain natural objects. Here we do not appreciate the objects *qua* art objects, but rather *qua* natural objects. We do not consider the rock on our mantel a ready-made sculpture, we consider it only an aesthetically pleasing rock. In such a case, as the example of non-representational sculpture suggests, our appreciation is limited to the sensuous and design qualities of the natural object and perhaps a few abstract expressive qualities: Our rock has a wonderfully smooth and gracefully curved surface and expresses solidity.

The above suggests that, even when it does not require natural objects to be seen as art objects, the object model imposes a certain limitation on our appreciation of natural objects. The limitation is the result of the removal of the object from its surroundings which the object model requires in order even to begin to provide answers to questions of what and how to appreciate. But in requiring such a removal the object model becomes problematic. The object model is most appropriate for those art objects which are self-contained aesthetic units. These objects are such that neither the environment of their creation nor the environment of their display are aesthetically relevant: the removal of a self-contained art object from its environment of creation will not vary its aesthetic qualities and the environment of display of such an object should not affect its aesthetic qualities. However, natural objects possess what we might call an organic unity with their environment of creation: such objects are a part of and have developed out of the elements of their environments by means of the forces at work within those environments. Thus the environments of creation are aesthetically relevant to natural objects. And for this reason the environments of display are equally relevant in virtue of the fact that these environments will be either the same as or different from the environments of creation. In either case the aesthetic qualities of natural objects will be affected. Consider again our rock: on the mantel it may seem wonderfully smooth and gracefully curved and expressive of solidity, but in its environment of creation it will have more and different aesthetic qualities – qualities which are the product of the relationship between it and its environment. It is here expressive of the particular forces which shaped and continue to shape it and displays for aesthetic appreciation its place in and its relation to its environment. Moreover, depending upon its place in that environment it may not express many of those qualities, for example, solidity, which it appears to express when on the mantel.

I conclude that the object model, even without changing nature into art, faces a problem as a paradigm for the aesthetic appreciation of nature. The problem is a dilemma: either we remove the object from its environment or we leave it where it is. If the object is removed, the model applies to the object and suggests answers to the questions of what and how to appreciate. But the result is the appreciation of a comparatively limited set of aesthetic qualities. On the other hand if the object is not removed, the model seemingly does not constitute an adequate model for a very large part of the appreciation which is possible. Thus it makes little headway with the what and how questions. In either case the object model does not provide a successful paradigm for the aesthetic appreciation of nature. It appears after all not a very "curious limitation" that when our attention is directed specifically toward the objects in the environment it is not called the love of nature.

The second paradigm for the aesthetic appreciation of nature I call the scenery or landscape model. In the artworld this model of appreciation is illustrated by landscape painting; in fact the model probably owes its existence to this art form. In one of its favored senses "landscape" means a prospect – usually a grandiose prospect – seen from a specific standpoint and distance; a landscape painting is traditionally a representation of such a prospect.[6] When aesthetically appreciating landscape paintings (or any representative paintings, for that matter) the emphasis is not on the actual object (the painting) nor on the object represented (the actual prospect); rather it is on the representation of the object and its represented features. Thus in landscape painting the appreciative emphasis is on those qualities which play an essential role in representing a prospect: visual qualities related to coloration and overall design. These are the qualities which are traditionally significant in landscape painting and which are the focus of the landscape model of appreciation. We thus have a model of appreciation which encourages perceiving and appreciating nature as if it were a landscape painting, as a grandiose prospect seen from a specific standpoint and distance. It is a model which centers attention on those aesthetic qualities of color and design which are seen and seen at a distance.

It is quite evident that the scenery or landscape model has been historically significant in our aesthetic appreciation of nature.[7] For example, this model was evident in the eighteenth and nineteenth centuries in the use of the "Claude-glass," a small, tinted, convex mirror with which tourists viewed the landscape. Thomas West's popular guidebook to the Lake District (first published in 1778) says of the glass:

> ... where the objects are great and near, it removes them to a due distance, and shews them in the soft colours of nature, and most regular perspective the eye can perceive, art teach, or science demonstrate ... to the glass is reserved the finished picture, in highest colouring, and just perspective.[8]

In a somewhat similar fashion, the modern tourist reveals his preference for this model of appreciation by frequenting "scenic viewpoints" where the actual space between the tourist and the prescribed "view" often constitutes "a due distance" which aids the impression of "soft colours of nature, and the most regular perspective the eye can perceive, art teach, or science demonstrate." And the "regularity" of the perspective is often enhanced by the positioning of the viewpoint itself. Moreover, the modern tourist also desires "the finished picture, in highest colouring, and just perspective"; whether this be the "scene" framed and balanced in his camera's viewfinder, the result of this in the form of a kodachrome slide, and/or the "artistically" composed postcard and calendar reproductions of the "scene" which often attract more appreciation than that which they "reproduce." R. Rees has described the situation as follows:

> . . . the taste has been for a view, for scenery, not for landscape in the original Dutch – and present geographical – meaning of the term, which denotes our ordinary, everyday surroundings. The average modern sightseer, unlike many of the Romantic poets and painters who were accomplished naturalists, is interested *not* in natural forms and processes, but in a prospect.[9]

It is clear that in addition to being historically important, the landscape model, like the object model, gives us at least initial guidelines as to what and how to appreciate in regard to nature. We appreciate the natural environment as if it were a landscape painting. The model requires dividing the environment into scenes or blocks of scenery, each of which is to be viewed from a particular point by a viewer who is separated by the appropriate spatial (and emotional?) distance. A drive through the country is not unlike a walk through a gallery of landscape paintings. When seen in this light, this model of appreciation causes a certain uneasiness in a number of thinkers. Some, such as ecologist Paul Shepard, seemingly believe this kind of appreciation of the natural environment so misguided that they entertain doubts about the wisdom of *any* aesthetic approach to nature.[10] Others find the model to be ethically suspect. For example, after pointing out that the modern sightseer is interested only in a prospect, Rees concludes:

> In this respect the Romantic Movement was a mixed blessing. In certain phases of its development it stimulated the movement for the protection of nature, but in its picturesque phase it simply confirmed our anthropocentrism by suggesting that nature exists to please as well as to serve us. Our ethics, if the word can be used to describe our attitudes and behaviour toward the environment, have lagged behind our aesthetics. It is an unfortunate lapse which allows us to abuse our local environments and venerate the Alps and the Rockies.[11]

What has not been as generally noted, however, is that this model of appreciation is suspect not only on ethical grounds, but also on aesthetic grounds. The model requires us to view the environment as if it were a static representation which is essentially "two dimensional." It requires the reduction of the environment to a scene or view. But what must be kept in mind is that the environment is not a scene, not a representation, not static, and not two dimensional. The point is that the model requires the appreciation of the environment not as what it is and with the qualities it has, but rather as something which it is not and with qualities it does not have. The model is in fact inappropriate to the actual nature of the object of appreciation. Consequently it not only, as the object model, unduly limits our appreciation – in this case to visual qualities related to coloration and overall design, it also misleads it. Hepburn puts this point in a general way:

> Supposing that a person's aesthetic education . . . instills in him the attitudes, the tactics of approach, the expectations proper to the appreciation of art works only, such a person will either pay very little aesthetic heed to natural objects or else heed them in the wrong way. He will look – and of course look in vain – for what can be found and enjoyed only in art.[12]

III

I conclude that the landscape model, as the object model, is inadequate as a paradigm for the aesthetic appreciation of nature. However, the reason for its inadequacy is instructive. The landscape model is inadequate because it is inappropriate to the nature of the natural environment. Perhaps to see what and how to appreciate in respect to the natural environment, we must consider the nature of that environment more carefully. In this regard there are two rather obvious points which I wish to emphasize. The first is that the natural environment is an environment; the second is that it is natural.

When we conceptualize the natural environment as "nature" I think we are tempted to think of it as an object. When we conceptualize it as "landscape" we are certainly led to thinking of it as scenery. Consequently perhaps the concept of the "natural environment" is somewhat preferable. At least it makes explicit that it is an environment which is under consideration. The object model and the landscape model each in its own way fail to take account of this. But what is involved in taking this into account? Here I wish initially to follow up some remarks made by Sparshott. He suggests that to consider something environmentally is primarily to consider it in regard to the relation of "self to setting," rather than "subject to object" or "traveler to scene."[13] An environment is the setting in which we exist as a "sentient part"; it is our surroundings. Sparshott points out that, as our surroundings, our setting, the environment is that which we take for granted, that which we hardly notice – it is necessarily unobtrusive. If any one part of it becomes obtrusive, it is in danger of being seen as an object or a scene, not as our environment. As Sparshott says, "When a man starts talking about 'environmental values' we usually take him to be talking about aesthetic values of a background sort."[14]

The aesthetic values of the environment being primarily background values has obvious ramifications for the questions of what and how to appreciate. In regard to what to appreciate this suggests the answer "everything," for in an essentially unobtrusive setting there seems little basis for including and excluding. I will return to this shortly. In regard to how to appreciate, the answer suggested is in terms of all those ways in which we normally are aware of and experience our surroundings. Sparshott notes that "if environmental aspects are background aspects, eye and ear lose part of their privilege" and goes on to mention smell, touch, and taste, and even warmth and coolness, barometric pressure and humidity as possibly relevant.[15] This points in the right direction, but as Sparshott also notes, it seems to involve a difficulty: that "the concept of the aesthetic tugs in a different direction" – the direction of the subject/object relation involving primarily the visual scrutiny of an aesthetic object.[16] However, I do not think this difficulty need be as serious as Sparshott seems to think. I suspect the apparent tension here is not due to the concept of the aesthetic being necessarily tied to the subject/object relation or to the visual, but rather is due to its being antithetical to the appreciation of anything only as unobtrusive background. To confirm this we need to consider the concept of the aesthetic as it is elaborated by John Dewey in *Art as Experience*.[17] Dewey's concept is such that anything which is aesthetically appreciated must be obtrusive, it must be foreground, but it need not be an object and it need not be seen (or only seen). Moreover, to assume that that which is aesthetically appreciated need be an object or only seen is to confine aesthetic appreciation to either the object model or the landscape model, which, as we have noted, impose unacceptable limitations on the aesthetic appreciation of the natural environment.

I suggest then that the beginning of an answer to the question of *how* to aesthetically appreciate an environment is something like the following: We must experience our background setting in all those ways in which we normally experience it, by sight, smell, touch, and whatever. However, we must experience it not as unobtrusive background, but as obtrusive foreground! What is involved in such an "act of aspection" is not completely clear. Dewey gives us an idea in remarks such as:

> To grasp the sources of esthetic experience it is . . . necessary to have recourse to animal life below the human scale. . . . The live animal is fully present, all there, in all of its actions: in its wary glances, its sharp sniffing, its abrupt cocking of ears. All senses are equally on the *qui vive*.[18]

And perhaps the following description by Yi-Fu Tuan gives some further indication:

> An adult must learn to be yielding and careless like a child if he were to enjoy nature polymorphously. He needs to slip into old clothes so that he could feel free to stretch out on the hay beside the brook and bathe in a meld of physical sensations: the smell of the hay and of horse dung; the warmth of the ground, its hard and soft contours; the warmth of the sun tempered by breeze; the tickling of an ant making its way up the calf of his leg; the play of shifting leaf shadows on his face; the sound of water over the pebbles and boulders, the sound of cicadas and distant traffic. Such an environment might break all the formal rules of euphony and aesthetics, substituting confusion for order, and yet be wholly satisfying.[19]

Tuan's account as to how to appreciate fits well with our earlier answer to the question of what to appreciate, viz. everything. This answer, of course, will not do. We cannot appreciate everything; there must be limits and emphasis in our aesthetic appreciation of nature as there are in our appreciation of art. Without such limits and emphases our experience of the natural environment would be *only* "a meld of physical sensations" without any meaning or significance. It would be a Jamesian "blooming buzzing confusion" which truly substituted "confusion for order" and which, I suspect contra to Tuan, would not be wholly satisfying. Such experience would be too far removed from our aesthetic appreciation of art to merit the label "aesthetic" or even the label "appreciation." Consider again the case of art. In this case, as noted in Section I, the boundaries and foci of aesthetic significance of works of art are a function of the type of art in question, e.g., paintings end at their frames and their colors are significant. Moreover, I suggested that our knowledge of such matters is due to art works being our creations. Here it is relevant to note the second point which I wish to emphasize about natural environments: they are natural. The natural environment is not a work of art. As such it has no boundaries or foci of aesthetic significance which are given as a result of our creation nor of which we have knowledge because of our involvement in such creation.

The fact that nature is natural – not our creation – does not mean, however, that we must be without knowledge of it. Natural objects are such that we can discover things about them which are independent of any involvement by us in their creation. Thus although we have not created nature, we yet know a great deal about it. This knowledge, essentially common sense/scientific knowledge, seems to me the only viable candidate for playing the role in regard to the appreciation of nature which our knowledge of types of art, artistic traditions, and the like plays in regard to the appreciation of art. Consider the aesthetic appreciation of an environment such as that described by Tuan. We experience the environment as obtrusive foreground – the smell of the hay and of the horse dung, the feel of the ant, the sound of the cicadas and of the distant traffic all force themselves upon us. We experience a "meld of sensations" but, as noted, if our state is to be aesthetic appreciation rather than just the having of raw experience, the meld cannot be simply a "blooming buzzing confusion." Rather it must be what Dewey called a consummatory experience: one in which knowledge and intelligence transform raw experience by making it determinate, harmonious, and meaningful. For example, in order for there to be aesthetic appreciation we must recognize the smell of the hay and that of the horse dung and perhaps distinguish between them; we must feel the ant at least as an insect rather than as, say, a twitch. Such recognizing and distinguishing results in certain aspects of the obtrusive foreground becoming foci of aesthetic significance. Moreover, they are natural foci appropriate to the particular natural environment we are appreciating. Likewise our knowledge of the environment may yield certain appropriate boundaries or limits to the experience. For example, since we are aesthetically appreciating a certain kind of environment, the sound of cicadas may be appreciated as a proper part of the setting, while the sound of the distant traffic is excluded much as we ignore the coughing in the concert hall.

What I am suggesting is that the question of *what* to aesthetically appreciate in the natural environment is to be answered in a way analogous to the similar question about art. The difference is that in the case of the natural environment the relevant knowledge is the common sense/scientific knowledge which we have discovered about the environment in question. This knowledge gives us the appropriate foci of aesthetic significance and the appropriate boundaries of the setting so that our experience becomes one of aesthetic appreciation. If to aesthetically appreciate art we must have knowledge of artistic traditions and styles within those traditions, to aesthetically appreciate nature we must have knowledge of the different environments of nature and of the systems and elements within those environments. In the way in which the art critic and the art historian are well equipped to aesthetically appreciate art, the naturalist and the ecologist are well equipped to aesthetically appreciate nature.[20]

The point I have now made about what to appreciate in nature also has ramifications for how to appreciate nature. When discussing the nature of an environment, I suggested that Tuan's description seems to indicate a general act of aspection appropriate for any environment. However, since natural environments differ in type it seems that within this general act of aspection there might be differences which should be noted. To aesthetically appreciate an environment we experience our surroundings as obtrusive foreground allowing our knowledge of that environment to select certain foci of aesthetic significance and perhaps exclude others, thereby limiting the experience. But certainly there are also different kinds of appropriate acts of aspection which can likewise be selected by our knowledge of environments. Ziff tells us to look for contours in the Florentine school and for color in a Bonnard, to survey a Tintoretto and to scan a Bosch. Consider different natural environments. It seems that we must survey a prairie environment, looking at the subtle contours of the land, feeling the wind blowing across the open space, and smelling the mix of prairie grasses and flowers. But such an act of aspection has little place in a dense forest environment. Here we must examine and scrutinize, inspecting the detail of the forest floor, listening carefully for the sounds of birds and smelling carefully for the scent of spruce and pine. Likewise, the description of environmental appreciation given by Tuan, in addition to being a model for environmental acts of aspection in general, is also a description of the act of aspection appropriate for a particular kind of environment – one perhaps best described as pastoral. Different natural environments require different acts of aspection; and as in the case of what to appreciate, our knowledge of the environment m question indicates how to appreciate, that is, indicates the appropriate act of aspection.

The model I am thus presenting for the aesthetic appreciation of nature might be termed the environmental model. It involves recognizing that nature is an environment and thus a setting within which we exist and which we normally experience with our complete range of senses as our unobtrusive background. But our experience being aesthetic requires unobtrusive background to be experienced as obtrusive foreground. The result is the experience of a "blooming, buzzing confusion" which in order to be appreciated must be tempered by the knowledge which we have discovered about the natural environment so experienced. Our knowledge of the nature of the particular environment yields the appropriate boundaries of appreciation, the particular foci of aesthetic significance, and the relevant act or acts of aspection for that type of environment. We thus have a model which begins to give answers to the questions of what and how to appreciate in respect to the natural environment and which seems to do so with due regard for the nature of that environment. And this is important not only for aesthetic but also for moral and ecological reasons.

IV

In this paper I have attempted to open discussion on the questions of what and how to aesthetically appreciate in regard to nature. In doing so I have argued that two traditional approaches, each of which more or less assimilates the appreciation of nature to the appreciation of certain art forms, leave much to be desired. However, the approach which I have suggested, the environmental model, yet follows closely the general structure of our aesthetic appreciation of art. This approach does not depend on an assimilation of natural objects to art objects or of landscapes to scenery, but rather on an application of the general structure of aesthetic appreciation of art to something which is not art. What is important is to recognize that nature is an environment and is natural, and to make that recognition central to our aesthetic appreciation. Thereby we will aesthetically appreciate nature for what it is and for the qualities it has. And we will avoid being the person described by Hepburn who "will either pay very little aesthetic heed to natural objects or else heed them in the wrong way," who "will look – and of course look in vain – for what can be found and enjoyed only in art."[21]

NOTES

1 Paul Ziff, "Reasons in art criticism," *Philosophy and Education*, ed. I. Scheffler (Boston, 1958). Reprinted in *Art and Philosophy*, ed. W. E. Kennick (New York, 1964), p. 620.
2 Ibid. Ziff is mainly concerned with the way in which knowledge of types yields different acts of aspection. For an elaboration of this point and its ramifications concerning what is and is not aesthetically significant in a work, see K. Walton, "Categories of art," *Philosophical Review* (1970), 334–67. How our knowledge of art (and the artworld) yields the boundaries between art and the rest of reality is interestingly discussed in A. Danto, "The artistic enfranchisement of real objects: the artworld," *Journal of Philosophy* (1964), 571–84.

3 F.E. Sparshott, "Figuring the ground: notes on some theoretical problems of the aesthetic environment," *Journal of Aesthetic Education* (1972), 13.
4 George Santayana, *The Sense of Beauty* (New York, 1961), p. 100.
5 Danto, op. cit., p. 579.
6 This favored sense of "landscape" is brought out by Yi-Fu Tuan. See *Topophilia: A Study of Environmental Perception, Attitudes, and Values* (Englewood Cliffs, 1974), pp. 132–3, or "Man and nature: an eclectic reading," *Landscape* 15 (1966), 30.
7 For a good, brief discussion of this point, see R. Rees, "The scenery cult: changing landscape tastes over three centuries," *Landscape* 19 (1975). Note the following remarks by E.H. Gombrich in "The Renaissance theory of art and the rise of landscape," *Norm and Form: Studies in the Art of the Renaissance* (London, 1971), pp. 117–18: ". . . I believe that the idea of natural beauty as an inspiration of art . . . is, to say the least, a very dangerous oversimplification. Perhaps it even reverses the actual process by which man discovers the beauty of nature. We call a scenery 'picturesque' . . . if it reminds us of paintings we have seen. . . . Similarly, so it seems, the discovery of Alpine scenery does not precede but follows the spread of prints and paintings with mountain panoramas."
8 Thomas West, *Guide to the Lakes* (London, 1778) as quoted in J.T. Ogden, "From spatial to aesthetic distance in the eighteenth century," *Journal of the History of Ideas* 35 (1974), 66–7.
9 R. Rees, "The taste for mountain scenery," *History Today* 25 (1975), 312.
10 Paul Shepard, *The Tender Carnivore and the Sacred Game* (New York, 1973), pp. 147–8. Shepard made this position more explicit at a lecture at Athabasca University, Edmonton, Alberta, 16 November 1974.
11 Rees, "Mountain scenery," op. cit., p. 312. Ethical worries are also expressed by Tuan, *Topophilia*, op. cit., chapter 8, and R.A. Smith and C.M. Smith, "Aesthetics and environmental education," *Journal of Aesthetic Education* (1970), 131–2. Smith and Smith put the point as follows: "Perhaps there is a special form of arrogance in experiencing nature strictly in the categories of art, for the attitude involved here implies an acceptance, though perhaps only momentarily, of the notion that natural elements have been arranged for the sake of the man's aesthetic pleasure. It is possible that this is what Kant had in mind when he said that in the appreciation of natural beauty one ought not assume that nature has fashioned its forms for our delight and that, instead, 'it is we who receive nature with favour, and not nature that does us a favour.'"
12 R.W. Hepburn, "Aesthetic appreciation of nature," *Aesthetics and the Modern World*, ed. H. Osborne (London, 1968), p. 53. Hepburn implicitly argues that our aesthetic appreciation of nature is enhanced by our "realizing" that an object is what it is and has the qualities which it has. See pp. 60–5.
13 Sparshott, op. cit., pp. 12–13. Sparshott also considers other possible relations which are not directly relevant here. Moreover, I suspect he considers the "traveler to scene" relation to be more significant than I do.
14 Ibid., pp. 17–18.
15 Ibid., p. 21.
16 Ibid., pp. 13–14, 21.
17 John Dewey, *Art as Experience* (New York, 1958), especially chapters 1–3.
18 Ibid., pp. 18–19.
19 Tuan, *Topophilia*, op. cit., p. 96.
20 I have in mind here individuals such as John Muir and Aldo Leopold. See, for example, Leopold's *A Sand County Almanac*.
21 Hepburn, op. cit., p. 53.

11

ON BEING MOVED BY NATURE: BETWEEN RELIGION AND NATURAL HISTORY

Noël Carroll

I Introduction

For the last two and a half decades – perhaps spurred onwards by R.W. Hepburn's seminal, wonderfully sensitive and astute essay "Contemporary Aesthetics and the Neglect of Natural Beauty"[1] – philosophical interest in the aesthetic appreciation of nature has been gaining momentum. One of the most coherent, powerfully argued, thorough, and philosophically compelling theories to emerge from this evolving arena of debate has been developed over a series of articles by Allen Carlson.[2] The sophistication of Carlson's approach – especially in terms of his careful style of argumentation – has raised the level of philosophical discussion concerning the aesthetic appreciation of nature immensely and it has taught us all what is at stake, logically and epistemologically, in advancing a theory of nature appreciation. Carlson has not only presented a bold theory of the aesthetic appreciation of nature; he has also refined a methodological framework and a set of constraints that every researcher in the field must address.

Stated summarily, Carlson's view of the appreciation of nature is that it is a matter of scientific understanding; that is, the correct or appropriate form that the appreciation of nature – properly so called – should take is a species of natural history; appreciating nature is a matter of understanding nature under the suitable scientific categories. In appreciating an expanse of modern farm land, for example, we appreciate it by coming to understand the way in which the shaping of such a landscape is a function of the purposes of large-scale agriculture.[3] Likewise, the appreciation of flora and fauna is said to require an understanding of evolutionary theory.[4]

Carlson calls his framework for nature appreciation the natural environmental model.[5] He believes that the strength of this model is that it regards nature as (a) an environment (rather than, say, a view) and (b) as natural. Moreover, the significance of (b) is that it implies that the appreciation of nature should be in terms of the qualities nature has (and these, in turn, are the qualities natural science identifies). Carlson writes "for significant appreciation of nature, something like the knowledge and experience of the naturalist is essential."[6]

My major worry about Carlson's stance is that it excludes certain very common appreciative responses to nature – responses of a less intellectual, more visceral sort, which we might refer to as "being moved by nature." For example, we may find ourselves standing under a thundering waterfall and be excited by its grandeur; or standing barefooted amidst a silent arbor, softly carpeted with layers of decaying leaves, a sense of repose and homeyness may be aroused in us. Such responses to nature are quite frequent and even sought out by those of us who are not naturalists. They are a matter of being emotionally moved by nature. This, of course, does not imply that they are noncognitive, since emotional arousal has a cognitive dimension.[7] However, it is far from clear that all the emotions appropriately aroused in us by nature are rooted in cognitions of the sort derived from natural history.

Appreciating nature for many of us, I submit, often involves being moved or emotionally aroused by nature. We may appreciate nature by opening ourselves to its stimulus, and to being put in a certain emotional state by attending to its aspects. Experiencing nature, in this mode, just is a manner of appreciating it. That is not to say that this is the only way in which we can appreciate nature. The approach of the naturalist that Carlson advocates is another way. Nor do I wish to deny that naturalists can be moved by nature or even to deny that something like our nonscientific arousal by nature might be augmented, in some cases, by the kind of knowledge naturalists possess. It is only to claim that sometimes we can be moved by nature – *sans* guidance by scientific categories – and that such experiences have a genuine claim to be counted among the ways in which nature may be (legitimately) appreciated.

Carlson's approach to the appreciation of nature is reformist. His point is that a number of the best-known frameworks for appreciating nature – which one finds in the literature – are wrongheaded *and* that the model of appreciation informed by naturalism which he endorses is the least problematic and most reasonable picture of what nature appreciation should involve. In contrast, I wish to argue that there is at least one frequently indulged way of appreciating nature which Carlson has not examined adequately and that it need not be abjured on the basis of the kinds of arguments and considerations Carlson has adduced. It is hard to read Carlson's conclusions without surmising that he believes that he has identified *the* appropriate model of nature appreciation. Instead, I believe that there is one form of nature appreciation – call it being emotionally moved by nature – that (a) is a longstanding practice, (b) remains untouched by Carlson's arguments, and (c) need not be abandoned in the face of Carlson's natural environmental model.

In defending this alternative mode of nature appreciation, I am not offering it in place of Carlson's environmental model. Being moved by nature in certain ways is one way of appreciating nature; Carlson's environmental model is another. I'm for coexistence. I am specifically *not* arguing that, given certain traditional conceptions of the *aesthetic*, being moved by nature has better claims to the title of *aesthetic* appreciation whereas the environmental model, insofar as it involves the subsumption of particulars under scientific categories and laws, is not an *aesthetic* mode of appreciation at all. Such an objection to Carlson's environmental model might be raised, but it will not be raised by me. I am willing to accept that the natural environmental model provides *an* aesthetic mode of appreciating nature for the reasons Carlson gives.

Though I wish to resist Carlson's environmental model of nature appreciation as an exclusive, comprehensive one, and, thereby, wish to defend a space for the traditional practice of being moved by nature, I also wish to block any reductionist account – of the kind suggested by T.J. Diffey[8] – that regards our being moved by nature as a residue of religious feeling. Diffey says, "In a secular society it is not surprising that there will be a hostility towards any religious veneration of natural beauty and at the same time nature will become a refuge for displaced religious emotions."[9] But I want to stress that the emotions aroused by nature that concern me can be fully secular and have no call to be demystified as displaced religious sentiment. That is, being moved by nature is a mode of nature appreciation that is available between science and religion.

In what follows I will try to show that the kinds of considerations that Carlson raises do not preclude being moved by nature as a respectable form of nature appreciation. In order to do this, I will review Carlson's major arguments – which I call, respectively: science by elimination, the claims of objectivist epistemology and the order argument. In the course of disputing these arguments, I will also attempt to introduce a positive characterization of what being moved by nature involves in a way that deflects the suspicion that it should be reduced to displaced religious feeling.

II SCIENCE BY ELIMINATION

Following Paul Ziff, Carlson points out that in the appreciation of works of art, we know what to appreciate – in that we can distinguish an artwork from what it is not – and we know which of its aspects to appreciate – since in knowing the type of art it is, we know how it is to be appreciated.[10] We have this knowledge, as Vico would have agreed, because artworks are our creations. That is, since we have made them to be objects of aesthetic attention, we understand what is involved in appreciating them.[11]

However we explain this feature of artistic appreciation, it seems clear that classifying the kind and style of an artwork is crucial to appreciating it. But with nature – something which in large measure it is often the case that we have not made – the question arises as to how we can appreciate it. By what principles will we isolate the appreciable from what it is not, and how will we select the appropriate aspects of the nature so circumscribed to appreciate? In order to answer this question, Carlson explores alternative models for appreciating nature: the object paradigm, the landscape or scenery model, and the environmental paradigm.[12]

The object paradigm of nature appreciation treats an expanse in nature as analogous to an artwork such as a nonrepresentational sculpture; as in the case of such a sculpture, we appreciate its sensuous properties, its salient patterns and perhaps even its expressive qualities.[13] That is, the object model guides our attention to certain aspects of nature – such as patterned configurations – which are deemed relevant for appreciation. This is clearly a possible way of attending to nature, but Carlson wants to know whether it is an aesthetically appropriate way.[14]

Carlson thinks not; for there are systematically daunting disanalogies between natural expanses and works of fine art. For example, a natural object is said to be an indeterminate form. Where it stops is putatively ambiguous.[15] But with artworks, there are frames or framelike devices (like the ropes and spaces around sculptures) that tell you where the focus of artistic attention ends. Moreover, the formal qualities of such artworks are generally contingent on such framings.[16]

Of course, we can impose frames on nature. We can take a rock from its natural abode and put it on a mantlepiece. Or, we can discipline our glance in such a way as to frame a natural expanse so that we appreciate the visual patterns that emerge from our own exercise in perceptual composition. But in doing this, we work against the organic unity in the natural expanse, sacrificing many of those real aesthetic features that are not made salient by our exercises in visual framing, *especially* the physical forces that make the environment what it is.[17] And in this sense, the object paradigm is too exclusive; it offends through aesthetic omission.

Thus, Carlson confronts the object paradigm with a dilemma. Under its aegis, either we frame – literally or figuratively – a part of nature, thereby removing it from its organic environment (and distracting our attention from its interplay with many real and fascinating ecological forces) *or* we leave it where it is, unframed, indeterminate, and bereft of the fixed visual patterns and qualities (that emerge from acts of framing). In the first case, the object model is insensitive; in the second, it is, putatively, inoperable.

A second paradigm for nature appreciation is the landscape or scenery model. This also looks to fine art as a precedent; it invites us to contemplate a landscape as if it were a landscape painting. Perhaps this approach gained appeal historically in the guidebooks of the eighteenth century which recommended this or that natural prospect as affording a view reminiscent of this or that painter (such as Salvator Rosa).[18] In appreciating a landscape as a piece of scenery painting, we attend to features it might share with a landscape painting, such as its coloration and design.

But this, like the object model, also impedes comprehensive attention to the actual landscape. It directs our attention to the visual; but the full appreciation of nature comprises smells, textures and temperatures. And landscape painting typically sets us at a distance from nature. Yet often we appreciate nature for our being amidst it.[19] Paintings are two-dimensional, but nature has three dimensions; it offers a participatory space, not simply a space that we apprehend from outside.

Likewise, the picture frame excludes us whereas characteristically we are included as a self in a setting in the natural expanses we appreciate.[20] Thus, as with the object model of nature appreciation, the problem with the scenery model is that it is too restrictive to accommodate all the aspects of nature that might serve as genuine objects of aesthetic attention.

Lastly, Carlson offers us the natural environment model of appreciation. The key to this model is that it regards nature as nature. It overcomes the limitations of the object model by taking as *essential* the organic relation of natural expanses and items to their larger environmental contexts. The interplay of natural forces like winds are as significant as the sensuous shapes of the rock formations that are subject to them. On this view, appreciating nature involves attending to the organic interaction of natural forces. *Pace* the scenery model, the totality of natural forces, not just those that are salient to vision, are comprehended. Whereas the scenery paradigm *proposes* nature as a static array, the natural environment approach acknowledges the dynamism of nature.

Undoubtedly the inclusiveness of the natural environment model sounds promising. But the question still remains concerning which natural categories and relations are relevant to attending to nature as nature. It is Carlson's view that natural science provides us with the kind of knowledge that guides us to the appropriate *foci* of aesthetic significance and to the pertinent relations within their boundaries.

In order to aesthetically appreciate art, we must have knowledge of the artistic traditions that yield the relevant classificatory schemes for artists and audiences; in order to aesthetically appreciate nature, we need comparable knowledge of different environments and of their relevant systems and elements.[21] This knowledge comes from science and natural history, including that which is embodied in common sense. Where else could it come from? What else could understanding nature as nature amount to? The knowledge we derive from art criticism and art history for the purpose of art appreciation comes from ecology and natural history with respect to nature appreciation.

Carlson writes:

> What I am suggesting is that the question of *what* to aesthetically appreciate in the natural environment is to be answered in a way analogous to the similar question about art. The difference is that in the case of the natural environment the relevant knowledge is the commonsense/scientific knowledge which we have discovered about the environment in question.[22]

The structure of Carlson's argument is motivated by the pressure to discover some guidance with respect to nature appreciation that is analogous to the guidance that the fixing of artistic categories does with works of art. Three possibilities are explored: the object paradigm, the scenery paradigm and the natural environment paradigm. The first two are rejected because they fail to comprehensively track all the qualities and relations we would expect a suitable framework for the appreciation of nature to track. On the other hand, the natural environment model is advanced not only because it does not occlude the kind of attentiveness that the alternative models block, but also because it has the advantage of supplying us with classificatory frameworks which play the role that things like genres do with respect to art, while at the same time these categories are natural (derived from natural history).

Stated formally, Carlson's argument is basically a disjunctive syllogism:

1   All aesthetic appreciation requires a way of fixing the appropriate *loci* of appreciative acts.
2   Since nature appreciation is aesthetic appreciation, then nature appreciation must have a means of fixing the appropriate *loci* of appreciative acts.
3   With nature appreciation, the ways of fixing the appropriate *loci* of appreciative acts are the object model, the scenic model and the natural environment model.
4   Neither the object model nor the scenic model suit nature appreciation.
5   Therefore, the natural environment model (using science as its source of knowledge) is the means for fixing the *loci* of appreciative acts with respect to nature appreciation.

Of course, the most obvious line of attack to take with arguments of this sort is to ask whether it has captured the relevant field of alternatives. I want to suggest that Carlson's argument has not. Specifically, I maintain that he has not countenanced our being moved by nature as a mode of appreciating nature and that he has not explored the possibility that the *loci* of such appreciation can be fixed in the process of our being emotionally aroused by nature.

Earlier I conjured up a scene where standing near a towering cascade, our ears reverberating with the roar of falling water, we are overwhelmed and excited by its grandeur. People quite standardly seek out such experiences. They are, pretheoretically, a form of appreciating nature. Moreover, when caught up in such experiences our attention is fixed on certain aspects of the natural expanse rather than others – the palpable force of the cascade, its height, the volume of water, the way it alters the surrounding atmosphere, etc.

This does not require any special scientific knowledge. Perhaps it only requires being human, equipped with the senses we have, being small and able to intuit the immense force, relative to creatures like us, of the roaring tons of water. Nor need the common sense of our culture come into play. Conceivably humans from other planets bereft of waterfalls could share our sense of grandeur. This is not to say that all emotional responses to nature are culture-free, but only that the pertinent dimensions of some such arousals may be.

That is, we may be aroused emotionally by nature, and our arousal may be a function of our human nature in response to a natural expanse. I may savor a winding footpath because it raises a tolerable sense of mystery in me. Unlike the scenery model of nature appreciation, what we might call the arousal model does not necessarily put us at a distance from the object of our appreciation; it may be the manner in which we are amidst nature that has moved us to the state in which we find ourselves. Nor does the arousal model of nature restrict our response to only the visual aspects of nature. The cascade moves us through its sound, and weight, and temperature, and force. The sense of mystery awakened by the winding path is linked to the process of moving through it.

Perhaps the arousal model seems to raise the problem of framing, mentioned earlier, in a new way. Just as the object model and the scenery model appeared to impose a frame on an otherwise indeterminate nature, similarly the arousal model may appear to involve us in imposing emotional gestalts upon indeterminate natural expanses. Nevertheless, there are features of nature, especially in relation to human organisms, which, though they are admittedly "selected," are difficult to think of as "impositions."

Certain natural expanses have natural frames or what I prefer to call natural closure: caves, copses, grottoes, clearings, arbors, valleys, etc. And other natural expanses, though lacking frames, have features that are naturally salient for human organisms – i.e., they have features such as moving water, bright illumination, etc. that draw our attention instinctually toward them. And where our emotional arousal is predicated on either natural closure or natural salience, it makes little sense to say that our emotional responses, focused on said features, are impositions.

An emotional response to nature will involve some sort of selective attention to the natural expanse. If I am overwhelmed by the grandeur of a waterfall, then certain things and not others are in the forefront of my attention. Presumably since I am struck emotionally by the grandness of the waterfall, the features that are relevant to my response have to do with those that satisfy interests in scale, notably large scale. But my arousal does not come from nowhere. The human perceptual system is already keyed to noticing salient scale differentials and the fact that I batten on striking examples of the large scale is hardly an imposition from the human point of view.

Suppose, then, that I am exhilarated by the grandeur of the waterfall. That I am exhilarated by grandeur is not an inappropriate response, since the object of my emotional arousal is grand – i.e., meets the criteria of scale appropriate to grandeur, where grandeur, in turn, is one of the appropriate sources of exhilaration. In this case, our perceptual make-up initially focuses our attention on certain features of the natural expanse, which attention generates a state of emotional arousal, which state, in turn, issues in reinforcing feedback that consolidates the initial selective gestalt of the emotional arousement experience. The arousal model of nature appreciation has an account of how we isolate certain aspects of nature and why these are appropriate aspects to focus upon; that is, they are *emotionally* appropriate.

Perhaps Carlson's response to this is that emotional responses to nature of the sort that I envision are not responses to nature as nature. This route seems inadvisable since Carlson, like Sparshott, wants us to think of the appreciator of nature as a self in a setting which I understand as, in part, a warning not to divorce human nature from nature.[23] Admittedly, not all of our emotional arousals in the face of nature should be ascribed to our common human nature, rather than to what is sectarian in our cultures, but there is no reason to preclude the possibility that some of our emotional arousals to nature are bred in the bone.

Conceding that we are only talking about *some* of our appreciative responses to nature here may seem to open another line of criticism. Implicit in Carlson's manner of argument seems to be the presupposition that what he is about is identifying the one and only form of nature appreciation. His candidate, of course, is the environmental model which relies heavily on natural science.

I have already argued that this model is not the only respectable alternative. But another point also bears emphasis here, namely, why presume that there is only one model for appreciating nature and one source of knowledge – such as natural history – relevant to fixing our appreciative categories? Why are we supposing that there is just one model, applying to all cases, for the appropriate appreciation of nature?

That the appreciation of nature sometimes may involve emotional arousal, divorced from scientific or commonsense ecological knowledge, does not disallow that at other times appreciation is generated by the natural environment model. Certainly a similar situation obtains in artistic appreciation. Sometimes we may be emotionally aroused – indeed, appropriately emotionally moved – without knowing the genre or style of the artwork that induces this state. Think of children amused by capers of *Commedia dell'arte* but who know nothing of its tradition or its place among other artistic genres, styles and categories. Yet the existence of this sort of appreciative response in no way compromises the fact that there is another kind of appreciation – that of the informed connoisseur – which involves situating the features of the artwork with respect to its relevant artistic categories.

I want to say that the same is true of nature appreciation. Appreciation may sometimes follow the arousal model or the natural environment model. Sometimes the two models may overlap – for our emotions may be aroused on the basis of our ecological knowledge. But, equally, there will be clear cases where they do not. Moreover, I see no reason to assume that these are the only models for the appropriate response to nature. In some cases – given the natural closure and salience of arrays in nature – the object model may not be out of place for, given our limited perceptual capacities, structured as they are, nature may not strike us as formally indeterminate.

My basic objection to Carlson is that emotional arousal in response to nature can be an appropriate form of nature appreciation and that the cognitive component of our emotional response does the job of fixing the aspects of nature that are relevant to appreciation. Here, I have been assuming that emotional arousal, though cognitive, need not rely on categories derived from science. But Carlson sometimes describes his preferred source of knowledge as issuing from common sense/science. So perhaps the way out of my objection is to say that with my cases of being moved by nature, the operative cognitions are rooted in commonsense knowledge of nature.

A lot depends here on what is included in commonsense knowledge of nature. I take it that for Carlson this is a matter of knowing in some degree how nature works; it involves, for example, some prescientific, perhaps folk, understanding of things like ecological systems. That I know, in my waterfall example, that the stuff that is falling down is water is not commonsense knowledge of nature in the way that Carlson seems to intend with phrases like common sense/science. For the knowledge in my case need not involve any systematic knowledge of nature's working of either a folk or scientific origin. And if this is so, then we can say that we are emotionally moved by nature where the operative cognitions that play a constitutive role in our response do not rely on the kind of commonsense systemic knowledge of natural processes that Carlson believes is requisite for the aesthetic appreciation of nature. And, perhaps even more clearly, we can be moved by nature where our cognitions do not mobilize the far more formal and recondite systemic knowledge found in natural history and science.

III THE CLAIMS OF OBJECTIVIST EPISTEMOLOGY

One reason, as we have just seen, that prompts Carlson to endorse natural history as the appropriate guide to nature appreciation is that it appears to provide us with our only satisfactory alternative. I have disputed this. But Carlson has other compelling motives for the type of nature appreciation he advocates. One of these is epistemological. It has already been suggested; now is the time to bring it centerstage.

Echoing Hume's "Of the Standard of Taste," Carlson's impressive "Nature, Aesthetic Judgment and Objectivity" begins with the conviction that certain of the aesthetic judgments that we issue with respect to nature – such as "The Grand Tetons are majestic" – are or can be appropriate, correct or true. That is, certain aesthetic judgments of nature are objective. Were someone to assert that "The Grand Tetons are paltry," without further explanation, our response would converge on the consensus that the latter assertion is false.

However, though the conviction that aesthetic judgments of nature can be objective is firm, it is nevertheless difficult to square with the best available models we possess for elucidating the way in which aesthetic judgments of art are objective. Indeed, given our best models of the way that aesthetic judgments of art are objective, we may feel forced to conclude that aesthetic judgments of nature are relativistic or subjective, despite our initial conviction that aesthetic judgments of nature can be objective.

So the question becomes a matter of explaining how our aesthetic judgments of nature can be objective. This is a problem because, as just mentioned, reigning accounts of how aesthetic judgments of art are objective have been taken to imply that aesthetic judgments of nature cannot be objective.

In order to get a handle on this problem, we need, of course, to understand the relevant theory of art appreciation which ostensibly renders nature appreciation subjective or relative. The particular theory that Carlson has in mind is Kendall Walton's notion of categories of art. This theory is an example of a broader class of theories – that would include institutional theories of art – which can be usefully thought of as cultural theories. Roughly speaking, cultural theories of art supply the wherewithal to ground aesthetic judgments of art objectively by basing such judgments on the cultural practice and forms – such as artistic genres, styles and movements – in which and through which artworks are created and disseminated.

On Walton's account, for example, an aesthetic judgment concerning an artwork can be assessed as true or false. The truth value of such judgments is a function of two factors, specifically: the non-aesthetic perceptual properties of the artwork (e.g., dots of paint), and the status of said properties when the artwork is situated in its correct artistic category (e.g., pointillism). Psychologically speaking, all aesthetic judgments of art, whether they are subjective or objective, require that we locate the perceived, nonaesthetic properties of the artwork in *some* category. For example, if an uninformed viewer finds the image in a cubist painting woefully confused, it is likely that that viewer regards the work in terms of the (albeit wrong) category of a realistic, perspectival representation.

However, logically speaking, if an aesthetic judgment is true (or appropriate), then that is a function of the perceived, nonaesthetic properties of the artwork being comprehended within the context of the *correct* category of art. In terms of the preceding example, it is a matter of viewing the painting in question under the category of cubism. Consequently, the objectivity of aesthetic judgments of art depends upon identifying the correct category for the artwork in question.

A number of circumstances can count in determining the category of art that is relevant to the aesthetic judgment of an artwork. But some of the most conclusive depend on features relating to the origin of the work: such as which category (genre, style, movement) the artist intended for the artwork, as well as cultural factors, such as whether the category in question is a recognized or well-entrenched one. These are not the only considerations that we use in fixing the relevant category of an artwork; but they are, nevertheless, fairly decisive ones.

However, if these sorts of considerations are crucial in fixing the relevant categories of artworks, it should be clear that they are of little moment when it comes to nature. For nature is not produced by creators whose intentions can be used to isolate the *correct* categories for appreciating a given natural expanse *nor* is nature produced with regard for recognized cultural categories. But if we cannot ascertain the correct category upon which to ground our aesthetic judgments of nature, then those judgments cannot be either true or false. Moreover, since the way in which we fix the category of a natural object or expanse appears to be fairly open, our aesthetic judgments of nature appear to gravitate towards subjectivity. That is, they do not seem as though they can be objective judgments, despite our starting intuition that some of them are.

The structure of Carlson's argument revolves around a paradox. We start with the conviction that some aesthetic judgments of nature can be objective, but then the attempt to explain this by the lights of our best model of aesthetic objectivity with respect to the arts, indicates that no aesthetic judgment of nature can be objective (because there are no *correct* categories for nature). Carlson wants to dissolve this paradox by removing the worry that there are no objective, aesthetic judgments of nature. He does this by arguing that we do have the means for identifying the relevant, *correct* categories that are operative in genuine aesthetic judgments of nature. These are the ones *discovered* by natural history and science.

For example, we know that the relevant category for aesthetically appreciating whales is that of the mammal rather than that of fish as a result of scientific research. Moreover, these scientific categories function formally or logically in the same way in nature appreciation that art historical categories function in art appreciation. Thus, the logical form, though not the content, of nature appreciation corresponds to that of art appreciation. *And* insofar as the latter can be objective in virtue of its form, the former can be as well.

Another way to characterize Carlson's argument is to regard it as a transcendental argument. It begins by assuming as given that nature appreciation can be objective and then goes on to ask how this is possible – especially since there does not seem to be anything like correct categories of art to ground objectivity when it comes to nature appreciation. But, then, the possibility of the objectivity of nature appreciation is explained by maintaining that the categories discovered by natural history and science are available to play the role in securing the objectivity of aesthetic judgments of nature in a way that is analogous to the service performed by art historical categories for art.

Thus, for epistemological reasons, we are driven to the view of nature appreciation as a species of natural history. Effectively, it is advanced as the only way to support our initial intuitions that some aesthetic judgments of nature can be objective. Moreover, any competing picture of nature appreciation, if it is to be taken seriously, must have comparable means to those of the natural environment model for solving the problem of the objectivity of nature appreciation.

Of course, I do not wish to advance the "being moved by nature" view as competing with the natural environment approach. Rather, I prefer to think of it as a coexisting model. But even as a coexisting model, it must be able to solve the problem of objectivity. However, the solution to the problem is quite straightforward when it comes to being emotionally moved by nature.

For, being emotionally moved by nature is just a subclass of being emotionally moved. And on the view of the emotions that I, among many others, hold, an emotion can be assessed as either appropriate or inappropriate. In order to be afraid, I must be afraid of *something*, say an oncoming tank. My emotion – fear in this case – is directed; it takes a particular object. Moreover, if my fear in a given case is appropriate, then the particular object of my emotional state must meet certain criteria, or what are called "formal objects" in various philosophical idioms.

For example, the formal object of fear is the dangerous. Or, to put the point in less stilted language: if my fear of the tank (the particular object of my emotion) is appropriate, then it must satisfy the criterion that I believe the tank to be dangerous to me. If, for instance, I say that I am afraid of chicken soup, but also that I do not believe that chicken soup is dangerous, then my fear of chicken soup is inappropriate. C.D. Broad writes: "It is appropriate to cognize what one takes to be a threatening object with some degree of fear. It is inappropriate to cognize what one takes to be a fellow man in undeserved pain or distress with satisfaction or with amusement."[24]

Of course, if emotions can be assessed with respect to appropriateness and inappropriateness, then they are open to cognitive appraisal. Ronald deSousa says, for example, that "appropriateness is the truth of the emotions."[25] We can assess the appropriateness of the emotion of fear for an emoter in terms of whether or not she believes that the particular object of her emotion is dangerous. We can, furthermore, assess whether the appropriateness of her fear ought to be shared by others by asking whether the beliefs, thoughts or patterns of attention that underpin her emotions are the sorts of beliefs, thoughts or patterns of attention that it is reasonable for others to share. Thus we can determine whether her fear of the tank is objective in virtue of whether her belief about the dangerousness of the tank, in the case at hand, is a reasonable belief for the rest of us to hold.

Turning from tanks to nature, we may be emotionally moved by a natural expanse – excited, for instance, by the grandeur of a towering waterfall. All things being equal, being excited by the grandeur of something that one believes to be of a large scale is an appropriate emotional response. Moreover, if the belief in the large scale of the cascade is one that is true for others as well, then the emotional response of being excited by the grandeur of the waterfall is an objective one. It is not subjective, distorted, or wayward. If someone denies being moved by the waterfall, but agrees that the waterfall is large scale and says nothing else, we are apt to suspect that his response, as well as any judgments issued on the basis of that response, are inappropriate. If he does not agree that the waterfall is of a large scale, and does not say why, we will suspect him either of not understanding how to use the notion of large scale, or of irrationality. If he disagrees that the waterfall is of a large scale because the galaxy is much much larger, then we will try to convince him that he has the wrong comparison class – urging, perhaps, that he should gauge the scale of the waterfall in relation to human scale.

In introducing the notion of the "wrong comparison class," it may seem that I have opened the door to Carlson's arguments. But I do not think that I have. For it is not clear that in order to establish the relevant comparison class for an emotional response to nature one must resort to scientific categories. For example, we may be excited by the grandeur of a blue whale. I may be moved by its size, its force, the amount of water it displaces, etc., but I may think that it is a fish. Nevertheless, my being moved by the grandeur of the blue whale is not inappropriate. Indeed, we may be moved by the skeleton of a *Tyrannosaurus rex* without knowing whether it is the skeleton of a reptile, a bird, or a mammal. We can be moved by such encounters, without knowing the natural history of the thing encountered, on the basis of its scale, along with other things, relative to ourselves.

Such arousals may or may not be appropriate for us and for others. Moreover, judgments based on such emotional responses – like "that whale excites grandeur" or "The Grand Tetons are majestic" – can be objective. Insofar as being moved by nature is a customary form of appreciating nature, then it can account for the objectivity of some of our aesthetic judgments of nature. Thus, it satisfies the epistemological challenge whose solution Carlson appears to believe favors only his natural environment model for the aesthetic appreciation of nature. Or, to put it another way, being moved by nature remains *a* way of appreciating nature that may coexist with the natural environment model.

At one point, Carlson concedes that we can simply enjoy nature – "we can, of course, approach nature as we sometimes approach art, that is, we can simply *enjoy* its forms and colors or *enjoy* perceiving it however we may happen to."[26] But this is not a very deep level of appreciation for Carlson, for, on his view, depth would appear to require objectivity. Perhaps what Carlson would say about my defense of being moved by nature is that being emotionally aroused by nature falls into the category of *merely* enjoying nature and, as an instance of that category, it isn't really very deep.

Undoubtedly, being moved by nature may be a way of enjoying nature. However, insofar as being moved by nature is a matter of being moved by appropriate objects, it is not dismissable as enjoying nature in whatever way we please. Furthermore, if the test of whether our appreciation of nature is deep is whether the corresponding judgments are susceptible to objective, cognitive appraisal, I think I have shown that some cases can pass this test. Is there any reason to think that being moved by nature must be any less deep a response than attending to nature with the eyes of the naturalist?

I would be very suspicious of an affirmative answer to this question. Of course, part of the problem is that what makes an appreciative response to nature shallow or deep is obscure. Obviously, a naturalist's appreciation of nature could be deep in the sense that it might go on and on as the naturalist learns more and more about nature, whereas a case of emotional arousal with respect to nature might be more consummatory. Is the former case deeper than the latter? Are the two cases even commensurable? Clearly, time alone cannot be a measure of depth. But how exactly are we to compare appreciative stances with respect to depth?

Maybe there is no way. But if the depth of a response is figured in terms of our intensity of involvement and its "thorough-goingness,"[27] then there is no reason to suppose that being moved by nature constitutes a shallower form of appreciation than does appreciating nature scientifically. The Kantian apprehension of sublimity[28] – and its corresponding aesthetic judgment – though it may last for a delimited duration, need not be any less deep than a protracted teleological judgment.

Again, it is not my intention to dispute the kind of appreciation that Carlson defends under the title of the natural environment model. It is only to defend the legitimacy of an already well-entrenched mode of nature appreciation that I call being moved by nature. This mode of nature appreciation can pay the epistemological bill that Carlson presupposes any adequate model of nature appreciation should accommodate. It need not be reducible to scientific appreciation, nor must it be regarded as any less deep than appreciation informed by natural history.

Of course, it may seem odd that we can appreciate nature objectively this way when it seems that a comparable form of appreciation is not available to art. But the oddity here vanishes when we realize that to a certain extent we are able to appreciate art and render objective aesthetic judgments of artworks without reference to precise art historical categories. One may find a fanfare in a piece of music stirring and objectively assert that it is stirring without any knowledge of music history and its categories. Being emotionally aroused by nature in at least certain cases need be no different.

Carlson may be disposed to question whether being emotionally moved by nature is really a matter of responding to nature as nature. Perhaps he takes it to be something like a conceptual truth that, given the culture we inhabit, attending to nature as nature can only involve attending to it scientifically. However, if I am taken with the grace of a group of deer vaulting a stream, I see no reason to suppose that I am not responding to nature as nature. Moreover, any attempt to regiment the notion of responding to nature as nature so that it only strictly applies to scientific understanding appears to me to beg the question.

IV ORDER APPRECIATION

The most recent argument that Carlson has advanced in favor of the natural environmental model of nature appreciation is what might be called the order argument.[29] In certain respects, it is reminiscent of his earlier arguments, but it does add certain new considerations that are worth our attention. Like his previous arguments, Carlson's order argument proceeds by carefully comparing the form of nature appreciation with that of art appreciation.

One paradigmatic form of art appreciation is design appreciation. Design appreciation presupposes that the artwork has a creator who embodies the design in an object or a performance, and that the design embodied in the artwork indicates how we are to take it. However, this model of appreciation is clearly inappropriate for nature appreciation since nature lacks a designer.

Nevertheless, there is another sort of art appreciation which has been devised in order to negotiate much of the *avant-garde* art of the twentieth century. Carlson calls this type of appreciation order appreciation. When, for example, we are confronted by something like Duchamp's *Fountain*, the design of the object does not tell us how to take it or appreciate it. Instead, we rely on certain stories about how the object came to be selected by Duchamp in order to make a point. These stories inform us of the ideas and beliefs that lead an *avant-garde* artist to produce or to select (in the case of a found object) the artwork.

These stories direct us in the appropriate manner of appreciating the object; they guide us in our selection of the relevant features of the work for the purposes of appreciation. They do the work with unconventional, experimental art that design does with more traditional art. For example, our knowledge, given a certain art historical narrative, of Surrealism's commitment to revealing the unconscious, alerts us to the importance of incongruous, dreamlike juxtapositions in paintings by Dali.

For Carlson, design appreciation is obviously ill-suited to nature appreciation. On the other hand, something like order appreciation appears to fit the case of nature appreciation. We can appreciate nature in terms of the forces that bring natural configurations about, and we can be guided to the relevant features of nature by stories. But where do these stories come from? At an earlier stage in our culture, they may have come from mythology. But at this late date, they come from the sciences, including astronomy, physics, chemistry, biology, genetics, meteorology, geology and so on. These sciences, and the natural histories they afford, guide our attention to the relevant forces that account for the features of nature worthy of attention.

Basically, Carlson's most recent argument is that art appreciation affords two possible models for nature appreciation: design appreciation and order appreciation. Design appreciation, however, is clearly inadmissable. That leaves us with order appreciation. However, the source of the guiding stories pertinent to the order appreciation of nature differ from those that shape order appreciation with respect to art. The source of the latter is art history while the source of the former is natural history.

But once again Carlson's argument is open to the charge that he has not canvased all of the actual alternatives. One's appreciation of art need not fall into either the category of design appreciation or order appreciation. We can sometimes appreciate art appropriately by being moved by it. Moreover, this is true of the *avant-garde* art that Carlson suggests requires order appreciation as well as of more traditional art.

For example, Man Ray's *The Gift* is an ordinary iron with pointed nails affixed to its smooth bottom. Even if one does not know that it is a specimen of Dada, and even if one lacks the art-historical story that tells one the ideology of Dada, reflecting on *The Gift* one may readily surmise that the object is at odds with itself – you cannot press trousers with it – in a way that is brutally sardonic and that arouses dark amusement. Similarly, one can detect the insult in Duchamp's *Fountain* without knowing the intricate dialectics of art history, just as one may find certain Surrealist paintings haunting without knowing the metaphysical, psychological and political aims of the Surrealist movement.

As it is sometimes with art, so is it with nature. In both cases, we may be emotionally moved by what we encounter without any really detailed background in art history or natural history. With respect to both art and nature, emotional arousal can be a mode of appreciation, and it is possible, in a large number of cases, to determine whether the emotional arousal is appropriate or inappropriate without reference to any particularly specific stories of either the art-historical or the natural-history varieties.

A parade or a sunset may move us, and this level of response, though traditionally well-known, need not be reduced to either design appreciation or order appreciation, nor must it be guided by art history or by natural history. Insofar as Carlson's approach to both art and nature appears wedded to certain types of "professional" knowledge as requisite for appreciation, he seems to be unduly hasty in closing off certain common forms of aesthetic appreciation. This is not said in order to reject the sort of informed appreciation Carlson advocates, but only to suggest that certain more naive forms of emotive, appreciative responses may be legitimate as well.[30]

I have argued that one form of nature appreciation is a matter of being aroused emotionally by the appropriate natural objects. This talk of the emotions, however, may seem suspicious to some. Does it really seem reasonable to be emotionally moved by nature? If we feel a sense of security when we scan a natural expanse, doesn't that sound just too mystical? Perhaps, our feeling, as Diffey has suggested, is some form of displaced religious sentiment. Maybe being moved by nature is some sort of delusional state worthy of psychoanalysis or demystification.

Of course, many emotional responses to nature – such as being frightened by a tiger – are anything but mystical. But it may seem that others – particularly those that are traditionally exemplary of aesthetic appreciation, like finding a landscape to be serene

– are more unfathomable and perhaps shaped by repressed religious associations. However, I think that there is reliable evidence that many of our emotional responses to nature have a straightforwardly secular basis.

For example, in his classic *The Experience of Landscape*,[31] and in subsequent articles,[32] Jay Appleton has defended the view that our responses to landscape are connected to certain broadly evolutionary interests that we take in landscapes. Appleton singles out two significant variables in our attention to landscape – what he calls prospect (a landscape opportunity for keeping open the channels of perception) and refuge (a landscape opportunity for achieving concealment).

That is, given that we are the kind of animal we are, we take a survival interest in certain features of landscapes: open vistas give us a sense of security insofar as we can see there is no threat approaching, while enclosed spaces reassure us that there are places in which to hide. We need not be as theoretically restrictive as Appleton is and maintain that these are the major foci of our attention to landscape. But we can agree that features of landscape like prospect and refuge may cause our humanly emotional responses to natural expanses in terms of the way they address our deep-seated, perhaps tacit, interests in the environment as a potential theatre of survival.

Thus, when we find a natural environment serene, part of the cause of that sense of serenity might be its openness – the fact that nothing can approach us unexpectedly across its terrain. And such a response need not be thought to be mystical nor a matter of displaced religion, if it is connected to information processing molded by our long-term evolution as animals.

Other researchers have tried to isolate further features of landscape – such as mystery and legibility[33] – that shape our responses to natural expanses in terms of a sense, however intuitive and unconscious, of the sorts of experiences we would have – such as ease of locomotion, of orientation, of exploration and so on – in the environment viewed. That is, our perhaps instinctive sense of how it would be to function in a given natural environment may be part of the cause of our emotional arousal with respect to it. A landscape that is very legible – articulated throughout with neat subdivisions – may strike us as hospitable and attractive in part because it imparts such a strong sense of how we might move around and orient ourselves inside of it.

Earlier I sketched a scene in which we found ourselves in an arbor, carpeted by layers of decaying foliage and moss. I imagined that in such a situation we might feel a sense of solace, repose, and homeyness. And such an emotional state might be caused by our tacit recognition of its refuge potential. On this view, I am not saying that we consciously realize that the arbor is a suitable refuge and appreciate it as such. Rather the fact that it is a suitable refuge acts to causally trigger our emotional response which takes the arbor as its particular object and responds to it with a feeling of repose and homeyness, focusing on such features as its enclosure and softness, which features are appropriate to the feeling of solace and homeyness.

Our feeling is not a matter of residual mysticism or religious sentiment, but is perhaps instinctually grounded. Moreover, if such a scenario is plausible for at least some of our emotional responses to nature, then it is not the case that being aroused by nature is always a repressed religious response. Some responses of some observers may be responses rooted in associations of nature with the handiwork of the gods. But other emotional responses, appropriate ones, may have perfectly secular, naturalistic explanations which derive from the kinds of insights that Appleton and others have begun to enumerate.

Admitting that our emotional responses to nature have naturalistic explanations, of course, does not entail a reversion to the natural environmental model of nature appreciation. For such explanations pertain to how our emotional responses may be caused. And when I appreciate a natural expanse by being emotionally aroused by it, the object of my emotional state need not be the recognition of my instinctual response to, for example, prospects. Perhaps one could appreciate nature *à la* Carlson from an evolutionary point-of-view in which the focus of our attention is the interaction of our emotions with the environment as that interaction is understood to be shaped by the forces of evolution. But this is not typically what one has in mind with the notion of being moved by nature.

In conclusion: to be moved by nature is to respond to the features of natural expanses – such as scale and texture – with the appropriate emotions. This is one traditional way of appreciating nature. It need not rely upon natural history nor is it a residual form of mysticism. It is one of our characteristic forms of nature appreciation – not reducible without remainder to either science or religion.

NOTES

1 R.W. Hepburn, "Contemporary aesthetics and the neglect of natural beauty," in his *Wonder and Other Essays* (Edinburgh University Press, 1984). This essay appeared earlier in *British Analytical Philosophy*, ed. B. Williams and A. Montefiore (London: Routledge & Kegan Paul, 1966).

2 See especially: Allen Carlson, "Appreciation and the natural environment," reprinted in this book. "Formal qualities in the natural environment," *Journal of Aesthetic Education* 13 (July, 1979); "Nature, aesthetic judgment and objectivity," *Journal of Aesthetics and Art Criticism* 40 (autumn, 1981); "Saito on the correct aesthetic appreciation of nature," *Journal of Aesthetic Education* 20 (summer, 1986); "On appreciating agricultural land-scapes," *Journal of Aesthetics and Art Criticism* (spring, 1985); "Appreciating art and appreciating nature," in *Landscape, Natural Beauty and the Arts*, ed. Salim Kemal and Ivan Gaskell (Cambridge University Press, 1993); Barry Sadler and Allen Carlson, "Environmental aesthetics in interdisciplinary perspective," in *Environmental Aesthetics: Essays in Interpretation*, ed. Barry Sadler and Allen Carlson (Victoria, British Columbia: University of Victoria, 1982); and Allen Carlson and Barry Sadler, "Towards models of environmental appreciation," in *Environmental Aesthetics*.

3 See Carlson, "Appreciating agricultural landscapes."

4 Carlson, "Appreciating art," in *Landscape, Natural Beauty and the Arts*, ed. Ivan Gaskell and Salim Kemal (Cambridge University Press, 1993).

5 Carlson, "Appreciation and the natural environment," p. 161.

6 Carlson, "Nature, aesthetic judgment and objectivity," p. 25.

7 See, for example, William Lyons, *Emotion* (Cambridge University Press, 1980), especially chapter 4.

8 T.J. Diffey, "Natural beauty without metaphysics," in *Landscape, Natural Beauty and the Arts*, ed. Ivan Gaskell and Salim Kemal (Cambridge University Press, 1993).

9 Ibid.

10 Carlson, "Appreciation and the natural environment," p. 155.

11 Ibid.

12 This is the way that the argument is set up in "Appreciation and the natural environment." In "Formal qualities in the natural environment," the object paradigm and the scenery model, it seems to me, both get assimilated under what might be called the formal-qualities model.

13 Carlson, "Appreciation and the natural environment," pp. 156–7.

14 Ibid.

15 Ibid.

16 Carlson, "Formal qualities," pp. 108–9.

17 Carlson, "Appreciation and the natural environment," p. 158.

18 See for example, Peter Bicknell, *Beauty, Horror and Immensity: Picturesque Landscape in Britain 1750–1850* (Cambridge University Press, 1981).

19 Carlson, "Appreciation and the natural environment," p. 160.

20 Carlson, "Formal qualities," p. 110.

21 Carlson, "Appreciation and the natural environment," pp. 164–5.

22 Ibid.

23 Francis Sparshott, "Figuring the ground: notes on some theoretical problems of the aesthetic environment," *Journal of Aesthetic Education* 6(3) (July 1972).

24 C.D. Broad, "Emotion and sentiment," in his *Critical Essays in Moral Philosophy* (London: Allen & Unwin, 1971), p. 293.

25 Ronald deSousa, "Self-deceptive emotions," in *Explaining Emotions*, ed. Amelie Oksenberg Rorty (Berkeley: University of California Press, 1980), p. 285.

26 Carlson, "Nature, aesthetic judgment and objectivity," p. 25.

27 A test suggested by Robert Solomon in his "On kitsch and sentimentality," *Journal of Aesthetics and Art Criticism* 49(1) (winter, 1981): 9.

28 See Immanuel Kant, *The Critique of Judgement*, trans. James Creed Meredith (Oxford: Clarendon Press, 1952), especially the "Analytic of the sublime."

29 See Carlson, "Appreciating art."

30 Towards the end of "Appreciating art," Carlson does refer to certain responses to nature, such as awe and wonder, which sound like the type of emotional responses I have been discussing. He thinks that even armed with the natural environment model, we may become aware that nature is still mysterious to us and *other*. And, in consequence, we feel awe and wonder. I do not want to deny that we may come to feel awe and wonder at nature through the process Carlson describes. However, I do not think that this is the only way that we can be overwhelmed with awe in the face of nature. We may, for example, be struck by the scale of nature, without any reference to scientific categories, and be overwhelmed by awe. Thus, though there may be a route to awe through the natural environment model, it is not

the only route. There are still other ways in which we may be moved to awe by nature *sans* natural history. Consequently, the account of awe that Carlson offers does not eliminate the more naive model of emotional arousal that I have been defending.

31 Jay Appleton, *The Experience of Landscape* (New York: Wiley, 1975).

32 Jay Appleton, "Prospects and refuges revisited," in *Environmental Aesthetics: Theory, Research & Applications*, ed. Jack L. Nasar (Cambridge University Press, 1988); and Jay Appleton, "Pleasure and the perception of habitat: a conceptual framework," in *Environmental Aesthetics: Essays in Interpretation*.

33 Stephen Kaplan, "Perception and landscape: conceptions and misconceptions," in *Environmental Aesthetics: Theory*, pp. 49–51. See also Kaplan's "Where cognition and affect meet: a theoretical analysis of preference," in the same volume.

SUGGESTIONS FOR FURTHER READING

Berleant, Arnold (1992) *The Aesthetics of Environment*, Philadelphia: Temple University Press.

Berleant, Arnold and Carlson, Allen (eds) (1998) Special issue on environmental aesthetics, *Journal of Aesthetics and Art Criticism* 56.

Budd, Malcolm (1996) "The aesthetic appreciation of nature", *British Journal of Aesthetics* 36: 207–22.

—— (2000) "The aesthetics of nature", *Proceedings of the Aristotelian Society* 100: 137–57.

Callicott, J. Baird (1983) "The land aesthetic", *Environmental Review* 7: 345–58.

Carlson, Allen (1981) "Nature, aesthetic judgment and objectivity", *Journal of Aesthetics and Art Criticism* 40: 15–27.

—— (1985) "On appreciating agricultural landscapes", *Journal of Aesthetics and Art Criticism* 43: 301–12.

—— (1986) "Saito on the correct aesthetic appreciation of nature", *Journal of Aesthetic Education*: 85–93.

—— (1997) "Appreciating Godlovitch", *Journal of Aesthetics and Art Criticism* 55(1): 55–7.

—— (1998) "Aesthetic appreciation of nature", *Routledge Encyclopedia of Philosophy*, ed. E. Craig, London: Routledge, vol. 6, pp. 731–5.

—— (2000) *Aesthetics and the Environment: The Appreciation of Nature, Art and Architecture*, London: Routledge.

—— (2001) "Environmental aesthetics", in *The Routledge Companion to Aesthetics*, ed. B. Gaut and D. Lopes, London: Routledge, pp. 423–36.

Eaton, Marcia (1998) "Fact and Fiction in the Aesthetic Appreciation of Nature", *Journal of Aesthetics and Art Criticism* 56: 149–56.

Godlovitch, Stan (1994) "Icebreakers: environmentalism and natural aesthetics", *Journal of Applied Philosophy* 11: 15–30.

—— (1997) "Carlson on appreciation", *Journal of Aesthetics and Art Criticism* 55(1): 53–5.

—— (1998) "Valuing nature and the autonomy of natural aesthetics", *British Journal of Aesthetics* 38: 180–97.

Hepburn, R.W. (1984) "Contemporary aesthetics and the neglect of natural beauty", in his *Wonder and Other Essays*, Edinburgh University Press.

—— (1996) "Landscape and the metaphysical imagination", *Environmental Values* 5: 191–204.

Jannaway, Christopher (1993) "Beauty in nature, beauty in art", *British Journal of Aesthetics* 33: 321–32.

Kemal, Salim and Gaskell, Ivan (eds) (1993) *Landscape, Natural Beauty and the Arts*, Cambridge: Cambridge University Press.

Leopold, Aldo (1949) *A Sand County Almanac*, New York: Oxford University Press.

Muir, John (1985) *The Mountains of California*, New York: Penguin.

Rolston, Holmes (1995) "Does aesthetic appreciation of nature need to be science based?", *British Journal of Aesthetics* 35: 374–86.

Saito, Yuriko (1984) "Is there a correct aesthetic appreciation of nature?", *Journal of Aesthetic Education* 18: 35–46.

—— (1998) "Appreciating nature on its own terms", *Environmental Ethics* 20: 135–49.

Sepanmaa, Yrjo (1993) *The Beauty of Environment: A General Model for Environmental Aesthetics*, 2nd edn, Denton: Environmental Ethics Books.

Stecker, R. (1997) "The correct and the appropriate in the appreciation of nature", *British Journal of Aesthetics* 37: 393–402.

Thompson, J. (1995) "Aesthetics and the value of nature", *Environmental Ethics* 17: 291–305.

Thoreau, Henry David (1947) "Walking", in *The Portable Thoreau*, ed. Carl Bode, New York: Viking Press.

Part 6

PHOTOGRAPHY AND REPRESENTATION

I am a camera with its shutter open, quite passive, recording, not thinking. Recording the man shaving at the window opposite and the woman in the kimono washing her hair. Some day, all this will have to be developed, carefully printed, fixed. . . .

They, and the people on the pavement, and the tea-cosy dome of the Nollendorfplatz station have an air of curious familiarity, of striking resemblance to something one remembers as normal and pleasant in the past – like a very good photograph.

Christopher Isherwood, A Berlin Diary

I have often thought that if photography were *difficult* in the true sense of the term – meaning that the creation of a simple photograph would entail as much time and effort as the production of a good watercolor or etching – there would be a vast improvement in total output. The sheer ease with which we can produce a superficial image often leads to creative disaster. We must remember that a photograph can hold just as much as we put into it, and no one has ever approached the full possibilities of the medium.

Ansel Adams, quoted in The Art of Photography

OF THE VARIOUS MEDIA DISCUSSED IN this book, photography is by far the youngest, and its claims to be a form of art have been hotly debated since its earliest days. The chapters in this part are concerned with a related but nonetheless distinct question, however: the question whether photographs are properly understood as *representations* of their subjects. In the first chapter, Roger Scruton argues that they are not. And in doing so, he raises one of the oldest questions in the philosophy of art: What sort of thing *is* an artistic representation?

At the heart of Scruton's argument lies the idea that there is an "*intentional*" relationship between a representation (for example, a painting) and what it represents (its subject). What he means by this is that a painting of a person, for instance, is more than simply an image of that person's appearance; it also expresses a *thought* about that person – "a thought embodied in perceptual form". So, for example, a portrait of George Washington might not only tell us what George Washington looked like, but also express the painter's thoughts of Washington as benevolent and fatherly.

By contrast, Scruton argues, the relation between a photograph and its subject is a *causal* relationship. And by this he means that a photograph is merely a record of how its subject looked at the time the photograph was taken. In Scruton's view, photography (unlike painting) is an essentially *mechanical* process. (This point comes out especially clearly when you think about vacation snapshots. Indeed, camera manufacturers often emphasize the causal and mechanical simplicity of photography when advertising their products: "Auto focus! Just point and shoot!") Because of its causal and mechanical nature, a photograph can express no thoughts about its subject – it "is not interesting as the realization of an intention", as Scruton puts it. Representations are essentially intentional – they express thoughts. Given that photographs are not intentional – they cannot express thoughts – photography cannot be a representational art. This is one of Scruton's conclusions.

Another conclusion, closely related to the first, is that photographs do not invite the kind of aesthetic interest that paintings characteristically do. An aesthetic interest in representation, he claims, is an "interest not in representation for the sake of its subject but in representation for its own sake". To be interested in a portrait solely as a record of what its subject looked like is not to be aesthetically interested in the portrait as a representation. It is to treat the portrait as a *surrogate* for its subject, to ignore "the way the painting presents its subject" and therefore to ignore the thoughts about the subject expressed by the painter. So we may be interested in a painting either as a surrogate for its subject *or* as a representation. By contrast, we can *only* be interested in a photograph as a surrogate. "If one finds a photograph beautiful, it is because one finds something beautiful in its subject. A painting may be beautiful, on the other hand, even when it represents an ugly thing." If we have an aesthetic interest in photographs, then, it is not the same as our aesthetic interest in paintings.

In the other chapters in this part, William L. King and Nigel Warburton take issue with Scruton's essay. King attempts to rebut Scruton's conclusion that photographs, being surrogates for their subjects, do not invite the kind of aesthetic interest that paintings characteristically do by showing that our reasons for looking at a photograph will often be different from our reasons for looking at its subject: in looking at a photograph, he argues, we may be interested in "*the manner of representing the subject*". Warburton suggests a different approach: if we are to understand the artistic possibilities of photographs, he argues, we need to give careful consideration to ways in which photographic artists create an individual style.

These chapters raise a number of important questions. Is it true that representation is essentially intentional? Is it true that photography is essentially causal, and thus that photography cannot represent things? Is an interest in a photograph *always* an interest in its subject, and never an interest in the way the subject is presented? Do we always treat photographs as surrogates for their subjects? Whatever the answers we give to these questions, the point is that in thinking hard about representation (as Scruton invites us to do), and about the nature of our aesthetic interest in photographs (as King and Warburton invite us to do), we are forced to ask exactly *what* kind of an art photography is. Is it an entirely new art form? Or is it just like painting, only less so?

12

PHOTOGRAPHY AND REPRESENTATION

Roger Scruton

Critics and philosophers have occasionally been troubled by the question whether the cinema is an independent art form – independent, that is, of the theatre, from which it borrows so many conventions.[1] This question can be traced back to a more basic one, the question whether photography is capable of representing anything. I shall argue that it is not . . .

It seems odd to say that photography is not a mode of representation. For a photograph has in common with a painting the property by which the painting represents the world, the property of sharing, in some sense, the appearance of its subject. Indeed, it is sometimes thought that since a photograph more effectively shares the appearance of its subject than a typical painting, photography is a better mode of representation. Photography might even be thought to have *replaced* painting as a mode of visual representation. Painters have felt that if the aim of painting is really to reproduce the appearances of things, then painting must give way to whatever means are available to reproduce an appearance more accurately. It has therefore been said that painting aims to record the appearances of things only so as to capture the experience of observing them (the *impression*) and that the accurate copying of appearances will normally be at variance with this aim. Here we have the seeds of expressionism and the origin of the view (a view which not only is mistaken but which has also proved disastrous for the history of modern art) that painting is somehow purer when it is abstract and closer to its essence as an art.

Let us first dismiss the word "representation". Of course this word can be applied to photography. We wish to know whether there is some feature, suitably called representation, common to painting and photography. And we wish to know whether that feature has in each case a comparable aesthetic value, so that we can speak not only of representation but also of representational art. (There is an important feature – sound – in common to music and to fountains, but only the first of these is properly described as an *art* of sound.)

1

In order to understand what I mean by saying that photography is not a representational art, it is important to separate painting and photography as much as possible, so as to discuss not actual painting and actual photography but an ideal form of each, an ideal which represents the essential differences between them. Ideal photography differs from actual photography as indeed ideal painting differs from actual painting. Actual photography is the result of the attempt by photographers to pollute the ideal of their craft with the aims and methods of painting.

By an "ideal" I mean a logical ideal. The ideal of photography is not an ideal at which photography aims or ought to aim. On the contrary, it is a logical fiction, designed merely to capture what is distinctive in the photographic relation and in our interest in it. It will be clear from this discussion that there need be no such thing as an ideal photograph in my sense, and the reader should not be deterred if I begin by describing photography in terms that seem to be exaggerated or false.

The ideal painting stands in a certain "intentional" relation to a subject.[2] In other words, if a painting represents a subject, it does not follow that the subject exists nor, if it does exist, that the painting represents the subject as it is. Moreover, if x is a painting of a man, it does not follow that there is some *particular* man of which x is the painting. Furthermore, the painting stands in this intentional relation to its subject because of a representational act, the artist's act, and in characterizing the relation between a painting and its subject we are also describing the artist's intention. The successful realization of that intention lies in the creation of an appearance, an appearance which in some way leads the spectator to recognize the subject.

The ideal photograph also stands in a certain relation to a subject: a photograph is a photograph *of* something. But the relation is here causal and not intentional.[3] In other words, if a photograph is a photograph of a subject, it follows that the subject exists, and if x is a photograph of a man, there is a particular man of whom x is the photograph. It also follows, though for different reasons, that the subject is, roughly, as it appears in the photograph. In characterizing the relation between the ideal photograph and its subject, one is characterizing not an intention but a causal process, and while there is, as a rule, an intentional act involved, this is not an essential part of the photographic relation. The ideal photograph also yields an appearance, but the appearance is not interesting as the realization of an intention but rather as a record of how an actual object looked.

Since the end point of the two processes is, or can be, so similar, it is tempting to think that the intentionality of the one relation and the causality of the other are quite irrelevant to the standing of the finished product. In both cases, it seems, the important part of representation lies in the fact that the spectator can see the subject *in* the picture. The appreciation of photographs and the appreciation of paintings both involve the exercise of the capacity to "see as", in the quite special sense in which one may see x as y without believing or being tempted to believe that x is y.

2

Now, it would be a simple matter to define "representation" so that "x represents y" is true only if x expresses a thought about y, or if x is designed to remind one of y, or whatever, in which case a relation that was *merely* causal (a relation that was not characterized in terms of any thought, intention, or other mental act) would never be sufficient for representation. We need to be clear, however, why we should wish to define representation in one way rather than in another. What hangs on the decision? In particular, why should it matter that the relation between a painting and its subject is an intentional relation while the photographic relation is merely causal? I shall therefore begin by considering our experience of painting and the effect on that experience of the intentionality of the relation between a painting and its subject.

When I appreciate a painting as a representation, I see it as what it represents, but I do not take it for what it represents. Nor do I necessarily believe that what is represented in the painting exists nor, if it does exist, that it has the appearance of the object that I see *in* the painting. Suppose that a certain painting represents a warrior. I may in fact see it not as a warrior but as a god. Here three "objects" of interest may be distinguished:

1 The intentional object of sight: a god (defined by my experience).
2 The represented object: a warrior (defined, to put it rather crudely, by the painter's intention).[4]
3 The material object of sight: the painting.[5]

The distinction between 1 and 2 is not as clear-cut as it might seem: it would become so only if we could separate the "pure appearance" of the painting from the sense of intention with which it is endowed. We cannot do this, not only because we can never separate our experience of human activity from our understanding of intention but also because in the case of a picture we are dealing with an object that is manifestly the expression of thought. Hence we will look for clues as to how the painting is intended to be seen and – such being the nature of "seeing as" – our sense of what is intended will determine our experience of what is there.

The "inference" view of perception, the view that there are certain things that we *basically* see (sense-data, etc.) from which we then *infer* the existence of other things, is wrong both as a matter of philosophical psychology, since there is no criterion for distinguishing datum and inference, and as a matter of epistemology, since it is only if we sometimes have knowledge of the "inferred" entities that we can have knowledge of the experience.[6] The point applies also to intention: we do not see the gestures and movements of another man and then infer from them the existence of intentions; rather, we see the gestures as intentional, and that is the correct description of what we see. But of course we cannot choose to see just what we will as a manifestation of intention. Our ability to see intention depends on our ability to interpret an activity as characteristically human, and here, in the case of representational art, it involves our understanding the dimensions and conventions of the medium. Art manifests the "common knowledge" of a culture;[7] as E.H. Gombrich has made clear, to understand art is to be familiar with the constraints imposed by the medium and to be able to separate that which is due to the medium from that which is due to the man. Such facts lead us to speak of understanding or misunderstanding representational painting.

Although there is not space to discuss fully the concept of "understanding" that is involved here, it is worth mentioning the following point: to understand a painting involves understanding thoughts. These thoughts are, in a sense, communicated by the painting. They underlie the painter's intention, and at the same time they inform our way of seeing the canvas. Such thoughts determine the perception of the man who sees with understanding, and it is at least partly in terms of our apprehension of thoughts that we must describe what we see in the picture. We see not only a man on a horse but a man of a certain character and bearing. And *what* we see is determined not by independent properties of the subject but by our understanding of the painting. It is the way the eyes are painted that gives that sense of authority, the particular lie of the arm that reveals the arrogant character, and so on. In other words, properties of the medium influence not only what is seen in the picture but also the way it is seen. Moreover, they present to us a vision that we attribute not to ourselves but to another man; we think of ourselves as sharing in the vision of the artist, and the omnipresence of intention changes our experience from something private into something shared. The picture presents us not merely with the perception of a man but with a thought about him, a thought embodied in perceptual form.[8] And here, just as in the case of language, thought has that character of objectivity and publicity upon which Frege commented.[9] It is precisely when we have the communication of thoughts about a subject that the concept of representation becomes applicable; and therefore literature and painting are representational in the same sense.

3

The ideal painting has no particular need for an identity of appearance with its subject. In order to present a visual account of the Duke of Wellington, it is not necessary for an artist to strive to present an exact copy of the Duke's appearance.[10] Indeed, it is tempting here to dispense with the notion of appearance altogether, to construe the painting as a conventional or even quasi-linguistic act which stands in a semantic relation – a relation of reference – to its subject, and which presents a visual appearance only as a means of fulfilling a referential function. Such a view would explain, perhaps better than all rival theories of representation, the role of intention in our understanding of art.[11]

I do not know how far those philosophers influenced by Gombrich's arguments – arguments emphasizing the place of convention in our understanding of visual art – would wish to take the analogy with language. I do not know, for example, whether a convention according to which colours were to be represented by their complements – a red object by a patch of green, a yellow object by a patch of blue – would be conceivable for such philosophers, conceivable, that is, as a mode of pictorial representation. It is undeniable, however, that such a painting would convey to someone who understood the convention as much information about its subject as another painting in which the colours copy the original. More bizarre conventions could also be imagined: a painting could be constructed entirely out of dashes and circles, arranged according to the grammar of a visual code. Given the right conventions, such a painting would count, according to the reference theory, as an extremely faithful representation of its subject. It would be read as a kind of scrambled message which had to be decoded in order to permit an understanding of what it says.

However, we cannot treat the visual connection between a painting and its subject as an entirely accidental matter, accidental, that is, to any process of representation that the painting may display. For we cannot deny that representational painting interests us primarily because of the visual connection with its subject. We are interested in the visual relation between painting and subject because it is by means of this relation that the painting represents. The artist presents us with a way of seeing (and not just any way of thinking of) his subject. (Hence the revolutionary character of such painters as Caravaggio and de la Tour.) It is this visual relation which seems to require elucidation. We cannot explain pictorial representation independently of the visual aspect of paintings and still expect our explanation to cast light upon the problem of the visual relation between a picture and its subject-matter. And yet it is that relation which is understood by the appreciative spectator.

That objection is of course not conclusive. It also seems to assume that a semantic theory of art (a theory which sees representation in terms of reference) must necessarily also be a linguistic theory. Surely there could be relations of reference that do not reflect the conventions of language, even relations that need to be understood in essentially visual terms. Let us, then, consider what such a conception of reference might be like.

It is no accident that language has a grammar. The existence of grammar is a necessary part of language and part of the all-important connection between language and truth. But there is a further significance in grammar, at least as grammar is now conceived. For the contemporary logician, grammar is primarily a "generative" function, a means of building complex sentences from the finite number of linguistic parts. Taken in conjunction with a theory of interpretation, a proper grammar will explain how speakers of a language understand an indefinite number of sentences on the basis of understanding only a finite number of words.[12] In this way we can show how the truth or falsehood of a sentence depends upon the reference of its parts, and the concept of reference in language becomes inextricably bound up with the idea that from the references of words we may derive the truth conditions of sentences. This "generative connection" between reference and truth is part of the intuitive understanding of reference which is common to all speakers of a language.

It is here, I think, that we find a striking difference between language and painting. While there may be repertoires and conventions in painting, there is nothing approaching grammar as we understand it. For one thing, the requirement of finitude is not obviously met. It is clearly true that we understand the representational meaning of, say, a Carpaccio through understanding the representational meaning of its parts. But the parts themselves are understood in *precisely the same way*; that is, they too have parts, each of which is potentially divisible into significant components, and so on ad infinitum. Moreover, there seems to be no way in which we can divide the painting into grammatically significant parts – no way in which we can provide a syntax which isolates those parts of the painting that have a particular semantic role. For in advance of seeing the painting, we have no rule which will decide the point, and thus the idea of syntactic or semantic rules becomes inapplicable. The means whereby we understand the total representation are identical with the means whereby we understand the parts. Understanding is not secured either by rules or by conventions but seems to be, on the contrary, a natural function of the normal eye. As we see the meaning of the painting, so do we see the meaning of its parts. This contrasts sharply with the case of reference in language, where we *construct* the meaning of the sentence from the reference of its parts, and where the parts themselves have reference in a way that is ultimately conventional.

There seems to be no justification, then, for thinking of representation in terms of reference. We could, however, insist that the relation of a painting to its subject is one of reference only by removing from "reference" that feature which leads us to think that an account of reference is also an account of understanding. To speak of the connection between a word and a thing as one of reference is to show how we understand the word, for it is to show how the truth conditions of sentences containing the word are determined. If we speak of reference in describing paintings, therefore, we should not think that we thereby cast any light on the *understanding* of representation. What representation is, how we understand it, and how it affects us – those questions seem to remain as obscure as ever. The only thing that remains to support the invocation of reference is the fact that paintings may be true or false. It is that fact which we must now consider.

4

The fact that a painting may be true or false plays a vital role in visual appreciation. We could not explain realism, for example, either in painting or in literature, unless we invoked the concept of truth. Again we must emphasize information (and therefore the concept of reference) in our understanding of the painter's art; or at least we are obliged to find some feature of the painting that can be substituted for reference and which will show how the connection with truth is established.

Such a feature, as a matter of fact, has already been described: we may describe realism in terms of what we see *in* the painting. We therefore analyse truth not in terms of a relation between the painting and the world but in terms of a relation between what we see in the painting and the world. Goya's portrait of the Duke of Wellington is realistic because the figure we see in the painting resembles the Duke of Wellington.[13] The truth of the painting amounts to the truth of the viewer's perception; in other words, the "intentional object of sight" corresponds to the nature of the subject. Those thoughts which animate our perception when we see the realistic painting with understanding are true thoughts.[14] Truth is not a property of the painting in the direct way in which it is the property of a sentence, and the possibility of predicating the truth of a painting does not open the way to a semantic theory of art any more than it opens the way to a semantic theory of, for example, clouds, or of any other phenomenon in which aspects may be seen.

Although distinctions may be made between true and false pictures, an aesthetic appreciation remains in one sense indifferent to the truth of its object. A person who has an aesthetic interest in the *Odyssey* is not concerned with the literal truth of the narrative. Certainly it is important to him that the *Odyssey* be lifelike, but the existence of Odysseus and the reality of the scenes described are matters of aesthetic indifference. Indeed, it is characteristic of aesthetic interest that most of its objects in representation are imaginary. For unless it were possible to represent imaginary things, representation could hardly be very important to us. It is important because it enables the presentation of scenes and characters toward which we have only contemplative attitudes: scenes and characters which, being unreal, allow our practical natures to remain unengaged.

If the concept of representation is to be of aesthetic importance, it must be possible to describe an aesthetic interest in representation. Only if there is such a thing as aesthetic interest which has representation as its object can there be representational art (as opposed to art that happens to be representational). It is commonly said that an aesthetic interest in something is an interest in it for its own sake: the object is not treated as a surrogate for another; it is *itself* the principal object of attention. It follows that an aesthetic interest in the representational properties of a picture must also involve a kind of interest in the picture and not merely in the thing represented.[15]

Now, *one* difference between an aesthetic interest in a picture, and an interest in the picture as a surrogate for its subject, lies in the kind of reason that might be given for the interest. (And to give the reasons for an interest is to give an account of its intentional object and therefore of the interest itself.) If I ask a man why he is looking at a picture, there are several kinds of reply that he might give. In one case his reasons will be reasons for an interest only in the things depicted: they will describe properties of the subject which make it interesting. Here the interest in the picture is derivative: it lies in the fact that the picture reveals properties of its subject. The picture is being treated as a means of access to the subject, and it is therefore dispensable to the extent that there is a better means to hand (say, the subject itself). With that case one may contrast two others. First, there is the case where the man's reasons refer only to properties of the picture – to pictorial properties, such as colour, shape, and line – and do not mention the subject. For such a man the picture has interest as an abstract composition, and its representational nature is wholly irrelevant to him. Second, there is the case where the reasons for the interest are reasons for an interest in the *picture* (in the way it looks) even though they make essential reference to the subject and can be understood as reasons only by someone who understands the reference to the subject. For example, the observer may refer to a particular gesture of a certain figure, and a particular way of painting that gesture, as revelatory of the subject's character (for example, the barmaid's hands on the counter in Manet's *Bar aux Folies-Bergère*). Clearly, that is a reason not only for an interest in the subject but also (and primarily) for an interest in the picture, since it gives a reason for an interest in something which can be understood only by looking at the picture. Such an interest leads naturally to another, to an interest in the use of the medium – in the way the painting presents its subject and therefore in the way in which the subject is seen by the painter. Here it could not be said that the painting is being treated as a surrogate for its subject: it is *itself* the object of interest and irreplaceable by the thing depicted. The interest is not in representation for the sake of its subject but in representation for its own sake. And it is such an interest that forms the core of the aesthetic experience of pictorial art, and which – if analysed more fully – would explain not only the value of that experience but also the nature and value of the art which is its object. We see at once that such an interest is not, and cannot be, an interest in the literal truth of the picture.

5

If I were to describe, then, *what I see* in a picture, I would be bound not merely to describe the visual properties of the subject but also to provide an interpretation of the subject, a way of seeing it. The description under which the subject is seen is given by the total thought in terms of which I understand the picture. In the case of portraiture, this interpretive thought need not be a thought about the momentary appearance of the subject: it need not be the thought "He looked like that". The thought may relate to the subject not as he appeared at any one moment but as he was or, rather, as the artist saw him to be. The appearance may be presented only because it embodies the reality, in which case it will be the reality that is understood (or misunderstood) by the spectator.

One of the most important differences between photography and portraiture as traditionally practised lies in the relation of each to time. It is characteristic of photography that, being understood in terms of a causal relation to its subject, it is thought of as revealing something momentary about its subject – how the subject looked at a particular moment. And that sense of the moment is seldom lost in photography, for reasons that will shortly be apparent. Portrait painting, however, aims to capture the sense of time and to represent its subject as extended in time, even in the process of displaying a particular moment of its existence. Portraiture is not an art of the momentary, and its aim is not merely to capture fleeting appearances. The aim of painting is to give insight, and the creation of an appearance is important mainly as the expression of thought. While a causal relation is a relation between events, there is no such narrow restriction on the subject-matter of a thought. This perhaps partially explains the frequently made comment that the true art of portraiture died with the advent of photography and that representational art, insofar as it still pursues an ideal of realism, is unable to capture, as the realist ought to capture, the sense of the passage of time.[16]

Of course a photographer can aim to capture that fleeting appearance which gives the most reliable indication of his subject's character. He may attempt to find in the momentary some *sign* of what is permanent. But there is a great difference between an image which is a sign of something permanent and an image which is an expression of it. To express the permanent is to give voice to a thought about its nature. To give a sign of the permanent is to create something from which its properties may be inferred. A man may remain silent when asked to defend his friend, and from that silence I infer his friend's guilt. Yet the man has certainly not expressed the thought that his friend is guilty. Similarly a photograph may give signs of what is permanent despite the fact that it is incapable of expressing it.

6

The ideal photograph, as I mentioned earlier, stands in a causal relation to its subject and "represents" its subject by reproducing its appearance. In understanding something as an ideal photograph, we understand it as exemplifying this causal process, a process which originates in the subject "represented" and which has as its end point the production of a copy of an appearance. By a "copy" of an appearance I mean an object such that what is seen in it by a man with normal eyes and understanding (the intentional object of sight) resembles as nearly as possible what is seen when such a man observes the subject itself from a certain angle at a certain point in its history. A person studying an ideal photograph is given a very good idea of *how something looked*. The result is that, from studying a photograph he may come to know how something looked in the way that he might know it if he had actually seen it.

With an ideal photograph it is neither necessary nor even possible that the photographer's intention should enter as a serious factor in determining how the picture is seen. It is recognized at once for what it is – not as an interpretation of reality but as a presentation of how something looked. In some sense, looking at a photograph is a substitute for looking at the thing itself. Consider, for example, the most "realistic" of all photographic media, the television. It seems scarcely more contentious to say that I saw someone on the television – that is, that in watching the television I saw *him* – than to say that I saw him in a mirror. Television is like a mirror: it does not so much destroy as embellish that elaborate causal chain which is the natural process of visual perception.

Of course it is not necessary to define the subject of a photograph in terms of this causal process, for the subject could be identified in some other way. But the fact remains that when we say that *x* is a photograph of *y* we *are* referring to this causal relation, and it is in terms of the causal relation that the subject of a photograph is normally understood. Let us at least say that the subject is so defined for my logical ideal of photography: that premise is all that my argument requires.

It follows, first, that the subject of the ideal photograph must exist; secondly, that it must appear roughly as it appears in the photograph; and thirdly, that its appearance in the photograph is its appearance at a particular moment of its existence.

The first of those features is an immediate consequence of the fact that the relation between a photograph and its subject is a causal relation. If *a* is the cause of *b*, then the existence of *b* is sufficient for the existence of *a*. The photograph lacks that quality of "intentional inexistence" which is characteristic of painting. The ideal photograph, therefore, is incapable of representing anything unreal; if a photograph is a photograph of a man, then there is some particular man of whom it is a photograph.

Of course I may take a photograph of a draped nude and call it *Venus*, but insofar as this can be understood as an exercise in fiction, it should not be thought of as a photographic representation of Venus but rather as the photograph of a representation of Venus. In other words, the process of fictional representation occurs not in the photograph but in the subject: it is the *subject* which represents Venus; the photograph does no more than disseminate its visual character to other eyes. This is not to say that the model is (unknown to herself) acting Venus. It is not she who is representing Venus but the photographer, who uses her in his representation. But the representational act, the act which embodies the representational thought, is completed before the photograph is even taken. As we shall see, this fictional incompetence of photography is of great importance in our understanding of the cinema; but it also severely limits the aesthetic significance of "representation" in photography. As we saw earlier, representation in art has a special significance precisely because of the possibility that we can understand it – in the sense of understanding its content – while being indifferent to, or unconcerned with, its literal truth. That is why fictional representation is not merely an important form of representational art but in fact the primary form of it, the form through which the aesthetic understanding finds its principal mode of expression.

One may wish to argue that my example is a special one, that there are other ways of creating fictional representations which are essentially photographic. In other words, it is not necessary for the photographer to create an independent representation in order for his photograph to be fictional. Suppose he were to take a photograph of a drunken tramp and label it *Silenus*. Would that not be a fictional photograph, comparable, indeed, to a painting of Silenus in which a drunken tramp was used as a model?

This example, which I owe to Richard Wollheim, is an interesting one, but it does not, I think, establish what it claims. Consider a parallel case: finding a drunken tramp in the street I point to him and say "Silenus". It is arguable that my gesture makes the tramp into a representation; but if it does, it is because I am inviting you to think of him in that way. I have expressed a representational thought: imagine this person as Silenus. And I have completed the thought by an act of ostension toward its dozing subject. The act of ostension might on some other occasion be accomplished by a camera (or a frame, or a mirror, or any other device which isolates what it shows).

The camera, then, is being used not to represent something but to point to it. The subject, once located, plays its own special part in an independent process of representation. The camera is not essential to that process: a gesturing finger would have served just as well. If the example shows that photographs can be representations, then it shows the same of fingers. To accept that conclusion is to fail to distinguish between what is accidental and what is essential in the expression of a representational thought. It is to open the way toward the theory that everything which plays a part in the expression of thought is itself a representation. Such a view does not account for the aesthetic significance of representations. It also, however, and far more seriously, implies that there is no distinction between representational and nonrepresentational art. The concept of representation that I am assuming makes such a distinction, and it makes it for very good reasons. I am not tempted by such dubious examples to abandon it. One might put the point by saying that a painting, like a sentence, is a *complete* expression of the thought which it contains. Painting is a sufficient vehicle of representational thought, and there may be no better way of expressing what a painting says. That is why representation can be thought of as an intrinsic property of a painting and not just as a property of some process of which the painting forms a part.

Consider also the second feature mentioned above: the subject of an ideal photograph must appear roughly as it appears in the photograph. By its very nature, photography can "represent" only through resemblance. It is only because the photograph acts as a visual reminder of its subject that we are tempted to say that it represents its subject. If it were not for this resemblance, it would be impossible to see from the photograph how the subject appeared, except by means of scientific knowledge that would be irrelevant to any interest in the visual aspect of the photograph. Contrast here the case of an electron microscope, which punches out on a ticker tape a codified indication of a crystal's atomic structure. Is that a representation of the atomic structure? If it is, then why not say that any causal relation which enables us to infer the nature of the cause from the properties of its effect provides us with a representation of the cause in the effect? Such a concept of representation would be uninteresting indeed. It is impossible, therefore, that the ideal photograph should represent an object except by showing how it appeared at a certain moment in its history and still *represent* it in the way ideal photography represents anything. How indeed could we make sense of an ideal photograph representing its subject *as* other than it appeared? We could do so only if we could also say that a photograph sometimes represents its subject as it appears; that is, if we could say that representation here is "representation as". But consider this sentence: x is an ideal photograph of y as z. It seems that we have no means of filling out the description "z", no means, that is, of filling it out by reference only to the photographic process and not, say, to some independent act of representation that precedes or follows it. One might say that the medium in photography has lost all importance: it can present us with what we see, but it cannot tell us how to see it.

We *must* be aware of the three features mentioned above if we are to appreciate the characteristic effects of photography. In looking at an ideal photograph, we know that we are seeing something which actually occurred and seeing it as it appeared. Typically, therefore, our attitude toward photography will be one of curiosity, not curiosity about the photograph but rather about its subject. The photograph addresses itself to our desire for knowledge of the world, knowledge of how things look or seem. The photograph is a means to the end of seeing its subject; in painting, on the other hand, the subject is the means to the end of its own representation. The photograph is transparent to its subject, and if it holds our interest it does so because it acts as a surrogate for the thing which it shows. Thus if one finds a photograph beautiful, it is because one finds something beautiful in its subject. A painting may be beautiful, on the other hand, even when it represents an ugly thing.

7

Someone might accept the general difference I have indicated between an aesthetic interest and an attitude of curiosity, and accept too the implication that something is a representation only if it is capable of carrying a reference to its subject without merely standing as a surrogate for it. He still might argue, however, that is possible to be interested in a photograph *as* a photograph and find it, and not just its subject, beautiful.

But what is it to be interested in a photograph as a photograph? Of course one might have a purely abstract aesthetic interest in a photograph – an interest in the photograph as a construction of lines and shapes (as one is intended to appreciate Man Ray's Rayogrammes, for example). One can have a purely abstract aesthetic interest in anything; photography is only a representational art if our interest in a photograph as a photographic "representation" is a type of aesthetic interest.

Let us return to the previous discussion of representation in painting. It appears that there is a prima facie contradiction between saying that I am interested in a thing for its own sake and saying that I am interested in it as a representation of something else. In attempting to reconcile these two interests, it is necessary first to restrict the place of truth in aesthetic interest. Truth is aesthetically relevant only insofar as it may be construed as truth to the situation presented rather than "truth to the facts". From the point of view of aesthetic interest, it is always irrelevant that there should be a particular object which is the object represented or, if there is such an object, that it should exist as portrayed. That is not to say, of course, that an aesthetic interest does not require things to be in general roughly as they are shown; but that is another matter.

As I have already said, this conflicts with the typical way in which we are interested in photographs. Knowing what we know about photographs, it is at least natural that we should be interested in them both because they are true to the facts and because they tell us useful things about their subject-matter. It seems, therefore, that the emotional or "aesthetic" qualities of a photograph tend to derive directly from the qualities of what it "represents": if the photograph is sad, it is usually because its subject is sad; if the photograph is touching, it is because its subject is touching, and so on. It is worth reflecting on why there could not be a photograph of a martyrdom that was other than horrifying. One's curiosity here would be no different from one's curiosity in the act itself. Hence it would be as difficult (and perhaps also as corrupt) to have an aesthetic interest in the photograph as it would be in the real situation. By contrast, a painting of a martyrdom may be serene, as is Mantegna's great *Crucifixion* in the Louvre. The painting has emotional qualities in defiance of the qualities of its subject. In the case of a photograph – say of the victim of some accident – one's attitude is determined by the knowledge that this is how things are. One's attitude is made practical by the knowledge of the causal relation between photograph and object. This is not to deny that one might be interested in a photograph for its own sake and at the same time maintain a proper distance from its subject, even when it depicts a scene of agony or death. But the real question is, Can we have such an interest in a photograph without having the same interest in its subject? Can I have an aesthetic interest in the photograph of a dying soldier which is not also an aesthetic interest in the soldier's death? Or, rather, can I maintain that separation of interests and still be interested in the "representational" aspect of the photograph? If we are distanced from the photograph only because we are distanced from its subject, then the important distinction that I wish to emphasize, between interest in the representation and interest in the subject, has still not been made. It seems necessary to show that photography *can* – by itself – create that sharp separation of interests which is everywhere apparent in serious painting. Consider too the photographs of old London. How is it possible to detach one's interest in their beauty from an interest in the beauty of London as it was? Regret is here the appropriate reaction to the photograph (as it is not – or at least not normally – an appropriate reaction to a Canaletto). "That is how it looked!" is the central index of one's emotion.

Consider, then, the reasons that may be given in answer to the question, "Why are you looking at that?" With a photograph, one mentions the features of the subject; with a painting, one mentions only the observable aspect captured in the picture. This essentially is what distinguishes an interest in a representation as a surrogate from an interest in a representation for its own sake. Suppose now that someone wishes to argue that it is *not* inevitable that we treat photographs, even ideal photographs, as I have described. Let us see what the consequences of such a position might be.

8

Imagine that we treat photographs as representations in just the same way that we treat paintings, so that their representational natures are themselves the objects of an aesthetic interest. What are the consequences if we study photography in such a way that it does not matter whether its subject actually existed or actually looked like the thing we see in the picture? Here we are interested not in the subject but in its manner of presentation. If there *can* be such an interest in a photograph, it suggests that a photograph may sometimes be the expression of a representational thought and not merely a simulacrum of its subject.

An interest in an object for its own sake, in the object as a whole, must encompass an interest in detail. For if there is nothing *for* which one contemplates an object, as has frequently been argued, there is no way of determining in advance of looking at it which features are, and which are not, relevant to one's interest.[17] It is for this reason that we cannot rest satisfied with nature but must have works of art as the objects of aesthetic judgment. Art provides a medium transparent to human intention, a medium for which the question, Why? can be asked of every observable feature, even if it may sometimes prove impossible to answer. Art is an expression of precisely the same rational impulses that find an outlet in aesthetic interest; it is therefore the only object which satisfies that interest completely.

The photographer, then, who aims for an aesthetically significant representation must also aim to control detail: "detail" being here understood in the wide sense of "any observable fact or feature". But here lies a fresh difficulty. The causal process of which the photographer is a victim puts almost every detail outside of his control. Even if he does, say, intentionally arrange each fold of his subject's dress and meticulously construct, as studio photographers once used to do, the appropriate scenario, that would still hardly be relevant, since there seem to be few ways in which such intentions can be revealed in the photograph. For one thing, we lack all except the grossest features of style in photography; and yet it is style that persuades us that the question, Why this and not that? admits such fruitful exploration in the case of painting. Style enables us to answer that question by referring solely to aspects of the painting rather than to features which are aesthetically irrelevant, or in no way *manifest* in what is seen.[18] The search for meaning in a photograph is therefore curtailed or thwarted: there is no point in an interest in detail since there is nothing that detail can show. Detail, like the photograph itself, is transparent to its subject. If the photograph is interesting, it is only because what it portrays is interesting, and not because of the manner in which the portrayal is effected.

Let us assume, however, that the photographer could intentionally exert over his image just the kind of control that is exercised in the other representational arts. The question is, How far can this control be extended? Certainly there will be an infinite number of things that lie outside his control. Dust on a sleeve, freckles on a face, wrinkles on a hand: such minutiae will always depend initially upon the prior situation of the subject. When the photographer sees the photographic plate, he may still wish to assert his control, choosing just this colour here, just that number of wrinkles or that texture of skin. He can proceed to paint things out or in, to touch up, alter, or *pasticher* as he pleases. But of course he has now become a painter, precisely through taking representation seriously. The photograph has been reduced to a kind of frame around which he paints, a frame that imposes upon him largely unnecessary constraints.[19]

In other words, when the photographer strives towards representational art, he inevitably seems to move away from that ideal of photography which I have been describing toward the ideal of painting. This can be seen most clearly if we consider exactly what has to be the case if photography is to be a wholly representational art – if it is to manifest all those aspects of representation that distinguish it from mere copying and which endow it with its unique aesthetic appeal. No one could deny that from its origins photography has set itself artistic ideals and attempted to establish itself as a representational art. The culmination of that process – which can be seen in such photographs as Henry Peach Robinson's "Autumn" – is to be found in the techniques of photo-montage used by the surrealists and futurists (and in particular, by such artists as László Moholy-Nagy and Hannah Höch). Here our interest in the result can be entirely indifferent to the existence and nature of the original subject. But that is precisely because the photographic figures have been so cut up and rearranged in the final product that it could not be said in any normal sense to be a *photograph* of its subject. Suppose that I were to take figures from a photograph of, say, Jane, Philip, and Paul, and, having cut them out, I were to arrange them in a montage, touching them up and adjusting them until the final result is to my mind satisfactory. It could very well be said that the final result represents, say, a lovers' quarrel; but it is not a photograph of one. It represents a quarrel because it stands in precisely the same intentional relation to a quarrel that a painting might have exhibited. Indeed, it is, to all intents and purposes, a painting, except that it happens to have employed photographic techniques in the derivation of its figures. Insofar as the figures can still be considered to be photographs, they are photographs of Jane, Philip, and Paul and not photographs of a lovers' quarrel. (Of course the fact of their *being* photographs might be aesthetically important. Some ironical comment, for example, may be intended in using figures cut from a medium of mass production.)

The history of the art of photography is the history of successive attempts to break the causal chain by which the photographer is imprisoned, to impose a human intention between subject and appearance, so that the subject can be both defined by that intention and seen in terms of it.[20] It is the history of an attempt to turn a mere simulacrum into the expression of a representational thought, an attempt to discover through techniques (from the combination print to the soft-focus lens) what was in fact already known.[21] Occasionally, it is true, photographers have attempted to create entirely fictional scenes through photography and have arranged their models and surroundings, as one might on the stage, in order to produce a narrative scene with a representational meaning. But, as I have argued, the resulting photograph would not be a representation. The process of representation was effected even before the photograph was taken. A photograph of a representation is no more a representation than a picture of a man is a man.

9

It might be felt that I have begged the question in allowing only one way in which photography may acquire representational meaning, a way which inevitably leads photography to subject itself to the aims of painting. One may argue that a photographer does not choose his subject at random, nor is he indifferent to the point of view from which he photographs it or to the composition in which it is set. The act of photography may be just as circumscribed by aesthetic intentions as the act of painting. A photograph will be designed to show its subject in a particular light and from a particular point of view, and by so doing it may reveal things about it that we do not normally observe and, perhaps, that we might not have observed but for the photograph. Such an enterprise leads to effects which are wholly proper to the art of photography, which therefore has its own peculiar way of showing the world. Why is that not enough to give to photography the status of a representational art?

I do not think that such an objection need cause me to revise my argument. For exactly the same might be said of a mirror. When I see someone in a mirror I see *him*, not his representation. This remains so even if the mirror is a distorting mirror and even if the mirror is placed where it is intentionally. This intention might even be similar to the intention in photography: to give a unique and remarkable view of an object, a view which reveals a "truth" about it that might otherwise have gone unobserved. One could even imagine an art of mirrors, an art which involves holding a mirror aloft in such a way that what is seen in the mirror is rendered by that process interesting or beautiful.

This art of mirrors may, like the art of photography, sometimes involve representation. It may, for example, involve a representation of Venus or of Silenus in the manner of the two types of "fictional" photographs considered earlier. But representation will not be a property of the *mirror*. It is impossible that I could, simply by holding a mirror before someone, make him into a representation of himself. For after all, whether I look at him or at the mirror, in either case it is *him* that I see. If the mirror is to become the expression of a representational thought, it too must be denatured; like the photomontage, it must be freed from the causal chain which links it to its subject. One can perhaps begin to see the truth in Oliver Wendell Holmes's description of the daguerreotype as a "mirror with a memory".[22] It was just such a mirror that led to the downfall of Lord Lambton.

It does not matter, therefore, how many aesthetic intentions underlie the act of photography. It does not matter that the subject, its environment, activity, or light are all consciously arranged. The real question is, What has to be done to make the resulting image into a representation? There are images which are representations (paintings) and images which are not (mirrors). To which class does the photograph belong? I have argued that it naturally belongs to the latter class. Photography can be *made* to belong to the former class by being made into the principal vehicle of the representational thought. But one must then so interfere with the relation between the photograph and its subject that it ceases to be a *photograph* of its subject. Is that not enough to show that it is not just my ideal of photography which fails to be a mode of representation, but also that representation can never be achieved through photography alone?

A final comparison: I mark out a certain spot from which a particular view of a street may be obtained. I then place a frame before that spot. I move the frame so that, from the chosen spot, only certain parts of the street are visible, others are cut off. I do this with all the skill available to me, so that what is seen in the frame is as pleasing as it might be: the buildings within the frame seem to harmonize, the ugly tower that dominates the street is cut off from view, the centre of the composition is the little lane between two classical façades which might otherwise have gone unnoticed, and so on.

211

There I have described an activity which is as circumscribed by aesthetic intentions as anything within the experience of the normal photographer. But how could it be argued that what I see in the frame is not the street itself but a representation of it? The very suggestion is absurd.

10

Here one might object that representation is not, after all, an intrinsic property either of a painting or of a description. Representation is a relation; an object can be described as a representation only if one person uses it to represent something to another. On this view, there is no such thing as "being a representation"; there is only "having a representational use." And if this were the case, my arguments would be in vain. Photographs are as much, and as little, representations as paintings, as gestures, as mirrors, as labels, and as anything else that can play its part in the process of communication.

The objection is more serious, and reflects a well-known dispute in the theory of meaning. Meaning, some say, is a property of a sentence; others, for instance, H. Paul Grice, argue that meaning is primarily a relation between utterance and speaker.[23] Now, even for Grice, there remains a distinction between utterances which are articulate and utterances which are not. Sentences are to be distinguished from nods of the head in that they participate in and exemplify a grammar, and through that grammar they can be understood independently of the context of their use. By being articulate, the sentence can stand alone as the principal expression of a thought. There arises a kind of interest in the sentence (and in its content) which is independent of any direct involvement in the act of communication. Meaning can be read *in* the sentence and need not be inferred from surrounding circumstances.

Similarly, painting, being fully articulate, can attract attention as the principal expression of a process of thought. It can be understood in isolation from the special circumstances of its creation, because each and every feature of a painting can be both the upshot of an intentional act and at the same time the creation of an intentional object. The interest in the intentional object becomes an interest in the thought which it conveys. A painter can fill his canvas with meaning in just the way that a writer may fill his prose. This is what makes painting and literature into representational arts: they are arts which can be appreciated as they are in themselves and at the same time understood in terms of a descriptive thought which they articulate.

In photography we may have the deliberate creation of an image. Moreover, I may use a photograph as a representation: I may use a photograph of Lenin as a representation of him, in the way that I might have used a clenched fist or a potato or a photograph of Hitler. The question is, What makes the image *itself* into the principal vehicle of representational thought? I wish to argue that an image can be deliberate without being properly articulate. The image becomes articulate when (a) the maker of the image can seriously address himself to the task of communicating thought through the image alone, and (b) when the spectator can see and understand the image in terms of the process of thought which it expresses. To satisfy (a) we require a painterly approach to detail; to satisfy (b) we must distract the spectator's attention from the causal relation which is the distinguishing feature of photography. Either way, the persistence of that relation – in other words, the persistence of the *photographic* image – can only hinder representation. It can contribute nothing to its achievement. This is perhaps what James Joyce meant when he wrote the following in his Paris notebooks of 1904:

> Question: Can a photograph be a work of art? Answer: A photograph is a disposition of sensible matter and may be so disposed for an aesthetic end, but it is not a human disposition of sensible matter. Therefore it is not a work of art.

If Joyce meant by "work of art" what I mean by "representation", then he was clearly getting at the same point. The property of representation, as I have characterized it, is the upshot of a complex pattern of intentional activity and the object of highly specialized responses. How can a photograph acquire that property? My answer is that it can do so only by changing in precisely those respects which distinguish photography from painting. For it is only if photography changes in those respects that the photographer can seriously address himself to the thoughts and responses of his spectators. It is only then, therefore, that the photograph becomes a proper *vehicle* of representational thought. . . .

NOTES

1 See for example, the discussions in Allardyce Nicoll, *Film and Theatre* (London, 1936; New York, 1972).
2 See Franz Clemens Brentano, *Psychology from an Empirical Standpoint*, ed. Linda McAlister (London and New York, 1973); Roderick M. Chisholm, *Perceiving* (London and Ithaca, NY, 1957), chapter 11; and G.E.M. Anscombe, "The intentionality of sensation", in R.J. Butler (ed.), *Analytical Philosophy*, second series (Oxford, 1965).
3 I think that in this area nonextensionality (intensionality) and intentionality should be sharply distinguished, so that the claim is not affected by any argument to the effect that causal relations are nonextensional.
4 I pass over the problem here of selecting and describing the appropriate intention.
5 For the material/intentional distinction, I rely on Anscombe.
6 The most famous arguments for this conclusion occur in Kant's *Critique of Pure Reason* (in particular in the "Transcendental deduction") and in Wittgenstein's *Philosophical Investigations*, part I.

7 The importance of "common knowledge", its complexity as a phenomenon, and its natural co-existence with conventions has been recognized in the philosophy of language; see especially the interesting discussion in David K. Lewis, *Convention: A Philosophical Study* (Cambridge, Mass., 1969; Oxford, 1972).

8 I have discussed elsewhere what I mean by the "embodiment" of thought in perception; see my *Art and Imagination*, Routledge & Kegan Paul, 1974, chapters 7 and 8.

9 G. Frege, *Translations from the Philosophical Writings*, Blackwell, 1952, p. 79.

10 There is a problem here about "identity of appearance" on which I touch again, pp. 116–17 in *The Aesthetics of Music*.

11 Nelson Goodman, the most important exponent of a semantic theory of art, manages to reconcile his approach with a view of photographs as representational; see his *Languages of Art*, Hackett, 1976, p. 9n.

12 I draw here on the now familiar arguments given by Donald Davidson in "Truth and Meaning", (reprinted in *Inquiries into Truth and Interpretation*, Oxford University Press, 1984, pp. 17–36) which originate with Frege and which were given full mathematical elaboration in Alfred Tarski's theory of truth.

13 That is, provided the painting is independently *of* the Duke of Wellington.

14 See n. 8, above.

15 Hence the tradition in philosophy, which begins with Kant, according to which representation constitutes a threat to the autonomy of art.

16 I am thinking of recent exercises in "photographic" realism by such painters as Ken Danby and Alex Colville. More traditional styles of realism have also emerged in open opposition to both the clinical lines of the photographic school and the contentless images of abstract expressionism. Witness here the paintings of David Inshaw and Robert Lowe.

17 See for example, Stuart Hampshire, "Logic and appreciation" in William Elton (ed.), *Aesthetics and Language* (Oxford, 1954; New Jersey, 1970).

18 See Richard Wollheim's interesting discussion "Style now" in Bernard William Smith (ed.), *Concerning Contemporary Art* (Oxford and New York, 1975).

19 This argument is hinted at in B. Croce, *Estetica*, 10th edn (Bari, 1958), p. 20.

20 See for example, Aaron Scharf, *Creative Photography* (London, 1975) and Rudolf Arnheim, *Film as Art* (California, 1957; London, 1958).

21 See especially Henry Peach Robinson, *The Elements of a Pictorial Photograph* (London, 1896).

22 Holmes, quoted in Beaumont Newhall, *History of Photography* (New York, 1964; London, 1972), p. 22.

23 'Meaning', *Philosophical Review*, LXVI (1957), pp. 377–88.

13

SCRUTON AND REASONS FOR LOOKING AT PHOTOGRAPHS

William L. King

I

In a provocative essay on the nature of photography,[1] Roger Scruton claims that photographs cannot be interesting in a way that paintings[2] can be. Paintings, because of their manner of representation, can possess qualities and evoke emotions not possessed by or evoked by their subjects. Thus Mantegna's *Crucifixion* in the Louvre evokes serenity, although the scene it portrays – a martyrdom – normally evokes horror: "The painting has emotional qualities in defiance of the subject".[3] Photographs, by contrast, seemingly lacking any manner of representation, can possess only the qualities and evoke the emotions possessed by and evoked by their subjects: "The photograph is transparent to its subject, and if it holds our interest it does so because it acts as a surrogate for the represented thing. Thus if one finds a photograph beautiful, it is because one finds something beautiful in its subject."[4] Photographs of old London are beautiful because old London was itself beautiful.[5]

Is this an accurate account of photographs? I shall argue that, at best, Scruton's account is applicable to photographs made as records, and to one way of seeing photographs. Otherwise, it is a distortion stemming from his initial claim that all photographs, since caused by their subjects, are copies of their subjects,[6] and his inclination to ignore the diversity of photographic practice.[7]

A way of testing his account is to develop one of its implications: that *the reasons we may give for looking at a photograph are the same reasons we may give for looking at the subject.*

Consider, then, the reasons that may be given in answer to the question, "Why are you looking at that?" With a photograph, one mentions the features of the subject;

215

with a painting, one mentions only the observable aspect captured in the picture. This essentially is what distinguishes an interest in a representation as a surrogate from an interest in a representation for its own sake.[8]

If one assumes that these reasons are the reasons *actually* given by viewers, then Scruton is off the mark in both cases. What is happening here, I suggest, is that he is employing specific, disparate models of the viewer for both paintings and photographs. The painting model constitutes relatively complex seeing, the seeing of mature viewers, including the seeing of representational painters in their non-technical moments. The photograph model constitutes relatively simple seeing, a seeing directed by historical or scientific concerns, certainly not the seeing of serious photographers, except in their historical or scientific moments.

II

To reveal the distortion in Scruton's monistic account of photographs – that the reasons for looking are all about the subject – I propose *assembling examples of reasons actually given by viewers*. Some of these reasons I have given myself; others I report from conversations with other viewers. Consider the following examples:

1   Here is an 1860 photograph of Abraham Lincoln. Now look at this 1865 photograph. The man was undergoing accelerated aging. The war.
2   Look at this satellite photograph of Hurricane Hugo (17 September 1989). You can see that Hugo is like a gigantic disc, spinning slowly counter-clockwise over the Caribbean. Awesome.
3   Want to see how some painters, for example, Géricault, misrepresented galloping horses? Look at Muybridge's photographs of Stanford's horse. All four hoofs *are* off the ground at one point, but never in the painter's "flying-gallop" position.

These remarks, functioning as reasons for looking at photographs, are consistent obviously with Scruton's account. And, of course, the list can be extended far beyond these representative cases. The interests are *cognitive*; they are interests in what the subjects looked, or look, like. Who would deny that these reasons are a dominant type of reason for looking at photographs?

Now consider another example similar to but different from the above:

4   Can you believe that I have been staring at this photograph of Paris's Notre Dame island, Ile de la Cité, for twenty minutes? It isn't that I don't remember what it looks like. I do. It's that sitting here alone, lingering over the details, I relive a pleasant May of wandering about the island, sunning along the river.

The dominant interest here is not in knowing the appearance of the subject. One remembers that. The interest is in memories that are stirred, feelings that are evoked. Again, as Scruton argues, the interest is in the subject, and – we add – *its emotional impact*, not in the photograph itself.

But there are other examples, different in another, significant way:

5   Students – look – here is what happens when you make a print from an overexposed, overdeveloped negative: a contrasty, grainy print. You may like that result; you may not.

6   This (colour) print has a weird look, yes? Look here by the window – it is faint pink all over. The exposing light is too green; that's the cause. Change the filter pack.

Here, of course, no subject is mentioned. The remarks are about the photograph – how it looks – and the causes. These reasons are clear-cut cognitive, but *technical* reasons: look at these photographs in order to learn about photographic processes, *not* about some subject. Such reasons constitute a type of counter-example to Scruton's viewer-model. Thus his phrase "reasons that may be given" excludes one type of actual reason, and his phrase "with a photograph, one mentions" excludes one type of viewer, namely, the photographer concerned about technical issues. However, these exclusions, while providing some evidence for the charge of distortion in Scruton's account, are relatively peripheral.

The exclusion that is central, and that is deliberate, is another type of reason, characterized by him as *aesthetic*: "It is commonly said that an aesthetic interest in something is an interest in it for its own sake: the object is not treated as a surrogate for another; it is itself the principal object of attention".[9] By restricting the reasons for looking at photographs to remarks about the subject, Scruton denies that photographs can be interesting in themselves or interesting aesthetically. His starting point – that photographs are caused by their subjects, and thus are copies of their subjects – is decisive here. Should it be? What about additional reasons actually given by viewers? To what extent are the following remarks *not* about the photograph itself?

7   You know why I'm still looking at that pink print? Well, I'm no longer looking to decide about a change; I'm looking because I like the bloody thing. That overall colour – rather subtle – in an otherwise almost black and white photograph seems to enhance the feeling of unity.

8   You just can't beat large format black and white for rich tonal values. Look at this 8 × 10 contact print, *Dunes, Oceano, 1936*, by Edward Weston. The whites are gleaming, the blacks compelling, the greys vibrant. The thing really glows. Stunning.

The interest here is in the photographs themselves, in the way they look, in part or overall. Traditionally, the features noted by these remarks – colour, luminosity – have been characterized as formal features or elements, and an interest in them has been called an *aesthetic* interest. Of course, some theorists, notably Clive Bell, have judged such an interest the *only* aesthetic interest. Do we have another set of counter-examples? Well, yes indeed, assuming Scruton's explicit reason-giving model for photographs, namely, that the reasons for looking are monistic, all about the subject. But – close by and unexpectedly – he admits that photographs *can* elicit this aesthetic interest since one can have a.purely abstract aesthetic interest in anything.[10] The implication here is that some reasons for looking *can* be aesthetic, namely those reasons about purely abstract features of a photograph. While annoying, and providing further evidence for Scruton's temptation to present a simplistic account, this problem should be distinguished from the following, main issue.

III

Can photographs elicit a *second type of aesthetic interest*, a non-formal interest that would involve an interest in manners of representation? Scruton's position on this issue is clear: repeatedly, photographs are denied the power to elicit this type of interest. A manner of representation presupposes an ability to control detail. The photographer, contrary to the painter, lacks this ability if the photograph is caused by the subject. Scruton's example of a picture that does elicit this interest is Manet's painting *Bar aux Folies-Bergère*. The barmaid's hands allegedly express Manet's way of seeing the subject.[11] This comment isn't developed, but any viewer can observe that the hands are almost invisible, gripping the back edge of the counter and extending down behind it. What is visible are rather long arms, extending to near the counter's edge. A point needing stress here, Scruton might say, is that Manet's ability to represent the barmaid in a certain manner presupposes his ability to control detail in the painting. Supposedly, the photographer's situation differs: "The causal process of which the photographer is a victim puts almost[12] every detail outside of his control."[13] A difference in kind? Or merely a difference in degree?

IV

Among the reasons given for looking at photographs we have distinguished several types: remarks about how the subject appears (examples 1–3); remarks about an evocative power of the subject (example 4); remarks about the cause of the photograph's formal appearance (examples 5–6); and remarks simply about the formal appearance of the photograph (examples 7–8). Contrary to Scruton, can one distinguish yet another type consisting of *remarks about the manner of representing the subject?* These remarks must be about observable features of the photograph which are controlled by the photographer, hence, are caused by the photographer, not by the subject.

Caution is needed in choosing examples, since some controls employed can pose a question about the nature of the result, namely, whether it remains a *photograph*. The techniques of photo-montage and multiple printing, Scruton argues, pose this question.[14] The results of employing these techniques, he concludes, are more accurately described as paintings and stand as evidence for the pollution of photography by photo-painters. Of course, *some* photography – traditionally called "Pictorialism" – has sought painterly qualities, frequently by employing non-photographic, even painterly, methods. We are seeking counter-examples that involve photographic controls only.

Must a photographer avoid the aims of painting also? Much painting, especially during the last century, has sought to be expressive. Is this aim forbidden for photographers? Forbidding expression – if photography *can* be expressive – must be purely arbitrary, since sculpture, architecture, literature, music, even weaving, share this aim with painting. To be sure, the solitary aim of what Scruton calls "ideal photography" – a logical construct allegedly capturing the "essential nature" of the medium – is recording, since nothing else is possible. Assume that the "ideal photograph" is a copy of the subject, assume that it is caused altogether by light reflected from the subject, assume that the photographer is a victim of this causal process, unable to control detail; assume all this, and of course, nothing else *is* possible.[15] But is the photographer so victimized? Does an expressive aim compel him to become a painter? As a matter of fact, some actual photography, while remaining photography, does aim at and succeed in being expressive. This is polluted photography? *That* is dogma.

Consider now these further examples of what one may see when looking at photographs:

9   Want to see a compelling photograph? Look here: William Klein's "Entrance to Beach, Ostia, Italy, 1956". I say "compelling"; I mean that it pulls me back repeatedly. Part of the explanation, of course, is the faces – three young male adults close up, unsmiling, staring directly at the camera. Curiosity? Hostility? Another factor, clearly, is the composition. The middle face is farther back, peering from between two uprights, one eye in shadow; two more young male faces, much farther back, peer around from the right. Additional glass door uprights contribute to a rectangular framing of the figures. Finally, the photograph is contrasty and grainy, enough in fact to impose a "photographic" texture throughout. This grain effect, especially, is most apparent in the light objects – a white shirt, human skin. These objects look like what they are, having the appropriate shapes; yet, in another respect, they don't look like what they are, lacking any visual clue suggesting smoothness. This texture – clusters of tiny black specks – can be interesting in itself.

Furthermore, it causes a slight distancing of the subject, seeming to contribute to an overall enigmatic, rather than threatening, quality.

10 Are you moonstruck? I am; and some photographers are, too. Ansel Adams was. Look here at his "Moon and Half Dome". A gibbous moon, showing surface detail, and appearing larger than normal in a darker than normal sky, has been placed slightly above a deep shadow on the top left edge of Half Dome, a massive granite cliff which occupies most of the picture space. This shadow is repeated by a much larger, equally dark, shadow on the right side and base of Half Dome. On the left edge of the photograph, a closer, smaller cliff is in total, almost featureless, shadow. Portions of the Dome's face, including snow patches, are gleaming in light from a low winter sun. The resultant contrast of rich blacks and whites, combined with a sense that the objects are closer than normal because larger than normal, gives the photograph a quality of unreality.

11 This photograph, "The Priest", by Ralph Gibson, is not the everyday head and shoulders photographic portrait. Look. The head above the chin, including the mouth, is missing; simply cut off. Perhaps *that* is enough to rivet one's glance; but there is more. One-half of his clerical collar, in direct sunlight, is an intense white, contrasting with his very dark, almost solid black vest and coat. The shadow cast by his chin forms a small, gleaming triangle at the front, widest portion of the collar. Most of the neck is in featureless shadow. Only the chin-shape and its skin-like texture suggest the presence of a living human. *Is* it a portrait, or merely a study in black and white? What is going on here?

Certainly, subjects are mentioned, even described, in these examples. And there are remarks about formal elements and relationships. What is new here are *remarks about the photographer's manner of representing the subject*: Klein has imposed a photographic texture, transforming the look of fabric and of human skin: Adams has juxtaposed, magnified, and heightened the contrast in monumental geologic forms; and Gibson has obliterated part of the subject – normally an important part – as well as obliterating shadow detail in the remainder. One would be hard pressed to understand how these examples differ *in kind* from Manet's handling of the barmaid's hands. Furthermore, the methods employed were altogether photographic.

Klein's transformation of values, but especially texture detail, is like a stylistic device, evident in the extensive body of his work focused on urban life.

Adams is recognized as the developer of a system of exposure called the "Zone System". Applying this system for the sake of an expressive purpose – his own purpose generally – entails deciding how we want the subject in a photograph to look *before* the subject is recorded on photographic film. He calls this act "visualizing"; it is the important initial step which guides exposing, developing, and printing. What is noteworthy here is that the photographer *systematically* becomes an additional causal agent of the photograph. The result, while an approximation of visual reality, is not a copy, nor is it intended to be:

> Many consider my photographs to be in the "realistic" category. Actually, what reality they have is in their optical-image accuracy; their *values* are definitely departures from reality . . . if it were possible to make direct visual comparison with the subjects, the differences would be startling.[16]

In "Moon and Half Dome" Adams visualized the objects larger than in normal vision, as if the viewer were closer, even above the valley floor looking straight on, rather than up, at Half Dome; and he visualized the shadows and sky much darker, seeking a heightened contrast. This rather radical transformation of reality was effected by using only photographic controls: a telephoto lens, an orange filter, longer-than-normal development, and burning-dodging manipulation during printing.[17]

That the photographer is doing something with the subject is most evident, perhaps, in the case of Gibson. His commentary:

> My primary concern in the photograph of the priest was to formalize the composition as rigidly as possible . . . [he] was posed in bright sun so that the geometric division of his collar would be intense . . . Of course I wanted to make a statement, both religious and photographic, in a tight structural way.[18]

Is the photographer trying to do something here that is photographically impossible? Saying this is baffling since a hidden half-head is more puzzling visually than hidden hands. If the latter is evidence for a manner of representing the subject, then the former, in conjunction with other details, seems to be even stronger evidence. Surely Gibson effects a manner of representation without becoming a photo-painter.

My conclusion, then, is that attention to detail in a photograph isn't necessarily attention to the subject as such. On the contrary, it may be attention to a manner of representing the subject. In other words, it can be attention to a quality possessed by the photograph that is *not* possessed by the subject. Commonplace subjects that are threatening can be made enigmatic (Klein), that are dramatically real can be made unreal (Adams), that are formally human can be made non-human (Gibson). Consequently, some photographs can be interesting in one way that paintings can be, namely, aesthetically interesting by virtue of the manner of representation.

NOTES

1 Roger Scruton, "Photography and representation", reprinted in this book.
2 For these comparative claims, and apparently by interest, Scruton's remarks about painting are restricted to representational paintings.
3 Ibid., p. 207.
4 Ibid., p. 206.
5 Ibid., p. 208.
6 Ibid., pp. 203–4.
7 Apart from the old London photographs his examples are few in number and similar in nature (hypothetical documentary).
8 Scruton, op. cit., p. 208.
9 Ibid., p. 201.
10 Ibid., p. 207.
11 Ibid., p. 202.
12 This qualification, potentially significant for Scruton's position, is pushed aside, undeveloped.
13 Ibid., p. 209.
14 Ibid., p. 210.
15 For an argument that something else is possible, that even Scruton's "ideal photograph" may serve an expressive purpose, see Robert Wicks, "Photography as a representational art", *British Journal of Aesthetics*, 29, (1) (Winter, 1989), pp. 1–9.
16 Ansel Adams, *The Negative* (Little, Brown & Co., 1981), p. ix.
17 Ansel Adams, *Examples: The Making of 40 Photographs* (Little, Brown & Co., 1983), pp. 133–5.
18 "Ralph Gibson: high contrast printing", *Darkroom*, E. Lewis, ed. (Lustrum Press, 1977), p. 68.

14

INDIVIDUAL STYLE IN PHOTOGRAPHIC ART

Nigel Warburton

Roger Scruton's controversial paper "Photography and Representation"[1] stirred a number of writers from their dogmatic slumber. They responded with horror to Scruton's claims that photography was never representational in any aesthetically relevant sense of the term. Scruton argued that photography is not representational because it can never be intentional. What he meant by this was that photographs can never embody thoughts about the objects they represent, nor can they represent anything that does not actually exist: they are transparent[2] and "fictionally incompetent". Actually Scruton never claimed to be talking about real photographs; his theory was about *ideal* photography, by which he meant "a logical fiction, designed merely to capture what is distinctive in the photographic relation and in our interest in it".[3] Ideal photographs are the result of an optico-chemical process, not an intentional one. This, he thought, made photography, in contrast with painting, incapable of evincing a way of seeing its subject matter: photographs are transparent, and so cannot exhibit anything but the grossest elements of style. They certainly do not merit the term "representational", not when compared with the paradigm representational art, painting. Scruton, of course, concedes that photographs are in ordinary language *called* representational, but denies that they exhibit anything of comparable aesthetic value to what is present in figurative painting. In other words he takes seriously Oliver Wendell Holmes's characterization of the daguerrotype as a "mirror with a memory". Indeed he explicitly compares photographic and mirror images at a number of points in his article.

Scruton's critics have typically replied that Scruton has misrepresented what actual photography is like. *Actual* photography involves all kinds of intentional input in terms of choice of camera, film, shutter speed, aperture and so on; it also involves choices of subject matter, framing and numerous other aesthetically relevant matters. The result, they claim, is that although perhaps fictionally incompetent, photography involves so many aesthetically relevant choices that it is perverse for Scruton to maintain that photographic representation is impossible and of less aesthetic relevance than representation in painting. I call this response the *weak response* to Scruton for reasons given below. Those who have given the weak response include R. A. Sharpe,[4] William L. King[5] and Robert Wicks[6] and myself.[7] The point of this article is to show why the weak position is weak and to present the outlines of a stronger response to Scruton's strong position.

For Scruton ideal photographs are always transparent to their objects, as he puts it:

> The photograph addresses itself to our desire for knowledge of the world, knowledge of how things look or seem. The photograph is a means to the end of seeing its subject; in painting, on the other hand, the subject is the means to the end of its own representation. The photograph is transparent to its subject, and if it holds our interest it does so because it acts as a surrogate for the thing which it shows. Thus if one finds a photograph beautiful, it is because one finds something beautiful in its subject. A painting may be beautiful, on the other hand, even when it represents an ugly thing.[8]

The appropriate attitude towards a photograph is one of *curiosity*: curiosity about the subject of the photograph. We should not be interested in the photographer's intentions, because the photographer's intentions are largely irrelevant to the finished object:

> With an ideal photograph it is neither necessary nor even possible that the photographer's intention should enter as a serious factor in determining how the picture is seen. It is recognised at once for what it is – not as an interpretation of reality but as a presentation of how something looked. In some sense, looking at a photograph is a substitute for looking at the thing itself.[9]

When actual photographers try to move away from this ideal of photography and achieve some kind of aesthetically relevant intentional input, Scruton accuses them of "polluting" photography with "painterly techniques". Indeed he claims that

> The history of the art of photography is the history of successive attempts to break the causal chain by which the photographer is imprisoned, to impose a human intention between subject and appearance, so that the subject can be both defined by that intention and seen in terms of it.[10]

The way in which Scruton has set up his argument leaves him vulnerable to the charge of having begged the very question that is at issue, namely whether or not photographic representation is possible. He has defined representation in terms of what occurs in painting and then declared that whenever actual photography achieves some modicum of representational significance, it has done so by borrowing the techniques of painting. However, it is fairly obvious that if you define representation purely in terms of what occurs in painting, then it is hardly surprising to find that the techniques of representation in other art forms are borrowed from painting.

The usual line of criticism, however, is to demonstrate that Scruton has a simplistic notion of what a photograph is like, and to demonstrate that real photographs involve all kinds of aesthetically significant decisions in the course of their making. For instance, we find William King drawing our attention to the fact that the photographer William Klein has, in a particular photograph, "imposed a photographic texture, transforming the look of fabric and of human skin".[11] This is supposed to show that the photographer's manner of representing the subject is relevant to a viewer's appreciation of it; in other words that photographers can and do exhibit aesthetically relevant intentions in their work. King writes "Klein's transformation of values, but especially texture detail, is like a stylistic device, evident in the extensive body of his work focussed on urban life."[12] Now, while this is undoubtedly true, it seems to play into Scruton's hands: Scruton never argued that photography is completely styleless, but only that photography lacks "all except the grossest features of style".[13] But surely what King has described here is precisely that. King's example is typical of those used by Scruton's critics: they all seem intent on drawing our attention to relatively crude photographic techniques which can scarcely merit the status of an individual style. Numerous photographers use a grainy finish for their images, but this certainly does not constitute a style. Style involves a far more sophisticated pattern of embodied intentions than this. Scruton's article is usually taken to be dismissive of the possibility of photographic art, and this sort of critic unwittingly gives him ammunition for this position.

Certainly it would not be unreasonable to conclude from Scruton's critics that even if photographic art is a possibility, it must be hamstrung by the crudity of stylistic choices available to the photographer. One reason why Scruton's critics have ended up with these apparently lacklustre conclusions is that they have focused on style within individual images. They have uncritically accepted Scruton's assumption that if style *can* be achieved within photography it *must* be achieved here and here alone. This is one of the assumptions that I wish to challenge. Another of Scruton's assumptions which they have uncritically accepted is that if style is achievable within photography, then it must be achieved in the act of representation rather than in some other way. A result of this is that the philosophical discussion of photography, at least that focused on the debate about Scruton's article, has presented a skewed picture of what is distinctive and important in photographic art. The truth is that photographic style is only in part achieved through the manner of taking photographs. There are numerous contemporary photographers, each with their own individual photographic style, but, it must be said, very little variety among the surface qualities of photographs. Most of Scruton's critics have concentrated on the *how* rather than the *what* of photographic image making. As a result they have tended to ignore the distinctive pattern of choices of subject matter and of image that for many photographers constitute their style. The way in which many photographers achieve an individual style in their photographic art is far more interesting than Scruton's critics allow. As I will show; the analysis of individual style in photographic art provides the material for a strong rebuttal of Scruton's implicit position on the possibility of photographic art; a far stronger response than the weak and ultimately unconvincing replies of the likes of Wicks, King and Sharpe.

First I should make clear what I mean by individual style.[14] Individual style is the style of an individual: it is a distinctive pattern of human intentions (or apparent intentions) communicated through works of art and revealing an apparent underlying artistic personality. Individual style is contrasted with general style. General style is usually the style of an epoch, such as the quattrocento, or of a self-conscious movement in art, for example the cubist style in painting. Individual style is frequently recognizable within a single work in painting. We can usually recognize the distinctive style of any of Van Gogh's paintings, for example, by his patterns of brush strokes, his use of colour, his choice of subject matter and so on. Now it may of course turn out that a painting which appears to be distinctively by Van Gogh was in fact painted by a clever forger. But even if forensic evidence were needed to decide whether or not it was a genuine Van Gogh, the painting would still be *in the style* of Van Gogh, i.e. in a style distinctive of paintings done by Van Gogh himself. The style would have had to have been established in order for it to have been imitated. "Style" in this individual sense is sometimes used to refer merely to whatever is distinctive of a particular artist's use of a medium. But a more important use of the term is to refer not just to what is distinctive but to those aspects of it that exhibit an aesthetically significant intention. Style in this sense is contrasted with mere "signature" or the use of "trademarks".

As Scruton rightly points out, our interest in style in works of art is largely an interest in human intention that allows us to understand what is chosen and what is accidental:

> it is style that persuades us that the question, Why this and not that? admits such fruitful exploration in the case of painting. Style enables us to answer that question by referring solely to aspects of the painting rather than to features which are aesthetically irrelevant, or in no way *manifest* in what is seen.[15]

Style in painting is typically achieved by control over detail. But, as Scruton argues, photographers do not have great control over the detail within their pictures; and, if they start exercising too much control over detail, they cease to be photographers, and become painters. Presumably Scruton would argue that the increased control of detail made possible by the new pixel technology and the so-called electronic darkroom are not really developments in photography, but in some other bastardized form of painting, or collage perhaps.[16]

Scruton's thesis that the photographer lacks intentional control over the image-making process, and particularly over detail, echoes the writings of the photographer and theorist P.H. Emerson, who as early as 1890 published his black-bordered pamphlet *The Death of Naturalistic Photography*. In this he retracted his former view that photography could in principle achieve artistic status, now arguing that photographs could never be works of art on the grounds that the photographer's choice of interpretation of subject matter was at the very least "cramped": "control of the picture is possible to a slight degree . . . but the all vital powers of selection and rejection are fatally limited".[17] Emerson's conclusions were in part based on his misunderstanding of the significance of certain findings in sensiometry, and it is undoubtedly true that new photographic technology has increased the scope of the photographer's control over the medium. Nevertheless there is certainly some truth in the claim made by both Emerson and Scruton that, in comparison with painting, photography is limited in choice of manner of representation. But representation is not a necessary feature of an artistic style; many non-representational art forms allow for the possibility of individual style. Nevertheless most writers on photography seem to have assumed that the only way in which style could be achieved in photography is in the manner of representation of its subjects.[18] My contention is that, while in certain cases the manner of photographic representation is important to understanding the individual style of the photographer, this is not true of the majority of cases. Faced with the relative intractability of the medium, photographic artists have found new ways of exhibiting complex patterns of human intentions through their images.

The automation in the photographic process makes it extremely difficult to tell what is due to the photographer and what simply to the uninterrupted causal optico-chemical operations of lens and camera. Consequently, when trying to understand a photograph as something more than a carrier of information about its subject matter, we characteristically need to go beyond what is visually given in the photograph. What this amounts to in the context of photographic art is at the very least looking at a series of images by the same photographer. It is only in a series of photographs that a photographer's choices can be made clear: this is an important feature of photography; because style can be achieved and demonstrated within an individual painting, there is in that art frequently less of a need to see a range of material by a particular artist in order to understand a particular work. What is more, two visually indistinguishable photographs by different photographers could have radically different meanings when inserted into their corresponding repertoires. For instance, Diane Arbus's photograph *A House on a Hill, Hollywood, Cal. 1963* is a photograph of part of a film set, a fake building, a façade held up with scaffolding. Her intentions in taking this photograph are not immediately obvious from considering it in isolation from the rest of her work. Precisely the same image within the output of a different photographer, one who was concerned simply to document Hollywood film sets, would embody intentions about appearances of film sets and would be correctly read as a record of an appearance. However, in Arbus's case, the photograph is best seen as exemplifying some of the themes apparent in her photographic portraiture. This is the only photograph of a film set in her published output, most of her images being photographs of people. Her portraits are almost always of outsider figures – transvestites, nudists, freak show performers, or else ordinary people looking strange because of their pose or dress. A common theme visible throughout her work is the concentration on unexpected self-revelation on the part of the subject. In the context of this repertoire, Arbus's film set photograph takes on a different meaning: it is not simply a documentary image of a building façade, but rather a metaphorical interpretation of the dominant theme in the rest of her photographic output. Seen this way, the photograph alludes to appearances and to the visible mechanisms that support them. The Hollywood façade is a façade meant for the camera; similarly the expressions of many of Arbus's subjects are poses for the camera which simultaneously reveal, though often unintentionally, the psychological equivalent of the scaffolding behind.[19] This is an extreme example, but it serves to demonstrate that the stylistic features of a photographer's output are best examined in a series of images rather than within a single image.

Everything I have said about photography could, making appropriate changes, also apply to painting. Even in painting, knowledge of an artist's repertoire is often the basic background necessary for an adequate appreciation of a particular work. There is, however, a difference in degree and emphasis: most works of photographic art would be completely unintelligible without some kind of contextualization within the photographer's output.

Actually, with photographic art the situation is more complex. Because, as we have seen, the nature of a photographer's repertoire conditions how an individual image is interpreted, the selection of what is to count as repertoire is itself an important intentional aspect of photographic art. Contingently photographers are capable of producing many thousands, if not millions, of images in a lifetime; however, very few of these are given the status of photographic art. Again, the same might be said of painting; however, it is just a fact about photography that it is remarkably easy to produce many thousands of images in a very short space of time. What usually happens is that a photographer implicitly dubs a selection of this output "personal work". This is achieved by such techniques as signing or stamping or making exhibition prints or exhibiting or perhaps including the relevant images in a photographic monograph. All these are signs that the photographer wants particular images to be considered part of a larger series. Without this sort of information about the status of particular photographs, it can be very difficult to discern the intentions behind an individual. This is in fact what often happens when, after a photographer's death, his or her estate releases numerous previously unseen images into the market place. Such acts, while they *may* be performed from the best motives (but usually are not), can seriously distort our understanding of what a photographer was trying to do, and thus of that photographer's style. Whilst it is not usually possible to say with certainty of every image that it was deliberately chosen as part of the photographer's artistic repertoire, usually there is relatively little controversy about which are the central artistic works of a particular photographer. Nevertheless, if exhibition curators and book compilers are interested in revealing a particular photographer's style and thus their most important intentional contributions within the medium, then they have a responsibility to examine the history of what has been done to these images or prints. We can only be certain that a photographer chose an image or print as part of his or her photographic repertoire if that photographer somehow indicated this. Similar considerations apply to some other kinds of visual art, but they are not usually so important. For instance, many artists produce large numbers of drawings or paintings, not all of which they wish to be included as part of their final output. In the case of painting or drawing, artists typically destroy those images they do not wish preserved. Photographers, however, because they frequently keep all or large numbers of their negatives, are particularly vulnerable to becoming prey to their photographic executors. Also it is true that photographers tend to produce many more images in a lifetime than any other kind of visual artist, and yet their intentions within individual images are far harder to discern. This has the consequence that some kind of implicit selection becomes necessary. A further reason why photographers need to dub their personal work to make it clear that it is such, is that, in the twentieth century at least, many of them have had to work commercially as photographers in order to make a living. Yet there may not be a clear division between artistic and commercial work: Bill Brandt, for example, recycled many of his commercially produced images originally made for commissions for *Picture Post*, *Lilliput* or *Harpers Bazaar* as part of his artistic output;[20] Diane Arbus worked as a magazine photographer,[21] but that did not stop her re-using some of the images made on assignment when it came to producing artistic work. To take an extreme example, Weegee worked as a passport photographer in his youth, but it would be ridiculous to consider these early Weegees as contributions to his mature photographic style.

Scruton's critics are entirely correct to take him to task for his misrepresentation of the sorts of choices that photographers make within individual images. However, this is only a small part of the story. A strong response to his strong position will have to take into account the fact that photographic artists actually create individual style through a number of techniques, predominant among which is the selection of particular photographs as part of their artistic output. And of course, selecting particular photographs involves selecting a particular subject matter. The reason why this can provide a stronger response to Scruton than the standard line is that even if we were to concede to Scruton that photography is not primarily a representational medium, we could still demonstrate that it is a medium which has the capacity to embody important and aesthetically relevant intentions. As such there is then no ground for saying that photographs cannot be works of art simply because they are causally and mechanically produced: all that is compatible with the expression of complex intentions of a kind typically found in paradigmatic works of art. If Scruton is prepared to bite the bullet and accept all this, then his focus on photography's alleged lack of representational potential appears simply beside the point.

My account of individual style in photographic art has several implications. First of all, for the philosophy of photography: it is time to broaden out the discussion of photographic art and to include consideration of non-representational (or at least non-pictorial) aspects of photography. Secondly, for critics: although they probably realize this anyway, photographic critics can only gain meaningful understanding of individual photographic images if they are placed within a context of a photographer's output. Thirdly, for photographic curators: exhibitions that present one or two images by each photographer are likely to be unintelligible to those without a background knowledge of these photographers' repertoires. Thematically arranged exhibitions are likely to have little to do with photographic art. Furthermore, when, as frequently happens in posthumous exhibitions, previously unknown images that had been discarded by the photographer in his or her lifetime are presented, these should be clearly labelled; if the viewer cannot tell the status an image had for the artist, then they will very likely get a misleading impression of that photographic artist's style. Lastly, with regard to photographic books: provided they are dubbed by the photographer, and meet up to his or her standards of production, they can be seen as the appropriate units for assessing photographic art. What I mean by this is that, as they provide a series of images, they are far more likely to reveal a photographer's individual style and thus his or her embodied intentions, than are single images.

What I have been describing is the ways in which photographic artists create an individual style. There is no reason why they should always continue to use these techniques. There are indeed signs that the new pixel technology will allow photographers so much control over the detail of their pictures that photography will become much closer to painting in the way that it achieves individual style. However, until that time, and when we are considering the photographic output of photographers working in a chemical rather than an electronic dark room, individual style in photography must be understood in more or less the way I have described it.

NOTES

1 Roger Scruton, "Photography and representation", reprinted in this volume.
2 Philosophers have, on the whole, been attracted to some version of the transparency thesis: the most influential statement of this is Kendall Walton's "Transparent pictures: on the nature of photographic realism", *Critical Inquiry*, 11 (December 1984), 246–77; this view is criticized in Nigel Warburton, "Seeing through 'Seeing through photographs'", *Ratio*

(New Series) 1 (June 1988), 62–74. For a critical overview of the debate, see Jonathan Friday's "Transparency and the photographic image", *British Journal of Aesthetics* 36(1) (January 1996), 30–42.

3 Scruton, "Photography and representation", p. 196.

4 R.A. Sharpe, *Contemporary Aesthetics* (Brighton: Harvester, 1983).

5 William L. King, "Scruton and reasons for looking at photographs", reprinted in this volume.

6 Robert Wicks, "Photography as a representational art", *British Journal of Aesthetics*, 29(1) (1989), 1–9.

7 Nigel Warburton, "Varieties of photographic representation", *History of Photography*, 15(3) (Autumn 1991), 203–10.

8 Scruton, "Photography and representation", p. 206.

9 Ibid., p. 204.

10 Ibid., p. 210.

11 King, "Scruton and reasons for looking at photographs", p. 220.

12 Ibid., p. 220.

13 Scruton, "Photography and representation", p. 209.

14 For a convincing account of the nature of individual style in terms of the expression of the artist's implied personality, see Jenefer M. Robinson, "Style and personality in the literary work," *Philosophical Review* 94(2) (April 1985), 227–47.

15 Scruton, "Photography and representation", p. 209.

16 For an interesting discussion of the impact of pixel technology on photo-journalism, see Fred Ritchin's *In Our Own Image* (New York: Aperture, 1990).

17 Emerson, quoted in Nancy Newhall, *P.H. Emerson: The Fight for Photography as Fine Art* (New York: Aperture, 1975), p. 93.

18 Jonathan Friday appears to be an exception to this trend when he points out that "aesthetic representation is not the only, or even the most important, source of aesthetic value" ("Transparency and the photographic image", p. 41). Unfortunately he takes the view that photography is not significant for its representational qualities; whereas I take it as obvious that it *can* be, but often is not.

19 For a discussion of Arbus's interest in the psychology of self-revelation, see Nigel Warburton, "Diana Arbus and Erving Goffman: the presentation of self", *History of Photography* 16(4) (Winter 1992), 401–4.

20 For further details of Brandt's output, see Nigel Warburton (ed.), *Bill Brandt: Selected Texts and Bibliography* (Oxford: Clio Press; New York: G.K. Hall, 1993), particularly the introductory essay, "Brandt's pictorialism".

21 For further details, see *Diane Arbus: Magazine Work* (New York: Aperture, 1984).

SUGGESTIONS FOR FURTHER READING

Arnheim, Rudolf (1974) "On the nature of photography", *Critical Inquiry* 1: 149–61.
Barthes, Roland (1981) *Camera Lucida*, New York: Hill & Wang.
Bazin, André (1967) "The ontology of the photographic image", in his *What Is Cinema?*, trans. Hugh Grey, Berkeley: University of California Press.
Blocker, Gene (1977) "Pictures and photographs", *Journal of Aesthetics and Art Criticism* 36: 155–62.
Brook, Donald (1983) "Painting, photography and representation", *Journal of Aesthetics and Art Criticism* 42: 171–80.
—— (1986) "On the alleged transparency of photographs", *British Journal of Aesthetics* 26: 277–82.
Carroll, Noël (1996) *Theorizing the Moving Image*, Cambridge: Cambridge University Press.
Cavell, Stanley (1979) *The World Viewed*, enlarged edn, Cambridge: Harvard University Press.
Currie, Gregory (1991) "Photography, painting and perception", *Journal of Aesthetics and Art Criticism* 49: 23–9.
Friday, Jonathan (1996) "Transparency and the photographic image", *British Journal of Aesthetics* 36: 30–42.
Martin, Edward (1986) "On seeing Walton's great-grandfather", *Critical Inquiry* 12: 796–800.
Maynard, Patrick (1983) "The secular icon: photography and the functions of images", *Journal of Aesthetics and Art Criticism* 42: 155–70.
—— (1989) "Talbot's technologies: photographic depiction, detection and reproduction", *Journal of Aesthetics and Art Criticism* 47: 263–76.
—— (1997) *The Engine of Visualization: Thinking Through Photography*, Ithaca and London: Cornell University Press.
Ross, Stephanie (1982) "What photographs can't do", *Journal of Aesthetics and Art Criticism* 41: 5–17.
Savedoff, Barbara (1999) *Transforming Images: How Photography Complicates the Picture*, Ithaca and London: Cornell University Press.
Scharf, Aaron (1968) *Art and Photography*, London: Allen Lane.
Sontag, Susan (1973) "Photography", *New York Review of Books* 20, October 18: 59ff.
—— (1977) *On Photography*, New York: Farrar, Straus & Giroux.
Snyder, Joel and Allen, Neil Walsh (1975) "Photography, vision, and representation", *Critical Inquiry* 2: 143–69.
Szarkowski, John (1975) "Photography – a different kind of art", *New York Times Magazine*, April 13: 16–19ff.
Walton, Kendall L. (1984) "Transparent pictures: on the nature of photographic realism", *Critical Inquiry* 11: 246–77.
—— (1997) "On pictures and photographs: objections answered" in Richard Allen and Murray Smith (eds), *Film Theory and Philosophy*, Oxford: Oxford University Press, pp. 60–75.
Warburton, Nigel (1988) "Photographic communication", *British Journal of Aesthetics* 28: 173–81.
—— (1988) "Seeing through 'Seeing Through Photographs'", *Ratio* (new series) 1: 64–74
—— (1991) "Varieties of photographic representation", *History of Photography* 15: 203–10.
—— (1997) "Authentic photographs", *British Journal of Aesthetics* 37(2): 129–37.
Wicks, Robert (1989) "Photography as a representational art", *British Journal of Aesthetics* 29: 1–9.

Part 7

FEELINGS AND FICTIONS

Dazzled by so many and such marvellous inventions, the people of Macondo did not know where their amazement began. . . . They became indignant over the living images that the prosperous merchant Bruno Crespi projected in the theater with the lion-head ticket windows, for a character who had died and was buried in one film and for whose misfortune tears of affliction had been shed would reappear alive and transformed into an Arab in the next one. The audience, who paid two cents apiece to share the difficulties of the actors, would not tolerate that outlandish fraud and they broke up the seats. The mayor, at the urging of Bruno Crespi, explained in a proclamation that the cinema was a machine of illusions that did not merit the emotional outbursts of the audience. With that discouraging explanation many felt that they had been the victims of some new and showy gypsy business and they decided not to return to the movies, considering that they already had too many troubles of their own to weep over the acted-out misfortunes of imaginary beings. . . . It was as if God had decided to put to the test every capacity for surprise and was keeping the inhabitants of Macondo in a permanent alternation between excitement and disappointment, doubt and revelation, to such an extreme that no one knew for certain where the limits of reality lay.

Gabriel Garcia Marquez, *One Hundred Years of Solitude*, pp. 185–6

WE OFTEN RESPOND TO NOVELS AND plays and movies in ways that go beyond the purely intellectual. They make us laugh and cry; we feel sorry for their characters, we fear for them, and sometimes even say that we are afraid *of* them. However, there is something puzzling about the fact that we are so often moved emotionally by characters and events that we come across in works of fiction. For these are characters who never existed as persons and events that never actually took place! And typically we are well aware that this is so as we read or watch such works.

But why does knowing that a work of fiction *is* fiction make our emotional responses to it puzzling? In the first chapter in this part, Colin Radford argues that it is largely because in everyday circumstances beliefs and judgements appear to play a crucial role in our emotional responses. Part of what it is to be afraid for oneself, for example, is to *judge* the situation one is in to be dangerous or threatening. Similarly, I cannot feel pity for others unless I *believe* them to be victims of misfortune. And beliefs of this sort would appear to depend on beliefs in the existence of the objects in question. For example, it will be difficult to make sense of my claim to be afraid of the burglar in the kitchen if I know that there is no such burglar. If I know that there is no burglar, how can I believe that a burglar (what burglar?) threatens me?

So there is something puzzling about the fact that we so often respond emotionally to what we know to be purely fictional characters and events. On the one hand, it seems that in many circumstances, at least, emotional response is in one way or another dependent on belief in the existence of what we are responding to: you cannot feel sorry for my sister if you know that I do not *have* a sister. On the other hand, it seems that we are often moved emotionally by what happens to fictional characters, knowing full well that they do not and never did exist.

Colin Radford takes the problem which arises here to concern the *rationality* of our responses to fiction. Radford argues that when we respond to novels by experiencing emotions such as pity for their characters, we are being *inconsistent*. In everyday life, he argues, we are not moved by what we know is not real; however, in responding to fiction we are moved by fictional characters and events which we know do not exist. After considering a number of possible "solutions" to the problem he raises, Radford concludes that our emotional responses to fictional characters and events are irrational.

A different approach is pursued by Alex Neill, in the second chapter. Neill argues that certain emotions depend on the adoption of a certain sort of perspective – they depend on "*seeing things from another's point of view*" – and that this perspective is one that readers may take on fiction, and indeed which fiction may demand of its readers. But Neill also holds that in thinking about these issues it is important to bear in mind the *variety* of our emotional responses. For example, he suggests, fearing for oneself and being jealous are very different sorts of emotional state from fearing for others and pitying them. Again, think of how different are the responses that Harlequin Romances aim at from the responses that a good horror movie can evoke in us. It may be that not all of the emotional responses that we can have to fiction are to be explained in the same way. Indeed, Neill suggests, not every sort of emotion can be experienced in response to fictional characters and events: for example, he claims that we cannot really be *afraid* of fictional characters.

A number of intriguing and difficult questions arise when we begin to think closely about the nature of our emotional engagement with the worlds of fiction. They are questions which bear directly on the wider issue of what it is to understand and appreciate fiction. And in addressing them, we also broach deep and important questions in the philosophy of mind and metaphysics. Aesthetics here as elsewhere can be seen to bear directly on some of the oldest concerns of philosophy itself.

15

HOW CAN WE BE MOVED BY THE FATE OF ANNA KARENINA?

Colin Radford

What's Hecuba to him, or he to Hecuba,
That he should weep for her?
Hamlet Act 2, Scene 2

1. That men feel concern for the fate of others, that they have some interest, and a warm and benevolent one in what happens to at least some other men, may be simply a brute fact about men, though a happy one. By this I mean that we can conceive that men might have been different in this respect, and so it is possible for us to be puzzled by the fact that they are not different. In a situation where men did not feel concern for others, children might be nurtured only because mothers could not stand the pain of not feeding them, or because it gave them pleasure to do this and to play with them, or because they were a source of pride. So that if a child died, a mother might have the kind of feeling the owner of a car has if his car is stolen and wrecked. He doesn't feel anything for the car, unless he is a sentimentalist, and yet he is sorry and depressed when it happens.

Of course there may be good biological reasons why men should have concern for each other, or at least some other men, but that is not to the point. The present point, a conceptual one, is that we can conceive that all men might have been as some men are, *viz.*, devoid of any feeling for anyone but themselves, whereas we cannot conceive, *e.g.*, that all men might be what some men are, chronic liars.

2. So concern and related feelings are in this sense brute. But what are they? What is it to be moved by something's happening to someone?

Anything like a complete story here is a very long one, and in any case I have a particular interest. Suppose then that you read an account of the terrible sufferings of a group of people. If you are at all humane, you are unlikely to be unmoved by what you read. The account is likely to awaken or reawaken feelings of anger, horror, dismay or outrage and, if you are tender-hearted, you may well be moved to tears. You may even grieve.

But now suppose you discover that the account is false. If the account had caused you to grieve, you could not continue to grieve. If as the account sank in, you were told and believed that it was false this would make tears impossible, unless they were tears of rage. If you learned later that the account was false, you would feel that in being moved to tears you had been fooled, duped.

It would seem then that I can only be moved by someone's plight if I believe that something terrible has happened to him. If I do not believe that he has not and is not suffering or whatever, I cannot grieve or be moved to tears.

It is not only seeing a man's torment that torments us, it is also, as we say, the thought of his torment which torments, or upsets or moves us. But here thought implies belief. We have to believe in his torment to be tormented by it. When we say that the thought of his plight moves us to tears or grieves us, it is thinking of or contemplating suffering which we believe to be actual or likely that does it.

3. The direction of my argument should now be fairly clear. Moving closer to its goal: suppose that you have a drink with a man who proceeds to tell you a harrowing story about his sister and you are harrowed. After enjoying your reaction he then tells you that he doesn't have a sister, that he has invented the story. In his case, unlike the previous one, we might say that the "heroine" of the account is fictitious. Nonetheless, and again, once you have been told this you can no longer feel harrowed. Indeed it is possible that you may be embarrassed by your reaction precisely because it so clearly indicates that you were taken in – and you may also feel embarrassed for the storyteller that he could behave in such a way. But the possibility of your being harrowed again seems to require that you believe that someone suffered.

Of course, if the man tells you in advance that he is going to tell you a story, you may reach for your hat, but you may stay and be moved. But this is too quick.

Moving closer still: an actor friend invites you to watch him simulate extreme pain, agony. He writhes about and moans. Knowing that he is only acting, could you be moved to tears? Surely not. Of course you may be embarrassed, and after some time you may even get faintly worried, "Is he really acting, or is he really in pain? Is he off his head?" But as long as you are convinced that he is only acting and is not really suffering, you cannot be moved by his suffering, and it seems unlikely as well as – as it were – unintelligible that you might be moved to tears by his portrayal of agony. It seems that you could only perhaps applaud it if it were realistic or convincing, and criticise if it were not.

But now suppose, horribly, that he acts or re-enacts the death agonies of a friend, or a Vietcong that he killed and tells you this. Then you might be horrified.

4. If this account is correct, there is no problem about being moved by historical novels or plays, documentary films, *etc*. For these works depict and forcibly remind us of the real plight and of the real sufferings of real people, and it is for these persons that we feel.[1]

What seems unintelligible is how we could have a similar reaction to the fate of Anna Karenina, the plight of Madame Bovary or the death of Mercutio. Yet we do. We weep, we pity Anna Karenina, we blink hard when Mercutio is dying and absurdly wish that he had not been so impetuous.

5. Or do we? If we are seized by this problem, it is tempting for us to argue that, since we cannot be anguished or moved by what happens to Anna Karenina, since we cannot pity Madame Bovary and since we cannot grieve at the marvellous Mercutio's death, we do not do so.

This is a tempting thesis especially because, having arrived at it, we have then to think more carefully about our reactions to and feelings about, *e.g.*, the death of Mercutio, and these investigations reveal – how could they do otherwise? – that our response to Mercutio's death differs massively from our response to the untimely death of someone we know. As we watch Mercutio die the tears run down our cheeks, but as O.K. Bouwsma has pointed out,[2] the cigarettes and chocolates go in our mouths too, and we may mutter, if not to each other, then to ourselves, "How marvellous! How sublime!" and even "How moving!"

"Now", one might say,

> if one is *moved*, one surely cannot comment on this and in admiring tones? Surely being moved to tears is a massive response which tends to interfere with saying much, even to oneself? And surely the nature of the response is such that any comments made that do not advert to what gives rise to the feeling but to the person experiencing it tend to suggest that the response isn't really felt? Compare this with leaning over to a friend in a theatre and saying "I am completely absorbed (enchanted, spellbound) by this!"

But although we cannot truly grieve for Mercutio, we can be moved by his death, and are. If and when one says "How moving" in an admiring tone, one can be moved at the theatre. One's admiration is for the play or the performance, and one can admire or be impressed by this and avow this while being moved by it.

6. So we cannot say that we do not feel for fictional characters, that we are not sometimes moved by what happens to them. We shed real tears for Mercutio. They are not crocodile tears, they are dragged from us and they are not the sort of tears that are produced by cigarette smoke in the theatre. There is a lump in our throats, and it's not the sort of lump that is produced by swallowing a fishbone. We are appalled when we realise what may happen, and are horrified when it does. Indeed, we may be so appalled at the prospect of what we think is going to happen to a character in a novel or a play that some of us can't go on. We avert the impending tragedy in the only way we can, by closing the book, or leaving the theatre.

This may be an inadequate response, and we may also feel silly or shamefaced at our tears. But this is not because they are always inappropriate and sentimental, as, *e.g.*, is giving one's dog a birthday party, but rather because we feel them to be unmanly. They may be excusable though still embarrassing on the occasion of a real death, but should be contained for anything less.

Of course we are not only moved by fictional tragedies but impressed and even delighted by them. But I have tried to explain this, and that we are other things does not seem to the point. What is worrying is that we are moved by the death of Mercutio and we weep while knowing that no one has really died, that no young man has been cut off in the flower of his youth.[3]

7. So if we can be and if some of us are indeed moved to tears at Mercutio's untimely death, feel pity for Anna Karenina and so on, how can this be explained? How can the seeming incongruity of our doing this be explained and explained away?

FIRST SOLUTION

When we read the book, or better when we watch the play and it works, we are "caught up" and respond and we "forget" or are no longer aware that we are only reading a book or watching a play. In particular, we forget that Anna Karenina, Madame Bovary, Mercutio, and so on are not real persons.

But this won't do. It turns adults into children. It is true that, *e.g.*, when children are first taken to pantomimes they are unclear about what is going on. The young ones are genuinely and unambiguously terrified when the giant comes to kill Jack. The bolder ones shout "Look Out!" and even try to get on the stage to interfere.

But do we do this? Do we shout and try to get on the stage when, watching *Romeo and Juliet*, we see that Tybalt is going to kill Mercutio? We do not. Or if we do, this is extravagant and unnecessary for our being moved. If we really did think someone was really being slain, either a person called Mercutio or the actor playing that rôle, we would try to do something or think that we should. We would, if you like, be genuinely appalled.[4]

So we are not unaware that we are "only" watching a play involving fictional characters, and the problem remains.

SECOND SOLUTION

Of course we don't ever forget that Mercutio is only a character in a play, but we "suspend our disbelief" in his reality. The theatre management and the producer connive at this. They dim the lights and try to find good actors. They, and we, frown on other members of the audience who draw attention to themselves and distract us by coughing, and if, during a scene, say a stage hand steals on, picks up a chair that should have been removed and sheepishly departs, our response is destroyed. The "illusion" is shattered.

All this is true but the paradox remains. When we watch a play we do not direct our thoughts to it's only being a play. We don't continually remind ourselves of this – unless we are trying to reduce the effect of the work on us. Nonetheless, and as we have seen, we are never unaware that we are watching a play, and one about fictional characters even at the most exciting and moving moments. So the paradox is not solved by invoking "suspension of disbelief", though it occurs and is connived at.

THIRD SOLUTION

It's just another brute fact about human beings that they can be moved by stories about fictional characters and events; *i.e.*, human beings might not have been like this (and a lot of them are not. A lot of people do not read books or go to the theatre, and are bored if they do).

But our problem is that people *can* be moved by fictional suffering given their brute behaviour in other contexts where belief in the reality of the suffering described or witnessed is necessary for the response.

FOURTH SOLUTION

But this thesis about behaviour in non-fictional contexts is too strong. The paradox arises only because my examples are handpicked ones in which there is this requirement. But there are plenty of situations in which we can be moved to tears or feel a lump in the throat without thinking that anyone will, or that anyone is even likely to suffer or die an untimely death, or whatever.

But are there? A mother hears that one of her friend's children has been killed in a street accident. When her own children return from school she grabs them in relief and hugs them, almost with a kind of anger. (Is it because they have frightened her?) Their reaction is "What's wrong with you?" They won't get a coherent answer perhaps, but surely the explanation is obvious. The death of the friend's child "brings home", "makes real", and perhaps strengthens the mother's awareness of the likelihood of her own children being maimed or killed. We must try another case. A man's attention wanders from the paper he is reading in his study. He thinks of his sister and, with a jolt, realises that she will soon be flying to the States. Perhaps because he is terrified of flying he thinks of her flying and of her 'plane crashing and shudders. He imagines how this would affect their mother. She would be desolated, inconsolable. Tears prick his eyes. His wife enters and wants to know what's up. He looks upset. Our man is embarrassed but says truthfully, "I was thinking about Jean's flying to the States and, well, I thought how awful it would be if there were an accident – how awful it would be for my mother." Wife: "Don't be silly! How maudlin! And had you nearly reduced yourself to tears thinking about all this? Really, I don't know what's got into you, *etc, etc.*"

In this case the man's response to his thoughts, his being appalled at the thought of his sister's crashing, *is* silly and maudlin, but it is intelligible and non-problematic. For it would be neither silly nor maudlin if flying were a more dangerous business than we are prone to think it is. Proof: change the example and suppose that the sister is seriously ill. She is not suffering yet, but she had cancer and her brother thinks about her dying and how her death will affect their mother. If that were the situation his wife would do well to offer comfort as well as advice.

So a man can be moved not only by what has happened to someone, by actual suffering and death, but by their prospect and the greater the probability of the awful thing's happening, the more likely are we to sympathise, *i.e.*, to understand his response and even share it. The lesser the probability the more likely we are not to feel this way. And if what moves a man to tears is the contemplation of something that is most unlikely to happen, *e.g.*, the shooting of his sister, the more likely are we to find his behaviour worrying and puzzling. However, we can explain his divergent behaviour, and in various ways. We can do this in terms of his having false beliefs. He thinks a 'plane crash or a shooting is more likely than it is, which itself needs and can have an explanation. Or his threshold for worry is lower than average, and again this is non-problematic, *i.e.*, we understand what's going on. Or lastly, we may decide he gets some kind of pleasure from dwelling on such contingencies and appalling himself. Now this is, logically, puzzling, for how can a man get pleasure from pain? But if only because traces of masochism are present in many of us, we are more likely to find it simply offensive.

The point is that our man's behaviour is only more or less psychologically odd or morally worrying. There is no logical difficulty here, and the reason for this is that the suffering and anguish that he contemplates, however unlikely, is pain that some real person may really experience.

Testing this, let us suppose first that our man when asked "What's up" says, "I was thinking how awful it would have been if Jean had been unable to have children – she wanted them so much." Wife: "But she's got them. Six!" Man: "Yes, I know, but suppose she hadn't?" "My God! Yes it would have been but it didn't happen. How can you sit there and weep over the dreadful thing that didn't happen, and now cannot happen." (She's getting philosophical. Sneeringly) "What are you doing? Grieving for her? Feeling sorry for her?" Man: "All right! But thinking about it, it was so vivid I could imagine just how it would have been." Wife: "You began to snivel!" Man: "Yes."

It is by making the man a sort of Walter Mitty, a man whose imagination is so powerful and vivid that, for a moment anyway, what he imagines seems real, that his tears are made intelligible, though of course not excusable.

So now suppose that the man thinks not of his sister but of a woman . . . that is, he makes up a story about a woman who flies to the States and is killed and whose mother grieves, and so on, and that this gives him a lump in his throat. It might appear that, if my thesis is correct, the man's response to the story he invents should be even more puzzling than his being moved by the thought of his sister's not having children. "Yet", one who was not seized by the philosophical problem might say, "this case is really not puzzling. After all he might be a writer who first gets some of his stories in this manner!"

But that is precisely why this example does not help. It is too close, too like what gives rise to the problem.[5]

FIFTH SOLUTION

A solution suggested by an earlier remark: if and when we weep for Anna Karenina, we weep for the pain and anguish that a real person might suffer and which real persons have suffered, and if her situation were not of that sort we should not be moved.

There is something in this, but not enough to make it a solution. For we do not really weep for the pain that a real person might suffer, and which real persons have suffered, when we weep for Anna Karenina, even if we should not be moved by her story if it were not of that sort. We weep for *her*. We are moved by what happens to her, by the situation she gets into, and which is a pitiful one, but we do not feel pity for her state or fate, or her history or her situation, or even for others, i.e., for real persons who might have or even have had such a history. We pity her, feel for her and our tears are shed for her. This thesis is even more compelling, perhaps, if we think about the death of Mercutio.

But all over again, how can we do this knowing that neither she nor Mercutio ever existed, that all their sufferings do not add one bit to the sufferings of the world?

SIXTH SOLUTION

Perhaps there really is no problem. In non-fictional situations it may be necessary that in order for a person to be moved, he must believe in the reality of what he sees or is told, or at least he must believe that such a thing may indeed happen to someone. But, as I concede, being moved when reading a novel or watching a play is not exactly like being moved by what one believes happens in real life and, indeed, it is very different. So there are two sorts of being moved and, perhaps, two senses of "being moved". There is being moved (Sense 1) in real life and "being moved" (Sense 2) by what happens to fictional characters. But since there are these two sorts and senses, it does not follow from the necessity of belief in the reality of the agony or whatever it is, for being moved

245

(S. 1), that belief in its reality is, or ought to be necessary for "being moved" (S. 2). So I have not shown that there is a genuine problem, which perhaps explains why I can find no solution.

But although being moved by what one believes is really happening is not exactly the same as being moved by what one believes is happening to fictional characters, it is not wholly different. And it is what is common to being moved in either situation which makes problematic one of the differences, *viz.*, the fact that belief is not necessary in the fictional situation. As for the hesitant claim that there is a different sense here, this clearly does not follow from the fact that being moved by what happens in real life is different from being moved in the theatre or cinema or when reading a novel, and I find it counterintuitive.[6] But even if the phrase did have different senses for the different cases, it would not follow that there was no problem. It may be that "being moved" (S. 2) is an incoherent notion so that we and our behaviour are incoherent, when we are "moved" (S. 2).

When, as we say, Mercutio's death moves us, it appears to do so in very much the same way as the unnecessary death of a young man moves us and for the same reason. We see the death as a waste, though of course it is really only a waste in the real case, and as a "tragedy", and we are, unambiguously – though problematically as I see it in the case of fiction – saddened by the death. As we watch the play and realise that Mercutio may die or, knowing the play, that he is about to die, we may nonetheless and in either case say to ourselves "Oh! No! Don't let it happen!" (It seems *absurd* to say this, especially when we know the play, and yet we do. This is part of what I see as the problem.) When he is run through we wince and gasp and catch our breath, and as he dies the more labile of us weep.

How would our behaviour differ if we believed that we were watching the death of a real young man, perhaps of the actor playing the part of Mercutio? First, seeing or fearing that the actor playing the part of Tybalt is bent on killing the other actor, we might try to intervene or, if we did not, we might reproach ourselves for not doing so. When he has been run through we might try to get help. But if we are convinced that we can do nothing, as we are when we watch the death of Mercutio or read about Anna, and if we thought that our watching was not improper, these irrelevant differences in our behaviour would disappear. Once again, we would say to ourselves – and, in this case also to each other since there is no question of aesthetic pleasure – "My God! How terrible!" And as the actor lay dying, perhaps delivering Mercutio's lines, either because he felt them to be appropriate or because, unaware that he was actually dying, he felt that the show must go on, we should again weep for the dying man and the pity of it. Secondly, but this is not irrelevant, our response to the real death is likely to be more massive, more intense and longer in duration for, after all, a real young man has been killed, and it will not be alloyed – or allayed – by aesthetic pleasure. But such differences do not destroy the similarity of the response and may even be said to require it.

So a similarity exists, and the essential similarity seems to be that we are saddened. But this is my difficulty. For we are saddened, but how can we be? What are we sad *about*? How can we feel genuinely and involuntarily sad, and weep, as we do, knowing as we do that no one has suffered or died?

To insist that there is this similarity between being moved and "being moved" is not to deny that there are other differences between them besides the necessary presence of belief in the one case and its puzzling absence in the other. Yet, as I have already indicated, some of the peculiar features of "being moved" add to the problem it presents. Not *any* difference between being moved and "being moved", over and above the difference in belief, has the effect of reducing the conceptual problem presented by the latter, as is suggested by this sixth solution. *E.g.*, when we hope that Mercutio will not get killed, we may realise, knowing the play, that he must be killed, unless the play is altered or the performance is interrupted and we may not wish for that. So not only is our hope vain, for he must die and we know this,[7] but it exists alongside a wish that he will die. After the death, in retrospect, our behaviour differs. In the case of the real man, we should continue to be moved and to regret that happened. With Mercutio we are unlikely to do this and, in talking about his death later, we might only be moved to say "How moving it was!" For we are no longer at the performance or responding directly to it. We do not so much realise later as appropriately remind ourselves later that Mercutio is only a character and that, being a character, he will, as it were, be born again to die again at the next performance. Mercutio is not lost to us, when he dies, as the actor is when he dies.

Our response to Mercutio's death is, then, different from our response to the death of the actor. We do not entirely or simply hope that it will not happen, our response is partly aesthetic, the anguish at his death is not perhaps as intense, and it tends not to survive the performance.

Perhaps we are and can be moved by the death of Mercutio only to the extent that, at the time of the performance, we are "caught up" in the play, and see the characters as persons, real persons, though to see them as real persons is not to believe that they are real persons. If we wholly believe, our response is indistinguishable from our response to the real thing, for we believe it to be the real thing. If we are always and fully aware that these are only actors mouthing rehearsed lines, we are not caught up in the play at all and can only respond to the beauty and tragedy of the poetry and not to the death of the character. The difficulty is, however – and it remains – that the belief, to say the least, is never complete. Or, better, even when we are caught up, we are still aware that we are watching a play and that Mercutio is "only" a character. We may become like children, but this is not necessary for our tears.

So the problem remains. The strength of our response may be proportionate to, *inter alia*, our "belief" in Mercutio. But we do not and need not at any time believe that he is a real person to weep for him. So that what is necessary in other contexts, *viz.*, belief, for being moved, is not necessary here and, all over again, how can we be saddened by and cry over Mercutio's death knowing as we do that when he dies no one really dies?

8. I am left with the conclusion that our being moved in certain ways by works of art, though very "natural" to us and in that way only too intelligible, involves us in inconsistency and so incoherence.

It may be some sort of comfort, as well as support for my thesis, to realise that there are other sorts of situation in which we are similarly inconsistent, *i.e.*, in which, while knowing that something is or is not so, we spontaneously behave, or even may be unable to stop ourselves behaving, as if we believed the contrary. Thus, a tennis player who sees his shot going into the net will often give a little involuntary jump to lift it over. Because he knows that this can have no effect it is tempting to say that the jump is purely expressive. But almost anyone who has played tennis will know that this is not true. Or again, though men have increasingly come to think of death as a dreamless sleep, it was pointed out long ago – was it by Dr. Johnson or David Hume?[8] – that they still fear it. Some may say that this fear is not incoherent, for what appals such men is not their also thinking of death as an unpleasant state, but the prospect of their nonexistence. But how can this appal? There is, literally, nothing to fear. The incoherence of fearing the sleep of death for all that it will cause one to miss is even clearer. We do not participate in life when we are dead, but we are not then endlessly wishing to do so. Nonetheless, men fear the endless, dreamless sleep of death and fear it for all that they will miss.

NOTES

1   Not for the performance which elicits this feeling or for the actor – for those we feel admiration, are impressed and so on. This may help to explain how we can enjoy tragedy. Besides the actor's skill and the producer's we also enjoy the skill of the writer. What is difficult is that we weep. This turns the usual problem upside down. People are more often puzzled about how we can enjoy a tragedy, not how it can harrow us, cf. Hume's essay, "On tragedy".

2   In "The expression theory of art", collected in his *Philosophical Essays*, Lincoln: University of Nebraska Press (1965); cf. p. 29.

3   Though why that should worry us is another worry. There may be some who still feel that there really is no problem, so consider the following case. A man has a genre painting. It shows a young man being slain in battle (but it is not an historical picture, that is, of the death of some particular real young man who was killed in a particular battle). He says that he finds the picture moving and we understand, even if we do not agree. But then he says that, when he looks at the picture, he feels pity, sorrow, *etc.*, for *the young man in the picture*. Surely this very odd response would be extremely puzzling? How *can* he feel sorry for the young man in the painting? But now suppose that the picture is a moving picture, *i.e.*, a movie, and it tells a story. In this case we *do* say that we feel sorry for the young man in the film who is killed. But is there a difference between these two cases which not only explains but justifies our differing responses? Is it, perhaps, simply because most of us do respond in this way to films that we do not find our doing so puzzling?

4   Cf. "The delight of tragedy proceeds from our consciousness of fiction; if we thought murders and treasons real, they would please no more." Johnson, *Preface to Shakespeare*.

5   Incidentally, and to avoid misunderstanding, I do not have a monolithic view about aesthetic response. I am not saying, for example, that we must believe a story about Harold Wilson to find it *funny*. I am saying that, with the paradoxical exception of watching plays, films, *etc.*, including those about Harold Wilson, we need to believe the story to weep for him, to feel pity for him.

6   Does "killed" have a different sense in "Nixon has been killed" and "Mercutio has been killed"?

7   Of course, seeing a clip from the newsreel of Kennedy's assassination may elicit the same response, "Don't let him get killed!", and here we do realise that our response is silly, is incompatible with our knowledge that he is dead and we are watching a film of his death. But there is in the theatre nothing analogous to actually witnessing Kennedy's death. The death of a character is always irrevocable, out of reach, and out of our control.

8   Either could have made such an observation, though Hume regarded death with phlegm, Johnson with honor. But in fact it was a contemporary, Miss Seward, "There is one mode of the fear of death which is certainly absurd; and that is the dread of annihilation, which is only a pleasing sleep without a dream." Boswell, *Life of Johnson*, for 1778.

16

FICTION AND THE EMOTIONS
Alex Neill

I

It is a fact about many of us that we can be moved by what we know to be fictional. But it is a fact that has been seen by philosophers as problematic in a variety of ways. Plato worried about the effect that responses of this sort have on our cognitive and moral development; Dr. Johnson wondered "how the drama moves, if it is not credited"; and more recently Colin Radford has started a small industry in philosophical aesthetics with a series of articles arguing that our emotional responses to what we know to be fictional are inconsistent, incoherent, and irrational.[1] In this article, I wish to focus on a question related to but nonetheless different from those raised by Johnson and by Radford: the question of what it is that we are moved *to* when we are moved by fiction. What *kind* of responses are our affective responses to what we know to be fictional characters and events?

This question is related to Dr. Johnson's "causal" question (*how*, or *why*, are we moved by what we know to be fiction?) and to Radford's question (is it *rational* to be so moved?) not least inasmuch as all three are motivated by the same thought – the thought that standardly, at least, we are moved by what we *do* "credit," that our emotional responses are typically founded on *belief*. This thought is central to the "cognitive theory" of emotion, which takes beliefs and judgments to be central to the emotions.[2] This theory of emotion has puzzling consequences with respect to our affective engagement with fiction. Given that I do not believe that Nosferatu the Vampire exists, I cannot believe that he poses any threat to me. And if such a belief is a necessary element of fear for oneself, as the cognitive theory of emotion holds that it is, it would appear to follow that I cannot be afraid of Nosferatu. Similarly, although what I feel for Conrad's character Winnie Verloc may *feel* very much like pity, I do not believe that Winnie ever existed, and hence do not believe that she underwent any suffering. And if pity conceptually involves a belief of this sort, as the cognitive theory suggests that it does, it would appear that I cannot properly be described as pitying Winnie. It is

250

important to notice that, *pace* Radford, the problem here does not, or at least does not initially, concern the *rationality* of our affective responses to fiction. If I lack the relevant beliefs, the question is not whether my "pity" for Winnie is *rational* or not, but rather whether my response is one of *pity* at all.

Several philosophers have come to the conclusion that my response cannot properly be described as one of pity, or at any rate not as pity for *Winnie*. Ryle, for example, wrote that "novel readers and theater-goers feel real pangs and real liftings of the heart, just as they may shed real tears and scowl unfeigned scowls. But their distresses and indignation are feigned."[3] And more recently Malcolm Budd has suggested that "it cannot be literally true that we pity Desdemona, or are horrified by Oedipus's self-blinding, or are envious of Orpheus's musical talent, or are distressed by the death of Anna Karenina – even if there should be tears in our eyes when we read the account of her suicide. For, as we know, these people never existed."[4] But if this conclusion is right, then how *are* we to describe those of our affective responses that appear to be "directed" at fictional characters and events? A number of strategies have been proposed in response to this question. One of the most popular involves attempting to redescribe what we are prereflectively inclined to describe as pity for Winnie Verloc (for example) as pity for real people who are brought to mind by Conrad's novel, about whom we do have the relevant beliefs.[5] Or (less plausibly) perhaps our affective responses to fiction can be adequately characterized in terms of states of feeling, such as moods, that do not depend on beliefs in the way that emotions do.[6] Or, again, perhaps they are to be understood as "imaginary" or "make-believe" emotions.[7]

However, leaving aside the difficulties involved in these strategies, it may be objected that their adoption would in any case be premature. As we have seen, our problem is generated by the claim that, given that we know that fictional characters *are* fictional, we cannot hold certain beliefs about them, such as a belief that they suffer misfortune. But this claim is, on the face of it, very odd. For surely we *do* believe, for example, that Emma Woodhouse was handsome, clever, and rich. Indeed, believing this would seem to be a criterion of having understood Jane Austen's novel. *Not* to believe it, or to disbelieve it, would suggest either that one has read *Emma* with so little attention that one could barely be described as having read it at all, or that one has simply got things very badly wrong.

One way of dispelling the mystery here, as a number of philosophers have noted, is by construing statements such as "Winnie Verloc had a pretty miserable time of things" as elliptical for statements of something like the form "it is *The Secret Agent*–fictional that Winnie Verloc had a miserable time of things." Thus while it is not true that Winnie had a miserable time, what *is* true is that it is *fictional* that she did; while we cannot (coherently) believe that Winnie had a miserable time, then, we *can* coherently believe that it is *fictional* that she did. And we can believe this without being committed to the belief that Winnie ever existed.[8]

Now if something like this is right, then a simple solution to the problem concerning our affective responses to what we know to be fictional suggests itself. For if those of our affective responses that seem to have fictional characters and events as objects *are* grounded on beliefs – beliefs about what is fictionally the case – then perhaps they *do* after all respect the constraints imposed by the cognitive theory of emotion, and hence *do* constitute emotions "proper". It is this possibility that I wish to consider in what follows.[9]

II

The question I shall be concerned with, then, is this: Can my belief that it is fictional that Winnie Verloc suffered (for example), together with certain other facts about me, make it true that I *pity* her?

But it may be objected at the start that this way of stating the question gets things wrong. After all, it may be said, in such cases we do not *actually* believe that anyone undergoes any suffering or misfortune at all. Some seeming support for this objection is offered by Bijoy Boruah, who characterizes attitudes of the kind we are concerned with here variously as "putative beliefs," as "insincere, hypothetical attitudes," as "no more than provisional assents to propositions about fictional phenomena."[10] But these characterizations are misleading. There is certainly nothing "putative," "insincere," "hypothetical," or "provisional" about my belief that Emma Woodhouse was handsome, clever, and rich. I *do, actually,* believe that (it is fictionally the case that) Emma had all of these attributes. There is nothing fictional about *beliefs* of this sort; it is their *content* that concerns the fictional. Beliefs about what is fictionally the case, that is, are just that: beliefs. They are not (as Flint Schier suggests)[11] "unasserted thoughts"; in believing that it is fictionally the case that *p* my attitude is one of judgment, the linguistic expression of which is assertion. In believing that it is fictional that *p*, I believe that it is *true* that it is fictional that *p*. Beliefs about what is fictional, like beliefs about the actual world, are open to assessment in terms of truth and rationality.

However, even if it is granted that beliefs about what is fictionally the case are genuine beliefs, it may be argued that this has little bearing on the real problem that we are faced with here. That problem, it will be said, arises not because in responding to *The Secret Agent* we do not *actually believe* that anything suffers – we do believe that (fictionally) Winnie suffers – but rather because in such cases we do not believe that *anything actual* suffers. The suggestion here is that in order to be correctly described as pitying someone or something, one must believe that the suffering or misfortune involved is actual, and thus that it is experienced by someone or something which actually exists. It is suggested that these beliefs are so central to pity that a person who does not hold them, a person who believes rather that it is fictional that the object involved suffers, and thus that it is fictional that the object exists, cannot properly be described as experiencing pity.

In support of this suggestion, it is sometimes held that beliefs about what is fictionally the case lack the *causal* power to move us. Thus Boruah suggests that such beliefs are no more than "mere recognitions on our part that, fictionally, something or other is the case," and that "mere recognition is not enough causally to explain why we feel any emotion towards fiction."[12] But this is unconvincing. For to the extent that my belief that fictionally Shylock is a victim of injustice can be construed as "a mere recognition that fictionally, something is the case," my belief that many Guatemalan refugees are victims of injustice can be construed similarly as "a mere recognition that, actually, something is the case." And there is no reason to suppose that "mere recognition" of what is fictional is any less causally efficacious with respect to emotion than "mere recognition" of what is actual.

In explaining the generation of many varieties of emotional response, a more helpful notion than those of "mere recognition" or bare belief is that of the adoption on the part of the subject of a certain sort of "perspective"; roughly speaking, one that involves *seeing things from another's point of view*. What makes my belief that many Guatemalan refugees are victims of injustice causally efficacious with respect to emotion, if it is, is the fact that in some way I can see what it must be like to be in their position; to some extent, at least, I can see things from their point of view. And there is no reason to suppose that we cannot adopt this kind of imaginative attitude with respect to fictional characters. Indeed, many works of fiction might plausibly be said to *demand* that we do so; the reader who doesn't see the world of *Tom Sawyer* through Tom's eyes will have understood the novel only in a very thin sense of "understand," if at all. And allowing the audience or reader to see and to understand his or her fictional world from a variety of perspectives and characters' points of view is a common criterion of an author's success.

The worry concerning the causal efficacy of our beliefs about what is fictionally the case thus looks misplaced. For on the one hand, if one takes belief to be the crucial factor in the production of emotion, there is no reason to suppose that our beliefs about what is fictionally the case will be any more causally impotent with regard to emotion than our beliefs about what is actually the case. On the other hand, if one takes the (I think more plausible) view that the crucial factor in the generation of emotion is something like the adoption of certain sorts of perspective, it seems clear that this factor can be present in (and indeed is arguably often central to) our dealings with fiction.

But we must not be too hasty here. Even if it is granted that many of our affective responses to fiction are caused in much the same way as many of our affective responses to what we take to be actual, the question I raised at the beginning of this article, that of what *sort* of responses these are, remains open. Furthermore, even if some emotions result from "seeing things from another's point of view," this is surely not true of all cases of emotional experience. As my neighbor's rabid dog charges toward me, slavering at the jaws, the only point of view with which I am likely to be concerned is my own! And as the spectator at the horror movie shrieks and sinks deeper into his seat, he is hardly interested in the perspective that the monster on the screen has on things. Not all emotions, that is, stem from adopting another's perspective. And this suggests that the various emotions to which we commonly appeal in attempting to describe our affective responses to fiction may not be amenable to treatment as a monolithic group, and hence that in discussing this issue we need to be wary of generalizing, and alert to the differences between various sorts of emotion and affective response.

III

Once again, then, the question I am concerned with is whether at least some emotions may be based on beliefs about what is fictionally the case as well as on beliefs about what is actually the case. In what follows, I shall argue that there is at least one emotion which can be based on beliefs about what is fictional. First, however, we should note that there is at least one variety of emotional response that is *not* of this sort; namely, fear for oneself. Central to fear for myself, as I noted earlier, is (roughly speaking) a belief that I am threatened by or in danger from the object of my response. And just as I cannot coherently believe that it is actually the case that I am threatened by something that I know to be fictional (for the only monsters who can threaten *me* are actual monsters) so I cannot coherently believe that it is fictionally the case that I am threatened by something that I know to be fictional (for the only people that Nosferatu and the like can threaten are fictional people).[13] Furthermore, because I do not believe that (it is either actually or fictionally the case that) I am threatened by Nosferatu, I do not have the sorts of *desire* characteristic of fear for oneself; I do not have any desire to escape his clutches, or to warn my friends and family, and so on. Hence I am not afraid of Nosferatu, nor of any creature whom I know to be a creature of fiction. Nor, I suggest, can I be *jealous* of what I know to be a fictional character. For central to jealousy are (once again, roughly speaking) a belief that the person of whom I am jealous has, or has designs on, something that is rightfully mine, and a desire to regain or retain whatever that is. And this belief/desire combination is not one that I can coherently have where I know that the object of my response is fictional. The ontological gap between fictional characters and ourselves precludes rivalry with them as well as being threatened by and escaping from them.

Fear for oneself and jealousy are both sorts of response that do not typically result from adopting another's perspective, from seeing things from another's point of view. However, it is not the *causes* of these sorts of response that are problematic here; it is rather the kind of beliefs and judgments that they involve. Fear for oneself and jealousy (and I do not suppose that these are the only responses of this sort) have the following feature in common: They both depend on the subject seeing him- or herself as standing in a certain sort of relation to the object of the response, a relation that cannot obtain between the inhabitants of different ontological "worlds."

The fact that we cannot fear or be jealous of what we know to be fictional characters accords well with our experience; how often, after all, do we really want to describe ourselves as feeling jealous of a fictional character? Fear for oneself may be less obviously dispensable within this context; however, I would suggest that in most if not all cases where we might be prereflectively inclined to describe ourselves as afraid of something that we know to be fictional, our response will on reflection turn out to be better characterized in terms of fear of actual counterparts of what is represented in the fiction, or in terms of non-belief-dependent reactive states. Thus, for example, seeing Spielberg's *Poltergeist* may make me afraid of *real* ghosts that may, for all I know, be lurking in my bedroom closet; or it may make me afraid *that* there are real ghosts after all. Alternatively, or perhaps additionally, my response to the film may be better described in terms of states such as shock and alarm; states which a good director will induce through the expert use of camera angle and editing and sound, and which may *feel* very much like fear. Furthermore, we should remember that not all fear is fear for oneself; we may also experience fear sympathetically, or *for* others, and empathetically, or *with* others. And it may be that although we cannot be afraid *of* what we know to be fictional characters, we can be afraid for and with them.

Both fear for and fear with others, unlike fear for oneself, are sorts of response that (typically, at least) we experience as a result of imaginatively adopting another's perspective on things. And in the remainder of this article I shall argue that at least one other emotion of this sort can be based on our beliefs about what is fictionally the case. The emotion in question is pity. Along with fear, pity has received the lion's share of attention in the contemporary debate on the issues with which we are concerned, not least because it is one of the emotions to which we appear to be most inclined to refer in describing our affective responses to fiction. For my purposes, pity is also a good "test case" here because it can plausibly be argued that a paradigmatic instance of pity will have all the features or "ingredients" that any emotion of this kind could have. (In this respect, pity may be contrasted with envy, for example, which often does not involve bodily feelings and sensations; and with certain sorts of grief, which may not involve desires of any kind.) I shall proceed, therefore, by considering whether there are any necessary or characteristic features of pity which are such that if a response is founded on beliefs concerning what is fictionally the case, rather than on beliefs about what one takes to be actual states of affairs, then those features of the emotion will be missing from that response. If there are no such features, I suggest, then there will be no reason not to describe certain responses based on beliefs about what is fictionally the case as responses of pity.

IV

A characteristic if not necessary feature of many emotions, including pity, is a physiological/phenomenological one. And it is undeniable that we can be moved to bodily feeling and sensation by what we know to be fictionally the case. As Radford says, "We shed real tears for Mercutio. They are not crocodile tears, they are dragged from us and they are not the sort of tears that are produced by cigarette smoke in the theatre. There is a lump in our throats, and it's not the sort of lump that is produced by swallowing a fishbone." The occurrence of feelings and sensations of this sort clearly does not depend on a belief that the situation witnessed or described is actual.

However, it must be granted that in general the feelings and sensations that we experience in response to fiction tend to be rather different from those that may issue from our beliefs about what is actually the case. As Hume puts it, "The feelings of the passions are very different when excited by poetical fictions, from what they are when they arise from belief and reality." A passion experienced in response to poetry, he suggests, "lies not with that weight upon us: It feels less firm and solid."[14] I shall have more to say about this later, but two points should be noted here. First, whatever Hume may have meant by "weight" and "firmness" and "solidity," the difference between the feelings I experience in responding to a fictional character or situation and those I experience in response to what I take to be actual cannot simply be understood in terms of *intensity*. What I feel for or about a fictional character may in fact be *more* intense than my feelings for or about the starving Ethiopians, or the Guatemalan refugees whose plight I hear about on radio or television. This may be morally worrying, but it appears nonetheless to be perfectly possible. Second, even if it could be established that beliefs about what is fictionally the case typically issue in "weaker" or less intense feelings than those that issue from beliefs about what is actually the case, it would not follow that responses founded on the former sort of belief cannot properly be construed as emotions. For the emotions cannot be defined in terms of the feelings and sensations that they may involve.[15] Whether or not it is a necessary part of pity, then, the "feeling" aspect of the emotion would appear to pose no difficulty for the position that I wish to defend here; namely, that a person may be correctly described as feeling pity for what he or she knows to be fictional.

However, Hume points to a further potential difficulty that we must address here. "A passion, which is disagreeable in real life," he suggests, "may afford the highest entertainment in a tragedy, or epic poem." Experienced as part of a response to what we know to be fictional, the emotion involved has "the agreeable effect of exciting the spirits, and rouzing the attention."[16] These remarks bring us up against a familiar problem in aesthetics, a problem which Hume addressed in more detail in his essay "Of Tragedy." His topic there is the "unaccountable pleasure which the spectators of a well-written tragedy receive from sorrow, terror, anxiety and other passions that are in themselves disagreeable and uneasy."[17] For our purposes, the problem that Hume is concerned with may be expressed with regard to pity as follows. A belief that the object of one's response is suffering is clearly not a sufficient condition of pity; in order to be correctly described as feeling pity, one must also be *distressed* by the suffering. If one reacts to the suffering of another with pleasure, one's response will be some form of *schadenfreude*; if one is simply indifferent to it, one will not be experiencing emotion at all. In responding to tragedy, however, we appear to take pleasure in experiencing emotions such as pity. And this raises the question (though it is not precisely Hume's question) of whether one's responses in such contexts really constitute *pity*.

In addressing this question, the first point to note is that our responses to the fictional depiction of suffering and distress do *not* always involve pleasure; what is depicted in a work of fiction may be so harrowing that we are forced to close the book or to leave the theater. And if we do not do so, it may be not because we take *pleasure* in what is depicted, but rather because we feel for one reason or another that we *ought* to endure it, as we may feel that we ought to suffer through Amnesty International's reports on torture and capital punishment. However, it seems clear that in many instances our experience of distressing fiction does involve pleasure; and it may be argued that in those instances, at least, our response is not correctly described in terms of intrinsically distressful emotions such as pity. For how can we be described as pitying something if we are taking pleasure in watching or reading about its suffering?

But this is unconvincing. For one thing, it is not clear that the pleasure that may be part of our response to a work of fiction even conflicts with, let alone rules out the possibility of, the distress that may *also* be a part of that response. In responding to a work of fiction as to anything else our attention may have more than one object; it may be, then, that our pleasure and our distress have different objects. (Thus we may be distressed by what is depicted in a work, yet be pleased by the manner of depiction.) If the object of the pleasure that we derive from a work of fiction really *is* the suffering depicted therein, then of course that will be a good reason for denying that our response is one of pity. But there is no reason to suppose that we are in general any more prone to take pleasure in fictional suffering than we are to take pleasure in actual suffering. Second, as Flint Schier remarked, the idea that we take *pleasure* in watching Oedipus or Gloucester with their eyes out (for example) is to say the least peculiar.[18] In discussions of this issue, that is, "pleasure" would appear to have a somewhat unusual sense, and one that needs to be spelled out. And the important point for our purposes here is that a major criterion of adequacy for any account of "tragic pleasure" is that it be able to show how this sort of pleasure is compatible with (and perhaps even involves) the distress that tragic fiction may also evoke in us.[19] The fact that we can take pleasure in tragic fiction, whatever "pleasure" may mean here, cannot plausibly be construed as ruling out the possibility that our responses to tragedy may also involve the distress that is an intrinsic part of emotions such as pity.

V

An examination of the feelings and sensations characteristic of pity thus supports, rather than casts doubt on, the suggestion that certain of our affective responses to fiction may in fact properly be described as responses of pity. The only element of pity that we have yet to consider is desire. If it can be demonstrated that a response founded on a belief that it is fictional that someone is suffering may involve the desires as well as the feelings and sensations that are characteristic of pity, then we shall have shown that there is every reason to describe such a response as one of pity.

It can plausibly be argued that a central and indeed necessary feature of pity is a want or desire that the misfortune suffered by the person or thing we pity should stop or could be avoided. It may then be argued further that we lack any such desire in responding to what we know to be fictional suffering, and that we do so precisely because we know that the suffering *is* fictional. Hence, it will be said, we cannot properly be described as pitying fictional characters. As it stands, however, this is unpersuasive. In responding to a work of fiction we may indeed desire that (fictionally) a character's suffering should come to an end, that (fictionally) his or her plight will be resolved happily. "How I hope that her father relents in time," we may think, or "How I wish that he didn't have to die." We sit tensed on the edges of our seats hoping that the heroine will get free of her bonds before the circular saw slices her up, wanting a character to realize his mistake before it is too late to rectify it, and so on.

However, with all but the most unsophisticated reader or spectator of fiction, the desires involves are likely to be more complex than this. Every time we see *Romeo and Juliet*, we may wish that Mercutio did not have to die; we may sit through many performances of *Lear*, wishing each time that Cordelia could survive. But suppose that one sees a performance of (what one initially took to be) *Romeo and Juliet* in which the director has obviously been so overwhelmed by the same desire that he arranges Mercutio's survival, letting him off with a minor flesh wound in the shoulder. Or suppose that one has not paid sufficient attention to the posters outside and realizes during a performance of *Lear* that one is watching Nahum Tate's version of the play, in which Cordelia survives. One's response in such situations is likely to be one of disappointment, if not outrage. It may be argued, then, that one does not *really* want Mercutio or Cordelia to survive; that at best one has conflicting desires with respect to the suffering of fictional characters: one both does and does not desire that their suffering should be prevented. Does this conflict of desire suggest that we are not properly described as pitying fictional characters?

Two points should be noted here. First, it is far from clear that we are in fact accurately described as having conflicting desires in cases such as those outlined above. We may genuinely and wholeheartedly wish that Mercutio *could* survive; our objection to the performance in which he does is not based on a conflicting desire that he should die, nor does it indicate that we do not really desire his survival. Rather, our objection is based on our knowledge that if Mercutio survives then we are no longer seeing *Romeo and Juliet* but another (and the chances are), inferior play. Our outrage at the "happy" ending, that is, need not conflict with our desire that the suffering involved could have been avoided, nor does it show that we do not really have any such desire. Second, even if we do have genuinely conflicting desires with respect to the suffering of a fictional character, this fact will not necessarily count against our being correctly described as pitying him or her. Our having mixed or conflicting desires with respect to another's suffering is not restricted to those cases in which the suffering involved is fictional; it is clear that we can also have conflicting desires with respect to suffering which we believe to be actual. Thus we may wish that the mental anguish and suffering undergone by a person recently bereaved could be ended, but also believe that this suffering has to be gone through if the person involved is to recover fully from his or her loss. Similarly, we might both wish that Lear's suffering could be avoided, and believe that for one reason or another he *should* undergo it. Indeed, there need be nothing altruistic about this conflict of desire; our pity may simply be mixed with a hint or more of *schadenfreude*. Whether or not we really *pity* Lear is to be decided in just the same way that we should decide whether or not we really pity the bereaved person; namely, by looking closely at the desires and beliefs that we have concerning them. The fact that we have conflicting desires concerning the suffering involved, if we do, no more rules out our being correctly described as feeling pity in one case than it does in the other.

A different aspect of the desires that are central to pity, and one that is more problematic, is pointed to by Charlton, who argues that "to be moved emotionally is to be moved to action. I am only moved by someone's plight if I want to help him."[20] (Here Charlton appears to construe "being moved" as synonymous with something like "feeling pity"; it is not true that all emotions conceptually involve some inclination to action – grief, for example, may well not.) Now the suggestion that a central component of pity is a desire to help the person whose suffering moves one does seem plausible. If it could be shown that it is in fact a *necessary* component of pity, then this would provide grounds for denying that any of our affective responses to fictional characters can properly be described as instances of pity. For typically we do *not* desire to come to the aid of what we know to be fictional characters. Indeed, it is arguable that we *cannot* have such a desire. For the "ontological gap" between fictional characters and ourselves is such that logically we *cannot* come to their aid, any more than we can escape from them or regain what is rightfully ours from them, and it can plausibly be argued that one cannot coherently desire what one knows to be logically impossible. However, even if desiring to help what we know to be fictional characters is possible, there would clearly be something odd about having such a desire. For if we understand that the characters that we are faced with are fictional, then we know that nothing that we could possibly do would *count* as helping them. This explains why it is that most of us do not, as a matter of fact, experience any desire to leap onto the stage in order to wrench Desdemona from Othello's grasp, and why it is that we regard those who write in to soap-opera characters offering sympathy and advice as having got something fundamentally wrong.

In assessing Charlton's suggestion, then, we must ask first whether a desire to help the person whose suffering moves one is in fact a necessary component of pity. The fact that I can explain an action intended to aid or to comfort another by saying that I pitied him or her shows that pity *may* involve such a desire.[21] However, *need* I have a desire to help the person whose suffering moves me if I am to be correctly described as pitying him? Consider a case in which you can see that someone is suffering, and where you believe (i) that you have the power to help him, and (ii) that there are no other and overriding reasons not to do so. (This excludes such cases as those in which you may have reason to believe that in some way or other the person in question will ultimately benefit from being left to cope on his own, or in which you believe that your coming to his aid will cause you far more discomfort than you could possibly save him.) In such a case, if you simply have no inclination to help the person in question, then you are probably not accurately described as pitying him. For your lack of any such desire or inclination strongly suggests that you are indifferent to (or perhaps even pleased by) the fact that he is in the plight that he is. Your reaction, that is, suggests (though of course it does not establish) that you are not *distressed* by his plight, and is thus a good *prima facie* reason to deny that you are correctly described as pitying him.

However, this way of setting the matter up does not show that a desire to help the person whose suffering moves one is a necessary component of pity as such, but at most that such a desire is a necessary component of pity in certain cases. In some instances of pity, I suggest, there is no question of the subject having a desire to help the object of his or her pity. Pity for people from the past appears to be perfectly coherent – I may genuinely feel sorry for my late uncle or for Lady Jane Grey – and yet it seems clear that our emotional experience in such cases does not involve a desire to help the figure in question; the point being, of course, that we *cannot* (in any straightforward sense, at least) help such figures. And it is because we know this that a desire to help plays no part in our emotional response. To take a rather different kind of case, I may know full well that I am utterly powerless to do anything to help a party of mountain-climbers caught in an avalanche, or a group of sailors trapped in a submerged submarine; and because I know this, my feelings with regard to them will typically not include any desire to help them. However, this does not in itself imply that I am indifferent to, let alone pleased by, their plight, and so that I do not pity them. As in the case of pitying historical figures, the distress I feel at their fate will be expressed in desires of a different form: broadly speaking, in a desire that their suffering should stop or could be ended (perhaps by someone who *can* do something to help); or, with respect to the suffering of an historical figure, a desire that it could have been avoided.[22] Although I know that

I cannot do anything to help, that I am (in the case of historical figures, logically) powerless to influence the state of affairs that they find or found themselves in, and so do not desire to do so, I *can* desire that things should be or could have been otherwise for them. And if I do have such a desire, then this will constitute good grounds for describing my response as one of pity.

Pace Charlton, then, the desire to help another is not a *necessary* condition of pitying him. Thus the fact that we have no such desire in responding to the sufferings of a character whom we know to be fictional does not in itself rule out the possibility of describing that response as one of pity; the fact that our responses to fictional characters (typically, at least) involve no desires of this sort simply reflects our awareness that we cannot – logically cannot – help, heal, soothe or comfort them. The desire that is necessary to pity must be construed more broadly than Charlton suggests; roughly, as a desire that things should be otherwise and better for the object of one's pity. The question that we must address here, then, is whether a desire of *this* sort is dependent on a belief that the object of one's response and his or her plight are (or were) actual. Is this a desire that we can have with respect to what we know to be a fictional character?

As I have formulated it above, it is not. I cannot desire that things should have gone differently and more happily for Anna Karenina, simply because I do not believe that Anna ever existed. However, I *can* believe that it is fictionally the case that Anna existed, and that it is fictional that she had a pretty miserable time of things. And given that I hold these beliefs, I may also desire that fictionally things should have gone differently and better for her. (It should be noted that there is nothing fictional about such a desire itself; as with beliefs about what is fictionally the case, "fictionality" attachs only to the *content* of such desires.) If I do have such a desire, and if it is founded on a belief that fictionally Anna suffered, and if the depiction of her suffering causes me to experience the feelings of distress characteristic of pity, then, I suggest, there are no good grounds for denying that my response to Anna Karenina is properly to be described as one of pity.

VI

At this point, however, it may appear that we are faced with a rather different problem.[23] For in wishing that fictionally things had gone differently for Anna, it would appear that I am in effect wishing that Tolstoy's novel had been written differently; that *Anna Karenina*, as well as Anna Karenina, were other than it is. Now I may, of course, wish just that. As a matter of fact, however, I do not; and it seems reasonable to assume that most of those who would describe themselves as pitying Mercutio or Winnie Verloc do not wish that *Romeo and Juliet* or *The Secret Agent* were other than they are. Indeed, it might plausibly be argued that to have such a desire would betoken a failing to engage with the work adequately and fully as a work of art, and hence that feeling pity for fictional characters, inasmuch as it involves having such a desire, is an inappropriate kind of response to them. Furthermore, we *value* certain works of fiction not least because they are capable of eliciting from us emotions such as pity for their characters. If responses of this sort involve our desiring that the work should be other than it is, however, we seem to be left with the very dubious conclusion that part of what we regard as valuable about certain works of fiction involves wishing that they were other than they are.

It would appear that we are faced here with two – equally unpalatable – alternatives. On the one hand, in pitying a fictional character, and hence wishing that fictionally things were otherwise with her, I also wish that the work of which she is a part were other than it is. And the fact that I have this desire suggests that my response to the work in question is in one way or another suspect. On the other hand, it may be that in pitying a fictional character I wish that fictionally things were different with her, and also want the work of which she is a part to be just as it is. And this latter scenario would appear to bring us very close to Radford's view that responses such as pity for fictional characters involve us in incoherence and irrationality. For it is logically impossible that (a) *Anna Karenina* (say) should be just as it is, *and* that (b) fictionally things should go differently for Anna Karenina. And if one cannot coherently desire what is logically impossible, our desiring both (a) and (b) above would involve us in incoherence.

However, this way of setting matters up neglects a third alternative available to us here; namely, the possibility that in pitying a fictional character we desire that fictionally things were otherwise for her, without having any desires at all with respect to the work of which she is a part. It is true that were it to be fictional that Anna escaped her fate, then *Anna Karenina* would not be the novel that it is. However, it does not follow that in *wishing* that fictionally things had gone differently for Anna, I am in effect *wishing* that Tolstoy's novel had been written differently. Similarly, even though it may be a necessary condition of my losing weight that I stop eating iced buns, my desire to lose weight is not in effect a desire to stop eating iced buns; I may desire to lose weight without having any desires with regard to iced buns at all.

The important point to recognize here is that when I feel pity for Anna, and hence wish that things could have gone differently for her, I am focusing on a particular aspect of *Anna Karenina*; roughly speaking, on the *story* that Tolstoy tells. And in focusing on this aspect, I do not have desires with respect to other aspects of the novel, such as its plot structure or its language. When I adopt a different stance toward the novel – when I consider it *as* a novel, or as a work of art, or as a part of Tolstoy's *corpus* – then my desires and my feelings are likely to change. In particular, in looking at the work from these sorts of perspective I am unlikely to have any desires with regard to Anna herself. Recognizing that we can adopt different perspectives in responding to a work of fiction, that we may focus on one or another aspect of that work, allows us to see that wishing that things were otherwise for a fictional character does not involve us in the dilemma outlined above. We can wish that things had gone differently and more happily for Anna Karenina without thereby either being involved in incoherence or responding to the novel in a fashion that is in one way or another suspect.

Recognizing this feature of our responses to fiction also allows us to bring out the truth in Hume's remark that an emotional response to fiction "lies not with that weight upon us"; to explain, that is, why it is that our emotional responses to fictional characters and events are typically (though not invariably) of shorter duration, and are often (though again not invariably) less intense, than are our emotional responses to similar actual persons and events. In responding to a work of fiction, we tend to adopt a variety of attitudes or stances toward the work; the focus of our concern shifts between various aspects of that work. Thus in watching a performance of *Lear*, I may experience a variety of more or less intense emotional responses to one or more of the characters; as the lights go up, however, my attention is forced back to the fact that what I have been watching is a *play*, and in this case a supreme work of art. And my responses then change; the focus of my attention gradually moves from Lear to *Lear*. If I am moved now, it will probably be the performance, or the play, or Shakespeare's art, that I am moved by. Similarly, when I am "caught up" in a good thriller or spy novel, my attention and affective responses will be focused on the characters and events depicted. When I put the book down, this focus shifts; I think of the work as a novel, or as the new Le Carré, or in terms of its structure. And I may now realize that my attention and responses were entirely unmerited, that what has occupied me so intensely for the last hour or so is simply not worth it. Certain writers and directors – John Fowles, for one – are able to force us continually to shift the focus of our attention from one aspect of the work to another, and the ability to make this an integral part of our experience of the work rather than an annoying distraction is one criterion of mastery of the art of fiction.

The fact that our emotional responses to fictional characters tend to be shorter in duration and less intense than our responses to actual people does not mean that we do not or cannot really *care* about fictional characters, then, nor that our beliefs or feelings or desires with respect to such characters are in some way "substandard." It rather reflects the fact that those fictional characters that we do care about are typically part of something else that also demands, and gets, our attention.

VII

At the beginning of this article I raised the possibility that certain emotions may be based on beliefs about what is fictional as well as on beliefs about what is actually the case. By way of an examination of the structure of pity, I have argued that for that emotion, at least, this is in fact the case. All those features which can plausibly be argued to be necessary to pity – certain feelings and sensations, an attitude of distress, and desire – may be involved in an affective response that is founded on beliefs about what is fictionally the case. And what has been argued here with respect to pity will also hold true with respect to certain other emotions. Just as we may properly be said to feel pity for fictional characters, I suggest, a detailed examination of the structures of the emotions in question will show that certain of our responses to fictional characters may also be properly described in terms of *schadenfreude*; that without distorting either the responses themselves or the concepts in question we may describe ourselves as envying and admiring fictional characters, and as fearing *for* and *with* them. However, we do need to be wary of generalizing here; our affective responses to fiction cannot usefully be treated monolithically, or as though they formed a homogeneous class. What has been argued here certainly does not show that *any* emotion, other than fear for oneself and jealousy, can be experienced for or about fictions. However, the discussion above strongly suggests that at least some emotions, along with pity, can be so experienced, and has demonstrated the kind of examination that is necessary if we are to get clear about this issue.

NOTES

1 See Plato's *Republic*, books III and X. Johnson's remarks on this issue are in his *Preface to Shakespeare's Plays* (Menston, England: The Scolar Press, 1969), pp. 26–8. Radford's first article on the topic was "How can we be moved by the fate of Anna Karenina?" reprinted in this book.

2 Recent versions of this theory (which goes back to Aristotle's *Rhetoric*) can be found in Anthony Kenny's *Action, Emotion and Will* (London: Routledge & Kegan Paul, 1963) and in William Lyon's *Emotion* (Cambridge University Press, 1980).

3 Gilbert Ryle, *The Concept of Mind* (Harmondsworth: Penguin Books, 1963), p. 103.

4 Malcolm Budd, *Music and the Emotions* (London: Routledge & Kegan Paul, 1985), p. 128. Similar conclusions are reached by Kenny in *Action, Emotion and Will*, p. 49, and by Kendall L. Walton in "Fearing fictions," *Journal of Philosophy* 75 (1978), 6.

5 Johnson advocates something like this in his *Preface to Shakespeare's Plays*; more recently versions of it have been advocated by Michael Weston, "How can we be moved by the fate of Anna Karenina? (II)," *Proceedings of the Aristotelian Society* supplementary volume 49 (1975); by Barrie Paskins, "On being moved by Anna Karenina and *Anna Karenina*," *Philosophy* 52 (1977); by Don Mannison, "On being moved by fiction," *Philosophy* 60 (1985); and by William Charlton, "Feelings for the fictitious," *British Journal of Aesthetics* 24 (1984).

6 As perhaps is suggested by Charlton's remark in his *Aesthetics* (London: Hutchinson, 1970) that "in general, works of art seem to affect our feelings more by putting us into a *mood* than by exciting a directed *emotion*" (p. 97).

7 Roger Scruton talks (very briefly) of "imaginary emotions" in "Fantasy, imagination and the screen," in his *The Aesthetic Understanding* (London: Methuen, 1983), p. 132. The role

of make-believe in our responses to and understanding and appreciation of fiction is a subject that Kendall Walton has made his own; see especially his *Mimesis as Make-Believe* (Cambridge, Mass.: Harvard University Press, 1990).

8 Derek Matravers offers an account of belief about what is fictionally the case in his "Who's afraid of Virginia Woolf?" *Ratio*, New Series, 4 (1991). I would emphasize that in what follows, I do not depend on any particular account of belief about fiction; I merely assume that a correct account is to be had.

9 I am not the first to consider this possibility. That affective responses grounded on beliefs about what is fictional can be emotions proper has been suggested by Eva Schaper in "Fiction and the suspension of disbelief," *British Journal of Aesthetics* 18 (1978); by R.T. Allen in "The reality of responses to fiction," *British Journal of Aesthetics* 26 (1986); and most recently by Derek Matravers in "Who's afraid of Virginia Woolf?" As should become clear, I am broadly speaking in agreement with their conclusion, but take a rather different route in reaching it.

10 Bijoy Boruah, *Fiction and Emotion* (Oxford University Press, 1988), pp. 60–3 and 68–70.

11 Flint Schier, "The claims of tragedy: an essay in moral psychology and aesthetic theory," *Philosophical Papers* 18 (1989), 13.

12 Boruah, *Fiction and Emotion*, p. 64. B.J. Rosebury makes a similar point in "Fiction, emotion and 'belief': a reply to Eva Schaper," *British Journal of Aesthetics* 19 (1979), 121–4.

13 In *Mimesis and Make-Believe* Kendall Walton argues that it may be fictional that I *believe* that I am threatened by a fictional character, if in responding to the work of which it is a part I play a game of make-believe using the work as a "prop." In which case, Walton argues, it may be fictionally rather than actually the case that I am afraid of the character. I have discussed Walton's account in my "Fear, fiction and make-believe," *Journal of Aesthetics and Art Criticism* 49 (1991), 47–56.

14 David Hume, *A Treatise of Human Nature*, ed. L.A. Selby-Bigge, 2nd edn, rev. by P.H. Nidditch (Oxford University Press, 1978), p. 631.

15 As is argued by George Pitcher, "Emotion," *Mind* 74 (1965); by Errol Bedford, "Emotions," *Proceedings of the Aristotelian Society* 57 (1956–7); and by William Alston, "Emotion and feeling," *Encyclopedia of Philosophy* vol. 2 (New York: Macmillan and The Free Press, 1967).

16 Hume, *A Treatise of Human Nature*, p. 631.

17 Hume, "Of tragedy."

18 Flint Schier, "Tragedy and the community of sentiment," in Peter Lamarque, ed., *Philosophy and Fiction* (Aberdeen University Press, 1983), p. 76.

19 The account that Schier began to develop in the two articles cited above is more successful in this respect than any other I have seen.

20 Charlton, "Feelings for the fictitious," p. 206. Similarly, Robert Solomon suggests that central to pity is a desire "to soothe, heal, or at least comfort the other." Solomon, *The Passions* (Notre Dame: University of Notre Dame Press, 1983), p. 344.

21 Indeed, the fact that emotions may function as motives to behavior is explained partly by the fact that they often involve desires of this sort in addition to beliefs and feelings and sensations.

22 My distress may also be expressed in a wish that I *could* help them (which of course is not the same as a desire *to* help them), but it need not be. Nor, *pace* Charlton (in "Feelings for the fictitious"), need my response involve a desire of the form, "Were anyone that I *could* help in Lady Jane Grey's situation, would that I might help them!"

23 I am very grateful to Aaron Ridley for pointing this out to me. A very illuminating discussion of this issue, to which I owe a great deal, can be found in his paper "Desire in the experience of fiction," *Philosophy and Literature* 16 (1992). This is a good place also to thank Curtis Brown and Marianne Melling for their help.

SUGGESTIONS FOR FURTHER READING

General background on emotion
Alston, William (1967) "Emotion and feeling", *Encyclopedia of Philosophy*, vol. 2. New York: Macmillan and The Free Press.
Lyons, William (1980) *Emotion*. Cambridge: Cambridge University Press.
Roberts, Robert C. (1988) "What an emotion is: a sketch", *Philosophical Review* 97: 183–209.
Solomon, Robert C. (1986) *The Passions*, New York: Doubleday.

On our emotional responses to fiction
Boruah, Bijoy (1988) *Fiction and Emotion*, Oxford: Clarendon Press.
Carroll, Noël (1990) *The Philosophy of Horror, or Paradoxes of the Heart*, London: Routledge. (See especially chapter 2.)
Charlton, William (1984) "Feelings for the fictitious", *British Journal of Aesthetics* 24: 206–16.
Currie, Gregory (1990) *The Nature of Fiction*, Cambridge: Cambridge University Press, chapter 5.
Dadlez, E.M. (1997) *What's Hecuba To Him?*, University Park: Pennsylvania State University Press.
Feagin, Susan L. (1996) *Reading With Feeling*, Ithaca and London: Cornell University Press.
Hanfling, Oswald (1983) "Real life, art and the grammar of feeling", *Philosophy* 63: 237–43.
Lamarque, Peter (1981) "How can we fear and pity fictions?", *British Journal of Aesthetics* 21: 291–304.
Levinson, Jerrold (1990) "The place of real emotion in response to fictions", *Journal of Aesthetics and Art Criticism* 48: 79–80.
Mannison, Don (1985) "On being moved by fiction", *Philosophy* 60: 71–87.
Mounce, H. O. (1980) "Art and real life", *Philosophy* 55: 183–90.
—— (1985) "Hanfling and Radford on art and real life", *Philosophy* 60: 127–8.
Neill, Alex (1991) "Fear, fiction and make-believe", *Journal of Aesthetics and Art Criticism* 49: 47–56.
—— (1995) "Emotional responses to fiction: a reply to Radford", *Journal of Aesthetics and Art Criticism* 53: 75–8.
Novitz, David (1980) "Fiction, imagination and emotion", *Journal of Aesthetics and Art Criticism* 38: 279–88.
Paskins, Barrie (1977) "On being moved by Anna Karenina and *Anna Karenina*", *Philosophy* 52: 344–7.
Radford, Colin (1977) "Tears and fiction", *Philosophy* 52: 208–13. (Response to Weston.)
—— (1979) "The essential Anna", *Philosophy* 54: 390–4. (Response to Paskins.)
—— (1982) "Philosophers and their monstrous thoughts", *British Journal of Aesthetics* 22: 261–3. (Response to Lamarque.)
—— (1982) "Stuffed tigers: a reply to H.O. Mounce", *Philosophy* 57: 529–32.
—— (1995) "Fiction, pity, fear and jealousy", *Journal of Aesthetics and Art Criticism* 53: 71–5.
Ridley, Aaron (1992) "Desire in the experience of fiction", *Philosophy and Literature* 16: 279–92.
Walton, Kendall. "Fearing fictions", *Journal of Philosophy* 75: 5–27.
—— (1978) "How remote are fictional worlds from the real world?", *Journal of Aesthetics and Art Criticism* 37: 11–23.
—— (1990) *Mimesis as Make-Believe*, Cambridge: Harvard University Press. (Especially relevant are chapters 5–7.)
—— (1997) "Spelunking, simulation and slime", in Mette Hjort and Sue Laver (eds) *Emotion and the Arts*, New York: Oxford University Press. (This volume contains a number of useful essays on the topic.)
Weston, Michael (1975) "How can we be moved by the fate of Anna Karenina?", *Proceedings of the Aristotelian Society* supplementary volume 49: 81–93.
Yanal, Robert (1999) *Paradoxes of Emotion and Fiction*, University Park: Pennsylvania State University Press.

Part 8

ENJOYING HORROR

I recognise terror as the finest emotion and so I will try to terrorise the reader. But if I find that I cannot terrify, I will try to horrify, and if I find that I cannot horrify, I'll go for the gross-out.

Stephen King, *Danse Macabre*, pp. 22-3

It seems an unaccountable pleasure which the spectators of a well-written tragedy receive from sorrow, terror, anxiety, and other passions that are in themselves disagreeable and uneasy. The more they are touched and affected, the more are they delighted with the spectacle; and as soon as the uneasy passions cease to operate, the piece is at an end. . . . The whole art of the poet is employed on rousing and supporting the compassion and indignation, the anxiety and resentment, of his audience. They are pleased in proportion as they are afflicted, and never are so happy as when they employ tears, sobs, and cries, to give vent to their sorrow, and relieve their heart, swoln with the tenderest sympathy and compassion.

David Hume, "Of tragedy"

IT IS A REMARKABLE FACT THAT works of horror – primarily in the form of films, novels and short stories – are as immensely popular as they are. For works of this sort have at least one feature in common: they are designed to produce a certain sort of reaction in their audiences – in short, to horrify. The better a work of this sort is, the more effectively it horrifies its audience.

But if this is true, we might ask why it is that works of this sort *have* an audience. For although there might be room for disagreement about just what sort of response "horror" is, it seems clear that it is not what might be called a positive emotion. Noël Carroll, for example, in the book from which the first chapter in this part is excerpted, characterizes it as involving a mixture of physical agitation, fear, and revulsion or disgust. And if we know that watching a film or reading a book or listening to a story is going to result in our feeling *that* sort of thing, why do any of us put ourselves through the experience? Again, then, why is it that there is an audience for horror?

This question concerning works of horror and our experience of them is analogous to – indeed, some might argue that it is just a version of – a much older question concerning our experience of works of tragedy. In the *Poetics*, Aristotle suggests that the function of tragedy is to give us a particular sort of pleasure. But the way in which he characterizes this pleasure looks very odd: "the tragic pleasure", he says, "is that of fear and pity". Part of what makes this odd is that in another work, the *Rhetoric*, Aristotle defines fear as "a *pain* or disturbance due to a mental picture of some destructive or painful event in the future", and pity as "*a feeling of pain* caused by the sight of some evil, destructive or painful, which befalls one who does not deserve it and which we might expect to befall ourselves or some friends of ours." So Aristotle holds that the emotions of pity and fear involve *painful* feelings. What can he mean, then, when he speaks of the *pleasure* of fear and pity? Assuming that the audiences of tragedies are typically not masochists, how is it that they can take pleasure in works that arouse in them painful or distressing responses?

In the first chapter in this part, Noël Carroll draws on some eighteenth-century discussions of the nature of our experience of tragedy to develop a theory of the appeal of works of horror. These works retain their audience, he suggests, because they provide us not only with experiences of revulsion and disgust, but also with pleasure, and specifically pleasure which derives from our engagement with their narrative structures. In Carroll's view, these stories of monsters, the uncanny, and the supernatural arouse our curiosity and interest, and are structured in ways that make the engagement and satisfaction of that curiosity and interest pleasurable. At the same time, however, given the subject matter of horror – what it is that we are interested *in* and curious *about* as we follow these stories – feelings of horror (fear, revulsion, disgust, and so on) are inevitable. The feelings of revulsion and horror that the works arouse are not *themselves* enjoyable, however, but are "the price to be paid" for the pleasure that we get from the engagement of our interest and curiosity.

Berys Gaut, in his chapter, disagrees. Gaut argues that part of what is puzzling about the audience of horror films and stories is precisely that this audience seems to take pleasure in the experience of what we ordinarily regard as "negative emotions" – that they appear to enjoy being frightened, disgusted and so on. In this Gaut echoes David Hume, who 250 years ago began his essay "Of tragedy "with the observation "It seems an unaccountable pleasure, which the spectators of a well-written tragedy receive from sorrow, terror, anxiety, and other passions, that are in themselves disagreeable and uneasy." According to Hume and to Gaut, that is, the apparently negative feelings aroused by works of tragedy and horror are not a negative *accompaniment* of pleasure, as Carroll holds, but are themselves somehow the *source* of the pleasure in question. This fact, if it is indeed a fact, clearly raises questions about the psychology of the audiences of horror and of tragedy, but it also raises questions about the nature and logic of the emotions, some of which Gaut takes up in the second half of his chapter.

Why do so many of us enjoy horror films and stories? How similar is our experience of works of this sort to our experience of works of tragedy, and for that matter to our experience of works of music which make us sad but which we value nonetheless? And does what we are asking here primarily concern human psychology or the forms of art in question? The questions raised in this part address one of the most enduring issues in the philosophy of art.

17

WHY HORROR?

Noël Carroll

In the ordinary course of affairs, people shun what disgusts them. Being repulsed by something that one finds to be loathsome and impure is an unpleasant experience. We do not, for example, attempt to add some pleasure to a boring afternoon by opening the lid of a steamy trash can in order to savor its unwholesome stew of broken bits of meat, moldering fruits and vegetables, and noxious, unrecognizable clumps, riven thoroughly by all manner of crawling things. And, ordinarily, checking out hospital waste bags is not our idea of a good time. But, on the other hand, many people – so many, in fact, that we must concede that they are normal, at least in the statistical sense – do seek out horror fictions for the purpose of deriving pleasure from sights and descriptions that customarily repulse them.

In short, there appears to be something paradoxical about the horror genre. It obviously attracts consumers; but it seems to do so by means of the expressly repulsive. Furthermore, the horror genre gives every evidence of being pleasurable to its audience, but it does so by means of trafficking in the very sorts of things that cause disquiet, distress, and displeasure. So different ways of clarifying the question "Why horror?" are to ask: "Why are horror audiences attracted by what, typically (in everyday life), should (and would) repel them?," or "How can horror audiences find pleasure in what by nature is distressful and unpleasant?"

In what follows, I will attempt to find a comprehensive or general answer to the question of what attracts audiences to the horror genre. That is, I shall try to frame a set of hypotheses that will supply a plausible explanation of the attracting power of horror in its many manifestations across the different centuries and decades, and across the different subgenres and media in which horror is practiced. However, in this regard it is important to emphasize that, though a general account of horror may be advanced, this does not preclude the possibility that it can be supplemented by additional accounts of why a particular horror novel or film, a particular horror subgenre, or a particular cycle within the history of horror also has some special levers of attraction over and above those that are generic to the mode of horror. That is, an explanation of basic pleasures or attractions of the horror mode is compatible with *additional* explanations of why, for example, *Rosemary's Baby* exercises its own particular fascination; of how werewolf stories, while sharing the allures of ghost stories and other horrific tales, have allures of their own; and of why horror cycles, like the Hollywood movie cycle of the thirties, gain attractive power by thematically developing concerns of especial appropriateness for the period in which they were made. . . .

The need to account for the peculiar nature of horror had already begun to strike writers in the eighteenth century. John and Anna Laetitia Aikin, in their essay "On the Pleasure Derived From Objects of Terror," write that ". . . the apparent delight with which we dwell upon objects of pure terror, where our moral feelings are not in the least concerned and no passion seems to be excited but the depressing one of fear, is a paradox of the heart . . . difficult of solution."[1] This question, of course, was not unique to tales of terror and horror. At roughly the same time, Hume published his "Of Tragedy," wherein he seeks to explain how the audiences of such dramas are "pleased in proportion as they are afflicted."[2] Hume, in turn, cites Jean-Baptiste Dubos and Bernard Le Bovier Fontenelle as earlier theoreticians concerned with the problem of how pleasure is to be derived from that which is distressful, while the Aikins themselves tackle this general problem in their "An Enquiry into those Kinds of Distress which excite agreeable Sensations."[3] And with reference to the sublime and objects of terror, Edmund Burke attempts to account for the way in which pain can give rise to delight in Part IV, Section V of his *A Philosophical Enquiry into the Origin of our ideas of the Sublime and Beautiful.*[4] Thus, the paradox of horror is an instance of a larger problem, viz., that of explaining the way in which the artistic presentation of normally aversive events and objects can give rise to pleasure or can compel our interests. . . . That is, encountering things such as ghosts or Desdemona's massacre in "real life" would be upsetting rather than entertaining. And, of course, what is disgusting on-screen or on the page is genuinely disgusting. It is something that we would ordinarily seek to avert. So why do we seek it in art and fiction? How does it give us pleasure and/or why does it interest us?

In order to answer these questions, I think that it is quite helpful to return to some of the very authors who first asked them – specifically, Hume and the Aikins – to see what they have to say. I will undoubtedly have to modify and amplify their accounts. However, a review of their thoughts will serve to orient us toward what I believe is at least part of a comprehensive answer to the paradox of horror. . . .

Speaking of the presentation of melancholy events by orators, Hume notes that the pleasure derived is not a response to the event as such, but to its rhetorical framing. When we turn to tragedy, plotting performs this function. The interest that we take in the deaths of Hamlet, Gertrude, Claudius, et al. is not sadistic, but is an interest that the plot has engendered in how certain forces, once put in motion, will work themselves out. Pleasure derives from having our interest in the outcome of such questions satisfied.

Hume writes:

> Had you any intention to move a person extremely by the narration of any event, the best method of increasing its effect would be artfully to delay informing him of it, and first to excite his curiosity and impatience before you let him into the secret. This is the artifice practiced by Iago in the famous scene of Shakespeare; and every spectator is sensible, that Othello's jealousy acquires additional force from his preceding impatience, and that the subordinate passion is here readily transformed into the predominant one.[5]

Hume's idea is that once a tragic, unsettling event is housed in an aesthetic context, with a momentum of its own, the predominant feeling response, in terms of pleasure and interest, attaches to the presentation as a function of the overall, narrative structure. That is, the ostensibly "subordinate passion," but the one keyed to the structure, becomes predominant. Hume notes:

> These instances (and many more might be collected) are sufficient to afford us some insight into the analogy of nature, and to show us, that the pleasure which poets, orators, and musicians give us, by exciting grief, sorrow, indignation, compassion, is not so extraordinary or paradoxical as it may at first sight appear. The force of imagination, the energy of expression, the power of numbers, the charms of imitation; all these are naturally, of themselves delightful to the mind: and when the object presented lays also hold of some affection, the pleasure rises upon us by the conversion of this subordinate movement into that which is predominant. The passion, though perhaps naturally, and when excited by the simple appearance of a real object, it may be painful; yet is so smoothed and softened, and mollified, when realised by the finer arts that it affords the highest entertainment.[6]

With tragedy, the "affection" Hume thinks takes hold is narrative expectation, which certainly harkens back to Aristotle's observations about the audience's anticipation of recognition and reversal in plays of that sort. Thus, it is not the tragic event in itself that imparts pleasure, but rather, the way it is worked into the plot.

Similarly, the Aikins look to the plot, in large measure, to account for the interest and pleasure taken in the objects of terror.[7] They think the question may be stated badly if we attempt to account for the pleasure derived from terror fictions solely in terms of saying how the objects – monsters, for our purposes – are attractive or pleasurable for their own sake. They write (in the first person, singular):

> How are we then to account for the pleasure derived from such objects? I have often been led to imagine that there is a deception in these cases; and that the avidity with

277

which we attend is not a proof of our receiving real pleasure. The pain of suspense, and the irresistible desire of satisfying our curiosity, when once raised, will account for our eagerness to go quite through an adventure, though we suffer actual pain during the whole course of it. We rather chuse to suffer the smart pang of a violent emotion than the uneasy craving of an unsatisfied desire. That this principle, in many instances, may involuntarily carry us through what we dislike, I am convinced from experience.[8]

One need not buy everything that Hume and the Aikins assert wholesale. I, personally, doubt that suspense is aptly described as painful, while the mechanics of Hume's transition of a subordinate passion to a predominant one are somewhat unfathomable, if not wrong (since the tragedy of the event and our predictably distressed reaction to it seems to me to be an inseparable element of the narration). However, their shared notion, that the aesthetic contrivance of normally upsetting events depends upon their contextualization in structures like narrative, is particularly suggestive with respect to the paradox of horror.

For . . . a great deal of the horror genre is narrative. Indeed, I think it is fair to say that in our culture, horror thrives above all as a narrative form. Thus, in order to account for the interest we take in and the pleasure we take from horror, we may hypothesize that, in the main, the locus of our gratification is not the monster as such but the whole narrative structure in which the presentation of the monster is staged. This, of course, is not to say that the monster is in any way irrelevant to the genre, nor that the interest and pleasure in the genre could be satisfied through and/or substituted by any old narrative. For, as I have argued earlier, the monster is a functional ingredient in the type of narratives found in horror stories, and not all narratives function exactly like horror narratives.

As we saw in my analysis of horror narratives, these stories, with great frequency, revolve around proving, disclosing, discovering, and confirming the existence of something that is impossible, something that defies standing conceptual schemes. It is part of such stories – contrary to our everyday beliefs about the nature of things – that such monsters exist. And as a result, audiences' expectations revolve around whether this existence will be confirmed in the story.

Often this is achieved, as Hume says of narrative "secrets" in general, by putting off the conclusive information that the monster exists for quite a while. Sometimes this information may be deferred till the very end of the fiction. And even where this information is given to the audience right off the bat, it is still generally the case that the human characters in the tale must undergo a process of discovering that the monster exists, which, in turn, may lead to a further process of confirming that discovery in an ensuing scene or series of scenes. That is, the question of whether or not the monster exists may be transformed into the question of whether and when the human characters in the tale will establish the existence of the monster. Horror stories are often protracted series of discoveries: first the reader learns of the monster's existence, then some characters do, then some more characters do and so on; the drama of iterated disclosure – albeit to different parties – underwrites much horror fiction.[9]

Even in overreacher plots, there is a question of whether the monsters exist – i.e., of whether they can be summoned, in the case of demons, or of whether they can be created by mad scientists and necromancers. Furthermore, even after the existence of the monster is disclosed, the audience continues to crave further information about its nature, its identity, its origin, its purposes, and its astounding powers and properties, including, ultimately, those of its weaknesses that *may* enable humanity to do it in.

Thus, to a large extent, the horror story is driven explicitly by curiosity. It engages its audience by being involved in processes of disclosure, discovery, proof, explanation, hypothesis, and confirmation. Doubt, skepticism, and the fear that belief in the existence of the monster is a form of insanity are predictable foils to the revelation (to the audience or to the characters or both) of the existence of the monster.

Horror stories, in a significant number of cases, are dramas of proving the existence of the monster and disclosing (most often gradually) the origin, identity, purposes and powers of the monster. Monsters, as well, are obviously a perfect vehicle for engendering this kind of curiosity and for supporting the drama of proof, because monsters are (physically, though generally not logically) impossible beings. . . . Many monsters of the horror genre are interstitial and/or contradictory in terms of being both living and dead: ghosts, zombies, vampires, mummies, the Frankenstein monster, Melmoth the Wanderer, and so on. Near relatives to these are monstrous entities that conflate the animate and the inanimate: haunted houses, with malevolent wills of their own, robots, and the car in King's *Christine*. Also many monsters confound different species: werewolves, humanoid insects, humanoid reptiles, and the inhabitants of Dr. Moreau's island.

Or, consider the conflation of species in these descriptions of the monster in Lovecraft's "The Dunwich Horror":

> Bigger'n a barn . . . all made o' squirmin ropes . . . hull thing sort o' shaped like a hen's egg bigger'n anything, with dozens o' legs like hogsheads that haff shut up when they step . . . nothin' solid abaout it – all like jelly, an' made o' sep'rit wrigglin' ropes pushed clost together . . . great bulgin' eyes all over it . . . ten or twenty maouths or trunks a-stickn' aout all along the sides, big as stovepipes, an'a-tossin' an' openin' an' shuttin' . . . all, with kinder blue or purple rings . . . *an' Gawd in Heaven – that haff face on top! . . .*

And:

> *Oh, oh, my Gawd, that haff face – that haff face on top of it . . . that face with the red eyes an' crinkly albino hair, an' no chin, like the Whateleys. . . . It was a octopus,*

279

centipede, spider kindo' thing, but they was a haff-shaped man's face on top of it,
an' it looked like Wizard Whateley's, only it was yards an'yards acrost. . . .

The creature in Howard Hawks's classic *The Thing* is an intelligent, two-legged, bloodsucking carrot. Now that's interstitial. Indeed, the frequent resort to referring to monsters by means of pronouns like "It" and "Them" suggests that these creatures are not classifiable according to our standing categories.[10] Moreover, this interpretation is also supported by the frequency with which monsters in horror are said to be indescribable or inconceivable. Recall . . . movie titles like *The Creeping Unknown*; while sometimes Frankenstein's creation is referred to as the "monster with no name." Again, the point would appear to be that these monsters fit neither the conceptual scheme of the characters nor, more importantly, that of the reader.

Horrific monsters often involve the mixture of what is normally distinct. Demonically possessed characters typically involve the superimposition of two categorically distinct individuals, the possessee and the possessor, the latter usually a demon, who, in turn, is often a categorically transgressive figure (e.g., a goat–god). Stevenson's most famous monster is two men, Jekyll and Hyde, where Hyde is described as having a simian aspect which makes him appear not quite human.[11] Werewolves mix man and wolf, while shape changers of other sorts compound humans with other species. The monster in King's *It* is a kind of categorically contradictory creature raised to a higher power. For It is a monster that can change into any other monster, those other monsters already being categorically transgressive. And, of course, some monsters, like the scorpion big enough to eat Mexico City, are magnifications of creatures and crawling things already ajudged impure and interstitial in the culture.

Categorical incompleteness is also a standard feature of the monsters of horror; ghosts and zombies frequently come without eyes, arms, legs, or skin, or they are in some advanced state of disintegration. And, in a related vein, detached body parts are serviceable monsters, severed heads and especially hands, e.g., de Maupassant's "The Hand" and "The Withered Hand," Le Fanu's "The Narrative of a Ghost of a Hand," Golding's "The Call of the Hand," Conan Doyle's "The Brown Hand," Nerval's "The Enchanted Hand," Dreiser's "The Hand," William Harvey's "The Beast With Five Fingers" and so on. A brain in a vat is the monster in the novel *Donovan's Brain* by Curt Siodmak, which has been adapted for the screen more than once, while in the film *Fiend Without a Face* the monsters are brains that use their spinal cords as tails.

The rate of recurrence with which the biologies of monsters are vaporous or gelatinous attests to the applicability of the notion of formlessness to horrific impurity while the writing style of certain horror authors, such as Lovecraft, at times, and Straub, through their vague, suggestive, and often inchoate descriptions of the monsters, leaves an impression of formlessness. Indeed, many monsters are literally formless: the man-eating oil slick in King's short story "The Raft," the malevolent entity in James Herbert's

The Fog and *The Dark*, in Matthew Phipps Shiel's *The Purple Cloud*, in Joseph Payne Brennan's novella "Slime," in Kate Wilhelm's and Ted Thomas's *The Clone*, and the monsters in movies like *The Blob* (both versions) and *The Stuff*.[12]

[Monsters thus] arouse interest and attention through being putatively inexplicable or highly unusual vis-à-vis our standing cultural categories, thereby instilling a desire to learn and to know about them. And since they are also outside of (justifiably) prevailing definitions of what is, they understandably prompt a need for proof (or the fiction of a proof) in the face of skepticism. Monsters are, then, natural subjects for curiosity, and they straightforwardly warrant the ratiocinative energies the plot lavishes upon them.

All narratives might be thought to involve the desire to know – the desire to know at least the outcome of the interaction of the forces made salient in the plot. However, the horror fiction is a special variation on this general narrative motivation, because it has at the center of it something which is given as in principle *unknowable* – something which, *ex hypothesi*, cannot, given the structure of our conceptual scheme, exist and that cannot have the properties it has. This is why, so often, the real drama in a horror story resides in establishing the existence of the monster and in disclosing its horrific properties. Once this is established, the monster, generally, has to be confronted, and the narrative is driven by the question of whether the creature can be destroyed. However, even at this point, the drama of ratiocination can continue as further discoveries – accompanied by arguments, explanations, and hypotheses – reveal features of the monster that will facilitate or impede the destruction of the creature.

To illustrate this briefly, let us consider Colin Wilson's novel *The Mind Parasites*. The story is presented as a compilation of the chronicle of humanity's confrontation with the mind parasites. This chronicle has been drawn from a number of sources. So, from the perspective of the order of the presentation of the fiction, it begins with the presupposition that the mind parasites – called Tsathogguans – exist. But the exposition proceeds by laying end to end successive discoveries of the existence of these creatures, among other things (such as the discovery of the ruins of an ancient city – a red herring, as it turns out). The major character, Gilbert Austin, first discovers his friend's – Karel Weissman's – discovery of the Tsathogguans, which itself comprises a narrative of discovery. Austin then goes through his own process of discovery. In the course of both discoveries the possibility that the discoverer is insane has to be disposed. Austin then proceeds to convince his colleague Reich of the existence of the mind parasites; this is not difficult, but it allows for more ratiocination and the compiling of a little more evidence.

Austin and Reich then impart their discoveries to a select group of other scientists, many of whom are killed by the mind parasites. But enough survive to share their discoveries eventually with the President of the United States. The plot, in other words, proceeds by means of the revelation of the existence of the Tsathogguans to increasingly larger groups of people. But even when Austin has secured sufficient government aid to confront the mind parasites, further discoveries are mandated by the story. Austin says:

> It was maddeningly frustrating. We possessed the great secret; we had warned the world. And yet, in a fundamental sense, we were as ignorant as ever. Who were these creatures? Where did they come from? What was their ultimate aim? Were they really intelligent, or were they as unintelligent as the maggots in a piece of cheese?

Of course, the reader wants to know the answers to these questions as well, and we stay on board to get them till the end of the plot. Moreover, it is not until then that we learn of the properties of the Tsathogguans (and their relations to the Moon) that make possible their final destruction.

The Mind Parasites contains a great deal more "philosophizing" than many horror fictions, employing a somewhat mystical brand of phenomenology as a weapon against the Tsathogguans in a way that ought to provoke Husserl's return from the dead. But by virtue of being what might be called a narrative of continuous revelation or disclosure, it is representative of a large body of horror fictions.

What is revealed and disclosed, of course, are monsters and their properties. These are appropriate objects of discovery and revelation, just because they are unknown – not only in the sense that the murderer in a detective fiction is unknown, but also because they are outside the bounds of knowledge, i.e., outside our standing conceptual schemes. This, as well, accounts for why their revelation and the disclosure of their properties is so often bound up in processes of proof, hypothesis, argument, explanation (including sci-fi flights of fancy and magical lore about mythological realms, potions, and incantations), and confirmation. That is, because horror fictions are predicated on the revelation of unknown and unknowable – unbelievable and incredible – impossible beings, they often take the form of narratives of discovery and proof. For things unknown in the way of monsters obviously are natural subjects for proof.

Applied to the paradox of horror, these observations suggest that the pleasure derived from the horror fiction and the source of our interest in it resides, first and foremost, in the processes of discovery, proof, and confirmation that horror fictions often employ. The disclosure of the existence of the horrific being and of its properties is the central source of pleasure in the genre; once that process of revelation is consummated, we remain inquisitive about whether such a creature can be successfully confronted, and that narrative question sees us through to the end of the story. Here, the pleasure involved is, broadly speaking, cognitive. Hobbes, interestingly, thought of curiosity as an appetite of the mind; with the horror fiction, that appetite is whetted by the prospect of knowing the putatively unknowable, and then satisfied through a continuous process of revelation, enhanced by imitations of (admittedly simplistic) proofs, hypotheses, counterfeits of causal reasoning, and explanations whose details and movement intrigue the mind in ways analogous to genuine ones.[13]

Moreover, it should be clear that these particular cognitive pleasures, insofar as they are set in motion by the relevant kind of unknowable beings, are especially well served by horrific monsters. Thus, there is a special functional relationship between the beings that mark off the horror genre and the pleasure and interest that many horror fictions sustain. That interest and that pleasure derive from the disclosure of unknown and impossible beings, just the sorts of things that seem to call for proof, discovery, and confirmation. Therefore, the disgust that such beings evince might be seen as part of the price to be paid for the pleasure of their disclosure. That is, the narrative expectation that the horror genre puts in place is that the being whose existence is in question be something that defies standing cultural categories; thus, disgust, so to say, is itself more or less mandated by the kind of curiosity that the horror narrative puts in place. The horror narrative could not deliver a successful, affirmative answer to its presiding question unless the disclosure of the monster indeed elicited disgust, or was of the sort that was a highly probable object of disgust.

That is, there is a strong relation of consilience between the objects of art-horror, on the one hand, and the revelatory plotting on the other. The kind of plots and the subjects of horrific revelation are not merely compatible, but fit together or agree in a way that is highly appropriate. That the audience is naturally inquisitive about that which is unknown meshes with plotting that is concerned to render the unknown known by processes of discovery, explanation, proof, hypothesis, confirmation, and so on.

Of course, what it means to say that the horrific being is "unknown" here is that it is not accommodated by standing conceptual schemes. Moreover, if Mary Douglas's account of impurity is correct, things that violate our conceptual scheme, by (for example) being interstitial, are things that we are prone to find disturbing. Thus, that horrific beings are predictably objects of loathing and revulsion is a function of the ways they violate our classificatory scheme.

If what is of primary importance about horrific creatures is that their very impossibility vis à vis our conceptual categories is what makes them function so compellingly in dramas of discovery and confirmation, then their disclosure, insofar as they are categorical violations, will be attached to some sense of disturbance, distress, and disgust. Consequently, the role of the horrific creature in such narratives – where their disclosure captures our interest and delivers pleasure – will simultaneously mandate some probable revulsion. That is, in order to reward our interest by the disclosure of the putatively impossible beings of the plot, said beings ought to be disturbing, distressing, and repulsive in the way that theorists like Douglas predict phenomena that ill fit cultural classifications will be.

So, as a first approximation of resolving the paradox of horror, we may conjecture that we are attracted to the majority of horror fictions because of the way that the plots of discovery and the dramas of proof pique our curiosity, and abet our interest, ideally satisfying them in a way that is pleasurable.[14] But if narrative curiosity about impossible beings is to be satisfied through disclosure, that process must require some element of probable disgust since such impossible beings are, *ex hypothesi*, disturbing, distressful, and repulsive.

One way of making the point is to say that the monsters in such tales of disclosure have to be disturbing, distressful, and repulsive, if the process of their discovery is to be rewarding in a pleasurable way. Another way to get at this is to say that the primary pleasure that narratives of disclosure afford – i.e., the interest we take in them, and the source of their attraction – resides in the processes of discovery, the play of proof, and the dramas of ratiocination that comprise them. It is not that we crave disgust, but that disgust is a predictable concomitant of disclosing the unknown, whose disclosure is a desire the narrative instills in the audience and then goes on to gladden. Nor will that desire be satisfied unless the monster defies our conception of nature which demands that it probably engender some measure of repulsion.

In this interpretation of horror narratives, the majority of which would appear to exploit the cognitive attractions of the drama of disclosure, experiencing the emotion of art-horror is not our absolutely primary aim in consuming horror fictions, even though it is a determining feature for identifying membership in the genre. Rather, art-horror is the price we are willing to pay for the revelation of that which is impossible and unknown, of that which violates our conceptual schema. The impossible being does disgust; but that disgust is part of an overall narrative address which is not only pleasurable, but whose potential pleasure depends on the confirmation of the existence of the monster as a being that violates, defies, or problematizes standing cultural classifications. Thus, we are attracted to, and many of us seek out, horror fictions of this sort despite the fact that they provoke disgust, because that disgust is required for the pleasure involved in engaging our curiosity in the unknown and drawing it into the processes of revelation, ratiocination, etc.

One objection to this line of conjecture is to point out that many of the kinds of plot structures found in horror fiction can be found in other genres. The play of discovery and confirmation, supported by ratiocination, can be found in detective thrillers. And the plots of the disaster movies of the first half of the seventies often also look like horror plots; but instead of ghouls and vampires calling for discovery and confirmation, potential earthquakes, avalanches, floods, and simmering electrical systems are the culprits.

Of course, with detective stones and disaster films, the evil that is disclosed is not impossible nor, in principle, unknown. This not only means that these narratives do not characteristically cause disgust, but that there is a qualitative difference in the kind of curiosity they invite and reward. My point here is not that one kind of curiosity is higher or lower than another kind; but only that there can be different kinds of curiosity engaged by plot structures that at a certain level of abstract description look formally equivalent, in terms of their major movements. However, it is one thing to be curious about the unknown but natural, and another thing to be curious about the impossible. And it is the latter form of curiosity in which horror fictions typically traffic.

Two other, I think, deeper objections to the preceding hypotheses about the paradox of horror are:

1   So far the conjecture only deals with horror narratives, indeed, only with horror narratives of a certain sort – namely those involving such elements as discovery, confirmation, disclosure, revelation, explanation, hypothesis, ratiocination, etc. *But* there are instances of the horror genre, e.g., paintings, that need not involve narrative; *and* there are, according to my review of characteristic horror plots, horror narratives that don't involve these elements. There may be, for example, pure onset or pure confrontation plots. Moreover, earlier hypotheses about the paradox of horror were rejected because they were not sufficiently comprehensive. But since there are instances of horror that are not narrative and since there may be horror narratives that do not deploy the elements of disclosure so far identified as the central source of attraction to horror, this conjecture must be rejected as failing its own standards of generality.

2   This conjecture seems to make the experience of being horrified too remote from the experience of the genre. The revulsion we feel at the horrific being is too detached from the source of attraction we find in the genre. This is peculiar, since it is the emotion of art-horror that differentiates the genre. Indeed, it is very often the expectation that a given fiction is defined by this emotion that leads us to select it over candidates from other genres. So one seems justified in supposing that what makes the genre special must have some intimate connection with what draws audiences to seek it out especially. But the account, thus far, falters in this respect.

The first criticism is absolutely on target about the limitations of my hypothesis *in its present state*. My view is not yet sufficiently comprehensive. The horror genre includes examples, like photographs and paintings, that do not involve sustained narration, especially sustained narration of the particular sort I have emphasized; and, there are horror narratives of the pure onset or pure confrontation variety that do not offer audiences the refined and sometimes intricately articulated stratagems of disclosure referred to above. However, I do not regard these observations as decisive counter-examples to my approach, but rather as an opportunity to deepen and expand it, indeed in ways that will also enable me to handle the second of the objections in the course of adjusting my position in order to accommodate the first objection.

I do think that the best account that can be given of the paradox of horror for the *majority* of works of horrific art will be very much like the one that I have already offered. However, it is true that it fails to cover non-narrative horror and horror fictions little concerned with the drama of disclosure. To deal with these cases more needs to be said; but the more-that-needs-to-be-said fits with what has already been said in a way that enriches while also extending the theory developed so far.

Central to my approach has been the idea that the objects of horror are fundamentally linked with cognitive interests, most notably with curiosity. The plotting gambits of disclosure/discovery narratives play with, expand, sustain, and develop this initial cognitive appetite in many directions. And as well, this is the way in which horror fictions usually go.

But it would be a mistake to think that this curiosity is *solely* a function of plotting, even if the plotting of certain types of fictions – namely those concerned with disclosure – brings it to its highest pitch. For the objects of art-horror in and of themselves engender curiosity as well. This is why they can support the kind of disclosure plots referred to above. Consequently, even if it is true that horrific curiosity is best expatiated upon within disclosure plots, and that, in its most frequent and compelling cases, it does mobilize such plots, it is also true that it can be abetted and rewarded without the narrative contextualization of disclosure/discovery plotting. Thus, it can be the case that while horror is most often, and perhaps most powerfully and most primarily, developed within narrative contexts of disclosure, it may also obtain in non-narrative and non-disclosure contexts for the same reason, viz., the power of the objects of art-horror to command curiosity.

Recall again that the objects of art-horror are, by definition, impure. This is to be understood in terms of their being anomalous. Obviously, the anomalous nature of these beings is what makes them disturbing, distressing, and disgusting. They are violations of our ways of classifying things and such frustrations of a world-picture are bound to be disturbing.

However, anomalies are also interesting. The very fact that they are anomalies fascinates us. Their deviation from the paradigms of our classificatory scheme captures our attention immediately. It holds us spellbound. It commands and retains our attention. It is an attracting force; it attracts curiosity, i.e., it makes us curious; it invites inquisitiveness about its surprising properties. One wants to gaze upon the unusual, even when it is simultaneously repelling.

Monsters, the anomalous beings who star in *The Philosophy of Horror*, are repelling because they violate standing categories. But for the self-same reason, they are also compelling of our attention. They are attractive, in the sense that they elicit interest, and they are the cause of, for many, irresistible attention, again, just because they violate standing categories. They are curiosities. They can rivet attention and thrill for the self-same reason that they disturb, distress, and disgust.

If these confessedly pedestrian remarks are convincing, three interesting conclusions are suggested. First, the attraction of non-narrative- and non-disclosure-type narration in horror is explicable, as is disclosure-type narrative, fundamentally by virtue of curiosity, a feature of horrific beings that follows from their anomalous status as violations of standing cultural schemes. Second, horrific creatures are able to contribute so well to sustaining interest in disclosure plots to an important degree just because in being anomalous, they can be irresistibly interesting. And lastly, with special reference to the paradox of horror, monsters, the objects of art-horror, are themselves sources of ambivalent responses, for as violations of standing cultural categories, they are disturbing and disgusting, but, at the same time, they are also objects of fascination – again, just because they transgress standing categories of thought. That is, the ambivalence that bespeaks the paradox of horror is already to be found in the very objects of art-horror which are disgusting and fascinating, repelling and attractive due to their anomalous nature.[15] . . . But at the same time that the breakdown of our conceptual categories disturbs, it also fixes our attention. It stimulates our cognitive appetite with the prospect of something previously inconceivable.

The fascination of the horrific being comes in tandem with disturbance. And, in fact, I would submit that for those who are attracted to the genre, the fascination at least compensates for the disturbance. This may be explained to a certain extent by reference to the thought theory of fictional emotion discussed earlier in *The Philosophy of Horror*. According to that view, the audience knows that the object of art-horror does not exist before them. The audience is only reacting to the thought that such and such an impure being might exist. This mutes, without eliminating, the disturbing aspect of the object of art-horror, and allows more opportunity for fascination with the monster to take hold.[16]

One supposes that fascination would be too great a luxury to endure, if one, against all odds, were to encounter a horrific monster in "real life." We, like the characters in horror fictions, would feel distressingly helpless; for such creatures, insofar as they defy our conceptual scheme, would leave us at a loss to think of how to deal with them – they would baffle our practical response, paralyzing us in terror (as they generally do to characters in horror fictions for the same reason). However, with art-horror, it is only the thought of the creature that is at issue; we know that it does not exist; we are not taxed literally by practical questions about what is to be done. So the fearsome and loathsome aspects of the monsters do not impinge upon us with the same practical urgency, allowing a space for fascination to take root. So, as a second approximation for resolving the paradox of horror, we can explain how it is that what would, by hypothesis, ordinarily distress, disturb, and disgust us, can also be the source of pleasure, interest, and attraction. With reference to art-horror the answer is that the monster – as a categorical violation – fascinates for the self-same reasons it disgusts and, since we know the monster is but a fictional confection, our curiosity is affordable.

This position enables us to give an answer to the justified objection to our first response to the paradox of horror, which response was so wedded to disclosure type narratives, to wit: non-narrative examples of art-horror, such as those found in the fine arts and narrative horror fictions that do not deploy disclosure devices, attract their audiences insofar as the objects of art-horror promote fascination at the same time they distress; indeed, both responses emanate from the same aspects of the horrific beings. The two responses are, as a matter of (contingent) fact, inseparable in horror. Moreover, this fascination can be savored, because the distress in question is not behaviorally pressing; it is a response to the thought of a monster, not to the actual presence of a disgusting or fearsome thing.

If it is true that fascination is the key to our attraction to the art-horror in general, then it is also the case that the curiosity and fascination that is basic to the genre also receive especial amplification in what I have referred to as narratives of disclosure and discovery. There curiosity, fascination, and our cognitive inquisitiveness are engaged, addressed, and sustained in a highly articulated way through what I have called the drama of proof and such processes of continuous revelation as ratiocination, discovery, hypothesis formation, confirmation, and so on.

At this point, then, I am in a position to summarize my approach to the paradox of horror. It is a twofold theory, whose elements I refer to respectively as the universal theory and the general theory. The universal theory of our attraction to art-horror – which covers non-narrative horror, non-disclosure horror narratives, *and* disclosure narratives – is that what leads people to seek out horror is fascination as characterized in the analyses above. This is the basic, generic calling card of the form.

At the same time, I should also like to advance what I call a general – rather than a universal theory – of the appeal of art-horror. The most commonly recurring – that is to say the most generally found – exercises in the horror genre appear to be horror narratives of the disclosure sort. The attraction of these instances, like all other examples of the genre, is to be explained in terms of curiosity and fascination. However, with these cases, the initial curiosity and fascination found in the genre are developed to an especially high degree through devices that enhance and sustain curiosity. If the genre begins, so to speak, in curiosity, it is enhanced by the consilient structures of disclosure plotting. In such cases, then, what attracts us to this sort of horror – which seems to me the most pervasive[17] – is the whole structure and staging of curiosity in the narrative, in virtue of the experience of the extended play of fascination it affords. That is, as Hume noted of tragedy, the source of our aesthetic pleasure in such examples of horror is primarily the whole structure of the narrative in which, of course, the apparition of the horrific being is an essential, and, as the universal theory shows, a facilitating part.

An earlier objection that I posed to my first approximation of the appeal of art-horror said it made the source of attraction in the genre too remote from the identifying emotion in the genre; it seemed to defer our pleasure into an exclusive concern with plot, which, of course, would also make it seem that similar plots without horrific beings – such as detective thrillers and disaster movies – could act as substitutes for art-horror. But I am now in a position to explain why it is not the case that explaining the appeal of the genre in terms of curiosity and fascination must detach that appeal from the central emotion of art-horror.

For I have argued that the objects of art-horror are such that they are both disgusting and fascinating, both disturbing and interesting, because they are classificatory misfits. The relation between fascination and horror here is contingent rather than necessary. That is, the objects of art-horror are essentially categorical violations and, as a matter of fact, categorical violations will quite regularly be the sorts of things that will command attention. Fascination and horror are not related by definition. Not everything that fascinates horrifies and not everything that horrifies fascinates. However, given the specific context of horror fiction, there is a strong correlation between fascination and horror due to the fact that horrific monsters are anomalous beings. That is, both fascination and art-horror converge on the same type of objects just because they are categorical violations. Where there is art-horror, there is likely to be at least the prospect of fascination. Fascination is not remote from art-horror, but is related to it as a probable recurring concomitant. Moreover, it is a recurring concomitant because the genre specializes in impossible, and, in principle, unknowable beings. This is the attraction of the genre. Detection thrillers and disaster films that mobilize analogous plot structures do not afford the same type of fascination, and, therefore, are not exact substitutes for horror fictions. We seek out horror fictions because the specific fascination they afford is bound up with the fact that it is animated by the same type of object that gives rise to art-horror.

A question raised by this account of the paradox of horror – in terms of the contingent relation of art-horror and fascination – is how, precisely, these two states are thought to relate to each other. Following Gary Iseminger, we may consider two possible relations between the distressful emotions provoked by a fiction (e.g., art-horror), on the one hand, and the pleasure derived from the fiction (e.g., fascination) on the other: namely, the integrationist view and the co-existentialist view.[18] According to the integrationist, when one derives pleasure from a melodrama, one is saddened by the events depicted and the very sadness contributes to the pleasure we take in the fiction. On the co-existentialist view, the feeling, of pleasure with reference to distressful fictions is a case of one feeling being strong enough to overcome the other, as in the case of "laughter through tears." In the case of a melodrama, the co-existentialist account says that sadness and pleasure exist simultaneously, with the pleasure compensating for the sadness.

It may not be the case that one can settle the issue between the co-existentialist and the integrationist hypotheses in a way that applies to all genres. One genre may be more susceptible to an integrationist account and another to a co-existentialist account. And, indeed, even within one genre, there may be co-existentialist and integrationist accounts depending upon the segment of the audience to which one refers. With respect to art-horror, the preceding explanation in terms of the contingent relation of fascination to fear and disgust leans more in the direction of the co-existentialist view.[19] This account is aimed at the average consumer of horror (in contradistinction to certain *specialized* consumers to be discussed below). In the case of the average consumer of art-horror, the claim is that the art-horror we feel is finally outweighed by the fascination of the monster, as well as, in the majority of cases, by the fascination engendered by the plot in the process of staging the manifestation and disclosure of the monster.

However, a critic of this solution would probably respond by saying that if we agree with the co-existentialist line of thought here, then it would seem to follow that if readers can have their quest for fascination satisfied by descriptions of monsters that are not horrifying, then they are likely to be satisfied by stories – like fairy tales and myths – in which the monsters are not horrifying. Moreover, if this is the case, then the pleasure to be had from horror fictions is not perfectly unique and does not individuate the genre. And, furthermore, if one could have the fascination without being horrified, i.e., by opting for a genre that delivered the same pleasure *sans*, for example, disgust, wouldn't it always make sense to choose the fairy tale?

To a qualified degree, I am willing to go along with part of this. But at the same time, I do not find it totally damning. It seems to me that consumers of horror are most often consumers of other sorts of monster fantasies as well.[20] The audience for the non-horror movie *Jason and the Argonauts* and the horror film *An American Werewolf in London* is probably roughly the same, and the pleasure it takes from the manifestation of monsters in each example is comparable. To a certain extent, such audiences may feel that with respect to pleasure, one movie might be as good as another on any given evening. However, it is also compatible with this that the pleasures to be had from many horror films, especially ones involving certain distinctive plot structures, may still equal or exceed the pleasure to be had from comparable fairy tales and myths, even subtracting the price being horrified exacts. So even though the pleasures to be had from these alternatives are of the same kind, there is no guarantee that an example of one genre provides a greater degree of it than another. Consequently, it would not make sense always to choose fairy tales and odysseys over horror fictions. Moreover, it does not seem to me to be a problem for the theory advanced in this book that certain genres that *obviously* belong to the same family – such as supernatural or monster fantasies – all deliver comparable pleasures; for example, this admission does not indicate that we cannot still differentiate these genres along other dimensions.

In general, I think that we can account for the pleasure that average consumers take in horror fiction by reference to the ways in which the imagery and, in most cases, the plot structures engage fascination. Whatever distress horror causes, as a probable price for our fascination, is outweighed for the average consumer by the pleasure we derive in having our curiosity stimulated and rewarded. However, even if this is the case for most consumers of horror, one could not deny that there may be certain audiences who seek horror fictions simply to be horrified. One suspects that some members of the audience for the *Friday the 13th* series may be like this; they attend simply for the gross-out. Horror films that have fascinating monsters but ones that are not very, very disgusting or revolting might be regarded as inferior by such connoisseurs of gore.

If this is an accurate description of some horror consumers, it would not seem captured by the co-existentialist account. For here the disgust engendered by the fiction appears to be essentially, rather than contingently, connected to the relevant audience's pleasure. So some kind of integrationist account of horror may be called for. One way of developing an integrationist account for these cases would be to extrapolate, following Marcia Eaton, from Susan Feagin's account of what she calls our *meta-response* to tragedy.[21] According to Feagin, the pleasurable response to tragedy is really a response to a response. That is, in a move reminiscent of the Aikins, Feagin thinks that the pleasure we take from responding with sympathy to tragic events in a fiction is a pleasurable response to finding ourselves the types of people who are morally and humanly concerned in this way. Analogously, it may be the case that those who savor the revulsion in art-horror – but not for the sake of fascination – are metaresponding to their own revulsion.

What could this response possibly be? Perhaps it involves a kind of satisfaction in the fact that one is capable of withstanding heavy doses of disgust and shock. Here, of course, it pays to recall that audiences for horror fictions are often adolescent males, some of whom may be using the fictions as macho rites of passage. For them, horror fictions may be endurance tests. Undoubtedly, this is not the brightest aspect of the horror genre, nor are horror fictions that are made exclusively to serve this purpose salutary. However, one must admit that the phenomenon exists, and that, in this particular case, an integrationist account, outfitted with the idea of metaresponses, may be necessary.

However, for most horror consumers, and judging by their construction, for most horror fictions, the co-existentialist hypothesis seems most accurate. It maintains that the pleasures derived from art-horror are a function of fascination, which fascination compensates for the negative emotions engendered by the fiction. This thesis can be applied to the manifestation of the monster pure and simple (the universal theory of horrific appeal); or it can be applied to the manifestation of the monster where this is embedded within a narrative context that orchestrates the manifestation of the monster in such a way that the whole process of narrative staging becomes the primary source of pleasure (the general theory of horrific appeal). As indicated earlier, the latter application seems to me to be the one that is most relevant and most closely suited to the largest number of cases, as well as to the most compelling cases, of art-horror that have so far been produced.

NOTES

1 John and Anna Laetitia Aikin, "On the pleasure derived from objects of terror; with Sir Bertrand, a fragment," in their *Miscellaneous Pieces in Prose* (London, 1773), pp. 119–37. John Aikin's sister also published under the name Anna Laetitia Barbauld.

In this article, it is true that the Aikens are not writing precisely about what I have called horror in this text; however, their questions are prompted by the kinds of writing that will give rise to the horror genre.

2 David Hume, "Of tragedy," in *Of the Standard of Taste and Other Essays*, ed. John W. Lenz (Indianapolis: Bobbs-Merrill, 1965), p. 29. This essay was first published in 1757 in Hume's *Four Dissertations*.

3 John and Anna Laetitia Aikin, "An enquiry into those kinds of distress which excite agreeable sensations; with a tale," in *Miscellaneous Pieces in Prose*, pp. 190–219.

4 Edmund Burke, *A Philosophical Enquiry into the Origin of our Ideas of the Sublime and Beautiful* (Notre Dame: University of Notre Dame Press, 1968), pp. 134–5. Burke's treatise was first published in 1757.

5 Hume, "Of tragedy," pp. 33–4.

6 Hume, "Of tragedy," p. 35.

7 With respect to some genres, like tragedy, the pleasure that the Aikins believe we have derives not from the distressful situation itself but from our response to the distressful situation. That is, we are distressed by the tragic event, and then we take pleasure in noting that we are the kind of morally concerned persons who are shaken by such events. Pleasure in the objects of terror seems more mysterious to them. For they do not see what it is about our terrified response and what having that response indicates about us that would give us satisfaction. This difficulty prompts them to search for an account of the pleasures of distressful, fictional events – of the terrifying variety – in terms of such narrative elements as suspense.

Interestingly, in a recent paper entitled "The pleasures of tragedy" – in *American Philosophical Quarterly* 20(1), January 1983 – Susan Feagin opts for a similar view of the pleasures of tragedy. The pleasure derived here, she believes, is a *metaresponse*, a satisfaction with the fact that we react sympathetically to tragic events. Later in the text we will take up the question of whether or not Feagin's idea of a metaresponse might not be useful in dealing with at least some aspects of the paradox of horror.

8 J. and A.L. Aikin, "Of the pleasure derived from objects of terror," pp. 123–4.

9 The special fermata over the discovery/disclosure of the monster in horror narratives is also in evidence in some of the most standardly employed expositional strategies in movies. For example, with respect to point of view editing in horror films, J.P. Telotte writes: "one of the most frequent and compelling images in the horror film repertoire is that of the wide, staring eyes of some victim, expressing stark terror or disbelief and attesting to an ultimate threat to the human proposition. To maximize the effect of this image, though, the movie most often reverses what is a standard film technique and, in fact, the natural sequence of events. Normally an action is presented and then commented upon with reaction shots; the cause is shown and then its effect. The horror film, however, tends to reverse the process, offering the reaction shot first and thus fostering a chilling suspense by holding the terrors in abeyance for a moment; furthermore, such an arrangement upsets our ordinary cause-effect orientation. What is eventually betrayed is the onset of some unbelievable terror, something which stubbornly refuses to be accounted for by our normal perceptual patterns." Though I do not agree with the analysis – in terms of identification – that Telotte appends to this description, the description itself is an apt one of a recurring cinematic

strategy in horror films, and it suggests the way in which this editing figure reflects, in the form of a "mini-narrative," the larger rhythms of discovery and disclosure in horror plotting. See J.P. Telotte, "Faith and idolatry in the horror film," in *Planks of Reason*, ed. Barry Keith Grant (Metuchen, New Jersey: The Scarecrow Press, 1984), pp. 25–6.

10 Consider the movie titles: *It Came From Outer Space, It Came From Beneath the Sea, It! The Terror From Beyond Space, It Conquered The World, It's Alive, It Lives Again, Them!*, and *They*. Titles like *The Thing, The Swamp Thing, The Creature from the Black Lagoon, Terror Out of the Sky, Monster, Monster from Green Hell, Monster from a Prehistoric Planet, Monster on the Campus, Monster from the Surf, Monster of Piedras Blancas, The Monster That Challenged the World* each in its own way bespeaks the theme of the lack of convenient linguistic categories with which to precisely label horrific beings. In a number of the preceding cases, the best we can do is to locate the monster in space (e.g., in *Piedras Blancas*).

11 In John Barrymore's 1920 version of *Dr Jekyll and Mr Hyde*, Hyde's make-up is designed to suggest that he is a cross between a man and a spider. See James B. Twitchell's analysis in his *Dreadful Pleasures: An Anatomy of Modern Horror* (New York: Oxford University Press, 1985), pp. 245–6.

12 Though not strictly horror images in the terms of my theory, Francis Bacon's paintings often evoke descriptions as horrifying because they suggest virtually *formless* mounds of human flesh. See his *Lying Figure with a Hypodermic Syringe*.

13 In claiming that the pleasures derived from horror are cognitive in the broad sense – of engaging curiosity – I am attempting to explain why the genre often engages us. I am not attempting to justify the genre as worthy of our attention because its appeal is cognitive. Nor by saying that it is cognitive, in the special sense of engaging curiosity, am I even implicitly signaling that I think it superior to some other genres whose appeal might be said to be exclusively emotive.

14 "Ideally" here is meant to take note of the fact that not all such horror fictions are successful.

15 This is not said to retract my earlier claim that with disclosure-type narration our fascination fastens primarily on the way in which our curiosity is orchestrated. However, in order to be orchestrated and to have that orchestration rewarded, the monster will ideally be capable of some independent source of fascination. And that source of fascination, I conjecture, is its anomalous nature.

16 In her article, "A strange kind of sadness," Marcia Eaton postulates that in order to appreciate distressing fictional events we must somehow be in control. As Gary Iseminger points out – in his "How strange a sadness?" – the idea of control here is a bit ambiguous. However, if the control that Eaton has in mind is self-control (rather than control over the events in the story), then adoption of the thought theory of fictional response with respect to horror could explain how we have this control, by virtue of the fact that we are knowingly only responding to the thought that some impure creature is devouring human flesh. Indeed, perhaps the very notion that I am merely *entertaining* this thought implies the requisite self-control. See Marcia Eaton, "A strange kind of sadness," in *The Journal of Aesthetics and Art Criticism* 41(1) (Fall 1982); and, Gary Iseminger, "How strange a sadness?" in *The Journal of Aesthetics and Art Criticism* 42(1) (Fall 1983).

In his "Enjoying negative emotions in fictions," John Moreall also cites the importance of control in enjoying fictions. He seems to suggest that such control enables us to vicariously feel the pleasure that the characters feel when they are angry or sad (p. 102). But I am not convinced that it is correct to say of the victims in horror fictions that they can feel pleasure in the state they are in. Perhaps some examples of anger and sadness have pleasureable dimensions. But surely not all the emotional states of fictional characters have such a dimension – surely, for example, horror does not. See John Moreall, "Enjoying negative emotions in fiction," in *Philosophy and Literature* 9(1) (April 1985).

17 If I am statistically wrong about the pervasiveness of disclosure narration in the genre, then I would probably want to rename the second part of my view *the special theory* of the appeal of horror. For I think the account of the appeal of disclosure narration offered above is right for that "special" group of horror narratives even if that group does not represent the most common formation in the genre. Needless to say, however, at present, I still am of the opinion that the drama of disclosure – in the ways discussed earlier in *The Philosophy of Horror* – is the most commonly practiced form in the genre.

18 See Iseminger, "How strange a sadness?," pp. 81–2; and Marcia Eaton, *Basic Issues in Aesthetics* (Belmont, California: Wadsworth Publishing Company, 1988), pp. 40–1.

19 Interestingly, I think that psychoanalytic accounts of horror also turn out to be co-existentialist, for the disgust and fear that the imagery elicits is the price that must be paid in order to have repressed wishes manifested without censorship.

20 Some informal evidence for this might include: 1) that within the fantasy movie cycles of the last decade and a half, there is an easy movement from the dominance of horror entries like the *Omen* series, to space odysseys, like *Star Wars*, to benign fantasies like *E. T.*, *Splash*, *Cocoon*, to sword and sorcery quests, like *The Never Ending Story*, *Willow*, *Labyrinth*, *Legend*, *Princess Bride*, *Dark Crystal*, etc. 2) that popular writers like King can move from horror to sword and sorcery without losing their following.

21 Feagin, "The pleasures of tragedy"; and Marcia Eaton, *Basic Issues in Aesthetics*, p. 40.

18

THE PARADOX OF HORROR

Berys Gaut

"It seems an unaccountable pleasure, which the spectators of a well-written tragedy receive from sorrow, terror, anxiety, and other passions, that are in themselves disagreeable and uneasy."[1] Thus did Hume open his classic discussion of the paradox of tragedy, and it can as properly serve as a statement of the kernel of the puzzle found in the closely related paradox of horror. We can approach this paradox by reflecting on the following statements, all of which seem to be true. (1) Some of us enjoy horror fictions. (2) Horror fictions characteristically produce fear and disgust in their audience. (3) Fear and disgust are intrinsically unpleasant emotions. The most straightforward explanation of these facts seems to be that we enjoy the fear and disgust the fictions produce in us. But to assert this yields the apparently paradoxical view that we enjoy intrinsically unpleasant emotions. So the paradox of horror rests on what might be termed the paradox of the enjoyment of negative emotions. However, there is another explanation of the phenomena available: we are enjoying not negative emotions, but rather some other feature of the situation, such as the curiosity we feel about what is going to happen. This is, roughly, the solution to the paradox that Noël Carroll defends.[2] I will criticize this solution, as well as an expressivist solution. I then examine several recent claims that there is nothing paradoxical about our enjoyment of negative emotions, and will show that a variation of this view can be defended against apparently decisive objections. Thus it transpires that we *can* enjoy fear and disgust, so there is nothing paradoxical about our enjoyment of negative emotions, nor about our enjoyment of horror fictions.

I

Carroll provides a cognitivist solution to the paradox of horror. Drawing on the work of the anthropologist Mary Douglas, he argues that monsters, such as werewolves or a man with a fly's head, are violations of our categorial schemes. Douglas argues that such violations are seen as threatening and impure, and this is Carroll's explanation of why works of horror generate fear and disgust. But because monsters are categorial violations, being physically impossible according to our conceptual scheme, we are also curious about them, and find them fascinating. This curiosity is heightened in the case of novels and films by the processes of narration, which entice us to wonder whether the monster exists and what it looks like, involve us in the question of whether the characters in the fiction will come to believe in its existence and can destroy it, and so on. Hence our enjoyment of horror arises from its exploitation and satisfaction of our curiosity about monsters and the narrational processes of their discovery, monsters being peculiarly suited to elicit our interest because of their status as categorial violations. But this status also explains why monsters produce fear and disgust in us. So we cannot have the enjoyment without the negative emotions: "the disgust that such beings [monsters] evince might be seen as part of the price to be paid for the pleasure of their disclosure" (p. 184). Moreover, because we know that the monsters are only fictional, the fear and disgust they arouse in us are muted in comparison with what they would be if we were to meet such monsters in real life, which allows the pleasures of curiosity more easily to outweigh the displeasures of fear and disgust.

Though Carroll demonstrates considerable skill in defending his solution, it is, I believe, unsatisfactory. His view depends crucially on claims about monsters, defined as beings not believed to exist now according to contemporary science (p. 27). Yet not all horror fictions involve monsters: an important and popular sub-genre of the modern horror film is the "slasher" movie, which deals with psychopathic serial killers.[3] Psychopaths are not monsters, they are instances of an all-too-real phenomenon. Carroll's response to this sort of objection is that some of these psychopaths are presented as having supernatural powers, and so are really monsters (p. 37); if the characters are human, but are akin to monsters, then fictions involving them are borderline cases of horror (p. 39); and otherwise we should regard the fictions as tales of terror (p. 15). But to take the latter course is simply to transform the paradox of horror into a paradox of tales of terror, where the solution involving appeal to monsters cannot work. On the other hand, to treat certain clearly human psychopaths as akin to monsters depends on a metaphorical extension of the term "monster", and to talk of psychopaths as categorial violations extends the notion of a categorial violation to the point where beings simply with unexpected or unusual traits will be counted as categorial violations: yet we clearly need not feel disgust at the unusual. Moreover, to hold a position from which it follows that films such as Demme's *The Silence of the Lambs* are borderline cases of horror marginalizes what look like paradigm examples of the modern horror film. Carroll's appeal to monsters disguises the simple point that we can be disgusted by and afraid of human beings because they do evil and awful things, and no mention of monsters or of categorial violations is needed to explain our reactions.

It might be thought that Carroll should drop his talk of monsters and his definition of horror in terms of them, and simply appeal to our curiosity about the extraordinary characters in horror fictions as overcoming the fear and disgust they produce in us. He is doubtless correct in holding that such fear and disgust are less intense than they would be if we thought these beings were real, but, even so, as his many examples and common observation show, we can feel great fear and disgust during horror films. The problem with Carroll's solution is that most horror films are so formulaic in their plots, and their monsters and killers so stereotypical, that it is difficult to believe that our curiosity could very often be sufficiently stimulated to overcome the purported disadvantages such works incur in producing disagreeable emotional states in us. The conventions of genre weigh too heavily on most horror fictions for Carroll's solution to be a plausible one.

Finally, and most simply, consider Norman, a disappointed spectator who comes out of a horror film and complains that it wasn't scary enough. He wanted to be *really* frightened, but the film hardly raised a mild tremor of apprehension in him. On Carroll's view Norman must really be complaining that his curiosity wasn't heightened enough. But that is not what he says, and indeed, he might say that the film was quite interesting. The problem was, he avers, that it wasn't *frightening*. We are back to the core of the paradox of horror again: people seem to enjoy experiencing negative emotions.

II

It is worth briefly exploring an expressivist solution to the paradox. This holds that we do not enjoy the negative emotions that horror engenders, but, rather, we enjoy the expression of these emotions, by which we relieve ourselves of them, or lighten the grip they have on us.[4] Collingwood usefully distinguishes two versions of expressivism: the simpler holds that the process is akin to unburdening oneself of emotions by engaging in acts of make-believe (for instance, getting rid of one's anger by imagining kicking someone), the more sophisticated overlaps with the cognitivist view, holding that one lightens one's emotion by coming to understand what was before an unknown perturbation.[5]

Carroll rejects expressivist solutions for horror, claiming that we cannot gain satisfaction from the expression of our fear of monsters, for there are none, so we have no antecedently felt fear of them (p. 246). However, this objection is too swift, for it fails to recognize that monsters can serve as metaphors for our fears. Interpretations of horror fictions as expressing covert sexual fears, or fear of death and the physicality of the body, or of loss of sexual identity, are legion, and are, in many cases, quite plausible. Carroll does acknowledge that the horror film cycle correlates quite well with periods of social tension (e.g., the 1930s cycle with the Great Depression), but he objects that horror had its *aficionados* even at times when there were no social anxieties, and that mere expression of social anxieties is not appealing, for otherwise public lectures on these topics would have mass appeal. Hence expressivism cannot provide a general solution to the problem of horror (pp. 206–14, 248). But this reply, too, succumbs to the objection that horror can express perennial personal anxieties, as well as social ones, and can do so in a powerfully metaphorical form.

However, I believe that Carroll is correct in rejecting the expressivist position, for, even as adumbrated above, it suffers from severe shortcomings. If we are attracted to horror for its cathartic effect, so that watching a horror film is the equivalent of "talking out" one's fears, it is odd that these films are least attractive if one is in an uneasy or fearful mood. One doesn't say "I'm scared, so I think I'll go to see a horror film." Rather, one needs to be in a fairly robust psychological state in order to enjoy these fictions at all. Further, these films not infrequently leave (and are designed to leave) a lingering sense of fearfulness in their audience: one may feel scared as one walks home, and uneasy going to sleep. This is precisely the opposite effect one would expect if one's fear had been "lightened". Instead, these fears have been induced and exacerbated, and then one is frequently left in a state of disquiet. Even if one has been given metaphors for the objects of one's fears, this has not resulted in a lightening of one's emotions, but rather provides new materials with which to produce these emotions at will. Finally, if the expressivist doctrine were correct, we should expect to dislike the arousal of our emotion of fear when watching a film, and then only start to enjoy ourselves when the emotion was dissipated at the end of the film, assuming that it has an end that did not further enhance our fear. But horror audiences can enjoy themselves throughout the film, and hence they cannot enjoy merely the "lightening" of the emotion.

III

It would be a Herculean task to examine the many possible variations of cognitivist and expressivist accounts of the paradox of horror. But I have shown that some simple versions of both are incorrect. However, the motivation to think that *some* version of these theories must be correct is presumably that otherwise we are left with the apparent paradox that audiences are enjoying the negative emotions of fear and disgust. If we can show that this is not paradoxical, then cognitivist and expressivist theories will be less compelling. Instead, we can endorse the enjoyment theory: horror attracts because people can enjoy being scared and disgusted. This thesis has the merit of simplicity, and it accounts for the intelligibility of Norman's complaint. It can also explain a salient fact about horror, of which it is easy to lose sight. The genre has as its self-conscious aim the production of fear and disgust in its audience, and it has become increasingly sophisticated and successful in achieving this effect. Moreover, the majority of horror works lack any serious artistic worth. They are pure entertainment: they aim simply at providing their audience with enjoyable experiences. Taking these points together, the simplest, most straightforward explanation of the phenomenon of horror is that sometimes people *enjoy* being scared.

Consider Suzy, a mountaineering enthusiast. She enjoys putting herself into dangerous situations, feeling the thrill of fear as she dangles over the edge, knowing that it is only her skill and equipment that save her from certain death. She finds life simpler, more elemental in such situations, her fear gives an acuteness and "edge" to her experience that is lacking in everyday life. She appreciates many aspects of the experience, and her fear is an inextricable part of the composite whole which she enjoys. Her motivations are not the stuff of psychopathology, still less are they unintelligible: the existence of many activities from sky-diving to motor racing testifies to the enduring attractions of danger. On a humbler level, even the pleasures of riding roller-coasters depend partly on the fear one feels as the car careers around the bend, and one is not entirely convinced that it will stay on the tracks.

Nor are such phenomena confined to fear alone. One can also enjoy other "negative" emotions. One can enjoy disgusting stories, and there is a minor genre, popular on college campuses, of "disgust" movies, pre-eminent amongst which is John Waters' *Pink Flamingos*. The negative emotion of anger can also be enjoyed: irascible individuals sometimes seek out situations in which they will have an opportunity to get angry. Likewise, it is possible to relish a feeling of quiet melancholy, dwelling on the sorrows and disappointments of life, and weeping for the sadness of the world.

Phenomena of this sort have been noted by several philosophers in the last decade, and have been seen as key ingredients in the solution of the paradoxes.[6] It would be tempting simply to cite such cases without explanation of how they are possible, and think that this would decisively show that one can enjoy negative emotions, and so dissolve the paradox of horror. But to do so merely opens one to the objection that they are not really possible at all, for they would involve the enjoyment of intrinsically unpleasant emotions. Hence, the objection continues, such cases are misdescribed, and what is enjoyed in them is something other than the presence of a negative emotion. For instance, Susan Feagin in her critique of Carroll's solution to the paradox discusses several examples, including the roller-coaster case, of the enjoyment of negative emotions and their associated sensations.[7] Carroll's response is that she simply ignores the paradoxicality of negative emotions, and what *he* enjoys about roller-coasting is not the queasiness, but the "novel way of moving through space" and the "overall thrill" of the ride.[8] This redescription strategy will be attractive only as long as we are unable to explain away the apparent paradoxicality of the enjoyment of these emotions.

Two kinds of theories have been advanced to explain how the enjoyment of negative emotions is possible, but neither is entirely satisfactory as it stands. The first is the "control thesis", developed by Marcia Eaton, and refined by John Morreall, on whose version I shall focus.[9] Morreall holds that one can enjoy negative emotions when one is "in control" of the situation which produces the emotions, where control is understood in terms of an ability to direct one's thoughts and actions. So Suzy can enjoy her mountaineering escapades because she knows that she is skilful enough to avoid coming to harm. It is peculiarly easy to enjoy negative emotions in the case of fiction, since the fiction has no practical consequences for its audience. In this case it is sufficient in order to be in control that one be able to direct one's attention and thoughts. However, if one loses this control, perhaps because the fiction depicts violence and suffering so graphically that one's negative emotions become too strong, then one will not enjoy the emotions.[10] Thus there is a ready explanation for how one can enjoy negative emotions, both in fiction and in real life.

This solution is ingenious, but inadequate. The paradox of negative emotions arises because, apparently, we are able to enjoy intrinsically unpleasant emotions. But the control thesis leaves it utterly mysterious how the mere fact that I can choose to attend or not to an otherwise unpleasant emotion, such as fear, could render that emotion pleasant. Further, the believer in the intrinsicality claim will hold that it is a necessary, conceptual condition of an emotion being fear that it is experienced as unpleasant, so that the psychic mechanism of hedonic transformation, to which the control theorist gestures, is a conceptual impossibility. There is thus a lacuna in the control theory, which owes us an account of how the apparent conceptual connection between fear and displeasure can be explained away, or how the connection can be construed so that it does not undermine the theory. But, in any case, the theory's linkage of the enjoyment of such emotions with the control of them seems straightforwardly false. People vary greatly and unpredictably as to whether or not they enjoy horror films. If Morag does not enjoy them, that need not be because she cannot adequately control her attention with respect to them. Rather, her reason for not enjoying the film is that when she *does* direct her attention to the bloody corpse, she does not like what she experiences. Conversely, Norman may believe that the very height of enjoyable fear is when his gaze is riveted to the gruesome spectacle, when he "cannot take his eyes off" the unfolding carnage. For, after all, if one is enjoying something, then one's attention tends to be drawn irresistibly to it.

IV

The second, more promising view of how it is possible to enjoy negative emotions has been developed by both Kendall Walton and Alex Neill. They deny that these emotional responses are intrinsically unpleasant. They both speak as if it is a purely contingent matter whether or not people enjoy the emotions themselves. It is not the emotions themselves that are intrinsically unpleasant, they hold, but, rather, it is the *objects* of the emotions which are unpleasant or disvaluable. Walton argues that Hume was wrong to think that sorrow is in itself disagreeable. Rather, "What is clearly disagreeable, what we regret, are the things we are sorrowful *about* – the loss of an opportunity, the death of a friend – not the feeling or experience of sorrow itself."[11] Neill, in a critique of Carroll's theory, similarly points out that the emotions of pity or fear aren't painful in the way that stepping on a thumb-tack is. Instead, he says,

> In describing an emotion as "painful" or "negative" or "unpleasant", I suggest, we are in fact saying something about the situations in response to which we typically experience those emotions: That is, it's the situations rather than the emotions which are distasteful or undesirable, which we (metaphorically?) describe as painful or unpleasant.[12]

However, this view encounters two serious objections as thus formulated. Firstly, the defender of the claim that negative emotions are intrinsically unpleasant will properly protest that it can't be a purely contingent matter that these emotions are felt as unpleasant. For imagine we came across a tribe who said that they felt a certain emotion at the death of their loved ones, and that this emotion was the most enjoyable one to be had. We would, I take it, be justifiably reluctant to translate the word they used to name this emotion as "grief". This suggests that there is a conceptual constraint on negative emotions being felt as unpleasant. Secondly, both Walton and Neill have a problem in so far as they appeal to a contrast between the unpleasantness of the emotion and the unpleasantness of the object of the emotion. For to say that something is unpleasant is to attribute to that thing a dispositional property: namely, the property of producing unpleasant experiences in people, and the salient experiences in the cases under discussion are those of sorrow and fear. Neill tries to counter his objection in a footnote by claiming that the unpleasantness may be in the situation itself rather than in the feelings I have towards the object. He gives the example of pity, which is an emotion directed towards others' suffering. So the painfulness figures here as something which the people whom I pity suffer, rather than as something which I experience.[13] As he admits, the suggestion needs further work, but it does not seem promising. For it is not sufficient for me to pity others that I think they are suffering: the sadist may believe the latter, without feeling any pity at all for them. If we have to appeal to unpleasantness here, it must be an unpleasantness which I also feel.

There is a more promising way to meet this second objection. Neill explicitly disavows a hedonistic theory of value,[14] and in the passage, which I quoted, he says that the situations towards which negative emotions are directed are distasteful *or undesirable*. Walton would doubtless take this position as well, and both he and Neill endorse versions of the evaluative theory of the emotions to be discussed in the next section. I suggest, then, that we drop talk of the pleasant and unpleasant here, and speak purely in general evaluative terms. This move would allow us to counter the objection I raised about the dispositionality of the unpleasant. Hence we could allow that when people are enjoying negative emotions it is not because they regard the objects of the emotions as unpleasant, even though they enjoy the emotions, but because they regard the objects of the emotions as undesirable, and to believe that something is undesirable, is not *ipso facto* to find it unpleasant. However, it will be replied, to drop the reference to pleasure, and merely to speak of the objects of the emotions as disvaluable, seems to make the first objection I considered even more devastating, for now the contingency of the link between the negativity of emotions and their unpleasantness is even more salient. But I will argue that one can meet this objection in a way that neither Walton nor Neill considers, by showing that there are conceptual connections between evaluation, desire and pleasure, but that these non-contingent links are of a sort which do not threaten the solution to the paradoxes defended here.

V

Hume was puzzled by how it is that the spectators of a tragedy can enjoy sorrow, terror and anxiety, since he held that such emotions essentially involve feelings of pain.[15] As Walton notes, we can dissolve the paradox by disputing Hume's analysis of the emotions. In fact, as I will now argue, the correct view of the emotions *entails* that negative emotions are such, not in respect of unpleasant feelings, nor even in respect of the unpleasantness of their objects, but, rather, in respect of the negative evaluative thoughts they incorporate.

Hume's theory is an instance of the "traditional" view of the emotions as phenomenologically characterized feelings. The dominant modern theory of the emotions, however, holds that emotions are cognitive, essentially incorporating evaluations.[16] Thus to fear something involves evaluating it as threatening, to be angry with someone involves evaluating her actions as wrong, to be sorrowful involves thinking that a loss has been suffered, and so on. What other factors must be present for an emotion to exist is a matter of dispute, but plausibly they include the requirement that the subject be in an abnormal physiological state caused by the evaluation. However, one emotion is to be individuated from another in terms of the evaluations involved, rather than by the particular features of the physiological state or of the associated bodily sensations, for there is no pattern of physiological changes or set of sensations peculiar to each emotion, and an emotion may be associated with different sensations in different people.[17] Now, if the emotions are to be individuated by the evaluations, then the difference between "positive" and "negative" emotions must consist in the difference between the evaluative thoughts. But there is no phenomenal character to a thought *per se*. So the difference between positive and negative emotions can only consist in the fact that the *evaluations* incorporated into the former are positive and those in the latter are negative. That is, what makes negative emotions negative is not the painfulness of either the emotional response or of the object. Rather, it consists in the fact that objects to which these emotions are directed are brought under negative evaluative concepts: the dangerous, the wrongful, the shameful, etc. Since we can disvalue something without finding it unpleasant, it follows that it is possible to find both negative emotional responses *and* their objects pleasant. Hence, by appeal to an evaluative theory of the emotions, we can show that there is nothing paradoxical about the enjoyment of negative emotions, for it is only required that one *disvalue* the *objects* of these emotions. Hence one can dissolve the paradoxes of horror and tragedy.

There is a certain irony in this solution, since Carroll is fully aware of the evaluative theory of the emotions. Indeed, his account of the emotions is based on the version of the evaluative theory due to William Lyons, which I have drawn upon in the preceding paragraph, and he elaborates his definition of the emotion of art-horror so as to conform to an evaluative analysis of the emotions (pp. 24–7). But he does not see in his book that the "abnormal, physically felt agitation" (p. 27), which he requires for fear to be present, need not be an intrinsically unpleasant state, for the negativity of the emotion can be explained in terms of the object of the emotion being negatively evaluated, rather than the emotion itself being unpleasant. Indeed, Carroll himself argues that what the agitation feels like can vary massively from person to person and from time to time in one person, so it is doubly puzzling why he assumes that the agitation must be experienced as unpleasant.

We now have to answer the objection that this solution allows it to be a contingent matter that we generally experience negative emotions as unpleasant. I am going to argue that the view of the emotions as evaluative does allow for the existence of a conceptual connection, but a conceptual connection of a sort that still allows us to dissolve the paradoxes. I will consider the connection in two stages: firstly, the conceptual link between evaluations and desire, and secondly, that between desire and pleasure.

Internalists about evaluation hold that there is a necessary connection between judging a situation to be good and having a motivating reason to bring it about (the reason need be only prima facie, and so may be overridden by other, conflicting reasons). This is so, because evaluations give us reasons for action: for someone to hold that an action is good, but that he has no reason to bring it about, shows that he has not grasped the meaning of the word "good". Further, people can be deceived about the contents of their beliefs, and if someone claims to believe that something is good, but it is apparent that he has no motivating reason to bring it about, that is defeasible evidence that he is mistaken about the content of his belief. Now internalism of this sort is too strong, for it is possible to be in a state of *anomie* or despair in which one can recognize that a course of action is a good one, yet not be motivated to pursue it. Further, it is at least conceivable that a moral pervert should be motivated by a course of action just because it is evil. But both sorts of cases are motivational deviations, which are specifiable as such only against a background of motivational normality. Hence a more modest internalism will claim that necessarily *typically*, if someone believes that something is good, then he will have a motivating reason to promote it.[18]

Secondly, there is a conceptual connection between having a motivating reason (a desire, in the broad sense in which philosophers use that term) and finding something pleasant. Hedonists try to capture this connection by claiming that the only thing desired for its own sake is pleasure. As many philosophers have argued, this is false, since I can, for instance, rationally choose to forego a life of pleasure if it is based on systematic deception.[19] But a more promising conceptual connection is captured by Mill's dictum that "to desire anything, except in proportion as the idea of it is pleasant, is a physical and metaphysical impossibility".[20] This is compatible with holding that we desire for their own sakes things other than pleasure, for instance, knowledge. For even if I desire knowledge for its own sake, I will find the idea of acquiring it pleasant. As J.C. Gosling has argued, Mill's dictum captures the characteristically human way of desiring things, one might say, passionately: if we *really* want something, we will be joyful at the prospect of achieving it, and downcast if we cannot obtain it.[21] This is supported by the fact that if one thinks that one desires something, yet feels no pleasure at the prospect of getting it, then that is strong, though defeasible, evidence that one does not desire it after all. So there is a conceptual connection between desire and pleasure. However, Mill, in holding that we always find the idea of the desired thing pleasant, makes the connection too strong, for one may, for instance, do one's duty without enjoyment. So we should adopt the same strategy as we used above and hold that necessarily *typically*, if someone desires something, then the idea of achieving it gives her pleasure.

Putting together these two conceptual connections, we have the conclusion that there is a conceptual connection between evaluation and pleasure: necessarily, typically if someone positively evaluates a state of affairs, then she will feel pleasure at the idea of achieving it. Now, if the individual has the relevant knowledge about the state of affairs concerned – if the state of affairs is as her idea represents it to be – then the state of affairs will be pleasant. Conversely, necessarily typically, if someone negatively evaluates a state of affairs and she is relevantly informed about it, she will find that state of affairs unpleasant. So it follows that, given that the agent is adequately informed, the view of the emotions as evaluative does place conceptual constraints on whether it is typically possible to enjoy being in the situations which are the objects of the emotions. Further, since the pleasant is a dispositional property, if the object is unpleasant, the experience of it (including one's affective experience of it) is unpleasant. Hence, in the case of negative emotions, the view of the emotions as evaluative entails that informed agents will typically experience the objects of their emotions and the emotions themselves as unpleasant.

So the evaluative theory of the emotions is not susceptible to the counter-example based on the unintelligibility of the tribal people who feel sorrow, yet find the emotion pleasant. For, we can note that the emotion concerned is not typically unpleasant for them, and therefore is not sorrow. But have we not now reproduced the paradox of horror, by showing that one cannot feel fear, and hence evaluate something as threatening, without experiencing the emotion as unpleasant? However, this is not so, for it was crucial to the conceptual connections discussed above that they were of the form "necessarily *typically*". This being so, there is plenty of scope for the enjoyment of these emotions in atypical situations or by atypical people. This allows Suzy to enjoy her fear, and it allows the *aficionados* of horror to enjoy their fear and disgust. The latter are helped by the fact that they know the film is fictional and that neither they nor the actors depicted are in real danger. But these atypical cases are only possible against a background in which people do not enjoy these negative emotions. The background of typical unpleasant responses is necessary for these emotions to be negative.

This itself might seem a paradoxical result, but it is not. It is, in fact, a perfectly familiar result of holistic theories about the mental. The position I defend here does not assume, or entail, the truth of functionalism. But like functionalism it is a holistic view, and functionalists similarly define mental states by means of a "typically" operator, in order to respect the holism of the mental. Functionalists seek to define mental concepts in terms of their functional role, and so hold, for instance, that pain is (roughly) that state which typically results from bodily damage, typically produces the desire to escape the source of the damage, and typically produces avoidance-behaviour. As David Lewis has pointed out, this allows for cases where atypical people may not be motivated to avoid pain (or, we can add, may even enjoy it): but it is only *pain* that they can enjoy because of the background of normal aversive reactions to that state in the (human) community of which they are members.[22] So the full solution to the paradoxes depends both on a view of the emotions as evaluative, and on the recognition of how mental holism presents itself in respect of emotions, desires and enjoyment.

Hence we can dissolve the paradox of horror. That paradox rests on the claim that the enjoyment of negative emotions, understood as intrinsically unpleasant emotions, is impossible. The paradox seems to arise only because we construe the negativity in terms of these emotions being intrinsically unpleasant, whereas we should really construe their negativity in terms of the fact that the emotions essentially incorporate negative evaluations. But this entails that typically people will find the objects of these emotions unpleasant *and* the emotions themselves are typically unpleasant. Thus it is wrong to hold that whether people enjoy these emotions or not is a merely contingent, non-conceptual matter. But because there is only a conceptual requirement that people *typically* don't enjoy them, that allows room for some individuals on some occasions to enjoy them. Moreover, this solution explains why it can seem so plausible to hold that these emotions are intrinsically unpleasant. For, while it is false that necessarily, if someone feels fear, she does not enjoy the experience, it *is* true that necessarily she or others of her community *typically* feel fear. It should be clear that this solution, being entirely general, also solves the paradox of tragedy.

Of course, why any particular individual enjoys feeling fear, and another doesn't, or why some horror films are enjoyable and others not, is an interesting and no doubt complex matter. But it is the proper subject of empirical, psychological investigation and it would be unproductive to engage in armchair speculation about why this is so. What I have shown here is that this empirical investigation is possible. For I have argued that there is no a priori, conceptual problem about the enjoyment of negative emotions in real life, or in fiction. There is no paradox of horror.[23]

NOTES

1 David Hume, "Of tragedy" in *Essays Moral, Political, and Literary*, eds T.H. Green and T.H. Grose (London: Longmans, Green and Co., 1907), pp. 258–65, at p. 258.

2 Noël Carroll, *The Philosophy of Horror or Paradoxes of the Heart* (New York: Routledge, 1990), portions of which are reprinted in this volume. Page references in the text are to the original book. In chapter 1 he defends the view, recorded in (2) above, that the horror genre produces not just fear, but also disgust in its audience.

3 See Carol J. Clover, "Her body, himself: gender in the slasher film", in James Donald (ed.), *Fantasy and the Cinema* (London: B.F.I., 1989), for some evidence of how widespread such films are.

4 This is, of course, a common, though perhaps incorrect, way of interpreting Aristotle's doctrine of *katharsis*. For a welcome scepticism about the possibility of establishing precisely what Aristotle meant by this term, see K. Bennett, "The purging of catharsis", *British Journal of Aesthetics* 21 (1981), 204–13.

5 R.G. Collingwood, *The Principles of Art* (Oxford U.P., 1938), pp. 109–11.

6 See the references below to Feagin, Eaton, Morreall, Walton, and Neill.

7 Susan L. Feagin, "Monsters, disgust and fascination", *Philosophical Studies* 65 (1992), 75–84, at p. 81.

8 Noël Carroll, "Disgust or fascination: a response to Susan Feagin", *Philosophical Studies* 65 (1992), 85–90, at pp. 87–8.

9 Marcia Eaton, "A strange kind of sadness", *The Journal of Aesthetics and Art Criticism* 41 (1982), 51–64; and John Morreall, "Enjoying negative emotions in fictions", *Philosophy and Literature* 9 (1985), 95–102.

10 Morreall, op. cit., pp. 99, 101.

11 Kendall Walton, *Mimesis as Make-Believe: On the Foundations of the Representational Arts* (Cambridge: Harvard U.P., 1990), p. 257.

12 Alex Neill, "On a paradox of the heart", *Philosophical Studies* 65 (1992), 53–65, at p. 62.

13 Ibid., p. 65, fn. 15.

14 Ibid., p. 61.

15 See Hume's discussion of the passions in *A Treatise of Human Nature*, book II, especially pp. 438–48, eds L. A. Selby-Bigge and P. H. Nidditch (Oxford U.P., 1978).

16 For an extremely useful overview of the modern debate, see Daniel Farrell, "Recent work on the emotions", *Analyse & Kritik* 10 (1988), 71–102.

17 See William Lyons, *Emotion* (Cambridge U.P., 1980), especially chapters 3, 7, and 8. Lyons

also thinks that the concepts of some, though not all, emotions involve reference to desires. But the internalism I argue for below will show that the concepts of all emotions implicitly incorporate reference to desires which are typically possessed by those experiencing the emotion.

18 The argument of this paragraph is that of James Dreier, "Internalism and speaker relativism", *Ethics* 101 (1991), 6–26, at pp. 9–14, though I have substituted "typically" for his "normally".

19 Robert Nozick, *Anarchy, State, and Utopia* (Oxford: Basil Blackwell, 1974), pp. 42–5.

20 J.S. Mill, *Utilitarianism*, ed. Mary Warnock (London: Fontana, 1962), p. 293. Mill, of course, endorses the dictum in the context of his defence of hedonism, but the dictum itself does not entail hedonism as formulated above.

21 J.C. Gosling, "Pleasure and enjoyment", in J.J. Macintosh and S. Coval (eds), *The Business of Reason* (London: Routledge & Kegan Paul, 1969), pp. 95–113, at pp. 111–13.

22 David Lewis, "Mad pain and Martian pain", in Ned Block (ed.), *Readings in Philosophy of Psychology*, vol. 1 (Cambridge: Harvard U.P., 1980), pp. 216–22.

23 I am grateful to John Haldane for his comments on this paper.

SUGGESTIONS FOR FURTHER READING

Aristotle (1941) *Poetics*, trans. by Ingram Bywater, in *The Basic Works of Aristotle*, ed. Richard McKeon, New York: Random House.

Carroll, Noël (1990) *The Philosophy of Horror*, New York: Routledge.

—— (1992) "Disgust or fascination: a response to Susan Feagin", *Philosophical Studies* 65: 85–90.

—— (1992) "A paradox of the heart: a response to Alex Neill", *Philosophical Studies* 65: 67–74.

—— (1995) "Enjoying horror fictions: a reply to Gaut", *British Journal of Aesthetics* 35(1): 67–72.

Eaton, Marcia (1982) "A strange kind of sadness", *Journal of Aesthetics and Art Criticism* 41: 51–63.

Feagin, Susan L. (1992) "Monsters, disgust and fascination", *Philosophical Studies* 65: 75–84.

Freeland, Cynthia A. (1996) "Feminist frameworks for horror films", in David Bordwell and Noël Carroll (eds), *Post-Theory: Reconstructing Film Studies*, Madison: University of Wisconsin Press.

Gaut, Berys (1995) "The enjoyment theory of horror: a response to Carroll", *British Journal of Aesthetics* 35(3): 284–9.

Heller, Terry (1987) *The Delights of Terror: An Aesthetics of the Tale of Terror*, Urbana: University of Illinois Press.

Hume, David, "Of tragedy", in his *Essays Moral Political and Literary*, many editions.

Iseminger, Gary (1983) "How strange a sadness?", *Journal of Aesthetics and Art Criticism* 42: 81–2.

Levinson, Jerrold (1982) "Music and negative emotion", *Pacific Philosophical Quarterly* 63: 327–46.

Markowitz, Sally (1992) "Guilty pleasures: aesthetic meta-response and fiction", *Journal of Aesthetics and Art Criticism* 50: 307–16.

Morreall, John (1985) "Enjoying negative emotions in fiction", *Philosophy and Literature* 9: 95–102.

Neill, Alex (1992) "On a paradox of the heart", *Philosophical Studies* 65: 53–65.

Packer, Mark (1989) "Dissolving the paradox of tragedy", *Journal of Aesthetics and Art Criticism* 47: 212–19.

Schier, Flint (1989) "The claims of tragedy: an essay in moral psychology and aesthetic theory", *Philosophical Papers* 18: 7–26.

—— (1983) "Tragedy and the community of sentiment", in *Philosophy and Fiction*, ed. Peter Lamarque, Aberdeen: Aberdeen University Press.

Walton, Kendall (1990) *Mimesis as Make-Believe*, Cambridge: Harvard University Press, chapter 7, section 3.

Williams, Christopher (1998) "Is tragedy paradoxical?", *British Journal of Aesthetics* 38: 47–62.

Part 9
SENTIMENTALITY

Part 3

SENTIMENTALITY

For she was dead. There, upon her little bed, she lay at rest. The solemn stillness was no marvel now.

She was dead. No sleep so beautiful and calm, so free from trace of pain, so fair to look upon. She seemed a creature fresh from the hand of God, and waiting for the breath of life; not one who had lived and suffered death.

Her couch was dressed with here and there some winter berries and green leaves, gathered in a spot she had been used to favor. "When I die, put near me something that has loved the light, and had the sky above it always." Those were her words.

She was dead. Dear, gentle, patient, noble Nell was dead. Her little bird – a poor slight thing the pressure of a finger would have crushed – was stirring nimbly in its cage; and the strong heart of its child-mistress was mute and motionless for ever.

Charles Dickens, The Old Curiosity Shop, chapter 71

One must have a heart of stone to read the death of Little Nell without laughing.

Oscar Wilde, quoted in The Wit and Humor of Oscar Wilde

Little Nell's death scene in The Old Curiosity Shop, which to many modern readers has seemed intolerably, soppily sentimental, may seem, to a reader who has lost a child of Little Nell's age, quite consoling and even restrained and justified by the facts – as it must have seemed to those Victorians who lost so many more children than we do.

Wayne C. Booth, The Company We Keep, p. 69

THE TERM "SENTIMENTAL" IS ONE THAT is often used in describing works of art and our responses to those works. But just what is it to be sentimental? The term has undergone a great change in meaning over the last two centuries. Originally, it meant something like "full of feeling", and indeed to describe a work of art as sentimental may still simply be to say that it tends to arouse responses full of feeling in us. However, the term "sentimental", especially when it is used to describe art and responses to art, has increasingly come to have a negative connotation. For example, the critic I.A. Richards wrote that sentimental responses are responses that are "too great", or "crude", or in one way or another "inappropriate". And Oscar Wilde suggested that sentimentality somehow involves dishonesty when he characterized a sentimental person as someone "who desires to have the luxury of an emotion without paying for it." At least some of our everyday uses of the term "sentimental" echo these negative characterizations of sentimentality. For example, to describe a person as sentimental about small children is to suggest that their responses to children are in some way inadequate: they (rightly) see toddlers as innocent and mischievously cute, but they consistently overlook such important features of toddlers as the dirty diapers they produce and their screaming fits and temper tantrums.

As the latter sort of case reminds us, the notion of sentimentality is not restricted to description and criticism of art and our responses to art. Sentimentality can be a feature of greetings cards, political conventions, ticker-tape parades, graduation ceremonies, news reporting, and indeed of more or less any aspect of public and private life. In attempting to understand how the term "sentimental" is typically used in art criticism, then, and in attempting to understand just what kind of flaw the term is intended to pick out, we shall also be exploring a phenomenon which extends beyond art into many aspects of our lives.

In the first chapter in this part, Anthony Savile suggests that "sentimentality is always open to criticism. There is always something wrong with it . . . There are no situations the proper perception of which demands a sentimental response." This is a striking claim, and one that should give pause for thought to anyone who has ever wiped a tear from their eye while reading Dickens, or who has sobbed their way through *Love Story*. What exactly can Savile mean by "sentimental" in order to hold that sentimentality is so objectionable?

What is wrong with sentimental responses, according to Savile, is that they are based on partial or selective views of what they are responses to. A sentimental response, that is, is a response that is based on a false picture of the world, and furthermore one which we adopt "under the guidance of a desire for gratification and reassurance". Thus Savile suggests that in responding sentimentally we are involved in a kind of self-deception. We *want* to feel in certain ways, and so we selectively and deliberately (though not necessarily consciously) misrepresent the world to ourselves so that we *can* feel in those ways. For example, a man may be so determined to feel superior to a female colleague that he deliberately misrepresents her to himself, refusing to recognize her strengths and abilities and exaggerating her weaknesses, so that he can regard her as less competent than he is. In effect, he *makes* himself believe what he *needs* to believe if he is to feel the way he wants to feel. His comforting feelings of superiority depend upon his deceiving himself about his colleague's true qualities. The common name for his attitude towards his colleague, of course, is "sexism". But if Savile is right, it is also a kind of sentimentality.

In the second chapter in this part, Ira Newman suggests that Savile's account, and others like it, may be too hard on sentimentality. Newman argues that the fact that a response is based on a deliberate misrepresentation of the way things really are, even if that means that the response in question is based on an act of self-deception, does not necessarily mean that the response in question must be flawed or objectionable. Indeed, Newman suggests that the idealization and self-deception characteristic of sentimental responses may sometimes be "psychologically practical": that without a certain measure of idealization and self-deception some aspects of our experience would not be tolerable at all. So perhaps it might be better sometimes to respond to the world sentimentally – to idealize it and deceive ourselves – than it would be to be broken by the world or to become incapable of responding to it at all. Sentimentality may always be objectionable, as Savile claims. But if Newman is right, it may nonetheless sometimes be the best mode of response available to us.

Is the attempt to offer us comfort against the often difficult and unpleasant realities of everyday life a respectable goal for art? Or should art be concerned with showing us the truth about ourselves and our world? In asking about the nature of sentimentality we are in effect asking very fundamental questions about the purpose of art and its proper place in our lives.

19

SENTIMENTALITY

Anthony Savile

An initial clue to the nature of sentimentality is that there is no distinct feeling or content of thought that passes under that name. What qualify are our standard feelings of grief, anger, pity, and so on, and the thoughts internally associated with them. This is not to say that every occurrence of such feelings and thoughts is sentimental. That would be absurd. They are sentimental when they are felt or entertained in a particular way. Sentimentality is properly seen as a *mode* of feeling or thought, not as a feeling of a particular *kind*. The task of elucidation is to characterize that mode by describing the way in which we sentimentally think and feel what we do.

Another thing we know is that sentimentality is always open to criticism. There is always something wrong with it. Whereas for any standard affect there will be situations in which it is quite appropriately felt or in which not to feel it requires explanation, in the case of sentimentality there are no situations the proper perception of which demands a sentimental response or in which its absence needs to be accounted for. The thought in which sentimental grief or pity about something is grounded will always be defective in some way, and I surmise that in its essential defectiveness we find a pointer to its nature.

One property that lays thought open to criticism is falsity. Another, quite compatible with thought's truth, is lack of evidential justification. Now while it is certainly true that when I sentimentalize an object something in my thought about it will be false or evidentially unjustified, these faults, either singly or together, do not capture its essence. If, seeing you knocked down by a car and mistaking you for your brother, I feel sympathy for him, I need not do so sentimentally. Again, if my love for you is rooted in the true but in fact unjustified thought that you cherish me, my love is not on that account a sentimental one.

These two defects of thought are naturally enough envisaged as arising in the course of truth-seeking enquiry. I have supposed myself to form the belief that your brother is hurt and that you cherish me under the guidance of a quite general desire to believe what is true. But we have only to remind ourselves that this is not the only desire that contributes to the formation of belief[1] to see that the deficiency of thought that is characteristic of sentimentality does not arise under the aegis of this particular overarching desire. For given that a belief of mine is so formed, when it is pointed out to me that it is false or that I am not justified in holding it, I shall abandon it or at least suspend belief. If nothing else sustains such errors than my desire rationally to believe what is true, they die a reasonably swift death. By contrast, a man whose grief, anger, or love is sentimental will tend to resist the correction of the thought on which his emotion rests, and this very recalcitrance suggests that what holds the thought in place is not a desire for truth and knowledge but something else – a desire that can be satisfied by seeing the object in a false light. Hence the crucial belief about it is not so much mistaken as arrived at as a result of active false-colouring. And we can perhaps descry the element of purposeful activity in the formation of feeling in the way we speak of ourselves actively *sentimentalizing* something rather than simply passively finding ourselves with a sentimental view of it.

What then is the desire under whose guidance sentimental thought is conducted? Doubtless there are several answers to this question. The most straightforward seems to be that what the sentimentalist seeks is the occurrence of certain enjoyable emotions. And since no emotion can be felt except as supported by a certain thought about its object, an appropriate thought has to be entertained for the sake of the pleasure. Where the object itself does not properly support that thought I shall have to contrive it by projection. Thus for instance I may sentimentalize a duckling before eating it by falsely representing it to myself as eagerly waiting for the pot, and in doing so make possible a gratifying feeling of benevolence towards the bird and the natural order to which the bird belongs.

A more interesting case – and surely as common in its occurrence – is that in which what is desired is not so much a gratifying feeling as a gratifying image of the self that is sustained by a fabricated emotion. As before, what makes the emotion possible is a thought about its object (which may or may not be the self). Take for instance those very common objects of sentimentalization, children and domestic pets. Projecting onto them an exaggerated vulnerability and innocence, I encourage myself to feel a tender compassion for them, one I may make use of to support a view of myself as a man of gentleness and fine feeling. And the temptation to sentimentality here is obvious, for it is far harder to be a man of fine feeling by proper response to the objects around me than it is to fabricate such a characterization of myself by some factitious projection. Indeed, provided that the feeling I generate is one that does underpin the character I want, sentimentality may offer me the added advantage that I may not need to go on and actually do anything about it. My aim is achieved in the feeling.

It must not be thought that only those emotions which we experience with pleasure make for sentimental thought, for once the structure of the phenomenon is clear it is evident that this will not be so. Even when we do not find them pleasing, anger or indignation for instance can easily be fitted into the pattern just illustrated. Thus a man who idealizes a distant political cause may be sentimentally angry or indignant when one of its exponents is extradited from the country, even though he does not experience these feelings with pleasure.[2] What may happen is that in demonstrating against the extradition he may sustain a view of himself as righteous and just. His anger is fed by his sentimental view of the cause, and while it may bring him distress, it also works to enable him to take a gratifying view of his own character. In the same vein it is no more difficult to imagine self-gratifying jealousy or hatred even though these emotions are far more painful to experience than anger or indignation. So my jealousy could support a pleasing view of myself as a man of grand passion, and my hatred for some luckless neighbour serve to endow me with a gratifying heroism that otherwise I would not take myself to possess.

What we see in these various cases is how the sentimentalist achieves a certain kind of gratification by false-colouring an object in his thought. A fuller description would undoubtedly attempt more precision. It would in particular tell us more about typical ways in which the sentimentalist acts, and would show how very often his activity has a protective function, so that what is achieved through the false-colouring of the world that he goes in for is reassurance in a world that is found unsettling. He tends to protect himself against the resistance of other things by softening them down, filing down their uncomfortable edges, or makes what is in truth rather alien and off-putting quite docile to his wishes and tastes. Thus when the advertizers of David Hamilton's *Le Jardin secret* hold out that book of popular photographs as containing "images d'un monde où le spectateur peut contempler la fragile beauté des jeunes filles aux premiers instants de leur éveil à la féminité; monde heureux qui ne connait ni violence, ni viellesse, monde d'élégance et de beauté, refuge contre les rigeurs de la realité," they collude with the photographer in offering the reader a world in which he is comfortably and protectively cocooned. The appeal of these popular shots would scarcely be comprehensible if they did not encourage fantasy to deny the reality of a world in just the odious ways the publicity so glutinously describes.

However, it may seem that the description of sentimentality I have offered is too wide, for it suggests that almost any gratifying self-protective fantasy projected onto the world will be a sentimental one. And that is surely wrong. For example I may find myself unable to understand the work of some difficult philosopher, Kant, say, or Wittgenstein, and rather than admit that the fault lies with me, rather than abandon my pride, I may accuse the author himself of bad faith and of passing off as deep insight what is in fact little more than empty babble. Here I protect my pride by discovering in imagination the confidence trick that has taken everyone else in. In consequence I represent the frustration arising from my own limitations as justified anger, and protect my self-esteem by detection of the intellectual fraud. Such a situation may appear to mirror those just set out, but it would scarcely be one in which I have sentimentalized the work of Kant or of Wittgenstein.

It is evident that this kind of case cannot be dealt with by pointing to some unacceptable harshness in the emotion that is involved. We have already noticed that *any* emotion can on occasion be sentimentally entertained – though it may well be that in some cases the object of the sentimentalization and the object of the emotion differ (as in the case of hatred that I mentioned). However, it may be right to suggest that what distinguishes the sentimental fantasy from the other one is its tendency to idealize its objects, to present them as pure, noble, heroic, vulnerable, innocent, etc., and that feature is quite absent in my mistreatment of Kant or Wittgenstein. There I went in for no idealization at all and have instead projected onto the obscure philosopher a kind of malevolent intent that permits me to divert frustration away from myself.

With this emendation made, my tentative suggestion is that a sentimental mode of thought is typically one that idealizes its object under the guidance of a desire for gratification and reassurance. Derivatively, emotion is sentimental which is supported by such as thought. And we can see that such an attitude is one that may be directed not only towards other people and abstract causes, as my illustrative examples have shown, but also towards the self and, at the other extreme, towards the inanimate natural world.

For an example of the former, consider Ruskin's remarks in 1865 to the cadets of the Royal Military Academy at Woolwich:

> You don't understand perhaps why I call you "sentimental schoolboys" when you go into the Army? Because, on the whole, it is love of adventure, of excitement, of fine dress and of pride of fame, all of which are sentimental motives, which chiefly make a boy like going into the Guards better than into a counting-house . . . So far then, as for your own honour and the honour of your families, you choose brave death in a red coat before brave life in a black one, you are sentimental.[3]

To put it more fully than Ruskin did, the young man will be sentimental in his action if he goes into the Guards because by doing so he sustains a picture of himself as grand, glorious, honourable, and dashing in contrast with the mediocre and drab fellow he may dimly suspect himself to be. The idealization of Army life makes it possible for him to love and admire himself and incidentally at the same time does something to ward off the uncomfortable prospect of banality which is the lot of most. To accept that lot, to accept what Ruskin calls life in a black coat, is what would be truly brave, for as Ruskin sees it it is based on fact and does not enjoy the support of illusion that the sentimental young guardsman relies on.

Exactly the same structure can be discerned in the other case too, in that of the sentimentalization of the natural world. Typically we find this when we project onto an inert and separately existing world a warm concern for our human welfare and a tender amenability to our desires and needs. Instances of the strategy are to be found throughout the work of the Romantic poets, and one instructively complex example is supplied by Matthew Arnold's "Dover Beach". There the poet, put in mind of the ebb of Christian faith by the grating of the pebbles on the shore, apostrophizes his mistress in the lines:

> Ah, Love, let us be true
> To one another! for the world, which seems
> To lie before us like a land of dreams
> So various, so beautiful, so new,
> Hath really neither joy, nor love, nor light,
> Nor certitude, nor peace, nor help for pain;
> And we are here as on a darkling plain
> Swept with confused alarms of struggle and flight
> Where ignorant armies clash by night.

Now undoubtedly it is sentimentalization of the ego, and not of Nature, that we first detect here. Lover and mistress are presented as engagingly forlorn and bereft of all comfort but what they offer each other. What makes them forlorn is the departure from the world of faith, whose presence we are given to understand previously extended to Nature herself. With its departure the natural world cannot but be bleak, alien, and comfortless. *This* view of nature is not sentimental. What is sentimental though is the view on which it relies for contrast; the view that when the tide of faith was full Nature did minister to our needs and desires, and that we are now to be pitied because this is no longer so. Here we have a case of one piece of sentimentality facilitating another. For if it were clearly recognized that Nature is unchangingly inert, and therefore just as much capable of attaching the poet now as before his loss of faith, its distance could not be made a source of self-pity. The poet would not be able to think of it as having abandoned him. It is the suggested breakdown of the first idealization that makes way for the second. Both are gratifying, and both give the poet an easy picture of himself that is insulated from the more precise and better sustainable – the painful – view.

NOTES

1   Cf. Freud, *Totem and Taboo*, chapter III, 2: "Our psychoanalytic work will begin at a different point. It must not be assumed that mankind came to create its first world system through a purely speculative thirst for knowledge. The practical need of mastering the world must have contributed to this effort." And Freud was no stranger to the idea that one way of mastering the world was to make it up.
2   The example comes from M. Tanner "Sentimentality", *Proceedings of the Aristotelian Society* (1976/7), 127–47.
3   Ruskin, *The Crown of Wild Olives*, §118.

20

THE ALLEGED UNWHOLESOMENESS OF SENTIMENTALITY

Ira Newman

Nearly all philosophers and literary analysts who have commented on the subject agree with Anthony Savile that sentimentality – whether in art or in life – is a defective condition that deserves our censure, if not outright contempt.[1] I shall oppose this position by challenging two arguments these critics have frequently used: first, the argument that sentimental objects and attitudes, because they are based on pleasing idealizations of reality, are false to the world; and second, the argument that sentimental persons, because of the way they form pleasing fantasies about bits of their lives, are false to themselves. I shall conclude that, although there may be unwholesome instances of sentimentality, there may be laudable ones as well. Underlying my account is the linguistic observation that the term "sentimentality" has not only an evaluative sense (as a term assessing fault), but also a descriptive sense, which is free of evaluation.

1 THE MEANING OF "SENTIMENTALITY"

The central idea in sentimentality is the evocation, by some aspect of the sentimental subject matter, of a tender emotion (for example, compassion, sympathy, or affection). This emotion, furthermore, is a response to a pleasing idealization, resulting from some degree of exaggeration or misrepresentation in the sentimental subject matter.[2] Thus when war veterans grow sentimental at a commemorative reunion, they may feel fondness for the drama of the great campaign in which they fought as young soldiers.[3] Their fondness may be described as "sentimental" because that emotion may be possible for them only if they idealize a battle that, at the time of engagement, they experienced as a repulsive series of disconnected events. Their idealization suppresses, to a certain degree, some of the important stressful, psychologically unassimilable features of combat.

When applied to art, "sentimentality" surfaces prominently as the name of a particular literary genre, style, or form. Thus a chapter of literary history is devoted to the appearance in the eighteenth century of the "sentimental novel," where characters such as Richardson's Clarissa and Sterne's Yorick exhibit a certain idealized portrait of virtue (in particular, an unwillingness to compromise with the world) in distress (due to their defeat by the world), and it is this idealized portrait that elicits our pity.[4] Subsequently, in the nineteenth century the fiction of Dickens and the Victorian novelists developed sentimental literary paradigms of innocent children, death and family separation, the poor, and moral conversion (such as Scrooge's). What distinguished these cases was their eliciting, from audiences, tender emotions of sympathy and affection, aimed at fictional objects that were shorn of the genuinely repugnant and dissonant features that their unidealized counterparts might be expected to exhibit.[5]

Whether applied to artworks in this way or to subjects in life, as outlined previously, the term "sentimentality" can be understood in a purely descriptive sense, as simply ascribing certain properties to a subject, without expressing any evaluation of the worth of the subject. Clearly, this evaluation-free sense is not the only way the term is used. "Sentimentality" may also be used as a term of evaluative abuse, when, for instance, we call something "sentimental nonsense" or "sentimental slop." I am neither denying that the latter usage exists nor legislating that it ought not exist. I am merely saying that the abusive sense is not the only legitimate sense, because – for one thing – there is nothing in any of the term's instantiations I have thus far mentioned that is obviously or inevitably faulty.[6] Surely sentimental subjects (in art and in life) can be burdened by faults, but upon further analysis these faults turn out to be attributable to aesthetic, psychological, or moral qualities that can plague any subject, not just, or even primarily, sentimental ones. My suspicion is that when "sentimentality" *is* used as an evaluative term of abuse, it is actually these other factors – such as poor aesthetic design, psychological shallowness, or moral insensitivity – that are being called to our attention, not the central ideas of sentimentality I have outlined above.[7] And finally, I suspect that the insults heaped on sentimentality, by a virtually unanimous chorus of critics in this century, have been the result of an illicit merging of the evaluative and descriptive senses of the term.[8] These critics have simply failed to recognize that there are two distinct senses here, not merely one.

In order to prove my point I shall outline some of the prominent arguments that have claimed sentimentality amounts to a flaw in a subject, and I shall then show why these arguments are themselves flawed.

2 BEING FALSE TO THE WORLD

If sentimentality is an idealization that suppresses many of the undesirable features in a subject matter, is this not a falsification of that subject matter? And if so, is this not a sufficient reason for condemning sentimentality, since being false to the world is either intrinsically or instrumentally bad? Such reasoning is one kind of attack perennially mounted against sentimentality. How valid is it?

A. Let us consider the claim, first, that there is something *intrinsically* bad about this kind of falsification. Underlying this view is a general presumption against falsification as a degenerate moral, aesthetic, or epistemological condition. When applied to art, this presumption leads to the view that although artworks may legitimately present fictional representations (for example, Scrooge is not a real person and the ghosts that visit him are incompatible with empirical views of reality), these fictional representations must be faithful, or true, to the psychology and morality of human beings and the events that befall them. Since the idealizing characteristics of sentimentality violate this requirement, sentimentality is intrinsically bad and deserves our censure.[9]

There are two reasons why this argument fails.

(i) Such falsification is not distinctive of sentimentality, but is found in many kinds of artworks and responses – even those of a clearly laudable nature. Thus Hector's tragic death in the *Iliad* is a blatant falsification, not simply because it is physiologically incredible that a man whose neck has just been speared could deliver a well-formed death speech, but because Homer purposely conceals from us the corporeal repulsiveness of blood and ripped flesh in order to cast a classical patina of grandeur on his warrior's death.[10] The butchery of death in war is purified by that remarkable Homeric light which converts the most vile act of violence into an epic tableau. In view of this sort of falsification, sentimental varieties, such as the antiseptic portraits of death by consumption in nineteenth-century romantic art, do not suffer for want of company.[11] There are plenty of targets around that are vulnerable to the same charge.

(ii) But is falsification of this sort – wherever it may be found – always a flaw? Perhaps not. There are times when we may regard competing values, such as kindness and concern for others, as more important than the value of telling the truth and, as a result, may come to view benevolent lies to a dying patient as morally appropriate in some cases. Examples like this suggest that truth telling and fidelity are only in *general* virtues; they are not virtues under *all* conditions.

We can extend such an analysis to the case of art, where the values of aesthetic excellence, audience pleasure, and cathartic release, and escapism often override (and quite properly so) the commitment to present the whole truth. One wonders what the story of the *Iliad* would look like if Homer were denied the authority to suppress the details that he did. There would be no epic or tragic quality to his tale, and it would thus be a disappointingly diminished aesthetic achievement. For although the *Iliad* would still retain its abundantly faithful psychological and moral observations (it is the intricate story, after all, of an angry man and his mistakes), it would lack that special transcendent vision of war, death, and human choices, which, however much larger than – and hence untrue to – life, nevertheless appeals to some deep and abiding need in our spiritual consciousness.

Therefore, basing a charge against sentimentality on its falsification of objects would once again be a confused accusation, because falsification is not always a flaw. In particular, it is not a flaw when aesthetic values deserve placement above truth in a ranking order.[12]

But, someone might object, falsification has its own dangers. It can lead to false or distorted beliefs and actions in those who encounter it. So while we might acknowledge the value of falsification to achieve some aesthetic ends, we would not be so generous toward it if we attended to many of the pathological beliefs and actions emerging in its wake. It is to these consequences that I shall now turn.

B. There are two kinds of consequentialist objections to falsification.

One kind claims that the falsifications in art generate false beliefs about reality and, consequently, unintelligent or ineffectual actions based on those false beliefs.[13] Dickens's novel *A Christmas Carol*, for instance, presents false views of the poor (their plight is attributed entirely to an immoral economic system, with surprisingly little responsibility given to their own character flaws); false views of moral improvement (Scrooge's miraculous conversion suggests nothing of the perseverance needed when the inevitable frustrations inherent in charitable giving surface); and false views of the solutions to social misery (a kind heart and distributed money, not basic changes in either the moral, educational, or social structures). Such false – and sentimental – views, the objection maintains, encourage audiences to acquire oversimplified beliefs and to act on these oversimplifications. Such actions, in all likelihood, will lack the sophistication to deal effectively with complex situations, such as social poverty. To compound matters, the defeated actors may become so resigned to their failure that they will be discouraged from attempting any further actions in the future.

While this first kind of objection addresses a person's inclinations to take action in the world, the second addresses a tendency found in many people to avoid action in the world altogether and to take refuge, instead, in a world of pleasing aesthetic fantasy. Sentimentality is conducive to such escapist inclinations because its falsifications involve projecting an appealing quality on its idealized subjects.[14] Thus if the Cratchits and Tiny Tim were presented as seething with resentment, or if Scrooge were not in the end presented as, in Chesterton's words, a "great furnace of real happiness"[15] – possibilities which would be, no doubt, psychologically and socially more true to life – we would probably not have the degree of fondness for them that we find ourselves so curiously possessing. This suggests the possibility that under some circumstances we might be tempted to remain within the aestheticized sanctuary of the sentimental "world" itself rather than deal with *real* poor people, whose intractable faults and problems may be the cause of deep discomfort to us.[16] For why bother with real poor people when we can deal exclusively with their more pleasing counterparts in art? But this spiral of thought clearly has a morally depraved character, which is forcefully illustrated by imagining a theatergoer who avoids encountering a homeless person, out of fear that this disturbing scene may ruin the delicious images of poor people he brings away with him from a dramatized performance of *A Christmas Carol*.[17]

What can we say in response to these consequentialist objections to sentimentality's falsification?

Based on my previous arguments, it is clear the response cannot be limited specifically to sentimentality, but must refer to the falsification found in art in general. This is because the falsifications of tragedy and epic poetry, for example, may be just as likely as those of sentimentality to lead to unwholesome consequences. Thus Hector's sanitized death may, in some way, lead to glamorized views of war, and, as a consequence, to an acceptance of or even eagerness for war. And reading the *Iliad* (as well as viewing its various reincarnations in contemporary war movies) may become a pleasing aestheticist alternative to the repellent, yet sometimes necessary, task of dealing with the psychological and moral horrors of real battlefield deaths.

Referring to the *Iliad* in this incidental manner, though, suggests an answer. Surely we do not condemn this work just because it may lead some audiences to develop undesirable beliefs or actions. While acknowledging that such effects do take place, we might also assert, quite legitimately, that blaming the *Iliad* would place far too much responsibility on the artwork itself. After all, audiences bring their own moral, intellectual, and psychological dispositions to artworks, and they should bear some of the responsibility for assessing the fidelity of various components of the artwork. An insensitivity to the realities of battlefield death, for example, reflects a shallow historical or intellectual background. The solution is to strengthen this background through an exposure to alternative reports of the sobering facts, such as photographs of war dead, or artworks expressing disillusionment with war (Wilfred Owen's poem "Dulce et Decorum Est," for instance). With this background, the *Iliad*'s narrative may be appreciated from a more balanced perspective, and those glorified views of dying on the battlefield can be taken for what they are: the transfigurations of art, not accounts of the truth. Much the same may be said about sentimentality's falsifications.

But isn't this reinstatement of falsification too sanguine in its expectations? Why should one assume that the audience can acquire the perspective needed to recognize the falsification for what it is? If the audience is fed a steady diet of such falsifications, or if a falsification is especially powerful (as it seems to be in Dickens), how is the audience to develop the resources to resist? The only answer to be given is that the match between artwork and audience is rarely an optimal one, and rarely a final one. Mistakes and misjudgments are bound to occur. The audience simply has to do its best to subject the artwork to various tests, and critics must continually prod the audience to persist in testing and to come up with the most balanced views. The fact that there is often failure is no justification for relieving the audience of its obligation.[18]

3 BEING FALSE TO ONESELF

There is another sort of falsification argument that has been used to discredit sentimentality. This sort of argument maintains that sentimentality involves the expression of responses that are false to the genuine traits of the person exhibiting the response, and false, moreover, in some normatively objectionable way.

In I.A. Richards's eyes, for example, the sentimental response can often be viewed as a contrived way of dodging certain unpleasant memories that the person is afraid to face, yet should.[19] There are hints of personal insincerity here: The person senses where the sources of disturbance are and simply avoids thinking of them, replacing them instead with the rosy idealizations that sentimentality brings. And if one thinks there might be some redeeming reasons for these evasive maneuvers, Richards reminds us that our personal development and "mental health" require us, sometimes, to "envisage" the painful aspects of experience we are so deviously trying to avoid.[20]

In contrast to Richards's emphasis on mental flabbiness, Oscar Wilde draws attention to the moral shabbiness of sentimentality. In Wilde's view, sentimental people want to appear good, both to themselves and to others, through exhibiting emotional expressions they have not earned the right to exhibit, simply because they have not made the sacrifices required for a genuine expression of the emotion. Thus they weep in sorrow and compassion without feeling the full pain or meaning of the sorrow and compassion they appear to have. Or they choose thoughtless (and hence easy to exhibit) forms of expression, such as commercial condolence cards. Like many hypocrites in the moral sphere they want to cash in on the rewards that moral sacrifice brings (the sense of nobility, the pride, the good name) without having paid the full moral price for these rewards. In Wilde's words, sentimentalists desire "to have the luxury of an emotion" (or the air of refinement that an act of moral loftiness brings) "without having to pay for it." It is a desire to look moral, even to feel moral, without really being moral.[21]

In a view reminiscent of both Richards's and Wilde's reflections, Anthony Savile calls attention to the desire, on the part of some sentimentalists, to maintain certain reassuring images of themselves even though such self-images are no more than pleasing fantasies, products of an often intricate set of fact-distorting manipulations. For example, a young man's sentimental attitude toward a military career may be traced to an initial, and distorting, idealization of army life, where he imagines adventure, fine dress, and bravery to rule the day, rather than the revulsion, humiliation, and terror that are often the soldier's true lot. When the young man, in a subsequent move, imagines *himself* to be a member of the military, his initial distortion of army life allows him to project a fantasy self he can love and admire, which in this case amounts to a "picture of himself as grand, glorious, honourable, and dashing in contrast with the mediocre and drab fellow he may dimly suspect himself to be." According to Savile, other sorts of sentimentalists may concoct still other kinds of pleasing fantasies: reassuring self-images, for instance, of compassion (on which Wilde seems to have focused), of righteousness, of forlornness, or of invulnerability to the assaults of a harsh reality.

To counter these stinging assessments, I shall contend that Richards, Wilde, and Savile are actually aiming their barbs at pathological or corrupt instances of sentimentality, and that not *all* instances of sentimentality are pathological or corrupt. My claim, then, is that there is more to sentimentality than the personal insincerity, hypocrisy, or fantasizing these writers attribute to it. Sentimentality can actually be displayed in circumstances where we might even heap praise on it for its exhibition of certain virtues – moral, aesthetic, and psychological.

For my support I shall return to Dickens, and this time to one of his acknowledged masterpieces, *Dombey and Son*. In that novel, chapter 16 is devoted to the death of Dombey's young son, little Paul. It is a scene of overwhelming sentimentality, where the young boy virtually presides over his own deathbed, attempting to comfort the grief-stricken adults with kind and judiciously expressed words ("Don't be so sorry for me, dear Papa! Indeed I am quite happy!"). The self-possession of little Paul – the absence of any public display of fear on his part, as well as any need for psychological support from the adult world – lends an idealized quality to Dickens's representation of him. This appears so because one source of our horror at a young child's death is the sense that adults are forced to abandon a vulnerable creature, possessing only minimal command of the mental and moral tools of life, to the intractable grip of death. Dickens denies all that in his description, in the interest of presenting Paul as a character for whom we feel sympathy and affection, yet whose death is not a source of unrelieved disturbance. It is in this way that Dickens has sentimentalized the death of his young character.[22]

Almost immediately the challenges of Richards, Wilde, and Savile can be heard. Is Dickens's portrayal a way of dodging the anguish implicit in such an unhappy event, as Richards might maintain? Or, to invoke Wilde's analysis, is the response elicited from readers, narrator, or author a falsely noble one, where we are caused no real pain by Paul's death, and where our expressive gesture of compassion – like some commercial sympathy card – is not thought out and is, therefore, superficial? Or to allude to Savile, does the sweetness of Paul's death lead us to fantasize a reassuring self-image, in which we see ourselves "cocooned" in a world where normally painful and uncontrollable events appear "quite docile to our wishes and tastes"?

To follow these lines of attack would be a mistake, however. While they clearly provide plausible analyses, and may even be applicable in some cases, they are not applicable in the case of little Paul's death. Actually it is just the reverse that seems true, based particularly on a reading of some personal letters Dickens wrote in a period before his creation of *Dombey*. In those letters (which announced how he planned to deal with the death of his young sister-in-law, Mary Hogarth), Dickens promised "never to shrink from speaking of her, as if her memory were to be avoided, but rather to take a melancholy pleasure in recalling the times when we were all so happy."[23] The suggestion here is that of encountering one's memories, not dodging them; of making oneself vulnerable to the pain of memory, rather than inuring oneself to loss by refusing to dwell on any thought of the dead; of loyalty, forbearance, and respect in relation both to the memory and to the lost person, rather than egoistic desensitization.

There clearly is something odd about nineteenth-century expressions of this sort, which differ so markedly from the more stoic, or reserved, attitudes toward death and sorrow that are the norm today. Such differences must not lead us to any smug conclusions about the cultural superiority of our own historical period, however. For a person living at the present time may still recognize such virtues as loyalty and forbearance in Dickens's letter, and this suggests that the oddness we detect in Dickens's response may reflect only our own unfamiliarity with a perfectly legitimate way members of another culture choose to react to misfortune.

If we now turn to little Paul's death scene, we can see how the pattern of ideas and responses associated with Dickens's letters is realized.

In the first place, the cheery idealization of Paul's death does not suggest a way for readers, narrator, or author to suppress the painful response to misfortune (as Richards might have thought). Nor does it suggest a way for the same individuals to maintain a reassuring self-image of invulnerability to pain (as Savile might have speculated). On the contrary, we can view Dickens's portrayal as a way of *recovering* the pain in question. For what the idealization achieves is a suppression not of *all* aspects of the pain, but only of those features that might prove to be most repugnant, and unbearably painful, to someone remembering them. It is these repugnant features – more precisely, the *anticipation* of having to remember them – that may drive a person toward fantasizing, in an effort to avoid recalling them altogether. But while avoiding the most repugnant features might be a rather innocent thing, the tendency for such forms of avoidance to include the person, thing, or quality of life whose absence gives rise to the pain, might not be: for by avoiding recall of these things, one becomes vulnerable to inappropriate levels of forgetfulness, apathy, or disloyalty. So in the interest of faithfulness to the memory of the loss, idealization, by making recall more palatable, proves to be a psychological ally, not an obstacle.

Second, the compassion extended to little Paul does not fit either of the Wildean signs of hypocrisy. For one thing, as we have just seen, the pain of the loss is not denied, but is genuinely felt. For another, the expressive response Dickens elicits is one requiring a certain degree of reflection and novelty for its formation. That response can best be described, in the telling phrase Dickens uses in his letter, as a "melancholy pleasure." Whatever that phrase signifies, it clearly is not reducible to the thoughtless and stock responses associated with commercial condolence cards.[24] This is because, at the very least, the phrase suggests that the person responding is trying to hold together emotional elements – of happiness and meditative sadness – in an extraordinary union, which extends well beyond what we would usually expect of these conflicting feelings.[25] And since it requires an *expense* of mental and moral energy for the person responding to resolve to hold these two in conjunction, how could Wilde's contemptuous assessment – that the sentimentalist is unprepared to "*pay*" for his emotions – still stand up? Wilde undoubtedly has his sights correctly targeted on many sentimentalists, but that may say more about them than about sentimentality. Dickens's sentimentality seems to have manifested itself in a different, and – by contrast – quite laudable, direction.

To conclude: I have claimed, in this paper, that the jeers almost everyone hurls at sentimentality spring from a fallacious set of arguments. First, while we may admit that sentimental objects and attitudes are false to the facts, it does not follow from this that sentimentality is flawed, for in many situations falsification may enable values such as aesthetic excellence or audience pleasure to be realized. Second, while some sentimental persons are false to themselves (through initiating fantasies about aspects of their lives), the same cannot be said of other sentimentalists, who may display personal virtues, such as loyalty and forbearance, in dealing with painful memories or possibilities. In the end, then, we can say that instances of sentimentality are susceptible of either praise or blame. But which assessment it is to be, is a matter to be decided by examining the particular contexts within which the sentimental instance emerges, not by complacently assuming a blanket evaluation of sentimentality itself.[26]

NOTES

1 Anthony Savile, *The Test of Time: An Essay in Philosophical Aesthetics* (Oxford: Oxford University Press, 1982), pp. 237–43.
2 A variation of this idea is expressed by R.A. Sharpe ("Solid joys or fading pleasures," in Eva Schaper, ed., *Pleasure, Preference and Value* [Cambridge: Cambridge University Press, 1983], pp. 86–98), who states that "sentimentality involves the taking of pleasure in an object without attending to the object in its comprehensive character" (p. 89). See also Mark Jefferson ("What is wrong with sentimentality?" *Mind* 92 [1983]: 519–29) for another variation: "[The sentimentalist's] trick is to misrepresent the world in order to feel unconditionally warm-hearted about bits of it." Components of the central idea are also found in the formulations of several other writers.
3 For other treatments of this example see I.A. Richards, *Practical Criticism* (1929; reprint, New York: Harcourt, Brace & Co., 1960). pp. 260–1, 267–8; and Robert C. Solomon, "In defense of sentimentality," *Philosophy and Literature* 14 (1990): 304–23 (see p. 321).
4 See R.F. Brissenden, *Virtue in Distress* (London: Macmillan, 1974), pp. 89–91; also pp. 159–86 (for an analysis of *Clarissa*) and pp. 218–42 (for an analysis of *A Sentimental Journey*).
5 In the late eighteenth century sentimental fiction was thought to require suppression of the repulsive. J.M.S. Tompkins (*The Popular Novel in England 1770–1800*, 1932; reprint [Lincoln: University of Nebraska Press, 1961], p. 104) quotes a critic of the day, when she

writes: "There was a crying need for a 'new torture or nondescript calamity' in the world of fiction, and the need was the more difficult to supply because distress, in order to be pleasing, must avoid awakening disgust. Pity must always be associated with love and esteem; no idea must be admitted which destroys 'the grace and dignity of suffering,' and even scenes of poverty must be so chastened as to leave the imagination an amiable figure to dwell upon."

6 Richards (op. cit., pp. 255–6) also wants us to know that there are different uses of "sentimentality" – in particular, an emotive use (lacking a descriptive core) and a descriptive use (which, contrary to Richards's label, is actually an evaluative use that merely presupposes, as any evaluation naturally must, a descriptive core). Thus, despite his linguistic interest, Richards fails to identify a purely descriptive and evaluation-free use of "sentimentality," as I am advocating. See also Solomon (op. cit., pp. 310–11) for ideas on how to define "sentimentality." One problem in Solomon's analysis is his having adopted a definition of "sentimentality" that is too weak ("an expression of and appeal to the tender emotions"). Without some further qualification, this definition articulates such a seemingly unobjectionable state of affairs that one may wonder where the fault in sentimentality is alleged to be found.

7 M.H. Abrams (*A Glossary of Literary Terms*, 3rd edn [New York: Holt, Rinehart & Winston, 1971], pp. 156–7) expresses similar thoughts: "A useful distinction between sentimental and nonsentimental is one which does not depend on the intensity or type of the feeling expressed or evoked, but labels as sentimental a work or passage in which the feeling is rendered in commonplaces and *clichés*, instead of being freshly verbalized and sharply realized in the details of the situation as represented."

8 Sentimentality's lone apologist, recently, is Solomon, who, in the article already cited and in "On kitsch and sentimentality" (*Journal of Aesthetics and Art Criticism* 49 [1991]: 1–14), argues that sentimentality is a virtue. While I sympathize with the attack on sentimentality's critics, Solomon's position, nevertheless, may tilt the balance too far in the direction of unqualified praise. That is one reason it is beneficial to carve out a descriptive, evaluation-free sense of "sentimentality."

9 See Sharpe (op. cit., pp. 88–9), where the contempt for this sort of falsification, in sentimentality, is suggested: "*The Merry Widow* is sentimental because it presents intrigues amongst the privileged with no hint of the exploitation needed to preserve that society, or even of its darker side. *The Marriage of Figaro* is unsentimental because it does not duck that issue; we see the depth of corruption that power creates in the privileged" (p. 88).

10 See Homer, *Iliad* (trans. W.H.D. Rouse), 22. Homer is careful to point out that Achilles' spear had not cut Hector's windpipe, and thus Hector "could still answer his foe." This may somewhat diminish our skepticism, but not by much.

11 See Sharpe (op. cit., p. 88): "Puccini presents us with the cliché of the lovers reunited just in time for the heroine to die of that romantic disease, consumption. The soprano lead will manage a discreet little cough but producers never give us blood and phlegm."

12 Solomon ("On kitsch and sentimentality," p. 12) asks a well-founded rhetorical question: "Should we insist that all paintings of young, adorable children be triptychs, an adorable centerpiece, perhaps, but two obligatory side panels displaying the child destroying a piece of furniture in one and throwing a temper tantrum in the other?" Solomon, however, attributes this all to a selective "focus" or "concern," rather than to "distortion" or falsification. I find Solomon's distinction unnecessarily coy here. The example *does* exhibit falsification, but there is nothing wrong with it in this sort of instance. See also Solomon, "In defense of sentimentality," pp. 318 and 321.

13 See Mary Midgley, "Brutality and sentimentality," *Philosophy* 54 (1979): 385–9; and Jefferson.

14 See note 5.

15 G.K. Chesterton, *Charles Dickens, a Critical Study* (1906; excerpt reprinted in George H. Ford and Lauriat Lane, Jr, eds, *The Dickens Critics* [Ithaca, N.Y.: Cornell University Press, 1961], p. 124).

16 For similar views, see Richard Shusterman, "Aesthetic education or aesthetic ideology: T.S. Eliot on art's moral critique," *Philosophy and Literature* 13 (1989), pp. 96–114; reprinted with some minor changes in his *Pragmatist Aesthetics: Living Beauty, Rethinking Art* (Oxford, England and Cambridge, Mass.: Blackwell, 1992), pp. 147–68.

17 This illustration is a slight modification of Shusterman's basic example ("Aesthetic education," p. 101 and *Pragmatist Aesthetics*, p. 155).

18 An audience, therefore, must grow to understand that Dickens's *Christmas Carol* is operating on several, often clashing, levels. There is, first, a good deal of truth in the novel: The poor under capitalism are in desperate straits and their problems need our attention; people can, and ought to, change their moral outlook if they are too egoistic and lack compassion; repentant sinners should be forgiven and welcomed back to the community. On the other hand, there is a good deal of pleasing untruth, some instances of which I have already mentioned. Added to this list is one overriding untruth which a judicious audience must acknowledge. That is the view that it is easy to be a benefactor: just be jolly, shed a tear for Tiny Tim, keep Christmas, and throw some money around. But giving is not easy. We have to decide what projects to support and how to support them. We have to distribute goods and energies according to a rational scheme. And we have to decide on a psychologically and morally plausible balance between helping others and satisfying ourselves. The truth is that we struggle with our benevolence as much as with our greed. But Dickens's novel, in the interest of aesthetic pleasure and escapism – which we can admit as worthwhile values – chooses to conceal all that. As responsible audience members, who are experiencing these delights, we cannot afford to collaborate completely in the concealment.

19 See Richards, op. cit., pp. 260–61, 267–70. "And those who contrive to look back to the War as 'a good time', are probably busy dodging certain other memories. . . . The sentimental response steps in to replace [a painful aspect of life] by some other aspect more pleasant to contemplate or by some factitious object which flatters the contemplator" (pp. 267–8).

20 Ibid., p. 268.

21 See Oscar Wilde, "De profundis," *The Letters of Oscar Wilde*, ed. Rupert Hart-Davis (New York: Harcourt, Brace & World, 1962), pp. 500–7. In this cryptic, but intriguing, section of a letter Wilde wrote from Reading Prison, Wilde accuses his lover, Lord Alfred Douglas, of hypocrisy and moral tackiness. According to Wilde, Douglas adopted a noble stance of charity toward his mother (whom he thought financially too strapped to be burdened by a son's request for money) while, at the same time, sponging funds from Wilde, in order to support his expensive lifestyle (pp. 500–1). From this situation of financial and moral irresponsibility, Wilde develops a metaphor for sentimentality. "A sentimentalist is simply one who desires to have the luxury of an emotion without having to pay for it. To propose to spare your mother's pocket was beautiful. To do so at my expense was ugly. You think that one can have one's emotions for nothing. One cannot. Even the finest and most self-sacrificing emotions have to be paid for. Strangely enough, that is what makes them fine" (p. 501). And immediately following this, Wilde lashes out at the willingness of "ordinary people" to settle for the convenience of adopting other people's stock emotional expres-

sions, rather than working out thoughtful expressions of their own. Their "intellectual and emotional life," says Wilde, "is a very contemptible affair. Just as they borrow their ideas from a sort of circulating library of thought – the *Zeitgeist* of an age that has no soul – and send them back soiled at the end of each week, so they always try to get their emotions on credit, and refuse to pay the bill when it comes in" (p. 501). For remarks about Wilde's ideas, in particular the costs required in understanding one's feelings, see Michael Tanner, "Sentimentality," *Proceedings of the Aristotelian Society* 77 (1976–7), pp. 142–3. For eighteenth-century critical ideas about the "luxury" of noble emotions and the possibility of hypocrisy, see Tompkins, op. cit., pp. 100–3, and Brissenden, op. cit., pp. 81–4. For similar ideas from the nineteenth century, see Walter E. Houghton, *The Victorian Frame of Mind, 1830–1870* (New Haven and London: Yale University Press, 1957), pp. 273–9.

22 For many readers, little Paul's death scene is a flawed literary performance, because of its sentimentality. See, for instance, H.M. Daleski, *Dickens and the Art of Analogy* (New York: Schocken Books, 1970), pp. 136–9. Other readers, however, argue persuasively for the death scene's considerable aesthetic merits, in terms of the overall structure of the novel and the subtlety of the psychological observations with which Dickens endows Paul. For some examples of critical praise, see Steven Marcus, *Dickens: from Pickwick to Dombey* (New York: Basic Books, 1965), pp. 322–9; Kathleen Tillotson, *Novels of the Eighteen-Forties* (Oxford: Oxford University Press, 1954), pp. 47–53; and Barbara Hardy, *Forms of Feeling in Victorian Fiction* (Athens, Ohio: Ohio University Press, 1985), pp. 63–77.

23 Charles Dickens, *The Letters of Charles Dickens*, ed. Madeline House and Graham Storey (Oxford: Clarendon Press, 1965), 1: 323. (The omission of a comma following "her" in the original text may suggest an ambiguity in meaning that is clearly not the intent of Dickens's statement. To avoid such a suggestion I have inserted a comma in my transcription.) For an illuminating discussion of the relationship between Dickens's personal letters of this period and his sentimental literature, see Marcus, op. cit., pp. 132–5, 158–61.

24 Dickens's "melancholy pleasure" is not to be confused with the "pleasures of melancholy." The latter refers to the popular eighteenth-century view of melancholic states as sources of wisdom and spiritual rapture. Dickens saw no such exalted dimension in melancholy. Instead, he seemed to view melancholy as one component in a complex mental state (along with pleasure as the other component), much as we might view bitter and sweet as components of a complex (and puzzling) experience we call "bittersweet." For the "pleasures of melancholy" see Louis I. Bredvold, *The Natural History of Sensibility* (Detroit: Wayne State University Press, 1962), pp. 53–73.

25 In commenting on another personal letter, Marcus (op. cit., p. 161) states: "With its distinctions that do not quite distinguish, with its qualifications that slide into blurred incertitude, this passage reveals Dickens' sentimentality as a condition of spirit in which doubt and pain and affirmation coexist, and in which affirmation is commanded forcefully, willfully, to prevail."

26 An earlier version of this paper was presented at both national and Eastern Division meetings of the American Society for Aesthetics in 1992, and at the 1993 meeting of the American Philosophical Association, Central Division. I am grateful to the respective commentators – Robert Solomon, Cynthia Grund, and Paul D. Eisenberg – for their provocative criticisms. Thanks are also extended to Ellen Blais, Bernard Koloski, Alex Neill, Richard Shusterman, and Kathleen Thompson for helpful suggestions, and to Mansfield University for research support.

SUGGESTIONS FOR FURTHER READING

Calinescu, Matei (1976) "The benevolent monster: reflections on kitsch as an aesthetic concept", *Clio* 6.

—— (1987) *Five Faces of Modernity: Modernism, Avant-Garde, Decadence, Kitsch, Postmodernism*, Durham: Duke University Press.

Crick, Philip (1983) "Kitsch", *British Journal of Aesthetics* 23: 48–52.

Dewey, John (1984) "Quest for certainty", in *John Dewey: The Later Works 1925–53*, vol. 4, ed. Jo Ann Boydston, Carbondale: Southern Illinois University Press.

Dorfles, Gillo (ed.) (1968) *Kitsch: The World of Bad Taste*, New York: Universe Books.

Eaton, Marcia Muelder (1989) "Laughing at the death of Little Nell: sentimental art and sentimental people", *American Philosophical Quarterly* 26: 269–82.

Greenburg, Clement (1965) "Avant-garde and kitsch", in his *Art and Culture*, Boston: Beacon Press.

Henry, Lyell D. Jr (1989) "Fetched by beauty: confessions of a kitsch addict", *Journal of Popular Culture* 13: 197–208.

Higgins, Kathleen (1992) "Sweet kitsch", in *The Philosophy of the Visual Arts*, ed. Philip Alperson, New York: Oxford University Press.

Jefferson, Mark (1983) "What is wrong with sentimentality?", *Mind* 92: 519–29.

Knight, Deborah (1999) "Why we enjoy condemning sentimentality: a meta-aesthetic perspective", *Journal of Aesthetics and Art Criticism* 57 (4): 411–20.

Kulka, Thomas (1988) "Kitsch", *British Journal of Aesthetics* 28: 18–27.

Kundera, Milan (1984) *The Unbearable Lightness of Being*, New York: Harper & Row.

Midgley, Mary (1979) "Brutality and sentimentality", *Philosophy* 54: 385–9.

Richards, I.A. (1929) *Practical Criticism*, New York: Harcourt, Brace & World Inc, pp. 242–3.

Solomon, Robert (1990) "In defense of sentimentality", *Philosophy and Literature* 14: 304–23.

—— (1991) "On kitsch and sentimentality", *Journal of Aesthetics and Art Criticism* 49: 1–14.

Tanner, Michael (1976–7) "Sentimentality", *Proceedings of the Aristotelian Society* 77: 127–47.

Wilde, Oscar (1962) Letter to Lord Alfred Douglas, 1897, in *The Letters of Oscar Wilde*, ed. Rupert Hart Davis, London: Hart-Davis, p. 501.

Part 10

ART AND MORALITY

When we admire aesthetically the marvellous masonry and architecture of the Great Pyramid or the exquisite furniture and jewellery of Tut-ankh-Amen's tomb, there is a conflict in our hearts between our pride and pleasure in such triumphs of human art and our moral condemnation of the human price at which these triumphs have been bought: the hard labour unjustly imposed on the many to produce the fine flowers of civilisation for the exclusive enjoyment of a few who reap where they have not sown. During these last five or six thousand years, the masters of the civilisations have robbed their slaves of their share in the fruits of society's corporate labours as cold-bloodedly as we rob our bees of their honey. The moral ugliness of the unjust acts mars the aesthetic beauty of the artistic results.

Arnold Toynbee, *Civilisation on Trial*, p. 26

What care I that some millions of wretched Israelites died under Pharaoph's lash or Egypt's sun? It was well that they died that I might have the pyramids to look on, or to fill a musing hour with wonderment. Is there one among us who would exchange them for the lives of the ignominious slaves that died? What care I that the virtue of some sixteen-year-old maid was the price paid for Ingres' *La Source*? That the model died of drink and disease in the hospital is nothing when compared with the essential that I should have *La Source*, that exquisite dream of innocence.

George Moore, *Confessions of a Young Man*, pp. 144–5

AESTHETIC JUDGEMENTS AND MORAL JUDGEMENTS have many points in common. Both are kinds of value judgement, and both express attitudes or views which may be of intense, and even overriding, significance to the person making them. For these reasons alone, the two would invite comparison. But understanding the relationship between them becomes urgent once one notes how often, historically, the two have been pitted *against* one another. Plato proposed the expulsion of art from his ideal state, largely on the grounds that it had the potential to corrupt the morals of the young. The reformers of the sixteenth century vandalized churches and cathedrals because they had moral objections to the ornamental and representational features to be found in them. The Nazis mounted an exhibition of so-called "Degenerate Art", selecting the exhibits for their supposed moral decadence (which, by a satisfying inversion of intent, succeeded in bringing together some of the finest works of art from the first part of the twentieth century). In each of these cases, considerations held by the protagonists to be moral ones were pitted against and allowed to override aesthetic considerations. (In each case, too, it seems likely that the judgement of posterity will be that the various protagonists backed the wrong horse.)

It is much harder, however, to think of cases where we allow our aesthetic values to outweigh our moral values. In the first of the chapters in this part, Kendall Walton suggests one set of reasons why that might be. Walton's basic idea is that in order to appreciate the aesthetic qualities of a work of art it is necessary to engage with the work imaginatively. The more a work of art distorts the moral world, Walton argues, the harder it will be to engage imaginatively with that work, and hence the harder it will be to appreciate it. So, for instance, the more loathsome the moral outlook expressed by a novel is, the harder imaginative engagement with and appreciation of it will be. This is why the moral trumps the aesthetic: the presence in a work of certain moral qualities may in effect simply obscure its aesthetic qualities, and so makes it difficult if not impossible to appreciate it. On this account, then, the sixteenth century reformers – say – simply couldn't *see* the beauty of the statuary they destroyed: their moral convictions made the beauty invisible to them.

In Walton's view it is much easier to engage imaginatively with works of art that distort or disregard things that we take to be factually true than it is to engage with works that distort the moral world. So, for example, it is easier to engage imaginatively with *Star Trek* than it is with Bret Easton Ellis's *American Psycho*, even though the latter is (in one sense, at least) much more realistic than the former. In the second chapter, however, Michael Tanner claims that Walton's position oversimplifies the relation between the moral and the aesthetic, and, in particular, underestimates the dependence of the moral on the factual. As Tanner puts it, "the most devastating critique we can mount of moral views" is often "the under-mining of the so-called factual beliefs on which they are based". So, for instance, undermining the moral view that slavery was acceptable depended not least on undermining the factual belief that the slaves in question were simply not fully human. Tanner argues that if the moral is bound up with the factual in this sort of way, then the question of what we can and can't engage with imaginatively, and hence of what we can and can't appreciate aesthetically, is considerably more complex than Walton suggests; and this opens up the possibility that the aesthetic may, sometimes, trump the moral. Tanner's fundamental point, then, is that since neither aesthetic nor moral values are unconstrained by other considerations, one should not expect either of them, always, to outweigh the other: the picture is more complicated than that.

The arguments in this area are difficult and demanding, but also fascinating; and in thinking about them seriously, we engage in a peculiarly direct way with what Friedrich Nietzsche – who defined man as "the valuing animal" – identified as "the fundamental problem" of philosophy: "man".

21

MORALS IN FICTION AND FICTIONAL MORALITY

Kendall L. Walton

I

Works of art from previous ages or from other cultures may contain or embody ideas that we find strange or disagree with. We take some differences in stride, but sometimes we object – the content we disagree with ruins our pleasure and we take it to be grounds for judging the work negatively. In the final five paragraphs of "Of the Standard of Taste",[1] David Hume attempts to locate this difference. We are not or shouldn't be bothered by representations of out of date fashions, he says. "Where any innocent peculiarities of manners are represented" – like princesses carrying water from the spring, or ruffs and fardingales in pictures of our ancestors – "they ought certainly to be admitted; and a man who is shocked with them, gives an evident proof of false delicacy and refinement." We are happy to overlook what we take to be factual mistakes. "Speculative errors . . . found in the polite writings of any age or country . . . detract but little from the value of those compositions." But moral differences are quite another matter, according to Hume. We do not, and should not, tolerate in a work "ideas of morality and decency" that we find repugnant. Although "I may excuse the poet, on account of the manners of his age, I never can relish the composition." Morally reprehensible ideas constitute deformities in the work.

Hume has a point here – actually more than one. That's the trouble. Our first task will be to disentangle them. I will begin with the simpler and more obvious strands and work toward the messier and more interesting ones. Some of the strands have clear affinities with the objections to painting and poetry that Plato expressed in the *Republic*, and have been much discussed since then; others are quite different from these. Questions will arise, as we sort things out, about what exactly Hume had in mind. Often there will be no clear answer. But there is a varied landscape richly deserving of exploration, in the general direction in which he gestured.

II

If someone advocates a moral position we find reprehensible or tries to get us to feel or to act in a way that violates our moral convictions, naturally we object. We refuse to think or feel or act in the way we are asked to, and we are likely to respond to the assertion or request or demand with disgust. The assertion or request or demand may come in an ordinary statement or a lecture or sermon or newspaper editorial. But people also make reprehensible claims or demands by writing poems, by telling stories, by creating fictions.[2] Hume says that "where vicious manners are described, without being marked with the proper characters of blame and disapprobation; this must be allowed to disfigure the poem, and to be a real deformity." His thought is probably that such a work in effect condones the vicious manners, that it condones behaving viciously in real life. If a story has as its moral or message the idea that the practice of genocide or slavery is morally acceptable, or that it is evil to associate with people of other races, of course we object, just as we would to a newspaper editorial that advocates genocide or slavery or condemns interracial friendships. Works of either kind will arouse disgust, and we will judge them negatively.

What kind of defect in the work is this? A moral one, obviously. But not, some would say, an *aesthetic* one. Hume doesn't speak specifically of "aesthetic" value. But he appears to have in mind values that are not themselves narrowly speaking moral, which the presence of morally repugnant ideas in a work may undermine. Morally repugnant ideas may so distract or upset us that we are unable to appreciate whatever aesthetic value the work possesses. Disgust with the celebration of the Nazi Party and its values in Leni Riefenstahl's *Triumph of the Will* may prevent us from appreciating or even noticing the film's cinematic "beauty". But maybe the beauty is there nonetheless; maybe the work's moral failings merely interfere with the enjoyment of its beauty. (They might outweigh its aesthetic value, if the two kinds of value are commensurable.) If so, we should consider it unfortunate that we are psychologically unable to bracket our moral concerns in order to appreciate the work aesthetically. Given that the work exists and has the moral deformities and aesthetic merits that it has, it is too bad that awareness of the former interferes with enjoyment of the latter.

In many instances we do not take this attitude, however. Rather than regretting our inability to appreciate the work aesthetically, we may feel that we don't *want* to; we may be unwilling even to try to look beyond our moral concerns in order to enjoy the work's beauty, as though the beauty itself is tainted. Perhaps our thought, sometimes, is that we don't want to profit (aesthetically) from moral depravity. (The realization that the pyramids were built by slave labour might ruin one's enjoyment of them.) This thought will make more or less sense depending on the extent to which we think the depravity contributes to our potential aesthetic enjoyment. If a work's "beauty" lies in the elegant manner in which it expresses certain thoughts, the thoughts provide the opportunity for the elegance, and to enjoy the beauty will be to profit from the expression of the thoughts.[3] But the cinematic or formal "beauty" of the shots of Hitler's airplane flying through the clouds, in *Triumph of the Will*, may be entirely independent of the film's moral depravity. They would be no less beautiful if they were embedded in an unobjectionable context, and a viewer who is somehow unaware of the film's message would have no difficulty appreciating them aesthetically.

In either case, the way still seems open to regard the work as *possessing* aesthetic value. But that is something we seem sometimes to deny, precisely because of moral failings. Compare a racist joke or a political cartoon that makes a point we find offensive. We may declare pointedly that it is *not* funny – precisely because its message is offensive. To laugh at it, we may feel, would amount to endorsing its message, so we refuse to laugh. Even judging it to be funny may feel like expressing agreement. Perhaps it isn't just that our disgust with the message of *Triumph of the Will* interferes with our ability to appreciate it aesthetically. To allow ourselves to enjoy even its cinematic or formal "beauty" may be to endorse or concur with its praise of Hitler and the Nazis, in this sense to "enter into" the sentiments Riefenstahl is expressing. We might express our unwillingness to do this by declaring that the film is *not* beautiful.

We must not simply assume that this declaration is to be taken literally (although I doubt that much is to be gained by deciding this question). One might reasonably hold that the film *is* beautiful and the cartoon funny, but that *admitting* this, as well as allowing ourselves to enjoy the beauty or the humour, amounts to subscribing to the work's evil message – so we don't admit it. Even so, there is a closer connection between moral and aesthetic value than some would allow. No amount of squinting or compartmentalizing could make appreciation of the aesthetic value morally acceptable. If the work's obnoxious message does not destroy or lessen its aesthetic value, it nevertheless renders this value morally inaccessible. That may be counted as an aesthetic as well as a moral defect; it is a circumstance that is unfortunate from a moral point of view.

What about the contrast that Hume insisted on between ideas concerning morality and ideas of other kinds, in works of art? Maybe works serve less frequently as vehicles for assertions about "factual" matters than moral ones. To describe "vicious manners" in a story without "marking them with the proper characters of blame and disapprobation" is not always to condone them, of course, but in stories of some kinds it is likely to be. Stories about fairy godmothers or time travel, however, rarely have as their messages the claim that there actually are fairy godmothers or that time travel is a real possibility, even if the story does not mark such ideas as not to be believed. Perhaps readers are more in the habit of looking for moral messages than for nonmoral ones in literature.

But fictions do sometimes serve to assert or convey information about nonmoral matters. An historical novel may be expected to get the historical events right, at least in broad outline, and it may have as one of its objectives informing readers about them.

If it gets things wrong we may complain. And we will not necessarily object less strenuously than we would to a work we take to be advocating a moral attitude we disagree with. The assertion of "factual" falsehoods is sometimes a serious matter (sometimes for moral reasons, sometimes for reasons that are not clearly moral). And we won't mind winking at what we take to be a relatively trivial moral claim with which we disagree.

The assertion of "factual" falsehoods in a story, when it matters, may distract us from appreciating the work aesthetically. I am less confident that appreciating the work aesthetically or judging it to be aesthetically good will often be felt as endorsing whatever factual claims we take it to be making.

III

Not all works have messages or morals (even on rather generous construals of these notions). Many contain or embody or express, in one way or another, ideas we may find morally repugnant, but without going so far as asserting or advocating them. The response some works call for is more one of imagining than one of acceptance or belief. A story might encourage or induce appreciators to imagine taking up a certain moral perspective or subscribing to certain moral principles without recommending that they actually do so. One obvious way to induce such imaginings is by portraying sympathetically and with understanding a character who accepts the perspective or principles in question. The story might at the same time encourage readers to disagree with the character; the author may make it clear in her story that she rejects the moral views her character subscribes to.

If we find the perspective presented in a story offensive enough, we may object even to imagining taking it up. We might refuse to empathize with a character who accepts it, to put ourselves imaginatively in her shoes. We usually don't flinch at imagining accepting as true nonmoral propositions that we firmly believe to be false: the proposition that there is a ring that makes its wearer invisible, or that a village in Scotland appears and disappears every hundred years. But the difference is not as large as it appears to be.

Why should we resist merely imagining subscribing to a moral perspective we consider offensive? One familiar explanation is that such imaginings may, subtly or otherwise, tend to encourage one actually to subscribe to it. I am sure there is some truth to this. Suppose I am taken to a cricket match. Finding the event disappointing as ballet, I think I would enjoy it more if I rooted for one team or the other. But I have no reason to prefer either team. Still I want to have a desire about the outcome. So I pick one of the teams arbitrarily, by flipping a coin, and then set out to *imagine* wanting it to win – pretending to myself that it matters. At first this isn't very satisfying and it doesn't help much to make the match exciting. My imaginings are too deliberate and artificial, and I am too vividly aware that I have no real reason for my imagined preference and that only a coin toss sent me in one direction rather than the other. But I follow the same team throughout the season, and my imaginings become less deliberate and seem more natural. Eventually, I find myself *actually* wanting my chosen team to win, and rather unaware of the fact that I have no good reason for wanting it to (although I may admit this if asked).[4]

If in an ordinary case like this, imagined experiences of believing, desiring, and feeling can, overtime, lead to the real thing, one should expect that, whatever combination of beliefs, desires, and feelings, or dispositions thereto, constitute accepting certain moral principles or a certain moral perspective, imagining accepting them can have some tendency to induce one actually to do so. So if a story presents, even just for imaginative understanding, a moral perspective we consider repugnant, we may rightly be wary about entering into the imagining.

We still do not have a very substantial difference between moral ideas in works of art that we disagree with and nonmoral ones, however. Advertisers and political propagandists know that getting people to imagine believing a factual proposition can nudge them toward believing it. We won't resist much if the matter is of little importance to us. It won't hurt me much to believe falsely that Brand A paper towels are softer and more absorbent than Brand X (if they are in fact comparable in quality and price). But when it does matter I do resist. I may want not to imagine that people of one race are genetically less capable in a certain respect than people of another. And I may object to a novel in which it is fictional that this is so, one that asks readers to imagine this. My objection in this case is based on moral considerations, although the proposition I avoid imagining is not itself a moral one. In other cases my concern is prudential. I might avoid reading an historical novel I know to be inaccurate, while preparing for a history examination, for fear it might confuse my knowledge of the historical events.

IV

Concern about being influenced to believe what we want not to believe does not explain very much of the resistance we feel to imagining contrary to our beliefs. Even when our convictions are so secure that there can be no real danger to them, we may strenuously resist imagining them to be mistaken. Hume seems to suggest that it is when we are sure of our moral convictions that we reject works containing contrary ideas.[5] Imaginings can have undesirable and even dangerous effects which, although cognitive in character, are not happily characterized, in ordinary folk psychological terms, as inducing false beliefs. Here is a distinctly nonmoral example.

I am lost in the woods and mistaken about which direction is which. A look at my compass sets me straight. But I am still *turned around*; it still seems to me that *that* direction is north, even though I know it is not. Let's say that I remain *disoriented*. In order to correct my orientation, to bring it into line with my knowledge and belief, I actively imagine north being the direction I know it to be, I picture to myself my house, New York, the Pacific Ocean where I know they are. Eventually my orientation, my "picture" of my surroundings, turns around to match reality.

Although one's orientation is distinct from one's beliefs and can vary independently of them, it has a lot to do with the organization, salience, and accessibility of what one believes. It is much easier for me to figure out which road leads home when I am correctly oriented than when I am not, even while I am looking at my compass. And if I walk without thinking when I am disoriented, my feet may take me in the wrong direction. So it is important that my orientation, as well as my beliefs, be correct.

Perhaps orientation is a matter of imagination, of possessing a certain imaginative picture or map of one's surroundings. In any case, explicit imaginings can affect one's orientation; it was by imagining things as they are that I corrected my orientation. Imagining what I know to be false can have the opposite effect. I may avoid imagining north to be where I think east is for fear doing so might disorient me, even if there is no danger to my knowledge of which direction is which.

We may have similar reasons to resist imagining accepting moral principles or perspectives which we consider mistaken or wrong. Even if we are entirely confident in our judgment and see no real possibility that any imagining will change our minds, we want our instincts to be in line with our convictions. That makes it easier to decide what actions accord with our convictions, and more likely that, when we act without thinking, we will do what we believe to be right. Adopting even in imagination a moral view that I reject in reality, allowing myself to think and feel in imagination as though my convictions were different from what they actually are, might change my moral orientation; it might in this sense "pervert the sentiments of my heart", even if it doesn't change my convictions. The more confident I am of my convictions, the more strenuously I will resist anything that might pry my moral orientation away from them.

Works of art may evoke imaginings which can affect one's orientation. If they threaten to induce an orientation that conflicts with what we believe concerning some matter we take to be important, we object. (We sometimes object to metaphors for similar reasons.)[6]

It is possible that this concern is especially important in the moral realm. I can certainly engage in a lot of imagining about fairies and goblins and time travel and magic rings without having to worry about my "orientation" with regard to these matters being distorted. (I suppose the child who finds himself afraid to walk home at night after watching a horror movie, though he knows full well that the monsters he saw are confined to the world of the movie, suffers such a distortion.) But the example of one's sense of direction shows that it is not only in moral instances that concerns about orientation apply.

V

It has not been hard to find explanations for appreciators' objections to works of art that contain ideas about morality they consider repugnant; the reasons I have mentioned are neither surprising nor unfamiliar. But we have not made much progress in validating the asymmetry that Hume insisted on between the moral and the nonmoral content of works of fiction. In *Mimesis as Make-Believe*[7] I suggested that such an asymmetry obtains at the level of mere representation, i.e. when it comes to ascertaining what is true-in-the-fictional-world, quite apart from what we might take to be the work's message or moral or any ambition or tendency it might have to change or reorganize our beliefs or attitudes or behaviour or instincts. My suggestion was, very briefly, that when we interpret literary and other representational works of art we are less willing to allow that the works' fictional worlds deviate from the real world in moral respects than in nonmoral ones. I associated this point with Hume's remarks in the paragraphs before us. But I have since come to think that, although some of what Hume says can be construed as aiming in this direction, my point in *Mimesis* is distinct from and independent of much of what Hume seems to be getting at. I suspect, however, that Hume had something like this point vaguely in mind when he contrasted objectionable moral ideas in literary works with nonmoral ones.

We go about deciding what is fictional, or true-in-a-fictional-world, in many instances, in much the way we go about deciding what is the case in the real world. We make similar inferences, utilizing much the same background information and exercising similar sensitivities and intellectual abilities. We often judge characters' feelings, motivations, and personalities on the basis of what they do and say, for instance, as though they were real people. We make use of whatever knowledge of human nature we may think we possess, and any relevant life experiences we have had. We sometimes put ourselves into characters' shoes to understand from the inside what they may be feeling or thinking, as we do in the case of real people.

This is what one would expect insofar as the construction of fictional worlds is governed by what I called the *Reality Principle* (RP). Crudely glossed, RP says that we are to construe fictional worlds as being as much like the real world as possible, consistent with what the work directly indicates about them. We are entitled to assume that fictional characters, like real people, have blood in their veins, that they are mortal, and so on – unless the story contains explicit indications to the contrary. On reading a story we note what it says explicitly about characters and events, and – insofar as the Reality Principle applies – ask what would be the case in the real world if all this were true.

The Reality Principle applies much less frequently than one might have supposed, and it is easy to underestimate the extent to which considerations special to the interpretation of works of fiction or certain genres of fiction, considerations without analogues in investigations of the real world, come into play when we decide what is fictional. Some exceptions to the Reality Principle occur when the author held beliefs about reality which we know to be mistaken. A medieval storyteller describes a character as recovering from disease after being treated by bloodletting, and expects listeners or readers to assume that (fictionally) the treatment cured him. Shall we disagree, since we know bloodletting to be ineffectual? I think we may well prefer to go along, to understand the story as we know the teller meant it to be understood. Otherwise it may lose its point. We may allow that, in the fictional world, bloodletting cures disease (even though the story does not directly or explicitly establish that this is so), despite our certainty that this is not so in the real world.[8]

When it comes to moral matters (moral principles anyway), however, I am more inclined to stick to my guns, and it seems to me that most interpreters are also. I judge characters by the moral standards I myself use in real life. I condemn characters who abandon their children or engage in genocide, and I don't change my mind if I learn that the author (and the society he was writing for) considered genocide or abandoning one's children morally acceptable, and expected readers to think this is so in the world of the story. If the author is wrong about life, he is wrong about the world of his story. I don't easily give up the Reality Principle, as far as moral judgments (moral principles) are concerned.

Can an author simply stipulate in the text of a story what moral principles apply in the fictional world, just as she specifies what actions characters perform? If the text includes the sentence, "In killing her baby, Giselda did the right thing; after all, it was a girl" or "The village elders did their duty before God by forcing the widow onto her husband's funeral pyre", are readers obliged to accept it as fictional that, in doing what they did, Giselda or the elders behaved in morally proper ways? Why shouldn't storytellers be allowed to experiment explicitly with worlds of morally different kinds, including ones even they regard as morally obnoxious? There is science fiction; why not morality fiction?

I am sceptical – sceptical about whether fictional worlds can ever differ morally from the real world. Of course people in fictional worlds can subscribe to moral principles we recognize as repugnant. Evil characters – characters who have by our lights twisted notions of morality – abound in the pages of fiction. An entire society in the world of a novel, the entire population of a planet, might accept the practice of genocide as legitimate or condemn interracial marriage as "contrary to nature". But can it be fictional that they are right? Can we reasonably judge it to be fictional that genocide is legitimate or interracial marriage a sin, while insisting that the real world is different? Can we accept that what would be virtue in the real world is, in a fictional world, vice, or *vice versa*?[9,10] I have learned never to say never about such things. Writers of fiction are a clever and cantankerous lot who usually manage to do whatever anyone suggests can't be done, and philosophers are quick with counterexamples. But in this instance counterexamples are surprisingly difficult to come by.

A reader's likely response on encountering in a story the words, "In killing her baby, Giselda did the right thing; after all, it was a girl", is to be appalled by the moral depravity of the *narrator*.[11] The sentence probably serves to express the narrator's moral sentiments, not the moral reality of the fictional world. If it were fictional that infanticide for the purpose of sexual selection is morally acceptable, readers would be called on to imagine that the sentiment expressed is proper, that Giselda did indeed do the right thing. They would be barred from imaginatively condemning either her or the narrator, although they might be aware of the repulsion they would feel concerning such practices in the real world. (A reader of science fiction may remind herself that demonic geniuses from outer space are not actually invading the earth and that travel in time is not possible, while imagining otherwise.) This strikes me as a seriously inadequate characterization of the experience a reader would be likely to have. The reader will imaginatively condemn the narrator's endorsement of infanticide, not allowing that he is right even in the fictional world in which he exists.

Some narrators are said to be "omniscient". This usually means that whatever, fictionally, they say is, fictionally, true. (It is usually *not* fictional that they are omniscient.[12]) Why shouldn't narrators sometimes be omniscient, in this sense, about morality? Then from the fact that fictionally the narrator declares infanticide or ethnic cleansing to be permissible we could conclude that, fictionally, it *is* permissible. In real life some people do sometimes accept another person's judgments about morality – children believe their parents, occasionally, the faithful trust religious leaders, disciples follow gurus. Why shouldn't there be conventions allowing a narrator this authority in certain instances? I am happy to go along with an "omniscient" narrator who informs me that there are griffins or fairies or that someone travels in time. But I jealously guard my right to decide questions of virtue and vice for myself, even in a fictional world. It is as though I would be compromising my actual moral principles, should I allow that different moral principles hold in a fictional world. The moral sentiments expressed by narrators are just that, it seems, their own personal moral sentiments; we are free to disagree, even though it is the moral nature of the fictional world, not the real one, that is in question.

Is there always a narrator to take the rap? If a literary fiction containing a statement in praise of ethnic cleansing has no narrator whose sentiments it can be understood to express, will there be any alternative to understanding it to characterize the fictional world itself? I do not rule out the possibility of narrator-less literary fictions, but it is not easy to find clear instances, even hypothetical ones. And the very fact that a text expresses a definite moral attitude may give us reason to recognize a narrator. Words expressive of praise or blame cry out to be attached to a (possibly fictional) person – anything, it seems, to avoid allowing them to characterize the moral nature of a fictional world.

A better place to look for narrator-less fictions is in pictorial representations. Pictures do not generally present someone's (fictional) report about events or states of affairs;

they portray the events or states of affairs themselves. The spectator, typically, imagines perceiving the events or states of affairs for herself, not being told about them (or even shown them) by someone. (There are exceptions, of course.) But how can a picture portray moral facts, the obtaining of certain moral principles, explicitly or directly? These aren't the sorts of states of affairs one perceives. A picture may depict a mixed race couple walking arm in arm, or a slave master beating a slave. But then it is up to us, the spectators, to decide on the moral attributes of these actions. I go by my own moral sense, the one I use in real life. I take it to be fictional that there is nothing wrong with the interracial friendship, and that the beating of the slave is abhorrent.

Suppose the picture of the interracial couple is titled "Shame!" or "Sin!" Here, finally, we have words in a work which probably are not to be attributed to a (reporting) narrator. The words of the title are not themselves part of the fictional world; it probably isn't fictional that anyone is using them to characterize the behaviour of the couple. But there is a tradition of allowing titles to contribute to what is fictional in the world of a picture. Paul Klee's "Singer of Comic Opera" (1923) depicts a woman, but the image itself doesn't establish that she is a singer, let alone a singer of comic opera. Only the title makes this fictional. Does the title of the picture of the interracial couple establish that it is fictional that the couple's behaviour is shameful or sinful? I doubt it. Maybe the artist, in giving the picture its title, intended or expected this to be fictional.[13] Even so, I will insist that it is not, that fictionally there is nothing shameful or sinful in what the couple is doing. The title amounts to an interpretation of the picture which we are free to disagree with, not an authoritative pronouncement establishing a feature of the fictional world. The disgusting sentiment expressed in the title can be attributed to the artist who chose it, or possibly to an implied or apparent or fictional artist (a storytelling narrator), rather than taking it to establish the moral reality of the fictional world.

VI

If fictional worlds ever differ morally from the real world, I suspect that this will be so when the moral character of the fictional world is presented implicitly or indirectly rather than by explicit stipulation, and when it is part of the background rather than the focus of the work.

I appreciate and value many works that in some way presuppose or are based on moral perspectives I don't entirely share. I think all of us do; otherwise there would be little for us to appreciate. Unlike *Triumph of the Will*, whose obvious main purpose is to further an obnoxious moral and political agenda and cannot but inspire disgust, some works merely presuppose or take for granted certain moral perspectives without in any way advocating them, or even addressing or intending to raise the question of their propriety. These moral perspectives then serve as a resource, as part of the setting in which the author pursues other, more specifically aesthetic objectives. If we disagree with the perspective, we might consider reliance on it to be a defect in the work, even an aesthetic defect, but this doesn't always prevent us from recognizing and appreciating the aesthetic qualities that result.[14]

I may understand a fictional event to be tragic, or ironic, or absurd, or poignant. I may think of a character as noble, or as ridiculous. The ending of a story may strike me as a happy one,[15] or as one of unmitigated tragedy, or as uncomfortably ambiguous, or as constituting a fitting denouement to the events that preceded it. I may think that a character does, or does not, in the end, get her comeuppance. Such aesthetically important perceptions are inevitably linked to certain values, often certain moral principles or perspectives; it is in light of a particular moral attitude that an event strikes me as tragic, or a character ridiculous, or an ending fitting.

The nature of the link is hard to pin down. Does it have to be fictional that the relevant moral principles are true in order for it to be fictional that certain events are tragic or ironic? Does appreciating the tragedy or irony commit us to recognizing the fictionality of those principles? If so, when we disagree with the principles we may have to judge that the fictional world differs morally from the real one. But there are other possibilities. The tragic or ironic nature of fictional events might derive from the fact that fictionally some or all of the characters (perhaps including the narrator) accept moral principles with which we disagree, without its being fictional that they are true. Appreciation might require respect or sympathy for the characters' moral attitudes. It might even require that we imagine agreeing with them, that we imagine sharing these attitudes ourselves without requiring us to judge it to be fictional that they are true. Perhaps we needn't even take it to be fictional that the events *are* tragic or ironic; it may be enough to realize that the author (or storytelling narrator) meant them to be so taken, and to respect or sympathize with him.

These are subtle and difficult questions which call for careful critical attention to examples of many different kinds. But we have a mystery on our hands in any case. Whether or not fictional worlds can ever differ morally from the real world, it seems clear that they don't as easily or as often as one might expect. We recognize the fictionality of ordinary empirical propositions and even propositions stating scientific laws, which we consider false, far more readily than we do that of moral principles which we reject. Authors just do not have the same freedom to manipulate moral characteristics of their fictional worlds that they have to manipulate other aspects of them. Why is this? The reader will not find a definitive answer in this essay. But progress can be made by ruling out some kinds of explanations which might initially seem plausible, and we will come to understand the puzzle better in the process.

VII

Propositions that are "true-in-the-world-of-a-story", ones I call *fictional*, are (in a nutshell) propositions readers of the story are to imagine.[16] We may find it distasteful, morally objectionable, to imagine that interracial friendships are sinful or that slavery is morally acceptable. I noted our resistance to imagining accepting moral principles we disagree with or disapprove of. Surely we would resist imagining those moral principles themselves, imagining them to be true. So we are unwilling to imagine what we are called upon to imagine, if it is fictional that interracial friendships are sinful or slavery acceptable.

This doesn't help. It does not explain why anyone should resist allowing that these propositions are fictional. To recognize it to be fictional in a story that slavery is morally acceptable would be merely to recognize that the story *calls* for imagining this. We don't have to go ahead and actually do the imagining. We might decide not to go along with the story, or not even to read it, precisely because it *does* ask us to imagine that slavery is acceptable, because it makes this fictional. A person who objects to imagining that the holocaust was a hoax, or that Abraham Lincoln was secretly a slave trader, may be unable or unwilling to appreciate a story in which this is so. But this won't prevent her from recognizing that it *is* fictional in the story that the holocaust didn't occur or that Lincoln traded in slaves. We might as well suppose that one cannot allow that a newspaper editorial advocates ethnic cleansing if one finds the practice of ethnic cleansing disgusting. It is not clear that moral objections to imagining moral principles we find repugnant have anything to do with the resistance I think most of us feel to recognizing such principles to be fictional.

VIII

Is this resistance essentially moral in character at all? Do we object *morally* to recognizing it to be fictional that slavery is morally acceptable? The resistance is of a piece, it seems to me, with an unwillingness to recognize the fictionality of certain propositions about matters we don't feel strongly about, including ones that do not involve morality.

Consider a really dumb joke, like this one: "Knock, Knock. Who's there? Robin. Robin who? Robbin' you! Stick 'em up!"[17] It is not easy to see how it could be fictional that this joke is hilariously funny (in circumstances just like ones in which, in the real world, it would be dumb), how one could reasonably allow it to be hilarious in a fictional world, while thinking that it is actually dumb. The same goes for a nonjoke like "A maple leaf fell from a tree" (said in no special context). This isn't funny in the real world, and it is not clear how one could create a fictional world in which it is funny (without supplying a special context which would make it funny in the real world as well). If in a story a comedian tells one or the other of these jokes and the author simply writes explicitly in the text that it is hilariously funny, I expect that I would attribute a juvenile or an incomprehensible sense of humour to the narrator, and stick with my own judgment that the joke is *not* funny. I insist on applying my own sense of humour, the one I use in the real world, to the fictional world, as I do my own standards of morality. It may be fictional that the comedian's audience and other characters in the fiction are amused, of course; they may be rolling in the aisles. I can admit that it is funny *for them* while judging that their reaction is inappropriate. I don't rule out the possibility of fancy counter-examples, cases in which there are special reasons for allowing fictional worlds to differ from the real one with respect to what makes for humour, but the fact that the counterexamples would have to be fancy needs explaining.

Whether either the dumb joke or the nonjoke is funny is hardly a question that arouses the passions or that we much care about, and it needn't have anything much to do with morality (although some jokes do). It is not passion, moral passion or any other kind, that drives my reluctance to let it be fictional that it is funny. I have no moral objection to recognizing this to be fictional. What is crucial, I believe, is that being funny or not funny supervenes or depends in a certain way on the "natural" characteristics of what is or isn't funny (the words of a joke and their meanings, the background and context, the joke teller's delivery); "natural" characteristics determine what is funny and what is not. I suspect that it is particular relations of dependence, which properties determine in the relevant manner which others, that cannot easily be different in fictional worlds and in the real one. Why this is so, and what kind of determination or dependence is involved, is still a mystery.

I invite readers to experiment with their intuitions about various other examples. Can different "aesthetic" principles obtain in fictional worlds as compared to the real one? Can what counts in the real world as a jagged or angular or awkward line be flowing or graceful in a fictional world (when relevant aspects of background and context are the same)? Can what in the real world makes for elegance or profundity or unity or bombast or delicacy be different in a fictional world? Those who take the mental to supervene on the physical may consider whether one might judge it to be fictional that a given mental state supervenes on certain physical ones, if one does not think it actually does.

Moral properties depend or supervene on "natural" ones and, I believe, in the relevant manner (whatever that is); being evil rests on, for instance, the actions constituting the practices of slavery and genocide. This, I suggest, is what accounts (somehow) for the resistance to allowing it to be fictional that slavery and genocide are not evil.

If I am right about this, the present point is very different from those I discussed earlier. We may judge a work to be morally defective if it advocates moral principles we find repugnant, or if it invites or has a tendency to induce us to imagine accepting them. (This moral failing might constitute or contribute to an aesthetic one.) If a novel endorses slavery or encourages even imaginative acceptance of it we will loathe it with something of the loathing we have for the institution of slavery. The more we abhor moral principles which a work promotes, the more objectionable we find it.

Refusing to understand it to be fictional that slavery is morally acceptable is not in itself to find the work defective. But if the author meant this to be fictional, her failure to make it so may be responsible for failings in the work. The very fact that an author tries to do something she can't bring off, if the attempt is evident in the work, can be disturbing or disconcerting to the appreciator. And insofar as other objectives the author meant to accomplish in the work depend on its being fictional that slavery is legitimate, she will have been unsuccessful in accomplishing them. We may be unable to regard the hero of the story as heroic or his downfall tragic if, contrary to the author's intentions, we judge him to be morally despicable.[18] This may not only destroy the story's excitement and dull our interest in it; it may also ruin the story's formal properties, the shape of the plot.

These are not *moral* defects in the work, however, but aesthetic ones, and we don't loathe it for failing to make it fictional that slavery is legitimate, with the loathing we direct toward slavery. Indeed, this failure is if anything a point in the work's favour, from a moral perspective. (But we may condemn the *author* for attempting to make this fictional in the work.) Our negative feelings about slavery do play an indirect role in the recognition of these aesthetic failings; it is because we find slavery repugnant that we judge it to be evil, that we recognize being evil to supervene on the practice of slavery. And that, I am suggesting, is why we disallow its being fictional that slavery is not evil.

Where do we stand in the attempt to find something special about our reaction to moral ideas that we disagree with in works of art? Our reluctance to allow moral principles we disagree with to be fictional is just an instance of a more general point concerning dependence relations of a certain kind. But it does distinguish moral principles from propositions about ordinary empirical matters of fact and also from scientific laws, which (usually) do not state dependence relations of the relevant kind.

IX

We still need an explanation of why we should resist allowing fictional worlds to differ from the real world with respect to the relevant kind of dependence relations. My best suspicion, at the moment, is that it has something to do with an inability to imagine these relations being different from how we think they are, perhaps an inability to understand fully what it would be like for them to be different.

This seems, initially, a most unpromising proposal. Some say that contradictions, logical or conceptual impossibilities, are unimaginable. Imaginability is supposed to be a test for possibility. But the propositions that slavery is just, and that the two jokes mentioned earlier are hilariously funny, are surely not contradictions. Moreover, even contradictions can apparently be fictional, although it takes some doing to make them so. The time travel portrayed in some science fiction stories is contradictory; there are pictorial contradictions in William Hogarth's *False Perspective*, in etchings of M.C. Escher, and in an assortment of familiar puzzle pictures.

How can contradictions be fictional? Sometimes a work makes it fictional that *p* (prescribes the imagining of *p*), and also makes it fictional that *not-p*. Then the conjunction, *p and not-p*, may be fictional by virtue of the fictionality of its conjuncts.[19] It is not clear that a similar strategy will work for the proposition that the institution of slavery is just and proper, that this can be separated into distinct components, each of which can unproblematically be made fictional. It might be fictional that a person's behaviour on a given occasion was morally acceptable, and also that her behaviour on that occasion consisted in beating a slave (just as it might be fictional that a person was simultaneously living in 20th century Chicago and in 16th century Italy). But this doesn't make it fictional that she was behaving morally *by virtue of* the fact that her behaviour consisted in beating a slave. It still may be difficult or impossible for *that* to be fictional, because it is difficult or impossible to imagine its being true.

Do contradictions or obvious conceptual impossibilities get to be fictional in other ways? If a work portrays Philip II of Spain and the Guises as a three-headed monster, or fascism as an octopus, it would not seem that the fictionality of these impossibilities derives from the fictionality of their components. But are these conceptual impossibilities fictional at all; are we to imagine that Philip and the Guises are (literally) a three-headed monster, or that fascism is an octopus? Perhaps what is fictional is merely that there is a three-headed monster, or an octopus, and in making this fictional the work expresses a thought about Philip and the Guises, or fascism – a thought one would express in uttering the obvious metaphor.

Is it difficult or impossible, for those of us who abhor slavery and genocide, to imagine engaging in these activities to be morally proper? We are capable of imagining *accepting* or *subscribing to* moral principles that in fact we reject, it seems. And we can imagine experiencing the feelings – feelings of disgust, or approval – that go with judging in ways we think mistaken. Most of us remember holding moral views we have since come to renounce. We know what it is like to subscribe to them, and we can still imagine doing so. A person who has undergone a conversion from one moral perspective to another may not *want* to put herself in her previous shoes; she may find it painful even to imagine thinking and feeling in the ways she previously did. She may be unable to *bring herself* to imagine this; it may require a "great effort" in this sense, just as sticking pins into a photograph of a loved one does. But certainly she could imagine this if she wanted to; otherwise why would she dread doing so? Sometimes we are able to understand and empathize with people who hold moral views we have never held or even been seriously tempted by, and this empathy is likely to involve imagining sub-scribing to these moral views ourselves. An important function of literary works is to facilitate such empathy by presenting characters with various moral perspectives in a sympathetic light.

But there are limits to our imaginative abilities. It is not clear that I can, in a full blooded manner, imagine accepting just any moral principle I am capable of articulating. I can't very well imagine subscribing to the principle that nutmeg is the *summum bonum* and that one's highest obligation is to maximize the quantity of nutmeg in the universe. (Some will put this by saying that I don't know what it would be like to hold this moral view.) I can *entertain the supposition* that I accept this principle, as one would in thinking about conditional propositions or in using *reductio ad adsurdum* arguments. But I have argued that fictionality involves a more substantial sense of imagining than this.[20] I have no difficulty imagining finding the "Knock Knock" joke related earlier funny. It is the sort of joke I once appreciated, and I know and empathize with people now who would appreciate it. But I have trouble with the nonjoke about the maple leaf. Perhaps with effort and ingenuity I could dream up a way of thinking about it in which it would strike one as funny. But there is a sense in which I can't now imagine finding it funny. People who do laugh at it would mystify me in a way that people who laugh at the "Knock Knock" joke do not.

I know what it is to be amused. Can't I just put that notion together in imagination with the idea of the story about the maple leaf, and imagine being amused by the story? I am suggesting that full blooded imagining of this may require not just conjoining these two thoughts but imagining a *way* in which the story amuses me. (Compare: a person may be incapable of imagining an instance of justified true belief which is not an instance of knowledge – until having read the Gettier literature he learns *how* this can be so, how to imagine it. And he might know, on authority, that this is possible and still not be able to imagine it. A contemporary of Columbus may be unable to imagine travelling west and arriving in the east, until she thinks of the possibility that the earth is round.)

We are still very far from the explanation we are after. For it is not only those propositions concerning morality or humour I have difficulty imagining accepting, that I am reluctant to recognize as fictional. I resist allowing it to be fictional that the "Knock Knock" joke is funny, or that moral principles I can, apparently, imagine accepting are true.

But can I imagine not only accepting or believing a moral principle which I actually disagree with and feeling appropriately – can I imagine being *justified* in accepting or believing it? Can I imagine its being *true*?[21] A work in which it is fictional that genocide is morally permissible would be one that calls for imagining that genocide *is* morally permissible, not just imagining accepting this to be so. I find myself strangely tempted by the thought that although I might imagine the latter, I cannot imagine the former.[22]

Alternatively, we might reconsider the idea that I can imagine believing, accepting as true, moral propositions I now reject. Maybe the attitude I imagine having, when I remember my earlier moral self or empathize with others, falls short of belief or acceptance. A sensitive portrayal of the Mafia or of colonial plantation owners might enable me to imagine desiring and feeling in many respects as they do. And I can imagine being amused by the "Knock Knock" joke. (This already distinguishes it from the maple leaf story.) But (first order) desires and feelings don't constitute moral commitments, and being amused does not itself amount to understanding the joke to be funny. On some accounts one needs to take a certain attitude toward one's desires or feelings or amusement, to endorse or desire them or regard them as proper or appropriate.[23] Perhaps one must also take an attitude of endorsement toward the second order attitudes, or at least not take a negative attitude toward them. At some point in the series one may find oneself able to imagine refusing to endorse an attitude but unable to imagine endorsing it; maybe this happens when I in fact reject the moral principles in question or consider the joke not to be funny. This inability may be akin to my inability to imagine being amused by the tale of the maple leaf. And perhaps it amounts to an inability to imagine accepting a moral position that I actually reject.

There are loose ends in this sketchy story, and insecure links. I don't know whether it can be made to work. And even if it were to succeed in establishing that people are, always or sometimes, unable to imagine, in a significant sense, accepting moral positions they reject, it may not be obvious how this explains our – or anyway my – reluctance to allow moral principles I disagree with to be fictional. The line of thought I have just outlined is worth pursuing, I believe, but I won't be too surprised if we find ourselves back on square one.

Hume had no idea how many worms lived in the can he opened. I have left most of them dangling, but at least I have begun to count them. That, I hope, is progress.[24]

NOTES

1 David Hume, "Of the standard of taste", in *Essays Moral, Political and Literary* (Indianapolis: Liberty Classics, 1987), pp. 245–9.
2 Hume mentions poetry specifically in these paragraphs, but his essay concerns works of other sorts as well, especially other works of literary fiction.
3 See my "How marvelous!: toward a theory of aesthetic value", *The Journal of Aesthetics and Art Criticism*, special issue on "Philosophy and the histories of the arts", LI(3), 1993.
4 David Lewis suggested to me that he had an experience something like this.
5 "Where a man is confident of the rectitude of that moral standard, by which he judges, he is justly jealous of it, and will not pervert the sentiments of his heart for a moment, in complaisance to any writer whatsoever." ("Of the standard of taste", op. cit., p. 247).
6 For an account of what a perspective induced by a metaphor might consist in, see my "Metaphor and prop oriented make-believe", *The European Journal of Philosophy* I(1),

April 1993. See also Richard Moran, "Seeing and believing: metaphor, image and force", *Critical Inquiry* XVI, Autumn 1989.

7 *Mimesis as Make-Believe: On the Foundations of the Representational Arts* (Cambridge, Mass.: Harvard University Press, 1990), pp. 154–5.

8 One might in this case prefer what I called the *Mutual Belief Principle* (which follows suggestions of David Lewis and Nicholas Wolterstorff). There is an enormous range of cases in which nothing even approximating either of these principles seems to apply. See *Mimesis as Make-Believe*, pp. 161–9.

9 Some may take the position that one has no right to pass judgment on the moral principles accepted in another society, that anthropologists, for instance, should not condemn practices that accord with the moral code of the agents' culture even if they conflict with the anthropologist's own moral code. Extending this tolerance to fictional as well as actual societies does not make the fictional world different morally from the real one.

10 I am using the language of moral realism here, but I do not mean to beg any questions in its favour. Anti-realists may insist on reformulating the problem, but that won't make it disappear. If there are no such things as moral propositions, it won't be fictional either that slavery is just, or that it is unjust. But anti-realists will have to explain what look like judgements readers make about the moral qualities of the actions of fictional characters. And they will have to make sense of the embedding of sentences expressing moral judgments in larger contexts, including "In the story . . ." contexts, as well as conditionals, etc. I do have hope that some variety of anti-realism will make the problem more tractable.

11 By "narrator" I mean a character in the work world who, fictionally, utters the words of the text. I have in mind what in *Mimesis as Make-Believe* I called *reporting* narrators, as distinguished from *storytelling* narrators.

12 See *Mimesis as Make-Believe*, §9.3.

13 This may be clear even if there is no title. Activities may be depicted in a glorified manner indicating the artist's approval, her belief that it is fictional that they are admirable, and her approval of similar behaviour in the real world. (Compare social realistic styles of depiction.)

14 I am indebted here to David Hills.

15 This doesn't mean simply that the characters end up happy. An unhappy villain doesn't prevent the story from ending happily.

16 *Mimesis as Make-Believe*, § 1.5.

17 Thanks to Jenefer Robinson.

18 "We are not interested in the fortunes and sentiments of such rough heroes: . . . And . . . we cannot prevail on ourselves to . . . bear an affection to characters, which we plainly discover to be blameable." "Of the standard of taste", op. cit., p. 246.

19 There may then be a prescription to imagine the conjunction, even if that can't be done. Some might prefer not to regard the conjunction as fictional at all, but the fictional world will still be contradictory in the sense that the conjunction of what is fictional is a contradiction.

20 *Mimesis as Make-Believe*, pp. 19–21.

21 Again, I am not committed to the propriety of this realist formulation.

22 Richard Moran raised this possibility in "Art, imagination, and resistance". Maybe it isn't quite as strange as it seems. It is arguable that I can imagine believing that Ortcutt is not identical with Ortcutt, or that water is not H_2O, but that, knowing what I know, I can't imagine either of these propositions being true.

23 See for instance Harry Frankfurt, "Freedom of the will and the concept of a person",

Journal of Philosophy 68(1), January 14 1971; Allan Gibbard, *Wise Choices, Apt Feelings* (Cambridge: Harvard University Press, 1990); and David Lewis, "Dispositional theories of value", *Proceedings of the Aristotelian Society*, supplementary volume 63, 1989.

24 I am grateful for conversations with Allan Gibbard, Daniel Jacobson, Eileen John, Richard Moran, Peter Railton, Gideon Rosen, Alicyn Warren, and especially David Hills. A talk by Richard Moran at the meetings of the American Society for Aesthetics in 1992 "Art, imagination, and resistance", on which I commented, was also very helpful, in addition to renewing my interest in this topic.

(In response to helpful conversations with Daniel Jacobson, I have made a couple of clarifying corrections in the text of this paper. Jacobson's "In praise of immoral art" (*Philosophical Topics* XXV (1) Spring 1997, David Hills, editor) explores perceptively, and more thoroughly than I do, the cluster of issues concerning relations between art and morality that occupy Parts I–IV of the present paper. See also the discussions by Noël Carroll, Berys Gaut, and Matthew Kieran that Jacobson cites. An important recent examination of the question which is the main focus of the present paper, whether fictional worlds can differ morally, i.e. with respect to what moral principles obtain, from the real world, is Tamar Szabó Gendler's "The puzzle of imaginative resistance", *The Journal of Philosophy* (2) 1997.)

22

MORALS IN FICTION AND FICTIONAL MORALITY – A RESPONSE

Michael Tanner

I

Kendall Walton begins his contribution with a quotation from Hume. I will begin with one from Nietzsche. It is, I think, comparatively well known, but it bears repeating, especially in the context of this subject. Characteristically it is both unfair and extraordinarily acute. It occurs in the section of *Twilight of the Idols* entitled "Skirmishes of an Untimely Man," and it is abruptly headed "*G. Eliot*". I will quote the first two paragraphs:

> They are rid of the Christian God and now believe all the more firmly that they must cling to Christian morality. That is an English consistency; we do not wish to hold it against little moralistic females à la Eliot. In England one must rehabilitate oneself after every little emancipation from theology by showing in a veritably awe-inspiring manner what a moral fanatic one is. That is the price they pay there.
>
> We others hold otherwise. When one gives up the Christian faith, one pulls the right to Christian morality out from under one's feet. This morality is by no means self-evident: this point has to be exhibited again and again, despite the English flatheads. Christianity is a *whole* view of things thought out together. By breaking one main concept out of it, the faith in God, one breaks the whole: nothing necessary remains in one's hands. Christianity presupposes that man does not know, *cannot* know what is good for him, what evil; he believes in God, who alone knows it. Christianity is a command; its origin is transcendent; it is beyond all criticism, all right to criticism; it has truth only if God is the truth – it stands and falls with faith in God.[1]

Despite its *ad feminam* tone, I hope that the bearing of this passage on the subject of fictional morality, as Walton has chosen to present it, is clear. In any case, I shall return to it. Hume, and Walton following him, make a firm distinction between those elements in a fictional work that concern matters of fact, and those that can be seen to be propounding or endorsing a morality. Hume's view is that, in general, we are, or should be, tolerant of factual errors or (in Walton's expansion) even of at least certain logical impossibilities in a work of art; beliefs, for example, in fairies, dragons, time-travel. But we should not, or maybe cannot, tolerate "ideas of morality and decency which we find repugnant". Walton goes on to discuss, first, to what extent moral failings in a work inhibit our pleasure in it, and second, why, granted that they do, that should be so. I shall deal with issues that are mainly relevant to the latter question first, and then move onto some considerations that bear on the former.

II

I detect in Walton's paper a strong tendency to think of "us" as sharing a set of moral values which we have difficulty in imagining not holding, though of course we know that most people in most places have not held them. It is this that creates his basic problem, so far as he is concerned. Thus the opening sentence of his paper runs "Works of art from previous ages or from other cultures may contain or embody ideas that we find strange or disagree with." True, perhaps, but one must have a very strong sense of belonging to a homogeneous moral community to confine that strangeness to works from other cultures and ages. So far as interesting moral issues are concerned which bear on our appreciation of works of art (among other things), we are more likely to find our imaginations stretched, engaged, stimulated, outraged, or what not, by works which don't flatly contradict the most basic views that "we", the morally correct majority, share. I feel that in only mentioning, at any point, slavery, genocide, killing female babies and disapproval of interracial marriage, Walton has made things in one respect easier, in another more difficult, for himself and us, for dealing with the grounds of our inability or unwillingness to imagine ourselves accepting repugnant moral views. It might have been better not to begin by quoting from that canonical text of aesthetics, "Of the Standard of Taste".

III

Hume's position, in many obvious ways, was very different from ours. Hume took it that there was a set of civilised values which everyone whom one could take seriously, not regarding them as barbarians or monkish, hare-brained fanatics, shares. And this set of values concerned not only the most basic matters, the ones which Walton mentions *passim* (though there is room for speculation on what Hume would have thought about interracial marriages), but also the overall way in which educated, rational, polite and elegant gentlemen would conduct themselves. I take it that there are many issues that we – I shall be investigating "we" shortly – are likely to be sharply divided about without our feeling that one side is thereby convicted of corrupt consciousness or a failure to qualify as members of the moral community. We, in other words, need to be perpetually braced for conflict about moral matters, though it would be surprising if it were about genocide or slavery, if the discussion were taking place in, say, a Joint Session in the United Kingdom; less surprising if it were among former Yugoslav philosophers, where the surprise would be rather that there was a Joint Session at all.

Hume strikes me, in his moral attitudes, as being quaint; Walton of living in a time-warp. Walton writes as if we share a set of moral views in the way that we share, more or less, a view of what the world consists of, at least in respect of what philosophers used to refer to as medium-sized specimens of dry goods. So fiction – though Walton doesn't go so far as to mention a single title – either expresses our moral views or else those that we find repugnant, to the point of being unwilling to imagine ourselves holding them. I use the term "holding" to bypass the issue of moral realism, which seems to me quite irrelevant to the matter under discussion. And when Walton talks about "the real world", as he does throughout his paper, he seems to be confident of what that is, and of course in some ways he is right to be. But in the ways that are relevant to his argument, he is not.

Morality concerns what has sometimes been called the human world, and there is a great deal of disagreement as to what that amounts to. Does the human world consist of free agents making choices for which they are to be held responsible, or are we automata? Is Freud right about the overdetermination of our actions by unconscious forces, or has psychoanalysis been a big mistake? Is there such a thing as a universal human nature, or are we products of the kind of social, political and economic circumstances in which we live? Are we to see ourselves as purely natural beings, part of a world which has evolved in one way or another, but not to be sharply separated from the rest of it? Or are we specially created beings, God having singled us out for glory or damnation to eternity, with this life as merely a testing-ground for that to come? And so on – there is still a wide assortment of *Weltanschauungen* to choose from.

IV

What are "our" answers to those questions? Fairly obviously, "we" don't have one single set of answers, yet what our answers are determines what we take "the real world" to consist of. It seems that when Walton talks of the real world as opposed to those fictional ones which harbour green slime and Martians he means roughly what one would perceive on an average day if one looked round one's room, took a stroll, got on an aeroplane, and so on, together with the kind of account that the natural sciences would provide of what that world consisted of. But fictions, in general, take that world for granted, sometimes adding to it, occasionally even subtracting from it (some of Beckett's later fiction).

And yet, if we think of some of the great novelists, for instance Jane Austen, Stendhal, Dickens, George Eliot, Melville, Henry James, Dostoevsky, Tolstoy, Proust, Thomas Mann, how differently that world appears in each of them, though for most of them the constituents of the real world are in one sense the same. If one finds some of these authors appealing and others repellent, some convincing and others implausible, what is it that makes them different? Not, surely, the moral judgments, certainly not merely those, that they advance or imply. Nor their inventories of what is to be found in the world; at least that would be a misleading way of putting it. They see what we may be inclined to call the same set of things in different ways.

When I think of what a "fictional world" is, as the title of this symposium leads me to, it is this kind of difference that I have in mind. Hume of course makes no reference to anything like this, yet when we brood on the morality of fiction with any degree of sophistication, surely that is what is most interesting. Of course if, like many people, I adore Jane Austen and abominate Dostoevsky, my reasons for doing so will be expressed partly in terms of the elements those authors select from what is certainly a capacious field. Even so, we do speak of their creating worlds, and it is easy to see why we should. Their concern, as usual with great novelists, is above all with how we should live, and they dwell on those aspects of the world which affect them most powerfully, seen in their sharply contrasting perspectives. In doing that they unquestionably concentrate on what they regard as permanent issues of attitude and conduct.

So they choose settings, characters, situations which they can explore in order to clarify, even to discover, what their values are. Revulsion from them is likely most often, though not always, to take the form of objecting to the kind of thing that exercises their moral imaginations. Thus a characteristic form of hostility to Jane Austen is her extreme provinciality, the feeling that she should have realised that there are more momentous things in life than who gets married to whom in an English village, while the Napoleonic Wars are raging. A defence of her is most likely to take the line that she has created an adequate microcosm of what preoccupies people enduringly, whether or not there are wars close at hand – I put this in brutally schematic form, clearly. But it is sufficient for me to establish that Hume and Walton would be wrong to say that we don't object to her selection of and concentration on natural qualities in her world, while finding her morality claustrophobic and banal. It seems, in fact, pointless if not impossible to make the distinction.

V

At this point I return to the opening quotation from Nietzsche. What he says of Christianity, that "it is a *system*, a whole view of things", clearly applies to many other sets of views too. Whatever one's line on the fact–value distinction may be, including naturally the one that it doesn't exist, it would be absurd to think that facts were irrelevant to values. And that is not an absurdity of which Walton is guilty. Indeed, he stresses the supervenience of moral properties on "natural" ones. Not only that, but, he writes, "This [supervenience], I suggest, is what accounts (somehow) for the resistance to allowing it to be fictional that slavery and genocide are not evil." I find this sentence puzzling, for two main reasons. The first is simply that whatever moral value we attach to something, we will take it that the value supervenes on the natural properties of the thing. The second is that I can't see how supervenience *could* provide the answer; Walton admits that it "is still a mystery" what kind of determination or dependence is involved, but my problem is with seeing how, whatever kind it is, it would deal with the fundamental question of his paper.

To return to the first reason: Those who practise slavery and genocide, no less than those who deplore them, think that their permissibility, or praiseworthiness, supervene on their natural properties, and might, if they were Waltonian philosophers, resist allowing it to be fictional that slavery and genocide are evil. They might, perhaps, characterise those practices differently, just as, in an aesthetic case, one man's vividness is another's garishness, one man's serenity another's tedium. But they might not, though of course they wouldn't simply say "We approve of genocide", but produce an account of the inequality of races such that the finer ones are at the gravest risk of being calamitously adulterated by contact with the degenerate ones. That, as we know, is what the Nazis did. Like Christians, they had a whole view of things, and among other bizarre activities, they attempted to isolate in laboratories those elements in Jewish blood which resulted in their pernicious qualities, to get empirical backing for their attitude.

One of the problems with taking genocide as an example to illustrate his general thesis is that Walton can count on our not taking seriously the whole world-view of which it was a part. Because the Nazi ideology was such an absurd rag-bag of bogus science and racial mysticism it is easy to discount that side of it altogether, and concentrate only on what its practical upshots were; which can give the impression that they weren't founded on *any* allegedly factual beliefs. And in a way they weren't. What came first was a loathing of the Jews, no doubt; what came in between was a set of beliefs about what the Jews were like which was claimed to validate that loathing; and what came last was genocide. The real contact, one may feel, was between the loathing and the extermination. And no doubt very many moral attitudes precede the attempted establishment of the natural facts on which it is claimed that they are based. One of the most important questions we can ask about moral views is why someone holds them –

something that tends to be concealed by the claimed autonomy of morality. Equally, the most devastating critique we can mount of moral views is not simply that they are so disgusting that no civilised person would even entertain them, but the undermining of the so-called factual beliefs on which they are based.

VI

But it is not as simple as I am making it sound. As I said about the great novelists, it is often impossible to separate the elements in a whole view of the world. Nazism again is not a good example, partly because of the uncouthness of its factual claims, partly because we have every right to think that they were manufactured for the most part in order to back up moral attitudes which had been arrived at first, which is a good reason for calling their total view irrational. Walton agrees with at least the first of these points. He writes

> I may not want to imagine that people of one race are genetically less capable in a certain respect than people of another. And I may object to a novel in which it is fictional that this is so, one that asks the reader to imagine this. My objection in this case is based on moral considerations, although the proposition I avoid imagining is not itself a moral one.

This is a rather odd way of putting it, though. We can't be as confident as we might like to be that the Creator of the world is as morally correct as we are. It may indeed be the case that people of one race are genetically less capable in a certain respect than people of another. It may be that we are not called on to imagine that, but to accept that it is true. Actually it would be rather odd if it weren't. Certainly the average height of the members of various races differs, which alone makes some "genetically less capable" in certain respects than others are. There doesn't seem to be much point in objecting morally to what is "naturally" the case.

VII

What we find with the great novelists (and some who aren't so great) is not so much assertions about genetic differences, though they can occur, as in some of the works of D.H. Lawrence, but rather depictions of the world which, if they compel us, do so by making us share their perspective, so that we find ourselves taking up moral positions which may surprise or even shock us, but which seem inevitable once we have agreed to imagine life on their comprehensive terms. That, I take it, is the source of Plato's deepest anxieties about the power of art. If we were able to separate the elements in a work of art which are concerned with natural features of the world, and those which are moral recommendations, Plato would have had far less cause for worry, and his objections to art would not have haunted us down the millennia. Once again, I find Walton coming close to recognising this point, but only in the context of art which is too vulgar to be taken seriously. He envisages a picture of a mixed race couple walking arm in arm, and entitled "Shame!" or "Sin!" and comments "The disgusting sentiment expressed in the title can be attributed to the artist who chose it, or possibly to an implied or apparent or fictional artist (a storytelling narrator), rather than taking it to establish the moral reality of the fictional world." So far, so simple – and this seems to be a paradigm, for Walton, of the relationship between depiction and moral judgments in works of art. But in a footnote to this passage he writes "Activities may be depicted in a glorified manner indicating the artist's approval, her belief that it is fictional that they are admirable, and her approval of similar behaviour in the real world. (Compare social realistic styles of depiction.)"

The rub comes in the parenthesis. We all know the kind of picture that Walton is referring to, of stern muscular men with jutting jaws leading the way to the fascist, or socialist, future, while flaxen-haired women stay at home smilingly looking after their healthy and happy children. But that is only a particularly crass way of proceeding, not different in kind from that which art at its most effective and sophisticated adopts all the time. The contrast between "Our Heroes defend the Motherland against the Fascist Invader" and Michelangelo's Last Judgment, or Raphael's Sistine Madonna, is only one of degree, though it remains prodigious.

Social realistic styles of depiction, whether in painting or in the novels of, say, Sholokhov, are not to be differentiated from those of other styles which we find more congenial because the latter are not trying to affect our attitudes. One might say, since the level is at this point elementary, that all art is propaganda. In the case of Fascist or Soviet art, both the message and the means by which it is transmitted are, for us, satisfyingly gross; it is a matter for speculation, but not here, of whether, had the Third Reich had a longer run for its money, any artists of stature would have appeared, who would have been equally dedicated to the cause, but subtler and more lastingly successful in their embodiment of it.

VIII

Which brings me back to Christianity. The world, as traditionally conceived by Christians, is for me without doubt a fictional one, ruled over by a God in whom I don't believe – so much, so far as I'm concerned, for Walton's ubiquitous "we". And, as I quoted Nietzsche saying, "By breaking one main concept out of it, the faith in God, one breaks the whole." And yet very much of the art to which I am most passionately attached is clearly Christian in its inspiration, its vision and its message. For most people in my position – hardly an unusual one – it tends to be the case that they find at least large areas of Christian morality more acceptable than the cosmology which supports them: that is Nietzsche's point. He, too, is stressing the supervenience of moral judgments on factual ones, and expressing his outrage that his contemporaries overlook that relationship. His complaint is evidently as relevant now as it was a century ago. For he continues, immediately after what I quoted at the start of this paper, by writing

> When the English actually believe that they know "intuitively" what is good and evil, when they therefore suppose that they no longer require Christianity as the guarantee of morality, we merely witness the *effects* of the Christian value judgement and an expression of the strength and depth of this dominion; such that the origin of English morality has been forgotten, such that the very conditional nature of its right to existence is no longer felt. For the English, morality is not yet a problem.

Overlooking Nietzsche's exclusive stress on the English, when many other nations seem equally culpable, we can share, I think, his bewilderment at the complacency with which people hold to moral views which then, as now, they credit their "intuitions" with – those dubious items which are strangely the last thing that contemporary philosophers are interested in investigating the status of. To explore this theme further would take me too far from the subject of this discussion. All I will add to what I have said already is that either all moral judgments are supervenient on factual ones, which is a kind of naturalism with a long and distinguished history; or else some are not, but are taken to be the basis upon which factual statements give rise to all other moral judgments. That view too has a parallel history; and the dispute remains very much where it has been for a long time. Genocide and slavery are taken by most people, I suspect, to be unarguably disgusting; in which case to say that they are evil is really to do no more than to specify, in part, the boundaries within which one is prepared to argue about moral issues. They are not so much activities upon which evil supervenes, as part of the definition of evil.

IX

Our relationship to art is not, I have suggested, the same as Hume's, partly because so many moral questions have entered, or re-entered, the area of contention since he wrote. We concentrate obsessively on the moral certainties we do have, because there are so many that we lack. The ones we have are, in the largest part, what remains of our

Christian inheritance. The ones we lack are those where we feel freed from it, but wonder what to put in its place. Christianity supplied its adherents with ideals, or really only one: to go to heaven. Since no-one is foolish enough to retain that ideal without the whole Christian package, we turn to works of the imagination with a zest or desperation previously unknown, to see what might be on offer instead. The variety is quite impressive, but for the restless seeker after happiness that is part of the trouble: it is in the nature of ideals, where one can expect their realisation to provide one with repose and fulfilment, that they are exclusive in their demands. But if they lack the alarming backing which the Christian ideal possessed, they also lack its coercive force, so it is tempting to shop around, giving them conditional allegiance. But to give conditional allegiance to an ideal which has claims to endow one's life with meaning is to come close to paradox.

That may seem questionable. Why, someone might ask, should I not try an ideal to see whether it works, and if it doesn't, discard it and try another one? The succinct answer is that, if one proceeds in that way, one is operating according to a standard which one applies from outside, and I take it as being criterial of an ideal that it dictates standards from within. Ideals demand commitment, and that in turn demands that one doesn't keep one eye on some external measure. If one does, that only shows that it is something else which is truly one's ideal – happiness, say, as a state which has form without content. The form is of the kind "I want to go on living like this", but this remains abstract, though that fact may be disguised by calling it happiness, since we think we recognise that state when we encounter it. In one way, of course, we do. But happiness which is experienced outside the context provided by a specific ideal is subject to fear, the fear of its cessation. That is one reason for the suspicion with which it is often regarded, particularly as an end in itself. Happiness can't sensibly be one's ideal, though an ideal which results in happiness, even an ideal pursued with the aim of being happy, can.

X

What bearing do these very general reflections have on our experience of fiction, and in particular on the relationship between fiction and morality? What bearing, especially, do they have now, since as I have indicated I think that the question must be historicised, to take account of the radical difference in our relationship to art as opposed to that of our ancestors, who at least officially shared a world-view and hence an ideal to which it led? A passage from Peter Strawson's paper "Social Morality and Individual Ideal" provides a good context for thought about this. He writes:

> As for the ways of life that may . . . present themselves at different times as each uniquely satisfactory, there can be no doubt about their variety and opposition.

The ideas of self-obliterating devotion to duty or to the service of others; of personal honour and magnanimity; of asceticism, contemplation, retreat; of action, dominance and power; of the cultivation of "an exquisite sense of the luxurious"; of simple human solidarity and cooperative endeavour; of a refined complexity of social existence; of a constantly maintained and renewed sense of affinity with natural things – any of these ideas, and a great many others too, may form the core and substance of a personal ideal. At some times such a picture may present itself as merely appealing or attractive; at others it may offer itself in a stronger light, as, perhaps, an image of the only sane or non-ignoble human reaction to the scene in which we find ourselves.[2]

It doesn't take much effort to assign names of works of art and of artists to any of these often conflicting ideals. Nor, for that matter, is it hard to think of philosophers, prophets, and assorted other non-artists who have espoused them. For some purposes the distinction between art and non-art here may not be important; for others it clearly is. Whether one is more likely to be captivated by a philosopher or a novelist is a matter of temperament. Both may be said, under some circumstances, to create fictional worlds which we then, if we are sufficiently impressed by them, elevate to the realm of truth. One may read Spinoza, at first, as presenting a fictional world which has an obscure fascination; by the time one gets to Book V of the *Ethics* one may have undergone a conversion, and embark on an existence of, to use the Strawsonian description which is most apt, "asceticism, contemplation, retreat". Equally one might steep oneself in what is known as "late James", and cultivate, again in Strawson's terms, "a refined complexity of social existence". In either case, beginning with a view of life which is remote from theirs, one might, thanks to the power they have to command our imaginations, gradually come to take up a series of different attitudes to phenomena with which one is familiar, as well as being introduced to others, and find that viewing the world from this new vantage point, or perspective, seems to give it more coherence, sense and therefore value.

XI

Both Spinoza and James, to stick for the time being with these two, are in an obvious sense moralists, though commentators on Spinoza's chief work surprisingly often seem to overlook its title. That is why they both give such elaborate accounts of the world as they see it. They take it that if we follow and agree with their presentations of life, we will find that we are resistlessly drawn into accepting their ideals. There is a famous passage in James's Preface to *The Portrait of a Lady* where he writes

There is, I think, no more nutritive or suggestive truth in this connexion than that of the perfect dependence of the "moral" sense of a work of art on the amount of felt life concerned in producing it. The question comes back thus, obviously, to the kind and degree of the artist's prime sensibility, which is the soil out of which his subject grows.

I take it that by "prime sensibility" James is referring to the impression made on him by the world, which, if he is a major artist, or (to keep Spinoza in the picture) a powerful communicator, in his chosen medium, he transmits to his audience. If the view he purveys is sufficiently surprising, as both late James and Spinoza tend to be for almost everyone at first reading, the effect will be one of bafflement and disbelief. It may even be – it often is – one of revulsion. But if one suffers that reaction, it has nothing to do with any Humean acceptance of manners and speculative errors, or repugnance towards ideas of morality and decency to be found in other ages and cultures. If anything, the more distant the culture represented, the less likely we are to read about it in any other than an anthropological spirit. Given the general view of life, and the circumstances in which it is endured, of, say, the *Saga of the Volsungs*, our reactions to the behaviour of the characters in it are certainly not those that we would experience to approximately similar behaviour on the part of people who inhabit "the real world".

XII

We are not, then, in any serious way challenged or offended in those cases where we can't make reasonably strong connections between a fictional world we encounter and our own. When we can't, it is unclear whether we have aesthetic or moral reactions of any significance. If it is to be the case that, as Walton puts it, "the content we disagree with ruins our pleasure and we take it to be grounds for judging the work negatively", then the work must in the first place have engaged us to a fairly impressive extent. That is why, I think, *Triumph of the Will* returns to haunt us. If we divide our responses to it into those that relate to its "beauty" (I put inverted commas around the word because Walton always does), and those that concern its moral message, then we are landed with the problem of whether it is aesthetically meritorious but morally odious, or whether the degree of its moral repulsiveness is such that we declare that the film is not beautiful. That we find the problem a vexing one, as also in the case of Dante's *Inferno* if we are non-Christians, is an index of some kind of success on Riefenstahl's part. It isn't a difficulty we have with *Der ewige Jude*. Walton's view is that "If the work's obnoxious message does not destroy its aesthetic value, it nevertheless makes it morally inaccessible. That must count as an aesthetic as well as a moral defect". Those are his last words on *Triumph of the Will*. The idea seems to be that if it is morally pernicious, and to a degree that interferes fatally with its aesthetic value, then it can be simply written off.

But surely there is *some* category in which it is successful, otherwise it would not have been the subject of such prolonged debate, which we may envisage continuing. Is there such a thing as a great bad work of art? Like Plato, we want to say No, on the grounds that the good and the beautiful are intimately connected. Unlike Plato, we don't have the confidence to approve only those works with whose morality we agree. So we allow works to be quite morally objectionable, but feel that we must draw the line somewhere. A work that is "morally inaccessible" is thereby aesthetically defective, which I think in Walton's terms means not beautiful. But in the first place I have to insist that *Triumph of the Will* is, in many places, beautiful, as in the sequence of Hitler's 'plane emerging from the clouds and casting its shadow on the streets of old Nuremberg, and in some of the spectacular operations in the stadium, involving huge collections of marchers in intricate balletic movements. In the second place there are other categories than the beautiful by which it may be judged an extraordinary success. As to the first point, one of the ingenuities of the film is to intertwine or juxtapose images of old Germany, half-timbered and peaceful, with parades and speeches, so that one loses one's sense of what is continuity and what is contrast, and the undeniable charm of Nuremberg is interfused with something that is starkly opposed to it, but is postulated as somehow emerging from it. As to the second, that is where one enters into the complex issue of the range of considerations which are relevant to assessing a work, especially one that straddles our usual categories to the extent that this film does. So this case is one which can't be dealt with summarily, and I shall leave discussion of it there, hoping nonetheless to have suggested that Walton's curt dismissal has an element of the disingenuous.

XIII

To return, finally, to those works which present us with a picture of life which challenges the view we (by which I mean "any one of us", not the Waltonian "all of us together") may initially have, but not in such a way as to incline us to outright or scornful rejection. It is they, surely, which preoccupy us most, leading us to enquire on many fronts. Perhaps most relevantly to this paper, the question arises as to the relationship between our imaginative absorption in them and what it would be actually to embrace the perspective on the world, and thus on how we should live, that they offer. We are the victims, often willing and eager ones, of two conflicting impulses. On the one hand there is the delight of expanding our imaginative lives by adopting one variety of what we think of as the aesthetic attitude, in which as appreciators of art we replicate Keats's "negative capability", rejoicing in the lack of an identity which he deplored, but as a

Romantic artist found it impossible to reject. On the other we are struck by, however much the details may alarm or amuse us, Tolstoy's late-found insistence that art should tell us the truth and that we should reject that which doesn't, which is bound to mean most of it – bound to, unless we are so committed to the first view that we end up regarding the adoption of ideals as something only to be undertaken in an imaginative mode. There is a central position, inherently unstable as they tend to be, which we find in the middle-period work of F.R. Leavis, where we judge art (specifically the novel) in terms of its possession of certain values, such as seriousness, maturity and depth, but allow that novels which manifest sharply different approaches to life may all possess them.

This last position, unstable though it may be, is in many respects the most attractive, since it does commit us, if we take it with Leavisian wholeheartedness, to an intensity of response to art which seems to do justice to its demands, at any rate when it is at its greatest. At the same time it encourages an imaginative freedom which we value so much that it is often built into the definition of art, if we allow ourselves such a thing. Yet in the end it is a cop-out, however furrowed-browed its expression may be. It not only postulates, but actively encourages a severance between our imaginative lives and our actual ones, which may give us a sense of possible liberation, but also a sense of final frustration at the gap that exists between the lives we lead and that which we might lead. That may be one reason, the most honourable, why as they grow older the most impressive critics tend to become narrower in their tastes, a phenomenon usually regarded with dismay and regretful sympathy. It can be seen, though, in quite a different light; not as one manifestation of the sclerosis which awaits us all if we survive long enough to suffer from it, but as a recognition that one can't permanently dwell among possibilities, for all their alluring variety. They make us think that we can lead several lives, but we all know that that may mean leading no life in particular.

Of course the merging of the actual and the imaginative in a person's life may mean that he has merely grown weary of the effort involved in exercising that faculty which, when it is not just a means of escape from the real, is exhausting in its demands for a special, rare kind of honesty. The merging may, however, register a triumph, though one which can look as though it is an abdication. Such is our approved promiscuity in aesthetic matters that it is likely that such a person will be said, as people regularly say of the old Tolstoy, to have given up art. I have tried to indicate, in the last part of this paper, that there is a sense in which that would not necessarily be a bad thing. I am thinking, as I hope is obvious, of the art which operates on us imaginatively; and there is a great deal of which that would be a very odd description, and to which my speculations would obviously not apply. Nor have I been concerned, in these last remarks, with green slime or genocide, because neither seems to me to be, in the appropriate sense, interesting. But whether I am right about that, or Walton is, is for others to decide.

NOTES

1   *Twilight of the Idols*, "Skirmishes of an untimely man", §5. Trans. Walter Kaufmann (*The Portable Nietzsche*, New York: Viking Press [1977], pp. 515–16).
2   *Freedom and Resentment* (London, Methuen & Co. Ltd, 1974), p. 26.

SUGGESTIONS FOR FURTHER READING

Barrett, Cyril (1982) "The morality of artistic production", *Journal of Aesthetics and Art Criticism* 41.

Beardsmore, R.W (1971) *Art and Morality*, London: Macmillan Press.

Bontekoe, Ron and Jamie Crooks (1992) "The interrelationship of moral and aesthetic excellence", *British Journal of Aesthetics* 32.

Booth, Wayne (1988) *The Company We Keep: An Ethics of Fiction*, Berkeley: University of California Press.

—— (1993) "On relocating ethical criticism", in *Explanation and Value in the Arts*, ed. Salim Kemal and Ivan Gaskell, Cambridge: Cambridge University Press.

Carroll, Noël (1996) "Moderate moralism", *British Journal of Aesthetics* 36.

Collinson, Diane (1985) " 'Ethics and aesthetics are one' ", *British Journal of Aesthetics* 25.

Crowther, Paul (1989) *The Kantian Sublime: From Morality to Art*, Oxford: Oxford University Press.

Currie, Gregory (1995) "The moral psychology of fiction", *Australasian Journal of Philosophy* 73.

Danto, Arthur (1994) "Beauty and morality", in *Embodied Meanings*, New York: Farrar, Straus & Giroux.

Diffey, T.J. (1975) "Morality and literary criticism", *Journal of Aesthetics and Art Criticism* 33.

Eaton, Marcia (1989) *Aesthetics and the Good Life*, Madison, N.J.: Fairleigh Dickinson University Press.

—— (1992) "Integrating the aesthetic and the ethical", *Philosophical Studies* 67.

—— (1998) "Aesthetics: mother of ethics", *Journal of Aesthetics and Art Criticism* 56.

Eldridge, Richard (1988) *On Moral Personhood: Philosophy, Literature, Criticism, and Self-Understanding*, Chicago: University of Chicago Press.

—— (1993) "Narratives and moral evaluation", *Journal of Value Inquiry* 27.

Fenner, David (ed.) (1996) *Ethics and the Arts*, New York: Garland.

Gardner, John (1978) *On Moral Fiction*, New York: Basic Books.

Goldman, Alan (1990) "Aesthetic versus moral evaluation", *Philosophy and Phenomenological Research* 50.

Guyer, Paul (1993) *Kant and the Experience of Freedom: Essays on Aesthetics and Morality*, Cambridge: Cambridge University Press.

Heinrich, Natalie (1993) "Framing the bullfight: aesthetics vs. ethics", *British Journal of Aesthetics* 33.

Hyman, Lawrence (1979) "Moral attitudes and literary experience", *Journal of Aesthetics and Art Criticism* 38.

—— (1984) "Morality and literature: the necessary conflict", *British Journal of Aesthetics* 24.

Janaway, Christopher (1995) *Images of Excellence: Plato's Critique of the Arts*, Oxford: Clarendon Press.

Jenkins, J. (1968) "Aesthetic education and moral refinement", *Journal of Aesthetic Education* 2.

Lamarque, Peter (1995) "Tragedy and moral value", *Australasian Journal of Philosophy* 73. Reprinted in his *Fictional Points of View*, Ithaca and London: Cornell University Press, 1996.

Levinson, Jerrold (ed.) (1998) *Aesthetics and Ethics: Essays at the Intersection*, Cambridge: Cambridge University Press.

McGinn, Colin (1997) *Ethics, Evil and Fiction*, Oxford: Oxford University Press.

Moore, Ron (1995) "The aesthetic and the moral", *Journal of Aesthetic Education* 29.

Palmer, Frank (1994) *Literature and Moral Understanding: A Philosophical Essay on Ethics, Aesthetics, Education, and Culture*, Oxford: Oxford University Press.

Parker, David (1994) *Ethics, Theory and the Novel*, Cambridge: Cambridge University Press.

Pole, David (1983) "Morality and the assessment of literature", in *Aesthetics, Form and Emotion*, London: Duckworth.

Robinson, Jenefer and Stephanie Ross (1993) "Women, morality and fiction", in *Aesthetics in Feminist Perspective*, ed. H. Hein and C. Korsmeyer, Bloomington: Indiana University Press.

Sankowski, Edward (1988) "Blame, fictional characters, and morality", *Journal of Aesthetic Education* 22.

Seamon, Roger (1989) "The story of the moral: the function of thematizing in literary criticism", *Journal of Aesthetics and Art Criticism* 47.

Sharpe, R.A. (1992) "Moral tales", *Philosophy* 67.

Tilghman, Ben (1991) *Wittgenstein, Ethics, and Aesthetics*, Albany, N.Y.: State University of New York Press.

Tirrell, Lynne (1980) "Storytelling and moral agency", *Journal of Aesthetics and Art Criticism* 48.

Wilde, Oscar (1907) *Intentions*, London: The English Library.

Williams, Bernard (1993) *Shame and Necessity*, Berkeley: University of California Press.

Zemach, Eddy (1971) "Thirteen ways of looking at the ethics/aesthetics parallelism", *Journal of Aesthetics and Art Criticism* 29.

Part 11
FEMINISM AND AESTHETICS

Not that [the fifth century BC Greek sculpture] the Esquiline Venus represents an evolved notion of feminine beauty. She is short and square, with high pelvis and small breasts, far apart, a stocky little peasant such as might be found still in any Mediterranean village. . . . But she is solidly desirable, compact, proportionate; and in fact her proportions have been calculated on a simple mathematical scale. The unit of measurement is her head. She is seven heads tall; there is the length of one head between her breasts, one from breast to navel, and one from the navel to the division of the legs. . . . [T]he sculptor has discovered what we may call the plastic essentials of the feminine body.

Kenneth Clark, *The Nude*, pp. 67–8

Yesterday we went to a show of the classical nude in marble form. It was nice to see some women looking so cool and neutral in the heat. They weren't quite in the altogether, though, these nudes, having been figleafed by a recent hand. It's ridiculous, said Martina, the tiny wraps and sprigs they've added on. Oh I don't know, I said: don't be too hasty – it's good to leave a little something to the imagination. She didn't agree. In my view, of course, the chicks would have looked even better if they'd added stockings and garter belts, G-strings and ankle-strapped shoes: but that's aesthetics for you. Tomorrow we go to the big new show by Monet or Manet or Money or some such guy.

Martin Amis, *Money*, p. 327

In the average European oil painting of the nude the principal protagonist is never painted. He is the spectator in front of the picture and he is presumed to be a man. Everything is addressed to him. Everything must appear to be the result of his being there. It is for him that the figures have assumed their nudity. But he, by definition, is a stranger – with his clothes still on. . . .

In the art-form of the European nude the painters and spectator-owners were usually men and the persons treated as objects, usually women. This unequal relationship is so deeply embedded in our culture that it still structures the consciousness of many women. They do to themselves what men do to them. They survey, like men, their own femininity . . .

[T]he essential way of seeing women, the essential use to which their images are put, has not changed. Women are depicted in a quite different way from men – not because the feminine is different from the masculine – but because the "ideal" spectator is always assumed to be male and the image of the woman is designed to flatter him. If you have any doubt that this is so, make the following experiment. Choose . . . an image of a traditional nude. Transform the woman into a man. Either in your mind's eye or by drawing on the reproduction. Then notice the violence which that transformation does. Not to the image, but to the assumptions of a likely viewer.

John Berger, *Ways of Seeing*, pp. 54, 63, 64

THROUGHOUT THE HISTORY OF AESTHETICS, and particularly of Anglo-American aesthetics, there has been a strong tendency to ignore, marginalize, deny, or condemn any connection between works of art and politics. It has often been felt that to acknowledge such connections would be to undermine the essential purity of art. It would be to surrender art to political interests, to a realm of experience in which concern for qualities such as beauty or craftsmanship would inevitably be lost. Above all, it would be to weaken drastically the assumption, central to much of traditional aesthetics, that *genuine* works of art stand apart from the currents of ideology – that genuine works of art speak to and for humankind as a whole, to persons of every condition, in every time and place. The capacity of art to be universal, then, its capacity to speak to and for all of us, has been thought to depend upon the segregation of art from politics.

But inevitably, in a century which has seen the expansion of political analysis into almost every aspect of life, this traditional conception of aesthetics has increasingly been interpreted as ideologically motivated. The self-image of aesthetics as the apolitical study of a body of works which stand above and beyond politics has been challenged. The very denial of political content has been construed as a political, and a very conservative, stance. It is no longer possible simply to *assume* that aesthetics can or should be a-political, any more than it is still possible to assume that the works of art which it studies are without political implications. Aesthetics has been politicized, and a variety of ideological perspectives now claim the right to pose *openly* political questions about the arts – questions of a kind which, it is argued, were previously excluded by the *covertly* political programme embodied in aesthetics as it has traditionally been understood. Aesthetics now finds itself facing serious and unfamiliar challenges to its assumptions, its methods, and even to its legitimacy.

Some of the most interesting of these challenges have come from feminist thinkers, and one of their central charges – briefly – is this. Most of the art considered "great" has been created by men, or has been created within a culture dominated by men. Much of that "great" art reflects, not a *human* view of the world, or a universal view, but an identifiably masculine view, which embodies and promotes a particular set of attitudes towards women. Feminist critics have argued that it does this at a number of levels: not only in its representation of women, but also at a deeper, more insidious level, by employing conventions (for instance, narrative conventions) whose apparent innocence masks an attempt to claim a monopoly on objectivity, on the power to "tell it like it is". As a result, the male-dominated view of the world, including its view of women, unjustifiably acquires the air of natural truth.

These charges are among those discussed by Mary Devereaux in the first chapter of this part, as she expounds and explores the feminist challenge to aesthetics. She does not conclude that "all traditional aesthetics is useless". But she does suggest that feminism points up a "cognitive dissonance which marks the current situation in aesthetics", and which deserves our attention. She goes on to describe various aspects of that dissonance, and to outline some of the changes which might be made in order to resolve it, both in the practice of philosophical aesthetics and in the production of new works of art.

Curtis Brown takes up Devereaux's suggestion that we need to address these questions in the second chapter. Brown explores in detail two "Principles of Autonomy", each of which holds that art and aesthetics are to some extent, at least, "insulated" from facts about the oppression of women. The first principle holds that facts about the history of production of a work can have no bearing on its aesthetic value. The second holds that a large body of works of art, namely fictions, say nothing about the real world. Both principles may *seem* to show that some feminist criticisms of art are misguided. If the history of a work of art is irrelevant to its value, then the fact that women were oppressed in its production is also aesthetically irrelevant. And if fictions say nothing about the real world, then the way women are portrayed in works of fiction cannot be oppressive. Brown uses pornography as a "test case" against which to assess these principles. He argues that, on the one hand, both principles, when properly understood, are correct, but that, on the other hand, the principles do not in fact protect art from feminist criticism.

Does the legitimacy of aesthetics as a responsible mode of inquiry depend upon a radical, feminizing overhaul of its basic methods and assumptions? Or should we conclude that, while it would benefit from including a number of questions and techniques which it has hitherto thought marginal, traditional aesthetics is essentially sound, and needs only to consider minor revisions to its presuppositions and procedures? Whatever conclusions we reach, one thing is certain: that aesthetics – whether it emerges feminized from its encounter with feminism, or merely somewhat altered – can hardly fail to benefit.

23

OPPRESSIVE TEXTS, RESISTING READERS AND THE GENDERED SPECTATOR: THE "NEW" AESTHETICS

Mary Devereaux

I

At the heart of recent feminist theorizing about art is the claim that various forms of representation – painting, photography, film – assume a "male gaze." The notion of the gaze has both a literal and a figurative component. Narrowly construed, it refers to actual looking. Broadly, or more metaphorically, it refers to a way of thinking about, and acting in, the world.

In literal terms, the gaze is male when men do the looking. Men look both as spectators and as characters within works. In figurative terms, to say that the gaze is male refers to a way of seeing which takes women as its object. In this broad sense, the gaze is male whenever it directs itself at, and takes pleasure in, women, where women function as erotic objects. Many feminists claim that most art, most of the time, places women in this position. In Laura Mulvey's words, man is the bearer of the gaze, woman its object.[1]

Feminist theorists, like many other theorists, take as basic the tenet that no vision, not even artistic vision, is neutral vision. All vision is colored by the "spectacles" through which we see the world. The notion that all seeing is "a way of seeing" contrasts sharply with the traditional realist assumption that observation can be cleanly separated from interpretation, at least under certain ideally specified conditions. In part, feminist theorists can be understood as reiterating a familiar, but still important, objection to the naive notion of the innocent eye. As E.H. Gombrich convincingly argues, observation is never innocent. In his words, "Whenever we receive a visual impression, we react by docketing it, filing it, grouping it in one way or another, even if the impression is only that of an inkblot or a fingerprint. . . . [T]he postulate of an unbiased eye demands the impossible."[2] Observation is always conditioned by perspective and expectation.

Yet, feminist claims that our representations inscribe a male gaze involve more than a denial of the eye's innocence. They involve asserting the central role that gender plays in formulating those expectations. Feminist theorists insist, moreover, that these expectations are disproportionately affected by male needs, beliefs and desires. Both men and women have learned to see the world through male eyes. So, for example, women throughout their lives expend enormous amounts of time and energy and money making themselves "beautiful." In undertaking this costly process, women judge themselves according to internalized standards of what is pleasing to men. As Sandra Bartky observes, adolescent girls "learn to appraise themselves as they are shortly to be appraised."[3] In this sense, the eyes are female, but the gaze is male.

Feminist theorists object to seeing the world "through male eyes." They equate the male gaze with patriarchy. The notion of patriarchy is key here. Defined as a social system structured upon the supremacy of the father and the legal dependence of wives and children, patriarchy makes women depend upon men not only for status and privilege, but for their very identity. The assumption is that this arrangement oppresses women. It also, as both feminists and non-feminists have argued, oppresses men, although not necessarily in the same way as it oppresses women.

This oppression occurs at the symbolic as well as the material level. Women, as the first editorial of the film journal, *Camera Obscura*, announced, "are oppressed not only economically and politically, but also in the very forms of reasoning, signifying and symbolical exchange of our culture."[4] Thus, to take a familiar but powerful example, in English "he" functions as the unmarked term, "she" as the marked term. "His" attributes define all humanity (i.e., "mankind"); "hers" define only women. The higher priority assigned to male attributes passes unnoticed because our language, like our thinking, equates "male" gender with "gender neutral."

Art, as another form of symbolical exchange, also participates in this oppression. In both its high and low forms, feminist theorists argue, art inscribes "a masculinist discourse" which we learn to reproduce in our everyday lives. Feminist theorists here draw on the insight that art both reflects the conditions of life and helps to establish and maintain them. The male gaze inscribed in art triggers what Elizabeth Flynn and Patrocinia Schweickart describe as a deep-seated impulse for women to adapt themselves to the male viewpoint.[5] Griselda Pollock goes further, arguing that the history of art itself is a series of representational practices which actively encourage definitions of sexual difference that contribute to the present configuration of sexual politics and power relations.[6]

For this reason, much of feminist theorizing about art is critical in tone. From its perspective, the artistic canon is androcentric, and hence, politically repressive. In Schweickart's words, "For a woman, then, books do not necessarily spell salvation."[7]

Briefly summarized, the feminist critique of representation rests on the equation: the medium = male = patriarchal = oppressive.

Some will greet this equation as exaggerated, even absurd. The idea that art is political or ideologically charged contradicts the deeply held belief that art speaks to and for all human beings. Socrates' charges against the poets notwithstanding, the Western European tradition characterizes art as liberating, enlightening, uplifting. Art's effects are positive; the experiences it offers intrinsically valuable. In categorizing art with other forms of patriarchal oppression, feminist theorists reject the division of art and politics basic to Anglo-American aesthetics.

The implications of this rejection are important and far-reaching. In dividing the artworld into male and female, feminist theorists irrevocably link the production and consumption of art with issues of power and control. Outside the Anglo-American paradigm, this linkage is not new. The Marxist tradition in aesthetics has long placed the concept of power at the center of the discussion of art. Marxism's emphasis on how class and other social forces and practices enter into the reading of any text lays the groundwork for feminist investigations of how gender enters the exchange with the text.

What is original to feminism is the linkage of art with sexual politics. Issues of sexual politics lie at the center of current academic debate in English Departments, Film Studies programs and feminist theory groups. Aesthetics, at least in America, has been slower to notice or respond to this debate. Although an occasional feminist paper has appeared on the program at the annual American Society for Aesthetics meetings, *The Journal of Aesthetics and Art Criticism* has prior to this writing never published a work of feminist theory. This omission is even more surprising given that philosophers from Plato to Nelson Goodman have been preoccupied with issues of representation – an issue that feminism, from another direction, centrally addresses.

This lack of attention to issues transforming the discussion of art in other disciplines is frequently attributed to a difference in vocabulary. Feminist theory has its roots in Foucault and Lacan, not in Plato, Aristotle and Kant. Confronted with talk of "mirror stages," voyeurism," and "difference," practitioners of traditional aesthetics may feel trapped by the jargon of a foreign discourse, one not bound by rules their own training insists upon. Stanley Cavell describes the experience of reading these works as involving a different set of satisfactions.[8] Whatever the promise of these satisfactions, some will maintain, it is difficult not to lose patience with contemporary writers whose texts demand the exegetical labors normally reserved for the dead and the "truly great."

On this account, feminist theories remain marginalized due both to their difficulty and unfamiliarity. But this explanation does not, I think, tell the whole story. Regular readers of the *Journal* have no doubt noticed the growing number of articles dealing with the latest developments in literary theory (the work of Stanley Fish, Jacques Derrida, Mikhail Bakhtin), hermeneutics (Hans-Georg Gadamer) and the philosophy of language (Donald Davidson). In each of these cases, vocabulary and methodology pose formidable challenges. Not every reader will find such challenges worth the time or effort. But dearly, in aesthetics, as in philosophy generally, difficulty alone never warrants exclusion.

The reason feminist theories of art and aesthetics have so long remained unmentioned lies deeper, I think. At stake in the debate over feminism are deeply entrenched assumptions about the universal value of art and aesthetic experience. The overthrow of these assumptions – linchpins of aesthetic theory since Kant – constitutes what art historian, Linda Nochlin, describes as a Kuhnian paradigm shift.[9] The new paradigm is a feminist paradigm and what we face is a conceptual revolution. If I am right, then the deeper explanation for the lack of attention to feminist theories lies in the natural resistance of those suddenly faced with the overthrow of an entrenched way of thinking.

As recent developments in the philosophy of science and ethics highlight, aesthetics cannot simply "add on" feminist theories as it might add new works by Goodman, Arthur Danto or George Dickie. To take feminism seriously involves rethinking our basic concepts and recasting the history of the discipline. And that requires more than adding women's names to the canonical list of great philosophers.

The requirement that we engage in such radical rethinking may seem burdensome and unnecessary. It is helpful to the self-esteem of women or to women who are feminists. But what of those who do not fit into either of these two categories? What, they may wonder, do they have to gain from feminist aesthetics?

In part to answer such questions, I want in the next section to return to the notion of the male gaze. In examining this key feminist notion more carefully, I hope to make clear the intrinsic interest of this approach to aesthetics and to suggest why its concerns merit serious consideration.

To this end, I want to investigate how gendered vision works in one specific representational practice, namely film. Film is a natural choice for such a study because it is a medium so fundamentally built around the activity of looking. It is also, not surprisingly, the medium where the male gaze has been most extensively discussed.

The relationship of gender and cinematic vision is extremely complicated. A complete analysis of this topic would require several hundred pages. In what follows, I focus on two key claims, namely, that in cinema the gaze is male and that the cinematic text is a male text. I seek to make clear how these claims should be understood and then to situate them philosophically. In confining myself to what I take to be the core claims of this debate, I will of necessity leave aside many important, but internal, issues in film theory.

II

Despite the extensive literature which refers to and relies upon it, the concept of the male gaze remains difficult to understand. It is so in part because, as noted above, the male gaze refers both to literal and metaphorical vision. A further difficulty in understanding the male gaze arises from the failure to distinguish three different gazes: that of film-maker, the characters within the film and the spectator. With each of these gazes, literal and figurative seeing interact in a variety of ways.

In the first case, that of the film-maker, someone looks through the viewfinder of a camera, someone (often the same person) looks at the rushes after the day's shooting and someone looks at the film's final cut. This person may be male, but need not be. Women, too, make movies and have done so since the early days of the medium (e.g., Maya Deren, Dorothy Artner, Leni Riefenstahl).

What does it mean then to say that at this level the gaze is male? It means that despite the presence of women directors and screenwriters, the institutions of film-making remain largely populated by men. Not all films have male authors, but whoever makes movies must work nonetheless within a system owned and operated by men. At the level of the filmmaker, then, men do not always do the looking, but they generally control who does. The male gaze is not always male, but *it is always male-dominated*.

By male-dominated, feminist theorists mean male-gendered, not simply possessed of male anatomy. A key move distinguishes sex from gender. A child is born sexed; through education and experience, it acquires gender. On this account, education and experience create the particular way of seeing which the term, "the male gaze," describes. Male institutional control thus refers not to the anatomy of film world personnel, which includes both men and women, but to the way film, however authored, contributes to the hegemony of men over women.

From a feminist point of view, this control matters because it "builds in" a preference for a particular type of film, i.e., one which positions women in ways consistent with patriarchal assumptions. Movies promote a way of seeing which takes man as subject, women as object. Simone de Beauvoir's *The Second Sex* puts the point succinctly. "Representation of the world, like the world itself, is the work of men; they describe it from their own point of view, which they confuse with absolute truth."[10]

As de Beauvoir explains, women, unlike men, do not learn to describe the world from their own point of view. As the "other," woman learns to submerge or renounce her subjectivity. She finds her identity in the subjectivity of the men to whom she is attached (father, husband, lover). In the eyes of men, she finds her identity as the object of men's desire.

In arguing that cinema, too, assigns woman this position, feminist theorists link male control of film institutions with a patriarchal way of seeing. At this point it should be clear that in attempting to describe the literal gaze of the film-maker, the question of whether men or women do the looking is not at root the issue. The real issue centers on whether, whoever stands behind the camera, a patriarchal way of seeing the world prevails. The discussion of the literal gaze thus very quickly becomes a discussion of the figurative gaze.

I do not want to deny the heuristic usefulness of talking about "literal" looking in film. Someone does look through the lens of the camera, and film-going is irrefutably a visual experience. Moreover, the medium itself offers a range of devices for representing what characters on screen themselves see, e.g., the long sequences in Alfred Hitchcock's *Vertigo* in which we see what the protagonist, Scottie, sees as he follows Madeleine.

A deeper and more damaging objection to the literal/figurative distinction emerges from the claim that literal seeing is always already figurative. Men – like women – do not simply look. Their looking – where and when they do it and at what – mimics a particular way of thinking about and acting in the world. So understood, seeing never escapes *a way* of seeing.

How then does the figurative way of seeing deemed "male" translate to the screen? How *are* women represented from the male point of view? And, with what effect on the spectator? To answer these questions requires shifting our attention from the film-maker's gaze to the manipulation of the gaze within film. At the textual level, feminist theorists have focused most directly on the story films of Hollywood as opposed to the international art cinema, experimental film or documentary film. Attention to the Hollywood film arose naturally from the broad popularity and profound influence which this tradition exercised on American cultural life.

Feminist theorists initially attacked the Hollywood film for its patriarchal content. Early feminist works such as Molly Haskell's *From Reverence to Rape*[11] examined how the portraits of the Good Girl, the Vamp and the Dutiful Wife presented so forcefully in westerns, detective films and melodramas reinforced a cultural mythology. In film after film, that mythology defined the value of women as their value to men. The good girl was a dutiful daughter who preserved herself (i.e., her virginity) for the right man "to take" from her. The bad girl, in contrast, flaunts her sexuality indiscriminately, "losing" her virginity or "giving it away."

Haskell's broadly sociological approach understood movies to tell the same stories we heard outside the theatre. In the movies, as in life, good girls were rewarded, bad girls punished. Any alternative point of view, one which might tell a different tale or the same tale differently, was effectively excluded. Put in the strongest terms, the charge was that the Hollywood film "belonged to patriarchy."[12] This commitment need not be intentional. Nor need it be confined to the works of male directors. Yet, as an institution, cinema, like television, was held to participate in and help to perpetuate a system of social organization which assigns power and privilege by gender.

Admittedly, not all films perpetuate patriarchy. Individual films may resist this arrangement. The strong-headed heroines typically played by Katharine Hepburn, Lauren Bacall and Bette Davis do not conform to this stereotype, nor do films such as Howard Hawks' *His Girl Friday*. As feminist critics themselves have demonstrated, the films of Hollywood evidence more variation and internal tension than a charge of monolithic patriarchy allows.

In speaking of Hollywood film as "belonging to patriarchy," something more subtle is at work than overt stereotyping. At the simplest level, Haskell and others had maintained, film reinforced women's dependence on men. As noted above, women on screen regularly won their happiness in the service of others (Griffith's Dear One, Marion as the amiable spouse in *Shane*). When they depart from societal norms, as Hepburn's high-level diplomat does in *Woman of the Year*, they are revealed to be cold-hearted and in need of "re-education." Tess learns from her husband Sam to place work second to companionate time with spouse and the duties of parenting. Those who refuse this role, find themselves alone and lonely (e.g., Tess' Aunt Ellen). Those who opt for illicit instead of married love, end up dead (e.g., Marion in *Psycho*, Alex in *Fatal Attraction*).

Thus, as Mary Ann Doane convincingly argues, at a more complex level, the Hollywood film functions as "a recuperative strategy" designed to return the wayward woman to the fold.[13] This return operates both within the narrative and externally, in the narrative's effect on its female audience. Internally, the Hollywood narrative typically charts the course by which a woman in a non-normative role cedes her control to a man.[14] The happy ending in which Tess returns to Sam serves externally to "recuperate" wayward members of the female audience as well. The message is that for a woman, unlike for a man, the satisfactions of solitude, work, or adventure cannot compare to those of caring for husband and children.

The classic Hollywood film reinforces this message stylistically by confining the spectator to the point of view of the narrative hero. In Tania Modleski's words, "the film spectator apparently has no choice but to identify with the male protagonist, who exerts an active, controlling gaze over a passive female object." By consistently stressing the man's point of view, the Hollywood film thus negates the female character's view.[15]

Stressing the male protagonist's point of view need not involve confining us consistently to his visual field. The one well-known experiment which confined us consistently to the first-person visual field of a character, Robert Montgomery's *The Lady in the Lake*, failed miserably to convey that character's figurative point of view. We saw what he saw, but we didn't feel what he felt. More typical narrative films, such as *The Big Sleep*, alternate between what the protagonist sees and what other characters see. Hawks gives us not only Marlowe looking at Vivian but Vivian looking at Marlowe. The gaze is thus not directly that of the protagonist.

Nevertheless, within the Hollywood film there is a long tradition of women performing for the camera. Women sing, dance, dress and undress, all before the steady, often adoring, gaze of an implied spectator. Frequently, female performance plays a role in the plot, as when Vivian sings for Marlowe and the audience at Eddie Mars' nightclub. But whether playing fictional characters who sing and dance before an audience or not, Marlene Dietrich, Marilyn Monroe, Ingrid Bergman and other female "stars," perform *for* the camera. As Stanley Cavell has pointed out, in photographing beautiful women, the cinema has found one of the subjects most congenial to it. But "congenial" here means the congeniality of men making films for men.

The male controlled institutions of film-making thus place women on screen in a particular position. As eroticized objects, women are doubly victimized. As Ann Kaplan argues, the male gaze involves more than simply looking; it carries with it the threat of action and possession. This power to act and possess is not reciprocal. Women can receive and return a gaze, but they cannot act upon it.[16]

To be fully operative as a mechanism of oppression, the male gaze depends upon a second condition. Not only must looking come with some "back-up" – physical, economic, social – but "being looked at" must also activate some level of female narcissism. Women themselves must not be indifferent to the gaze turned upon them; they must have internalized a certain assignment of positions.[17]

It is this disequilibrium in power both inside and outside the arena of looking which makes the male gaze different from what some have called a female or gender-neutral gaze. Consider the oft-cited cases where men serve as the object of the gaze, as in the recent spate of Richard Gere movies (*Breathless*, *American Gigolo*). Despite the "role reversal," the degradation which women suffer in occupying the role of "looked at" is not matched by their male counterparts.

It would be useful at this point to make a distinction, one between objectification, aestheticization and degradation.[18] "Objectification," as I am using the term, means no more than to make someone or something the object of my gaze. There is nothing inherently oppressive about objectification understood in this way. Nor is the filmic male gaze any more objectifying than any other gaze. Aestheticization, defined here, means simply treating people or things as objects of aesthetic contemplation. There is nothing inherently oppressive about aestheticization. Both objectification and aestheticization may be degrading, but they need not be. "Degradation" is a complex notion, associated with such concepts as respect, human dignity and worth. To degrade is to demean or debase someone, where this involves not only failing to respect, but also, in some sense, actively diminishing the value or dignity of the person. Rape, slavery and torture provide three obvious examples of degradation.[19]

Given these distinctions, it is easy to see that male characters, like their female counterparts, may be objectified or even, as in the case of Richard Gere, aestheticized (or eroticized). And they, like women, may also be portrayed in degraded or less than fully human ways. It is with respect to actual degradation that the asymmetry between men and women reappears. For in the case of women, unlike that of men, real life degradation often runs parallel to portrayals of degradation. Because women frequently lack power off screen, they are more likely to be degraded by their portrayals on screen. Even if men are portrayed in degrading ways, their real life power shields them from actual degradation.

As I've said above, objectification and aestheticization are not in themselves degrading. Nevertheless, feminist theorists are correct that Hollywood films reflect and encourage a cultural proclivity to treat the female body and the female self *only* as objects of aesthetic contemplation. And they are also correct in suggesting that this way of treating women *is* degrading. While, as I have argued, movie-making and movie-watching cannot be held solely responsible for the oppression of women, feminist theorists rightly emphasize the connection between how we represent our lives and lived experience itself.

In turning, finally, to the effect of the film text on its spectators, I want first to consider the means by which the gender bias of many Hollywood films remains hidden. The Hollywood film conventionally presents its telling as, to quote Beauvoir again, "absolute truth." It depends for its effect upon creating a narrative illusion. The film story must unfold transparently, as though happening before our very eyes. It is crucial to such film-making that it proceed without calling attention to itself as a story. In this, the stylistic conventions of Hollywood follow those of the 19th century realist novel. For a film to acknowledge its status as a story or fiction admits a point of view, a place from which its story gets told. Devices such as Godard's use of stop-action and words written across the screen aim to resist narrative illusionism. They announce the film as a film, as a fiction, a construct.[20]

For many feminists, as for many Marxists, the narrative illusion central to the classic Hollywood film is politically compromised. Hollywood films are said to foster strong character identification and full absorption in the action. This absorption in turn is believed to encourage viewer passivity. At its worst, warned Max Horkheimer and Theodor Adorno, such film-making undermines individual autonomy. It renders its audience a "mass" easily manipulated in the interests of the status quo.

In an effort to encourage active, critically engaged spectatorship, feminist theorists often exaggerate the connection between conventional Hollywood techniques of storytelling and passive spectatorship. Passive spectatorship is not, however, restricted to Hollywood narratives, nor do all such films aim for, or achieve, such an effect, e.g., Spike Lee's *Do the Right Thing*. To the extent that the average Hollywood product *does* encourage passivity, it renders *both* male and female spectators passive. Unfortunately, feminist critics often lose sight of this point.

In calling for active reading to replace this passivity, feminist critiques of the Hollywood film here parallel Brecht's critique of Aristotelian drama. Both denounce what they see as efforts to elicit the passive empathy of the spectator; both ask for art to break the narrative illusion. However, feminist theorists go beyond Brecht's analysis to examine how identification differs in male and female spectators. Gender, they rightly assert, plays a key role in eliciting the empathy and identification typical of narrative film.

The analysis of film's effects on the spectator brings us to the third and, I would argue, most important site at which the male gaze operates. In developing a theory of spectatorship, feminist theorists move beyond an initial concern with film content and style to explore the mechanisms of viewing. To the question "how does film represent women?" is added the question "what sources of satisfaction do these representations of women offer the spectator?" At what many now call its second stage, feminist film theory shifts attention from the literary critical and sociological reading of individual films to the more broadly theoretical project of describing the unconscious mechanisms involved in watching movies.[21]

Primary among these mechanisms is voyeuristic pleasure. In this view, enormously influential among film theorists, spectators derive erotic pleasure through the opportunities for looking which the cinema affords. As Christian Metz argues in *The Imaginary Signifier* (1975), the darkened theatre, the absence of the object viewed, and its inability to return the gaze all contribute to the idea that film viewing constitutes unauthorized looking.[22] From its early association with the Nickelodeon, the motion picture has come to function as a metaphor for the illicit activity of the voyeur, as Alfred Hitchcock's 1954 film, *Rear Window*, illustrates. Lest one miss the point, Hitchcock makes L.B. Jeffries – an inveterate voyeur – a photographer.[23]

The question of how film plays to our already existing desires, fantasies, and fears received one of its most influential treatments in Laura Mulvey's now classic, "Visual Pleasure and Narrative Cinema." Mulvey begins from the premise that film reflects the psychical obsessions of the society which produces it. In making this assumption, Mulvey, like most other second wave theorists, draws heavily on psychoanalysis, particularly Freud and Lacan. She sets out to analyze the characteristic sources of pleasure and unpleasure offered by the cinema.

Narrative cinema, by which she means narrative in the unself-conscious mode described above, provides the spectator with two sources of pleasure. First, it provides what Freud calls "scopophilic" pleasure, the pleasure of viewing another as an erotic object. As we saw above, this pleasure characteristically takes the form of looking at women. In film after film, women function both as erotic objects for characters within the movie, as Vivian does for Marlowe, and as erotic objects for the spectator in the movie-house, as Lauren Bacall does for us. Thus, women's presence on screen presupposes the appreciative glance of a male spectator.

Men, in contrast, only rarely function as eroticized objects for female (or male) spectators. Men, Mulvey points out, feel uncomfortable in such a role. Neither the ruling assumptions of patriarchy "nor the psychical structures that back it up" encourage the male "to gaze at his exhibitionist like."[24] Instead, man's role is to function as the locus of narrative action. His role, on screen as off, involves shooting the bad guys and blazing the trails. The male movie star attracts our admiration and respect by his deeds. We are encouraged to *identify with* him, to imagine ourselves doing what he does.

In Freudian terms, the male functions as an "ego-ideal," not as an object of erotic desire. The possibility of identifying with this ego-ideal offers the spectator a second, contrasting source of pleasure, i.e., the pleasure of identifying with the characters projected on screen. Since, on Mulvey's analysis, it is the male hero who makes things happen and controls them, we typically identify with him. Thus, the spectator's gaze is male in two senses, both in its direction at women as objects of erotic fascination and in its identification with the male protagonist. The division of male and female roles on screen mimics traditional gender roles: women functioning as the passive objects of the viewer's gaze; men functioning as the active subjects of the viewer's imagination.

In playing to our existing desires, fantasies and fears, film also offers what Mulvey calls unpleasure. In the patriarchal unconscious, woman represents the threat of castration. This threat the Hollywood film typically meets in one of two ways. It may contain the threat posed by the mystery and fearsomeness of women by domesticating them, typically through marriage (e.g., *Notorious*), or, more drastically, by killing them off, as in *Fatal Attraction*. Alternatively, the threat may be denied altogether by elevating the woman to the status of a fetish. In the latter case, the woman becomes reassuring instead of dangerous.[25]

To summarize, then, the male gaze refers to three interlocking forms of control. With respect to the film-maker, it refers to male control of the practices of film-making. This control leads, at the level of the film text, to a product whose content and style inscribe the patriarchal unconscious of the culture at large. Lastly, these devices position the male or female audience member to find in film a way of seeing which calms our fears and satisfies our desires.

This is a provocative account of film spectatorship. To ask who is doing the looking assumes all spectators are not similarly positioned, i.e., that factors such as gender have a role to play in structuring – maybe even in constituting – what we see. Mulvey's original analysis, however, leaves the *female* spectator with no active viewing position except to identify with the male protagonist. In identifying with the women on screen, the female spectator is assumed to align herself with the female-as-object.[26] More recent feminist theory rightly inquires how Mulvey's account explains the pleasure which women derive from going to the movies. As Ann Kaplan has asked, is the female spectator's pleasure, like the man's, the pleasure of looking at women, the masochistic pleasure of enjoying objectification, or the sadistic pleasure of identifying with the men who oppress her?[27]

In "Afterthoughts on Visual Pleasure and Narrative Cinema," Mulvey herself proposes, more positively, that identification with the male allows the female spectator to revert, at least imaginatively, to the active independence of what Freud termed the female child's "early masculine period." In this "tomboy" phase, she takes pleasure in a freedom that correct femininity will later repress.[28]

In moving beyond the static model of active male/passive female, current theories of spectatorship acknowledge women's resistance to the position assigned to them in patriarchal culture. There remains, however, a tendency to speak of *the* female spectator as if all women shared the same aims and aspirations and came to film texts similarly equipped. To make these assumptions overlooks important differences between women of color and white women, rich and poor, women and feminists and different varieties of feminists.

Similarly, feminist theories of spectatorship tend to speak of *the* male spectator as though all men's gazes are male. This assertion assumes, unjustifiably, that all men are equally powerful and that they stand equally to gain from the arrangements of patriarchy. Such assumptions contradict feminism's own insistence on the relationship between power and variables such as economic standing, education, ethnic identity, sexual orientation and so on. Thus, for example, in feminist terms, the male gaze is not only sexist but also heterosexist. Should not then an adequate theory of spectatorship also include an account of how the male gaze operates when the spectator is not heterosexual?

As these objections suggest, a more fine-grained analysis of spectatorship undermines the easy identification of male viewer with "the male gaze." The characterization of the male gaze as "totally active" is, I suggest, difficult to sustain once we move beyond the assumption that all men occupy the same position in a patriarchal social system. Moreover, the assumed activity and control of the male spectator is at odds with the widespread notion that the Hollywood film monolithically encourages a form of passive spectatorship. Equating the male gaze with the active gaze ignores the passive element involved in looking at movies. The male spectator, whatever his real political and social power, cannot interact with the on-screen woman. She appears, but is physically absent.

As I hope to have made clear, the notion of the male gaze cannot simply be identified with the way men see the world. The gaze, properly understood, has undergone certain refinements. It describes a way of seeing the world which is typically male. But it is not a way of seeing confined to men nor is it the province of all men.

Part of what makes feminist theories interesting and powerful is their attention to factors which affect how we see and respond to texts. Gender is one of these factors. As they evolve, feminist film theories, like feminist theories more generally have, however, increasingly recognized the necessity to move beyond a simple binary analysis of gender. In articulating the interconnections between gender and other variables, such as sexual orientation, race, and class, a feminist orientation serves to fine-tune our understanding of art and its effects upon us.

III

What general conclusions can we draw from this analysis of the male gaze? That film works to reinforce societal norms? That it is male? That film, like art generally, may be harmful to women? Such conclusions are now common in film studies. As noted earlier, we find similar arguments in older, more entrenched, fields such as literature and art history. As a body of theory, feminism has succeeded in placing the question of gender at the center of contemporary literary and artistic theory. As I suggested earlier, this new agenda has unsettling consequences for traditional aesthetics. The new agenda seeks not only to have us surrender certain longstanding assumptions, but to replace them with whole new ways of thinking about art and our relationship to it. I want to conclude therefore by sketching briefly some of these changes and raising several questions for us to consider.

First, feminist theorists ask us to replace the conception of the artwork as an autonomous object – a thing of beauty and a joy forever – with a messier conception of art. Seen in these terms, the artwork moves from an autonomous realm of value to the everyday realm of social and political praxis. It gains a history which overflows the former bounds of "art history." Who makes art and what type of art gets made depend, we learn, on the interaction of the artworld with other worlds.

In drawing our attention to culture in the broadest sense, feminist theorists rely on an alternative, European view of art. In this, feminist aesthetics constitutes part of a larger movement away from "autonomous" aesthetics. Even within Anglo-American aesthetics, the old paradigm no longer holds the place it once did. Our understanding of representation, of the pleasures and powers of art, and of spectatorship have been immeasurably enriched by the expanded context in which we now look at art. Yet, in this enlarged context, how does a concept of the "aesthetic," if by that we mean the *purely* aesthetic, function? Is the discipline of aesthetics possible apart from sociology, cultural studies, identity politics?

Second, feminist theorists propose that we re-examine art's claim to speak for all of us. Does art speak in a gender-neutral voice or does it privilege some experiences and ways of seeing over others? Traditional aesthetics inherits from Aristotle belief in a universal human condition of which art, at least great art, speaks.

Feminist theorists challenge the adequacy of the classic, Aristotelian model not only with respect to the Hollywood film (which some might argue is not great enough to qualify as "great" art), but with respect to all art. The films of Sergei Eisenstein and Jean Renoir, like the plays of Shakespeare, all speak in "particular" voices. On the new view, the artwork, like the generic pronoun, speaks for "mankind," but mankind includes only some of us.[29]

To question art's autonomy and universality, need not imply that these artworks are without value – quite the contrary – although their value may differ from what we once supposed. Nothing in feminist theory precludes ranking Henry James a more important novelist than Jane Austen or Alice Walker a greater writer than John Steinbeck.

In making these evaluative rankings, feminist theorists do insist, however, that we acknowledge the criteria used in defining "important" and "great." Does "great" mean the forcefully written or the spare, the heartfelt or the coolly reasoned, the typical or the innovative? When is a text forcefully written and who decides? Feminist theorists offer a framework from within which we may – indeed, should – raise such questions. Only when we explicitly acknowledge the criteria used in making these judgements do we create space for competing criteria.

In denying that artworks or the criteria we use to judge them are value-neutral, feminist theorists also urge a third proposal. We are asked to reconsider our relationship to established artistic traditions. The canon, still heralded by some as a reservoir for the best of human thinking, is accused of excluding and silencing women (among other groups). At the very least, a feminist perspective requires that we rethink our relationship to the artistic tradition in terms which do not assume a monolithic "we." Describing existing artistic traditions as uniformly enlightening and liberating ignores those for whom the authority of those traditions is unquestionably problematic. Thus, we must ask whether the coming of age stories of Holden Caulfield and David Copperfield affect adolescent girls in the same way as adolescent boys, and what significance this difference, if any, makes. Being willing to ask *who* is doing the reading forces us to question whether the pleasures of art are invariant and impervious to factors such as class, race and gender.

Fourthly, feminist theorists alter the characterization of reading or viewing as neutral activities. Like hermeneutics and reader-response theories, they seek to explain how the social and historical placement of the spectator affects the meaning derived from the text. Meaning is no longer determined exclusively by the text. Aside from emphasizing the social and historical context in which interpretation occurs, feminist theorists break new ground in demonstrating how texts themselves "assume" a particular reader through narrative and stylistic devices. The best of feminist theorizing executes this demonstration through a careful analysis of texts.

In advancing new theories of readership, however, what justifies feminist theorists in assigning "the woman reader" a central place in the analysis of texts? If it is meaningful to think in terms of "the woman reader," then why not in terms of "the lesbian reader,"[30] "the adolescent reader," "the ideal reader," "the over-educated reader"? Are all of these categories equally important, and according to what theoretical or political criteria?

Lastly, feminist theorists, like other post-structuralist theorists, endeavor to make the unnoticed noticed. They adopt from the Frankfurt School the belief that the informed spectator is a more critical spectator, and the critical spectator is one less likely to be victimized by the text.

Calls for critical reading are unlikely to meet resistance among aestheticians. But what of claims that art may not be good for us? – At the very least, not all art and not for all of us. In adopting a *politics of art*, feminist theorists confront Anglo-American aesthetics head-on. They replace reverence for art with skepticism. They ask that we be willing to rethink what we value and the reasons we value it.

In suggesting that this challenge deserves serious consideration, I might be understood to claim that all traditional aesthetics is useless, that the accomplishments of the last century are a chimera. This is not my intent. My intent is instead to describe the cognitive dissonance which marks the current situation in aesthetics. If feminism constitutes a new paradigm, then we may wish to ponder how far the old model of aesthetics and the new are commensurable. Is traditional aesthetics contingently or necessarily associated with patriarchy? Can the "gender-neutral" aesthetics of the traditional model be reformed or must it be rejected?

Aside from these theoretical issues, feminist theory raises several practical issues which demand attention. If art contributes to the disequilibrium in power between the sexes, then what should we do? Should we simply quit going to the movies?

Raising such questions returns us to the Socratic tradition which urges caution in the face of art's power. Socrates followed that warning with a call for censorship. With this suggestion, however, many feminists would not agree. Feminist theory confronts the ancient problem of art's potential for harm with two other, far more promising, strategies. Neither appears to have occurred to Socrates. I want therefore to conclude by looking very briefly at these solutions.

IV

The first proposed solution consists in a call for a new type of art. Some feminists, Claire Johnson for example, have proposed the creation of a counter-cinema to compete with the mainstream Hollywood cinema.[31] This strategy, like establishing public radio and television stations aims to offer an alternative to the usual fare.

The suggestion to create an alternative art might please Socrates. It would allow him to replace Homer's epics with his own, more philosophically informed, tales. This so-called revision of the canon would meet the Socratic objections to art whose content and form encouraged a weakening of the requisite moral virtues.

Creating new artistic traditions provides an alternative to the passive reception of dominant traditions. This strategy is most often described as creating a female voice or female gaze. It allows women to write their own texts, their own history. Achieving such a "female gaze" requires more than simply providing women with access to the means of filmmaking. As Diane Waldman correctly argues, women don't make better, less "patriarchal" films simply because they are women, as if women automatically had access to resources not available to the male psyche. The required transformation of film depends not upon some female essence, but upon a consciously adopted political perspective.[32]

Adopting such a perspective has resulted in interesting films by Mulvey, Sally Potter, Lizzie Borden, Barbara Hammer and others. These films strive in a variety of ways to disrupt or rework the narrative conventions of the dominant cinema. Sally Potter's *Thriller*, for example, retells the story of *La Bohème*. In Potter's *film noir* version of the doomed love affair, Mimi investigates her own death. Her voice-over and the fragmented narrative through which her story unfolds resist the character identification and narrative closure typical of traditional narrative. Films such as *Thriller* strive to critique the dominant moods of cinematic representation by privileging heterogeneity and multiplicity of meaning. In this, these films aim to free the spectator to engage more actively with the text. Other films, such as those of Barbara Hammer, seek alternatives to the forms of cinematic pleasure provided by the glossy image of the professional photographer. The range and variety of feminist film-making far exceeds what I can survey here. However, these films are shown primarily in film courses and private film societies. Thus, despite their importance in providing an alternative tradition, their influence on mainstream audiences and film-practices is limited.

The second feminist strategy consists in developing methods of dealing with existing texts. This strategy is variously described as re-reading, as reading against the grain, or as "re-vision." It involves active readership, where I mean reading in the broad sense to include both visual and written texts. These strategies have in common the aim of critique and reappropriation. Thus, they do what good criticism always does. But more than this, they involve learning to see through what Kuhn calls a "new pair of spectacles."[33] This new pair of spectacles provides an education not in *what* to think but *how*. Reading against the grain is a strategy designed by out of power groups to counterbalance the dominant textual traditions by offering alternative interpretations of works within those traditions.

Thought of in these terms, feminist theories offer a different critical perspective. They provide a means of resistance, and an alternative to, the male gaze. Admittedly, just as the male gaze involves a distinct political position, so too a feminist perspective is not, nor should it be regarded as, politically neutral.[34] Yet, as a way of seeing, it importantly differs from its male counterpart in acknowledging itself *as* a way of seeing.

The possibility of such textual strategies is politically important not only for feminists but for others concerned with "neutralizing" the effects of certain artworks or forms of art within a cultural setting committed to the protection of free speech. Reading "against the grain" offers an alternative to the passive readership which censorship assumes, and in its paternalism, encourages.

As an interpretative strategy, it opens to all of us – male and female – the possibility of finding our own way through the text. For various historical and cultural reasons, feminist theorists look more optimistically than did Socrates on the capacity of each of us to find that way. Yet, producing new forms of art and reading against the grain of the old will not by themselves topple the existing gender hierarchy. For that, women must also have power off-screen.

NOTES

1 Laura Mulvey, "Visual pleasure and narrative cinema," in *Film Theory and Criticism*, 3rd edn, eds Gerald Mast and Marshall Cohen (Oxford University Press, 1985), pp. 803–16.

2 E.H. Gombrich, *Art and Illusion: A Study in the Psychology of Pictorial Representation* (Princeton University Press, 1960), pp. 297–8.

3 Sandra Bartky, "Women, bodies and power: a research agenda for philosophy," *APA Newsletter on Philosophy and Feminism* 89 (1989), p. 79.

4 Robert Lapsley and Michael Westlake, *Film Theory: An Introduction* (Manchester University Press, 1988), p. 23.

5 Elizabeth A. Flynn and Patrocinio P. Schweickart, eds, *Gender and Reading: Essays on Readers, Texts, and Contexts* (Johns Hopkins University Press, 1986), xix.

6 Griselda Pollock, *Vision and Difference* (New York: Routledge, 1988), p. 11.

7 Patrocinio Schweickart, "Toward a feminist theory of reading," in *Gender and Reading*, p. 41.

8 Stanley Cavell, *In Quest of the Ordinary: Lines of Skepticism and Romanticism* (University of Chicago Press, 1988), p. 131.

9 Linda Nochlin, *Women, Art and Power and Other Essays* (New York: Harper & Row, 1988), p. 146.

10 Simone de Beauvoir, *The Second Sex*, trans. and ed. H.M. Parshley (New York: Vintage Books, 1974), p. 134.

11 Molly Haskell, *From Reverence to Rape: The Treatment of Women in the Movies* (Harmondsworth: Penguin Books, 1974).

12 B. Deidre Pribram, ed., *Female Spectators: Looking at Film and Television* (New York: Verso, 1988), p. 1.

13 See Mary Ann Doane, *The Desire to Desire: The Woman's Film of the 1940s* (Indiana University Press, 1987), chapter 2.

14 Mary Beth Haralovich, cited in Annette Kuhn, *Women's Pictures: Feminism and the Cinema* (London: Routledge & Kegan Paul, 1982), p. 34.

15 Tania Modleski, *The Women Who Knew Too Much: Hitchcock and Feminist Theory* (New York: Methuen, 1988), p. 73.

16 E. Ann Kaplan, "Is the gaze male?" in *Women and Values: Readings in Recent Feminist Philosophy*, ed. Marilyn Pearsall (Belmont, California: Wadsworth Publishing Co., 1986), p. 231.

17 The idea that women's oppression depends upon the fulfillment of both of these conditions I owe to a conversation with Tim Gould.

18 I base these distinctions on Lydia Goehr's helpful commentary on an earlier version of this paper. Her comments were presented at the American Society for Aesthetics, Eastern Division Meeting. State College, Pa., 16 March 1990.

19 In saying that acts such as rape degrade their victims, I do not mean to endorse the conventional view of women according to which rape is degrading because it destroys or damages a woman's "purity." I do, however, want to maintain that there is a sense in which rape (along with slavery and torture) is truly degrading. The notion of degradation is complicated and we are likely to have conflicting intuitions. Many of us would like to uphold the Kantian idea that human dignity is inviolable. In this view, human dignity is such that no act can diminish it. On the other hand, there is the also compelling view that certain acts are such that they do degrade and diminish persons. In this latter view, it is the potential for real degradation that makes the rapist's acts so horrible.

20 Interestingly, what is termed the "new" Hollywood cinema has adopted some of the techniques and self-conscious strategies of the international art cinema.
21 This division of feminist film theory into first and second stages can be found, for example, in Lapsley and Westlake, *Film Theory*, p. 25. The same division emerges less explicitly in Claire Johnson, "Women's cinema as counter-cinema," in *Movies and Methods*, ed. Bill Nichols (University of California Press, 1976), pp. 209–15.
22 Christian Metz, from *The Imaginary Signifier, Film Theory and Criticism*, 3rd edn, ed. Gerald Mast and Marshall Cohen (Oxford University Press, 1985), pp. 799–801.
23 See Modleski's chapter on *Rear Window* for a discussion of the film's critical reception.
24 Mulvey, "Visual Pleasure and Narrative Cinema," p. 810.
25 Ibid., p. 811.
26 Pribram, *Female Spectators*, pp. 1–2.
27 Kaplan, "Is the gaze male?" p. 252.
28 Laura Mulvey, *Visual and Other Pleasures* (Indiana University Press, 1989), p. 37.
29 For a more detailed analysis of the concepts of art's autonomy and universality, see my "The philosophical and political implications of the feminist critique of aesthetic autonomy," in *Turning the Century: Feminist Criticism in the 1990s*, Glynis Carr, ed., *The Bucknell Review*, xxxvi (2) (Cranbury, NJ: Associated University Presses, 1992).
30 Jean E. Kennard, "Ourself behind ourself: a theory for lesbian readers," in *Gender and Reading*, p. 63.
31 Johnson, "Women's cinema as counter-cinema" (work referred to in note 21).
32 Diane Waldman, "Film theory and the gendered spectator: the female or the feminist reader?" *Camera Obscura* 18 (1988), p. 81.
33 Kuhn, *Women's Pictures*, p. 70.
34 Ibid.

24

ART, OPPRESSION, AND THE AUTONOMY OF AESTHETICS

Curtis Brown

I INTRODUCTION

Mary Devereaux has suggested, in an overview of feminist aesthetics,[1] that feminist aesthetics constitutes a revolutionary approach to the field: "Aesthetics cannot simply 'add on' feminist theories as it might add new works by [Nelson] Goodman, Arthur Danto or George Dickie. To take feminism seriously involves rethinking our basic concepts and recasting the history of the discipline." In particular, feminist theory involves a rejection of "deeply entrenched assumptions about the universal value of art and aesthetic experience." Overthrowing these assumptions "constitutes what art historian, Linda Nochlin, describes as a Kuhnian paradigm shift."[2] Near the end of her essay, Devereaux returns to this theme:

> If feminism constitutes a new paradigm, then we may wish to ponder how far the old model of aesthetics and the new are commensurable. Is traditional aesthetics contingently or necessarily associated with patriarchy? Can the "gender-neutral" aesthetics of the traditional model be reformed or must it be rejected?

At first glance, we may be uncertain why feminist aesthetics should *either* replace traditional aesthetics *or* be added to it. Concerns about the relation between art and women's oppression seem to be broadly speaking *moral* concerns rather than aesthetic ones, and we may wonder why aesthetics cannot acknowledge that the concerns are important and interesting, but deny that they ought to form part of the subject matter of aesthetics itself. This is precisely the attitude we take toward many other concerns that are germane to issues about art: the economics of the art market, however interesting to aestheticians, is thought of as part of economics, not as part of aesthetics; the interpretation and evaluation of particular works of art are a matter for art criticism rather than for aesthetics; the chemistry of pigments is part of natural science rather than of aesthetics; and so on. From the point of view of traditional aesthetics, one might well wonder what makes feminist aesthetics *aesthetics* at all, rather than ethics, social and political theory, or art criticism.

In order to regard feminist aesthetics as aesthetics, it may seem, we need to show that aesthetics is not, or should not be, as isolated from other subject matters as much modern aesthetics has taken itself to be. A good deal of modern aesthetics has taken itself to be *autonomous*. The term "autonomy" here is broad and not terribly clear. I shall use it to describe the general view that artworks may and should be studied and appreciated as objects in their own right, without regard to the causes of their production, their historical context, their effects on an audience, or even their relation to the (rest of the) real world, and, moreover, that the contemplation or study of artworks should appeal only to some of the properties of the artwork, namely its aesthetic properties – as opposed especially to its moral properties, but also to its economic or physical or practical properties.[3] Harold Osborne describes the view as involving:

> the concentration of attention on the work of art as a thing in its own right, an artifact with standards and functions of its own, and not an instrument made to further purposes which could equally be promoted otherwise than by art objects. . . . A work of art, it is now held, is in concept an artifact made for the purpose of being appreciated in the special mode of aesthetic contemplation; and although particular works of art may be intended to do other things and may in fact serve other purposes as well as this, the excellence of any work of art *as art* is assessed in terms of its suitability for such contemplation. This is what is meant by claiming that art is autonomous: it is not assessed by external standards applicable elsewhere, but by standards of its own.[4]

As this quotation suggests, the doctrine in question is often described as the doctrine that *art* is autonomous, but this is misleading. The artwork *itself* is not held to be independent of its context, its causes and effects, and so on. Rather, the point is that the appropriate *examination* of art *as art* is an examination which abstracts from or ignores these factors. That is, what is held to be independent of external factors is not the artwork itself, but rather its appropriate study or contemplation. In short, it is *aesthetics* rather than art which is held to be autonomous.

It is no accident that feminists have attacked the view that aesthetics is an autonomous discipline.[5] For the autonomy of aesthetics seems to show that any relation art might bear to the oppression of women is irrelevant to its aesthetic value. Were women oppressed in the production of the work, or by the actions of people influenced by the work? No matter; the concern of aesthetics is the work itself, not its causes or effects. Are women represented by an artwork in false and degrading ways? Again, no matter, for, first, the work says nothing about the real world but merely sets up a fictional world; or, second, if the work can be construed as saying something about the world, nevertheless its representational content is irrelevant to its aesthetic value; or, third, even if representational content is relevant to aesthetic value, *moral* evaluations of this content are irrelevant to the artwork's value *as art*. To make the case that the oppressive character of some artworks is aesthetically relevant, it seems, feminist aesthetics will have to challenge the doctrine of aesthetic autonomy.

I will be arguing in this essay in favor of two specific kinds of insulation of the aesthetic, two ways in which aesthetics is autonomous. I will suggest, first, that the history of production of a work of art is relevant to its artistic value only by way of its effects on the work's sensory properties or its content, and second, that the content of a fictional work of art says nothing about the real world, but only describes a fictional world. Both of these doctrines threaten to render at least some facts about women's oppression irrelevant to the philosophy of art. But I will also argue that the insulation provided by these principles is not as thick as might at first appear: Feminist criticisms of art are sometimes legitimate aesthetic criticisms despite the fact that in the respects I have mentioned aesthetics is autonomous.

This conclusion opens up the possibility of a kind of reconciliation between feminist aesthetics and traditional aesthetics. Feminist aesthetics need not overthrow the two autonomy doctrines I will defend in order to legitimize itself, and at the same time traditional aesthetics cannot employ the doctrines in question to dismiss feminist aesthetics as an impostor. Of course, the two doctrines I will discuss express only two of the many ways in which aesthetics has been held to be autonomous, and the doctrine of autonomy is only one of many traditional doctrines of aesthetics called into question by feminists. But my admittedly limited conclusion may give some reason to hope that feminist aesthetics and traditional aesthetics will in the end turn out to be more compatible than many have thought.

II OPPRESSION AND THE PRODUCTION OF ART

Can oppressive treatment of women in the production of a work of art affect the artistic value of the work of art itself? The view that aesthetic value is autonomous, that we can and should determine an artwork's aesthetic value without considering such external facts as how the work came to be, seems to provide a powerful reason for insisting on a negative answer to this question. In this section I will defend a restricted version of the independence of aesthetic value from history, while arguing that this principle is compatible with the view that in some important cases, oppression of women in the production of art is aesthetically relevant.

Benvenuto Cellini (1500–71): *Nymph of Fontainebleau*, Louvre, Paris.
Courtesy of Scala group.

A The Nymph of Fontainebleau

Let us begin with an example from the realm of sculpture. The following memorable
account may be found in the autobiography of the sixteenth-century Italian goldsmith
and sculptor Benvenuto Cellini. Cellini describes asking one Pagolo Micceri to keep
watch both over Cellini's property and over "that poor young girl Caterina; I keep her
principally for my art's sake, since I cannot do without a model; but being a man also,
I have used her for my pleasures, and it is possible that she may bear me a child."[6]
Pagolo later sleeps with Caterina. Enraged, Cellini at first threatens to kill him, then
forces him to marry Caterina. There follows the incident in which I am principally
interested. Cellini writes:

> If I did not confess that in some of these episodes I acted wrongly, the world might
> think I was not telling the truth about those in which I say I acted rightly. Therefore
> I admit that it was a mistake to inflict so singular a vengeance upon Pagolo Micceri.
> . . . Not satisfied with having made him take a vicious drab to wife, I completed my
> revenge by inviting her to sit to me as a model, and dealing with her thus. I gave

her thirty sous a day, paid in advance, and a good meal, and obliged her to pose for me naked. Then I made her serve my pleasure, out of spite against her husband, jeering at them both the while. Furthermore, I kept her for hours together in position, greatly to her discomfort. This gave her as much annoyance as it gave me pleasure; for she was beautifully made, and brought me much credit as a model. At last, noticing that I did not treat her with the same consideration as before her marriage, she began to grumble and talk big in her French way about her husband. . . . [T]he wretch redoubled her insulting speeches, always prating big about her husband, till she goaded me beyond the bounds of reason. Yielding myself up to blind rage, I seized her by the hair, and dragged her up and down my room, beating and kicking her till I was tired. . . . When I had well pounded her she swore that she would never visit me again. Then for the first time I perceived that I had acted very wrongly; for I was losing a grand model, who brought me honour through my art. Moreover, when I saw her body all torn and bruised and swollen, I reflected that, even if I persuaded her to return, I should have to put her under medical treatment for at least a fortnight before I could make use of her. [The next morning Caterina returns.] Afterwards I began to model from her, during which occurred some amorous diversions; and at last, just at the same hour as on the previous day, she irritated me to such a pitch that I gave her the same drubbing. So we went on several days, repeating the old round like clockwork. There was little or no variation in the incidents.

(pp. 344–7)

Let us ignore questions about Cellini's reliability as a source.[7] And let us pass over a number of disturbing features of this story – the way in which Cellini regards his torment of Caterina as an injury to her husband rather than to her; the fact that he apparently believes he acted wrongly only because he placed himself at risk of "losing a grand model"; the fact that his sexual relationship with Caterina consists, as he cheerfully writes, in his having "used her for my pleasures"; his apparent failure to see anything out of the ordinary in his becoming furious because Caterina brags about her husband, or in his acting on this fury by beating her.

B First autonomy principle: the independence of value from history

The incident is useful for my purposes because during the modeling sessions in question, Cellini was sculpting what has come to be a famous work, the *Nymph of Fontainebleau*, designed to appear over a doorway but now on display in the Louvre. The question I want to ask is whether Cellini's mistreatment of Caterina while producing the *Nymph* has any aesthetic significance. Does it affect the way we ought to see the work? My own view is that it does not. Granted, it has had an effect on the way I *do*, in fact, see the work: I cannot now look at photographs of the *Nymph* without thinking about Caterina, and without trying to glean from the *Nymph*'s features some sense of what Caterina herself might have been like. But isn't this strictly irrelevant to the properties the object has *as an artwork*? Examining the *Nymph* to discover what Caterina looked like seems exactly on a par with, say, studying ancient Greek statues of athletes to glean information about the sports popular at the time[8] – both endeavors may be intrinsically interesting, but they are at best indirectly relevant to the way in which we view the object as a work of art. The artistic value of the *Nymph*, I would suggest, is unaffected by Cellini's mistreatment of Caterina in producing the work.

This conclusion is underwritten by a version of the autonomy doctrine which holds that the history of production of a work can affect its value only indirectly, by virtue of affecting properties of the work itself. If this is correct, then oppressive treatment of women in the production of a work will affect the artistic value[9] of the work only to the extent that it leads the artist to produce a work which is, say, uglier or tawdrier or more vacuous or inane than it would otherwise have been.

This formulation of the doctrine will not do, however. It is completely empty to say merely that the history of production of a work is relevant to its value only to the extent that it affects properties of the work itself. *Which* properties of the work itself? After all, *having a certain history* is a property of the *Nymph*, and Caterina's beatings certainly affect *that*! We could say that a work's history affects its value only to the extent that the history affects the work's *artistically relevant* properties. If "artistically relevant" merely means something like "relevant to artistic value," however, the doctrine has an unpleasantly circular character. If the principle is to have any content, we need an independent way of specifying which properties are artistically relevant. I suggest that there are really two such properties. First, there is the work's *appearance*, including under this heading the way the object appears to any of the senses, not just its appearance to the sense of sight. In the case of a sculpture, for example, such properties as shape and texture are directly relevant to the appearance of the sculpture. Second, in addition to the work's appearance, its meaning or *content* is artistically relevant.[10] This second artistically relevant property, content, does not reduce to the first, appearance, since content may be affected by features of the work's history or context that do not directly affect the work's appearance. We know for example that the *Nymph* illustrates a legend about the origin of Fontainebleau.[11] But this fact is not completely determined by the shape, size, texture, and so on of the work. It depends as well on facts about the legends of the region and their influence on Cellini's creation of the work.

We are left, then, with the following version of the principle that value is independent of history: Facts about a work's history are irrelevant to its artistic value *unless* they affect either its appearance *or* its content. I think that, provided we construe the notion of "content" broadly, this principle is correct – though it must be admitted that the notion of content, so construed, is not as clear as one might wish.[12] I intend the notion to include *at least* linguistic representation, pictorial depiction, and the expression of emotion.

The autonomy principle I have just formulated has affinities with more radical principles which have been widely accepted. The New Critical doctrine that the artist's intention is irrelevant to the interpretation of a work of art,[13] and the poststructuralist doctrine of the "death of the author,"[14] may both be seen as effecting a similar, though more extreme, separation of the work from its genesis. These affinities may or may not be seen as support for the principle. Affinities aside, why should we accept the principle? The main attraction of the view, I think, is simply the thought that, if the notion of a discipline devoted to the study of art as art is to make any sense at all, there must be some way of discriminating between features of artworks which are the proper concern of that discipline and features which are not. Indeed, if the notion of an artwork itself is to have any content, there must be a distinction between features of an object which are relevant to its status as an artwork, and features of the object which have nothing to do with that status. If so, then there must be some autonomy principle which states that certain features of artworks are not related to their status as artworks. Any particular proposal about how to distinguish relevant from irrelevant features will be more controversial than the simple claim that some such principle is true. But I offer my principle as a reasonable first approximation, since appearance and content are the features which figure most prominently in discussions of art in criticism and in aesthetics. In particular cases, the clearly relevant facts I can think of all seem to pertain either to a work's appearance or to its content.[15]

C Pornography

I think that our first autonomy principle is correct: The artistic value of a work *is* independent of its history of production. I am quite content to accept the consequence that the artistic value of the *Nymph* is unaffected by Caterina's mistreatment during its production. I turn now, however, to a second example in which women are oppressed in the production of works of art – an example which I find more troubling and more puzzling than that of Cellini and Caterina. The example I have in mind is that of certain sorts of pornography – namely pornographic films depicting abusive treatment of women, produced by recording on film acts which are genuinely abusive of women.[16] Of course the abusive acts performed in the course of making such a film are objectionable. But what effect does their existence have on the artistic value of the resulting pornographic film?

Feminist critics of pornography often stress that pornographic films at least sometimes are produced in ways that abuse women.[17] Here is Catherine MacKinnon: "Pornography is . . . routinely defended as 'fantasy,' meaning not real. It is real: the sex that makes it is real and is often abuse, and the sex that it makes is sex and is often abuse."[18] And compare this vivid passage from Andrea Dworkin's book *Pornography: Men Possessing Women*:

> This book is distinguished from most other books on pornography by its bedrock conviction that the power is real, the cruelty is real, the sadism is real, the subordination is real: the political crime against women is real. . . . In this book, I wanted to dissect male dominance; do an autopsy on it, but it wasn't dead. Instead, there were artifacts – films, photographs, books – an archive of evidence and documentation of crimes against women. This was a living archive, commercially alive, carnivorous in its use of women, saturating the environment of daily life, explosive and expanding, vital because it was synonymous with sex for the men who made it and the men who used it – men so arrogant in their power over us that they published the pictures of what they did to us, how they used us, expecting submission from us, compliance; we were supposed to follow the orders implicit in the pictures.[19]

This passage raises more issues than I will be able to discuss. But at this point, notice that Dworkin, like MacKinnon, stresses that the acts which pornographic films record are real acts between real people. The films are typically, of course, fictions; the characters in the films are imaginary, the plots invented. Nevertheless, these fictional characters and events are portrayed on film by recording real events involving real people. So, for example, Linda Marchiano, who appeared in the infamous pornographic movie *Deep Throat* under the name Linda Lovelace, has claimed that her treatment in the production of the film was deeply abusive – indeed, that "every time someone watches that film, they are watching me being raped."[20]

The principle of the independence of value from history would seem to suggest that the reality of the abuse involved in producing a film is irrelevant to the artistic value of the film. Given two similar films of fictional abusive scenes, one of them produced by filming real abuse and one of them produced by filming feigned abuse, the autonomy principle suggests that, so long as their content is the same, this difference between the two has no bearing on their relative artistic merit, though of course it has a great deal to do with the relative *moral* status of the two filming episodes. What matters to the artistic merit of the film is only the features of the fictional scene it depicts, not the features of the real scene the cameras recorded. (One might argue – perhaps Dworkin and MacKinnon would – that the filming of pornography is *always* abusive of women. I am skeptical about this, but my point does not depend on denying it. The same point could be made with respect to nonpornographic fictions which portray abusive treatment, and it surely is not the case that *any* depiction of abuse must itself be abusive.

Moreover, even in the pornographic case, there are presumably *more* and *less* abusive ways of depicting abuse; the disturbing point about the autonomy principle is that it seems to imply that this difference is irrelevant aesthetically.)

This view leads to consequences I find it difficult to accept. Suppose that a filmmaker wants to make a fictional film about a male character, "Bill," who beats a female character, "Jane." He has in his studio two actors named, coincidentally, "Bill" and "Jane." (Or maybe it isn't a coincidence; these are not experienced actors, and it may be easier for them to remember their characters' names if they coincide with their own.) He makes his movie by having Bill actually beat Jane, and recording the beating on film. Suppose that the same filmmaker also wants to make a documentary film recording the beating. He can set up a second camera (call it "camera B," and call the first one "camera A") and record the very same scene through it. Now, although cameras A and B are recording the same scene, the film produced by camera A is a fiction, while the film produced by camera B is a documentary. Isn't there something odd about this? Odder still, suppose it occurs to our filmmaker that it is a needless waste of resources to have two cameras recording the same scene. Why not make do with one? Then two copies of the same film can be made, one a documentary and one a fiction. In a final burst of economy, the filmmaker may even make do with a single copy of the film, simply changing the way he labels it depending on where it is to be shown.

It seems a cruel joke to suggest that a film of a beating can, by a simple relabeling, be turned into a harmless fiction. And it is precisely this cruel joke that feminists like Dworkin and MacKinnon argue is being told by many pornographic filmmakers. What the pornographers claim are harmless fictions are precisely what Dworkin insists are in fact "an archive of evidence and documentation of crimes against women."

D A way out: films as recorded performances

What shall we say about this? We have three choices. First, we might bite the bullet and concede that, odd as it may seem, there is a world of difference between the films recorded by camera A and camera B – one is a fiction, the other not – while at the same time insisting that there is no artistic difference between the fictional beating produced by recording a real beating, and the fictional beating produced by recording a feigned beating. Second, we might give up the principle of autonomy. Perhaps the two fictions are different in some artistically relevant way, despite being the same in appearance and content. Or, third, we might give up the idea that the content of a film is separable from the facts about the actual scene the camera records. Perhaps you cannot prevent a film from representing or being about a real beating simply by relabeling it as about a fiction. In that case we can preserve the principle of autonomy while still insisting that the two fictional films are as different as can be, and that the products of cameras A and B are

407

alike in that each represents a real beating (though one of them *also* represents a fictional beating).

I think that the third option is the correct one. The autonomy principle is correct: The only things relevant to an artwork's aesthetic value are its appearance and its content. But the content of the film cannot be insulated from the difference between a real and a feigned beating. A film is not *just* a presentation of fictional characters engaged in fictional actions. It is also a recording of a performance. The artistically relevant features of the film include features of the performance. In criticizing the film, we quite legitimately talk not only of the characters, but also of the actors who play them, and we distinguish between the traits of the two: It's one thing to say that a particular character was inexpressive and unemotional; it is another to say that an actor's performance was wooden.

In this respect, films are like stage productions, and unlike novels (and unlike some painting, sculpture, and poetry). When we watch a stage play, the aesthetic object to which we attend is not simply the fiction presented, but also the presentation, the way that flesh-and-blood actors portray the fictional characters they represent. I want to suggest that in some ways, a fictional film is like a documentary film which records a stage production. (The thinness of the line between the two may perhaps be suggested by a film like Bergman's *The Magic Flute*, which is a kind of borderline case.) There is more to a film than this, of course. Many of the aesthetic features of the film will not have been present in the performance: The cinematography, the editing, the special effects are all aesthetically relevant features of the film which have little or nothing to do with the recorded performance. But the addition of these features does not erase the film's documentary character, does not negate the fact that among the functions of the film is to record performances, which are real actions of real people.

Now, let us return to the difference between real and feigned abuse in the production of what is claimed to be a work of art. But let us shift the scene for a moment: Consider now a stage production. We are sitting in the audience watching a play in which a woman is beaten. In version one of this example, the actors perform the fictional beating by feigning a beating. In version two, the beating is not feigned but genuine: The woman is genuinely being beaten before our eyes. Now, in this second case, we are liable to refuse to take the real beating as just part of the play. We will want to call the police, or to jump up on stage and stop the beating. But suppose we are somehow convinced to take the real beating as just a particularly vivid way of performing a fictional beating. Perhaps all the actors, including the victim, have agreed beforehand that the performance will be conducted in this way. (If Chris Burden can have himself shot as part of a work of "body art," surely a beating can also be part of a work of art. And if actors can portray fictional walking and talking by means of real walking and talking, surely it is possible in principle to portray a fictional beating by means of a real beating.) Despite our acceptance of the beating as part of the performance, however, we will legitimately feel not only moral indignation at the beating, but also that the resulting artwork is aesthetically inferior.

In saying this, I am explicitly rejecting one doctrine which has sometimes been described as the autonomy of art, namely the doctrine that aesthetic value is independent of moral value. This is the idea that art "might draw off by itself and be content with an emphatic assertion of autonomy – its own kind of intrinsic worth . . . apart from, and perhaps in defiance of, the rival norms of ethics and politics."[21] To show that real abusive treatment is explicitly represented in a film is not enough to show that the film is *aesthetically* inferior; one must also show that our negative moral evaluation should carry over to our aesthetic evaluation. I wish I had more to say in defense of this view; all I can offer at present is that some moral views are not just false but ugly, and some actions are not just immoral but repulsive. Of course, under some circumstances even ugliness and repulsiveness can be turned to worthwhile artistic purposes. But in the absence of a rather special redeeming context, they are likely to be aesthetically debilitating. As much as I would like to have more to offer on this point, perhaps in the present dialectical context I need no more, since my main purpose is to defend and discuss the consequences of two principles of aesthetic autonomy; my dialectical opponents, the critics of autonomy, may reasonably be presumed to grant the relevance of moral to aesthetic concerns.

The point I have been making about the difference between two staged portrayals of a fictional beating applies as well to films. Recall Linda Marchiano's claim that she was raped in the production of *Deep Throat*. When we reach the scene in the movie in which this occurs, we cannot leap onto the stage and stop the rape. We might take the view that the movie stops being an artwork at that point, just as we might regard the play as effectively over when the real beating commences. But suppose that we are persuaded to take the film as an art object. It remains the case that it records a real rape, and this fact is not only morally relevant but also aesthetically relevant.[22]

Let us return to our original question: Can oppressive treatment of women in the production of a work of art affect the artistic value of the work of art itself? It now appears that we can answer this question in the affirmative *even if*, as our first autonomy principle maintains, the artistic value of a work is independent of its history of production except insofar as that history affects the work's appearance or content.

III OPPRESSION AND THE CONTENT OF ART

Let us turn now to a second question: Can fictional artworks be oppressive by virtue of their content? I will defend a second principle of autonomy which may seem to show that they cannot. I will then argue that in fact, the truth of the principle is compatible with the view that artworks may constitute assertions of oppressive claims.

A Second autonomy principle: the independence of fiction from reality

As in our previous section, a fairly plausible autonomy principle would seem to insulate fictions from the real world in such a way that they could not possibly be oppressive. The principle is this: Fictions represent fictional worlds; they do not represent the actual world. Fictions may of course *resemble* the actual world in various ways, and our efforts to discover their similarities to and differences from the actual world may lead us to surprising discoveries. But fictions do not *say* anything about the real world, so they cannot be oppressive or libelous or slanderous or defamatory or degrading – nor can there be "orders implicit in the pictures," as Dworkin puts it.

In defense of the independence of fiction from reality, I would offer the following argument. No one will maintain that *every* representation in a fiction is to be taken to be an accurate portrayal of the world. At most, the defender of the view that fictions should be taken to represent the world accurately may hold that some represented features are to be taken to be accurate and some are not. This raises the problem of how we can determine which features are which. I take the following to be a useful way to think about this problem. Works of history or science carry a kind of implicit "It is true that . . ." operator. We are to take the representations they contain to be at least attempts at an accurate portrayal of the world. Similarly, works of fiction carry an implicit "It is fictional that . . ." or "It is true in this fiction that . . ." operator. Now, there *can* be mixed cases – cases in which some sentences of a work[23] are to be taken to be fictional and others to be truthful. For example, it is common for philosophical essays to include brief fictional examples designed to illustrate a point. (For concreteness, consider Judith Jarvis Thomson's famous essay on abortion, in which the following interjection occurs: "It sounds plausible. But now let me ask you to imagine this. You wake up in the morning and find yourself back to back in bed with an unconscious violinist . . . [whose] circulatory system [has been] plugged into yours."[24] The phrase "imagine this" notifies the reader that what follows will be a fictional interlude in a largely nonfiction piece.) But it is *very* difficult to imagine a mixed case which is predominantly fiction rather than predominantly nonfiction. In the philosophical case, we have a work we take to be implicitly prefaced with "It is true that. . . ." Within this work, we hit a paragraph or two implicitly prefaced with "It is fictional that. . . ." Now we have one operator embedded inside the scope of another, yielding "It is true that it is fictional that. . . ." If it is true that it is fictional that a violinist is plugged into you, then it is fictional that a violinist is plugged into you. So far so good: A little fiction within a nonfiction work seems entirely possible.

But now consider a predominantly fictional case. The entire fiction is implicitly prefaced with "It is fictional that. . . ." Now the author attempts to insert some material we are to take to be factual. How can the text indicate that this material is to be taken to be factual? It must include something tantamount to the "It is true that . . ." operator. The result is again that one operator is embedded within the scope of another, yielding "It is fictional that it is true that. . . ." But to say that it is fictional that something is true is precisely *not* to say that it is true! Any claim to truth *within* a fiction is just one more part of the fiction. And of course creators of fictions take advantage of this fact all the time, producing fictionally true prefaces, fictionally true footnotes, fictionally true dictionary or encyclopedia entries, and so on. These fictionally true items may happen also to be actually true, but it cannot be part of the content of the fiction that they are (really) true.[25]

B Devereaux on movies

If this second autonomy principle is correct, then some of Devereaux's criticisms of Hollywood movies must be questioned. Devereaux distinguishes between different levels of feminist criticism of the content of movies. At the simplest level, feminists "attacked the Hollywood film for its patriarchal content." These films perpetuated a "mythology [which] defined the value of women as their value to men." In particular, these films portrayed women as falling into one of several stereotypical categories, such as "the Good Girl, the Vamp, and the Dutiful Wife."

This indictment is problematic even apart from considerations of autonomy. In the first place, a particular film cannot be said to imply that all women fall into one of these categories simply because it portrays women who do. No doubt there are real women who fit these stereotypes reasonably well, women who value themselves largely in terms of their value to men. So a particular film, in portraying women who fit the stereotypes, may simply be presenting fictional characters who in fact are significantly like (some) real women. Presumably, then, the indictment must be an indictment, not of any particular film taken in isolation, but of "the Hollywood film" taken as a whole: The objection must be that since all (most? many?) movies present women only in terms of their value to men, the body of Hollywood films taken as a whole implies that this is women's only value. But this would be a difficult claim to defend, as Devereaux herself recognizes. Although she writes at one point that "any alternative point of view, one which might tell a different tale or tell the same tale differently, was effectively excluded," by the next paragraph she is acknowledging that "not all films perpetuate patriarchy. . . . The strong-headed heroines typically played by Katharine Hepburn, Lauren Bacall and Bette Davis do not conform to this stereotype, nor do films such as Howard Hawks' *His Girl Friday*."

What we are left with is the claim that many or most Hollywood films, though not all, present their female characters from a masculine perspective according to which their chief, perhaps only, value is their value to men. This will permit us to say neither that any particular film endorses the view that all (real) women are valuable only insofar as they are valuable to men, nor that "the Hollywood film" as a whole endorses this view. This is not to say that frequent stereotyping is innocent or innocuous. (A very plausible account of what precisely is wrong with it has been offered by Noël Carroll.)[26] But the problems with stereotyping do not have to do with what films say, or film in general says, about women.

If the content of a fictional artwork says nothing about the real world, as the autonomy principle claims, however, then an even stronger conclusion is possible: Not only is it unlikely on empirical grounds that "the Hollywood film" asserts or implies that women's only value is their value to men, but no (fictional) film or set of films *could* assert or imply this. Characters in the film may assert, or reveal by their actions that they believe, that women are valuable only insofar as they are valuable to men, but that is not the same thing as the film itself endorsing this view. And, according to the defender of autonomy, this is what the film cannot do. All it can do is to present an imaginary world, and let viewers connect this imaginary world to the real one in any way they like.

The insulation of fictional content from claims about the real world also bears on other criticisms Devereaux offers. Citing the work of Mary Ann Doane, Devereaux writes that "at a more complex level, the Hollywood film functions as a 'recuperative strategy' designed to return the wayward woman to the fold." She goes on to say that in such films, "The message is that for a woman, unlike for a man, the satisfactions of solitude, work, or adventures cannot compare to those of caring for husband and children." But if films are insulated from the real world in the way the autonomy principle suggests, then they cannot carry "messages" about the real world. Again, Devereaux suggests that Hollywood films degrade women by portraying them "*only* as objects of aesthetic contemplation." This complaint too seems to presuppose that such films make general assertions about actual women. Portraying fictional characters as only objects of aesthetic contemplation may be degrading to the fictional characters, but cannot be degrading to actual women unless portraying fictional characters in this way expresses something about actual women rather than about fictional women – and this is precisely what the second autonomy principle says cannot happen.

C Pornography again

Some feminist discussions of pornography also take the view that fictional material may nevertheless make assertions about real people. Helen Longino, in fact, *defines* pornography in a way which presumes this:

> Pornography . . . is verbal or pictorial material which represents or describes sexual behavior that is degrading or abusive to one or more of the participants *in such a*

way as to endorse the degradation. . . . Pornography communicates its endorsement of the behavior it represents by various features of the pornographic context: the degradation of the female characters is represented as providing pleasure to the participant males and, even worse, to the participant females, and there is no suggestion that this sort of treatment of others is inappropriate to their status as human beings.[27]

Many other writers make similar claims, usually without doing as much as Longino to explain on what basis pornography is said to communicate an endorsement. Susan Brownmiller: "Pornography is the undiluted essence of anti-female propaganda."[28] Ann Garry: "Some pornographic films convey the message that all women really want to be raped, that their resisting struggle is not to be believed."[29] And we remember Dworkin's reference, quoted earlier, to "the orders implicit in the pictures."

All these claims are, I think, deeply problematic. Let us distinguish between two slightly different kinds of things pornography is supposed to assert. First, it is claimed to assert falsehoods about women, for example that all women want to be raped, or that women exist only for the satisfaction of men. Second, it is claimed to assert pernicious value judgments: that rape is a good thing, that women ought to be bound and tortured, and so on.[30] I claim that pornography does, and can do, neither of these things. Consider as an analogy the case of action films – the sort of films that star Arnold Schwarzenegger or Jean-Claude Van Damme or Sylvester Stallone. In these films, people often move their limbs through the air so fast they make a whistling sound, and blows to the face or body typically make a loud thwacking noise. Do the movies therefore represent the real world as working this way? Hardly! At most, they depict a world in which hitting someone in the face makes a thwacking noise, but they cannot assert that the world they depict is the actual world, or is like the actual world in this particular way.[31] The same point applies to moral features of the fictional world as well as to factual ones. In the world of action heroes, it may be an appropriate response to a perceived insult to punch the offending person in the face. I for one am quite prepared to cheer when a Schwarzenegger character punches an offensive boor for making an inappropriate remark. But although I accept this as appropriate behavior in the fictional world of certain films, I would be horrified if someone acted that way in the real world.[32] As I experience and interpret action films, the moral values presupposed in the fictional world are just further elements of the fiction; they may correspond to real values, but they need not. I believe this to be a common experience. And unless this common experience is missing something rather important, a film's acceptance of a particular set of values does not represent an implicit claim to the *truth* of the values it accepts. I would argue that, similarly, a pornographic film's depiction of a world in which it is a good thing to rape women does not constitute an assertion that in the actual world it is a good thing to rape women. Indeed, if the autonomy principle is correct, as I believe it to be, a film *could* not make this assertion, or any other.

Even films which may appear to be commentaries on the relation between fiction and reality cannot really be said to represent the real world. Consider *The Last Action Hero*, a Schwarzenegger movie in which an action hero is transported from his fictional world into the "real" world, and is surprised by the differences between the two. In such a film, what we really have is a commentary on the relation between two fictional worlds, one of them a fiction "inside" the other. The relation between the fictional fiction and the fictional reality is, to be sure, analogous to the relation between fictional reality and real reality. But there is no way for a fiction to specify the respects in which it is like the real world and the respects in which it is not, so there is no way for a fiction to assert anything about reality.

The second autonomy doctrine, although I believe it to be correct, is bound to sound rather hollow in some contexts. Let me offer one example among many. In the movie *I Posed for* Playboy, several women decide to pose for *Playboy* magazine.[33] One of these women is the editor of the Yale student newspaper, a woman who has recently written an editorial protesting the presence of *Playboy* photographers on campus and urging students not to be photographed. She comes to realize that posing for the magazine can be a valuable affirmation of her independence and her femininity; in a monologue addressed directly to the audience, with the camera in a tight close-up on her face, she explains the reasons for her choice to pose and her satisfaction with that decision. It seems clear that the audience is supposed to find her reasons convincing. Moreover, it also seems clear that, in finding her reasons convincing, the audience is also supposed to recognize the potential value to real women of really posing for the real magazine. The movie, in short, seems to be more than a mere portrayal of a fictional world: It seems to make value judgments about the real world, and in fact to be a bit of propaganda for *Playboy* magazine.

Wayne C. Booth expresses a similar sense of the hollowness of appealing to the autonomy principle in his discussion of John Donne's "Song," which includes these lines: "Ride ten thousand daies and nights,/Till age snow white haires on thee,/Thou, when thou retorn'st, wilt tell mee/All strange wonders that befell thee,/And sweare/No where/Lives a woman true, and faire." Booth describes discussing the poem with "a large group of English teachers" and finding some of the women present defending something very like the autonomy principle we have been discussing:

> Some of those who thought of themselves as professional critics scoffed at the very idea of worrying about "message." Why should we let annoyance at the male poet's direct assertion that women are inherently false and fickle interfere with our aesthetic responses? One said, "I can enter imaginatively into the world of the poem just as well as any man. Besides, Donne is not speaking in his own person – he is

creating a persona." Uh huh. Perhaps. Nobody could ever disprove the claim. But meanwhile we do know one thing for sure: many male readers, including at least one young male English teacher (myself years ago), have found in the poem a delightful reinforcement, from "high culture," of our "natural" sense of male superiority. Can we really claim that such a fact is irrelevant to critical talk about the poem's true worth *"as poetry"*?[34]

D A way out: semantics and pragmatics

It can seem obvious that fictions do not say anything about the real world. Indeed, a number of accounts of the nature of fiction define fiction in terms of this sort of independence from reality.[35] On the other hand, it can seem equally obvious that the author of a fiction may, in creating the fiction, be asserting all sorts of things about the real world. As Kendall Walton notes:

> There is no reason why, in appropriate circumstances, one should not be able to make an assertion by writing fiction. Indeed there is a long tradition of doing just that. There is what we call didactic fiction – fiction used for instruction, advertising, propaganda, and so on. There is the not uncommon practice, even in ordinary conversation, of making a point by telling a story, of speaking in parables.[36]

Is there any way to reconcile these obvious, but apparently conflicting, views? Is there any way to account for our feeling that fictions can reinforce disagreeable values, or false beliefs, without abandoning the autonomy principle? I think that there is. What I would like to appeal to is a distinction analogous to the linguistic distinction between *semantics* and *pragmatics*.[37] We need to distinguish between the content of a film or other fiction, on the one hand, and the information it may be used pragmatically to express, on the other. To borrow Nathan Salmon's terminology,[38] we need to employ a distinction analogous to that between *semantically encoded* information and *pragmatically imparted* information.

Consider some straightforward examples to get a sense for this distinction. If I say, to someone who has telephoned me, "Well, I don't want to run your phone bill up," my words do not have the semantic content "I would like to stop talking now," but they may pragmatically impart that information. If I say "Good question!" to a student in class, I have not said that I don't know the answer, but I may have pragmatically imparted the information that I do not. If, in response to the question, "Don't you think he's smart?" I respond, "He works very hard," my words do not mean that he isn't all that smart, but in all likelihood I do, by uttering them, impart the information that I don't believe he is smart.

Many literary devices rely on the distinction between pragmatics and semantics for their success. Consider, for example, Jonathan Swift's essay "A Modest Proposal." This essay is a textbook example of irony. But irony is a pragmatic, not a semantic, phenomenon.[39] Semantically, the piece expresses the view that eating children is an appropriate response to famine. But the view pragmatically imparted by the piece is quite the opposite. Again, metaphor is best understood pragmatically rather than semantically.[40] "Richard is a lion" semantically expresses only the proposition that Richard is a lion – an obvious falsehood. But this sentence may be used to pragmatically impart the proposition that, for example, Richard is brave.

The crucial distinction between semantic and pragmatic phenomena is that the semantic content of an expression is determined by general linguistic conventions about the meaning of expressions, while what is pragmatically imparted by a given utterance depends upon features of the context of the utterance. The semantic content of the same expression will remain the same from one use to the next, but its pragmatic content will vary with the context of the particular use. Thus the movie *Reefer Madness* presents a fictional world in which a few puffs of marijuana suffice to induce instant addiction and all sorts of bizarre behavior. It was originally used to pragmatically impart the idea that marijuana is a deeply dangerous drug which should be scrupulously avoided. By the time I was a college student, screenings of the movie were often used instead to pragmatically impart the idea that antidrug propaganda is often factually inaccurate and absurdly overstated.[41] The fictional world of the movie remains the same from screening to screening, but the relations between that fictional world and the real world which are pragmatically suggested may vary widely from one context to another.

The implication of this view for our evaluation of pornography is this. We cannot indict a *work* for its degrading or defamatory treatment of women. But we can indict an artist, or a producer or curator or anyone else for *using* a work to pragmatically impart a message which is defamatory or endorses degradation. This is, I think, a result feminists ought to applaud; it has the consequence that one may criticize a pornographer for using pornography to propagate falsehoods about women, while not criticizing a feminist who shows all or part of the pornographer's work in a critical context. Fictional works are not intrinsically truthful or untruthful any more than technological innovations are intrinsically good or bad: Everything hinges on how they are used.

IV CONCLUSION

Devereaux suggests in her penultimate section that feminist aesthetics radically challenges a number of features of traditional aesthetics, and thus constitutes "a new paradigm" in aesthetics. My own suspicion is that Devereaux overstates the incompatibility of traditional and feminist aesthetics.

One of the challenges Devereaux notes is that "feminist theorists ask us to replace the conception of the artwork as an autonomous object . . . with a messier conception of art." My essay has largely been an attempt to take Devereaux's advice to "ponder how far the old model of aesthetics and the new are commensurable." I have tried to explore the extent to which two versions of the doctrine that aesthetics is autonomous protect art from feminist criticism. A diehard traditionalist might argue that these autonomy doctrines show that feminist aesthetics is simply not aesthetics at all; rather, it is "merely" social and political philosophy, or sociology, or art criticism. On the other hand, some feminists will insist that the autonomy doctrines are simply false; traditional aesthetics, which is committed to these doctrines, is moribund and needs to be replaced with feminist aesthetics. I hope to have shown one way to avoid both extremes, at least with respect to these two specific doctrines. The autonomy principles are correct, I have suggested, so at least two of the challenged doctrines of traditional aesthetics survive criticism. But the autonomy principles do not do as much as one might have thought to protect art from feminist criticism. The survival of traditional aesthetics may yet leave room for feminist aesthetics.[42]

NOTES

1 Mary Devereaux, "Oppressive texts, resisting readers and the gendered spectator: the 'new' aesthetics," reprinted in this volume.

2 This attribution could be a little misleading, since Nochlin (a) is not talking about the overthrow of quite these assumptions; (b) does not mention Kuhn; and in fact (c) doesn't even explicitly mention paradigm *shifts*. But she does say that "the so-called woman question . . . can become a catalyst, an intellectual instrument, probing basic and 'natural' assumptions, providing a paradigm for other kinds of internal questioning, and in turn providing links with paradigms established by radical approaches in other fields" (Linda Nochlin, "Why have there been no great women artists?" in Nochlin, *Women, Art, and Power and Other Essays* [New York: Harper & Row, 1988], p. 147).

3 The doctrine of aesthetic autonomy seems to have its origins in the eighteenth century, especially in the work of Kant; it is closely related to the nineteenth-century notion of "art for art's sake," and versions of it have played a role in the twentieth century in the "New Criticism" and, more recently, in poststructuralist criticism. For the early history of the notion, see the interesting chapter 22, "Art for art's sake," of William K. Wimsatt and Cleanth Brooks, *Literary Criticism: A Short History* (New York: Random House, 1957).

4 Harold Osborne, *Aesthetics and Art Theory: An Historical Introduction* (New York: Dutton, 1970), pp. 262–3.

5 Devereaux's brief discussion of this topic in "Oppressive texts" is much amplified and developed in her helpful article "The philosophical and political implications of the feminist critique of aesthetic autonomy," in Glynis Carr, ed., *"Turning the Century": Feminist Theory in the 1990s* (Lewisburg, Pa.: Bucknell University Press, 1992). The specific doctrines I will describe as "autonomy principles," however, are different from any Devereaux discusses.

6 Benvenuto Cellini, *Autobiography of Benvenuto Cellini*, trans. John Addington Symonds (New York: Modern Library, n.d.), p. 334.

7 Much of Cellini's autobiography seems incredible to the contemporary reader. But John Pope-Hennessy, observing that the book's credibility is often questioned, indicates his own belief that "almost every direct statement in the *Life* (direct as distinct from reported statement) is correct." John Pope-Hennessy, *Cellini* (New York: Abbeville Press, 1985), p. 13.

8 Of course, the knowledge thereby gleaned might be *indirectly* relevant to the aesthetic properties of artworks; for instance, once we learned from whatever source about sports and the way they were practiced, such knowledge might enable us to characterize particular sculptures as realistic or idealized.

9 I use the terms "artistic value" and "aesthetic value," and the terms "artistic property" and "aesthetic property," interchangeably. The term "aesthetic" in these contexts has the virtue of greater familiarity, but runs the risk of misleading, since historically and etymologically "aesthetic" properties have been understood to be restricted to properties of a work's appearance. The terms "artistic value" and "artistic property," though they sound a bit unnatural, have the virtue of suggesting precisely the notions I have in mind: "Artistic value" is the value of a work as art; an "artistic property" is a property relevant to a work's status as a work of art.

10 This has of course been denied, notably by Clive Bell: "If a representative form has value, it is as form, not as representation. The representative element in a work of art may or may not be harmful; always it is irrelevant" (Bell, *Art* [New York: Capricorn Books, 1958], p. 27). On Bell's view, aesthetic value is independent not only of history, but also of representational content. But for rhetorical purposes, I need not defend my view that content is relevant, since I am defending a less extreme autonomy principle against those who would reject the autonomy of aesthetics altogether.

11 Pope-Hennessy, op. cit., p. 137.

12 It is also not clear to me precisely what sort of effect on the content of a work its history must have in order to be relevant to its artistic worth. For instance, suppose that Cellini had mistreated Caterina deliberately in order to produce a certain kind of expression which he could then sculpt, as the photographer Karsh is reported to have stolen Churchill's cigar just before photographing him to produce the precise look of outrage he wanted for the portrait. Would this affect the artistic value of the *Nymph*? If so, how?

13 The classic source is of course William K. Wimsatt and Monroe C. Beardsley, "The intentional fallacy," in Wimsatt, *The Verbal Icon: Studies in the Meaning of Poetry* (Lexington, Ky.: University of Kentucky Press, 1954).

14 See Roland Barthes, "The death of the author," in Barthes, *Image-Music-Text*, trans. Stephen Heath (London: Fontana, 1977), pp. 142–8. In the context of film criticism, see the discussion in chapter 4, "Authorship," of Robert Lapsley and Michael Westlake, *Film Theory: An Introduction* (Manchester: Manchester University Press, 1988).

15 I don't mean to be dogmatic about this. There *may* be further kinds of facts which are relevant. For example, the *originality* of a work may be germane to its value; originality clearly isn't a matter of appearance, and perhaps is also not a feature of the work's content. Similarly, in the performing arts, difficulty of execution may be an aesthetically relevant quality which does not affect the appearance or content of a work. The crucial thing is that there must be a distinction between relevant and irrelevant facts. My suspicion is that, whatever the right account of the distinction turns out to be, it will classify Caterina's oppression on the "irrelevant" side.

16 One might insist that pornography is not art. Perhaps some of it is not. But I don't see how

one could describe, say, a typical Hollywood movie as art and still insist that the better productions of the pornographers are not. At any rate, precisely the same points I will be making about pornographic films could be made about nonpornographic films. For example, it may be that the fictional mistreatment of the Peruvian Indians who pushed a steamboat over a mountain in Werner Herzog's movie *Fitzcarraldo* was produced in part by filming real mistreatment. (See "Art of darkness," *The Progressive* 46 [August 1982]: 20–21; George Dolis and Ingrid Weiland, "The floating opera," *Film Comment* 18 [September–October 1982]: 56–9.)

17 It may be that radical feminist critics overestimate the proportion of pornography of which this is true. For some relevant data, see Ronald J. Berger, Patricia Searles, and Charles E. Cottle, *Feminism and Pornography* (New York: Praeger, 1991), pp. 95–6.

18 Catherine MacKinnon, "Sexuality, pornography, and method," *Ethics* 99 (1989): 314–46, at 342.

19 Andrea Dworkin, *Pornography: Men Possessing Women* (New York: E.P. Dutton, 1989), pp. xxxvii–xxxviii.

20 Quoted in Dworkin, *Pornography*, p. xvi.

21 Wimsatt and Brooks, op. cit., p. 476.

22 I suspect that this fact is not of much interest to Dworkin – nor is there any reason it should be. For Dworkin does not take herself to be doing aesthetics; she is interested in moral and political issues rather than artistic ones. Regardless of one's view about whether the artistic content of a film includes facts about the real people and events filmed, a film which records real abuse will constitute evidence of that abuse in the way that footprints or tire tracks constitute evidence of the presence of people or automobiles.

23 I take a literary work as my example here because it is difficult to formulate the point in a general enough way to be neutral as between literary fiction, cinematic fiction, painted fiction, and so on.

24 Judith Jarvis Thomson, "A defense of abortion," *Philosophy and Public Affairs* 1 (1971), reprinted in Marshall Cohen, Thomas Nagel, and Thomas Scanlon, eds, *The Rights and Wrongs of Abortion* (Princeton: Princeton University Press, 1974), pp. 3–22, at pp. 4–5.

25 There may be special cases in which we have conventions dictating that certain portions of a predominantly fictional work are to be taken to be factual. Easy cases are prefaces and postscripts to literary works; consider Henry James's long introductions to the New York edition of his novels. This is an easy case because the introductions are outside the fiction proper; the initial "It is fictional that . . ." operator does not take effect until *after* the introduction. A little more difficult is a case like Eliot's footnotes to *The Waste Land*, but again we may take the notes as simply external to the work itself. A very puzzling case is Henry Fielding's essays in *Tom Jones*. Perhaps we are to take them as nonfiction intermingled with the fiction. But it is very hard to be certain; for all we can glean from the work itself, they may be intended to be taken as the product of a fictional narrator, and so to be just more fiction. The only case I can think of in which clearly nonfictional bits occur within a predominantly fictional work is the case of fables in which a little story ends with an explicitly stated "moral." But this is surely a very special case.

26 Noël Carroll, "The image of women in film: a defense of a paradigm," *The Journal of Aesthetics and Art Criticism* 48 (1990): 349–60.

27 Helen E. Longino, "Pornography, oppression, and freedom: a closer look," in Laura Lederer, ed., *Take Back the Night* (New York: Morrow, 1980), reprinted in Marilyn Pearsall, ed., *Women and Values: Readings in Recent Feminist Philosophy* (Belmont, Cal.: Wadsworth, 1986), pp. 167–76, at p. 169.

28 Susan Brownmiller, *Against Our Will: Men, Women and Rape* (New York: Simon & Schuster, 1975), p. 374, quoted in Ann Garry, "Pornography and respect for women," *Social Theory and Practice* 4 (1978): 395–421, reprinted in Jeffrey Olen and Vincent Barry, eds, *Applying Ethics*, 4th edn (Belmont, Cal.: Wadsworth, 1992), pp. 127–35, at p. 128.

29 Garry, "Pornography and respect for women," op. cit., p. 128. Garry also writes that included among the most objectionable pornography are "movies which recommend that men rape women, molest children and puppies, and treat nonmasochists very sadistically" (p. 131).

30 This is virtually the same distinction drawn by Alan Soble between the criticism of pornography that it defames women and the criticism that it endorses the degradation of women. Soble offers some valuable arguments against both of these criticisms – without, however, going quite as far as I would: Soble stresses that "I have not claimed that depictions . . . never implicitly or explicitly endorse." Alan Soble, "Pornography: defamation and the endorsement of degradation," *Social Theory and Practice* 11 (1985): 61–87, at p. 79.

31 Alex Neill has suggested to me that the thwacking noises are not even part of the fictional world, but function rather like the lines trailing behind an object in a cartoon which indicate that the object is moving quickly. The suggestion is that the thwacking noises, like the cartoon lines, are part of the representation, but not part of the fictional world represented. I would be surprised to discover, however, that this is a common way of "reading" action films.

32 In fact, I *was* horrified when I read that Texas congressman Henry B. Gonzalez had in fact responded to a perceived insult in a restaurant near my university by punching the offender off his seat at the counter. I might add that I am puzzled by Thomas Nagel's remark that there's something peculiarly appropriate about a punch to the nose as a response to insult – footnote 6 of "War and massacre," in Nagel's book *Mortal Questions* (Cambridge: Cambridge University Press, 1976), p. 66.

33 I saw parts of this movie on network television. In what I would be surprised to learn was a coincidence, the movie played at the same time that another channel was showing a Miss Texas pageant.

34 Wayne C. Booth, *The Company We Keep: An Ethics of Fiction* (Berkeley: University of California Press, 1988), p. 393.

35 See especially Monroe C. Beardsley's account in *Aesthetics: Problems in the Philosophy of Criticism* (Indianapolis: Hackett, [1958] 1981), pp. 419–23. See also Beardsley's updating of his view in his 1980 postscript to this book, at pp. xliv–xlviii.

36 Kendall Walton, *Mimesis as Make-Believe: On the Foundations of the Representational Arts* (Cambridge: Harvard University Press, 1990), p. 78.

37 The distinction we need is only analogous to the semantics/pragmatics distinction, since many fictions are presented largely in media which lack precise semantic rules. Paintings and movies may be fictional, but there isn't literally a semantics of painting or cinema. Nevertheless, there are general conventions which enable us to extract from a painting or a movie a description of a fictional scene or world, and there is a genuine distinction between these general conventions and the context-dependent ways in which such a painting or movie may be used to impart propositions which are not a part of its content.

38 Nathan Salmon, *Frege's Puzzle* (Cambridge: MIT Press, 1986).

39 See H.P. Grice's brief discussion of irony in "Logic and conversation," reprinted in Steven Davis, ed., *Pragmatics: A Reader* (New York: Oxford University Press, 1991), pp. 305–15, at p. 312; and Dan Sperber and Deirdre Wilson, "Irony and the use-mention distinction," in Davis, ed., *Pragmatics*, pp. 550–63.

40 There are by now a number of detailed accounts of metaphor which take it to be a prag-
matic phenomenon. Two early and very influential pieces in this vein are Donald Davidson,
"What metaphors mean," in Sheldon Sacks, ed., *On Metaphor* (Chicago: University of
Chicago Press, 1979), pp. 29–46, and John R. Searle, "Metaphor," in Andrew Ortony, ed.,
Metaphor and Thought (Cambridge: Cambridge University Press, 1979), pp. 92–123. Both
essays are reprinted in Davis, ed., *Pragmatics*, op. cit., along with relevant essays by Merrie
Bergman and A.P. Martinich.

41 Soble, in "Pornography: defamation and the endorsement of degradation," cited above,
also discusses *Reefer Madness* (p. 79). He uses the example to support the claim that
"whether an item of pornography implicitly endorses degradation is partially a function of
the nature of the audience" (p. 80). I would want to suggest instead that pornography itself
never endorses anything, but that it can be *used* to pragmatically impart an endorsement.
This view avoids the awkwardness of Soble's apparent view that content depends on features of the audience.

42 I am indebted to Alex Neill for detailed and very helpful comments.

SUGGESTIONS FOR FURTHER READING

Barwell, Ismay (1995) "Who's telling this story, anyway? Or, how to tell the gender of a storyteller", *Australasian Journal of Philosophy* 73: 227–38.

Battersby, Christine (1989) *Gender and Genius: Towards a Feminist Aesthetics*, Bloomington: Indiana University Press.

Beauvoir, Simone de (1987) "Women and creativity", in *French Feminist Thought*, ed. Toril Moi, Oxford: Blackwell.

Berger, John (1973) *Ways of Seeing*, New York: Viking Press.

Brand, M. and Korsmeyer, C. (1990) *Feminism and Traditional Aesthetics*, special Issue of the *Journal of Aesthetics and Art Criticism* 48.

Broude, Norma and Garrard, Mary D. (eds) (1992) *The Expanding Discourse: Feminism and Art History*, New York: Harper Collins.

Case, Sue-Ellen (1989) "Toward a butch-femme aesthetic", in *Making a Spectacle*, ed. L. Hart, Ann Arbor: University of Michigan Press.

Carroll, Noël (1990) "The image of women in film: a defence of a paradigm", *Journal of Aesthetics and Art Criticism* 48: 349–60.

Devereaux, Mary (1993) "Protected space: politics, censorship, and the arts", *Journal of Aesthetics and Art Criticism* 51: 207–15.

—— (1992) "The philosophical and political implications of the feminist critique of aesthetic autonomy", in *Turning the Century: Feminist Criticism in the 1990s*, ed. Glynis Carr, *Bucknell Review* 36: 164–86.

Ecker, Gisela (ed.) (1986) *Feminist Aesthetics*, Boston: Beacon Press.

Felski, Rita (1989) *Beyond Feminist Aesthetics: Feminist Literature and Social Change*, Cambridge: Harvard University Press.

Freeland, Cynthia A. (1996) "Feminist frameworks for horror films", in David Bordwell and Noël Carroll (eds), *Post-Theory: Reconstructing Film Studies*, Madison: University of Wisconsin Press.

Haskell, Molly (1974) *From Reverence to Rape: The Treatment of Women in the Movies*, Harmondsworth: Penguin Books.

Hess, Thomas and Baker, Elizabeth (eds) (1973) *Art and Sexual Politics*, New York: Macmillan.

Kaplan, E. Ann (1983) "Is the gaze male?" in *Powers of Desire*, ed. Snitow, Stansell, and Thompson, New York: Monthly Review Press.

Korsmeyer, C. (1993) "Pleasure: reflections on aesthetics and feminism", *Journal of Aesthetics and Art Criticism* 51: 199–206.

Korsmeyer, C. and Hein, H. (eds) (1993) *Aesthetics in Feminist Perspective*, Bloomington: Indiana University Press.

Kuhn, Annette (1982) *Women's Pictures: Feminism and the Cinema*, London: Routledge & Kegan Paul.

Lauretis, Teresa de (1987) *Technologies of Gender: Essays on Theory, Film, and Fiction*, Bloomington: University of Indiana Press.

Leibowitz, Flo (1996) "Apt feelings, or why 'women's films' aren't trivial", in David Bordwell and Noël Carroll (eds), *Post-Theory: Reconstructing Film Studies*, Madison: University of Wisconsin Press.

Lippard, Lucy (1990) *Mixed Blessings: New Art in a Multicultural America*, New York: Pantheon.

McClary, Susan (1991) *Feminine Endings: Music, Gender, and Sexuality*, Minneapolis: University of Minnesota Press.

Mulvey, Laura (1989) *Visual and Other Pleasures,* Bloomington: Indiana University Press. (Includes her article "Visual pleasure and narrative cinema", discussed in Devereaux's article in this book.)

Nochlin, Linda (1988) *Women, Art and Power, and Other Essays*, New York: Harper & Row.

Owens, Craig (1982) "The discourse of others: feminists and postmodernism", in *The Anti-Aesthetic: Essays on Postmodern Culture*, ed. Hal Foster, Port Townsend, WA.: Bay Press.

Shrage, Laurie and Tuana, Nancy (eds) (1990) *American Philosophical Association Newsletter on Feminism and Philosophy* 89(2 and 3).

Part 12

PUBLIC ART

Standing where it does, *Tilted Arc* is the metal grin of the art world having bitten off a piece of the public world, which it means to hold in its teeth forever, the public be damned.

Arthur Danto, *The State of the Art*, p. 94

If we leave the selection of public art to the residents of a community – or even permit their strong influence on the process – we will end up with an aesthetic common denominator of sterile, benign and conventional art that will neither offend nor stimulate anyone.

Alvin Lane, writing in the *New York Times*, 13 July 1985

Richard Serra: *Tilted Arc*, 1981. Weatherproof steel. 12' × 120' × 2½". Collection: General Services Administration, Washington DC. Installed: Federal Plaza, New York. Destroyed 1989. Photograph: Ann Chauvet. Courtesy of Richard Serra.

Maya Lin: Vietnam Veterans Memorial, Washington Mall, Washington, DC.
Photo: AKG London, by Keith Collie, 1996.

THE DEBATE OVER RICHARD SERRA'S SCULPTURE *Tilted Arc* – which was commissioned by the US Federal Government to stand in the plaza of the Jacob Javits Federal Building in Manhattan, installed in 1981, and eventually, after much public controversy, removed in 1989 – suggests a number of interesting questions concerning the very idea of public art. To begin with, following Hilde Hein in her chapter in this part, we might ask what it is for art to *be* public art. In part, this is to ask about the relation between public art and the tastes of the public: should the selection of public art be driven by public taste, or does it rather represent an opportunity to educate and shape public taste? If a piece of public art is widely disliked by the community it is in the midst of, need that mean that the art work in question is a failure? If so, what kind of failure would that be? (It seems clear that it would not necessarily be an aesthetic or artistic failure, since the public in question may simply have bad taste.) And however we answer these questions, it still remains to be asked who exactly the public in question are – everyone? Everyone who lives or works nearby and hence regularly comes into contact with the work in question? Or might the public for a particular work consist of some other subset of the community as a whole?

Michael Kelly takes up some of these questions concerning the relation between a work of public art and its public in his discussion of the commissioning and reception of Maya Lin's Vietnam Veterans Memorial in Washington D.C. as well as *Tilted Arc*. The differences between the works Kelly discusses serve to remind us that it may not be possible to answer questions

427

like those posed in the paragraph above without being more specific about the nature of the public art at issue. Thus, for example, there are differences between works whose function appears to be primarily decorative, others whose function is to celebrate something, others whose function is to memorialize, and doubtless others with different functions still, and it seems likely that different questions will be raised, and different answers required, by each of these. For example, it is highly unlikely that the notion of the public in these different cases will be usefully understood in the same way.

In his chapter, Gregg Horowitz considers the character of the debate leading up to the removal of *Tilted Arc*, suggesting that what may at first sight appear to be a triumph of the public will over an elitist and patronising art world – a triumph of democracy, in effect – was in fact a victory of "regressive political strategy" over genuine "democratic discourse". The removal of the sculpture may have been in some sense a response to public demand – though Horowitz questions how real a sense that was – but its effect was to deprive the public of the opportunity to engage in precisely the kind of critical discussion of the nature of public space that *Tilted Arc* had the potential to provoke. Horowitz's suggestion, then, is that a work's being responsive to its public may involve its making demands on that public, and that this sort of responsiveness may be at least as valuable, in the appropriate context, as a responsiveness that consists in being to the public's liking. (In this context, we might ask whether graffiti, no less than *Tilted Arc*, might have the potential to provoke genuinely democratic discourse. And in doing so we should come up again against the question of just what it is for a work to be a work of public art.)

As Hilde Hein emphasizes, the very idea of public art is a puzzling one. And yet the sponsoring and production of public art appears to be a central characteristic of civil society wherever the latter appears. Questions about the nature and function of public art thus have a place in a much wider context having to do with our conception of ourselves as social and political beings.

25

TRANSCRIPT OF A HEARING TO DECIDE THE FUTURE OF *TILTED ARC*

Representative Ted Weiss: Imagine, if you will, this curved slab of welded steel twelve feet high, 120 feet long, and weighing over seventy-three tons bisecting the street in front of your house, and you can imagine the reaction to *Tilted Arc* of those who live and work in the area.

Adding to the shock effect is the sculpture's natural oxide coating, which gives it the appearance of a rusted metal wall. Many who first viewed *Tilted Arc* regarded it as an abandoned piece of construction material, a relic perhaps too large and cumbersome to move.

The artist is said to have intended with this piece to "alter and dislocate the decorative function of the plaza." If that was the intent, one may conclude from the sculpture's harsh, disorienting effect that the artist has eloquently succeeded.

But what of those who live and work nearby? The sculpture cuts a huge swath across the center of the plaza, dividing it in two and acting as a barrier to the building's main doorways. Access to the building is awkward and confusing, and the normal walking patterns of those who enter and exit the building are disrupted.

The time has come to find a new location for *Tilted Arc*.

Mr. Serra argues that because his work is site specific, moving it to another location would destroy it. It has, he maintains, a proprietary claim upon the plaza just as real as that of a painting to its canvas. I suggest that there are other valid claims upon the plaza that conflict with Mr. Serra's, and that the scales tip in their favor. The community – those thousands of people who live and work in the area – has the right to reclaim this small oasis for the respite and relaxation for which it was intended.

Mr. Serra, I do not wish to see your work destroyed. I simply would like to see it in a more felicitous location.

Richard Serra: My name is Richard Serra and I am an American sculptor.

I don't make portable objects. I don't make works that can be relocated or site adjusted. I make works that deal with the environmental components of given places. The scale, size, and location of my site-specific works are determined by the topography of the site, whether it be urban, landscape, or an architectural enclosure. My works become part of and are built into the structure of the site, and they often restructure, both conceptually and perceptually, the organization of the site.

My sculptures are not objects for the viewer to stop and stare at. The historical purpose of placing sculpture on a pedestal was to establish a separation between the sculpture and the viewer. I am interested in creating a behavioral space in which the viewer interacts with the sculpture in its context.

One's identity as a person is closely connected with one's experience of space and place. When a known space is changed through the inclusion of a site-specific sculpture, one is called upon to relate to the space differently. This is a condition that can be engendered only by sculpture. This experience of space may startle some people.

When the government invited me to propose a sculpture for the plaza it asked for a permanent, site-specific sculpture. As the phrase implies, a site-specific sculpture is one that is conceived and created in relation to the particular conditions of a specific site, and only to those conditions.

To remove *Tilted Arc*, therefore, would be to destroy it . . .

It has been suggested that the public did not choose to install the work in the first place. In fact, the choice of the artist and the decision to install the sculpture permanently in the plaza were made by a public entity: the GSA. Its determination was made on the basis of national standards and carefully formulated procedures, and a jury system ensured impartiality and the selection of art of lasting value. The selection of this sculpture was, therefore, made by, and on behalf of, the public.

The agency made its commitments and signed a contract. If its decision is reversed in response to pressure from outside sources, the integrity of governmental programs related to the arts will be compromised, and artists of integrity will not participate. If the government can destroy works of art when confronted with such pressure, its capacity to foster artistic diversity and its power to safeguard freedom of creative expression will be in jeopardy.

Judge Dominick DiCarlo: I had my first encounter with *Tilted Arc* after learning that I was being considered for appointment to the United States Court of International Trade. I was driving on Centre Street when I saw it. What is it? It's a 120-foot-by-twelve-foot rusted piece of iron. Having just returned from visiting our embassies in Rome, Islamabad, Rangoon, and Bangkok, I concluded that this rusted iron object was an anti-terrorist barricade, part of a crash program to protect United States government buildings against terrorist activities. But why such a huge barricade? Was this an overreaction? Why in cities where terrorist activity is much greater are comparatively attractive highway dividers and concrete pillars sufficient to do the job?

After my appointment to the court, I was told that this was art. Was it a thing of beauty? Could be, since beauty is in the eyes of the beholder. Could its maker be making a political statement? Perhaps it was a discarded and rusted piece of the iron curtain. Or perhaps its author was expressing his views on trade policy. This is the Court of International Trade. Was his iron barrier symbolic of a protectionist viewpoint?

We don't have to guess why the iron wall was placed in the plaza. Those responsible have told us. It was to alter and dislocate the decorative function of the plaza, to redefine the space, to change the viewers' experience of that plaza. Simply put, their intention was to destroy the plaza's original artistic concept, the concept of its architects.

To object to the removal of the iron wall on the basis of an honest, moral right to preserve the integrity of the work is astounding, since the sculptor's intent was to destroy another artistic creation . . .

Peter Hirsch: I am the research director and legal counsel for the Association of Immigration Attorneys. We are constantly at 26 Federal Plaza, since that is where the Immigration Service is located.

My membership has authorized me to say that we are entirely opposed to *Tilted Arc*. My own personal view is that a good place to put *Tilted Arc* would be in the Hudson River. . . . I am told that they are going to have to put artificial things in the river to provide shelter for the striped bass. I think *Tilted Arc* would make a very fine shelter.

Fred Hoffman: I am an art historian and curator of contemporary art associated with many of the leading cultural organizations in Los Angeles.

We can learn more about ourselves, about the nature of our social relations, and about the nature of the spaces we inhabit and depend upon by keeping *Tilted Arc* than we ever could by languishing in the alleged pleasures of a Serra-less plaza.

One of the fundamental realities about an important work of art such as *Tilted Arc* is that it does not simply sit down, roll over, and play dead. This work does not have as its intention pleasing, entertaining, or pacifying. By structuring an experience that is continually active, dynamic, and expansive, *Tilted Arc* makes sure that we do not fall asleep, mindless and indifferent to our destiny and to the increasing scarcity of freedom in an increasingly banal, undifferentiated, and style-oriented world. . . .

William Rubin: I am director of the Department of Painting and Sculpture at the Museum of Modern Art.

Like many creations of modern art, *Tilted Arc* is a challenging work that obliges us to question received values in general and the nature of art and of art's relation to the public in particular.

About one hundred years ago the Impressionists and post-Impressionists (Monet, Gauguin, Cézanne, for example), artists whose works are today prized universally, were being reviled as ridiculous by the public and the established press. At about the same time, the Eiffel Tower was constructed, only to be greeted by much the same ridicule. Leading architects of the day as well as writers and philosophers, to say nothing of the man on the street, condemned the tower as a visual obscenity.

As these examples suggest, truly challenging works of art require a period of time before their artistic language can be understood by the broader public.

I must say that I have never heard of a decision to remove a public monument being settled by popular vote. If that is what is being contemplated here, it seems to me a most dangerous precedent. Moreover, the decision should, it seems to me, involve the sentiments of a much wider circle than simply those who work in the immediate neighborhood. For society as a whole has a stake in such works of art.

Certainly the consideration of any such move should not be a response to pressure tactics and, above all, should not take place before the sculpture's artistic language can become familiar.

I therefore propose that a consideration of this issue be deferred for at least ten years.

Joel Kovel: I am a writer and a professor at the New School for Social Research.

This very hearing proves the subversiveness, and hence the value, of *Tilted Arc*. Its very tilt and rust remind us that the gleaming and heartless steel and glass structures of the state apparatus can one day pass away. It therefore creates an unconscious sense of opposition and hope.

This opposition is itself a creative act, as, indeed, this hearing is a creative act. I would submit that the true measure of a free and democratic society is that it permits opposition of this sort. Therefore, it is essential that this hearing result in the preservation of Serra's work as a measure of the opposition this society can tolerate.

Joseph Liebman: I am the attorney in charge of the International Trade Field Office, Civil Division, U.S. Department of Justice, with offices located at 26 Federal Plaza.

I have worked at 26 Federal Plaza since 1969. While the plaza never fulfilled all my expectations, until 1980 I regarded it as a relaxing space where I could walk, sit, and contemplate in an unhurried manner. Every now and then rays of sunshine bathed the plaza, creating new vistas and moods for its vibrant, unchallenged space.

I remember those moments. I remember the cool spray of the fountain misting the hot air. I remember the band concerts. I remember the musical sounds of neighborhood children playing on the plaza while their mothers rocked baby carriages. I remember walking freely in the plaza, contemplating the examination of a witness, undisturbed by the presence of other people engaged in conversation or young lovers holding hands. I also remember my dreams of additional seating areas, more cultural events, temporary outdoor exhibits of painting and sculpture, and ethnic dance festivals.

All of those things are just memories now.

Regardless of the thoughtfulness and artistic accomplishment of its creator, *Tilted Arc* fails to add significant value to the plaza. The arc has condemned us to lead emptier lives. The children, the bands, and I no longer visit the plaza. Instead, the arc divides space against itself. Whatever artistic value the arc may have does not justify the disruption of the plaza and our lives.

The arc, a creation of mortal hand, should yield. Relocate it in another land. Reprieve us from our desolate condemnation . . .

Donald Judd [sculptor]: We need to revive a secular version of sacrilege to categorize the attempt to destroy Richard Serra's work in Federal Plaza in Manhattan.

Art is not to be destroyed, either old or new. It is visible civilization. Those who want to ruin Serra's work are barbarians . . .

Holly Solomon: I have a gallery in SoHo and now I've moved to Fifty-seventh Street. I don't feel qualified to discuss the law part of this and I don't feel I have time to discuss the taste or the art historical importance of this piece. I can only tell you, gentlemen, that this is business, and to take down the piece is bad business. Mr. Serra is one of the leading sculptors of our time. I sell many paintings. I try very hard to teach people about contemporary art, but the bottom line is that this has financial value, and you really have to understand that you have a responsibility to the financial community. You cannot destroy property.

Phil La Basi: I have been a federal employee for twenty-two years, about eleven years in this building.

First of all, I would like to say that I really resent the implication that those of us who oppose this structure are cretins or some sort of reactionaries.

It seems to be very typical of self-serving artists and so-called pseudointellectuals that when they disagree with something someone else has to say, they attack the person. So I am not going to attack the artist.

What I see there is something that looks like a tank trap to prevent an armed attack from Chinatown in case of a Soviet invasion. In my mind it probably wouldn't even do that well, because one good Russian tank could probably take it out.

To be very serious, I wouldn't call it *Tilted Arc*. To me it looks like crooked metal or bent metal. I think we can call anything art if we call that art. I think any one of these people here could come along with an old broken bicycle that perhaps got run over by a car, or some other piece of material, and pull it up and call it art and name it something. I think that was what was done here . . .

Frank Stella [painter]: In the matter under discussion here the government and the artist, Richard Serra, have acted in good faith and have executed their responsibilities in exemplary fashion.

The objections to their efforts are without compelling merit. The objections are singular, peculiar, and idiosyncratic. The government and the artist have acted as the body of society attempting to meet civilized, one might almost say civilizing, goals – in this case, the extension of visual culture into public spaces.

The attempt to reverse their efforts serves no broad social purpose and is contrary to the honest, searching efforts that represent the larger and truer goals of society.

Satisfaction for the dissenters is not a necessity. The continued cultural aspirations of the society are a necessity, as is the protection of these aspirations.

The dissenters have accomplished enough by having their objections heard, discussed, and publicized. Whatever merit their case may have, it is now part of the public record and will have its proper influence in future decisions involving matters of this kind.

To destroy the work of art and simultaneously incur greater public expense in that effort would disturb the status quo for no gain. Furthermore, the precedent set can only have wasteful and unnecessary consequences.

There is no reason to encourage harassment of the government and the artist working toward a public good. There are no circumstances here to warrant further administrative or judicial action. If the matter stands as it is, no one will experience any serious harm or duress and one more work of art will be preserved.

This dispute should not be allowed to disrupt a successful working relationship between government agencies and citizen artists.

Finally, no public dispute should force the gratuitous destruction of any benign, civilizing effort.

Danny Katz: My name is Danny Katz and I work in this building as a clerk. My friend Vito told me this morning that I am a philistine. Despite that, I am getting up to speak. Listen fast, because I hear seconds being counted and tempers are high.

The blame falls on everyone involved in this project from the beginning for forgetting the human element. I don't think this issue should be elevated into a dispute between the forces of ignorance and art, or art versus government. I really blame government less because it has long ago outgrown its human dimension. But from the artists I expected a lot more.

I didn't expect to hear them rely on the tired and dangerous reasoning that the government has made a deal, so let the rabble live with the steel because it's a deal. That kind of mentality leads to wars. We had a deal with Vietnam.

I didn't expect to hear the arrogant position that art justifies interference with the simple joys of human activity in a plaza. It's not a great plaza by international standards, but it is a small refuge and place of revival for people who ride to work in steel containers, work in sealed rooms, and breathe recirculated air all day. Is the purpose of art in public places to seal off a route of escape, to stress the absence of joy and hope?

I can't believe that this was the artistic intention, yet to my sadness this for me has been the dominant effect of the work, and it's all the fault of its position and location.

I can accept anything in art, but I can't accept physical assault and complete destruction of pathetic human activity.

No work of art created with a contempt for ordinary humanity and without respect for the common element of human experience can be great. It will always lack a dimension.

I don't believe the contempt is in the work. The work is strong enough to stand alone in a better place. I would suggest to Mr. Serra that he take advantage of this opportunity to walk away from this fiasco and demand that the work be moved to a place where it will better reveal its beauty.

26

WHAT IS PUBLIC ART?

Time, place, and meaning

Hilde Hein

I A PUBLIC ART OF PLACE AND TIME

Public art is an oxymoron according to the standards of modernist art and aesthetic theory. Modern philosophical aesthetics focuses almost exclusively on subjective experience and a commodified work of art. Art is taken to be the product of an individual and autonomous act of expression, and its appreciation is, likewise, a private act of contemplation. By contrast, as a public phenomenon, art must entail the artist's self-negation and deference to a collective community. It is interesting to observe that the recognized art of nearly all cultures, including that of the western European tradition prior to the late Renaissance, embraces just such a collective model, indulging the differences among individuals as variant manifestations of a common spirit. The celebrated treasures of Greece and Rome, as well as the Christian works of the Middle Ages and the age of the fresco that succeeded them, do not exalt the private vision of individual artists so much as they bespeak the shared values and convictions of cultural communities, and are accordingly to be found in those edifices and open places where people regularly gather to commemorate those same values and convictions. Privacy was for centuries a privative concept, demarcating the dissociated and limited experience of persons cut off from and below the level of full social humanity.[1]

Modernism, with its glorification of the individual, has reversed that order, investing personhood with uniqueness and regarding the social as a derivative aggregate. Its representation of art, correspondingly, gives pride of place to that which is irreducibly personal. The aesthetic of modernism has yoked art with subjective consciousness and expression, and with a new construction of freedom based on the possession of libertarian rights. In its defense, partisans, from Kant to the present, have endowed art with a liberatory function conceptually constructed out of a fusion of artistic independence (the unregulated genius) with political autonomy (the absence of heteronomous coercion). The autonomous individual, glorified in the person of the artist and secondarily in the created object, transcends the public, whose emancipatory benefit is vicarious and derivative.[2] The art denoted, however, is explicitly not that of the self-effacing tribal or (public) artist who reflects the culture of the community, but that of the self-affirming (private) individual.

Strictly speaking, no art is "private." Even those abortive essays consigned to flames in frustration by their authors were, presumably, made for, but withheld from, publication. But neither does art become "public" simply in virtue of its exposure and accessibility to the world. Publicity has social and political connotations that are untranslatable to public access. Conventionally, the term "public art" refers to a family of conditions including the object's origin, history, location, and social purpose. All of these conditions have changed their meanings in a world of evolving technology, secularization, cultural migration, and economic restructuring. Yet today's public artworks still have conceptual links with such traditional art forms as the medieval cathedral and the mural and temple ruins of ancient Mexican and Latin American civilizations.[3]

Like many complex social ideas, the concept of public art has undergone radical changes, and recent public quarrels which focus on an instance at hand – a current scandal or judicial decision – scarcely reveal the pluralization and polarization that both art and the notion of public art have withstood. The monolithic cultural assumptions implicit in Roman forum statuary or an altar triptych or even the typical town square equestrian statue are no longer viable. The supposition that a visual form, an anthem, or a text might express its deepest values or unify a coherent social group has become a relic of romantic history.[4] Instead, the concept of *a* public has become so problematized that putative works of public art demand justification in terms of qualitatively unrelated analyses of public space, public ownership, public representation, public interest, and the public sphere. Rarely does a work satisfy in all of these dimensions. Indeed, few works address or embody all of these aspects of publicity, and their selective attention to one or more of them – frequently conflict-ridden – accounts for the baffling variety of items proffered as public art.

What, then, remains to render an object a work of public art, if neither collective origin nor spiritual cohesiveness nor central placement nor even popularity serves to determine it? A crudely pragmatic and narrow definition of public art equates it with art installed by public agencies in public places and at public expense.[5] But this is hardly sufficient to encompass the explosion of non-traditional projects that now lay claim to designation as public art. The two cases discussed in this symposium by Horowitz and Kelly, though superseded by more recent examples, lay the ground of disputation over contemporary public art. Both Richard Serra's *Tilted Arc* and Maya Lin's Vietnam Veterans Memorial were produced by artworld figures whose design proposals were selected from among other submissions by boards of artworld judges; thus from the vantage of the Institutional Theory of Art, both indisputably qualify as works of art.[6] The Vietnam Veterans Memorial's construction was funded entirely by private donations (solicited from individual veterans); only its (public) placement on the Washington Mall required Congressional approval. Its location and explicit memorializing mission, however, would surely warrant its public designation by traditional standards. Ironically, the memorial's formal independence of government is what protected it from official intervention when a group of opponents objected to what they perceived to be its disrespectful and negative tone.[7] Had it been publicly funded, they might have been able to intervene more destructively. Instead, (also at private expense) the opposition succeeded only in winning the installation of a conventionally realist representation, complete with flagpole, nearby.

Tilted Arc was publicly funded and was also placed on a federally owned site. But, Serra's claims to First Amendment protection notwithstanding, the fact that the *Arc* was initiated by the government did not ensure against its destruction. Both its erection and its subsequent demise were presided over by decisions of the United States General Services Administration. Although the sculpture belonged to the United States government and was displayed on government property, the judge who condemned the sculpture to removal declared it a privatization of public space.[8] Neither location in a public place nor inception by a state agency sufficiently identified it as public art in Judge Pollack's estimation. That alone might not have warranted its removal, but many critics from within and without the artworld agreed with him that, whether or not that was tantamount to its destruction, the sculpture should be removed from its site.[9]

Public art today seems to engage more abstract concerns and more ephemeral interpretations of site, memory, and meaning. Space and time continue to play a definitive part, but like most philosophical categories, their meaning has grown attenuated. They no longer refer simply to "where" and "when," but have become symbolic and relational indicators, far removed from the coordinates that once sufficed to situate things. Today's public artworks may be impermanent and discontinuous, like the installations of Suzanne Lacy. They may subsist only momentarily or in multiple instantiations, immaterially suspended, like the projections of Krzysztof Wodiczko. They may be unheroically unspectacular, like the neighborhood sculptures of John Ahearn or like the local landscapes of Sondquist. And they may be realized exclusively in discrete mental spaces, like some of the exhortations of the Guerrilla Girls. How then do they qualify as public art?

II A PUBLIC ART OF MEANING

Modernism and its formalist aesthetic dictated a stripped-down public as well as a minimalist private art. Site-specificity took on a spatial and architectural rather than occasional meaning, and with the demise of content, public art became first an object in public space, and then a sculpting of that space as objects too evaporated, leaving only relations behind. And, since relations exist in the eye of the beholder, the audience (before it too was eliminated) became a necessary ingredient in the work of art, rendering it public in a new and non-ceremonial sense. Public art became vernacular, having to do not with a spirit that magnifies as it collectivizes, but with ordinary, unmythicized people in ordinary places and with the ordinary events of their mundane lives.[10]

At the same time that it became more abstract, public art also became more explicitly communitarian. The audience no longer figured as passive onlooker but as participant, actively implicated in the constitution of the work of art. Effectively, the work's realization depends on the audience's bestowal of meaning upon it, a contentious social and political undertaking. The integration of the public into the work of art is inherently political, and is as such equally congenial to both conservative and revolutionary ideology. Public art has been used to great effect promotionally and oppositionally by all political persuasions. Nazi architecture, designed by Albert Speer and gorgeously displayed in Leni Riefenstahl's film *Triumph of the Will*, complements the political *bon mot* of Joseph Goebbels: " ' "The statesman is an artist too. For him the people is neither more nor less than what stone is for the sculptor." ' "[11] The same sentiment, directed toward more benign ends, is intended in the work of Vito Acconci, Siah Armajani, Beverly Pepper, Mierle Ukeles, and Christo, among many others who strive to arouse and capture the social conscience of a passive public. Sometimes despairing, sometimes hortatory, and sometimes uplifting, all these artists agree in stating that human beings are not and shall not be detached from the social and natural world. Hostile or harmonious, the world resonates with the human presence, intrudes upon it, and will not be denied.

Perhaps the very lability of social and aesthetic interactions and their receptivity to multiple interpretations accounts for the difficulty the public sometimes experiences "reading" public works. As Michael North points out in comparing what he calls the "modest populism" of Siah Armajani with the "bleak puritanism" of Lauren Ewing, "The very techniques [s/]he chooses to represent commonality can also represent the conformity that [the artist] means to expose."[12] It is interesting that opposite reasons can be given for identical judgments of a single work, just as different works may be oppositely judged for the same reasons. The cases discussed by Horowitz and Kelly involve just such interpretive ambiguity. *Tilted Arc*, avowed by its author to be politically motivated, was denounced by a number of critics for its elitist aestheticism; while the overtly apolitical Vietnam Veterans Memorial narrowly avoided destruction by opponents who called it a subversive "wailing wall for anti-draft demonstrators." Both works are formally abstract, minimalist in design, and both were selected by artworld juries, presumably on the basis of their aesthetic merit alone.

Both works profess a site-specificity that is neither purely spatial nor locally commemorative. Serra maintained that the site-specificity of *Tilted Arc* was determined as much by material social conditions as by aesthetic exigency. He meant to confront the public in *behavioral space* "in which the viewer interacts with the sculpture in its context. . . . to engage the public in a dialogue that would enhance, both perceptually and conceptually, its relation to the entire plaza." The sculpture would not literally interdict movement, but it would (and did) cause the viewer to feel blocked. The experience of oppression was real enough, but Serra wanted it to redirect attention to its actual source in the mechanisms of state power. He hoped that the sculpture would redefine the space in terms of itself; and so it did – even beyond his expectation. The crusade for the removal of the sculpture was initiated by a federal judge and federal employees who protested the affront committed by the *Arc* and the aggression it might inspire, but in their testimony some revealed a deeper sensibility – a consciousness raised and smothered by oppression from elsewhere. Far from letting aesthetic considerations recede into irrelevancy, they had read them rightly as inseparable from deepest values. *Tilted Arc* evoked the pressure of coercion. Only the source of that unwelcome feeling was ambiguous.[13]

In their analyses for this symposium, Horowitz and Kelly disagree over the meaning of site-specificity. Kelly holds that *Tilted Arc* fails to be site-specific, since "the public" is reduced to the abstraction of "traffic" and was excluded from consultation regarding the sculpture's selection. In other words, the piece does not inhabit the public sphere. Horowitz, on the other hand, claims that the managed opposition to *Tilted Arc* was a cynical subversion of its deliberately achieved menace, converting the aesthetic dis-ease it provoked into mistrust of the work as an actual threat. His survey of circulation notwithstanding, Serra certainly did mean to disrupt the specious openness of Federal Plaza, but the dialogue that ensued did not have the political outcome he anticipated.

It may be that, whether with persons or with places, dialogue does not always end happily. If the aim of site-specific art (which, by the way, is not coextensive with public art) is to evoke "critical adjustment" to a place, that can end with its acceptance or rejection. Another alternative is that it sustain attention to a subject that is enlightened but remains unresolved.[14]

The Vietnam Veterans Memorial seems to engage its visitors in just such a critical colloquy. Constrained by the conditions of the contest she won to make a design that was contemplative, harmonious with its site and surroundings, and that would make no political statement about the war, Maya Lin produced a work that evokes profound emotions in viewers, whatever their political sympathies.[15] The Vietnam Veterans Memorial manages to work as public art both in the traditional sense that it occupies public space and memorializes a public event, and in the current sense that it questions the meaning of that space and that event and draws the public into intelligent discourse with it. In doing this, it brings an additional aspect of publicity into focus, that it is multiform and multivalent, recalling that the forum is a place for debate – and not just a site for communion or collective affirmation. Speaking of the work of Lin (and Hans Haacke), Michael North says:

[I]t is not the public experience of space but rather public debate that becomes a work of art. They make manifest an important truth about public space, that unless it is embedded in a larger public sphere that values debate, a public sphere like that defined by Jürgen Habermas in which private people use their reason to discuss and reach conclusions, then it will always be decorated by mass ornaments, no matter what sort of art is put into it.[16]

Despite its nonrepresentational modernist aesthetic, the Vietnam Veterans Memorial is not a "mass ornament"; neither is it "nihilistic."

It is clear that location and accessibility are misleading parameters of publicity. Sizable works of art are now commonly commissioned for such semipublic places as university grounds, hospitals, housing developments, and bank lobbies. Government subsidy often mandates the inclusion of artworks under percent-for-art regulation, and private corporations receive tax benefits for the cultural contribution they make in the form of artistic embellishment. But the sheer presence of art out-of-doors or in a bus terminal or a hotel reception area does not automatically make that art public – no more than placing a tiger in a barnyard would make it a domestic animal. The object, artwork or animal, does not derive its identity from the character of the place in which it is found. Public placement does, however, make the work available to more people than might otherwise experience it, and, depending upon the extension of legal coverage to it, the freedom of expression of the artist(s) who made it is more or less protected.[17]

No more than does its location, the mere integration of art into the ordinary life of people fails to bestow social meaning upon it and does not render it public. Collaborations that include artists along with architects and engineers in the landscape design and planning of office or housing projects often end with what have been called "corporate baubles." These are public in the sense that they are inscribed in spaces not usually set aside for private art experiences; and they are art in the sense that their function is chiefly aesthetic, but they neither satisfy the traditional memorializing criteria of public art nor engage citizens in any but the most superficial social and aesthetic interactions of the public sphere.[18]

It must be recalled that the very places paradigmatically designated for private aesthetic viewing, museums and galleries, are public in that, discounting the increasingly prohibitive price of entry, they are open to anyone. Yet, even were this to guarantee universal access to their contents, the items contained in museums would not be public art. Although museums were founded to liberate objects previously confined in private treasuries and to place them in the public sphere by declaring them national property, those objects became "privatized" and extracted from the public sphere by virtue of the very aesthetic appropriation that made them "museum pieces."[19]

Being museum art, with all the artworld anointment that this entails, appears to bar the way to an object's having public art status, but even that qualification is dissipating.

There is burgeoning interest now among private museums and publicly funded art institutions to display self-designated public art. The exhibits are mostly descriptive and conceptual, involving verbal or pictorial records and documentation of ephemeral events that are somewhere else, did happen, or cannot be reproduced. Their publicity is a matter of faith and Xerox machines. Do these representations become private art when they are mounted on the walls of the Whitney Museum or the Institute of Contemporary Art? Has the public sphere lost its claim to them or has it too been assimilated into the sanctum of the private?[20]

The presence or absence of walls, doors, and columns no longer separates private from public space.[21] Indeed, space itself no longer attaches to materiality; and thus whatever material displacement might have marked their difference no longer distinguishes public from private space. Meanings occupy virtual spaces, and traffic through them is subject only to the limits of fantasy. In fantasy, as Horowitz suggests, a space can represent powerlessness or liberation, and an ambiguous object can challenge power or dissolve a dream. The creative display of objects and their deployment for aesthetic pleasure are revealed as politically significant acts. This is no less true of art heretofore cordoned off as private than of avowedly public art. Both share as art in a designation meant to depoliticize the concept. By declaring itself "public," public art points to the impropriety of that characterization and reclaims the political status of all art.

Who speaks for the public? There are many who position themselves in that role – judges, government officials, corporate moneymakers, social scientists, and philosopher-critics. Artists, despite their professed asocial status, are as deeply engaged in the public sphere as those whose civic function is ordained by definition. Artists do not have privileged vision, but they do have a practiced eye and the ability to speak in a rich variety of languages – verbal, visual, conceptual, sensual, serious, humorous, figurative, and rational. Sometimes and somehow they break through ordinary expectation and cause people to venture upon new perspectives. This is not because they have made an orbital leap from private to public, but because their insightful expression ignites response. Public art cannot promise public understanding, any more than private art assures private salvation, whatever these might be. We have turned to artists in moments of distress as we formerly turned to religion, and then to science, for public enlightenment and private satisfaction. Each has stirred up its own problems and given us some gratification in return. We should not expect consensus. To cite Patricia Phillips's appreciation of public art: "It is an art which is absolutely engaged with the world and this engagement often invokes spirited disagreement. . . . Absolute consensus is not necessarily a happy state."[22] But perhaps it is a better state than one that constructs mutual destruction or mutual avoidance as the only alternatives.

To revert to my initial dilemma, I suggest that it is private – not public – art that evokes contradiction. Exceeding even the error of aesthetic enshrinement is the political wrong of negating art's publicity as a site of multiple meaning and communicative exchange. But art is escaping its confinement to private sensibility. It is descending into the streets once more and reclaiming its place in the public realm.[23]

NOTES

1 Hannah Arendt describes the public realm as conceived in antiquity as the common world of reality, in which human beings coexist in freedom, a world of politics, history, and continuity. The private realm is privative. To enter it is to be imprisoned in the subjectivity of singular experience (no matter how often it is replicated by the identical experience of others). It is to be "deprived of things essential to a truly human life . . . of the reality of being seen and heard by others . . . to be deprived of the possibility of achieving something more than life itself." See Arendt, *The Human Condition* (University of Chicago Press, 1958), p. 58.

   Jürgen Habermas describes a later (seventeenth century) sense of public realm that refers to permanent structures of communication and authority. In this sense, "public" connotes state related and controlling, while "private" is a correlative concept referring to those socially significant functions (and persons who enact them) that are regulated. "The relationship between the authorities and the subjects thereby assumed the peculiar ambivalence of public regulation and private initiative." As with Arendt, privacy is conceived privatively. The private person lacks perspective and knowledge, and is therefore unqualified to take part in social decision-making. Habermas, *The Structural Transformation of the Public Sphere: An Inquiry Into a Category of Bourgeois Society*, trans. Thomas Burger and Frederick Lawrence (MIT Press, 1989), p. 24.

2 Possibly the most explicit and stirring expression of this view appears in Friedrich Schiller, *On the Aesthetic Education of Man*, trans. Reginald Snell (Yale University Press, 1954).

3 The Bulgarian artist, Christo, likens his wrapping of public buildings and landscapes to the construction of the cathedrals. See his video interviews in "Islands," produced by the Maysles Brothers. See also Timothy W. Drescher, *San Francisco Murals: Community Creates Its Muse, 1914–1990* (St Paul: Pogo Press, 1991) for an analysis of contemporary Latino mural art.

4 Emblems such as these have been displaced by the purely visual logo, unencumbered by historical associations or significance.

5 W.J.T. Mitchell, "The violence of public art," in *Art and the Public Sphere*, ed. W.J.T. Mitchell (University of Chicago Press, 1992), p. 38.

6 Maya Lin, though only twenty-one at the time and as yet unknown, was an art student at Yale University, well-versed in the same modernist tradition as her older and more established compatriot, Richard Serra.

7 Detractors took umbrage at its black color, the fact that it "sinks" into the ground, its "unheroic" mass, and the reflective surface that confronts viewers with their own images superimposed upon the names of the dead.

8 "The sculpture as presently located has features of a purpresture . . . [:] 'An inclosure by a private person of a part of that which belongs to, and ought to be free and open to the enjoyment of the public at large,'" Judge Milton Pollack, *Richard Serra v. United States General Services Administration*, 667 F. Supp. 1042, 1056, n. 7 (S.D.N.Y 1987), cited in Barbara Hoffman, "Law for art's sake in the public realm," in Mitchell, ed., *Art and the Public Sphere*, p. 116.

9 Arthur Danto is a case in point. Writing in favor of the removal of *Tilted Arc*, he says: "The public has an interest in the existence of museums, but it also has an interest in not having all of its open spaces treated as though they were museums, in which esthetic [i.e., private] interests rightly dominate. The delicate architectural siting of *Tilted Arc* in Federal Plaza ignores the human realities of the place. Were he not blind to everything but the esthetic, Serra could learn something about human orientation to space and place. Standing where it does, *Tilted Arc* is the metal grin of the art world having bitten off a piece of the public world, which it means to hold in its teeth forever, the public be damned." Danto, *The State of the Art* (New York: Prentice-Hall Press, 1987), pp. 93–4.

10 Of course there are exceptions. Much of fascist public art preserves the heroic sublation of "the folk." It was the genius of Leni Riefenstahl to create of film an art form that exalted the ordinary to heroic proportions, inspiring people to identify with a non-individuated ideal whose magnificent "*Uebermenschlichkeit*" did not seem a contradiction.

11 From Goebbels's novel, *Michael* (1929), cited by Michael North, in "The public as sculpture: from heavenly city to mass ornament," from a prior citation in Elizabeth M. Wilkinson and L.A. Willoughby's introduction to Friedrich Schiller, *On the Aesthetic Education of Man* (Oxford: Clarendon Press, 1982), p. cxlii. See "The public as sculpture," in Mitchell, ed., *Art and the Public Sphere*, pp. 9–28.

12 North, "The public as sculpture," p. 23.

13 Douglas Crimp, "Redefining site specificity," in *On the Museum's Ruins* (MIT Press, 1993). Another discussion of a similar instance of site-displaced hostility may be found in James E. Young's account of Sol Lewitt's *Black Form*, an installation in Germany's "Skulptur Projekte 87" to commemorate the missing Jews of Münster. Like *Tilted Arc*, this work attracted graffiti and political slogans and many complaints that it obstructed traffic, and it too was removed barely a year after its dedication. See Young, "The counter-monument: memory against itself in Germany today," in Mitchell, ed., *Art and the Public Sphere*, pp. 49–79.

14 This, after all, is how most of Plato's dialogues do end.

15 Charles L. Griswold, "The Vietnam Veterans Memorial and the Washington Mall: philosophical thoughts on political iconography," in Mitchell, ed., *Art and the Public Sphere*, pp. 79–111.
   The response is sometimes unsympathetic to Lin. Frederick Hart, the producer of the "counter" memorial *Three Fighting Men*, which was installed a year afterward, said of Lin's memorial that it is "intentionally not meaningful. . . . a serene exercise in contemporary art done in a vacuum with no knowledge of the subject. It's nihilistic – that's its appeal," "An interview with Frederick Hart," inset in Elizabeth Hess, "A tale of two memorials," *Art in America* 71(4) (1983): 124.

16 North, "The public as sculpture," p. 28.

17 Courts do not regard all places where people gather as equally public. Streets and parks have "immemorially been held in trust for the use of the public," but even where theaters or other assembly sites are owned by governments, courts have found that public communication in them may be controlled by different standards. Not every open plaza is also a public forum and not every form of expression is equally permitted (Hoffman, "Law for Art's Sake").

18 There are, of course, exceptions to this superficiality. The waterfront development of New York's Battery Park City enlisted artists to create an environment that would foster neighborly interaction, and a community of sorts has in fact been produced.
   Another example of a project that builds civic consciousness is New York City's Arts for Transit program. Established in 1985, this program renews a principle intended by the

planners of the transportation system in 1899: "The railway and its equipment . . . constitute a great public work. All parts of the structure where exposed to public sight shall therefore be designed, constructed and maintained with view to the beauty of their appearance, as well as their efficiency" (cited from the initial construction contract in the brochure for the *Art en Route* exhibition, PaineWebber Art Gallery, New York, 1994). The contemporary mandate is to provide the public with an experience that is "interesting, stimulating and aesthetically pleasing." The public is in fact involved in a variety of ways:

    (a) By sometimes taking part in the selection of projects from among those submitted by artist proposals.

    (b) By sometimes contributing to the creative design or participating in its execution.

    (c) Through commemorative reference to local inhabitants, culture, history.

    (d) By responsiveness of the art to expressed neighborhood needs and interests (environmental, political, educational).

    (e) Through promotion of public awareness of the art and identification with it.

19 Napoleon created the first public museum, the Louvre, by nationalizing the formerly private palace and declaring its treasures national property. Citizens thereby gained access to the collection and could take pride in it, but it was the museum and not the art that was rendered public. If anything, the privacy of the aesthetic experience was intensified by the new emphasis on aesthetic sensibility and the educability of individual taste.

20 The complexity of this question is multiplied when the exhibiting institution does not even have the public status of a museum, but is a privately owned corporation, e.g., Paine-Webber, which opens its reception space to the public for an artistic display of artworks – models, maquettes, photographs, and drawings of works of (public) art whose realized embodiment as public art can be discovered simply by taking a ride on the (public) transportation system.

21 The critic, Patricia Phillips, observes that the millions of television viewers of the lighted apple's descent in New York's Times Square New Year's Eve celebration are as much a part of the public spectacle as are the thousands of witnesses on the street. Only the meaning of the word "public" has changed, becoming more "psychologically internalized" as a result of developments in urban and information systems. See Phillips, "Public art's critical condition," *On View* 1(1) (1990): 12.

22 Cited in Pam Korza, "Evaluating artistic quality in the public realm: a report of the *On View* symposium on public art, May 1989, Harvard University," *On View* 1(1) (1990): 76.

23 I would like to thank my co-symposiasts Gregg Horowitz and Michael Kelly, as well as the anonymous readers and the editor of the *Journal of Aesthetics and Art Criticism* for their helpful and incisive criticism.

27

PUBLIC ART/PUBLIC SPACE

The spectacle of the *Tilted Arc* controversy

Gregg M. Horowitz

On the night of March 15 1989, after a battle that lasted, not coincidentally, almost exactly as long as the Reagan presidency, Richard Serra's sculpture *Tilted Arc* was removed from Federal Plaza in lower Manhattan.[1] Because *Tilted Arc* was designed specifically for, and so in part derived its identity from, its site, its expulsion from Federal Plaza was at the same time its destruction. The agent of *Tilted Arc*'s demolition, the General Services Administration (GSA), was also the agent of its installation. The GSA is the federal agency responsible for the construction and maintenance of United States government property. Part of its mandate, the Art-in-Architecture program (AIA), is to devote one-half of one percent of the cost of the construction or repair of federal property to the funding of public art. After a standard procedure of proposal and review, *Tilted Arc* was installed in 1981. A few objections were raised immediately, but since expressions of displeasure are typical at first when any public art is installed, nothing came of them. However, in 1984, William Diamond, the Reagan appointee as GSA New York Regional Administrator, began to take an interest in the matter and provided a legitimating platform for the opponents of the sculpture. Diamond himself, despite having already spoken out against the work, convened a hearing at which the issue of *Tilted Arc*'s removal was aired publicly; 58 people testified in favor of removal, 122 against.[2] Nonetheless, the panel voted four to one for eviction. Serra fought the GSA in the courts until 1989, at which point, his appeals exhausted, the GSA was permitted to destroy *Tilted Arc*.

While *Tilted Arc* was by its nature a public spectacle, so too was the making of the decision about its fate. Serra's substantial reputation warranted coverage both by the general and the art media, and further attention was garnered by the oddity of the federal government pressing for a work of art to be destroyed. Ultimately, however, the essentially public nature of the dispute was guaranteed by Diamond's insistence on a public decision-making process. It was a quasi-democratic procedure at best, since

Diamond ignored the "polling" he himself initiated, but it was nevertheless a staged performance of democratic public deliberation over the fate of a work of public art. Much ink was spilled and many voices raised because the battle was propelled by the GSA into public scrutiny, and it is the public discourse about the fate of public space – specifically, the discourse of the protection of public space from public art – that is my central focus here.

Since so much has already been said about *Tilted Arc*, another analysis may not seem necessary. Nonetheless, in the years since the sculpture's destruction, events have occurred and trends have solidified which allow us to see more clearly what was at stake in getting rid of it. The battle over *Tilted Arc* was not simply a fight over a public artwork. It was also a piece of the struggle over the fate of public space in the American city, over its existence, the legitimation of claims upon it, and the role of art and aesthetic experience in opening up or closing down reflection on these issues. In addition, it was also an early version of the strategy of censorship-as-liberation used by regressive political forces in other antidemocratic projects. It is in light of these larger concerns that the public spectacle of the debate over *Tilted Arc* may be seen to be as significant as the spectacle of the sculpture itself. In a controversy in which public art was pitted against public space, with the federal government depicting itself as the defender of public space, we can see how the destiny of the very idea of public space and of certain forms of democratic political practice was being contested and also how opposition to critical art came to be a cover for antidemocratic tendencies.

Before beginning my discussion; let me stress again that my aim is to analyze the then-current opposition to *Tilted Arc* in order to reveal how it functioned or was made to function as part of a specific sociopolitical tendency (and a tendency which, once made explicit, might, in fact, not be endorsed by any particular opponent). Of course, establishing this point could not support, nor is it intended to support, the claims to permanency offered on behalf of *Tilted Arc* by Serra or his allies. As Michael Kelly argues elsewhere in this symposium, the arguments for those claims might well be defective. I will remain silent regarding that issue (although the silence ought not to be construed as backhanded derogation of those claims, either).

It follows from my self-imposed limits that I do not rule out the possibility of arguments in favor of the destruction of *Tilted Arc* other than those analyzed here. In a less charged and tendentious context, more subtle arguments about the relation between public art and urban public space might have been brought to bear; indeed, my analysis is offered in the hope of bringing to the surface some of the issues such arguments would have to confront. However, that the considerations I offer were not addressed is a constitutive feature of the spectacle of deciding *Tilted Arc*'s fate. The hearings convened by Diamond served to suppress the underlying issue of the disposition of public space, and it is along the tracks of that suppression that my discussion runs. Hence, although other arguments against *Tilted Arc*'s permanency are possible, unless they were to address the construction of the idea of "the public" used against the sculpture, they would remain irrelevant to my concerns here.[3]

Perhaps one final word is required in defense of returning to this case. After all, since *Tilted Arc* is a thing of the past, why dredge up old hurts yet again? Might not living in the distant past of the 1980s open us to the charge of a certain lugubrious fascination with dead issues? However, aside from the fact that similar cases continue to arise and that 1989, the year of *Tilted Arc*'s destruction, is really not so very long ago, the desire to move on to new cases which do not raise a ruckus is, I suggest, inappropriate. We should not treat the successful opposition to *Tilted Arc* as irrelevant to the relatively uncontroversial operation of some later AIA or percent-for-art programs; to do so would be to think as if the criteria for "successful" public art have developed innocently of the threat forged as the idea of "the public" in the Serra case. The papers in this symposium by Kelly and by Hilde Hein address the implications of this case for other instances of public art; nonetheless, if my analysis of the tone and nature of the opposition to *Tilted Arc* is correct, then any discussion of public art which does not wrestle with the issues raised by this case runs the risk of unconscious complicity with the enemies of democratic public space. In short, turning away from the Serra controversy, either in weariness or in an effort to be rigorously up-to-date, would be forward-looking only if a vision of the future of public art depends, as I think it does not, on turning a blind eye even to the recent past. Compliance with the imperative of progress is philosophically unbecoming when that imperative demands the public sacrifice of criticism in the name of reconciliation.

Diamond held his public hearings March 6–8, 1985. Three kinds of objections were raised: (1) *Tilted Arc* was an improper symbol of the functions housed in the courthouse, in the adjacent Jacob Javits Federal Building, and in the plaza itself; (2) the sculpture destroyed the original beauty of the plaza; and (3) it prevented the plaza from being used for other purposes. On the basis of these objections, the complainants entreated the government to remove *Tilted Arc* from their sight.[4]

I will begin with the objection that *Tilted Arc* was an improper symbol. In a November 1984 letter, Judge Edward Re of the United States Court of International Trade said that "this rusted steel barrier" undermines the goals of "provid[ing] proper identification for the Courthouse" and "generat[ing] respect for its symbol of justice" (p. 28). This political objection was seconded by Congressman Ted Weiss when he described the goal of AIA as "seeking to enhance the image of America through its government buildings by placing distinctive works of contemporary American art in public view" (p. 112). At first this objection seems much like the one that led to the erection of a realistic statue in the precinct established by Maya Lin's Vietnam Veterans Memorial in Washington, and perhaps this was what Re had in mind. As the Vietnam Veterans Memorial example demonstrates, the taste for affirmative symbols of grandeur grows in direct proportion to insecurity about the grandeur itself. And for Judge Re, an executive of the very justice he wanted to see respected in statuary, an affirmation of the glory of American justice might well also be a self-affirmation.

However, the second part of Weiss's gloss suggests a deeper and, in fact, more widely shared objection, that *Tilted Arc* was an improper symbol not of justice but of the beneficence of the federal government in providing something like amenities for the public. This objection, it should be noted, is different from another which I will consider, that *Tilted Arc*, in fact, fails to be an amenity or prevents the use of the plaza as an amenity. The issue Weiss raised has to do not with the usefulness of works of art but rather with their symbolism, a distinction that can be obscured too easily when what is being symbolized is the benevolent paternalism of providing objects for use. In this light, we might see the symbolic objection as directed at *Tilted Arc*'s obscuring of the liberal intentions of AIA itself.

The most revealing expression of the symbolic objection came in the decision handed down by Dwight Ink, Acting Administrator of the GSA, to remove *Tilted Arc*. In his summary, Ink observed that "those testifying in favor of relocation regarded the Plaza and the open space it symbolized much more highly than did those who favored retention" (p. 156). Notice the odd phrasing: not "the open space the plaza is" but "the open space it symbolized." At one level a plaza is by definition an open space in the sense that it has no enclosing structure on it. However, what Ink reveals here is that the plaza is not just an open space but is also a symbol of openness, of a freedom of movement provided by a benefactor. The openness of Federal Plaza is supposed to stand at the symbolic level for the real thing, real open space, and so for a kind of democratic accessibility. This symbolic displacement is especially important, since in a deeper sense of open, it is precisely open space that is tendentially absent from the postmodern city.

It is useful to consider how the plaza-as-symbol played a role in several fantasies about public life. Joseph Liebman, who worked in Federal Plaza, testified at the hearing in favor of removal by speaking not of what the plaza was before the arc was installed but rather of what it might have been. He needs to be quoted at length because of the stark intertwining in his remarks of fantasy and reality characteristic of attendance on the symbol.

> I have worked at 26 Federal Plaza since 1969. While the plaza never fulfilled all my expectations, at least until 1980, I regarded it as a relaxing reflective space where I could walk, sit, and contemplate in an unhurried manner. Every now and then, rays of sunshine bathed the plaza, creating new vistas and moods for its vibrant and unchallenged space.
>
> I remember those moments: I remember the cool spray of the fountain misting the hot air; I remember the band concerts; I remember the musical sounds of neighborhood children playing on the plaza, while their mothers, sheltered under the courthouse, rocked baby carriages, still minding their children at play. I

remember walking freely in the plaza, contemplating the examination of a witness, undisturbed by the presence of other people engaged in conversation or young lovers holding hands. I also remember my dreams of additional seating areas, of more cultural events, temporary outdoor exhibits of sculptures and paintings, ethnic dance festivals and children's shows.

(p. 111)

When we consider that in the seventeen years of the plaza's existence prior to *Tilted Arc* there were fewer than twenty public events, that other than the steps into the buildings there was no public seating except, of course, for the lip of the fountain because the fountain was usually dry, that the plaza is a notoriously windy site, we can see that Liebman's dream was blocked not by the sculpture but by the space itself. Liebman envisioned a festive, multiuse space which never existed, but for its nonexistence he blames the arc. Immediately following his list of what he calls dreams, he says, "All of those things are just memories now, ending with the installation of the *Tilted Arc*" (pp. 111–12). This was a typical response: the arc itself became a focal point not as a disturbance in public space but as a disturbance in the transparency of the plaza's symbolic effect.

Norman Steinlauf, another worker in the complex, made a similar point. Public art is an excellent idea, he said, because art transports us, if only for a moment, into a realm of personal meaning, but *Tilted Arc* "represent[s] an irritant and an impediment" (pp. 109–10). We should take Steinlauf's and Liebman's attention to representation literally, for it is closely attuned to the symbolic function of the plaza as a substitute for real public space, a function disturbed at the level of the symbol by the arc. *Tilted Arc* is not the cause of the deathliness of Federal Plaza, nor is it itself an impediment – instead, it prevents viewers of it from using the plaza merely to imagine the existence of an alternative public space. That *Tilted Arc* deprived people of the privilege of their illusions is, I believe, the reason it became a focus of dispute.

That Federal Plaza became the focus of fantasies about public space after the installation of *Tilted Arc* can also be seen in the second objection, that the sculpture destroyed some specific and concrete beautiful aspect of the plaza. While there might be a reasonable version of this objection which first identifies some such aspect and then demonstrates how *Tilted Arc* negated or attenuated it, it seems unimaginable that such an argument could be developed for this site (although, as I will show, whether there is a reasonable version is, in any case, irrelevant to the functioning of this objection). Federal Plaza is one of the ugliest projects in lower Manhattan, a final excrescence of the design standards characteristic of the federally funded urban renewal projects which destroyed several downtowns while trying to revalorize them economically. The ugliness of the complex is doubly determined. First, it has all the features of the degenerate utopianism of urban renewal; it is a set of building-machines, an efficiently organized office complex, plunked down in the middle of a mockery of a streetscape as if visible devotion to productivity at the office were in itself a human good. Federal Plaza, in other words, looks like government-corporate power in barely aestheticized form. Second, Federal Plaza was a late urban renewal project. It was completed in 1968, that fateful year when the combination of urban insurrection and student and labor unrest on the one hand and the expenses of overseas American adventurism on the other were leading toward reevaluations of the entire idea of federal urban "renewal." As the goal of the beautiful open city receded from view, so too did the money required for achieving it, and the ugly incompleteness of Federal Plaza is a result. Indeed, no public art was installed until 1981 precisely because no funds were available as construction was finished in 1968. Even if Federal Plaza had had the possibility of being beautiful, the commitment to making it so had vanished by the time it was built.

It is in light of the failure to beautify Federal Plaza that we can best grasp the insistent fantasies about its beauty. The plaza was held to be beautiful not because it is but because it had to be. As with so many of the urban revitalization projects of the 1950s and 1960s, unless there were spaces where the workers could sit during lunch hour to imagine release and relief, the brutality of the complexes would be overwhelmingly manifest. The open space was intended to provide the imaginary alternative to the utter routinization of work life, as Steinlauf's comment reveals. In the real absence of such an alternative, the insistence on the right to imagine it intensified. Only in this context can we make any sense at all of Re's objection that *Tilted Arc* "eliminated . . . the aesthetic vista of the plaza for thousands of New Yorkers, many of whom toil in windowless offices" (p. 28). Surely the aesthetic vista was eliminated by the lack of windows. However, rather than address the painful reality of the spatial brutalization effected by slotting people into blind office blocks, Re and others displaced what must have been a long-standing grievance onto a sculpture which highlighted the vistalessness of the space it occupied. One can only imagine thousands of New Yorkers sitting in windowless offices imagining not seeing the sculpture that is blocking their now merely aesthetic satisfaction.

At this point the argument seems to have returned to *Tilted Arc*'s primary crime in the eyes of its attackers, that it is an obstacle to imagining the existence of nonexistent public space. However, this return has a twist. The conception of publicity which played such a crucial ideological role in postwar urban renewal underwent a tendential transformation in the 1980s; public space, for many and complex reasons, went from being the civic center of urban life to a zone of danger and threat. The traditional ideal of a space of democratic public encounter evaporated in the movement to the cities of indoor malls, commercial theme parks, and inward-turning multiblock developments. The ideal of public space did not disappear – it just went private and so reappeared in a simulacrum. In a sense, then, the only public space many complainants against the arc wanted was a symbolic one, a space which, in its public nonpublicity, could serve as a comforting reminder of dangers avoided. Thus, one of the objections which hovered around the edges of the complaint that the plaza was rendered less useful by the sculpture is, in its phantasmic exaggeration, at the very heart of the matter. Margo Jacobs, a self-identified horse breeder, begins her testimony by dismissing the question of the aesthetic value of *Tilted Arc* as irrelevant to the issue at hand, since not only does it make the plaza less effective as a public space, it also makes it "possibly a dangerous place to be when a large number of people congregate at once, as they do in the political demonstrations we have all seen on the seven o'clock news" (p. 124). Jacobs apparently does not take part in the televisual demonstrations she watches at home; they are congregations of other people, people who use the space differently from her, people who, when in the plaza in the presence of the arc, constitute not a legitimate public but a danger. The crossing of the political and the public, just that intermingling blocked by the pseudo-public spaces of the 1980s metropolis, is here presented as a threat.

The fantasy of political danger crystallizing around the arc was most paranoiacally detailed by Vickie O'Dougherty, a GSA security specialist, who claimed that *Tilted Arc*'s curvature made it a blast wall for explosives. Perhaps so, but notice the remarkable slippage in O'Dougherty's testimony from activism to terrorism, from graffiti to violence, from the arc's possible use by terrorists to its being pro-terrorism:

> Now in past experience we have had several explosions on federal property by terrorists, activists. The principles that they used were twofold: they used many times this type of device – a wall or something like that to vent the explosion against the building. . . . It would, of course, take a larger bomb than which has been previously used to do this kind of, to destroy enough for their purposes; but it is possible, and lately we are expecting the worst in the federal sector. . . . Yes – most people do express their opinions against us in either violent ways or with graffiti and those other types of ways. We are considering right now many, many antiterrorist types of devices to install in the building, but we already have some that exist that are proterrorist.
>
> (p. 116)

As in Jacobs's objection, but in a more delirious form, the political use of public space, which is to say its use as public space, is systematically conflated with violence and terror. What is expelled as outside the protected precincts of urban enclosures, what in being expelled becomes alien, here returns already inflated into a danger as such and a danger to "legitimate" use.

A less fantastic dream of symbolic utilization can bring out how *Tilted Arc* could be made such a lightning rod. O'Dougherty and Jacobs express their fears of the urban directly and so overtly manifest an utter loss of the political desirability of public space, but Paul Goldstein, representative of Manhattan Community Board #1, exhibits a more subtle symptom of this loss:

This potentially wonderful area, which could easily be brought to life with more trees and benches, a working fountain, and lunchtime entertainment, has instead been turned into a virtual no-man's-land, and it must be recognized that Mr. Serra's sculpture has regrettably contributed to the public's rejection of this space. Many people are even bewildered when they are told that this large metal structure is not a piece of leftover construction material, but is, in fact, a piece of art. Its overwhelming size prevents the free-flowing circulation that the plaza was built to enhance, and in the minds of many the piece constitutes both a safety and a fire hazard.

(p. 126)

Goldstein's gentler and more carefully spoken objection acknowledges that Federal Plaza was a dead space even before the arc's installation; it was never useful, had never provided what it promised. His complaint, however, issues in a demand for a space of entertainment, not a public space but a space of private pleasure that happens to be in the middle of the city, and in this sense Goldstein's imagination is bound by the ideological transformation of the city characteristic of the 1980s. Nonetheless, in his barely audible utopian demand we can hear the tattered remains of a striving for alternatives, a signal that the cauterization of desire implicit in the malling of public space was, in 1985, still incomplete and unstable. But in directing this distorted utopian complaint not against the GSA or the general trends of 1980s urbanism but rather against *Tilted Arc*, Goldstein reveals the one legitimate use to which Federal Plaza could still be put, as an occasion to imagine alternatives. Caught between the abandonment of public space it now cannot be and its replacement by pseudo-public simulacrum, Federal Plaza becomes at most a site of desire and fantasy.

It is the use of Federal Plaza as a site of urban fantasy against which *Tilted Arc* offends. One complaint against the arc was that it interrupted free passage through the plaza. However, prior to the design's approval, Serra did studies requested by the GSA in which he chalked out various sitings to examine whether the arc would interfere with the routine passages from street to building and discovered that it would not. Furthermore, he left half the plaza open for social functions and gave the non-working fountain a wide berth.[5] *Tilted Arc* did not interfere at all with paths of transit; rather, it appeared to do so, but in the domain of fantasies of easy use that was exactly the problem. Serra did not cause the deadness and unusability of Federal Plaza, but he did make it manifest. As Roberta Smith observed in defending *Tilted Arc*, "It is not wide entertainment and it is not an escape from reality, but it does ask you to examine its own reality, its scale, its material, its tilted sweep, and so the other things around it" (p. 103). This may well be a proper function of a public artwork, to provoke critical reflection and dialogue on the space it occupies,[6] but at a moment when that space is both a sign of the powerlessness of those who pass through it and a focus for distorted

453

fantasies of liberation from potentially unpleasant encounters, the demand for critical reflection is sure to elicit hostility. *Tilted Arc* did not destroy a plaza, but it did, in its aggressive site-specificity, destroy a dream.

The demand for a usable public space expressed in the opposition to *Tilted Arc* was thus really a demand for a symbolic space, a fantasy center of an imaginary city, secured, mall-like, and heavily surveilled. It was this demand, so useful to an urban policy leaning toward privatization, the abandonment of the city to a destiny determined by corporate and financial capital, and the elimination of, precisely, spaces for criticism of that tendency, which was staged as a public outcry. Diamond convened a panel stacked with his own employees, sent out fliers inviting testimony at the supposedly neutral hearing, and so gave a platform to the heretofore random pleading for federal relief. Finally, despite the two-to-one ratio in favor of retaining *Tilted Arc*, Diamond recommended its destruction, defending his decision in a letter to Ink by presenting himself as a protector of the public interest. In a precursor to the surreal presidential campaign of Ross Perot, Diamond built himself a "public" he could then answer to responsibly. As Clara Weyergraf-Serra bitterly asked, "Where is direct democracy used other than to get rid of art?" (p. 88).

In short, the opposition to *Tilted Arc* was not just organized into a movement by a Reagan bureaucrat but was also then staged by him. The form of the drama was a contest between the public interest, represented by opposition to the arc, and the artworld, between the concern for open space and effete aesthetic concerns; this is a drama we have seen staged with increasing frequency and ferocity in the years since. In this conflict between a people and art, the government presents itself as an impartial mediator attempting to be fair to all and, in its "fairness," it then grants the request of that very public it had constructed for release from the obligation to criticize, in this case, the shape of urban policy. Diamond positioned himself as an ally of this public and, by removing *Tilted Arc*, doing the public the favor of saving it from art. In the process, he also "saved" the public from the critical reflection that would have led to a different, dangerous, more democratic discourse. Diamond's staging of the struggle over *Tilted Arc* forged an ideological alliance between the people and the processes of urban restructuration, between the demos and the tendential elimination of the space of democracy, at a moment when that alliance was necessary but still unsecured. Insofar as it was a critical work of art that was promoted to the status of the common enemy binding this alliance, the staging instantiated a regressive political strategy of censorship-as-liberation with the likes of which we are not yet done.[7]

NOTES

1   For helpful commentary and discussion on this essay, I would like to thank Idit Dobbs-Weinstein, Lydia Goehr, Thomas Huhn, Ellen Levy, and the anonymous referees for this journal.

2   These numbers are inherently misleading. Some of those who testified did so as representatives of groups. John Guare and Betty St. Clair, for instance, supported Serra as spokespeople for the Municipal Arts Society and the National Emergency Civil Liberties Committee, respectively, while Peter Hirsch and Paul Goldstein testified in favor of removal as representatives of the Association of Immigration Attorneys and Manhattan Community Board #1, respectively. Several others who testified invoked their titles and affiliations but noted that they were speaking as private citizens, as if there were some officially sanctioned alternative way to speak. Hence, the official numbers seem to represent larger constituencies, but they do so opaquely insofar as we do not know how to sum personal, semi-public, and institutional preferences.

3   It is for this reason that I will not discuss the published opposition to *Tilted Arc* of the several commentators and critics whose views, despite the more tempered tone made possible by written presentation, still did not get behind the veil of "the public." Arthur Danto, for example, argued in favor of the destruction of the sculpture in his typically urbane manner but nonetheless assumed just that integrity of the idea and fact of the public I am challenging. "Public art is the public transfigured: it is us," Danto wrote, "in the medium of artistic transformation," from which it follows that Serra's claims for the artistic integrity of *Tilted Arc* must take second place to the claims of the work's subject. This sentiment may be true. However, until we unpack the putatively integral "us" in the name of whom Danto speaks and, in so speaking, constructs as much as reports, it is not a counterargument to the analysis which follows. Arthur Danto, "*Tilted Arc* and public art," in *The State of the Art* (New York: Prentice-Hall Press, 1987), pp. 90–4.

4   The references in this essay are to original testimony and documents collected in *Richard Serra's* Tilted Arc, ed. Clara Weyergraf-Serra and Martha Buskirk (Eindhoven: Van Abbemuseum, 1988). Further citations will be referenced in the text.

5   A number of people testified at the hearing about Serra's having satisfied the concerns of the AIA review panel regarding these issues before *Tilted Arc*'s installation. See especially the testimony of Julia Brown, who had been the project manager for the GSA's AIA program, in Weyergraf-Serra and Buskirk, eds, *Richard Serra's* Tilted Arc, pp. 83–5. A detailed chronology of the proposal and review process can be found in Sherrill Jordan, project coordinator, *Public Art, Public Controversy: The* Tilted Arc *on Trial* (New York: ACA Books, 1987), pp. 49–56. It should be noted that Judith Balfe and Margaret Wyszomirski argue that neither Serra's pole-and-string sitings nor the model of *Tilted Arc* put on display prior to installation gave "an accurate impression of the mass and solidity of the artwork itself." However, if it is granted that such preliminary investigations did ascertain that pedestrian flow was not impeded, then "mass and solidity" here must mean perceived mass and solidity. The perception of mass and solidity, however, does not impede traffic. Balfe and Wyszomirski, "The commissioning of a work of public art," in Jordan, *Public Art and Public Controversy*, pp. 18–27.

6   Serra writes of site-specificity: "Based on the interdependence of work and site, site-specific works address the content and context of their site critically. A new behavioral and perceptual orientation to a site demands a new critical adjustment to one's experience of the place. Site-specific works primarily engender a dialogue with their surroundings." See Richard Serra, "*Tilted Arc* Destroyed," *Art in America* 77(5) (1989): 41.

7   In late 1993, Frank Stella's *The Town-Ho's Story* in the Robert Metcalfe Federal Building
    in Chicago became the object of protest. A petition complained that the work was com-
    missioned without proper community input despite the fact that the arts panel which
    approved it included local residents and officials. See "Stella sculpture prompts protest,"
    Art in America 81(12) (1993): 27. In 1994, Serra himself resigned a commission by the
    Fine Arts Museum of San Francisco after abusive commentary in the local press and his
    inability to gain assurances about the permanent siting of the as-yet unnamed sculpture.
    The attacks in this case began even before Serra had developed detailed proposals or ren-
    derings. Whether genuine *public* opposition killed this public artwork will have to be
    decided by the metaphysicians. See Patricia Failing, "An unsitely mess," *ARTnews* 93(8)
    (1994): 150–3.

28

PUBLIC ART CONTROVERSY

The Serra and Lin cases

Michael Kelly

The identity of the public in contemporary public art is amorphous, yet strong-willed and divisive. As a result, public art is riddled with controversy which is as perilous as it is vital for today's pluralistic culture. While some might want to argue that public art can serve only the ideological purpose of propagating a false sense of consensus in a society deeply divided about art, we need not aim toward consensus.[1] Discussions of public art might rather start from the recognition that complete consensus is impossible because the public comprises many different subspheres, organizations, and institutions, each with many voices in terms of race, gender, ethnicity, sexuality, and class. In Thomas Crow's words, the public is "nothing more nor less than a series of representations" laying claim to "the public."[2] Instead of consensus, debate and dialogue about these representations should be the mandate in public art.

This view of public art makes it difficult, however, to know who should make judgments when the inevitable controversies arise. According to what procedures and criteria should we judge? How are the public's manifold identities best represented while the commitment to pluralism is respected? Two recent examples of public art – Richard Serra's *Tilted Arc* and Maya Lin's Vietnam Veterans Memorial – provide some guidelines – negative and positive, respectively – about how these controversies might be adjudicated without compromising or abandoning public art. My aim here is to explore the middle ground between crippling controversy and concocted consensus in contemporary public art.

Although both examples stem from the 1980s, they have radically transformed, in ways Hilde Hein discusses above, how public art is now understood, created, and treated in the United States. Since these transformations have not been fully comprehended philosophically, it is still important to examine the arguments underlying the cases that provoked them, as Gregg Horowitz does above in the case against Serra. Finally, while I am critical of Serra's legal defense against the removal of *Tilted Arc* from Federal Plaza, I will not comment on whether it should have been removed; there may be reasons why it should have remained even if his site-specificity defense is unconvincing, as I will argue it is. My interest here, which explains my preference for Lin's public art, is to see how we might better understand the "public(s)" of public art.

I

Serra's *Tilted Arc* was commissioned by the General Services Administration (GSA), selected by a National Endowment for the Arts panel, and installed in the public plaza of a federal office building complex in downtown Manhattan in 1981.[3] Backed by people who worked in the buildings around the plaza, a judge and a GSA administrator initiated a legal battle in 1985 to have *Tilted Arc* removed because its 12-foot height and 120-foot length of cortan steel obstructed the public's use of the open plaza. After numerous public hearings and court sessions over several years, which Horowitz analyzes above, the final judgment in 1988 was that the sculpture could be removed since the concerns of the public who lived and worked near the plaza had more legal weight than those of a single artist or the professional artworld. Thus it could be said that a conflict between two publics – the artworld and the people who use Federal Plaza – was resolved in the latter's favor. Serra has subsequently retreated from public art projects, at least in the United States.[4]

When Lin won the 1981 veterans-sponsored national competition for the design of the Vietnam Veterans Memorial in Washington, DC, some other veterans and members of the public (for example, some in Congress) vigorously objected to the choice of her design (from among 1,421 alternatives), arguing that it was nonrepresentative and unheroic, and thus would remind citizens more of individual death and national defeat than of the war's mission. These critics preferred a more traditional war memorial promoting patriotism. Since the Vietnam Veterans Memorial was unveiled in 1982, however, it has been overwhelmingly supported by the viewing public at large, making it year after year the most visited monument in Washington. While these visitors have judged the memorial largely on the basis of personal experiences of the Vietnam War rather than in terms of issues about public art, their experiences at the memorial have been occasioned by the artist's handling of its public site. Since she completed the Vietnam Veterans Memorial, Lin has created other equally successful, if less grand, public artworks.[5]

What the Serra and Lin cases have in common is that a small group of people selected a work of art and, in effect, decided in the name of the public what its art should be. The public disagreed among itself, with different groups testifying on behalf of competing interpretations of the public's identity (interests and rights).[6] If the controversies about public art always involve such interpretive conflict, how can they be adjudicated without imposing a singular identity on the public or indulging in the mere play of multiple identities? Moreover, what is the relationship between this issue of "the public" and the rights and responsibilities of the artist engaged in public art? Because of the way the design for the Vietnam Veterans Memorial was selected, and especially because of the way Lin understood the public(s) with which she was dealing, I think her example of public art remains a positive model for thinking about these questions. And because the notion of site-specificity can serve as a link between the two questions, it will be the focus of my analysis of the Serra and Lin cases.

II

According to Barbara Hoffman, a legal theorist and practicing attorney specializing in art law, Serra alleged in federal district court in New York City that

> the GSA's decision to remove the sculpture violated his rights under (1) the Free Speech Clause of the First Amendment, (2) the Due Process Clause of the Fifth Amendment, (3) federal trademark and copyright laws, and (4) state moral rights law.[7]

Judge Milton Pollack, who presided over this case, dismissed (3) and (4) for lack of subject matter jurisdiction; and he granted summary judgment to the appellees on (1) and (2) because the decision to relocate *Tilted Arc* was deemed content neutral. In his appeal, Serra emphasized (1) and (2) again after abandoning a moral rights appeal at the last minute. He argued that once *Tilted Arc* was installed, it was protected by the First Amendment. The New York Supreme Court adjudicated the appeal by deciding (a) that Serra's free-speech rights were not violated because he relinquished them voluntarily when he sold *Tilted Arc* to the GSA and (b) that, again, the GSA's decision was content neutral since its concern was to restore public space, not to restrict individual artistic expression.

The linchpin of Serra's defense throughout the proceedings was – in the court's eyes and Serra's words (and those of his defenders) – the notion of site-specificity: "the existence of a cognizable legal relationship between the site and the artwork, which prevented its relocation or removal."[8] If *Tilted Arc* were site-specific, to remove it would be to destroy it. The presiding judge argued in the end, however, that *Tilted Arc* was not site-specific, because to be specific to Federal Plaza, it had to be public, but it was not:

> The sculpture as presently located has features of a purpresture . . . [:] "An inclosure by a private person of a part of that which belongs to, and ought to be free and open to the enjoyment of the public at large."[9]

Tilted Arc was merely a private sculpture located in a public space, rather than a work public art specific to a particular public site; that is, Serra privatized a public space instead of creating a public sculpture in it. Since *Tilted Arc* was not site-specific, the court judged that the public was not destroying it by removing it; rather, the public was merely reclaiming a site for its own purposes.[10] Serra thus undermined his own case by not securing the linchpin – site-specificity – of his defense.[11]

The defense of *Tilted Arc* based on site-specificity depended on the meaning of "public" in the senses of both the people and the space of Federal Plaza. Because of Serra's treatment of these two senses, however, *Tilted Arc* was not public and not site-specific. Such treatment reveals in more detail the inadequacy of Serra's understanding of site-specificity. It is not that he had to appease all the publics of Federal Plaza, but that he deliberately ignored and even defied them by the way he practiced site-specificity. This attitude – only implicit in the trial but, I think, embodied in *Tilted Arc* – added further support to the court's judgment.

Serra did not regard the public who experienced *Tilted Arc* as people who had legitimate, aesthetic and other claims on Federal Plaza. He was actually rather candid on this issue: "If you are conceiving a piece for a public place, a place and space that people walk through, one has to consider the traffic flow."[12] So Serra thought of the "public" as "traffic," as anonymous people who were taken into consideration only insofar as they could be expected to have peripatetic perceptual experiences of his sculpture in a behavioral space of his design: "The work I make does not allow for experience outside the conventions of sculpture as sculpture."[13] *Tilted Arc* was situated to encompass "the people who walk on the plaza as *its* volume . . . to bring the viewer into the sculpture."[14]

While it is difficult to define the public in this or any other case of public art, the court deemed it reasonable to regard the public, whoever it is, as more than traffic. The identity of this "more" is, of course, the issue. We enter here the explicitly public level of public art. Serra refused to consider this level at all; for he did not want to "worry about the indigenous community, and get caught up in the politics of the site."[15] That is, he refused to deal with the public on whose behalf the GSA implicitly acted when it commissioned him to create a sculpture for Federal Plaza.[16] But as the court argued, the minimum – and, I should think, noncontroversial – point is that to be public, art must be created with a recognition on the artist's part of the people who constitute the "public" of public art, whoever they are. For Serra, this would have meant recognizing the identities and rights of the different publics associated with Federal Plaza in various ways (working, living, visiting). He defiantly did not recognize the public in any of these senses.[17] So again, *Tilted Arc* was not public and not site-specific.

Serra treated Federal Plaza itself as a space constituted more by aesthetic than by public issues. He stated, for example, that the purpose of *Tilted Arc* was not only to redefine people's experience of Federal Plaza by the placement, size, and tilt of the sculpture, but to alter the space itself: "After the piece is created, the space will be understood primarily as a function of the sculpture."[18] While the redefinition of a space by a sculpture may be consistent with the idea of site-specificity (at least if it is understood primarily, if not exclusively, in formal-aesthetic terms, as it was by Serra and his defenders), it alone is not sufficient to make art site-specific; for the sculpture, in turn, has to be shaped by this same space in order to be considered specific to its site.[19] That is, while the idea of site-specificity implies a reciprocity between space and sculpture, Serra's understanding of this idea was one-sided, judging by his own statements: "in my urban site-specific works the internal structure responds to external conditions, but ultimately the attention is focused on the sculpture itself."[20]

What was deficient about Serra's idea of site-specificity was not only its one-sidedness, however, because there were also problems with the way he understood the one side of site-specificity to which he confined his energies. For in making *Tilted Arc* for Federal Plaza, he had something else in mind other than the public nature of that space. His stated goal was to dislocate the decorative aspects of Federal Plaza as designed by architects: "I've found a way to dislocate or alter the decorative function of the plaza and actively bring people into the sculpture's context."[21] He wanted to challenge the tendency within architecture at the time to treat public sculpture as mere decoration for buildings. If this was Serra's concern, however, then his claim about site-specificity was rather a claim about the autonomy of sculpture vis-à-vis architecture. Though this claim is legitimate, it had little, if anything, to do with *public* art. For even though Serra's battle with architecture took place in public in this case, it could have taken place in a private space just as easily, whether indoors or outdoors.

Moreover, in the context of this same battle, Serra consciously adopted a posture of avant-garde art toward the public of Federal Plaza. He hoped to enlighten people about public space by insisting that they recognize his sculpture separate from the architecturally defined space of Federal Plaza. His strategy backfired. The public – as amorphous as it was – rejected Serra's offer to be enlightened and reciprocated the confrontational gesture by blocking his efforts to redefine their space without being consulted. In effect, there was a conflict between Serra's commitment to site-specificity and his avant-garde campaign for autonomous sculpture, and he unequivocally privileged the latter.

A further problem with Serra's understanding of the notion of site-specificity was that, for him, it may have had more to do with a critique of the commodification of art galleries than with public art.[22] He thought that if his art were taken out of commercial art galleries and museums and repositioned in the public sphere using site-specificity as its theoretical basis, it would no longer be a commodity: "Urban and landscape work built in place [i.e., site-specific] by-passes commerce and cultural institutions by not being available for secondary sales or confinement in the ahistorical space of the museum."[23] Serra was right that there is generally no resale market for public art and that museums are typically understood as ahistorical spaces. But he was mistaken in thinking that by relocating his art to the public sphere he escaped the commodification of art. Artists do not receive a percentage of the resales of their art, but they do benefit concretely, if indirectly, because the resales can escalate the future prices of their art in the primary market (of galleries). Similarly, there are escalating fees or increased opportunities for artists who do public art and who are at the same time successful in the primary market. Serra is, in fact, a perfect example of this: he has had the best of both markets. He need not be faulted for this, but he should not confuse the issue of commodification with that of site-specificity. Serra's confusion here was due to his overconfidence in art's ability to overcome commodification simply by being placed in public spaces.[24]

A final weakness of Serra's understanding of site-specificity concerns his view of the process for making decisions about public art. He seems to prefer to work in countries with strong governments which are not directly responsible to the public, that is, which are less democratic than the United States, the home of the public expected to live with *Tilted Arc*. This preference has led him to work and live mostly in Europe, especially in Germany and France, where there is, by his account, less democracy, at least in dealing with public art.[25] Since the public sphere in the United States is defined by a commitment to democracy – whether that commitment is always fully and fairly adhered to is another question – Serra's lack of respect for democracy with regard to matters of public art demonstrates once again that his public art was not site-specific, for he did not take the specificity of his public into consideration in defining his "site."

All the above problems with Serra's notion of site-specificity, the linchpin of his legal defense, had the serious consequence of weakening his claim that his First Amendment right to free speech was violated by the GSA when it removed the sculpture. For if *Tilted Arc* was not site-specific, then Serra's freedom of speech was not violated when the sculpture was removed. The court decided that while Serra had every right in principle to express himself, he had no particular right to do so in Federal Plaza, which was deemed a "limited public forum" where restrictions on speech are allowed so long as they are content neutral.[26]

III

In contrast to Serra's *Tilted Arc*, the entire process surrounding Lin's Vietnam Veterans Memorial was a much more promising model of how to deal with public art and all its attending controversies. Veterans, members of the using public, were the memorial's principal organizers from the first initiatives through the dedication. They raised the money, arranged the architectural competition, chose the jury that selected Lin's design, oversaw the construction, and led the dedication ceremony. In all these steps, official

Washington politicians were left out of the picture so that the veterans would not be dependent on Congressional approval, and thus would not have to resolve the deeply partisan debates among veterans, members of Congress, and the general public about the wisdom of the Vietnam War. Congressional approval was required only for the land on the Mall where the memorial is now situated, and it was mainly at that stage of the process that the public debate heated up. Some critics tried to stop the project by challenging its funding, but they were unable to do so because funding was provided largely by "private" (nongovernmental) sources through a direct-mail campaign to the general "public."[27] But the organizers and the designer of the Vietnam Veterans Memorial were attuned to their using public from the start, putting them in a good position to defend the memorial to the public before, during, and after it was built.

Lin and the organizers of the Vietnam Veterans Memorial were not politically neutral or naive in treating the controversy about the Vietnam War. On the contrary, they were politically astute in recognizing just how complex the American people's feelings are about that war. Evidence of this astuteness is that one of the veterans' conditions on the design of the memorial was that it "make no political statement regarding the war or its conduct,"[28] but rather dedicate the memorial to the veterans, not to the war itself – hence the name, Vietnam *Veterans* Memorial. Another principal condition was that it "be reflective and contemplative in nature,"[29] allowing the surviving veterans to meditate on the Vietnam War, individually and collectively, in all its tragic complexity.

There are, of course, many reasons why the Vietnam Veterans Memorial has been so successful. Most important is undoubtedly the architectural and sculptural ingenuity with which Lin transformed the conditions of the veterans committee into a sublime memorial. A contributing factor to its success, however, is certainly the process through which it was selected; for in contrast to the Serra case, the public generally feels that the memorial is its own rather than a sculpture belonging to an artist who regards them as traffic. Another reason for this success, which is related to the other two reasons – and may help to clarify them – is that the Vietnam Veterans Memorial is site-specific in precisely the senses that *Tilted Arc* was not.

The first sense in which the Vietnam Veterans Memorial is site-specific is that because Lin designed it without presuming to resolve the debate about the Vietnam War, many individuals and "publics" are duly represented by her memorial. In Michael North's words, "to view the piece is not simply to experience space," as was the case with *Tilted Arc*, "but also to enter a debate."[30] If the task of public art is to keep debate alive, allowing it to be as rational as it is impassioned and open-ended rather than aimed at consensus, Lin has succeeded in creating exemplary public art.[31]

The second sense of site-specificity, having more to do with space than with people, is that the Vietnam Veterans Memorial's two granite walls, which cover 450 feet and meet at an apex, were veneered so that they could reflect the surrounding space: the Lincoln Memorial on one side, the Washington Monument on the other, linking the

Vietnam Veterans Memorial with two other memorials commemorating divisive wars in American history.[32] The surface of the memorial also reflects the individuals looking at it, which, though it could easily intimidate people, seems to make the memorial more intimate by projecting living bodies onto the 58,196 names of dead soldiers. At the same time, Lin accentuated the time frame of the war by listing the names chronologically according to when the soldiers died, rather than alphabetically, so that the inscribed walls stretch from the first (1959) to the last (1975) death.[33] Visitors' experiences of this time frame are further heightened by the fact that the names start from the middle of the apex, go out to the right end, then continue back in the middle, concluding at the left end. This orchestration of the visitors engages them more directly by drawing them back into the apex rather than letting them file past the names. In addition, the walls are sunken so that people have to walk below grade into the earth to visit the names of the dead, bringing them down as many as ten feet into a site that is part of a larger sacred memorial ground.

It is important to note that, in contrast to Serra again, who brought viewers of *Tilted Arc* into its space so that they could experience *his* sculpture and *his* idea of architectural space,[34] Lin brings viewers in so that they can experience the *subject matter* of the memorial both individually and collectively, personally and publicly.[35] And whereas Serra set up an opposition between sculpture and architecture, Lin approached her site as an architect would, according to Judith E. Stein, "by creating space and place, providing a physical context for viewers' experience."[36] In addition, while art experts were involved in the selection of Lin's design, they were chosen and guided by the veterans. So the public guided the artist here, whereas the artist insisted on maneuvering the public in the Serra case. In short, Lin's sensitivity to the memorial's site, as well as to the issue that occasioned its being built, allows visitors to revisit the Vietnam War on their own terms.

Of the three senses of site-specificity that arose in the Serra case – legal, and the two senses of public: people and space – Lin has been more successful than Serra in dealing with all three, though the second two have been more prominent in her case since there were no legal proceedings.[37] Lin worked with rather than against the people and space of the memorial site; in her own words, she was "not combative but additive."[38] She recognized that there were already enough memories of combat for the American public to deal with and that her task was to design a site that would provide these memories a public space to breathe without her or anyone else pretending to reach a consensus on the war. This, it seems to me, is a much more constructive way to handle divisive issues in and about public art.

IV

In W.J.T. Mitchell's recent discussion of public art, he, too, focuses on the Serra and Lin cases, offering two conflicting types of interpretations for each case which are helpful in summarizing and concluding my analysis.[39] He suggests that Serra's *Tilted Arc* can be seen *either* as "a classic instance of the high modernist transformation of a utilitarian public space into an aesthetic form" *or* as "a signal that modernism can no longer mediate public and private spheres on its own terms, but must submit itself to social negotiation."[40] Mitchell believes that the first interpretive option is a form of critique; in trying to transform a (dysfunctional) utilitarian Federal Plaza into an aesthetic space, for example, Serra was engaged in a critique of that particular public space. Many of Serra's advocates in the court hearings made claims of this sort, arguing that *Tilted Arc* had the *effect* of criticizing Federal Plaza – regardless of Serra's intentions, designs, or words – by revealing its dysfunctional state.[41] While exposing these problems, however, *Tilted Arc* also compounded them and soon became the scapegoat when people decided to do something about them. What they achieved by removing *Tilted Arc*, on this account, was at best a restoration of Federal Plaza to a more tolerable, but still dysfunctional state. All this may be true, but it does not make *Tilted Arc* critical; for only if it had been site-specific to Federal Plaza could it have functioned as a critique of it.[42] Neither Serra's words nor *Tilted Arc* itself support this interpretation, if, as I have argued, it was not site-specific because he did not take the public as people and space into consideration.

I would rather agree with the second of Mitchell's two ways of interpreting *Tilted Arc*. What we have learned about public art from the Serra case is that artists working on public art can no longer mediate their relations with the public on their own (modernist aesthetic) terms (which, as Hein argues above, privilege the "private" over the "public"). They must now submit themselves to negotiations with the public, as Serra now acknowledges,[43] about what is, after all, its art. This is precisely what happened in the Lin case. And it is certainly how public art has been practiced since these two cases first unfolded, which is why they remain relevant to public art today.

Lin's Vietnam Veterans Memorial is poised, according to Mitchell, between the utopian and the critical;[44] for "it can be experienced both as an object of national mourning and reconciliation that is absolutely inclusive, embracing, and democratic, and as a critical parody and inversion of the traditional war memorial."[45] I agree with Mitchell that Lin's memorial is utopian, but only with this important qualification: it does not achieve nor even aspire to reconciliation. In fact, its strength depends, I think, on the lack of public reconciliation about the Vietnam War. Were the American public ever to come to a consensus about that war, the Vietnam Veterans Memorial would possibly become merely a large tombstone.

But I disagree that the Vietnam Veterans Memorial is critical in the way he describes.

Rather, I think it is critical by being utopian; that is, contrary to Mitchell, I do not think critique here involves parody. Parody typically ends without offering an alternative, which would mean in the Lin case that a parody of war memorials would expose the patriotic ideology our war memorials traditionally embody, but would do so without suggesting an alternative to that tradition. This would not be an accurate description of the Vietnam Veterans Memorial, however, for it is a counter*monument*, not just *counter* monuments. That is, while Lin is indeed critical of other memorials, she is so only by showing what else a memorial can be, by raising the standards for future public art projects in a pluralistic culture, several of which Lin herself has already created. The Vietnam Veterans Memorial is not a public statement about individual artistic rights or about the rights of sculpture in relation to architecture (Serra), but rather is a site for public and personal expression about Vietnam, for the public(s) to exercise its right to express itself on this issue in different and competing ways.

In conclusion, Lin's understanding and practice of public art is preferable to Serra's, because she has helped to guide us out of the modernist impasse in dealing with public art by showing how controversy can be handled without imposing any one set of aesthetic principles or political beliefs on the public(s).[46]

NOTES

1 See, for example, the articles in *The Phantom Public Sphere*, ed. Bruce Robbins (University of Minnesota Press, 1993).

2 Thomas Crow, *Painters and the Public Sphere in Eighteenth-Century Paris* (Yale University Press, 1985), p. 102.

3 For documentation, see *Richard Serra's* Tilted Arc, eds Clara Weyergraf-Serra and Martha Buskirk (Eindhoven: Van Abbemuseum, 1988).

4 A relevant and recent exception was the commissioned but then canceled project in San Francisco. See Horowitz, chapter 27 above, note 7.

5 The Civil Rights Memorial in Montgomery, Alabama; and the *Women's Table* at Yale University. By her own account, however, Lin has now retired from public memorials; see her comments in *Maya Lin: Public/Private* (Columbus: Wexner Center for the Arts, 1994), p. 29.

6 In the Serra case: his wife; the people from GSA; art professionals; lawyers; politicians; people living near Federal plaza; employees of the Federal office building. In the Lin case: mostly veterans groups and members of Congress.

7 Barbara Hoffman, "Law for art's sake in the public realm," in *Art and the Public Sphere*, ed. W.J.T. Mitchell (University of Chicago Press, 1992), pp. 113–46, here pp. 121–2.

8 Hoffman, "Law for art's sake," p. 122. Clara Weyergraf-Serra, Serra's wife, also identifies site-specificity as the pivotal point in Serra's defense.

9 Judge Milton Pollack, *Richard Serra v. United States General Services Administration*, 667 F. Supp. 1042, 1056, n. 7 (S.D.N.Y 1987) – quoted by Hoffman in "Law for art's sake," p. 116.

10 Cf. Horowitz's analysis above, in which he distinguishes between the real and the imagined purposes of Federal Plaza as expressed by the opponents of *Tilted Arc.*

11 Despite Serra's apparent commitment throughout his career to the notion of site-specificity, the judge's finding should not have surprised him, for he once said: "Ideally, I suppose, I would prefer to have a private space in a public situation." See Richard Serra, *Writings Interviews* (University of Chicago Press, 1994), p. 106. Perhaps this is why Serra's major "public" art project to date is in a remote part of Iceland where there is no public to conflict with his art.

12 Ibid., p. 49.

13 Ibid., p. 117. According to Eleanor Heartney, *Tilted Arc* was, as a piece of public art, "the product of the artist's desire to treat the plaza as an abstract space regardless of its function and meaning within the urban fabric," in *Culture Wars: Documents from the Recent Controversies in the Arts*, ed. Richard Bolton (New York: New Press, 1992), p. 141.

14 Serra, *Writings Interviews*, p. 127, emphasis added.

15 Ibid.

16 As Virginia Maksymowicz has argued in connection with this case, "[w]hen such considerations are sidestepped, public art ceases to be public." See "Alternative approaches to public art," in Mitchell, ed., *Art and the Public Sphere*, pp. 147–57, p. 155. See also Patricia C. Phillips, "Temporality and public art," in *Critical Issues in Public Art: Content, Context, and Controversy*, eds Harriet F. Senie and Sally Webster (New York: HarperCollins, 1992), pp. 295–304, esp. pp. 297–8: "public art is not public just because it is . . . in some identifiable public space . . .; it is public because it is a manifestation of art activities and strategies that take the idea of public as the genesis and subject for analysis."

17 In a public hearing in 1985, Serra claimed that in his original design he explicitly addressed the types of concerns the public eventually raised in their opposition to *Tilted Arc*. But I think the quotes from Serra in the last few pages make it clear that his claim was inaccurate.

18 Serra, *Writings Interviews*, p. 127.

19 Cf. Rosalyn Deutsche, "Public art and its uses," in Senie and Webster, eds, *Critical Issues in Public Art*, pp. 158–70, p. 160: "It is . . . insufficient to support site specificity by simply stating that a work like Richard Serra's *Tilted Arc* intervenes in the city in order to redefine space as the site of sculpture. . . . For in its own way *Tilted Arc* still floats above its urban site."

20 Serra, *Writings Interviews*, p. 138.

21 Ibid., p. 127; cf. also Weyergraf-Serra and Buskirk, eds, *Richard Serra's* Tilted Arc, p. 189. This point potentially undercuts Serra's procedural claim that, based on his contract with the GSA, *Tilted Arc* should be permanent. His attitude about permanence is deeply ambiguous; elsewhere, he says that "Permanence implies value, and notions of value tend to reinforce the trustees' thinking about the potential of money," *Writings Interviews*, p. 108. He is against this kind of permanence, but for the permanence of his own artwork, at least in this case.

22 Serra was also critiquing the minimalist notion of site-specificity for being limited to galleries and museums.

23 Serra, *Writings Interviews*, p. 117.

24 There is an important distinction concerning public art and the issue of commodification, namely, that public art monies are handled largely by governmental agents rather than by private citizens. At the same time, however, these monies come from taxes on those same citizens who, in turn, make decisions, directly or indirectly, about which public art is funded (often by supplementing public money with private donations).

I do not mean to suggest here that art cannot critique its commodity status. There are several strategies for doing so which are, I think, more effective than Serra's; for example, see *Hans Haacke: Unfinished Business*, ed. B. Wallis (MIT Press, 1986).

25 Serra, *Writings Interviews*, pp. 225–7. See John Rockwell, "An artist a lot more at home away from home," in *The New York Times*, Monday, 14 June 1993, section C, pp. 11, 14, in which Clara Weyergraf-Serra (who speaks for Serra on occasion as his manager) says: "I have come to realize that democracy doesn't work all that well when it comes to integrating art and the public." "I don't think you can include a community in that kind of decision-making process. But a government can educate a community. That's almost non-existent in America, but they have been very good at it in France."

26 That is, having rejected Serra's claim that *Tilted Arc* was site-specific the court also rejected his point that he could express himself through *Tilted Arc* only in Federal Plaza. His right to free expression and speech as well as his particular expression in the form of *Tilted Arc*, therefore survived the removal of the sculpture from Federal Plaza. As far as I know, however, *Tilted Arc* is in a warehouse somewhere in the New York City metropolitan area.

Hoffman clarifies the governmental limits on free speech as follows: in a *public forum*, such as a street or park, content-based speech can be restricted only to serve a compelling state interest and then only in the least restrictive manner; in a *limited public forum*, i.e., areas dedicated to speech such as city theaters, objections to content cannot be raised; a *nonpublic forum*, on the other hand, is subject to content and speaker-identity restrictions in light of the purpose the forum is intended to serve. See "Law for art's sake," p. 133.

27 The opponents of the Vietnam Veterans Memorial, led by Ross Perot, did succeed in having a second memorial built on the Washington Mall: *Three Fighting Men*, designed by Frederick Hart. This helped to diffuse the opposition to the Vietnam Veterans Memorial.

28 *Maya Lin: Public/Private*, p. 31.

29 Ibid.

30 Michael North, "The public as sculpture: from heavenly city to mass ornament," in Mitchell, ed., *Art and the Public Sphere*, pp. 9–28, here p. 25.

31 According to the American cultural historian Michael Warner, there are a number of ways to describe public subjectivity or identity: "as a universalizing transcendence, as ideological repression, as utopian wish, as schizocapitalist vertigo, or simply as a routine difference of register." See Warner, "The mass public and the mass subject," in Robbins, ed., *The Phantom Public Sphere*, pp. 234–56, here p. 234.

32 For a lengthy analysis of this memorial in relation to the others around it, see Charles L. Griswold, "The Vietnam Veterans Memorial and the Washington Mall: philosophical thoughts on political iconography," in Mitchell, ed., *Art and Public Sphere*, pp. 79–111.

33 The reflective quality of the walls was linked to this time frame. Lin says she wanted "to return the vets to the time-frame of the war and in the process, I wanted them to see their own reflections in the names," *Maya Lin: Public/Private*, p. 31.

34 According to Douglas Crimp, Serra's "egotism" here is merely a reflection of "the truth of our social condition." See Crimp, "Redefining site specificity," in his *On the Museum's Ruins* (MIT Press, 1993), p. 179. But if this is true, he is simply part of the problem, not a critic of it.

35 In the two essays in the Mitchell volume in which the Serra and Lin cases are discussed – by Griswold and by Mitchell himself – Serra's name is always and often mentioned in connection with *Tilted Arc*, while Lin's name is rarely if ever mentioned in connection with the Vietnam Veterans Memorial, except in footnotes. While this difference in how the two artists are mentioned may reflect the gender prejudice in how male and female artists are treated in art-critical literature, it also reveals these two artists' distinct attitudes about public art.

36 Judith E. Stein, "Space and place," *Art in America* 82(12) (1994): 67.

37 The legal issue came up briefly when there was an effort made by opponents to Lin's design to make some changes in it (cf. note 27 above); the threat of such changes, which were not made, raised the issues of the artist's freedom of expression and the art object's integrity which, as we saw, also arose in Serra's case.

38 *Maya Lin: Public/Private*, p. 26.

39 Mitchell, "Introduction: Utopia and critique," in Mitchell, ed., *Art and the Public Sphere*, pp. 1–5.

40 Ibid., p. 3. To explain what Mitchell means by modernism's "own terms," its presumption of autonomy, we need only quote from Serra: "I've never felt, and I don't now, that art needs any justification outside itself." See Serra, *Writings/Interviews*, p. 41.

41 Cf. the Weyergraf-Serra volume. And see Crimp's "Redefining site specificity": "The genuine importance of *Tilted Arc* can best be understood through an analysis of the crisis that it precipitated within established cultural policy" (p. 176), namely, "to insist on the necessity for art to fulfill its own functions rather than those relegated to it by its governing institutions and discourses" (p. 179). While Crimp's article, originally published in a catalog in 1986 for a Serra exhibition at the Museum of Modern Art, is perhaps the most extensive argument for the site-specificity of *Tilted Arc* in terms of "the public," he tends to understand by "the public" only the state powers that occupied the buildings around Federal Plaza. But *Tilted Arc* was not threatened by "governing institutions and discourses." For while it is true that some of the people who opposed *Tilted Arc* were indeed federal and state employees, they were not the majority, and most of those employees spoke as individuals rather than as officials of the government. My main response to Crimp's analysis, however, is that although important issues about art and public policy were raised in the course of the proceedings surrounding the removal of *Tilted Arc*, those issues say nothing about the site-specificity of *Tilted Arc*. Serra's sculpture was merely an occasion around which those issues were raised, but some might never have been raised, and some would have been more convincing, had *Tilted Arc* been site-specific.

42 Could it be that the opponents of *Tilted Arc* who had vivid, if inaccurate, memories of what Federal Plaza was before it was installed were actually the critics here instead of Serra?

43 Serra, *Writings Interviews*, pp. 221, 227.

44 In "Introduction: Utopia and critique," p. 3, Mitchell introduces a dialectic between the *utopian* and *critical* relations between art and its public: "on the one hand, art that attempts to raise up an ideal public sphere, a nonsite, an imaginary landscape . . .; on the other hand, art that disrupts the image of a pacified, utopian public sphere, that exposes contradictions and adopts an ironic, subversive relation to the public it addresses, and the public space where it appears."

45 Ibid.

46 I would like to thank the referees and the editor of the *Journal of Aesthetics and Art Criticism*, as well as Hilde Hein and Gregg Horowitz, for their critical and constructive comments on earlier versions of my article.

SUGGESTIONS FOR FURTHER READING

Crimp, Douglas (1993) "Redefining site specificity", in *On the Museum's Ruins*, MIT Press.

Danto, Arthur (1987) "*Tilted Arc* and Public Art", in *The State of the Art*, New York: Prentice-Hall.

Finkelpearl, Tom (ed.) (2000) *Dialogues in Public Art*, MIT Press.

Hess, Elizabeth (1983) "A tale of two memorials", *Art in America* 71(4).

Jordan, Sherrill (1987) *Public Art, Public Controversy: The* Tilted Arc *on Trial*, New York: ACA Books.

Korza, Pam (1990) "Evaluating artistic quality in the public realm: a report of the *On View* symposium on public art, May 1989, Harvard University", *On View* 1(1).

Mitchell, W.J.T. (ed.) (1992) *Art and the Public Sphere*, Chicago: University of Chicago Press.

Robbins, Bruce (ed.) (1993) *The Phantom Public Sphere*, Minneapolis: University of Minnesota Press.

Senie, Harriet (1992) *Contemporary Public Sculpture: Tradition, Transformation, and Controversy*, New York: Oxford University Press.

Senie, Harriet and Sally Webster (eds) (1992) *Critical Issues in Public Art: Content, Context and Controversy*, New York: Harper Collins.

Serra, Richard (1989) "*Tilted Arc* Destroyed", *Art in America* 77(5).

—— (1994) *Writings Interviews*, Chicago: University of Chicago Press.

Weyergraf-Serra, Clara and Martha Buskirk (eds) (1991) *The Destruction of* Tilted Arc: *Documents*, MIT Press.

INDEX